The Material World of
Eyre Hall

The Material World of Eyre Hall

FOUR CENTURIES OF CHESAPEAKE HISTORY

Carl R. Lounsbury, Editor

With an introduction by Cary Carson, and contributions by
Laura Pass Barry, Bennie Brown, Edward A. Chappell, Sam Florer, Erik Goldstein,
Haley Hoffman, Robert Hunter, Neal T. Hurst, Angelika R. Kuettner, Mark B. Letzer,
Carl R. Lounsbury, George W. McDaniel, Katie McKinney, Elizabeth Palms,
Sumpter Priddy, Margaret Pritchard, Will Rieley, Alexandra Rosenberg,
J. Thomas Savage, Gary Stanton, Robert Watkins,
and John Watson

MARYLAND CENTER FOR HISTORY AND CULTURE, BALTIMORE
In association with
D GILES LIMITED

© 2021 Maryland Center for History and Culture

First published in 2021 by GILES
An imprint of D Giles Limited
66 High Street,
Lewes BN7 1XG, UK
gilesltd.com

Library of Congress Cataloging-in-Publication Data

Names: Lounsbury, Carl, editor. | Barry, Laura Pass, author. | Carson, Cary
  writer of introduction.
Title: The material world of Eyre Hall : four centuries of Chesapeake
  history / Carl R. Lounsbury, editor ; with an Introduction by Cary
  Carson, and contributions by Laura Pass Barry [and nineteen others]
Description: [Baltimore, Maryland] : Maryland Center for History and
  Culture in association with D Giles Limited, [2021] | Includes
  bibliographical references and index.
Identifiers: LCCN 2021011553 | ISBN 9781911282914 (cloth)
Subjects: LCSH: Eyre Hall (Va.)--History. | Northampton County
  (Va.)--Biography. | Ayers family. | Plantations--Virginia--Northampton
  County--History. | Material culture--Chesapeake Bay Region (Md. and
  Va.)--History. | Slaves--Virginia--Social conditions. | Eyre, Thomas,
  -1657--Family.
Classification: LCC F232.N85 M38 2021 | DDC 975.5/15--dc23
LC record available at https://lccn.loc.gov/2021011553

ISBN: 978-1-911282-91-4

For Maryland Center for History and Culture:
Project Manager: Martina Kado

For D Giles Limited:
Copy-edited and proof-read by Sarah Kane
Designed by Helen Swansbourne
Produced by GILES, an imprint of D Giles Limited
Printed and bound in China
All measurements are in inches

Front cover:
Aerial view of Eyre Hall looking north

Back cover:
Eyre Hall gardens, detail of fig. 43, detail of fig. 95, cat. 64,
detail of cat. 137, detail of fig. 56, detail of cat. 82

Frontispiece: Library/chamber looking southeast. Detail of fig. 98.

Opposite: Entrance hallway looking north. Detail of fig. 95.

Pages 32–33: Parlor looking east. Detail of fig. 96.

Pages 186–187: Eyre Hall, exterior view

Pages 238–239: Eyre Hall, aerial view

Pages 282–283: "Morningstar" punch bowl. Cat. 64.

Unless cited from a published source, all references to Northampton
County orders, wills, inventories, tax lists, and court of chancery records
were taken from the original books in the Northampton County Clerk's
Office, Eastville, Virginia. References to the records of other Virginia
counties were taken from the microfilm reels at the Library of Virginia,
Richmond. The U.S. Census records, which are held by the National
Archives and Records Administration, Washington, D.C., were sourced
online, at http://FamilySearch.org.

Contents

I

THE CHANGING FORTUNES OF THE EYRE FAMILY THROUGH FOUR CENTURIES

Acknowledgments

RESEARCH AND WRITING ABOUT THE MATERIAL world of Eyre Hall has been a pleasure, in part because at every stage of the four-year process it kept getting better. I had known the house for many years as an architectural gem on the Eastern Shore, but knew very little about the family or the society that built and sustained it for several centuries. I was flattered to be invited by its long-time owner Furlong Baldwin to explore the history of his family and their material legacy. I took up his challenge and was given the freedom to organize the investigation of Eyre Hall and to find the right people to collaborate in turning this project into the scholarly interpretations and historical narratives of the book. As an architectural historian, I could tell part of that story, but understood full well that I would have to draw upon the special skills of many different people to capture its complexity. I was lucky to convince a number of friends and colleagues who have those talents to join in this undertaking and am grateful to all of them for accepting my invitation to participate without hesitation. This work is made richer for their contributions.

One of the first things I decided to do was to run the basic research through the NIAHD (National Institute of American History and Democracy) program at William and Mary, which allowed me to involve undergraduate and graduate students from this public history program. NIAHD students are introduced to the kinds of research practiced by educators, curators, conservators, architectural historians, and archaeologists who are employed for the most part outside academic institutions. I was fortunate that many were quick to take the bait and found that their interests in Eyre Hall ranged widely. Some chose to study the fine collection of decorative arts scattered throughout the house while others became interested in documentary research. They enjoyed their frequent trips to the clerk's office in Eastville where they learned the tricks of decoding colonial handwriting as they transcribed material from court records books that spanned more than three centuries. Still others tracked down primary sources associated with the Eyre family in libraries and archives across the region, helped excavate a domestic quarter, and measured and produced digital drawings of service and farm buildings. I have been buoyed by their enthusiasm as they discovered the individuals and stories that have enriched our understanding of the history of this place. Many thanks to Rebecca Albers, Joe Bailey, Mackenzie Coker, Wyatt Falcone, Jay Feyerabend, Sam Florer, William Gaskins, Zach Harris, Haley Hoffman, Elizabeth Kenison, McKenzie Long, Franklin Lowe, Hunter McKinney, Claire Nevin, Deeno O'Connell, Elizabeth Palms, Alexandra Rosenberg, Annie Shirley, Samantha Slusher,

Shea Simmons, Josie Sneed, Robert Watkins, Ann Waters, and Ying Zhang. Many engaging discussions of discoveries made at Eyre Hall or in the clerk's office in Eastville transpired over frequent dinners at Stingrays, a roadhouse restaurant with generous portions that provided a welcoming haven as we waited for rush-hour traffic to thin out at the Hampton Roads tunnel.

I would like to acknowledge the important role that the William and Mary NIAHD program played in administering the research grant for Eyre Hall. Thanks to Julie Richter, its director, for overseeing the budget and keeping the various deans apprised of the contributions the students made. This project has given the opportunity for five of them to publish their findings in special focus essays that intersperse the first section of the book. Thanks as well to administrative assistants Jennifer Fox and Maggie Henson for keeping the project running smoothly. Jay Gaidmore, the director of Special Collections at William and Mary's Swem Library, kindly agreed to host a collection of Eyre Hall documents provided by owner Furlong Baldwin so that students could review them in a secure and climate-controlled environment.

I would like to recognize the help of many others for their time, advice, and access to materials, including Traci L. Johnson, the clerk of the Northampton County Circuit Court in Eastville, who welcomed us in to dig through records that dated back to 1632. At the Virginia Department of Historic Resources, Quatro Hubbard, Elizabeth Lipford, Calder Loth, and Marc Wagner provided information, site reports, and images of Eastern Shore structures that help place the architecture of Eyre Hall into a state and regional context. A number of years ago, Michael Bourne conducted invaluable research into the fabric of Eyre Hall that culminated in a Historic Structures Report that formed the basis of the research done for this project. His measured drawings of the house in the early 2000s were extremely useful, as was his work and those of others that culminated in Eyre Hall being made a National Historic Landmark in 2012. Susan Buck kindly provided a copy of her paint report on the house and enriched my understanding of the changing paint schemes. Michael Worthington furnished a copy of the dendrochronological report on Eyre Hall and undertook the analysis of Elkington, a nearby house whose plan was based on Eyre Hall. Special thanks to Nick Luccketti and the crew of the James River Institute of Archaeology for their work excavating a quarter, tracing fence lines, and searching for evidence of quarters. During a few hot summer days in 2017 and 2018, my old colleagues from Colonial Williamsburg— Cary Carson, Edward Chappell, and Jeff Klee—were joined by Wies Erkelens, Susan Kern, Reavis Lounsbury, and students Joe Bailey, Sam Florer, Elizabeth Palms, and Robert Watkins to help record the outbuildings and overseer's house at Eyre Hall, the main house at Eyreville, and Elkington. Fine meals and agreeable dinner talk at Eyre Hall hosted by Furlong Baldwin and Louise Hayman helped repay our gratitude for their hard work.

I would like to recognize the work of the photographers Gavin Ashworth, Jeff Klee, and Dennis McWaters who were commissioned to photograph the house and many of the extraordinary objects at Eyre Hall. Their handsome images enhance the book immeasurably. I appreciate the special cartographic skills of Richard Britton, who produced the maps that orient readers to the landscape of Eyre Hall and the Eastern Shore and greater Chesapeake. Will Rieley, landscape architect, devised the drawings showing the development of the gardens and buildings of the Eyre Hall curtilage. Thanks to Michael Bourne, Jeff Klee, Marianne Martin, Laurie Klingel, Michael Lavin, Jamie May, Elizabeth Palms, Robert Watkins, and Ron Wrucke for their help and generosity in creating, loaning, scanning, and restoring images used in the book. I would also like to recognize the assistance of several people and institutions that provided images that illustrate various aspects of the Eyre family history and interests; these include the Eastern Shore Public Library, Marion Naar of the Cape Charles Historical Society,

Gordon Campbell of At Altitude Gallery in Cape Charles, the Colonial Williamsburg Foundation, Special Collections at the University of Virginia, the Virginia Museum of Fine Arts, Special Collections in Swem Library at William and Mary, and the personal photographic collections of DeCourcy McIntosh, Furlong Baldwin, Joyce Ramassar, Robert Curtis, Jr., Helen Burton, and George McDaniel. Thanks also to Mark Atkinson for some eleventh-hour photography.

Not only was Eyre Hall a collective research project, but, as the table of contents suggests, the task of writing was shared by many. Besides the William and Mary students, my former colleagues at the Colonial Williamsburg Foundation contributed their expertise. I would like to thank Ron Hurst for allowing his curators a busman's holiday to write about the objects that they know so well. Thanks especially to Laura Barry, Angelika Kuettner, Katie McKinney, Neal Hurst, Erik Goldstein, Margaret Pritchard, and John Watson for their catalogue essays. My thanks also to outside specialists including Sumpter Priddy, Mark Letzer, Rob Hunter, Bennie Brown, and Gary Stanton for their expertise in their fields of scholarship. Former director of Drayton Hall, George McDaniel, has spent a career listening and recording the voices of those who have often been overlooked in history. At the urging of Louise Heyman and DeCourcy "Dick" McIntosh, I engaged George to search out descendants of those African American families who had worked for two and three generations for the Baldwin family at Eyre Hall, to tell their stories of life in a rural community in the era of the Great Depression and Jim Crow social barriers. Thanks to Joyce Curtis Ramassar, Robert Curtis, Jr., Paulette Curtis, Helen Burton, Jane Fair, and Anthony Foeman for sharing their memories of their parents, grandparents, and siblings who knew this place intimately. McDaniel's work also draws upon Furlong Baldwin's memories of Eyre Hall that were recorded in a series of interviews with Elaine Eff more than a dozen years before.

I was also fortunate to tap into the knowledge of scholars who have had a long working relationship with the Baldwins at Eyre Hall. Tom Savage, a man raised not far from Eyre Hall and who had spent many hours listening to Margaret Taylor Baldwin's stories of the place, kindly contributed the foreword to the book. A number of years ago, Will Rieley was called on to oversee the stabilization of the green-house ruins and took that time to explore the actual mechanics of the heating system that allowed the Eyres to grow exotic tropical plants and trees. I was fortunate that he decided that he needed to learn more about the garden and shared with him the pleasure of analyzing many old grainy photographs to tease out new information about the grounds and buildings. Margaret Pritchard had long been involved with helping Furlong Baldwin grow his collection of maps and prints and steered him to the conservationists at Colonial Williamsburg when he needed help in conserving his collection of objects. Margaret, along with Cary Carson, my mentor in graduate school and my boss at Colonial Williamsburg, and Mark Letzer of the Maryland Center for History and Culture, long-time friend of the family and a silver specialist in his own right, originally conceived of this research project and convinced Furlong Baldwin that it would be an important contribution to his family's history as well as an unparalleled opportunity for scholars interested in the study of early Chesapeake material culture.

In providing a home for the publication of the book, I am thankful to Mark Letzer of the Maryland Center for History and Culture for stepping forward and offering the kind offices of his organization and staff including Martina Kado, the director of publications. Thanks to Jamie Bosket of the Virginia Museum of History and Culture for recommending our publisher Dan Giles of D Giles Limited. Dan has been a great partner in this task, and I would like to thank him and his staff including Allison McCormick, Louise Parfitt, Sarah Kane, Helen Swansbourne, Louise

Ramsay, and Harry Ault for transforming the manuscript and images into a book with efficiency and good cheer.

I would like to thank my family, Susan Kern, Reavis Lounsbury, and Anne Lounsbury, for their contributions to this project at home and in the field, and for their patience during those long months of close quarters brought on by the pandemic quarantine, when I spent most waking hours working on this task. At the same time, it saddens me to note the death of my dear friend Edward Chappell in the summer of 2020. I had known Ed since I first met him on an archaeological site in York, England, in the summer of 1974, and worked with him in the Architectural Research Department at Colonial Williamsburg for 35 years. I look upon his essay on the English architectural hardware at Eyre Hall as his farewell gift. I will deeply miss his passion for architectural fieldwork and will recall with pleasure the many adventures that we shared in that endeavor.

Finally, I am deeply indebted to Furlong Baldwin and members of his family for making me feel at home at Eyre Hall over the past four years. I am grateful to Louise Hayman for her warm smile and generous hospitality as well as her sustained contributions to this project, from helping to underwrite the archaeology of the quarter site and chasing down photographs to providing many helpful research leads. Thanks to Eyre Baldwin, Grace Baldwin, and Molly Baldwin for sharing with George McDaniel their memories of Eyre Hall, as well as to Dick McIntosh, whose grandmother Mary Eyre Wright was the last Eyre to be born in the ancestral home. Dick very kindly underwrote much of the cost of the catalogue photography, supplied many personal photographs of his grandmother's generation, and was instrumental in broadening the scope of this project by covering the expenses of McDaniel's interviews and transcriptions of his conversations with former residents on the Eyre Hall estate.

I cannot thank Furlong enough for giving me the opportunity to share the history of Eyre Hall with a wider audience. In my many years of working in the field of early American architecture, I have rarely met an individual who has spoken so passionately about the importance of history in the lives of ordinary Americans or has made such considerable effort to share the treasures that he has inherited with scholars and the public. Thanks, friend, for all that you have done.

CARL R. LOUNSBURY

A Note from Henry Furlong Baldwin

THIS BOOK IS NOT WHAT I IMAGINED WHEN THE idea was first presented to me. I grew up with the conviction that Eyre Hall was worthy of the best stewardship I could provide, but only because the house and property descended to me after nine generations before me had done their part to maintain it, its setting, and its collections. Now it was my turn. So I would first like to thank the countless craftsmen and contractors who have contributed to the upkeep of the place, each adding their skill and taking pride in the part they have played in the enormous collective enterprise of Eyre Hall.

Gradually, I began to suspect I was the custodian of a treasure larger than any preceding generation had recognized. With encouragement from many who became contributors to this book, I began to see the importance in Eyre Hall beyond maintaining it for the next generations of my family or simply describing its architecture and contents. I came to realize that it is in fact a living laboratory for the study of the history of the Chesapeake region.

It was not only experts in the fields of history and historic preservation who influenced my decision to authorize this book. That was equally informed by the thousands of visitors to Eyre Hall in my lifetime, many during decades of participating in Virginia's Historic Garden Week, but also the random visitors who wander through the gardens nearly every day, some leaving notes of appreciation and encouragement for our efforts.

I am pleased that my view of Eyre Hall expanded to encompass its value as a teaching tool for scholars and researchers, a destination for those wishing to experience all the facets of its history, and an oasis from the turmoil of the present.

My family and I are fortunate to have developed an unparalleled network of the most talented and engaged historians, with national reputations in their field. I am particularly pleased that representatives of the next generation of these giants also participated in this publication. It is not possible to thank them individually though, happily, Carl Lounsbury, in the acknowledgments, has done a thorough job in naming them. Already respectful of Carl's abilities, four years after engaging him to lead this work I hold him in ever higher esteem.

The preparation of this book, and the discoveries and documentation brought to light during the course of it, have been some of the most interesting and enjoyable experiences of my life. Indeed, *The Material World of Eyre Hall* fulfills my original intent and more, allowing me to share my good fortune in being the latest steward of Eyre Hall with all those who appreciate its educational significance and its rarity.

Eyre Hall
September 2020

Fig. 1. Portrait of Henry Furlong Baldwin by Peter Egeli, 1994.

Foreword

J. THOMAS SAVAGE

I WILL ALWAYS BE GRATEFUL FOR A CHILDHOOD spent on Virginia's Eastern Shore, that rural paradise cradled by the Atlantic Ocean and the Chesapeake Bay. Memories of fishing and crabbing, of swimming and water skiing, and of family boat trips to "maroon" and gather sea shells on deserted barrier islands remain vivid more than half a century later. Here my culinary preferences were developed. Long before any slow food movement, Eastern Shoremen savored the regional pleasures of outdoor oyster roasts, freshly caught fish, steamed Cherrystone clams dived for the same afternoon, and, on holidays, local turkey stuffed with oyster dressing, Crab Imperial, and yellowish green "Hayman" sweet potatoes, a delicacy unique to the lower Delmarva peninsula.

For a little boy obsessed with history, antiques, and old houses, the Eastern Shore offered much to engage the senses and fire the imagination. Dotting the agrarian landscape were abundant architectural survivals from the eighteenth and early nineteenth centuries, some beautifully restored and some abandoned, others gently and simply occupied and some collapsed or on the verge. I explored them all, in Sunday finest during Historic Garden Week and in protective gear for the abandoned and collapsed. The best visits were with patient owners who tolerated, fostered, and encouraged my interests, and I remain indebted to them

to this day. In particular I recall many a happy hour with Helen Hollerith at Warwick, an Upshur place with ties to Eyre Hall; with Florence Upshur Mears at Wainhouse, where my paternal grandparents had lived; and with Margaret Eyre Taylor Baldwin, the mistress of her ancestral home, Eyre Hall. Having been introduced to Mrs. Baldwin during numerous childhood Garden Week pilgrimages, my visits became more frequent after acquiring my driving permit. While at St. Andrew's School, I could always find a way to incorporate Eyre Hall and its contents in a paper or project, and Mrs. Baldwin was gracious and welcoming with every new request. I treasure the memory of those delightful and informative visits with her particularly as they turned out to be a preamble to a closer relationship with the house and its next owner, her son Furlong Baldwin.

One would be hard-pressed to name an owner who derives more pleasure from historic house stewardship than Furlong Baldwin. Over the decades, Furlong has welcomed countless groups I have brought to Eyre Hall during Williamsburg Antiques Forum as well as Collectors groups from both Winterthur and Williamsburg. For him, the greatest joy of stewardship is sharing the property with others, be they scholars or enthusiasts, or, in one case, a knowledgeable English couple of mutual acquaintance who could not be on the Eastern Shore during Garden Week and found themselves treated to a private invitation the day before. His joy in extending hospitality has long been shared by Louise Hayman, a passionate and experienced preservationist and the best ally a country house owner could hope for. I recall the mutual excitement of giver and receiver during a recent Christmas when Louise gifted Furlong a scientific paint and finishes analysis for an Eyre Hall interior. My life has been greatly enriched by their friendship and support and the many happy times spent together in New York, on Christmas night at Eyre Hall, and in England where we rendezvoused for country house visits while they explored ancestral churches and houses of the Eyre family.

A dozen years ago, Furlong and the late Wendell Garrett invited me to write an article on Eyre Hall for *The Magazine Antiques*, fulfilling a long-held dream to have a house from the Eastern Shore of Virginia represented within the pages of that storied publication. Of necessity, its scope touched the tip of the iceberg but introduced the historic property to a wider audience. In this publication, the brightest and best—seasoned scholars and in-process graduate students alike—have come together to record the totality of an extraordinary survival. It is certain to set a new standard for the documentation of historic places, their contents, and lives lived both within and outside the great house. The Eyre Hall project has been a labor of love for all involved, and Carl Lounsbury has coordinated a team of contributors whose numbers and expertise constitute a powerhouse of knowledge. From inception to completion, the vision has been Furlong Baldwin's. He inherited a legacy and left it far richer and better documented for his presence. This volume is his present to us all.

Eyreloom

AN INTRODUCTION

CARY CARSON

N O SMALL NUMBER OF GENTLEMEN'S SEATS once dotted the Virginia countryside. Virginia was, after all, Mother Country Britain's largest and wealthiest colony in mainland North America. That said, gentry houses like Eyre Hall were always outnumbered—hundreds of times over—by a multitude of commonplace dwellings, home to dirt farmers, tenants, enslaved workers, hangers-on. Those structures have all but disappeared since the eighteenth century. But so have most big planters' houses. Today, the Virginia Landmarks Registry lists fewer than a hundred prodigy houses built before 1800. Of those, an even smaller number—a dozen plus—are still owned by the original families. Eyre Hall is one of these (Fig. 2).[1] Actually, not just one; it is among the rarest of the rare. While some of the others can justly point with pride to collections of paintings, furnishings, and other decorative arts objects acquired by generations of owners, it is also true that house fires, neglect, divided inheritances, Yankees, and other mishaps have over the years severely reduced many of these ancient patrimonies.

Not Eyre Hall's. Slip a bookmark between the pages here to save your place, then turn to the catalogue raisonné

behind. There you will find, described and illustrated, a trove of prints and paintings; books and papers; musical instruments; silver plate; glass and ceramic tablewares; and roomfuls of furniture that have survived the vicissitudes of fortune for two and a half centuries. In all, the house that Littleton Eyre built in 1759 is home today to over 1,500 objects that he and succeeding generations acquired and have preserved to the present day.[2] Not everything has been saved of course. Two household and plantation inventories drawn up in 1769 and 1774 record many things, now gone, that later Eyres used up, wore out, broke, discarded, and replaced. Likewise, a cache of sherds found some years ago under a porch floor is a fortuitous reminder that once fashionable table settings and teawares fell prey to changing tastes in this household as elsewhere.[3]

It would be easy to confuse this book with a conventional museum catalogue. The finest pieces seen in these pages certainly could be found there, too. The catalogue entries here read like they were written by specialist curators; they were. The illustrations look like the work of professional museum photographers; they are. Do not be misled. The similarities end there. The Eyre Hall collection is a *domestic*

Fig. 2. Aerial view of Eyre Hall looking north. Cherrystone Creek is to the northwest in this view while Eyreville is to the north, on the other side of the smaller Eyreville Creek.

collection. All its pieces belong together. While they were acquired over many years by generations of family, they all furnished one place only, Eyre Hall. They come therefore with their original context intact, which is to say, with a setting they all share, with known owners and users we can identify, and therefore in circumstances that raise far-reaching questions about the role that the house and its furnishings played in the lives of Eyres and Baldwins from 1759 until now. This opening chapter will make the necessary introductions, then show where such a rare domestic collection can lead readers who are curious to see Eyre Hall in a broader historical perspective (Fig. 3).

* * *

The reasons for Eyre Hall's unusual endurance emerge in Carl Lounsbury's history of the Eyre family and their Baldwin descendants in Part I. The newly built house and its newly installed furnishings remained bright and shiny during the short ownerships of the first three Eyres: Littleton, his son, and eldest grandson. Together their tenure lasted only 30 years. John Eyre, a younger grandson and fourth in line, inherited the property in 1789 at age 21. He managed the plantation for the next 66 years, and, when it passed to his grandnephew Severn in 1855, it enjoyed another uninterrupted title until 1914. In all, the house and its contents remained in the possession of only these two men for 125 years, both young adults when they assumed their inheritance and both prosperous.

Very prosperous. John Eyre, planter, slave owner, landlord, and investor, was the wealthiest man in Northampton County. His fortune was firmly grounded on the land. That world soon turned topsy-turvy for Severn. Five years after he took over the plantation, "Rebellion," as he called it, plunged the country into civil war. His workforce of enslaved Black people, 90 strong at the outbreak of hostilities, shrank to a handful of domestic servants, farm laborers, and superannuated retainers by the conflict's end. In consequence, "I have been made poor," he declared, styling himself as "a sufferer by the war" in an appeal to Abraham Lincoln. Regardless, he made astute choices to protect his assets at Eyre Hall. When Union troops garrisoned the Eastern Shore in November 1861, he proclaimed himself a loyal Unionist, exciting "execration" among some of his neighbors. Having never supported the secession, "or been in any way connected with it," he managed to shield his house and farm from the depredations that many less prudent southerners soon suffered. In the end, Eyre Hall glided through the Civil War unscathed.[4]

All the same, agriculture per se ceased to be the prime engine of wealth that it once had been. Again Severn made shrewd adjustments. Increasingly, he turned farming over to leaseholders, not just the Eyre Hall acres, but additional tenanted properties that he both inherited and bought and sold himself. "Sufferer" or not, he, like John before him, was reckoned to be the wealthiest landowner in the county by the end of the century, a reputation partly owing to his considerable real estate holdings.[5] The larger part of his fortune, though, came from a new source: from investments in the new postwar economy that flourished in America's burgeoning cities. Baltimore fast became the center of Severn's world, financially at first, then socially. He invested heavily in railroads and steamship lines; he subscribed to public works projects and hazarded venture capital on private development schemes. Finally, in 1882, he moved his entire family from the ancestral seat in the country to a brand-new permanent residence on West Monument Street. From that time forward the whirlwind lives of Mr. and Mrs. Severn Eyre and their three children made frequent "News of the Fashionable World" in the pages of the Baltimore *Sun*.[6]

The transformation of this once-upon-a-time "Farmer" into a big city "Capitalist" aided the preservation of Eyre Hall in two important ways.[7] The new money, added to the old, kept the house repaired and even modestly modernized, with a newer kitchen and indoor plumbing. Better yet, the move to Baltimore shifted to the townhouse all the Eyres' ambitions to redecorate a fashionable showplace for the endless round of receptions, dinners, debutant parties, and weddings frequently announced and glowingly acclaimed in the city's society pages. Meanwhile, down on the Eastern Shore, Eyre Hall settled into a contented retirement as the family's country house, a summer retreat, a comfortable old shoe regarded somewhat quizzically from the city as "a noted place of horticultural interest." Patriarch Severn, it was generally understood, "spends his summers at Eyre Hall with his family . . . and makes his home in Baltimore during the winter."[8] Having long ago finessed a Yankee occupation, the old house and by now its quaint interiors paid almost no heed whatsoever to the invasion of Victoriana.

Severn's death in 1914 put Eyre Hall at risk for the first time since the eighteenth century. His only son and heir apparent having died prematurely years earlier, Severn next intended to bequeath his estate to his two daughters. But Grace, the eldest, passed away shortly before her father. In the end he deeded the property to his surviving daughter, Mary, and to his 16-year-old granddaughter, Margaret, Grace's daughter. The division between aunt and niece hung in the balance for 15 years. Finally, on the eve of Margaret's marriage to Henry duPont Baldwin in

Fig. 3. Map of the
Chesapeake region.

1928, Eyre Hall came face to face with the hazard that had scattered the movable patrimony of many other ancient families in Virginia. The settlement awarded the house and most of the furnishings (but not all) to the newlywed Mrs. Baldwin. Various gilded mirrors, card tables, a sideboard, some fancy chairs, parts of two porcelain dinner services, and a selection of eighteenth-century silver serving dishes and accessories were left to Mary.[9]

That division might well have brought another sad end to an all-too-familiar story. Except that Eyre Hall was fortunate again. Where longevity, prosperity, benign neglect, and a dash of luck had kept the house and its interiors together for 170 years, now it was Margaret's admiration for her forebears and her youthful zeal for stewardship that came to the rescue. She had just turned 30 when she married and came into her inheritance. Immediately she took up residence in the ancestral home, the first owner to live there year-round in almost 50 years. She had been born and bred at a time when many old families along the East Coast, anxious about the rapidly changing world around them, sought tangible ways to reaffirm the traditional values and immortalize the staid aesthetics of their forefathers. Saving and preserving old buildings and collecting early American antiques were favorite projects for promoters of this Colonial Revival movement, among them many energetic women. In Virginia, women were the driving force behind the veneration and preservation of Washington's Mount Vernon and the Lee family's Stratford Hall. Margaret, the new mistress of Eyre Hall, had no need to enlist helpmates to secure the future of her family seat and no need to seek out and acquire appropriate furnishings to summon up a semblance of times past. Instead, she found her lifework ready and waiting on her doorstep—a venerable plantation house still in family hands—and, everywhere she looked, family treasures—*Eyrelooms* emphatically!—already collected and still in everyday use. Family tradition remembers that the first words she spoke on returning from her honeymoon

proclaimed both her duty and her destiny. "I'm home," she promised, a promise she kept for 50 years.

At once the new Mrs. Baldwin set about making overdue repairs and improvements to a house that seasonal use had left outdated and run-down. She built a service wing, including another, more modern kitchen, introduced electric lights, and installed central heating. Like many of her generation, she admired the good taste that had prevailed in those ages past when Littleton Eyre built the house and John Eyre and his wife Ann furnished it so stylishly. Mercifully, Severn Eyre's move to the big city had spared the homeplace much fussy Victorian design. Margaret was not of a mind to redecorate the house as a museum piece dedicated to an older romanticized aesthetic. She did make additions to the gallery of family portraits, namely the likenesses of men and women from the Taylor side of her father's family, as Laura Barry discovered and explains in her catalogue essay on paintings and portraiture. Otherwise, Margaret added few new things to the many attractive and still serviceable household possessions that she and her young family now put comfortably to use again.

Her decision to make Eyre Hall her year-round residence settled its future for the time being. But her greater contribution to its long-term preservation was her gift for inspiring others to consider it *their* home and *their* life's work as well as hers. George McDaniel's concluding chapter to Part I draws on oral interviews he conducted with, among others, men and women who had worked there as kitchen help, housekeepers, and farmhands—just as had many of their parents, grandparents, and various aunts and uncles going back to the early decades of the twentieth century. All were African Americans, but none seem to have descended from the enslaved workers who disappear from the census records for Eyre Hall following emancipation. The hired help Margaret employed were generally newcomers to the property. They show up in the records about the same time she took over the farm. Those who stayed intermarried, and,

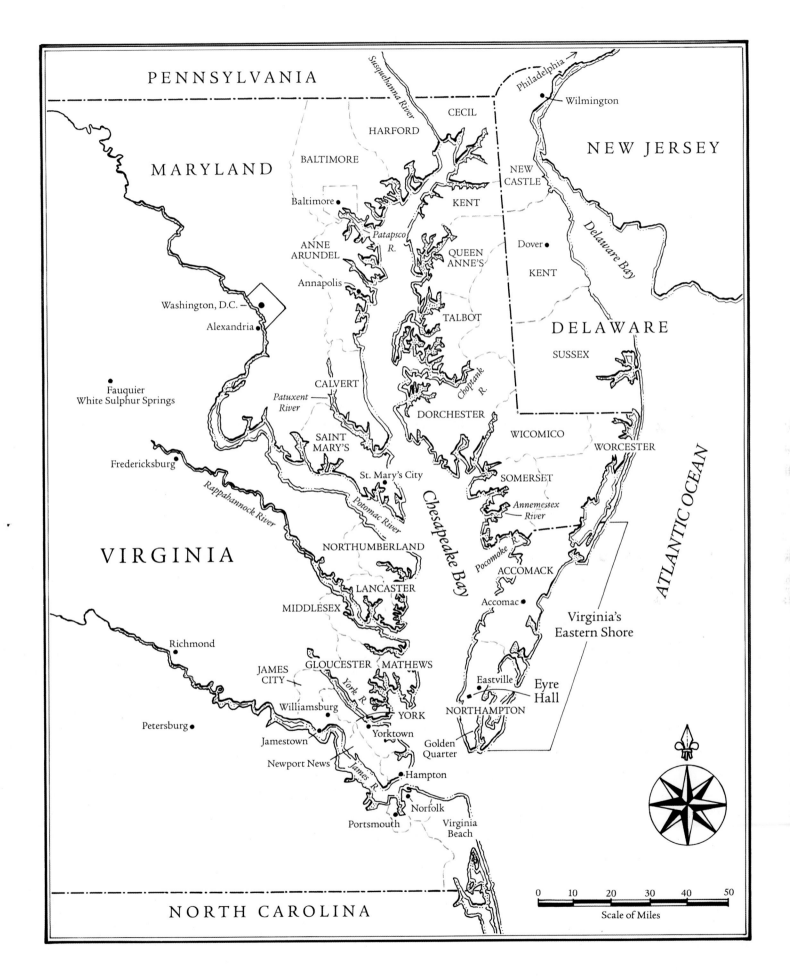

PENNSYLVANIA

Susquehanna River

Philadelphia

Wilmington

CECIL

HARFORD

NEW JERSEY

BALTIMORE

NEW
CASTLE

MARYLAND

KENT

Baltimore

Patapsco R.

DELAWARE Bay

ANNE
ARUNDEL

QUEEN
ANNE'S

Dover

KENT

Annapolis

Washington, D.C.

TALBOT

DELAWARE

Alexandria

SUSSEX

Fauquier
White Sulphur Springs

CALVERT

Choptank R.

*Patuxent
River*

DORCHESTER

WICOMICO

WORCESTER

SAINT
MARY'S

Fredericksburg

SOMERSET

St. Mary's City

*Annemessex
River*

Rappahannock River

Potomac River

Chesapeake Bay

ATLANTIC OCEAN

Pocomoke R.

NORTHUMBERLAND

VIRGINIA

ACCOMACK

LANCASTER

Accomac

MIDDLESEX

Virginia's
Eastern Shore

Richmond

GLOUCESTER MATHEWS

JAMES
CITY

York R.

Eastville

Eyre
Hall

Williamsburg

YORK

NORTHAMPTON

Petersburg

Yorktown

Jamestown

Newport News

James R.

Golden
Quarter

Hampton

Norfolk

Portsmouth

Virginia
Beach

0   10   20   30   40   50

Scale of Miles

NORTH CAROLINA

as time passed, Foemans and Bagwells became an extended clan of intermingled kinfolk lasting well into the 1970s (see Fig. 70). This was, of course, still an era in the South when whites and Blacks knew each other's place. McDaniel's informants made no secret of the bigotry they encountered at school and on the streets of nearby Cheriton. Back home on the Eyre Hall farm things were easier. They remember having pretty much the run of the place as kids, even in and around the main house. These were domains where their parents, aunts, and uncles worked every day, used their skills, and exercised considerable authority. In their telling, Mrs. Baldwin comes across as a kind and thoughtful employer. She was, to be sure, a southern lady of the old school, with everything that label implies about racial attitudes. But over and over again the people whom McDaniel interviewed used the words considerate, respectful, honest, and hard-working to describe her daily management of the kitchen, household, garden, and farm. They said that she herself set a steady pace and maintained high standards. Getting a job done right, whether polishing silver or mowing the lawn, became a habit that elders passed on to rising generations. This shared pride kept Eyre Hall going when Margaret's otherwise modest resources were stretched to the limit. From the early 1960s until her grown son began conferring regularly with the farm manager, Eyre Hall's first and only female owner ran the entire operation herself with hired help whose loyalty she earned with kindness and by her own tireless example.[10]

Besides fostering this partnership with staff, her other important convert to the preservation cause was her own son. In truth, both her children formed strong ties to the place; both daughter and son returned to live on the property in retirement. But it was her son Furlong Baldwin who committed himself and dedicated his career to building a financial safety net to secure the future of Eyre Hall forever, or for as much of forever as was consistent with his strong preference that it should always remain a family home. By

happenstance Furlong followed in his great-grandfather Severn's footsteps. He sought his fortune in Baltimore, in banking. He too prospered, and, while several institutions in that city and beyond enjoyed his generosity, Eyre Hall was always his first love and chief philanthropic cause. Looking back many years later, he told George McDaniel, "You either love this place or hate it." He laughed. It was always tempting you to hate it, he allowed, because ignored "it will take you down. There is always something—a tractor needs repair, roofs need to be fixed, pipes to be replaced. Fortunately, I love it. Always have."

This book is testament to what his devotion accomplished. Littleton Eyre's 260-year-old house is shipshape again; its merit acknowledged as a National Historic Landmark; his mother's garden a popular Historic Garden Week perennial; the landscape and water views protected by acquisitions and scenic easements; and the remarkably intact collection of paintings and decorative arts widely shared and much studied by curators and historians from Colonial Williamsburg, the Winterthur Museum, and the Maryland and Virginia historical societies among others.[11] Now, with this publication, Furlong shares his family's legacy further afield with collectors, scholars, students, art lovers, and fans of American history everywhere. That too is a canny hedge against an unknowable future. Like landmarked buildings, coherent collections with acknowledged reputations enjoy an extra margin of protection against piecemeal dismemberment.

Ultimately, though, it was their dedication, imagination, and grit that Eyres and Baldwins drew on repeatedly to beat the odds and bring their ancient homeplace into the twenty-first century safe and sound. Furlong has placed a bet on the next generation too. Again after the manner of Severn before him, he has deeded the property to his granddaughter. The bequest will someday be her opportunity to live modern at Eyre Hall while remaining faithful to a treasure that has few equals in Virginia or beyond.

* * *

The exceptional survival of Eyre Hall and its collections is reason enough for publication. That said, the value of reading this book need not stop there. Much more can be learned from so special a collection of material things accumulated by one family in one place over five or six generations.

First of all, information about the Eyre family's possessions, richest in the period from 1750 to about 1830, can be pushed back more than 50 years to the late 1600s using early probate records. Taken together, they encompass almost the whole of a seminal time span in the cultural history of Britain, northern Europe, and the faraway places those nations colonized. It was a moment in Western history when people learned a new kind of visual literacy. That is to say, people who had once acquired one kind of useful information from the physical things they saw around them eventually came to view the places and spaces they inhabited in more complicated ways. The house and service buildings that Littleton Eyre built and furnished in 1759 enclosed architectural spaces and defined work yards that his family and slaves used quite differently than had his father and grandfather on their farms farther down the peninsula. The difference was not one of resources: the Eyres had been well-to-do planters and slaveholders since the seventeenth century. No, times and expectations had changed, as they were to change again when they prompted Littleton's son Severn to make a dining room addition to the house before 1774 and later still when they induced another Severn to indulge his family's appetite for stylish city living by moving to a townhouse in Baltimore. The buildings and collections at Eyre Hall are therefore more than just a chronicle of architectural and decorative arts styles. Viewed more broadly, they reflect changing house habits that prompted Eyres, like gentlefolk elsewhere, to make adjustments to the buildings and landscapes that gave their lives physical form

and the material things that assisted their daily interactions with others.

A probate inventory compiled in 1698 provides a glimpse into an Eyre ancestor's household where a family's possessions were still prized mainly for their intrinsic value or as badges of rank. This document records the combined belongings of a father and son, distant kin to Littleton Eyre by two and three generations. The checklist opens the door into the older man's dwelling, which by then the son had inherited, moved into, and furnished with a few newer things before his own death. Taken together, the Kendalls' possessions usher us into a domestic interior fitted out for comfortable living at the end of the seventeenth century.[12] As such it becomes a useful starting point from which to watch how the Eyre family's possessions became more numerous and complicated generation after generation over the next 150 years. Not only did they elaborate the daily lives of the Eyres themselves, but, as you will find on reading the recollections compiled in the following scrapbook, their care and continued use into modern times defined many daily chores and employed the special skills of the housekeepers, cooks, and yardmen who kept Eyre Hall running for Margaret and Furlong Baldwin until only recently. It can be said with absolute confidence that old Colonel Kendall and his son could hardly have named, let alone guessed the use of, many things featured in the catalogue raisonné at the end of this book. Eyre Hall and its collection stand astride a period of years in the cultural history of Europe and America when our modern notion of a furnished house emerged recognizably from its bygone ancestry.

The inquiring reader asks *how that happened and why*. The Kendalls' inventoried possessions offer clues. They tell us that traditional social distinctions and old-fashioned ways of life still held sway in the Kendalls' households, but here and there they were beginning to give way to new ideas and habits around the turn of the century. For instance, it is easy to picture the "one long table with a carpet on it" recorded in the hall and the "two long forms [benches] to the long table" as pieces of furniture handed down from father to son. His had been a time, back in the 1660s and '70s, when diners sat down at table according to their rank—masters, fathers, or sometimes both parents at the head typically in armchairs, children and servants along the sides on stools and benches. The dinner table mirrored their social universe in miniature. Furniture and its placement gave physical form to age-old notions about family hierarchy; they showed who was master (or mistress) and who ranked lower. Possessions also gave measure to a traditional householder's standing among his neighbors in the world outside. Notable were treasured objects valuable in and of themselves, tablewares made of silver for example and expensive textiles. A chest of drawers stored safely in Kendall's hall chamber held a trove of silver spoons, plates, salts, drinking vessels, a sugar dish, and a porringer. Turkeywork carpets covered his tables and upholstered another set of chairs; old-fashioned chests and presses were stuffed with napkins, sheets, coverlets, pillows and pillowcases, and a miscellany of bulk yard goods. These and other things, which the son inherited from his father in all likelihood, harked back to a time when furnishings—tools for living—signified to the tool-users where they belonged in the pecking order and how to behave toward everybody else who shared their domestic space.

And so such objects continued to do into the early eighteenth century, but somewhat differently and with a few novel additions. Some of these changes were already afoot by 1698. Significantly there were two tables in Kendall's hall, the long rectangular one and another, a round table also draped with a turkeywork carpet. Furthermore, by then, diners could be seated individually on a matching "dozen new Russia leather chairs," replacements for the older communal benches.[13] These were significant differences that connote a profoundly altered consciousness among people of means in England and the colonies. Little by little they were coming to regard themselves as a class apart: ladies

and gentlemen who were better bred, more refined, and ultimately superior to the menials they employed. Slavery drew this distinction sharper still.[14] Notions of superiority sorted people into separate groups. It followed further that sorting encouraged a radically new fashion-consciousness among these self-styled gentlefolk. They now deployed their personal possessions in support of social hierarchies built not upon rank but on the specialized knowledge and the practice of good manners they shared with others so privileged and disposed.[15] Obviously, more was changing than just the shape of tables and the seating furniture around them. Servants and often even children were dismissed from the formal dining table; they ate elsewhere. The convivial round table and the matching individual leather-bottom chairs were reserved for a company of social equals, more or less. The degree of more or less mattered little compared to the attention now paid to etiquette and refined table manners. Those patterns of behavior are very hard to detect in a mere list of inventoried tablewares and household furnishings. But there is one entry in the younger Kendall's listing that leaves no doubt that this Eyre forebear could already entertain with a nod to fashion. He had further furnished his hall with an up-to-the-minute glass case, a newfangled piece of case furniture specifically designed to store and display the individual beer and wine glasses that were fast replacing cups, tankards, and communal drinking vessels at stylish tables. Sure enough, here too the inventory-takers recorded "about one dozen glasses in the glass case," the same number as the new Russia leather chairs, doubtless no coincidence.

Fast-forward another generation to 1728. Littleton Eyre's father had died, and his executors had drawn up a list of the goods and chattels belonging to the plantation house and farm where Littleton spent most of his boyhood.[16] We need take only passing notice of this domestic setting as we follow the ongoing elaboration of the Eyre family's material world. Nothing about the furniture and textiles inventoried here makes them sound either outmoded at one extreme or modish at the other. The executors did call out a set of "blue & white Earthen ware," no doubt tin-glazed tablewares painted to look like Chinese porcelain. They assigned a high value to a suite of calico bedcurtains, but dismissed a second set as "Motheaten & Rotten." Even an oval table could already be counted "old fashion" by the 1720s. One indisputable heirloom was certainly that, a "Coat of Arms wth a Golden frame." This hatchment was a clear throwback to an age when ancestry not fashion bore out a family's reputation.

Another generation passes. Littleton has come of age, married, bought the Eyre Hall property, and built and furnished his new plantation house. He dies in 1768. The probate inventory of his estate is our Rosetta Stone; it is the key to understanding the material life of a mid-eighteenth-century country squire in Virginia, it and one more document in the case of Eyre Hall.[17] A second exhaustive list of the contents of house and farm was prepared only five years later following the premature death of Littleton's grownup but sickly son.[18] The two inventories give us our earliest close look inside Eyre Hall itself. The sheer number of entries is the first sign that father and son had acquired a great many more things than their Kendall forebears or even Littleton's father and mother had found necessary and useful. By the third quarter of the eighteenth century, architectural refinements, wall treatments, and a multitude of room furnishings and table settings were sending many more visual signals to people far more attuned to them than ever before. Gentlefolk generally—family, friends, neighbors, travelers—looked for and now took as a matter of course pieces of customized furniture and specialized tablewares needed to engage in the special leisure-time activities that set them apart from those who were not genteel. Dressing and grooming, tea taking, card playing, punch drinking, reading, sophisticated music making, just plain lounging around, and of course polite dining were impossible without the proper accessories. No surprise, then, that the 1769 and 1774 inventories are replete with dressing tables and dressing glasses, tea tables, card tables, sideboards, and easy chairs.

Littleton could set his dining table with a large collection of earthenware (unspecified) and pewter plates. His son Severn dramatically upped the ante. He not only built a brand-new dining room off the back of the house, but also laid his elegant table with two new sets of china. One was blue-and-white and enameled Chinese porcelain; the other a sensational new import from Britain: 13 serving dishes and three dozen plates, all "Queen's china," the highly refined Queen's Ware that Josiah Wedgwood had launched on a worldwide market not ten years earlier. The leftover service Severn inherited from his father's estate was quietly retired and part of it written off simply as "67 lb old Pewter." Besides the new ceramics, Severn added more silver plate to the already considerable family trove, notably a full complement of table spoons in the latest style, candlesticks, and pairs of matching sugar casters. Genteel dining at the son's table called for special-purpose accoutrements as well. They included decanters, fruit dishes, glass salts, a custard bowl, a butter boat, and a china tureen, many making their appearance at Eyre Hall for the first time. Politeness and hospitality further required the serving of tea, coffee, and sometimes chocolate in sets of matching cups and saucers, each beverage prepared in its own distinctive pot, both now in silver.

Suddenly there was much more to be seen in a fully furnished gentry house, at Eyre Hall and everywhere. Domestic settings presented many more attention-getters for knowledgeable, well-bred people to take in at a glance, understand, navigate, and respond to appropriately. The fashion-bearing objects they chose to furnish their own homes, or expected to find in public rooms in other ladies' and gentlemen's houses, had become as fine-tuned to class as old-time furnishings had once signified rank.

Fashion—cool-today-uncool-tomorrow—was the new coin of the realm in the modern world of the eighteenth century. Precious metals, still mainly silver, continued to hold intrinsic value, and doubtless Severn proudly displayed his collection of inherited family plate, as Furlong Baldwin does today. But mahogany and walnut chairs and tables, refined china, crystal stemware, polished brass hardware, and printed wallpaper, while expensive to buy, were esteemed for their style first and foremost—for the rake of a chair leg, for the delicacy of a sauceboat, for a teacup's subtle difference from a chocolate cup. Attention to fashion and adherence to good taste set the rules that transformed Littleton and all later Eyres into modern men *à la mode* and, in so doing, men *du monde* as well. Their acquisition and cultivated use of these truly worldly possessions endowed them with a visual lingua franca that was understood far and wide by a multitude of cognoscenti likewise conversant.

The storyline we have followed through these Eyre family documents is complete, but not finished, in the inventoried lists of Littleton's and Severn's goods and chattels. They bring to a close this account of the transformation of consumer behavior from its ancient practice supporting hierarchy to its fusion with late seventeenth-century notions of gentility to its explosive elaboration into fashion-consciousness by the middle of the eighteenth century. Carried forward from that moment, the story at Eyre Hall is a repetitive story of once fashionable things replaced again and again by other, more fashionable things. Few objects featured in the catalogue raisonné at the end of this book can be traced back to the 1769 and 1774 inventories. Silver plate, showpiece ceramics, prints, and books are the exceptions. Almost everything else that makes the collection so notable today was acquired shortly before and after 1800, much of it by John Eyre and his wife Ann Upshur Eyre. When Severn, the next owner, moved his family to Baltimore in 1882, modern taste followed them there. Fashion—long since *old-fashion*—was left behind to mothball at the summer house in the country, an unintended legacy to posterity, thank goodness.

John and Ann Eyre's considerable contribution to the surviving decorative arts collection, the library, the sheet music, and the picture gallery is fully described and illustrated by the curators, bookmen, and historians who carefully studied these materials in preparation for this book. They explain that the family's acquisition of household furnishings from the 1790s through the Civil War changed their basic lifestyles very little, that is to say, it did not alter their social behavior appreciably. Much more significantly, it served to keep their all-important fashionable appearance au courant. This onrush of fashionableness was accelerated by several forces that gathered strength as the century progressed: the advent of new manufacturing technologies, new trade patterns, new marketing strategies, and cultural influences from an ever more connected, ever shrinking world. The catalogue essays take note of the impact that these developments made, or did not make, on the collections at Eyre Hall. But the fundamental social reshaping of consumer behavior had mostly been completed by the turn of the nineteenth century. The surprising result is that young granddaughter Grace Baldwin, today the Eyre in waiting, has more in common with à-la-mode Littleton Eyre, the builder, than he had with the old Colonel and Captain Kendalls with whom this account began.

* * *

The Eyre family tree reaches further back than their time, of course. To start at the very beginning and trace the family's fortunes across a span of 275 years, Carl Lounsbury, the book's editor, has written three opening chapters. These are accompanied by two special focus sidebars, one reporting on archaeological excavations at the Kendall homestead at Eyreville and another looking closely at the plantation economy before and after it was powered by slave labor.

From there George McDaniel brings the history forward another 100 years, this time in company with several African American families who lived on the farm and came to regard it as their home as much as their employers'. Long before that, and years before emancipation freed the workforce of enslaved Africans, we catch glimpses of the genteel pleasures and pastimes afforded to slave owners who enjoyed the wealth and leisure to indulge their cultivated tastes. Those that the collections speak to include light reading, music making, poetry recitals, and print collecting, not to mention Virginians' baser passions for horseracing, cockfighting, and the inveterate gambling those sports inflamed. A catalogue and careful study of the surviving book collection shows, says bibliographer Bennie Brown, how the Eyres' reading habits followed fashions of the day from books of instruction, edification, and self-improvement in the eighteenth century to a torrent of "belles lettres" that poured off American and British presses in the next.[19] Print curator Katie McKinney explains that three rare sets of prints still in their original frames—portraits of famous English racehorses, views of Roman antiquities, and British landscape perspectives—illustrated Eyre pastimes both real (horseracing) and imagined (grand touring in Italy and sightseeing in the British Isles). Curator of musical instruments John Watson and musicologist Gary Stanton teamed up to discover that Ann Upshur was the music lover in the family. Her voice and pianoforte accompaniment sounded through the house for three decades from 1800, when John married her, until her death in 1829. Her at-home performances for and with a circle of like-minded friends, mostly women, were sight-read from loose-leaf sheet music, much of it popular pieces drawn from the comic-opera stage in Britain.

The largest category of objects in the collection—ceramics—and the most valuable—silver plate—furnished still other pastimes that gentlefolk indulged almost daily, the consumption of food and drink. Formal dining, punch drinking, and tea taking were full-dress occasions when ladies and gentlemen showed off their good manners and, not coincidentally, displayed the fashionable accessories needed to perform them. Hollowwares in the collection gauge the Eyres' changing tastes and dining habits more precisely than anything else. As Mark Letzer explains in his catalogue essay, the hallmarks stamped on many pieces give us dates and makers' names. When set alongside the family history, this information can tell us who the tastemakers were who bought and first used these beautiful utensils. The silver at Eyre Hall tracks the family's lifestyles across two centuries from 1704 to the end of the nineteenth century—from tankards and punch bowls to elaborate silver tea sets to fish platters and a plethora of highly specialized table gadgetry whose proper use only Victorians could or cared to fathom.

These insights into some of the pleasurable activities that animated everyday life for the Eyres themselves, their friends, and neighbors come from accurately identifying and dating surviving objects and understanding their original use. That was the assignment given to the knowledgeable specialists who were invited to study these materials and write the catalogue essays and entries. You will learn still more from the essays that describe furniture, glass and ceramics, arms and ironwork, and (least well preserved) clothing and textiles, again each essay the work of someone at Colonial Williamsburg or elsewhere who has studied such materials for a lifetime.

Of course, some leisure-time activities worthy of note left behind no physical evidence whatsoever. Lounsbury's students found clues to some of these in the archive of family papers. They are presented in these pages as two more special focus sidebars: the first looks at horse breeding and racing, especially by Littleton's son Severn, who owned a fine English racer almost twice the value of any other steed in his stable; the second follows the Eyres on frequent excursions to spa towns across Virginia and resort hotels farther away.

Imagine for a minute that this entire decorative arts collection had been saved, but not at the house. Pretend instead that it had been given to a museum, intact, and was now shown to the public in conventional exhibit galleries. It would still be wonderful and important, but not in the same way and, frankly, not quite so wonderful or quite so important. That difference accounts for the special significance of this book. The complete collection still preserved in the house for which it was acquired, where it has always been used, and is now presented as such in this publication, enjoys two, exceptional, value-added enhancements—places and faces. The places—the house and its outbuildings, the celebrated garden and a greenhouse, a family cemetery, and the home farm itself—are the subjects of Parts II and III. Lounsbury, wearing his architectural historian's hat, describes the house and service buildings as first built and then with alterations and additions made by later owners. He collaborates with two former colleagues from Colonial Williamsburg. Edward Chappell is surprised to find that the super-elegant, British-made brass hinges, locks, and latches installed throughout the house are as fine as hardware found anywhere else in the region, even in larger, more ambitious gentlemen's mansions. Wallpaper too, three layers of it, was exceptionally chic, Margaret Pritchard reports, especially the scenic paper hung in the entry and stair hall. Landscape historian Will Rieley will walk you through a garden behind the house that you must picture in your mind's eye. He believes that Littleton Eyre envisioned and built house and garden as a unified design, which only later John and Ann Eyre expanded with the parterred boxwood garden so popular today.

The faces belong to Eyres and Eyre relations. Since Severn (d. 1773) sat for his portrait, his likeness and those painted later have hung on the walls where still today they introduce to us the very same men and women who exclaimed over the new queensware dinner service or curled up with a copy of *Tristram Shandy* in the chamber-cum-library off the parlor.

In her catalogue entries curator Laura Pass Barry hails these family portraits as rare survivors from one of the last Virginia collections still in private hands. They were painted by some of the most notable portraitists of the age, among them Benjamin West, Thomas Sully, and James Peale. When studio photography replaced painted faces, Baldwin likenesses, framed in silver, convened atop the piano in the parlor where they remain today.

The house and the catalogue raisonné are the heart of this book. But as the project took form, a second central focus came into view. From the start the editor wanted to include a scrapbook of snapshots showing ordinary, everyday life on the farm. To find them and collect material for captions he and Furlong's cousin Dick McIntosh asked George McDaniel to interview people who had grown up there as kids, anybody with memories they were willing to share. The photos and the recollections gave names, faces, and eventually real-life oral histories to Blacks as well as whites, to Margaret Baldwin's son, his cousin Dick McIntosh, and her grandchildren, but also to the children and grandchildren of the cooks, gardeners, housekeepers, and farmhands whom she employed well into the 1960s.

The result is a rarely seen group portrait of countryfolk, two races sharing the same place, at a pivotal moment in mid-century rural America before the full awareness of rights and opportunities denied and the onrush of mechanized farm work uprooted the last generation of African Americans to grow up at Eyre Hall and scattered them far afield. The scrapbook is a powerful reminder that the probate inventories that tell us so much about material culture are a record of goods and chattels, lawyers' lingo for personal property. It must never be forgotten or carelessly ignored that for generations the Eyres' personal property included *human chattels*. The enslaved men, women, and children whose lives they ruled over absolutely numbered in the hundreds, starting as early as the turn of the eighteenth century with the first known slave-owning Eyre, Thomas II

(d. 1715). By 1773, 37-year-old Severn Eyre owned no fewer than 163 living souls; his widow acquired 15 more.[20]

When taking inventory, court-appointed executors usually named the deceased person's slaves one by one; sometimes they gave their age and, most important, always their monetary value. Beyond that, little else is usually known about this almost invisible plantation population. Occasional reference is made to husbands and wives, to hiring out idled workers temporarily, and to trade skills that added to someone's appraised value and expected sale price. Only rarely was record made of an Eyre slaveholder's treatment of his or her slaves. John Eyre is an exception. He drew up his will in 1855, eight years before the Emancipation Proclamation.[21] He ordered the executors to sell all the bondsmen he inherited from his wife's estate, but he directed them to let individuals make their own choice of future masters, "provided good ones be selected." Buyers were even to be offered a 25 percent discount to ease the transaction. But sell his chattels he most certainly did.

Rarer still is any evidence of Blacks' feelings about their unfree condition. Except here again there is, remarkably! In 1832, three of John Eyre's slaves conspired with 15 neighbors to steal a whaleboat and sail down the bay and up the Atlantic coast to the promise of freedom in New York City. Alexandra Rosenberg writes about their escape and its tragic outcome in another sidebar essay, this one appended to Chapter 3. This singular incident only underscores how seldom historians can peer into the desperate hopes and dreadful fears of people who lived and died as other men's disposable human property.

The modern-day Foemans, Bagwells, Curtises, and other African American men and women whom you now meet in the pages of the scrapbook were no one's property, it goes without saying. It seems they were not even descendants of those Eyre slaves freed at the end of the Civil War, at least not most of them. Margaret Baldwin's workforce came from elsewhere, from many elsewheres, the scrapbook tells

us. Nor, of course, did the people she employed suffer the cruel treatment that countless bondsmen had endured in earlier times. "Actually," recalled Joyce Ramassar, one of McDaniel's most thoughtful informants: "I didn't even know I was living on a plantation, because my definition of a plantation was quite different from living here."[22] Yet, while she and her Black family, friends, and neighbors were certainly not unfree, the Virginia Eastern Shore was still the American South in the 1930s, '40s, '50s, and '60s. "They're not like us" was a truth that each race understood about the other implicitly. How each then behaved toward the other based on that conviction spelled the difference between the trust and openness that Margaret Baldwin practiced and the bigotry and discrimination that African Americans often experienced beyond the farm gate.

Thus, interview by interview, the scrapbook assembles another kind of catalogue raisonné, in a sense a parallel catalogue. It too comes with portraits, the snapshots yes, but more vividly McDaniel's lively sketches of his informants and, in turn, their recollections of their parents and grandparents whose memories they and the Baldwin children kept alive with such epigraphs as "She was the strongest woman I ever knew" (Pinky Foeman) or "She clearly understood that we lived in a racist world, but believed in humanity and in justice" (Georgia Curtis). The oral histories are full of real places, too. They enlarge the landscape. The houses where Black families lived and their daily workplaces can be plotted on a map of the property (see Fig. 66). More revealing are the mental maps that both white kids and Black kids learned and remembered for the rest of their lives: "I could walk from my house to his in about five minutes" or "I would be at my grandfather's house, maybe a quarter of a mile away, and you could smell that pig being smoked." Finally, the scrapbook is richest where residents on the Eyre Hall acres or neighbors describe and reflect on the many everyday activities that, recorded now, make this account of their overlapping lives an unusually redolent vignette of a rural American community on the cusp of events that would change it forever.

At first the collection of antique family heirlooms, safeguarded in the house that Littleton Eyre built two and a half centuries ago, seemed reason enough to write a book that shared that legacy with art and architecture lovers far and wide. Along the way, however, the authors discovered eyewitnesses to another treasure, this one preserved as living memory. Actually, it would be more accurate to say that that treasure was *rediscovered*. Lounsbury's family history research led eventually to the will and testament that John Eyre drew up shortly before his death in 1855. It did not just direct his executors to sell excess slaves quartered on farms he had inherited from his wife. "It is further my desire," his instructions continued, that so long as two elderly retainers, Nat and Nancy, may live, "they shall be considered as attached to and pass *as heirlooms of the said Eyre Hall Estate.*" The words were those of an unabashed chattel owner; their tenor betrays a streak of kindliness.[23] Two generations later, Margaret Baldwin's friendship with the Black people she employed and their respect for her produced an important second Eyre Hall heirloom legacy worthy of the book that now is yours to explore.

NOTES

1. Others include Shirley Plantation, Charles City Co. (1738, 1772); Sabine Hall, Richmond Co. (1738); Hillsborough, King and Queen Co. (1750s); Mount Airy, Richmond Co. (1760–64); Harewood, Berkeley Co., now Jefferson Co., W.Va. (1770); Elmwood, Essex Co. (ca. 1774); Blenheim, Westmoreland Co. (1781); Stuart House, Staunton, Augusta Co. (ca. 1790); Redlands, Albemarle Co. (1792); Totomoi, Hanover Co. (1795); Burnt Quarter, Dinwiddie Co. (eighteenth-century core). Courtesy Calder Loth and Edward Chappell.

2. Estimate does not separately count individual pieces in sets and services.

3. For the most informative artifacts, see the essays on ceramics and glass in the catalogue raisonné. The tip underneath the north porch floor was excavated in 2000 by Colonial Williamsburg archaeologists Kelly Ladd and Mark Kostro; see their typescript report, "Eyre Hall, Eastern Shore, Virginia: Archaeological Investigation," August 2001, Colonial Williamsburg Foundation archives. The midden was a curious miscellany of ceramic and glass tableware fragments and table scraps, notably bones. There were no coarse kitchen wares. The archaeologists surmised that it had accumulated piecemeal over time, maybe when servants clearing the table broke things and threw them away on the sly using a loose floorboard in the porch after it was rebuilt about 1806. Kelly Ladd-Kostro to Cary Carson, email communication, November 17, 2019.

4. Severn Eyre to Abraham Lincoln, March 3, 1864, Abraham Lincoln Papers Series 1: General Correspondence, 1833–1911, Library of Congress, Washington, D.C.; Eighth U.S. Census, Population Schedule, 1860, Northampton County, Virginia, Eastville District; Ninth U.S. Census, Population Schedule, 1870, Northampton County, Virginia, Eastville District.

5. "One of the largest real estate owners and wealthiest men" of Northampton County, *Sun* (Baltimore), September 15, 1899, 7; *Virginian-Pilot* (Norfolk), February 25, 1900, 14.

6. *Sun* (Baltimore), September 14, 1899, 7.

7. Nine and Tenth U.S. Censuses, Population Schedules, 1870 and 1880, Northampton County, Virginia, Eastville District; Virginia, Deaths, 1912–2014, Virginia Department of Health, Richmond, Virginia.

8. *Sun* (Baltimore), September 14, 1899, 8; September 15, 1899, 7.

9. See the silver essay in the catalogue raisonné; also "Eyre China & Furniture Belonging to Madeline Eyre McIntosh," typed list, 2 pages, n.d., file copy with DeCourcy McIntosh, New York City.

10. The only other woman manager (but not owner) had been Margaret, the wife of Severn Eyre (d. 1773) and mother and guardian of 12-year-old Littleton (d. 1789). She ran the plantation for nine years until he came of age in 1782.

11. Michael Bourne, Marilyn Harper, Virginia B. Price, and James A. Jacobs, "Eyre Hall, Cheriton, Virginia," National Historic Landmark nomination report, National Park Service, Washington, D.C., 2012. Based on a historic structures report by Michael Bourne, "A Description of Eyre Hall, Cheriton, Northampton County, Virginia," unpublished report undertaken as part of a recording project for the Historic American Buildings Survey, Library of Congress, Washington, D.C., December 2004, Colonial Williamsburg Foundation archives.

12. Inventory of the estate of Capt. William Kendall (d. 1696) appears to include property inherited from his father, Col. William Kendall (d. 1686): July 28, 1698, Northampton County Orders & Wills, No. 13, 1689–1698, 499–505 (transcript courtesy of Jenean Hall). Merged into one estate, the inventoried possessions of both Kendalls may have been acquired over a 40-year period from the 1660s to 1698.

13. Unless genteel dining was already a tradition with the Kendalls and these 12 new Russia leather chairs simply upgraded eight others described as "pretty old." In that case, were the long table and benches used for everyday meals for the larger household including servants and the formal table and chairs reserved for special occasions and guests? It should further be noted that two more tables and five "old chairs" (but no stools or benches) were located in the parlor, traditionally the best chamber and often the room to which the family proper withdrew to dine separately from the servants' mess in the hall.

14. How slaveholding hastened the spread of genteel consumption in the region is the subject of Cary Carson, "Banqueting Houses and the 'Need of Society' among Slave-Owning Planters in the Chesapeake Colonies," *William and Mary Quarterly*, 3rd ser., 70, no. 4 (October 2013): 725–80.

15. For general treatments of this theme see, in particular, Carole Shammas, *The Pre-Industrial Consumer in England and America* (New York: Oxford University Press, 1990); Richard L. Bushman, *The Refinement of America: Persons, Houses, Cities* (New York: Knopf, 1992); Cary Carson, *Face Value: The Consumer Revolution and the Colonizing of America* (Charlottesville: University of Virginia Press, 2017).

16. Inventory of the estate of Severn Eyre (d. 1728), August 14, 1728, Wills, Deeds, etc., Northampton County, Virginia, 1725–1733, 151–54. The list of goods is not organized room by room and mingles stocks of merchandise, especially dry goods, with household possessions. Severn wore many hats—planter, lawyer, magistrate, and, not least of all, merchant.

17. Inventory of the estate of Littleton Eyre (d. 1768), October 14, 1769, Northampton County Wills & Inventories, No. 24, 1766–1772, 224–26. Littleton's father, Severn (d. 1728) had divided his valuable plate and perhaps other bequests between his two sons. When the younger son died soon afterwards, his inheritance passed to the older brother, Littleton, bringing the family's possessions back into single ownership again. It was only the first in a long string of lucky breaks that kept the collection largely intact.

18. Inventory of the estate of Severn Eyre (d. 1773), February 27, 1774, Northampton County Wills & Inventories, No. 25, 1775–1777, 390–400.

19. The catalogue was prepared by McKenzie Long, "Eyre Family Library Catalogue," typescript report (2017), William and Mary Eyre Hall Project archives.

20. A tally is appended to Sam Florer, "Land and People: The Foundational Elements of the Wealth and Influence of the Eyre Family," typescript report (2018), William and Mary Eyre Hall Project archives.

21. Will of John Eyre, February 21, 1855, Northampton County Wills, No. 39, 1854–1897, 22–25.

22. Joyce Curtis Ramassar, interview with George McDaniel, July 30, 2019, William and Mary Eyre Hall Project archives.

23. Will of John Eyre (my italics). He further provided "that my aged servants Nat and Nancy shall be permitted to reside in a house on the Eyre Hall estate, whereon I now reside, to be designated for that purpose, and be permitted to occupy and cultivate one acre of ground to be annexed to such house. And I further direct, that these aged servants be not required to perform any service by any legatee of mine; and in the event of their standing in need of any of the ordinary comforts of life, I request that the same shall be furnished by my grandnephew Severn Eyre." Nat is identified as John Eyre's butler by Fanny Fielding [pseud.], "Southern Homesteads. Eyre Hall," *The Land We Love* 3, no. 6 (October 1867): 507–11.

THE
CHANGING
FORTUNES OF
THE EYRE FAMILY
THROUGH FOUR
CENTURIES

Golden Quarter

CARL R. LOUNSBURY

THE EASTERN SHORE IN THE MID–SEVENTEENTH CENTURY

IN 1657 SURGEON THOMAS EYRE AND HIS WIFE SUSANNA Baker Eyre and their three young children—John, Thomas, and Daniel—lived on a two-hundred-acre plantation near the southern tip of Virginia's Eastern Shore in an area known as Magothy Bay. They were part of a dispersed rural community of first- and second-generation immigrants who faced enormous hardships in such an isolated place. A series of low-lying, sandy barrier islands on the east buffered the narrow peninsula from the full force of Atlantic storms, but the shallow waters around them provided difficult access and anchorage for large ocean-going vessels (Fig. 4). On the Chesapeake Bay side to the west, a number of small inlets and creeks provided welcoming havens for smaller ships, which had attracted the first handful of English colonists to the Eastern Shore in the 1620s. In the following decades settlers and speculators patented and occupied lands along Hungars Creek and Cherrystone Creek in the north, King's Creek, Old Plantation Creek, and Magothy Bay 20 miles to the south.[1] They cleared forests and scrubland to scratch out a living on tobacco plantations worked by family members, indentured white servants, some Native Americans, and a few Africans whose legal status was yet to be clearly determined. By mid-century, perhaps a thousand people occupied this wind-swept land, most of whom, like Thomas Eyre, were relatively recent arrivals.[2]

Thomas Eyre's plantation stood approximately halfway between the eight miles that separated Old Plantation Creek in the north and Cape Charles in the south. The waters of the bay formed the western edge of the Eyre farm, which extended eastward beyond the clearing containing the house lot, garden, and small fields where hills of corn and tobacco grew. Further inland, there may have been marshes where cattle grazed, and on the farm's periphery there were stands of woodlands where hogs rooted, wild game roamed, and predators such as panthers and wolves lurked.[3] Emanating from Eyre's small frame dwelling, a path may have led to a nearby boat landing and others would have wound through the woods to the homes of neighbors.

Overland travel was difficult. To get anywhere, most people walked—to their neighbor's house, to an alehouse, to church, to a tobacco landing, or to the place where the county court convened. Before mid-century, horses were few; Thomas Eyre owned one, which he bought from a neighbor. With a medical bag filled with instruments and nostrums saddled to his horse, Eyre could reach people more quickly, especially when he was called upon to administer "physic" to those who fell ill. Even so, accessible horse paths were far from common, bridges few, and marshes, bogs, and broad and deep creeks created obstructions. In 1673 George Fox, the inveterate English Quaker proselytizer, spoke of being habitually soaked as he traveled through the "many bad watry swamps and marshy ways" in the region.

Travel by water was far more common. Ferries existed in some places. People used canoes, boats, and small ships to get around the peninsula or "across the water" to the western shore of the colony. The water provided faster movement but could also prove perilous, as Fox discovered. One day, he sailed 50 miles from Annemessex River in Somerset County to Hungars Creek but had "rough weather in our passage to this place and were in great danger, for the boat . . . turned over; and I lost my hat and cap."[4]

Though the absence of roads and bridges and the relative scarcity of horses in the first decades of settlement prevented convenient overland travel and the bay limited contact for many residents of the Eastern Shore with colonists across the bay, they were far from being cut off from communication with the outside world. In fact, trade connections opened up the Eastern Shore to the Atlantic world.[5] Its merchants and great tobacco planters developed business links with a wide variety of partners who came calling in their sloops and brigantines. English merchants supplied the colonists with essential manufactured goods, organized the transportation of emigrants, and collected hogsheads of tobacco to ship home to a market that at mid-century seemed insatiable.

As early as the 1630s there was an active intercolonial trade with New England, New Netherlands, and the Caribbean. From bayside landings, ships loaded with corn, livestock, tobacco, and naval stores embarked for Boston, New Haven, New Amsterdam, and islands in the Caribbean. By 1643 trade was so brisk that the Dutch in New Amsterdam erected a stone inn "to accommodate the English who daily passed with their vessels from New England to Virginia."[6] Mariners from New England often stopped in the bay to pick up corn and pork as well as lumber, pitch, and tar, which they carried southward to Barbados, Antigua, and Jamaica (after 1655). One of them who plied this route regularly in the 1640s was Captain William Strangridge of Boston, who partnered with local merchants like Edward Drew. Strangridge sailed into the Chesapeake with cargoes of rum, sugar, brandy, and slaves from Caribbean islands and carried Eastern Shore tobacco and corn northward to New Amsterdam and Boston on his return. After Edward Drew's death in 1652, the Boston mariner married Mary, his widow, and moved into Drew's house on land that would become known as Eyre Hall Neck.[7] When Strangridge died two years later, the web of commercial ties developed by Drew and Strangridge were taken over by Drew's former trusted servant and business agent, William Kendall, who not only maintained but increased the business established by his predecessors.

Dutch ships filled the Chesapeake Bay from the 1630s through the early 1650s, when the first of the Anglo-Dutch wars disrupted bonds of trade between the English colonists and Dutch merchants and mariners. The Dutch exchanged household wares including pottery, textiles, and ironware, consumer items such as clay pipes, as well as luxury goods like glassware and books, for tobacco. Even manufactured building materials found eager customers. Each fall, the Dutch competed for this tobacco crop with English and colonial ships. In 1643, 30 English ships and four Dutch ones gathered at the mouth of the bay to begin lading their holds with hogsheads of tobacco. Matching planters with ships was something of a scramble, and mariners who had established relations with planters often fared better than those who arrived without them. David Peterson DeVries, a Dutch captain active in the Chesapeake trade, observed in 1635 that those Dutch merchants "who wish to trade here, must keep a home here, and continue all year, that he may be prepared, when the tobacco comes from the field, to seize it, if he would obtain his debts. It is thus the English do among

Fig. 4. Detail of a map drawn by Augustine Herrman, ca. 1670.

themselves; so that there is no trade for us, unless there be an overplus of tobacco, and few English ships."[8]

For the Dutch to have an impact on the Chesapeake tobacco trade, they needed to develop a network of local agents, which became more feasible when the English Civil War disrupted shipping between London and Virginia. At the height of the conflict—between 1643 and 1649— some 33 Dutch ships were active in that tobacco trade.[9] Some importers who had operated from Rotterdam, Amsterdam, and New Amsterdam realized the wisdom of DeVries's observation and immigrated to the source of their business. Dutch merchants John Cornelius, John

Michael, and William Westerhouse traded for a number of years from Amsterdam before they, alongside John Custis, the Rotterdam-born son of English parents, settled permanently in Northampton County, strengthening those connections.[10] A few arrived in a roundabout manner. Born and trained in his native city of Cologne, Dr. George Hack moved to Amsterdam where he became engaged in business ventures and married a Dutch woman, Ann Varlet. The couple immigrated to New Amsterdam in 1646 where he resumed his mercantile activities. Five years later, they settled on the Eastern Shore and raised tobacco, which he exported successfully on the strength of the commercial ties that he had established in both cities. Ann's sister Jane married Augustine Herrman, a German-speaking native of Prague who was also a merchant and cartographer. They lived in New Amsterdam where Herrman worked for the Dutch West India Company before moving to the upper Eastern Shore of Maryland. Like his brother-in-law, Herrman continued to trade with his erstwhile employers in New Amsterdam as well as practice his skills as a mapmaker (see Fig. 4).

Until he tangled with the Dutch in the early 1650s—when relations between the English Commonwealth government and the Dutch Republic moved from maritime rivalry to open warfare as London merchants tried to recover their once dominant position in the tobacco trade—Edmund Scarburgh II, one of the most entrepreneurial of the planter-merchants to settle on the Eastern Shore, had extensive connections with New Amsterdam besides his links to New England merchants. His father, Edmund I, was a native of East Anglia and trained as a barrister in London, where Edmund II was born in 1617. Edmund Scarburgh I and some of his family emigrated to Virginia in the late 1620s with considerable resources at their disposal. He patented many acres on the Eastern Shore around Magothy Bay and was a commissioner of the county court and a member of the House of Burgesses at the time of his death in 1635.[11] His son Edmund II stepped into his father's role as one of the leading merchant-planters of Eastern Shore society and aggressively expanded his business contacts in the New World. He purchased slaves in Manhattan and transported them to the Eastern Shore where he claimed their headrights, which allowed him to obtain additional land.[12]

Not only did Scarburgh grow tobacco for export to the Dutch and other trading partners, but he diversified the local economy by setting up salt-making and shoe-making operations. His investment in the latter business was extensive. In 1663 he fretted about the quality and limited supply of hides being produced by local tanners that prevented his nine shoemakers from being fully employed

in their trade.[13] Archaeological excavations in the late 1980s along the shoreline of Stephen Charlton's Church Neck plantation just south of the mouth of Nassawaddox Creek revealed the remains of eight wells used in the mid-century manufacture of leather products including shoes (Fig. 5). The shoes may have been fabricated for a colonial market across the bay, but some may have been destined for the Caribbean plantations.[14] Like Scarburgh, Charlton loaded his ships and those of English, Dutch, and Virginia merchants with his workmen's goods in addition to tobacco, corn, wheat, and peas that his servants and slaves raised in nearby fields.

Despite the efforts of merchant-planters such as Scarburgh and Charlton to diversify the economy of the Eastern Shore, tobacco remained its driving force through the third quarter of the seventeenth century, when the price of tobacco began to slump and poor soils and exhausted fields made its production less competitive with other parts of the tobacco coast. Like most colonists in Virginia who staked their economic livelihood on the production of tobacco, those who wished to profit by the trade required lots of laborers beyond household members to cultivate and harvest their crops. They found their source in the hundreds of English men and women who sought better prospects in the colonies. Although a few families emigrated to the Chesapeake together, most of those who sailed to the New World came individually, and of these, boys and young men far surpassed women in number.[15] With few kinsmen to welcome them, most had only their labor to offer. And there were many rapacious men waiting to exploit their one asset once they stepped ashore. As one Dutch mariner observed, "the English are a villainous people, and would sell their own fathers for servants."[16]

Merchants, ships' captains, and middlemen paid for the transportation of most servants to Virginia, and in exchange these passengers contractually bound themselves to planters for a set number of years of servitude. They were required to

Fig. 5. Detail from 1987 excavation of one of the barrel wells and a well-preserved shoe associated with Stephen Charlton's shoemaking operations (ca. 1650) at his Church Neck plantation on the bay.

work the tobacco fields, grow corn, manage livestock, and perform other farm duties and received in turn "sufficient meat, drink, apparel, washing and lodging"; at the end of their term, they were given a suit of clothes, a few barrels of corn, and perhaps some tools. Servants became integral members of a planter's household, living, working, eating, sleeping, and socializing in small cramped dwellings; they either gained by these circumscribed arrangements or else endured the petty and more consequential tyrannies of masters and mistresses. At the time of his death in 1665, the 30-year-old planter John Severn, Jr. lived in a two-room house along with his younger brother Peter and two servants. A widower, Severn and perhaps his brother slept in a bed in the hall, while John Farthing and Nicholas Barnes occupied the smaller, unheated inner "room where the servants lye." Members of this household cooked over the hearth in the hall, took their meals at a table seated in leather chairs, and stored household items in trunks and a gun and their plantation tools in corners of the crowded room.[17]

Some servants were treated well by their employers during the time when they were put to the hoe. When a servant girl who worked for Thomas Leatherberry died, his wife wept at her funeral at the "loss of soe good a servant that was good natured & soe good company."[18] A few individuals were remembered in the wills of their masters, often receiving livestock, clothing, or a reduction in their terms of service. When Edward Brunt completed his servitude with John Severn, Jr., his former master offered to

continue his "diet & lodging till such tyme as by his striving he might be able to provide for himself."[19] But others suffered grievously by hard-driving and grasping men who thought little of exploiting their labor. A jury of inquest, convened in December 1653 to ascertain the cause of death of Christopher Corke, a servant who worked for surgeon John Billyotte and his wife Bridget, discovered that he fled his master and mistress's household after they had beaten him. Corke hid in the wilds where he suffered from the cold and eventually starved to death. The jury determined that he died from his own negligence.[20]

The chances of this large population of freed English male servants setting up as small planters themselves on land of their own, getting married, and raising a family on the Eastern Shore were relatively slim. For one thing, an unbalanced sex ratio made finding marriage partners difficult, even if these servants survived their indentures and gained their freedom. Women who lost their husbands seldom remained widows for long. Landless laborers won few hands. Many former servants could not afford to buy land and became long-standing tenants rather than freeholders. Without money to purchase land or labor and expand their own plantations, tenants rarely ascended the social scale, but eked out a living on the margins.

All of those who chose to live in this land faced a harsh reality. The Chesapeake was as much a death trap as a beacon of opportunity. Diseases such as small pox, malaria, dysentery, and other fatal disorders struck all members of colonial society with a disturbing frequency that even surprised many in an era when early death was commonplace. Some may have brought their disease with them to the New World—such was the case of Richard and Edward Newport, two gentlemen who soon after landing were quarantined at Argall Yeardley's house where they were attended by surgeon John Stringer for eight days before they died of the "contagious disease called the plague." Although Stringer became sick in the performance of his duties, he survived and was rewarded the dead men's clothing as part of his compensation.[21] Accidents, the wear and tear of hard toil, and irresponsible behavior took their toll on many. The waters that surrounded and bisected this land could prove fatal for those who were caught in storms or others who could not swim. Nicholas Spratlen died from falling off his horse; orphan Elizabeth Pope was killed in the house of her master when a gun was "unintentionally discharged" by a young servant; Irish servant Ellinor Cowell died as a result of being accidentally hit with a stone thrown by her mistress Katherine Pannuell; and after a night of drinking, John Cottman suffered a nasty end when, lying face down, he "merely suffocated in his own vomit."[22] Perhaps more common was the fate of William Williams who had been weakened by disease, but tainted food and improper care by his mistress finished him off.[23]

Unfortunately, many healthy newcomers perished within a year of landing. Yet even those who withstood this period of "seasoning" were not guaranteed a long life whether rich merchant or poor laborer. Life expectancy in the Chesapeake during this period was about 40 years. Most marriages dissolved within a decade with the death of the wife or husband. Second marriages of surviving spouses created mixed families of half-siblings, uprooting children from familiar patterns and thrusting them into new households. Childbirth too often proved fatal to mother or offspring. A quarter of the children born perished before they reached their first birthday, and half of those who

survived infancy died before they reached their twentieth birthday.[24] After a clandestine affair with John Kendall, the nephew of her employer, Colonel William Kendall, Bristol-born servant Anne Orthwood died very shortly after giving birth to twins, one of whom did not survive.[25] Although the circumstances were sordid, the fate of Orthwood and her unnamed child was all too common.

To sustain its population growth, Chesapeake society depended upon the continued influx of newcomers. A boom in tobacco prices from the late 1630s through the middle of the 1650s encouraged men of means, including a number of long-time residents, to patent additional tracts often based on headrights, which granted 50 acres of land for every new immigrant sponsored or purchased by the patentee. By mid-century, many of the great planters like Edmund Scarburgh had begun to purchase African laborers (some of whom were indentured for life, that is were considered slaves, but others of whom were granted or were able to purchase their freedom and lived precariously within the legal margins of local and provincial laws that had yet to set inflexible codes of racialized slavery).[26] By these means, the complexion of Eastern Shore society was transformed, as new faces replaced those who had died or moved away. With such instability, merchants and planters of substantial means could quickly take their place among the leaders of this plantation society by patenting large tracks of land and assembling a large force of indentured laborers. In 1640, one of the earliest great planters on the Eastern Shore, Nathaniel Littleton, patented 3,500 acres "for his own personal adventure and Anna his wife" whose father, Henry Southey, was granted 900 acres in 1627. For this land on Magothy Bay, Littleton was responsible for the transportation of 15 Africans. Among the 36 whites who were claimed by Littleton in the patent were Daniel Baker, the brother of Eyre's wife Susanna. Even men of far more modest means could assemble a plantation through the transportation of family members and servants. In the same year that Littleton took up his substantial landholdings, a neighbor, Dr. John Severn, who had been in Northampton County since at least 1638, was granted 300 acres for the transportation of himself, his wife Bridgett Severn, son, John Severn, Jr., William Stephens, Abraham Merifield, and John Pott, a nephew of his wife.[27]

ESTABLISHING COMMUNITY: THE FIRST THREE GENERATIONS OF EYRES, ca. 1650–1728

Despite their geographic isolation, the overweening dependence upon tobacco—which required a constant supply of a large underclass of servant and slave labor—the deadly, disease-ridden environment in which they worked, and the consequent flux in population, the mid-seventeenth-century inhabitants of Northampton and Accomack Counties slowly began to construct familial, social, economic, and institutional bonds that would tie them together. This process of creating a community out of a disparate group of settlers is most evident at the neighborhood level and can be pieced together from the county court records—the best evidence to survive, conveying, in fragmented and often incomplete details, how that process evolved.[28] The first documents for Northampton County (which originally included all the peninsula south of Maryland before the northern part was split off in 1663 to form Accomack County) begin in 1632. These books contain not only legal disputes about land and property, but the transcriptions of depositions in civil and criminal cases, wills, deeds, and inventories that minutely list all the goods and chattels of the deceased. They provide the raw material from which to weave a history of the Eyre family and their contemporaries. In a largely illiterate society where letters were few and surviving personal papers rare, these records sometimes captured the opinions of the powerless and the beliefs of the long-forgotten.

Freighted with experiences, customs, and prejudices about work, land, authority, community, and family formed in England, Europe, Africa, in colonial settlements stretching from New England to the Caribbean, and in Native American lands, Northampton inhabitants discovered that this isolated environment reshaped many of those perceptions and expectations. Whereas some thrived, others floundered in frontier conditions where many traditional material comforts were severely circumscribed. Living conditions for many were far more marginal than English and European standards that they had left behind. The traditional arrangements of domestic space in English farmhouses according to gender and status could not be fully replicated in small, rudely finished dwellings such as the two-room structure occupied by people like John Severn, Jr. and his servants.[29]

Settlers faced disruptive breaches and distortions in their accustomed social order in this frontier, where Old World tailors with a bit of good fortune might find themselves sitting as judges in the county court, much to the annoyance of those who thought themselves better-born. The privilege of superior status was hard earned. Harsh words spoken in haste sometimes escalated into violent confrontations in a culture where the line between discipline and abuse was narrowly drawn. Cruelty to servants was commonplace. Because of the appalling death rate, an orderly hierarchy of society based on wealth and land ownership—which passed from one generation to the next—was slow to mature. All newcomers needed to assert their right to land and labor based on what personal capital they brought with them rather than what they had inherited in this place. Africans and Native Americans stood outside early modern European cultural norms, and the idea of slavery—with its degradation of individuals based on their race—was justified and took root in a place where success became vested in those who could command a perpetual workforce of laborers.

THOMAS AND SUSANNA BAKER EYRE: THE FIRST GENERATION

The world that Thomas and Susanna Eyre had created for their family on Magothy Bay came to a shattering end in November 1657. Having become "dangerous sicke & weake," Thomas prepared his will on November 18, making his wife the sole executrix of his estate. He died shortly thereafter, and on November 30 his will was presented in the Northampton County court by neighbors "Thomas Harmar, gent. & Stephen Costen, planter" for probate by the magistrates, which included Captain Francis Pott and Mr. William Kendall.[30]

The few items enumerated in the will reveal a family of modest means. Thomas Eyre bequeathed his house and plantation to his eldest son John, who was to inherit it when he turned 18. John also received five head of cattle and the "breeding horse" that his father bought from his neighbor Stephen Costen. The two-hundred-acre plantation was all the land that Thomas owned, so his two younger sons, Thomas II and Daniel, received no land. Instead, their father left them the remainder of the herd of cattle that he possessed. The only other chattel mentioned in the will was Thomas's red suit and leather stockings and common wearing clothes, all of which he gave to his "friend" Stephen Costen along with his fishing line, shot, and his "great gun."[31] There is no mention of other lands in his possession, slaves, or indentured servants. Nor are there references to any family members beyond the immediate household in the county, colony, or England who would be legatees. Outside the farm on Magothy Bay and a little more than a dozen cattle and a horse, there was no great estate that would sustain his children. Such was the legacy of Thomas Eyre to the second generation of young boys, the oldest of whom, John, was no more than eight or nine.[32]

The recording of Thomas Eyre's will in probate in the Northampton County courtroom in November 1657 reveals nearly everything we know of his life. The progenitor of the Eyre family is little more than a cipher, for there is so much about his origins and life that is lost. We do not know how old he was when he died; we do not know how long he was married to Susanna Baker or where he met her; we do not know when he arrived in Virginia or why he chose to settle where he did; we do not know where he trained or practiced as a surgeon; we do not where he was born and raised; and we know nothing of his parentage.

Of Thomas Eyre's English origins, a number of genealogies have asserted his connection to various branches of the Eyre family that had thrived in many parts of England since the Middle Ages, but none have proven conclusive. The two most prominent branches resided in northwest Derbyshire (Jane Eyre country of Charlotte Brontë) and in Wiltshire, while there were also Eyres in the rapidly expanding metropolis of London in the late Elizabethan period.[33] Eyres, spelled variously as Ayers, Ayres, Aires, Eyers, and Eires (as in Thomas's will of 1657), show up in New England and Virginia in the seventeenth century but none appear to be linked to Thomas.[34]

At the beginning of the twentieth century, historian Lyon G. Tyler alleged that Thomas Eyre had a brother named Robert and that the two men "may have been sons of Thomas Ayres or Eyres who was one of the company to settle at Warrascoyack in Isle of Wight County in 1622" under the leadership of the Puritan merchant Edward Bennett.[35] However, subsequent research failed to confirm this supposition, and Thomas Ayres does not appear in Virginia records. He seems to have been a business associate of Bennett and an investor in the settlement scheme rather than an actual colonist. A William Ayres may have been related to the London businessman Thomas Ayers. William Ayres patented land in Isle of Wight County in 1635 and Lower Norfolk County in 1642. He eventually wound up in Maryland, settling with other Bennett Puritans from Virginia in the town of Providence in what would later become Anne

Arundel County. In 1655 Ayres died at the Battle of the Severn, a skirmish between the Puritan settlers, who refused to swear allegiance to Lord Baltimore, the proprietor of the colony, and a Catholic militia from St. Mary's City led by Governor William Stone.[36]

Robert Eyre, the man whom Tyler thought may have been Thomas Eyre's brother, first appears in Virginia documents in 1638, where he is described as a tobacco planter living on the Elizabeth River in Lower Norfolk County.[37] Born between 1609 and 1612 in England, Eyre must have been a planter of some means since he was elected to represent the county in the House of Burgesses in 1646 and then again in 1648.[38] By 1649 he is cited with the honorific title "Gent." Robert's only relative noted in the court records was an older cousin, Peregrine Bland, a Cambridge graduate, who represented Charles River (York County) in the House of Burgesses in the 1639–40 session. If Robert Eyre had any familial connection to the Eastern Shore, it was established posthumously. When he died in 1651 his widow, Elizabeth Robinson Eyre, married John Custis, who had recently moved from Rotterdam to Northampton County where his sister Ann Custis Yeardley lived with her husband Argall Yeardley, a large landowner and son of Sir George Yeardley, an early governor of the colony.[39]

One further genealogical origins story has clouded Thomas Eyre's beginnings in Northampton County. Before he died in 1691, Thomas's youngest son Daniel had become a Quaker, as did a number of settlers on the Eastern Shore in the second half of the seventeenth century. Mary, one of Daniel's daughters, married into the prominent Littleton family of Magothy Bay in 1712. Her husband, Southey Littleton, had converted to Quakerism when he married. Sadly, Littleton died within the year, leaving his young widow with more than 4,050 acres in the region as well as other land in Accomack County. By 1714 she had met and married Edward Mifflin, the scion of a prominent Quaker family of Philadelphia.[40] In the genealogical history of the Mifflin family published in 1905, Hilda Justice repeated a traditional story that tied the first Thomas Eyre to the Quaker cause. She noted that Thomas "was sent down by William Penn, commissioned to aid in establishing Quaker Meeting Houses on the peninsula. He was a man of some wealth, and bequeathed lands to his sons, John, Thomas and Daniel."[41] Unfortunately, this story stretches credulity since Thomas died in 1657 when William Penn was only 13 years old and still an Anglican. The Quakers had barely consolidated their identity and principles under the dynamic leadership of George Fox in the early 1650s. Quakers appeared in the colonies in the 1650s and suffered grievously in New England among the Puritan faithful; unwelcome in Virginia, they did however make inroads in Maryland where, except for Catholic strongholds around the capital of St. Mary's City, organized denominational religion had scarcely taken root. This posthumous anointment of Thomas Eyre as a Quaker has muddied genealogical studies for more than a century. And as Thomas Eyre's will makes clear, he was not a wealthy man when he died. He left land to his eldest son, John, but not to Thomas and Daniel. The Eyre family route to wealth and power did not start in Jamestown in the earliest decades of the colony; it did not spring from an extended family or a powerful patron, nor was it part of an early wave of Quaker migration. Thomas Eyre's origins remain obscure.

The Northampton County court documents do little to shed light on Thomas Eyre's life on the Eastern Shore. Though among the most complete records of any county in Virginia for the seventeenth century, Eyre hardly left a trace in them. The earliest dates to 1643 when a merchant's invoice included payment of £4 for a book for "Mr. Tho: Eyres," which indicates not only his presence in Northampton County for the first time, but, because of its high value, perhaps relates to his practice of medicine.[42] The courtesy appellation "Mr." also suggests the social status of a "chirurgeon," as his occupation was spelled at the time, a measure of respect not usually given to servants. Even so, Eyre does not show up in the county records in his capacity as a medical practitioner. He apparently did not make house calls on behalf of the court as did others in his profession.

Eyre's appearance in the county records is rare. His name is not among those of the 180 men in Northampton who swore allegiance to the English Commonwealth in late March 1651.[43] Perhaps he was ill at home, harbored loyalty to the martyred king, or was out of the county when his neighbors appended their names to the petition declaring their fealty to the new government. Eyre seems to have been neither a litigious man who took any grievances against his patients or neighbors to court nor an active speculator in land transactions.[44] In fact, he may not have settled on his bayside plantation until 1654. The 200 acres had been patented in 1636 by Robert Drake of Merstham, Surrey. After his death the same year, members of his family continued to reside there, including his daughter Jane Drake, who had married Thomas Parramore, an early settler on the Eastern Shore who had arrived in Virginia in 1622. Parramore continued overseeing the farm for the Drake family until he was ordered by Robert Drake, Jr. to surrender the plantation in 1654 to Captain Richard Hill.[45] Presumably, Robert Drake, Jr., who was living in London, arranged through Hill to sell the property to Thomas Eyre, though no deed of such a transaction has been traced.

Perhaps because of his recent arrival in the community, Eyre did not serve as a witness to wills or deeds, nor was he selected to inventory the goods of deceased neighbors. Outside his own immediate household, Thomas Eyre does not appear to have had siblings, cousins, or other relatives on the Eastern Shore—at least, none are mentioned in his will. Unlike her husband, Susanna did have a family member nearby. Her brother Daniel had emigrated to Northampton County, perhaps from London, at least by 1640, when he was named as one of the individuals in Nathaniel Littleton's headright grant of land that year. He may have accumulated some land in the ensuing years, but he seems to have been a trusted tenant or perhaps an overseer for Littleton and subsequently for other important planters in the area, including Francis Pott followed by William Kendall.[46]

In the little community of Magothy Bay, neighbors looked after one another in small ways and large. Taking care of orphaned children was one of them. In making her will in 1656, Ann Littleton, the widow of the wealthy Colonel Nathaniel Littleton, specified that their daughter Esther, then age eight, was "to be with Mrs. Eyres until 10, and Mrs. Ayres to have 800 lbs. tob. as formerly paid her yearly." Following those two years in the Eyre household, Ann stipulated that her daughter was to be looked after until she was 14 by Mrs. Isabella Douglas, another neighbor and wife of a justice in Magothy Bay, Edward Douglas.[47] The will suggests that Esther Littleton had already resided with the Eyre family and, if the terms of the will were kept, she may have been some help and comfort to Susanna when Thomas Eyre died the following year.

Those who lived in the neighborhood were also cognizant of behavior that sometimes warranted intervention by parish and county authorities from petty crimes of theft to the mistreatment of servants and spouses. When Elizabeth Lewis Spratt and John Stephens were presented by the churchwardens to the court for prosecution for scandalous sexual relations in 1654, Thomas Eyre and his neighbors Mathew Gethings and Nicholas Bernard testified to their misconduct, which resulted in the couple's public shaming by being whipped on their "naked shoulders."[48]

Three years later, Susanna Eyre was examined by magistrate Edward Douglas whose task it was to investigate the suspicious death of her neighbor Elizabeth Severn. In her deposition, made in July 1657, she recalled that "Elizabeth ye wife of Mr. Jno Severne" told her "that Mathew Gethinges & Ellynor his wife were ye occasion of difference, & chiefe cause of the disagreement of ye sd Mr. John Severne & his late wife." Susanna went on to describe how Elizabeth "hath complained to me that her husband thrust her out of doors & beat her." Susanna had advised her to complain about the abusive behavior to their neighbor, a magistrate and John Severn, Jr.'s uncle, Francis Pott, "which she sd Elizabeth did; & acquainted him wth ye hard usage she had from her husband; but after yt (as ye woman hath told your deponent) her husband (Mr. Severne) used her worse." Elizabeth Severn spoke several times to her neighbor Susanna Eyre of how her husband not only "expressed himself very harsh, & violent towards her both in words and actions; but procured & made most of his Neighbors her adversaries," and used such calumny in trying to turn Susanna and her husband Thomas against her, whom she hoped would "still be my friends." Susanna sympathized with her plight and worried that through her "words & signes" the "poor woman . . . was intending either to drowne, or other ways make away herself." Susanna believed that she dissuaded "her from yt intent & practice; Telling her that she ought to have respect & regard to her Soule, rather than her body, and take some better course than bring her life to an untimely end."[49]

John Stephens, the man who had been punished for his sexual misconduct three years previously, confirmed the ill-usage of Elizabeth Severn by her husband "who would not allow her Cloathes (fit for a woman to goe amongst her Neighbors)" and reiterated the fact that "Mathew Gethinge & his wife were ye chiefe cause of ye bad usage she recd from her husband (as testified by Mrs. Susanna Ayres) and may be further witnessed by other of our Neighbors, att Maggottey baye."[50] Despite these testimonies before the local magistrate, there is no evidence that John Severn, Jr. was brought to trial for the untimely death of his wife nor that was he ostracized by his neighbors for his unconscionable treatment of her.[51] Within three years, Severn had remarried. His new wife was Damaris, the daughter of Mathew and Eleanor Gethings, the couple who had spoken so ill of Severn's first wife. On May 13, 1661, Damaris gave birth to a daughter, Jane Severn.[52]

Susanna had scarcely the time to absorb the death of her maligned neighbor Elizabeth Severn when her husband Thomas died in November 1657. Perhaps in her late twenties or early thirties with three young children and a small farm, Susanna needed help holding her family and its livelihood together.[53] In the small world of Magothy Bay, Susanna's loss would have been well known, and there were many men willing to take on the responsibility of looking after this widow and her children. Her neighbor, Captain Francis Pott, was quick to offer his hand; Susanna accepted, and the two were married early in the new year. It was a fortuitous match for Susanna and her sons. Francis Pott was a wealthy and well-connected man. He had been in Virginia for many years. His brother, Dr. John Pott, briefly served as governor of the colony, from 1629 to 1630. In the early 1630s Francis was commander at Old Point Comfort until he and his brother had a falling-out with Governor John Harvey in 1635 and spent a number of years thereafter in England. When John Pott died childless in the early 1640s, Francis inherited his lands in Virginia and returned to settle as a planter in Northampton County, perhaps to be near one of his sisters, Bridget Pott Severn, who had married Dr. John Severn, and was the mother of the odious John Severn, Jr.[54] Between then and his marriage to Susanna Eyre a dozen years later, Francis purchased or patented additional lands on which English servants and African slaves planted tobacco and raised livestock.[55] As he prospered in his business ventures, Pott was selected as a justice on the county court and served as its sheriff in 1655.

In August 1658, after only a few months together in their new domestic arrangements, Pott said goodbye to his "dear friend and my entirely loved wife" Susanna and traveled to the colony's mainland, "having taken a sudden resolution to go over the Bay about some urgent occasions." Realizing that he had not put his affairs at home in order, he hastily wrote a will. With no children of his own, Pott devised to his nephews John Pott, John and Peter Severn "all my lands contained in 2 patents, one for 1500 acres and the other for 1000 acres." He left various sums of money to friends in England and Virginia as well as to his godchildren, cousin, and three sisters. The rest of his personal estate, including slaves, he left to his wife, along with "all my land in Magattbay, viz. Golden Quarter [1,500 acres] and lands bought of Mr. Edmond Scarburgh and 1000 acres" at Mockhorn Island on the seaside of the lower Eastern Shore. Pott designated Susanna as executrix. His foreboding proved prescient. Within a few weeks of making his will, Pott died. On October 28, 1658, the will was proved in court.[56] Less than a year after the death of her first husband, Susanna Baker Eyre Pott found herself a wealthy widow, but her life and those of her children were turned upside down once again, if only briefly.

By late December 1658, Susanna had remarried, this time to another prominent merchant-planter and magistrate of the Northampton County court, Colonel William Kendall.[57] The family left Magothy Bay and moved north to Kendall's plantation on a branch of the Cherrystone Creek now known as Eyreville. John, Thomas, and Daniel had to adjust to a new home and their second stepfather in a little over a year. They also became members of an expansive household that included Colonel Kendall's nephew, John Kendall, Susanna's brother Daniel Baker, as well as a number of indentured servants and slaves. The family expanded when Susanna Kendall gave birth to a daughter named Mary in 1661 and a son William in 1664.[58] A heady businessman, Kendall fulfilled his role of straightening out and overseeing the settlement of the estate of his former colleague on the bench, John Pott, as he sold some of the land Susanna inherited with her agreement and made sure that her children would be provided for from the lands that Pott had left to her and the slaves that came with his estate.[59]

Over the next decade and a half, as they reached their majority and took control of their inheritance, John, Thomas, and Daniel were educated in the ways of plantation management and mercantile practices. Kendall amassed thousands of acres of land through patents and purchase, much of which he resold. He owned several plantations beyond the immediate home farm at Eyreville on which he grew cash crops and raised livestock for export and domestic consumption. In the 1660s there were sometimes as many as 20 tithables associated with his household including indentured servants, slaves, and sailors.[60] As a merchant, he imported goods from abroad and owned interests in several ships as his trading connections extended to New England, New Amsterdam, and England. As a politician, Colonel Kendall succeeded not only in the county ranks—becoming the senior magistrate and head of the militia—but as a member of the House of Burgesses, culminating in his selection as the speaker of that body in 1685.

Not only did the Eyre boys receive practical instruction in plantation affairs and politics, but they became acquainted with a variety of new consumer goods in a house that was expanded twice during Kendall's lifetime. Maps, books, furniture, silver, ceramics, and other luxury items imported from abroad filled the rooms. Susanna and her husband may have taken up the latest fashions in dress, deportment, and social customs that were spreading among the newly affluent planters of the Chesapeake, though the new English fashion for taking tea does not appear to have reached the Kendall household by this time.[61] The material welfare of the inhabitants of the Eastern Shore, the amount of things in a household, and the number of specialized objects used to clothe, cook, dine, and entertain increased markedly. Indeed, the three Eyre sons may have reflected on the differences between the conditions of their earliest childhood and the comforts and opportunities afforded to them in their stepfather's house. William Kendall did his best for his stepsons in preparing them to take their place as leaders of the next generation of slave-owning planters and merchants. Their mother Susanna sustained them through a difficult period and lived long enough to see them married and heads of their own households before she died in 1683, three years before her third husband.

THE SECOND GENERATION OF EYRES

Susanna Baker Eyre Pott Kendall's fortuitous second and third marriages insured the success of the second generation of Eyres. Although her marriage to Francis Pott was short-lived, her much longer one to William Kendall provided a stable environment in which to raise her three boys to adulthood and launch them successfully into an Eastern Shore society that was becoming more hierarchical in structure. Marriages between members of leading planter and merchant families helped consolidate their social positions, and their wealth enabled them to acquire land and purchase slaves to labor in their tobacco and grain fields and manage livestock, which enhanced their economic dominance at the expense of smaller landowners and white tenants who could not compete on such a scale. As white Virginians embraced racialized slavery expressed in the passage of a series of proscriptive acts of the provincial assembly, those free Black people who had managed to maneuver through the intricacies of race and bondage in earlier decades found their prospects severely curtailed by the end of the century.

Although there was still room at the top for a few well-connected newcomers to find a place among the elite families of Northampton and Accomack Counties, the sons and grandsons of Anglican vestrymen, court officials, and militia officers assumed the places held by their grandfathers, fathers, uncles, and cousins. No more would upstart tailors or indentured servants find these offices open to them by dint of their personality, perspicuity, or luck. Though not quite a closed shop, the elite families that emerged in the late seventeenth and early eighteenth centuries would remain at the forefront of county society for the next century.

John, Thomas, and Daniel Eyre were groomed to take their place among the emerging gentry of Northampton County. As they reached their majority, Colonel Kendall provided additional slaves, livestock, and money to help sustain their own plantations when they left his household, first John in 1669, then Thomas by 1676, followed by Daniel a few years later.[62] Kendall also actively promoted their advancement into leadership positions. With his patronage, John became a justice of the Northampton County court in 1677, an office in which he served for more than twenty years.[63] His younger brother Thomas was selected to accompany Colonel Kendall and Southey Littleton, who had been appointed in 1679 as commissioners to represent Virginia in discussions with northern Indians in Albany, New York, sponsored by New York Governor Edmund Andros.[64] Thomas later became a member of the vestry of Hungars Parish. Daniel probably learned surveying while in his stepfather's household and was responsible for surveys of county property and tracts for important landowners in the 1680s.[65]

One after another, the three Eyre brothers took up their Pott inheritance at Golden Quarter, more than 2½ square miles of land that began on the seaside of Magothy Bay near the lower end of the peninsula and extended inward to the west for a little more than a mile and northward along the tidal or "sunken marshes" along the ocean for nearly three miles (Fig. 6). Much of this area is now protected as a national wildlife refuge and state natural area preserve. After Pott's death, William Kendall had the patent reissued in his name in 1668, adding another 100 acres to the total. In 1670 the patent went directly to John, Thomas, and Daniel Eyre.[66] In 1688, after a number of years settled on their plantations, the three brothers formally exchanged deeds, which laid out the boundaries of their three shares.[67] Their inherited 1,600 acres were not contiguous, but a small section of 223 acres at the northern end was separated from the rest by a patent of 600 acres that had been granted to

Fig. 6. View looking south towards the lower end of the Eastern Shore of Virginia. The Golden Quarter plantation inherited by the second generation of Eyre brothers stretched along the seaside.

someone else.[68] Thomas took possession of 310 acres at the bottom of the peninsula where he made his home. He also took the northernmost piece of 223 acres at the top of Golden Quarter.[69] Older brother John claimed possession of 533 acres above Thomas's lower land.[70] The youngest brother Daniel received 533 acres above John's tract and was bordered on the north by the parcel of land that was not part of the Pott patent.

In addition to Pott's Golden Quarter, stepfather William Kendall supplemented their holdings (Fig. 7). In 1669, he added 40 acres to the land that John had inherited from his father in 1657, giving him 240 acres of the old Drake patent on the bayside.[71] In 1681 Kendall gave Thomas 289 acres south of Golden Quarter at the tip of the peninsula that encompassed Long Point (now an island). This gift meant that Thomas owned 599 acres at the southern tip of the county in addition to the 223 acres of discontiguous land at the north end of the Pott patent.[72] Kendall also added 200 acres to Daniel Eyre's holdings immediately to the south, bringing his total number of acres to 733.[73]

The extensive landholdings provided the means for the Eyre brothers to succeed in this maturing agricultural society in the late seventeenth century. With the land came the necessity of laborers to work the fields. Although tobacco remained a prominent staple on the Eastern Shore, the agricultural economy became more diversified as planters grew corn, oats, and wheat and raised livestock for export. The Pott and Kendall legacies also included slaves and servants to work the land and look after the animals in the fields, forests, and marshes of the Golden Quarter plantations. In addition, harvesting the bounty of the ocean and bay and shipping their produce became integral to their livelihoods.

In the late seventeenth century, racial slavery became increasingly intertwined with the tobacco economy of the Chesapeake. At mid-century many of the large planters had turned to the use of imported Africans or Caribbean-born Black people to work their tobacco fields, finding the investment in enslaved people and their offspring a much more stable and long-term profitable source of investment than the short-term indentures of British-born immigrants. In 1664 the list of tithables (white men over the age of 16 and Black men and women of or above that age) enumerated 62 Black people, which made up about 14 percent of all tithables.[74] The Pott and Kendall inheritance

Fig. 7. Detail of Herrman map of 1673 showing the location of Golden Quarter at the extreme south end of the peninsula.

two grandsons of his two daughters, who maintained the family plantations at Golden Quarter until after the Revolution.[75]

Despite his early death in 1691, Daniel Eyre left his wife and three children 733 acres and a handful of slaves. Daniel and his wife Anne Neech Eyre had become Quakers, but there were few moral qualms among this sect at this time concerning the ownership of slaves. Daniel mentions two slaves in his 1690 will. His daughter Sarah was bequeathed a boy named George and his daughter Mary received a boy named Daniel. Others were not enumerated, but, when Anne Eyre drew up her will 30 years later, there were at least a dozen enslaved members of the household. Anne gave to each of her seven grandchildren one enslaved child apiece. Her daughter Mary Mifflin received a slave woman and her children. Anne bequeathed to her son Daniel II a slave man named Daniel and a woman named Betty. Her slave Sembore was "to have liberty to go with which of my children he pleases."[76]

THOMAS II AND JANE SEVERN EYRE

The builder and subsequent owners of Eyre Hall traced their branch of the family through Thomas Eyre II, the middle son of Thomas and Susanna Baker Eyre (Fig. 8). Once established on his own in Golden Quarter in the mid-1670s, Thomas Eyre II's economic and social prospects mirrored those of his two brothers; he was endowed with land and a small number of slaves to work his plantation successfully, and he enjoyed the patronage of his stepfather William Kendall for a decade. For example, white tenant Walter Mannington had been employed for Colonel Kendall for ten years when he moved to Golden Quarter to work for Thomas in the mid-1670s.[77]

included some of those Black tithables, who became integral to the establishment and operation of the Eyre plantations at Golden Quarter in subsequent years.

The general trend among the leading families of Northampton County in the late seventeenth and early eighteenth century was the increasing use of enslaved labor for domestic service and agricultural work. The second generation of Eyres were deeply invested in this system. At the time of his death in 1719, John Eyre owned ten slaves valued at £208, which accounted for half the value of his inventoried estate. He had acquired no more land than the 774 acres that had been the legacy of his father and his stepfathers, but he divided this land and the slaves between

Fig. 8. Eyre family tree.

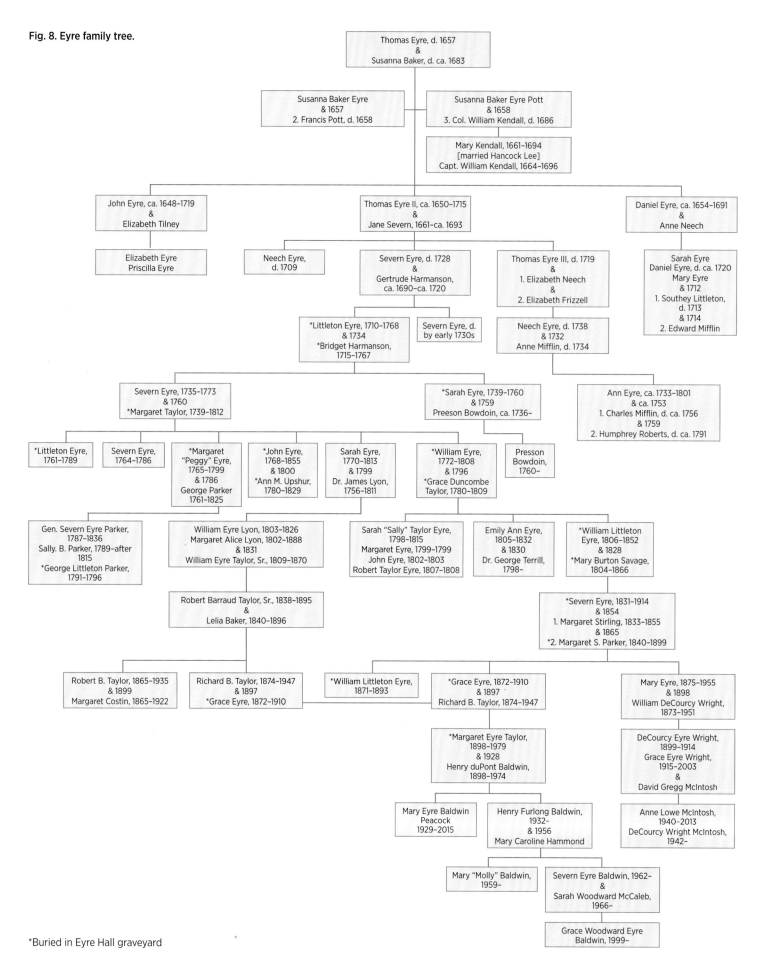

*Buried in Eyre Hall graveyard

Although few details survive to document the path and extent of his mercantile ventures, Thomas II became more than a tobacco planter, dependent upon the fluctuations in the price of this cash crop to sustain his livelihood. Like his stepfather, William Kendall, Thomas not only imported and exported goods but joined in partnerships to own ships. Located at the bottom of the peninsula, Eyre's wharf was well placed for ships to load and unload their goods. Like other merchants, he may have had a warehouse or store to house a variety of commodities or keep for display and sale in his own dwelling.

Eyre understood that there was money to be made not only in raising tobacco, grains, and livestock but in transporting them around the Chesapeake, the northern colonies, the Caribbean, and England. One of his closest business associates was Daniel Neech, a neighbor who also served as clerk of the Northampton County court for 30 years from the 1670s until his death in 1703. Fragmentary records indicate that Eyre and Neech had invested in the ownership of one or more ships. In 1692, one of their sloops was commandeered by the sheriff to transport Major John Robins and Thomas Harmanson, the two burgesses who represented Northampton County in the General Assembly, across the water so that they could attend the legislative session in Jamestown.[78] Another partner or investor in Thomas Eyre's mercantile enterprises was Captain Isaac Foxcroft.[79] Like many of those who lived on the Eastern Shore, Thomas probably fished the waters of the ocean and bay. He may have been the original owner of an oared whaleboat, iron harpoons, and lances that appeared in his son Thomas III's inventory in 1719 that also contained nearly 100 pounds of whale bones.[80]

Although he never achieved the political pinnacle of serving as a justice of the peace on the county court like his older brother John, Thomas II nonetheless became an influential leader in county society as a member of the vestry of Hungars Parish, which was composed of merchants and leading planters. His elevation to vestry can be attributed in no small part to his marriage into interconnected families of large landowners, which provided him with additional social and economic benefits.

By the early 1670s, Thomas would have been in his early twenties and of suitable age for marriage for men. In 1674 he was still listed as a tithable in William Kendall's household, but by the following year he had established his own household in Golden Quarter. Yet he appears to have put off marriage until 1677 when he married Jane Severn, the 16-year-old daughter of John Severn, Jr. What Susanna Kendall made of this union between her son Thomas and the daughter of the man she had held in such contempt in her deposition to the local magistrate some 20 years earlier is unknown.

In the small planter-merchant community of Northampton County in the second half of the seventeenth century, Thomas Eyre II would have known Jane for most of her life. Born in 1661, Jane was very young when her mother Damaris Gethings Severn died and was only four when she was orphaned by the death of her father in 1665.[81] After the death of her mother, Jane had been placed in the home of Elias Hartree and his wife Jane for a few years before their deaths.[82] Thomas Eyre's stepfather, William Kendall, intervened on behalf of Jane to administer John Severn's estate after his father-in-law Mathew Gethings had refused. After Gethings died in the late 1660s, Thomas Eyre's friend Daniel Neech, clerk of the Northampton court, married the widow Eleanor Gethings, Jane's grandmother. After her marriage to Eyre, Jane acquired the land and household goods from her grandmother as well as land devised to her on the deaths of her father and grandfather. In 1679, after Eleanor Gethings Neech had died, her husband Daniel turned over to Jane items willed to her by her grandmother, which included a variety of household goods, livestock, her clothing, her rings, and "one silver & gilt Bowle."[83] Household objects, wearing apparel, and jewelry were common items passed down through the female line, but the silver and gilt bowl was unusual in this respect and the earliest known silver that came into the Eyre family. Without male heirs, the land owned by Jane's father and her grandfather Mathew Gethings came into her possession on the death of her grandmother and her marriage to Thomas II. Jane and her husband inherited her grandfather's 175-acre patent north of Thomas Eyre I's old plantation on the bayside of Magothy Bay, which they sold in 1686.[84]

Jane and Thomas II were married for perhaps a little more than a dozen years. Jane Eyre died sometime between 1686 and 1693. From their marriage in 1677 until that time they had at least three children, all boys, who lived into adulthood—Neech, Severn, and Thomas. The youngest, Thomas III, was named for his father or grandfather. Neech, the oldest, appears to have been named after Daniel Neech. Daniel Neech lived near the family, had purchased land from Thomas and Jane, served as a witness to a number of wills of neighbors in the area along with either John, Thomas, or Daniel, all of whom were described as his good friends in documents in later years. One of Neech's children from an earlier marriage, Anne, married Daniel Eyre in the late 1670s or early 1680s.[85] That bond with the Eyres was further solidified when Thomas III married Elizabeth Neech, Daniel Neech's daughter by Margaret Saunders, his third and last wife.

Jane and Thomas's third son Severn was named after his mother's family. It was the Severn side of the family rather than the Gethings that enhanced the fortunes of Thomas Eyre II and his children. Although John Severn, Jr. proved to be an unscrupulous rascal his entire life, his mother's relatives were more reputable. The road to wealth from this side of the family was more indirect but had a much greater impact on the Eyres in the third generation by way of Thomas and Jane's middle son, Severn, through whom the Eyre Hall line of the family descended.

John Severn, Jr.'s mother was born Bridget Pott and was a sister of Captain Francis Pott, Susanna Baker Eyre's second husband. After the death of her husband Dr. John Severn in 1644, Bridget Pott Severn married Stephen Charlton. Charlton had emigrated to Northampton County sometime before 1635 and must have had some financial wherewithal when he arrived in the colony; indeed, he patented and amassed many acres of land along the Nassawadox Creek on the bayside of the county, where he planted tobacco, set up a shoemaking business, owned interests in ships, and imported goods to sell to fellow planters (see Fig. 5). He served on the parish vestry by the mid-1630s; became a justice on the county court by 1640; and sat as a member of the House of Burgesses in successive sessions from 1644 to 1652.[86]

Bridgett Pott Charlton brought her two young sons, John Jr. and Peter, into the new Charlton household, which grew with the birth of two daughters, Bridget around 1645 and Elizabeth four years later. Weakened perhaps by the birth of her second daughter at the end of January 1649, Bridgett Pott Severn Charlton died early the following year. With a house filled with young children, Charlton remarried in 1651.[87] In late 1654 he died a wealthy man and left his sizable estate, which included ships, land, and slaves, to his two young daughters Bridget and Elizabeth, each of whom were to inherit one half of it when they turned fourteen. A good Anglican, Charlton also set aside one of his tracts of land as a glebe to sustain the ministry of Hungars Parish if his two daughters had no children.[88]

Soon after Charlton's death, his widow dispatched her stepchildren Bridget and Elizabeth to a neighboring plantation where they were to be taken care of and educated through funds set aside from their father's estate. In the early 1660s the two daughters were living with planter William Jones, a colleague who had served on the county bench with their father. On April 23, 1661, a few weeks before their half niece Jane Severn was born, 16-year-old Bridget married Captain Isaac Foxcroft, a merchant and planter.[89]

With her sister Bridget married off to Isaac Foxcroft, Elizabeth Charlton quickly fell vulnerable to the machinations of her half-brother John Severn, who devised a perfidious scheme with his wife's brother, John Gethings. In August 1661, Severn kidnapped his half-sister, Elizabeth, then only 12 years old, from her guardian's plantation with the intent of having her marry Gethings.[90] Knowing that no local minister or magistrate would consent to this sordid plot, they whisked her away to a justice of the peace "on the other side of the water" who unwittingly consented to marry the fugitive couple. In December 1661, Gethings, supported by Severn and a few others, staked his claim in court to the Charlton inheritance of his new child bride, which was provisionally granted. Elizabeth died sometime in the first half of 1662 and in December the court acceded to Gethings petition to take possession of his wife's substantial estate.[91] Bridget Charlton Foxcroft and her husband Isaac disputed the validity of the action and the following month, one the most powerful men on the Eastern Shore, Edmund Scarburgh took up their cause. Captain Scarburgh not only argued about the immorality of the forced marriage of someone so young for which the governor's council had previously declared unlawful and ordered her return to the custody of Captain Jones, her guardian, but challenged the legitimacy of turning over Charlton's estate to Gethings based on a technicality in the will. He noted that one of its provisions stated that the daughters would not inherit their part of his property until they turned 14. The exact date of Elizabeth's birth was verified by two midwives who were present on the occasion, each recalling that it coincided with a memorable event. She was delivered either on or right before the day that King Charles I was beheaded in London (January 31, 1649).[92] Since Elizabeth was only 13 when she died, her husband was not entitled to his wife's estate. The court agreed with Scarburgh and Gethings lost all claims to his wife's property.[93]

With most of the Charlton inheritance now securely reunited in the hands of Bridget and Isaac Foxcroft, the couple were wealthy. Isaac Foxcroft was a relatively recent immigrant who profited by his mercantile connections with his kinsmen of the same name, a mariner from Hull, when he started exporting tobacco from his Northampton County plantation in the 1660s.[94] In the same decade he was elevated to the court and some years later became sheriff. Foxcroft represented the county in the House of Burgesses during the 1677 and the 1685–86 sessions. For many years, he was also a member of Hungars Parish vestry, where he worked alongside and became friends with Thomas Eyre II.

During the forty years of their marriage, the Foxcrofts accumulated land, slaves, and acquired many valuable possessions including silver. They had no children so in their old age they began to plan for the distribution of their estate to their relatives. Among their closest kin were Thomas and Jane Eyre and their children. In 1693 Isaac Foxcroft, "out of the love and Affection I have and beare to Severn Eyre the Son of Thomas Eyre . . . Gent. and Jane Severn late his wife decd: who was the Daughter of John Severn Gent. also decd. and Kinsman to my present Deare and Lovinge wife Bridget Foxcroft," deeded 400 acres of land near Hungars Creek to his wife's grandnephew Severn Eyre when he turned 21. If Severn died before then, the gift would go to "his youngest brother Thomas Eyre, Junr., the son of the abovesaid Thomas Eyre and Jane his wife."[95] Isaac died in 1702 leaving his estate to his wife Bridgett.[96] When she drew up her will two years later, she gave many things to her beloved kinsmen Severn Eyre including livestock, linen, "the silver punch bowl, sugar box ditto and the silver cup thereto belonging, the new silver tankard, twelve spoons ditto, two porringers ditto" and "one brass kettle containing twenty five or thirty gallons now in his father Mr. Thomas Eyre possession (see Cat. 64)."[97]

Thomas II survived his wife Jane by more than two decades. Although Jane died when her children were still relatively young, her husband surprisingly never remarried.

When Thomas II died in 1715 he had already outlived one of his sons, Neech Eyre of whom little is known. Neech became the de facto executor of Daniel Neech's estate for his widow Margaret Neech when the former clerk of court and friend of the older generation of Eyre brothers died in 1703. This implies that Neech Eyre had reached his majority around the turn of the century and was considered a trusted individual who could handle the responsibilities of sorting out his namesake's financial affairs.[98] Over the next half dozen years he brought cases to court against those who were indebted to the estate. His status as the nephew of a former justice, John Eyre, and the eldest son of a successful merchant father, Thomas II, prompted the magistrates of Northampton County to recommend Neech Eyre to the justices' bench in 1706. Yet he served on the bench for only a few sessions before he ceased attending and was summons by the sheriff in August 1707 to take the oath of office.[99] Perhaps he had become a Quaker or a member of another dissenting sect; he could have been a Jacobite sympathizer who wanted no part in swearing allegiance to Queen Anne; or maybe he suffered from a chronic illness that made it difficult for him to assume his duties. Bad health would plague many generations of Eyres. His name appears sporadically over the next few years in cases that he had pursued as executor of Daniel Neech's estate, but they were either continued or dismissed because of his failure to appear in court. In a suit brought in 1710 by Thomas Eyre III as an administrator of an estate, which was argued in court by his attorney and older brother Severn Eyre, Severn produced an account book that chronicled the transactions that were in contention in the case, which, he noted, had been in the possession of "Neech Eyre deceased."[100] This laconic remark is the last time that Neech appears in the county records. When and where he died is unknown nor is there any trace of an estate that he may have left to his brothers, or a spouse and children if he had married.

When Thomas II died in 1715, there is no mention of Neech Eyre in his father's will though there is reference to

a namesake, Neech Eyre, a grandson, who was either named after his uncle by his father Thomas Eyre III or for his mother, Elizabeth Neech, the daughter of Daniel Neech. Grandson Neech received £40 for his education and upbringing as well as a "Negro boy called Daniel." Of Thomas II's two surviving sons, Severn the oldest received £20, a "Negro man James," and half of his father's "goods" that were "not cut up of Linnen & Woolen," a reminder of the goods sold in Thomas II's mercantile business. Severn received no land, presumably because he had already taken possession of the 400 acres of land on a tributary of Hungars Creek that he had inherited from Isaac Foxcroft. The remainder of the Thomas II's estate including slaves and the plantation at the lower end of the peninsula went to Thomas III, his youngest son.[101] When Thomas III died four years later, his son Neech Eyre inherited his grandfather's portion of Golden Quarter.[102]

SEVERN AND GERTRUDE HARMANSON EYRE: THE THIRD GENERATION

The prospects of the earliest generations of the Eyre family depended as much upon strategic marriages and healthy children as it did business acumen. This is especially true of Severn Eyre, the first of that name, who married Gertrude Harmanson in the first decade of the eighteenth century. Not only did that union tie him to one of the leading families of planters and merchants on the Eastern Shore, but it also shifted his interests and those of his descendants beyond the Golden Quarter northward to land along the bayside creeks of Hungars and Cherrystone and the area around Eastville, which became the county seat of government in 1690.[103]

By the early eighteenth century, the Harmanson family was large, and their extensive landholdings spread across the middle part of Northampton County. The patriarch of the family, Thomas Harmanson, who died in 1702 only a few years before his granddaughter Gertrude married Severn Eyre, had been born in 1631 in the eastern German province of Brandenburg. Trained as a tailor before emigrating to the Eastern Shore in the early 1650s, Harmanson must have had a number of social and political skills and the financial resources to survive and thrive in this foreign land. Although he fell in with the likes of John Severn, Jr. early on, he managed to impress important leaders of the county and married Joan Andrews in the mid-1650s, the daughter of Major William Andrews, a magistrate and one of the earliest settlers on the Eastern Shore who had arrived in Virginia on the same ship that brought Captain Samuel Argall to Jamestown in 1617 to serve as governor.[104] Through the connection with Andrews and his own perspicuity, Harmanson began amassing sizable tracts of land including a patent of 1,300 acres for transporting 26 people in 1654.[105] From the late 1650s through the early 1670s, Joan and Thomas had nine children who lived into adulthood, and many of these siblings married into prominent families such as the Andrews, Kendalls, Littletons, Waters, Yeardleys, and Savages, all of whom had sizable landholdings and kinsmen who had served as justices, vestrymen, and officers in the county militia.

One measure of the position of the Harmansons and the Eyres in Northampton County society appears in the 1704 quit rent rolls. Every year those who held land in the colony, which technically belonged to the Crown, were obliged to pay a tax on every 50 acres of land in their possession. Although a yearly tax, only the tax rolls for 1704 survive for the entire colony, providing the most comprehensive survey of the division of land ownership in Virginia at the beginning of the century. The 1704 rent rolls for Northampton County list 257 individuals and one institutional owner, Hungars Parish glebe, which contained 1,500 acres that had been donated for that purpose in Stephen Charlton's will. The size of landholdings by individual ownership can be divided into roughly four categories (Fig. 9).

The average-size holding of the 257 listed owners was 389 acres. Although not every acre was of equal value, those individuals who owned more than 501 acres were most likely to command a labor force that included enslaved Africans and to hold positions of leadership in the county. They composed just 17 percent of landowners. At the lowest range were men who owned just 25 acres. At the apex was Susanna Andrews Littleton, the sister of Thomas Harmanson Sr.'s wife Joan and the widow of Nathaniel Littleton II, who had died the previous year. She owned 4,050 acres. The next most substantial landowners were Colonel John Custis III, who held 3,400 acres mainly on Wilsonia Neck on the bayside (in addition to 5,950 acres in neighboring Accomack County), and his son John Custis IV, who inherited his grandfather's estate at Arlington on the south side of Old Plantation Creek and controlled 3,250 acres. After the final division of their father's property two years earlier, three of the five living Harmanson sons owned estates of more than a thousand acres: John possessed 1,600 acres, Henry 1,250, and George 1,586. The other two sons, Captain William Harmanson and Thomas Harmanson Jr., had 308 and 400 acres respectively. The second generation of the Eyre family, who lived at Golden Quarter, were also among the elite, thanks to the Pott and Kendall legacies. John owned 774 acres, Daniel's widow Anne 773, and Thomas II 1,133.[106]

With their familial connections and success as planters and merchants, the Harmansons progressed up the political ladder. Thomas Harmanson, Sr. became a magistrate in the 1670s, serving on the bench with Severn Eyre's uncle John Eyre for many years along with William Kendall and Isaac Foxcroft. Harmanson, the German-born tailor, was naturalized in 1680 and was elected to represent the county in the House of Burgesses in the 1688 and 1691–92 sessions.[107] His sons followed his political footpath.[108] At the time of Thomas Sr.'s death in 1702, two of his sons, William and George, sat on the Northampton County bench and were followed two years later by a third, John. In 1706, not only did the three Harmanson brothers take their seats on the justices' bench, but so too did two of their brothers-in-law, William Waters who had married Isabel Harmanson and Thomas Savage whose wife was Alicia Harmanson.[109] Severn Eyre's older brother Neech sat briefly as a judge in 1706, which meant that, when Severn started to appear before the Northampton County court as a practicing attorney around the time he married Henry and Gertrude Littleton Harmanson's daughter Gertrude, the body of magistrates who sat in judgment was almost entirely composed of his extended family. Late in his life, Severn finally took his place on the bench, firmly ensconced as a member of the county's ruling elite.[110]

Though Severn Eyre's participation in court business is well documented, next to nothing is known about his domestic life and business activities. His wife, Gertrude Harmanson, is no more than a name. She was one of several daughters of Henry and Gertrude Littleton Harmanson, but little is known of her life—not even when she was born or when she died. Circumstantial evidence suggests that she was probably born in the early 1690s, and she seems to have married Severn in the last years of the first decade of the eighteenth century, when she was in her late teens. Her son Littleton (named in honor of her mother Gertrude Littleton's family) was born in 1710, and a second son, Severn, was born a few years after that.[111] If there were other children, they did not survive childhood. Gertrude died either in the late 1710s or early 1720s. Severn Eyre does not mention her in his will of 1728. Both boys were underage, and Severn named his mother-in-law, Gertrude Littleton Harmanson, and his brother-in-law, Henry Harmanson, as co-executors of his estate and charged with their care and education until they reached their majority.[112]

Severn left the "Plantation whereon I live," which was the Foxcroft legacy of 400 acres near Hungars Creek, along with "Two hundred & thirty acres on Hog Island" on the seaside, to his eldest son Littleton. He provided no land for his son Severn, but stipulated that the executors were to sell the nearby plantation that he purchased to help settle outstanding debts as well as pay for his namesake's education. He specified an "Equall Devision of my Negroes between my Two Sons to them & their heirs when my Son Severn Shall attain att ye age of Eighteen." At his death, Severn Eyre owned 21 slaves, almost half of whom he had inherited from his father, Bridget Foxcroft, and a merchant colleague, Robert Howson.[113] Finally, he carefully divided the silver that he had inherited from Bridget Foxcroft in addition to one or two other pieces that he and his wife had acquired between the two and allowed them to claim their inheritance when they turned 19, which for Littleton was the following year.[114] Severn Jr. died within a few years, and all the silver, slaves, and residue of the estate came into Littleton's sole possession.

The inventory taken of Severn Eyre's possessions in August 1728 suggests a modest level of comfort for a rising member of the gentry class. His domestic possessions included a greater quantity and variety of furnishings than were common a few decades earlier. Nothing is known about the house itself, but its rooms were filled with a number of tables, leather and matted chairs, a chest of drawers, a cupboard with folding doors, cupboard cloth, several bedsteads, bolsters, good sets of sheets and pillows, linen table cloths, napkins, and other textiles, candlesticks, and sconces. Bridget Foxcroft's "great looking glass" still held its value. Severn and Gertrude had a leather case containing knives and forks, blue-and-white earthenware, pewter, glassware, and other dining accoutrements that were increasingly seen as necessary possessions. The inventory also noted several pieces that had outlived their usefulness; among them were an oval table and a large table described as "old fashioned," a "much worn rug," "3 old chairs without bottoms," a set of calico bed curtains "Motheaten & Rotten," and the 25-gallon brass kettle given to Severn by Mrs. Foxcroft two decades earlier, which was now "full of holes" and of little use. Other items indicated a man of business including

Number of acres	Number of landowners	Percentage of landowners
1–100	60	24%
101–500	150	59%
501–1,000	27	10%
1,000+	20	7%
Total: 99,966 acres Average: 389 acres	Total: 257	Total: 100%

Fig. 9. Size of landholdings in Northampton County, 1704.

a pair of money scales and weights, a "pair of stilliards," "3 Money purses & Several bags with money," a chest with lock and key, and £571.19.5, an extraordinary amount of cash in a specie-starved colony. Severn owned an *Abridgement of the Laws of Virginia* and Michael Dalton's instructive *The Country Justice*, which must have been well thumbed from his work as an attorney and a magistrate. There were "9 small books" and "1 Large book Titld the new Testam^t according to the Catholick Church," perhaps a curious presence in an Anglican household. Less surprising was "1 Large Bible," most likely the surviving seventeenth-century Bible that remains in the family's possession, pages of which were inscribed five years later by Severn's son Littleton Eyre. Then there were the status symbols including gold rings, parcels of old silver, as well as the Foxcroft collection of silver including the large punch bowl, tankards, cup, sugar box, porringer, and spoons (though two were broken by this time). Finally, the enumerators noted hanging on one of the walls "1 Coat of Arms with a Golden Frame," a none-too-subtle assertion of the family's social standing.[115]

With its accounting of numerous horses, cattle, hogs, and sheep, wagons, hoes, axes, and barrels, Severn Eyre's inventory describes a working farm where more than 20 enslaved people worked tending livestock and raising crops such as corn, wheat, tobacco, and vegetables. The inventory makes clear that the plantation was a place of production, with implements and machines such as sheers, wool cards, tow cards, flax hakes, hackles, cider presses, tanning troughs, mill stones, wool wheels, and spinning wheels, which slaves employed to turn crops and animal fleeces and hides into items to clothe and feed not only those who worked the fields but also those who were sold to neighbors and others in the region. With few exceptions, Eyre's itemized list of more than 60 types of textiles consisted of hard-wearing materials, typical of what was used to clothe enslaved field hands and household servants. Because the inventory is so voluminous, it is possible that some of this material was sold by Eyre to local planters. The inventory also reveals evidence of the commercial production of candles. It lists more than 100 pounds of tallow from animal fat, a large supply of beeswax, and more than 1,200 pounds of wax produced by the boiling, skimming, and straining of the liquid produced by the fruit of an evergreen shrub known as a wax myrtle or bayberry. The myrtle wax was valued at more than £30, the highest valued item in the entire inventory. Eyre's workmen loaded his shallop—a two-masted, shallow-bottomed vessel suitable for sailing coastal waters—to deliver these and other goods he manufactured at his plantation to customers on the Eastern Shore and perhaps across the bay.[116] It was a modest operation that would be eclipsed in the following decades by that of his son Littleton Eyre, who set his sights on a much larger market that spanned Britain's Atlantic world.

NOTES

1. According to the mid-twentieth-century historian of Virginia's Eastern Shore, Ralph Whitelaw, in the earliest records "Magothy Bay" was used to describe the lower bayside of the peninsula. The name later came to designate the seaside, but sometimes referred to all land south of Plantation Creek. Since the twentieth century, it has denoted the southernmost seaside waterway. Ralph T. Whitelaw, *Virginia's Eastern Shore: A History of Northampton and Accomack Counties* (Richmond: Virginia Historical Society, 1951), 1:55.

2. On settlement patterns and population estimates, see James R. Perry, *The Formation of a Society on Virginia's Eastern Shore, 1615–1655* (Chapel Hill: University of North Carolina Press, 1990), 28–69.

3. On August 4, 1674, John Eyre brought a panther head to magistrate John Custis in order to claim a bounty paid to inhabitants of the county for killing predatory animals. Howard Mackey and Marlene Groves, eds., *Northampton County, Virginia, Record Book: Deeds, Wills, &c. vol. 10, 1674–1678* (Rockport, Maine: Picton Press, 2003), 109.

4. George Fox, *A Journal; or, Historical account of the life, travels, sufferings, Christian experiences, and labour of love in the work of the ministry, of that ancient, eminent, and faithful servant of Jesus Christ, George Fox* (London: Thomas Northcott, 1694), 381.

5. April Hatfield, *Atlantic Virginia: Intercolonial Relations in the Seventeenth Century* (Philadelphia: University of Pennsylvania Press, 2004).

6. David Peterson DeVries, *Voyages from Holland to America, A.D. 1632–1644*, trans. Henry C. Murphy (New York: Billin and Brothers, 1853), 148.

7. Perry, *Formation of a Society on Virginia's Eastern Shore*, 153–54.

8. DeVries, *Voyages from Holland to America*, 112.

9. John R. Pagan, "Dutch Maritime and Commercial Activity in Mid-Seventeenth-Century Virginia," *Virginia Magazine of History and Biography* 90, no. 4 (October 1982): 485–91.

10. Perry, *Formation of a Society on Virginia's Eastern Shore*, 152.

11. Jennings Cropper Wise, *Ye Kingdome of Accawmacke; or, The Eastern Shore of Virginia in the Seventeenth Century* (Richmond, Va.: The Bell Book and Stationery Co., 1911), 85–86.

12. Susie M. Ames, *Studies of the Virginia Eastern Shore in the Seventeenth Century* (Richmond, Va., 1940; reissued New York: Russell & Russell, 1973), 95.

13. Howard Mackey and Marlene Groves, eds., *Northampton County, Virginia, Record Book vol. 8, 1657–1664* (Rockport, Maine: Picton Press, 2002), 270, January 28, 1663.

14. Timothy Morgan, Beverley Straub, and Nicholas Luccketti, "Archaeological Excavations at 44NH8: The Church Neck Wells Site, Northampton County, Virginia," Virginia Department of Historic Resources Technical Report Series No. 4, 1997, 6, 39–40. Some of the shoes produced by Charlton's workmen may have remained on the plantation. Charlton was the guardian of his teenage stepson, John Severn, who was chafing to be free of his oversight. Until Severn reached his majority at 21, the court ordered that Charlton provide his ward yearly with proper clothing including "four pair of shoes." Howard Mackey and Marlene Groves, eds., *Northampton County, Virginia, Record Book: Orders, Deeds, Wills &c. vol. 5, 1654–1655* (Rockport, Maine: Picton Press, 1999), 3, March 28, 1654.

15. Historian Lorena Walsh estimated that free families with enough resources to pay for their transportation to the New World comprised approximately 20 percent of the total number of immigrants who came to the tobacco colonies in the seventeenth century. Of the vast majority of those who could not afford their passage, male servants outnumbered female servants by three to one. Lorena Walsh, "Migration, Society, Economy, and Settlement, 1607–1830," in *The Chesapeake House: Architectural Investigation by Colonial Williamsburg*, ed. Cary Carson and Carl Lounsbury (Chapel Hill: University of North Carolina Press, 2013), 49–50.

16. DeVries, *Voyages from Holland to America*, 113.

17. Mackey and Groves, *Northampton County, Virginia, Record Book vol. 8, 1657–1664*, 358, 1664 list of tithables; Howard Mackey and Marlene Groves, eds., *Northampton County, Virginia, Record Book: Court Cases vol. 9, 1664–1674* (Rockport, Maine: Picton Press, 2003), 21–23, April 19, 1665.

18. Mackey and Groves, *Northampton County, Virginia, Record Book vol. 8, 1657–1664*, 265, February 4, 1663.

19. Unfortunately, Brunt failed to take advantage of the generous offer made by Severn. Thomas Evans, a surgeon called by a jury to explain Brunt's untimely death observed the former servant was diseased and that by his "obstinate slothfulness and perverse disposition" probably hastened his demise. Mackey and Groves, *Northampton County, Virginia, Record Book vol. 8, 1657–1664*, 261, December 4, 1662.

20. Northampton County Deeds, Wills, etc., No. 4, 1651–1654, 189, December 7, 1653. Such brutality was not an isolated incident. A jury inquest into the death of John Tems, a "servant lad" to George Corbin, determined that his death was a result of having been beaten by his master and froze to death overnight due to the bad weather. Northampton County [Wills] Order Book, No. 10, 1674–1679, 231, January 29, 1678.

21. Susie Ames, ed., *County Court Records of Accomack-Northampton, Virginia, 1640–1645* (Charlottesville: University Press of Virginia, 1973), 257–59, March 6, 1643.

22. Northampton County Order Book, 1657–1664, November 3, 1661; Northampton County Deeds, Wills, etc., No. 3, 1645–1651, 197, January 9, 1650; Northampton County Order Book, 1657–1664, 62–64, February 13, 20, 28, 1660; Mackey and Groves, *Northampton County, Virginia, Record Book: Orders, Deeds, Wills &c. vol. 5, 1654–1655*, 150, November 12, 1654.

23. Frank V. Walczyk, ed., *Northampton County, Va., Orders, Deeds, & Wills 1651–1654, Book IV* (Coram, N.Y.: Peter's Row, 1998), 224, March 8, 1654.

24. T. H. Breen and Stephen Innes, *"Myne Owne Ground": Race and Freedom on Virginia's Eastern Shore, 1640–1676* (New York: Oxford University Press, 1980), 44–45.

25. John R. Pagan, *Anne Orthwood's Bastard: Sex and Law in Early Virginia* (New York: Oxford University Press, 2003), 88.

26. In a colony where holding Black people in permanent bondage was commonly accepted from the very beginning of settlement, the Eastern Shore stood out as a place where some masters chose to manumit their slaves or allowed them to purchase their freedom. John Coombs argues that enslavement was a more permeable condition here than in the rest of the colony. He notes that more than a quarter of slave owners made provisions in their wills to free some or all of their slaves in the years between 1640 and 1675, compared to only 6 percent of masters who resided "across the water." John Coombs, "'Others Not Christian in the Service of the English': Interpreting the Status of Africans and African Americans in Early Virginia," *Virginia Magazine of History and Biography* 127, no. 3 (2019): 228–29.

27. Ames, *County Court Records of Accomack-Northampton, Virginia, 1640–1645*, 42, 50, November 23, 1640.

28. For a comprehensive history of an early Virginia county based on a close reading of court records, see Darrett and Anita Rutman, *A Place in Time: Middlesex County, Virginia, 1650–1750* (New York: W. W. Norton and Company, Inc., 1986).

29. For a comparative analysis of living conditions in the west of England near Bristol and the Chesapeake colonies, see James P. P. Horn, "'The Bare Necessities': Standards of Living in England and the Chesapeake, 1650–1700," *Historical Archaeology* 22 (1988): 74–91.

30. Northampton County Deeds, Wills, etc., No. 7, 8, 1655 [1654]–1657, 72, November 30, 1657. Thomas Harmar was the son of Dr. John Harmar, Greek Reader at Oxford University. James Handley Marshall, *Abstracts of Wills & Administrations of Northampton County, Virginia, 1632–1802* (Camden, Maine: Picton Press, 1994), 37.

31. Northampton County Deeds, Wills, etc., No. 7, 8, 1655 [1654]–1657, 72, November 30, 1657.

32. In 1668 John Eyre is referred to as an "orphan" in a complaint made by his guardian Lt. Colonel William Kendall to the county court. Eyre must have been 18 or 19 years old at that time, for two years later he assumed a role in county government, serving on an inquest jury. Mackey and Groves, *Northampton County, Virginia, Record Book: Court Cases vol. 9, 1664–1674*, 162, August 28, 1668.

33. J. B. Firth, *Highways and Byways in Derbyshire* (London: Macmillan and Co., 1920), 330 (for the connection of Jane Eyre with Hathersage and North Lees); Mary Richardson-Eyre, *A History of the Wiltshire Family of Eyre* (London: Mitchell & Hughes, 1897).

34. For New England see, for example, John Camden Hotten, *The Original Lists of Persons of Quality, Emigrants, Religious Exiles, Political Rebels, Serving Men Sold for a Term of Years, Apprentices, Children Stolen, Maidens Pressed, and Others who Went from Great Britain to the American Plantations, 1600–1700* (London: John Camden Hotten, 1894; reprinted New York: Empire State Book Co.), 66.

35. Lyon G. Tyler, *Encyclopedia of Virginia Biography* (New York: Lewis Historical Publishing Company, 1915), 1:231.

36. John Bennett Boddie, *Seventeenth Century Isle of Wight County, Virginia* (Chicago: Chicago Law Printing Company, 1938), 34–35, 54.

37. Alice Granbery Walter, ed., *Lower Norfolk County, Virginia Court Records: Book A, 1637–1646, and Book B, 1646–1551/2* (Baltimore: Clearfield Company, 1994), 12; John A. Brayton, *Transcription of Lower Norfolk County, Virginia, Records, Volume One: Wills and Deeds, Book D, 1656–1666* (Memphis: John A. Brayton, 2007), 31–32.

38. Charles McIntosh, "Ages of Lower Norfolk County People," *William and Mary Quarterly*, 1st ser., 25, no. 1 (July 1916): 36–40; H. R. McIlwaine, ed., *Journals of the House of Burgesses, 1619–1658/59* (Richmond, Va.: The Colonial Press, E. Waddey Co., 1915), xix.

39. Walter, *Lower Norfolk County, Virginia Court Records*, 41–42, 182; John A. Brayton, *Transcription of Lower Norfolk County, Virginia, Records, Volume Two: Record Book C, 1651–1656* (Memphis: John A. Brayton, 2010), 7.

40. Warner Mifflin, a grandson of Edward Mifflin and Ann Eyre Littleton Mifflin, became a prominent Quaker abolitionist in the second half of the eighteenth century. Gary Nash, *Warner Mifflin: Unflinching Quaker Abolitionist* (Philadelphia: University of Pennsylvania Press, 2017), 19–21.

41. Hilda Justice, *Life and Ancestry of Warner Mifflin: Friend, Philanthropist, Patriot* (Philadelphia: Ferris & Leach, 1905), 11.

42. Howard Mackey and Marlene Groves, eds., *Northampton County, Virginia, Record Book: Orders, Deeds, Wills &c. vol. 3, 1645–1651* (Rockport, Maine: Picton Press, 2000), 194, June 29, 1646.

43. Marshall, *Abstracts of Wills & Administrations of Northampton County, Virginia, 1632–1802*, 34–35.

44. In 1654 Eyre's name showed up in a rare court action when "the difference between Jno Parramore plt & Mr. Th: Ayres deft" was "referred to ye next Court." Mackey and Groves, *Northampton County, Virginia, Record Book: Orders, Deeds, Wills &c. vol. 5, 1564–1655*, 150, November 12, 1654.

45. Whitelaw, *Virginia's Eastern Shore*, 1:25, 71; John Frederick Dorman, *Adventurers of Purse and Person, Virginia, 1607–1624/5*, 4th ed. (Baltimore: Genealogical Publishing Co., Inc., 2005), 2:776.

46. For example, Daniel Baker served as a witness, along with Captain Francis Pott, to Ann Littleton's will in 1656. Northampton County Deeds, Wills, etc., No. 7, 8, 1655 [1654]–1657, 24, October 28, 1656.

47. Northampton County Deeds, Wills, etc., No. 7, 8, 1655 [1654]–1657, 24, October 28, 1656. Ann Littleton named Edward Douglas, Francis Doughty, the minister of the parish, and Capt. Francis Pott, as her administrators. Presumably after the age of 14 Esther would have been taught the basics of housewifery and thought suitable for marriage. In 1663, when Esther was 15, she married John Robins, the son of Colonel Obedience Robins, one of the major planters of the Eastern Shore. Dorman, *Adventurers of Purse and Person, Virginia, 1607–1624/5*, 2:703.

48. Mackey and Groves, *Northampton County, Virginia, Record Book: Orders, Deeds, Wills &c. vol. 5, 1564–1655*, 58, September 4, 1654.

49. Howard Mackey and Marlene Groves, eds., *Northampton County, Virginia, Record Book: Deeds, Wills &c. vol. 6, and 7–8, 1655–1657* (Rockport, Maine: Picton Press, 2002), 161, July 27, 1657.

50. Mackey and Groves, *Northampton County, Virginia, Record Book: Deeds, Wills &c. vol. 6, and 7–8, 1655–1657*, 162, July 27, 1657.

51. Edward Douglas, the magistrate who took these depositions, became ill shortly thereafter and died in November 1657, which may have delayed or deterred any case against John Severn that might have been brought before the Northampton County court. Northampton County Deeds, Wills, etc., No. 7, 8, 1655 [1654]–1657, 76, November 12, 1657.

52. The lower parish register recorded her birth, which was transcribed into the court record book. Howard Mackey and Marlene Groves, eds., *Northampton County, Virginia, Record Book: Deeds, Wills &c. vol. 7, 1657–1666* (Rockport, Maine: Picton Press, 2002), 172.

53. Although Susanna's age and place of birth are unknown, some chronology can be established by what we know of her two brothers, Daniel and Edward. Daniel must have been about 18 to 20 years old when he emigrated to Virginia around 1640 or slightly earlier. He appears regularly in court documents from that time, suggesting that he was of age. His younger brother, Edward, does not appear in Virginia records until about 1662 and his will of 1664 noted that he was "late of London." It is possible that this was the place of nativity for Elizabeth and Daniel, but Edward may have only been a transient in London, coming from somewhere else in England before taking his chances in Virginia like his two siblings. Susanna may have been slightly younger than Daniel, which would place her birth somewhere in the early to mid-1620s. It is not clear when she came to Virginia, but she may have been in her early twenties when she met and married Dr. Thomas Eyre. If this chronology is correct, then in 1657 she would have been in her early to mid-thirties. Ames, *County Court Records of Accomack-Northampton, Virginia, 1640–1645*,

42, November 23, 1640. On Edward Baker, see Accomack County Deeds and Wills, 1663–1666, 79, November 16, 1664.

54. Dorman, *Adventurers of Purse and Person, Virginia, 1607–1624/5*, 2:311.

55. On Potts's involvement with the Severn family, see Mackey and Groves, *Northampton County, Virginia, Record Book: Orders, Deeds, Wills &c. vol. 3, 1645–1651*, 31, January 28, 1646; Mackey and Groves, *Northampton County, Virginia, Record Book: Orders, Deeds, Wills &c. vol. 3, 1645–1651*, 305, September 6, 1648. On the purchase of slaves and selling them to his brother-in-law Stephen Charlton, see Northampton County Deeds, Wills, etc., No. 4, 1651–1654, 81, May 25, 1652.

56. The will was proved in court on October 28, 1658. Marshall, *Abstracts of Wills & Administrations of Northampton County, Virginia, 1632–1802*, 58–59.

57. Mackey and Groves, *Northampton County, Virginia, Record Book: Deeds, Wills &c. vol. 7, 1657–1666*, 43, December 29, 1658.

58. William Kendall was born in the village of Brinton in Norfolk, England, in 1621, the son of a tailor. He developed his commercial skills when he worked as a clerk for a merchant. Nearly 30, he emigrated from England to Virginia and served as an indentured servant to Eastern Shore planter Edward Drew. He soon became his indispensable clerk. After Drew's death his wife married mariner William Strangridge and Kendall fulfilled the same role as he did for his former master. When Kendall received his freedom in 1654, he took over much of the commercial network that he had been running for his previous masters. For a summary of Kendall's career see Pagan, *Anne Othwood's Bastard*, 27–37.

59. William Kendall acknowledged in court that he had married Susanna, "ye Executx & relict" of John Pott. Mackey and Groves, *Northampton County, Virginia, Record Book: Deeds, Wills &c. vol. 7, 1657–1666*, 43, December 29, 1658; Northampton County Deeds, Wills, etc., 1657–1666, 32, November 29, 1659; Mackey and Groves, *Northampton County, Virginia, Record Book: Deeds, Wills &c. vol. 7, 1657–1666*, 296, August 17, 1666; Mackey and Groves, *Northampton County, Virginia, Record Book: Deeds, Wills &c. vol. 6, and 7–8, 1655–1657*, 205, December 21, 1666; Mackey and Groves, *Northampton County, Virginia, Record Book: Court Cases vol. 9, 1664–1674*, 162–63, August 28, 1668.

60. John B. Bell, *Northampton County, Virginia, Tithables, 1662–1677* (Bowie, Md.: Heritage Books, Inc., 1993), 11, 18, 25, 30, 36, 44, 48, 63.

61. No inventory was taken when Susanna Kendall died around 1683, nor even following the death of her husband, Colonel William Kendall, in 1686. After their son William Kendall died, a room-by-room inventory was made of the objects in the old and new house, kitchen, and store. No items related to tea or tea drinking were listed. Inventory of the estate of William Kendall, July 28, 1698, Northampton County Orders & Wills, No. 13, 1689–1698, 485–505.

62. In 1671, John Eyre recorded in court that he had received £100 sterling from his stepfather William Kendall, which "hee freely did give unto mee also I doe acknowledge to have recd all ye Estate both Lands & goods & chattels that was left mee by

mr. Tho: Eyre my Divine & honored Father decd & all other things mentioned by the said Kendall gift upon word, for wch hee . . . is fully discharged from mee . . . fore ever fourteen pounds Sterling money for a mare & mre foale sold to him & one mare to bee delivered mee att ye age of one & Twenty only Excepted." Northampton County Deeds, etc., 1668–1680, 19, February 26, 1671. In 1685 Daniel Eyre acknowledged in court that he had received from his stepfather William Kendall "full satisfaction for all things & any ways did to me by Gift on Record or otherwise all of which I am fully contented and paid. . . . I doe also Acknowledge to have recorded full satisfaction . . . for other Negroes." Northampton County Deeds, Wills, etc., No. 11, 1680–1692, 111, January 28, 1685.

63. On November 22, 1677, John Eyre "was Sworne as Justice of the Peace of this County of Northampton by virtue of a Commission of the Rt. Honble Governor." Mackey and Groves, *Northampton County, Virginia, Record Book: Deeds, Wills &c. vol. 10, 1674–1678*, 297.

64. Thomas Eyre II witnessed the will drawn up by Southey, Littleton, who died while at the meeting with the northern Indians in Albany, New York, in 1679. Marshall, *Abstracts of Wills & Administrations of Northampton County, Virginia, 1632–1802*, 117.

65. For Daniel Eyre's role as a surveyor, see Frank V. Walczyk, ed., *Northampton County, Virginia: Orders & Wills 1683–1689*, vol. 1, *1683–1686* (Coram, N.Y.: Peter's Row, 2001), 90, January 28, 1685. He was also responsible for the survey and partition of a large tract of land for the Harmanson family. Frank V. Walczyk, ed., *Northampton County, Virginia: Orders & Wills 1698–1710*, vol. 1, *1698–1703* (Coram, NY: Peter's Row, 2001), 92, November 28, 1702.

66. Whitelaw, *Virginia's Eastern Shore*, 1:64.

67. Northampton County Deeds, Wills, etc., No. 11, 1680–1692, 172–74, May 28, 1688.

68. Whitelaw, *Virginia's Eastern Shore*, 1:63–64, 72–73.

69. Whitelaw, *Virginia's Eastern Shore*, 1:64.

70. Whitelaw, *Virginia's Eastern Shore*, 1:72.

71. Northampton County Deeds, etc., 1668–1680, 19, February 26, 1671.

72. Northampton County Deeds, Wills, etc., No. 11, 1680–1692, 20–21, August 5, 1681.

73. Whitelaw, *Virginia's Eastern Shore*, 1:72.

74. Breen and Innes, *"Myne Owne Ground,"* 68.

75. Will of John Eyre, April 21, 1719, Northampton County Deeds, Wills, etc., 1718–1725, 24–25. Eyre left the 534 acres of the seaside plantation at Golden Quarter where he resided to his grandson John Burton, the son of his daughter Procilla Burton, who predeceased her father. He also bequeathed to him "my Negro woman Betty and my Girle Grace and my Girle Ester and my boy James" after the death of his other daughter Elizabeth Stockley. Eyre gave the 240 acres that was the original Thomas Eyre I property on the bayside to his grandson John Bagwell. The Golden Quarter plantation remained in the hands of the Burtons until 1791, when John Burton's granddaughter Esther Parramore and her husband sold the remainder of it out of the family. In 1729, John Bagwell and his wife

Sarah exchanged the original 240-acre bayside plantation with Gertrude Harmanson for land elsewhere. Whitelaw, *Virginia's Eastern Shore*, 1:66–67, 72.

76. Will of Daniel Eyre, December 31, 1690, Northampton County Orders & Wills, No. 13, 1689–1698, 96–97; Will of Anne Eyre, May 15, 1720, Northampton County Deeds, Wills, etc., 1718–1725, 146–47.

77. Bell, *Northampton County, Virginia, Tithables, 1662–1677*, 18, 25, 38, 48, 58, 64.

78. Frank V. Walczyk, ed., *Northampton County, Virginia: Orders and Wills 1689–1698*, vol. 1, *1689–1693* (Coram, N.Y.: Peter's Row, 2000), 105, March 29, 1692.

79. Frank V. Walczyk, ed., *Northampton County, Virginia: Orders and Wills 1689–1698*, vol. 2, *1693–1698* (Coram, N.Y.: Peter's Row, 2000), 179, March 4, 1698.

80. Northampton County Wills, etc., No. 15, 1717–1725, 73–76, October 28, 1719.

81. Mackey and Groves, *Northampton County, Virginia, Record Book: Deeds, Wills &c. vol. 7, 1657–1666*, 172, June 4, 1662. "The Register of ye lower parish of Northampton County for the year Adm 1661 . . . Births . . . Jane ye Daughter of John & Dammerons Sevorne born ye 13th of May." Mackey and Groves, *Northampton County, Virginia, Record Book: Court Cases. vol. 9, 1664–1674*, 10–11, 21, April 10, 1665, April 19, 1665.

82. Marshall, *Abstracts of Wills & Administrations of Northampton County, Virginia 1632–1802*, 75–76.

83. Northampton County Deeds, etc., 1668–1680, 197, December 29, 1679.

84. Whitelaw, *Virginia's Eastern Shore*, 1:76.

85. Daniel Neech had another daughter, Elizabeth, with a later wife named Margaret Melling. Elizabeth married Thomas Eyre III and had several children including Neech Eyre, probably named for his uncle who was mentioned as the godson of his grandfather Daniel Neech.

86. Susie Ames, ed., *County Court Records of Accomack-Northampton, Virginia, 1632–1640* (Washington: American Historical Association, 1954), 39, September 14, 1635; Mackey and Groves, *Northampton County, Virginia, Record Book: Orders, Deeds, Wills &c. vol. 3, 1645–1651*, 47, February 25, 1646; McIlwaine, *Journals of the House of Burgesses, 1619–1658/59*, xviii, xix, xxi.

87. Marshall, *Abstracts of Wills & Administrations of Northampton County, Virginia 1632–1802*, 32.

88. A glebe was land owned by an Anglican parish for the use of its minister. Although some ministers resided in a church-owned dwelling on the glebe, in some parishes the house and land were rented and the income was applied to the maintenance of the living or the church fabric. Northampton County had one of the earliest parsonages built to house a minister. In 1635, the vestry agreed to build a frame house that was 42 by 18 feet. Mackey and Groves, eds., *Northampton County, Virginia, Record Book: Orders, Deeds, Wills &c. vol. 5, 1564–1655*, 112–14, October 28, 1654; Carl Lounsbury, *An Illustrated Glossary of Early Southern Architecture and Landscape* (New York: Oxford University Press, 1994), 162–63.

89. Mackey and Groves, *Northampton County, Virginia, Record Book vol. 7, 1657–1666*, 170.

90. Mackey and Groves, *Northampton County, Virginia, Record Book vol. 8, 1657–1664*, 181, September 4, 1661.

91. Mackey and Groves, *Northampton County, Virginia, Record Book vol. 8, 1657–1664*, 254, December 4, 1662.

92. Mackey and Groves, *Northampton County, Virginia, Record Book vol. 8, 1657–1664*, 260–61, 275, December 4, 1662, January 28, 1663.

93. Apparently, the case was taken to the General Court in Jamestown, which agreed with the count court's decision to award the entire Charlton estate to Isaac and Bridget Foxcroft. Mackey and Groves, *Northampton County, Virginia, Record Book: Deeds, Wills &c. vol. 7, 1657–1666*, 233, April 9, 1663.

94. Northampton County Deeds, Wills, etc., 1657–1666, 117, December 12, 1661.

95. Isaac Foxcroft deed of gift to Severn Eyre, September 28, 1693, Eyre Hall Family Papers, Virginia Historical Society, Richmond.

96. Marshall, *Abstracts of Wills & Administrations of Northampton County, Virginia 1632–1802*, 168.

97. Frank V. Walczyk, ed., *Northampton County, Virginia: Orders & Wills 1698–1710*, vol. 2, *1704–1710* (Coram, N.Y.: Peter's Row, 2001), 3, January 13, 1704.

98. Walczyk, *Northampton County, Virginia: Orders & Wills 1698–1710*, vol. 1, *1698–1703*, 128, September 29, 1703. Even earlier, Neech Eyre appears in the records in 1701 when he accompanied John Custis, Jr. surveying cattle that had been turned loose on Smith Island that may have been part of Custis's father's estate. Walczyk, *Northampton County, Virginia: Orders & Wills 1698–1710*, vol. 1, *1698–1703*, 66, September 29, 1701.

99. Walczyk, *Northampton County, Virginia: Orders & Wills 1698–1710*, vol. 2, *1704–1710*, 43, March 28, 1706; 45, June 28, 1706; 46, July 16, 1743; and 74, August 28, 1707.

100. Walczyk, *Northampton County, Virginia: Orders & Wills 1698–1710*, vol. 2, *1704–1710*, 2, March 29, 1704; 7, May 31, 1704; 10, July 28, 1704; 50, November 28, 1706; 56, December 30, 1706; 59, January 28, 1707; 145, September 30, 1709; 152, November 30, 1709; and 160, March 1, 1710.

101. Will of Thomas Eyre, January 23, 1714, Northampton County Wills, Deeds, etc., 1711–1718, 104.

102. When Neech Eyre died in 1738, he left his estate to his only child, Ann Eyre, the daughter of Neech's first wife and cousin Anne Eyre Mifflin. Ann held on to her part of Golden Quarter until the beginning of the nineteenth century when her son William Roberts sold it out of the family. Marshall, *Abstracts of Wills & Administrations of Northampton County, Virginia 1632–1802*, 299–300; Whitelaw, *Virginia's Eastern Shore*, 1:64–65, 68. For Ann Roberts's tribulations during the Revolution and her effort to manumit the slaves she inherited, see Nash, *Warner Mifflin*, 110–19.

103. Carl Lounsbury, *The Courthouses of Early Virginia: An Architectural History* (Charlottesville: University of Virginia Press, 2005), 92–97.

104. Whitelaw, *Virginia's Eastern Shore*, 1:25.

105. Nell Marion Nugent, *Cavaliers and Pioneers: Abstracts of Virginia Land Patents and Grants, 1623–1800* (Richmond, Va.: Dietz Press, 1934), 1:294.

106. 1704 Northampton County Rent Rolls, Clerk's Office, Eastville, Virginia, transcribed by Julie Richter, Colonial Williamsburg Foundation. See also Annie Laurie Wright Smith, compiler, *The Quit Rents of Virginia, 1704* (Baltimore: Genealogical Publishing Co., 1977).

107. "The Harmanson Family," *Virginia Magazine of History and Biography* 37, no. 4 (October 1929): 379; on naturalization registered in Northampton County, see loose papers, June 24, 1684, Eyre Hall Family Papers.

108. Both John and George Harmanson were elected to represent Northampton County in the House of Burgesses in a number of sessions in the 1710s and early 1720s. H. R. McIlwaine, ed., *Journals of the House of Burgesses, 1712–1726* (Richmond: Virginia State Library, 1912), viii, x, xi, 364, 401.

109. Walczyk, *Northampton County, Virginia: Orders & Wills 1698–1710*, vol. 2, *1704–1710*, 46, July 16, 1706.

110. By 1726, if not earlier, Severn had been selected to serve as a magistrate on the Northampton County bench. *Virginia Magazine of History and Biography* 48, no. 2 (April 1940): 148.

111. Severn's father, Thomas Eyre II, had been a witness to the will of Gertrude Littleton's father, Colonel Southey Littleton, who died in Albany, New York, in 1679 while on a mission to negotiate with northern Indians.

112. Will of Severn Eyre, February 28, 1728, Eyre Hall Family Papers.

113. The enslaved people listed in Severn Eyre's 1728 inventory were "James, Subb, Mingo, Zacharia, Little James, Miney, Esau, Jacob, Eli, Stephen, Benjamin, Sis, Indea, Bridget, Sarah & Betty, Negro's of Jno Matthews Marlborough, Sam, Susse, Tom, & George." Many of these individuals were enumerated in Severn Eyre's lists of tithables from 1720 through 1725, though there were other names of people who appeared and disappeared over this time. Thomas Eyre II left James to his son in his 1714 will. In 1704 Bridget Foxcroft had devised to her kinsman five individuals: Subwell, Benjamin, Zachariah, Jenny, and Sis. Finally, in 1720, merchant and clerk of the court Robert Howson promised George, Mingo, and Sam to his colleague and executor if his grandson John Custis Matthews died before he turned 21. Although Matthews lived until the late eighteenth century, Eyre's inventory notes the presence of five "Negro's" in his estate. Slaves with those names appear later in Littleton Eyre's list of tithables in the 1730s and early 1740s. Whether some of them are the same individuals is unknown. Inventory of the estate of Severn Eyre, August 14, 1728, Northampton County Wills, Deeds, etc., No. 26, 1725–1733, 151–54; Marshall, *Abstracts of Wills & Administrations of Northampton County, Virginia 1632–1802*, 175, 206, and 230; John B. Bell, *Northampton County, Virginia, Tithables, 1720–1769* (Bowie, Md.: Heritage Books, Inc., 1993), 3, 15, 26, 40, 55, 77, 258, 303, 356.

114. Will of Severn Eyre, February 28, 1728.

115. Inventory of the estate of Severn Eyre, August 14, 1728; Addenda to the inventory of Severn Eyre, April 9, 1735, Northampton County Wills & Inventories, No. 18, 1733–1740, 82.

116. The shallop was valued at £23. Inventory of the estate of Severn Eyre, August 14, 1728.

EYREVILLE: ARCHAEOLOGY OF THE LATE SEVENTEENTH CENTURY

HALEY HOFFMAN

Recent archaeological discoveries at Eyreville reveal the transformation of Eastern Shore society from a rough-and-tumble frontier to a more settled agricultural society in the second half of the seventeenth century. Life for a number of second- and third-generation residents and newcomers, especially large planters and merchants, was not quite as harsh and rudimentary as it had been in the first half of the century. This shift is evident in the material goods found in the archaeological and documentary record of the site. Excavations have uncovered the physical remains of several generations of buildings and objects associated with the merchant-planter Colonel William Kendall, his family, and his servants, and slaves who lived on this site in the second half of the seventeenth century (Fig. 10). Although the archaeology of the site is far from complete, a few recovered artifacts indicate that the Kendalls had a wider variety of personal and household items than most of their contemporaries. The following sample of artifacts unearthed at Eyreville is indicative of the trade patterns that tied the Eastern Shore settlers to a host of merchants and suppliers from Europe and other colonies who were eager to sell them the latest consumer goods in exchange for tobacco, grains, corn, and livestock. These items are emblematic of the emergence of a planter elite and the tentative beginnings of a gentry society that would dominate the region in the coming century.

Ceramics

Wooden bowls, pewter dishes, mismatched drinking vessels, and communal pots were among the common implements used by families and servants at mealtimes in early Chesapeake households. By the last quarter of the seventeenth century, dining among the elite took on more formal rituals through the use of new, specialized goods. The rudimentary wooden trenchers of the past were slowly replaced by matching dinnerware and silver, and kept in cabinets designed for their display.[1] One Eyreville artifact that speaks to the Kendalls' participation in this shift is Chinese porcelain. Its pearly white, almost opalescent complexion and vitrified body, coupled with its dainty hand-painted designs, became a status symbol across Europe when it was first introduced by the Portuguese in the sixteenth century.[2] Porcelain's popularity, and the high cost of its importation, led Europeans to emulate it. Among the most popular types were Dutch tin-glazed earthenwares in the seventeenth century and English soft-paste porcelains and tinted iron-glazed earthenware.[3] Not surprisingly, numerous sherds of porcelain teaware and flatware were recovered at Eyreville (Fig. 11). Chinese porcelain was also seen as a sign of status due to its use in tea ceremonies. A novel practice at the end of the seventeenth century, tea drinking became a high-status custom due to the rarity of imported tea and sugar and the necessary and costly equipage needed for the ceremony.

As domestic preparations became more elaborate, with different ways to prepare and cook meals, new ingredients were also introduced. Through the Kendalls' mercantile connections, new ingredients such as spices, coffee, tea, and chocolate were brought from afar. There are three references to chocolate in the 1698 inventory of Colonel Kendall's son, Captain William Kendall. Two relate to the production of chocolate, "one stone chocolate grater" and "two tin chocolate pots," and the third involves a consumable product, "one bag chocolate nuts."[4] The earliest reference to chocolate in North America is a 1641 account of the Spanish bringing crates of chocolate to Florida. The earliest record of chocolate being consumed in the colonies is from 1670 in Boston.

Fig. 10. Aerial view of brick foundations of a house at Eyreville. Colonel William Kendall probably built this house in the third quarter of the seventeenth century.

Fig. 11. Porcelain sherd with hatched flower design.

Fig. 12. English and Dutch white clay tobacco pipes and local red clay tobacco pipes found at Eyreville.

Fig. 13. Local red clay tobacco pipe with "running deer" design.

Furthermore, in 1742, a recipe for chocolate almonds was included in an elite Williamsburg cookbook.[5] The fact that Captain Kendall obtained chocolate and/or cacao beans, items of wealth and status, is no doubt associated with his widespread mercantile connections with merchants in Britain, the Netherlands, and other American colonies on the mainland and the Caribbean.

Tobacco Pipes

While tobacco production and consumption are some of the signature features of the Chesapeake colonies, they also represent the globalization of a social practice whose origins were in the New World. Originally a Native American crop, the production of tobacco to satiate local, English, and European demand led to a thriving transcontinental market. Its labor-intensive cultivation was also responsible for the devastating importation of African slaves to work in its fields in the Chesapeake and the concomitant institutionalization of slavery in America.

Tobacco pipes have been found in great number and variety at Eyreville. The pipes recovered are mainly of Dutch and English origin, but there are also a number of locally made pipes (Fig. 12). A stark contrast to the European white ball-clay pipes, local pipes, also known as Chesapeake pipes or terracotta pipes, are produced with local clay and therefore range in color from red to brown. These pipes usually have incised decorations such as geometric patterns and motifs depicting plants, animals, and stars.[6] The local pipes found at Eyreville include multiple examples of the "running deer" pattern, as well as botanical designs that most likely represent corn or tobacco (Fig. 13). Although it is unclear who was producing these pipes and why, archaeologists have speculated that the pipes were made by a variety of manufacturers including Native Americans, African slaves, and white colonists.[7] This further raises the question

of who was using them. Did they express status? Were European white clay pipes reserved for the use of white planters and local pipes for the use of natives, slaves, and indentured white servants? Did smoking the more fragile white clay pipe imply a sort of status, a signal that its user could afford to replace a more costly implement as opposed to red clay pipes?[8] Or, did the smoker choose it based purely on availability and accessibility? If, in fact, there is some overarching trend of pipe usage based on ethnicity, the pipe type distribution at Eyreville may be quite telling. From early analyses of artifact distribution at the site, archaeologists have discerned a correlation between the locations of European pipes and local pipes, possibly suggesting a commingling of their users.[9] Additionally, considering the use of tobacco for leisurely activities, this may also suggest the casual interaction of people of different classes and ethnicities.

Books

Books were not a common household object in seventeenth-century Virginia. Most estate inventories from the first century of settlement on the Eastern Shore rarely contain them, in part because such imported items were expensive, but also because literacy was still a rarity among most inhabitants.[10] If a household possessed a book, it was most likely a Bible, an essential buttress of protestant religiosity. According to the probate inventory of 1698, Captain Kendall had 31 books "great and small" and a law book belonging to Major Custis.[11] The latter may have been a primer on legal procedure that provided guidance for justices who presided over the county court sessions.

Unfortunately, due to the friable nature of their materials, books do not preserve well in the archaeological record. Fortunately, not all traces of Kendall's books were lost. Excavations revealed two small oxidized fragments of metal that, when mended together, formed a beautiful book clasp (Fig. 14). The clasp, made of a cupric material,

Fig. 14. Book clasp with stamped designs including a *fleur de lis* pattern.

Fig. 15. Detail of furniture hardware with an Amsterdam maker's mark, early 1600s.

bears a floral design in the center and a *fleur de lis* at the top. This small fragment is yet another indication that the Kendalls were leaders of their community and versed in the intellectual and economic currents of the time.

Hardware

As Cary Carson observes in the introduction, the possessions listed in Kendall's inventory offer clues into the life and success of Colonel Kendall and his son, who inherited the estate from his father in 1686. One final clue is a seemingly mundane object, devoid of the beauty of porcelain and the sophistication of literature. It is a small iron artifact, rectangular in shape with a screw-like fastener on the front side. From the shape, material, and fastener, it can be surmised that this object was once a type of hardware for a piece of furniture or storage chest (Fig. 15). Changes in furniture were another cultural and economic marker for colonists. Moving on from the basic stool and bench of the early years, furniture increased in both quality and quantity, further exemplifying the character of its owner. As Carson mentions, the Kendalls had accrued an impressive collection of furniture by the time of the 1698 inventory, demonstrating to their contemporaries the extent of their accomplishments.

What truly catches the eye with this artifact, however, is the small stamped mark above the fastener. Encased in three Xs and topped with a crown, this specific mark was the hallmark of Amsterdam in the early 1600s.[12] The fact that the artifact and

its corresponding host were produced in Amsterdam and shipped to Virginia confirms the strong Dutch trade connections that were present on the Eastern Shore throughout the seventeenth century.[13]

The Wealth of Things

The Kendalls' level of wealth is evident in the four types of artifacts found in the archeological record and can also be corroborated by documentary evidence. Historians Lois Green Carr and Lorena Walsh examined the material wealth of seventeenth- and eighteenth-century Chesapeake colonists by tracking the prevalence of 12 specific items in probate inventories.[14] The study looked at approximately 7,500 probate inventories in Maryland and Virginia from 1643 to 1777. The selection of items ranged from basic household and sanitation objects such as beds and chamber pots, to luxury and leisure commodities such as spices, pictures, and books. The results of the study varied slightly according to location, but ultimately showed that most households possessed about two of the 12 signature goods during the seventeenth century and approximately five by the time of the American Revolution. In Captain Kendall's 1698 probate inventory, the family possessed all but one of the 12 items, placing them in the elite rank and head and shoulders above the average household at the end of the century. The Kendalls were thus part of the emerging gentry class that would dominate the Chesapeake world in the eighteenth century.

NOTES

1. Lois Green Carr and Lorena S. Walsh, "Changing Lifestyles and Consumer Behavior in the Colonial Chesapeake," in *Consuming Interests: The Style of Life in the Eighteenth Century*, ed. Cary Carson, Ronald Hoffman, and Peter J. Albert (Charlottesville: University Press of Virginia, 1994), 66–67.
2. Charlotte Wilcoxen, *Dutch Trade and Ceramics in America in the Seventeenth Century* (Albany, N.Y.: Albany Institute of History and Art, 1987), 67.
3. Wilcoxen, *Dutch Trade and Ceramics*, 67–71.
4. Inventory of the estate of Captain William Kendall (d. 1696), July 28, 1698, Northampton County Orders & Wills, No. 13, 1689–1698, 499, 502, 504.
5. James F. Gay, "Chocolate Production and Uses in 17th and 18th Century North America," in *Chocolate: History, Culture and Heritage*, ed. Louis Evan Grivetti and Howard-Yana Shapiro (Hoboken, N.J.: Wiley, 2009), 281–300.
6. Kathryn Sikes, "Stars as Social Space? Contextualizing 17th-Century Chesapeake Star-Motif GG Pipes," *Post-Medieval Archaeology* 42, no. 1 (June 1, 2008): 75–103.
7. Anna S. Agbe-Davies, *Tobacco, Pipes, and Race in Colonial Virginia: Little Tubes of Mighty Power* (Walnut Creek, Calif.: Left Coast Press, 2015).
8. On the status and social significance of white and red clay pipes on Chesapeake sites, see Willie Graham, Carter Hudgins, Carl Lounsbury, Fraser D. Neiman, and James Whittenburg, "Adaptation and Innovation: Archaeological and Architectural Perspectives on the Seventeenth-Century Chesapeake," *William and Mary Quarterly*, 3rd ser., 54 (July 2007): 486–93.
9. Jim Gloor and Carol Reynolds, "Preliminary Analysis of Tobacco Pipes Recovered from Newport House Site 44NH0507," unpublished site report, 2017.
10. F. W. Grubb, "Growth of Literacy in Colonial America: Longitudinal Patterns, Economic Models, and the Direction of Future Research," *Social Science History* 14, no. 4 (1990): 451–82.
11. Inventory of the estate of Captain William Kendall, 499.
12. *Hallmarks Encyclopedia*, http://hallmarkwiki.com/?country=Netherlands&province=Amsterdam, accessed July 2020.
13. For more on Dutch relations on the Eastern Shore, see April Lee Hatfield, *Atlantic Virginia: Intercolonial Relations in the Seventeenth Century* (Philadelphia: University of Pennsylvania Press, 2007); James R. Perry, *The Formation of a Society on Virginia's Eastern Shore, 1615–1655* (Chapel Hill: University of North Carolina Press, 1990).
14. Carr and Walsh, "Changing Lifestyles and Consumer Behavior," 59–166.

Eyre Hall: Power House

CARL R. LOUNSBURY

LITTLETON EYRE: MAN OF BOUNDLESS AMBITION

THE FAMILY BIBLE WAS THE MOST COMMON AND SOMETIMES the only book in the homes of colonial Americans. Not only did reading and discussing its passages form one of the core responsibilities of Christian education, but stories from the Old and New Testaments provided readers with examples of how People of the Book struggled with issues that they too faced in their lives: from birth, love, illness, death, and grief to the promise of life everlasting. They took solace in these narratives of biblical times, and, just as they turned to its verses to find names to call their own children, so they began to use it to keep a record of their lives—the births, baptisms, marriages, deaths, and other major family events. The Bible became the repository for documenting the names, dates, and relationship of family members through the generations, chronicling in microcosm their own genesis stories.

Not surprisingly, the oldest object associated with the Eyre family at Eyre Hall is the family Bible. Unfortunately, the first few pages including the title page of the Old Testament were ripped out at some time, leaving the date of its publication uncertain and removing any genealogical inscriptions that may have been recorded by the family. However, it was bound at an early point with a copy of the Anglican Book of Common Prayer, the Book of Psalms, and the New Testament. The latter two retain their title pages with their publication place and date: Cambridge, England, 1638 (see Cat. 122). Old enough to have been in the possession of Thomas Eyre, the first of the family in Virginia, who died in 1657, it seems highly likely that it was in the possession of his grandson Severn Eyre when he died in 1728. On his death, the Bible was inherited by his son Littleton Eyre and has remained at Eyre Hall ever since.

Littleton Eyre may have continued the habit of inscribing his family's life events in the missing front pages, but he also found it an appropriate place to record his own particular achievements. Five years after his father's death, the 23-year-old Littleton boldly inscribed in youthful script, along the outer margin of one of the pages in the Book of Common Prayer: "Littleton Eyre his Name 1733 He being Sheriff that year." It was the declaration of an aspiring man eager to make his mark in the world (Fig. 16). What had precipitated this extraordinary outburst of pride was his selection on

65

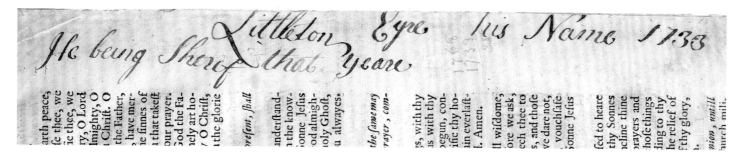

Fig. 16. Littleton Eyre's inscription on a page of the Book of Common Prayer in the family Bible.

June 12, 1733 by the Northampton County magistrates to be a sub-sheriff, a minor position whose incumbent was tasked by the sheriff with doing all the routine work of apprehending petty thieves, remanding debtors to prison, serving writs, and maintaining order in the courtroom.[1] On taking the oath of sub-sheriff before the justices that day in the courthouse in Eastville, Littleton Eyre took the first step in his rise to political prominence, which culminated two short decades later when he became the most powerful official in the county and a significant player in provincial affairs who would challenge the prerogative of crown authority in the late colonial period. The inscription in the family Bible was but the first of many symbols of Littleton Eyre's driving ambition.

In this family story, Littleton Eyre, the fourth generation of Eyres on the Eastern Shore, is the first individual whose personality traits are evident not in his words but in his actions. With no surviving personal letters, it is hard to read his attitudes toward his wife and family and those who worked for him; it is also difficult to imagine his inter-actions with his friends, neighbors, business associates, and colleagues who served with him as magistrates, or indeed with those more famous Virginians of the late colonial period alongside whom he worked as a member of the House of Burgesses in Williamsburg for 20 years. Few left their candid impressions of him. We know next to nothing of his religious beliefs, other than that he served faithfully as churchwarden and vestryman of Hungars Parish for many years, looking out for the interests of the Anglican church. Though he had a propensity to scribble his name in the margins of the Bible and even sketched a profile of a ship on one page, we don't know how frequently he opened it to read and take comfort in its words.

It is from the success of his varied business interests and his many public offices—which he held from the early 1730s until his death in June 1768—that we can catch a glimpse of a man who worked hard, was fair in his dealings, and earned the trust and respect of his friends, associates, and common folk. The encomium published in the *Virginia Gazette* a couple of weeks after his death spoke of those virtues. He was "a Gentleman whose amiable qualities in private life will ever endear his memory to those who had the happiness of his acquaintance. In friendship he was open, generous, and sincere; as a parent and husband, kind, tender, and affectionate." In his public life "he always distinguished himself by an uprightness of heart, and firm attachment to the interests of his country."[2] He may have harbored doubts in his mind, but he comes across as a man who was confident in his judgment and comfortable with the responsibilities and the perquisites of his class.

Although Littleton Eyre was orphaned at 18, he was not at a loss for family members to look after his welfare. His mother's large family, the Harmansons, took him under their wing and provided for him until he reached his majority. Named in honor of his grandmother's family, Littleton probably spent much time in her household as a child, and it was to her and her son, Henry Harmanson, that Severn Eyre had entrusted the wellbeing of his two sons, Littleton and Severn, as executors of his estate. Gertrude Littleton Harmanson, a formidable widow in her sixties when Littleton's father died in 1728, took control of their lives. We don't know how much longer the younger son Severn lived, for no mention of him is made in records after his father's death. By 1732, when Littleton had reached his majority and was about to embark on his career as a merchant-planter and public servant, Gertrude Harmanson confirmed in court that she had assumed the responsibility of providing him with the educational necessities of "Reading, Writing and Arithmetick" requisite for someone of his status, as well as the basic needs of "Sufficient Cloathing [and] Dyet" derived from the profits of his estate that she and her son Henry had managed.[3] There is no evidence that reveals whether this education was received at a private academy in the county or across the water or whether a private tutor had been hired, but Littleton was to be the last generation of Eyres who did not receive formal instruction at a college.[4]

Gertrude Harmanson may have played some role in orchestrating her ward's matrimonial prospects, but even if not, she would not have been too displeased to find Littleton betrothed to her brother-in-law George Harmanson's daughter Bridget, who was also a younger first cousin of Littleton's mother. Born around 1708, Bridget was the third of six daughters and one son born to George Harmanson and his wife Elizabeth Yeardley, the daughter of Argall Yeardley II, scion of one of the most distinguished Virginia families, which had deep roots, landholdings, and wealth on the Eastern Shore.[5] In the vast Harmanson cousinage, Bridget and Littleton had probably known each other since they were children, and, given marriage patterns among the elite, this was a typical match. On January 15, 1734, Bridget and Littleton married. William Tazewell, Gertrude Littleton Harmanson's son-in-law who had married her daughter Sarah, sister to Littleton's mother Gertrude II, posted the security for the marriage bond. Littleton's grandmother gave her consent to the marriage. The two witnesses were Henry Harmanson, Gertrude Littleton Harmanson's son who married Bridget's younger sister, Rose, two years later, and Neech Eyre, Littleton's first cousin (son of Thomas Eyre III), who married Isabel Harmanson, Bridget's older sister, in March 1734.[6] Once married, Bridget and Littleton took up residence at Broad Creek plantation: 360 acres of land on the ocean side of the peninsula that George Harmanson had given to the couple.[7] In 1735 Bridget and Littleton's first

child Severn was born, named after his grandfather. Four years later, on September 28, 1739, Sarah Eyre was born. There may have been other children, but none survived into adulthood.

What Littleton Eyre learned from his grandmother was a passion for land. Since the 1640s the Littletons had been among the largest landowners on the Eastern Shore. As a girl, Gertrude Littleton had inherited 380 acres of land at Swans Gut Creek in Somerset County, Maryland, from her father Southey Littleton. What other land she may have inherited came to her husband Henry Harmanson when she married him in the early 1690s. In the 1704 rent rolls for the county, Harmanson owned 1,250 acres. After his death in 1709, Gertrude continued to purchase land in her own right, amounting to at least 1,351 acres. Writing in 1823, one of her descendants, United States senator Littleton Waller Tazewell, described her as a highly intelligent woman of will who "managed all her estates herself, with as much industry and skill and attention as any man could have done—Mounted on horseback she rode from one end of the Eastern Shore to the other without any attendant visiting different estates; and was reputed the best manager they had."[8] Her expanded landholdings insured that the three principal benefactors in her will—her son Henry, her daughter Sophia Tazewell, and her grandson Littleton Eyre—would receive an ample legacy. She devised to Littleton the land in Maryland and 207 acres on Hog Island, which nearly doubled the amount of grazing land that he had inherited from his father on this low-lying barrier island on the seaside.[9] In addition he later received an additional 350 acres from her estate.

Over the next 30 years Littleton followed his grandmother's predilection for playing the real estate market in Northampton and Accomack Counties, buying and selling more than 30 parcels amounting to more than 5,000 acres. His holdings on Hog Island alone amounted to nearly 850 acres (Fig. 17). When a whale washed up on its shore in 1764,

Fig. 17. View of Hog Island on the seaside.

the collector of customs for the district had to warn smugglers against taking away any parts of the whale from its rightful owner, who happened to be Littleton Eyre.[10] With land given to him by his father, grandmother, and father-in-law, Littleton amassed nearly 2,000 acres spread across the middle of Northampton County from the bayside to the seaside (see Fig. 26).

The most significant land acquisition in Littleton Eyre's career was the purchase of 700 acres on Cherrystone Creek, which belonged to distant kin. In the late seventeenth century, this parcel was the possession of William Kendall, who lived on the north side of the creek. In 1658 he married the widow Susannah Baker Eyre Pott, who was Littleton Eyre's great-grandmother. Shortly thereafter, Susannah and William Kendall had a daughter named Mary, who married Hancock Lee around 1680. In 1685 her father gave them the 700-acre tract on the south side of the creek where they were then living and entailed the land to their daughter Anna, who was born in 1682. Sometime after Mary's father died in 1686, she and her husband moved across the bay to Ditchley in Northumberland County on the Northern Neck. The land remained entailed until Anna, now an old woman, and her grandson, John Armistead, who was in financial straits and looking for ways to raise money, found a willing buyer in Littleton Eyre.

Through an act of the General Assembly, the Armisteads had the entail docked in the fall of 1754 and sold the 700 acres to Eyre for £850: a substantial amount for the period, but which must have seemed worth the cost as it was a very large tract in a choice location in the middle of the county surrounded on three sides by water.[11] One last hurdle for the transaction was the approval of the act by the Board of Trade in London. In order to sway its members to view it favorably, Governor Robert Dinwiddie wrote in February 1755 to James Abercromby, Virginia's colonial agent, "to use Y'r Int't to get Assent thereto, and I here send you a Let'r to Mr. Jas. Buchanan [London merchant] to Supply you with Money to pay the necessary Exp's thereof."[12] Abercromby submitted it to the Board with "Expedition & dispatch" in April and recommended confirmation to the Lords Justices, who approved it in August 1755.[13] Perhaps Eyre understood that a financial incentive to the right people would expedite the matter in the council, which readily gave its assent.

Christened Eyre Hall, the land became the home plantation of the Eyre family when workmen completed the gambrel-roofed, two-story, framed 40-foot-square mansion house in 1759. As plainly as the scribbled inscription in the family Bible announced Littleton's first steps in his political ascent to power, this well-finished and well-stocked house, with its two-story pedimented porch on the west side facing the waterside approach from Cherrystone Creek, proclaimed his arrival at its pinnacle (Fig. 18). An influential merchant, planter, and politician, Littleton built a power house that matched his ambitions. In a display of costly signaling understood by the ruling elite in Britain and replicated by the gentry of colonial Virginia, those who aspired to be leaders in county or provincial politics demonstrated this theory by

Fig. 18. Eyre Hall, view looking southeast.

constructing grand houses on well-tended estates to convey their natural predisposition toward those positions of authority. Building well in colonial Virginia was undeniably a costly endeavor, and therefore an efficacious signal of status. A grand house advertised the permanence of the Eyre family who had long-term interests in the community and could be trusted to manage its affairs. From 1759 onwards, Eyre Hall became the beacon of the family's identity and the locus of its power. It was home.

At his death in 1768 Littleton Eyre owned 4,395 acres including six major parcels of more than 500 acres apiece, four of which—Hungars Plantation, Broad Creek Plantation, Seaside Plantation, and Eyre Hall, the new home plantation— were working farms sustained by enslaved laborers who were quartered on them.[14] In addition to these agricultural lands, Eyre leased 517 acres and raised crops at Townfields, known as the Secretary's Land, one of the sinecures of the office

of the secretary of the colony, which was held by Thomas Nelson.[15] The Ferry Land property on Hungars River was the center of his shipping operations and ferry service, and Hog Island was reserved for fattening livestock.

As Littleton Eyre expanded his agricultural holdings from the 1730s to the 1760s, the number of people he held in bondage increased as well. On his father's death, he had inherited 21 slaves, and, by the late 1730s and early 1740s, there were between 18 and 22 Black tithables (men and women above the age of 16) enumerated in the list compiled each year for tax purposes. Since the list did not include Black children under 16, the total number of enslaved people owned by Eyre was probably well over 30 by this time. In addition, between five and ten white servants or tenants worked for Eyre as laborers or in other capacities on his farms in the 1730s and early 1740s.[16] Over the next two decades, the number of slaves in his possession

Fig. 19. Hungars Parish Church, Northampton County, 1742, altered 1851.

probably grew threefold, both by natural increase as well as the demand for specialized labor in his business enterprises, which expanded beyond agriculture into trade and services. Besides the small number who worked for Littleton Eyre as cooks, coachmen, stable hands, and body servants, African Americans worked at his grist mill, served as ferrymen transporting people and animals across the bay to Norfolk, Yorktown, and Hampton, and loaded and manned his merchant ships that sailed the Chesapeake and the Atlantic. Some fished the waters and harvested oyster beds; others trained in the building trades constructed and repaired housing and fencing across the family's several plantations. As his many enterprises expanded, so did the demand for labor. In his will of May 1768, Littleton Eyre gave all his slaves "to my Son Severn amounting to, with what he has now in possession, to about one hundred and five," which made him among the largest slave owners in the county.[17]

PUBLIC LIFE

Littleton Eyre's appointment as sub-sheriff of the county in 1733 signaled his assumption of the public duties expected of young men with ambition and ability from leading planter and merchant families. Their economic and social status positioned them for parochial, county, and provincial offices where they were expected to fulfill the many responsibilities of governing their community. For 35 years, Eyre served the inhabitants of Northampton County as a churchwarden and vestryman of his parish of Hungars, worked his way up the ranks in the county court in Eastville to become the senior magistrate, sheriff, and the chief military officer or lieutenant of the county, and represented his community in the House of Burgesses in Williamsburg from 1742 until 1761 before relinquishing the position. For

years these offices overlapped: he spent much of his time in meetings in Eastville or Williamsburg, or traveling on official business within the community inspecting roads, wharves, and public buildings or inventorying the goods and chattels of deceased neighbors or kinsmen. His time spent away from home was substantial.

In the year 1755 Littleton's public obligations revolved around regular meetings of Hungars Parish vestry, the Northampton County court, and sessions of the House of Burgesses. Following in the footsteps of his grandfather and possibly his father, Littleton had first been selected as a member of Hungars vestry in the 1730s and may have been deeply involved in the construction of an imposing brick church on Hungars Creek in 1742 (Fig. 19).[18] Although the vestry book for that year does not survive, the average number of meetings in subsequent years ranged from six to eight, including the invariable Easter Monday gathering, sometimes held at the brick church or at the courthouse in Eastville. In 1755 Littleton was selected once again as one of the two churchwardens, which meant that the time devoted to parish affairs was far greater than when he served only as vestryman.[19]

The county court sat every month with a docket that filled one or two days. In 1755 Littleton was present on January 14, February 12, March 11, April 8–9, June 10, August 12–13, September 9, October 14–15, and December 9.[20] His absence from the bench at the May, July, and November court sessions was due to his obligations in Williamsburg as a member of the House of Burgesses, which had much on its agenda with raising money, materiel, troops, and other preparations for a war against France and its Indian allies on the colony's western frontier. The opening session ran from May 1 to June 2 when it adjourned for a three-week break. It was during this time that General Edward Braddock's regiments of British troops, supported by American militia led by George Washington, marched across the Allegheny Mountains into western Pennsylvania. This hiatus in the House's schedule allowed Eyre to cross the bay and attend the June court session in Northampton. Two weeks later he was back in Williamsburg, as the legislature resumed its deliberations on June 24 and was prorogued on July 9, the very day that Braddock's army suffered a crushing defeat at the Battle of the Monongahela. News of the debacle must have been especially heartbreaking to Littleton as he had been appointed leader of the county militia in 1754. He had helped recruit and send volunteers from the Eastern Shore at the beginning of the year to support the British regulars in their march into the wilderness. Governor Dinwiddie had thanked him for his war efforts and the money that he had advanced to a recruitment officer, as well as for the supplies of "weathers and Fowles" that Eyre had shipped to Hampton for the cause.[21] Although he never came close to battle during the French and Indian War, Colonel Eyre proudly wore the silver-hilted smallsword now hanging over the south-passage doorway at Eyre Hall when he later inspected the mustered militiamen of Northampton County (see Cat. 151).

The panic caused by Braddock's defeat forced Governor Dinwiddie to recall the House of Burgesses on August 5 for a three-week session that lasted until August 23. Eyre crossed the bay for a fourth time two months later to attend the recalled assembly that met from October 27 through adjournment on November 8.[22] By the end of the year, Littleton had spent more than 100 days conducting public business, with an additional ten days or so devoted to traveling to Williamsburg and back to the Eastern Shore. Add to this the time that he spent on public correspondence and impromptu meetings with constituents, and it is hard to imagine too many days that went by in which he was not involved in some aspect of public business. Although 1755 was a particularly momentous year because of the war—with more trips to Williamsburg than usual—Eyre's hectic pace never slowed from year to year.

As vestryman, justice, provincial legislator, and lieutenant of the county, Eyre dealt with major issues such as overseeing the construction of a large brick church for the parish, sitting in judgement of slaves accused of capital offenses in so-called oyer and terminer courts, overseeing militia training, or declaring in court that acts of Parliament were not valid in his jurisdiction. He also dealt with the mundane realities of life, the foibles and mendacities of his neighbors, and the requests and demands of his constituents. He examined the purported lewd conduct of his fellow parishioners. Blasphemers and bastard-bearers would be presented in court and, if found guilty of immoral behavior, subjected to public shaming through corporal punishment or monetary penalties. He weighed the selection of a new minister to fill the pulpit, purchased pewter vessels and cloth for the church's communion table, and made sure that paupers had decent burials. In court he was frequently called upon to serve as a guardian for orphans and as an executor of estates. He superintended the repair of the county courthouse and jail, managed the construction of a tobacco warehouse, and directed the dumping of ships' ballast and animal carcasses in a convenient place to keep the channels of Hungars Creek clear. For his trouble in overseeing the construction of the warehouse, his fellow magistrates granted him the right to build "a corn room above the joists" to store his grain before it was loaded onto his ships.[23]

Public weal yielded private perks. With responsibilities of office came power and influence, and Littleton Eyre used his positions to protect and boost the prospects of family members, safeguard and expand his business interests, and promote the welfare and prosperity of his parish and county at the provincial level. As a member of the Burgesses, Littleton insured that bills were passed that allowed

Fig. 20. William and Mary, ca. 1740. Brafferton, 1723, left; College Building, 1695–97, center; President's House, 1732, right.

Hungars to sell off 87 of the 1,600 acres appropriated for the glebe land that had been given in Stephen Charlton's will 90 years previously—in order that the parish might purchase additional slaves to work the remaining land to raise revenue to support the minister.[24] He managed to secure sole proprietorship for the ferry service between Hungars and the ports of Yorktown, Hampton, and Norfolk in 1745.[25] Twenty years later, Littleton and his son Severn, who had now taken his father's seat in the Burgesses, fought strenuously and successfully to ward off competition from others who were bidding to break this lucrative monopoly when it came up in the legislature in 1766 and 1767.[26] When a vacancy opened for a collector of customs on the death of William Fairfax in 1757, Littleton wrote to his son George William Fairfax and offered him £100 to use his influence to secure the position of collector of the Eastern Shore for himself or his son Severn, who had just come into his majority.[27]

SEVERN EYRE, THE HEIR

Groomed to take his father's place in the family business and public offices, Severn Eyre spent his late teens receiving a formal education, something that his father probably recognized as a valuable asset to have in order to take his place in provincial politics. While serving in the House of Burgesses, Littleton may have gotten advice from his fellow legislators about schools and academies led by prominent tutors that attracted the sons of the gentry. After a long session in the capitol, it is easy to imagine him chatting over a bowl of punch in one of Williamsburg's taverns with representative Beverley Whiting of Gloucester County

whose two sons John and Peter Whiting attended a nearby private grammar school run by the Reverend William Yates, the minister of Abingdon Parish, who later served as the fifth president of William and Mary. Littleton chose to enroll his son in Reverend Yates's academy, which was held in the brick glebe house a few miles north of the church. It is not clear how long Severn attended the school, which was limited to 12 pupils. However, when John Page of Rosewell arrived in 1752 at the age of nine, he noted that Severn Eyre was one of the older boys who was soon to leave. Other classmates included Charles and Edward Carter of Shirley, Francis Willis of Whitehall in Gloucester, Thomas Nelson of Yorktown, Robert Tucker of Norfolk, and John Fox, Augustine Cooke, and Christopher Robinson, all sons of the gentry.[28] Yates instructed his pupils in grammar, mathematics, and the rudiments of Latin.

The Gloucester grammar school served as a conduit for further education at the College of William and Mary. In the fall of 1753, Severn Eyre traveled to Williamsburg accompanied by a young body servant to join more than one hundred other students at William and Mary, including at least a half dozen of his former grammar school classmates including the Carters, Fox, Cooke, the Whitings, and Tucker. More than 50 students lodged in the college building itself and took their meals in the great hall in its north wing (Fig. 20). In the two years that Severn was enrolled at the college, there were at least eight other students who also had body servants in attendance with them.[29] Although the name of Eyre's servant is unknown, he was responsible for taking care of his master's daily needs and probably slept in a passage outside his door if not inside the same room. The servant probably took his meals in the kitchen beneath the great hall.

Fig. 21. Portrait of Severn Eyre by Benjamin West, ca. 1757–59.

Under the direction of President William Stith, the college offered two courses of related subjects of study. Eyre attended classes in natural philosophy, which included physics, metaphysics, and mathematics. He also studied moral philosophy that covered rhetoric, logic, and ethics.[30] His two years at the college and in Williamsburg allowed him to get the kind of education that he needed to thrive in the wider world of provincial society, culture, and politics. He also developed friendships with the future leaders of the colony. More than a dozen of his collegiate classmates or their siblings would serve alongside Severn in the provincial assembly in the late 1760s and early 1770s.[31]

After completing his education in 1755, Severn Eyre probably returned to the Eastern Shore to help his father run his extensive agricultural estates and business interests. As the only male heir, he would also be expected to master these responsibilities. As a planter, he learned the seasonal patterns of raising crops and overseeing the labor of an enslaved workforce on several discontiguous plantations. His interest in trade and shipping may have drawn him to the work of his father's commercial partners at Bowdoin, Eyre, and Smith. John Bowdoin was only a few years older than himself, but the two had known each other since childhood. He would have also begun to take the first steps in the public sphere by serving on juries or inventorying estates of neighbors.

However, few documents reveal how Severn Eyre spent these early years. He shows up in the public record for the first time on the wrong side of the law for a minor indiscretion. In 1758 he was presented by the churchwarden of Hungars Parish along with John Bowdoin and Custis Kendall and several others for cursing, no doubt brought on by a boisterous night of drunken revelry after which 15 young men were summoned to appear in court to answer the charges.[32] It may have been a little awkward for Bowdoin who was a magistrate. Early the following year, Preeson Bowdoin married Severn's sister Sarah on February 19, 1759. Severn

served as security for the license. The marriage sealed the union between the families. In June, with the construction of Eyre Hall on its way to completion, Littleton and Bridget took a major step in recognizing the independence of their son by deeding him the 468-acre plantation where they were then living on Old Town Neck, which was bounded on the west by the bay and Hungars River and on the east by Mattawoman Creek. They also gave him the Broadwater Creek plantation on the seaside of the peninsula that had been presented to Bridget and her husband by her father George Harmanson when they were married. Witnesses to the deed included John Bowdoin and his brother Preeson, the Eyres' new son-in-law.[33]

One thing expected of Severn was to find a helpmeet. In his search for a suitable matrimonial partner, Severn could have followed the pattern that had become standard among the gentry of colonial Virginia and looked to his extended cousinry or to neighboring families of similar social status, as had his sister Sarah in marrying Preeson Bowdoin. Being the son of a leading member of the gentry with a college education and friends that stretched beyond the Eastern Shore, Severn may have taken advantage of his wealth and position to travel to visit people across the Tidewater and perhaps even further afield. It seems highly likely that he journeyed to Philadelphia during this period where he had his portrait painted by a young Benjamin West whom he probably met through Preeson Bowdoin (Fig. 21).

Old school friends or business may have been the lure for Severn to visit the port of Norfolk where he met Margaret, the daughter of Margaret and John Taylor. A Scots merchant who had settled in Norfolk, John Taylor was one of the biggest dealers in manufactured goods and had the largest assortment of dry goods for sale in his store in Norfolk in the 1740s. He had been an alderman and served as mayor of the port from 1739 until his death in 1744. Taylor and his wife Margaret had three children: daughter Margaret and two sons named James and John. John became a merchant like his father; James, having studied medicine in Scotland and then practiced as a doctor on his return to Norfolk, eventually became involved in commerce like his brother.[34]

The brothers may have been the intermediaries through whom Margaret and Severn met; if not, then they met through other commercial, familial, or social connections that remain obscure. No matter how they came to know one another, their friendship blossomed. Severn and Margaret married in Norfolk on January 28, 1760. He would turn 25 that year and she celebrated her 21st birthday a few months after their wedding. A little over a year later, on March 15, 1761, Margaret gave birth to their first child in Norfolk. Named after his grandfather, Littleton would be the first of five more children. The others were Severn, 1764; Margaret, called "Peggy," 1765; John, 1768; Sarah or "Sally," 1770; and finally William, 1772, who was born less than a year before his father died in January 1773.[35] If there were any still births or infant mortalities in this succession of children, they do not appear in family records. If none, then the fact that six children survived into adulthood was an unusual occurrence among most families.

Established on his own land with a growing family, Severn Eyre's future seemed assured. But like many in his family before and after him, he suffered debilitating pulmonary illnesses. Although we know little about the causes of his poor health or whether it afflicted him earlier in his life, in June 1762 he sought a remedy for his pain by traveling more than two hundred miles from the Eastern Shore to the Warm Springs and Hot Springs in Augusta County on the edge of the western mountains. With a weak constitution, the journey must have been arduous. Staying overnight in taverns and in private homes, Severn took two weeks to ride from Williamsburg to the Hot Springs (see Fig. 49). His cryptic diary entries covering the two weeks at the hot springs are a litany of miseries—rainy most of the time he was there; frequent entries noting he was "sick" or "very sick," interspersed by days when he was "sweated"; and a laconic statement recording "nothing but bread to eat with some butter" over a five-day period. He set off for home near the end of the month and was back in Norfolk in early August, returning to his wife and young son who were staying with her relatives and feeling probably no better from his sojourn and regimen of sweats and purges at the mountain springs.[36]

Although this is the most detailed account of his effort to find relief in travel, there may have been many more trips in the coming years, all of which have left little documentary evidence except one tantalizing episode. In August 1770 Severn and the Reverend Richard Hewitt, his old college friend and the minister of Hungars Parish, were traveling in New England where they met with John Adams, John Hancock, and a number of other distinguished gentlemen in Boston. They visited Cambridge where they spent "a very agreeable day" with their hosts touring Harvard College. Eyre and Hewitt were also accompanied by Paul Trapier and William Bull, two young men from prominent families in South Carolina. Adams observed that these southern "Gentlemen are all Valetudinarians and are taking the Northern Tour for their Health." He described Eyre as "very full, and zealous in the Cause of American Liberty," and noted that he was "an intimate Friend of Mr. Patrick Henry . . . and is himself a Gentleman of great fortune, and of great Figure and Influence in the House of Burgesses. Both He and Mr. Hewitt were bred at the Virginia Colledge, and appear to be Men of Genius and Learning."[37]

Between his trip to the Hot Springs and his conversations in Harvard Yard with John Adams and John Hancock nearly a decade later, Severn Eyre had assumed the mantle of public office that his father had prepared for him. Before he set out on his journey to Augusta County in 1762, Severn was elected to the vestry of Hungars Church where he joined his father, John Bowdoin, Custis Kendall, a couple of Harmanson cousins, and Thomas Dalby, who had taken Littleton's place in the House of Burgesses in 1761. On May 22, 1762, Severn and members of the vestry selected Richard Hewett to be the minister of the parish.[38]

The most important moment in Severn's time as a county magistrate occurred on the first day he was sworn as a full justice of the peace for Northampton County on February 11, 1766. It was on this day that the court decided to weigh in on a controversy that had generated increasing tensions between American colonists and the British government over the previous couple of years. In 1763 the British had successfully concluded a global war against their old enemy France, which resulted in the expulsion of the French from Canada. The end of the Seven Years' War put a serious strain on British finances, and ministers believed that, since much of the war had been fought in America to protect colonial interests, it only seemed fair to get the Americans to shoulder some of the expenses. Parliament passed several acts imposing indirect and direct taxes on the colonies. Particularly infuriating was the Stamp Act passed by Prime Minister George Grenville's government in 1765. Outrage over the Stamp Act reverberated throughout the colonies because it threatened to bring public affairs and private business to a standstill if colonists refused to pay the tax on paper. Although there is no record of what Severn may have said in public about the act, in private he was disgusted with the actions of Grenville, going so far as to describe him in his private notebook on three occasions as "the American

Gump," for his doltish policies. He even sketched him as a stick figure with a noose around his neck between two posts of a gallows with these words below: "George Grenville the American Gump, an infernal, hellish Tyrant" (Fig. 22).[39]

This imperial debate over the right of Parliament to tax its American constituents without their representation in that body came to a head that day in the courthouse in Eastville. The justices of Northampton County, led by Littleton Eyre as the presiding magistrate, unanimously declared that this act of Parliament "did not bind effect or concern the Inhabitants of this Colony," deeming "said Act ... to be unconstitutional" and suggesting that the officers of the court were free to go about their duties without incurring any penalty by ignoring it.[40] This small act of defiance played no role in parliamentary debate one month later when the House of Commons voted to repeal the Stamp Act. However, at the same time it passed the Declaratory Acts, which affirmed that its authority to levy taxes extended to the American colonies.

In 1766, Severn was elected to the House of Burgesses and traveled to Williamsburg in November to deal with the aftermath of the repeal of the Stamp Act; over the next six years, he would face a series of other parliamentary acts that would continue to tear at the imperial bonds between America and Britain. It was during this period in the late 1760s that Eyre became known for his forceful position as a zealous defender of American liberty, as John Adams observed of him in their encounter in Boston and Cambridge in 1770. Not only did he consider the issues of empire, but he focused on the nitty-gritty of provincial legislation. Along with Patrick Henry, Richard Henry Lee, and Benjamin Harrison, Eyre was part of a committee that examined irregularities found in the late treasurer John Robinson's accounts. During his time in the House, he submitted a bill for the construction of a new lighthouse at Cape Henry, one to encourage the further settlement of Alexandria, another to promote the making of hemp, and amendments to the laws to prevent unlawful hunting and ranging. He brought constituent bills to the floor including one to vest the entailed lands of his friend Nathaniel Littleton Savage in fee simple and another to empower the churchwardens and vestry of Hungars Parish to lease certain lands. He was added to the committee for religion and the committee for trade, two of his most passionate interests.[41]

He worked hard during General Assembly sessions in Williamsburg, but his frail constitution gradually wore him down. On April 7, 1772 he was granted leave "to be absent from the Service of this house til the End of this session of the General Assembly."[42] He never returned. Severn died on January 25, 1773 in Norfolk from what was described as "pleuritick Disorder."[43] He was 37 years old and was buried in Norfolk, his wife's hometown, rather than at Eyre Hall, the only owner not to be buried in the family graveyard.

It is difficult to know what role he might have played when the long simmering colonial disgruntlement turned to open rebellion. His contemporaries knew that they had lost an exceptional leader. The *Virginia Gazette* described him as "a Gentleman of Abilities, a warm Friend of his Country, and greatly esteemed."[44] Poems published in the newspaper in the following weeks extolled his virtues: "Patriot full well his grateful County knows/ What to his Wisdom and his Love she owes/ Each Friend to Freedom can attest the Zeal/ That fir'd his Bosom for the general Weal."[45] Another praised his passion for liberty and his contempt for tyrants "from Nimrod down to Grenville's based Name."[46] Burgess member Benjamin Harrison of Charles City County wrote to a friend in Boston a couple of months after Eyre's death that "our Country has sustained a great loss in this Gentlm., we had few men of more Sense amongst us, nor had it one more attached to its interest or that would have gone greater Lengths to have supported the Liberties of America." On a personal note, Harrison mourned his loss, because the two men shared similar sentiments that "Cemented a Friendship."[47]

MERCHANTS OF EMPIRE

The Eyre family had been merchants as much as planters since the time of Thomas Eyre II in the late seventeenth century. His son Severn Eyre had combined his legal career with planting and the production of goods that he marketed among his neighbors in Northampton County and perhaps across the bay in parts of the Tidewater. Both Thomas II and Severn owned or had invested in ships to transport their goods to markets. Littleton Eyre followed in their mercantile footsteps but expanded the horizons of his business operations to reach across the Atlantic to England and Madeira off the northwest coast of Africa. He traded with merchants in New England and in the Caribbean. In the home waters of the Chesapeake Bay and the rivers that fed it, smaller vessels sailed from his docks at Hungars to deliver produce raised on neighboring plantations and products procured from rum distillers in the Caribbean and wine merchants in Madeira to Virginians eager to buy consumer goods and necessary staples grown, manufactured, and made in this Anglo-American empire. From the late 1740s through the middle of the 1770s—when revolution disrupted these trade routes—Littleton Eyre and his son Severn Eyre, in partnerships with a few other like-minded neighbors, profited from their expansive commercial ventures. Planting made them well-off, but trade made them wealthy. Eyre Hall and the homes of their neighbors filled with these goods of empire.

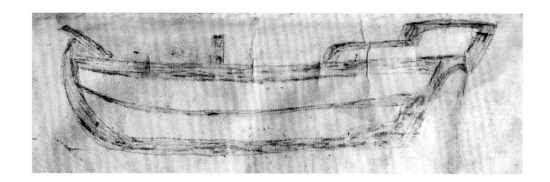

Fig. 23. Sketch of a ship's hull from a page of the family Bible.

Without business records from the early years of Littleton Eyre's mercantile career in the 1730s and '40s, it is hard to determine just when and how extensive was his engagement in the importation of English and colonial-made goods that he sold to the inhabitants of the Eastern Shore. He operated a mill by the early 1740s, and at the end of the decade he owned a schooner capable of transporting goods to foreign destinations. The extent of his trade and the type of goods he dealt with are not clear, but presumably he exported local produce including some tobacco, corn, oats, and peas.

Port records for the district of Accomack from the early 1750s survive in part and shed light on the extent of his carrying trade from his landing at the Ferry Land on Hungars Creek. Between 1749 and 1753, Littleton Eyre was the part owner of at least six ships.[48] Most of his partners were Eastern Shore merchants but some were ship's masters (Fig. 23). The largest was the *Sally*, a fifty-ton, square-stern sloop with a crew of five or six, which was built in Accomack in 1750 and co-owned by merchant Richard Drummond.[49] In the fall of 1751 it returned from a trip to the Caribbean, including its last stop in Dutch-owned Curaçao, with a hold full of ballast and £536.5.8 in currency. A few months later, in the new year, master George Scott sailed to Barbados carrying nearly 2,000 pounds of tobacco, 2,350 bushels of corn, 316 bushels of oats, 250 bushels of peas, 9,000 wood shingles, and 120 feet of scantling. In October 1752, the *Sally* returned from another voyage to Boston laden with 1,000 gallons of rum, 2,000 gallons of molasses, and one barrel of loaf sugar. Another Eastern Shore merchant, Peter Hogg, became Littleton's partner in the 40-ton sloop the *Severn*, which was also built in Accomack in 1750. Mariner Samuel Tomkins made trips to Barbados, Antigua, and Jamaica carrying corn, oats, potatoes, and pork and returning with rum, molasses, and sugar.[50]

Littleton also invested in smaller, square-sterned sloops of 10 to 20 tons, which appear to have kept to coastwise routes destined for northern ports and within the Chesapeake Bay. In the summer of 1749, the *Elizabeth*, of which he was co-owner with Northampton County resident John Haggoman, transported a load of grain to Maryland along with "some loose European goods, some stoneware, 1 Negro man and 1 Negro woman." After making its initial delivery, the ship continued to Philadelphia where it unloaded 700 bushels of oats and 200 pounds of feathers. The 12-ton *Ann of Northampton* made numerous runs to Rhode Island carrying corn, staves, and black walnut planks, and usually returned with a hold filled with barrels of rum and molasses.[51]

In smaller sloops Littleton Eyre also transported goods around his home waters in the bay and its large rivers. He shipped 250 bushels of oats to William Lightfoot of Yorktown in 1754.[52] Three years later, his enslaved ship's captain, Stephen Booker, transported a load of oats and several canoes to George William Fairfax and Scots merchant John Carlyle in Alexandria for their disposal.[53] He also shipped 900 bushels of corn and 615 bushels of wheat to George Washington in 1758 or 1759.[54]

In late 1754 Eyre formed a partnership with John Bowdoin, a Northampton County man in his early twenties who had been trained in the business in Boston where he was apprenticed for seven years to merchant Stephen Boutineau, a family relative. Like Boutineau, John Bowdoin was a descendant of a Huguenot family that had fled France after Louis XIV revoked the Edict of Nantes in 1685. The patriarch, Pierre Baudouin, ended up in Boston where the former physician turned to trade and made a fortune in the 15 years before he died in 1706. Two of his sons, James and John Bowdoin, sailed for the Eastern Shore in the first years of the eighteenth century where they forged ties with local merchants and planters. James returned to New England but John stayed and grew wealthy with those trade connections, purchased land in Northampton County, and operated a mill.[55] John's son Peter Bowdoin married Adah Harmanson, the daughter of John Harmanson and Susannah Kendall Harmanson. He took over his father's business and milling operations but died in 1746 when he was 40, leaving behind two sons, John, age 14, and his half-brother Preeson, who was 10. John chose Littleton Eyre as his guardian, and, in accordance with his father's will, was sent to Boston where he apprenticed with Stephen Boutineau. Peter Bowdoin also stipulated that his younger son Preeson was to be trained in the profession when he turned 14, but was to be sent to Philadelphia rather than Boston to be apprenticed with either merchant William Allen or Andrew Hamilton II, who were both distantly connected to the Bowdoins by marriage. Hamilton was the son of Andrew Hamilton, the Scots-born lawyer who had first settled on the Eastern Shore and had been the legal adviser and estate executor of Bridget Foxcroft. In 1706 Hamilton married Quaker Anne Preeson, the widow of planter Joseph Preeson, who was the brother of Peter Bowdoin's second wife Susannah.[56] Allen, a wealthy merchant, had married Margaret, the daughter of Andrew Hamilton I and Anne Preeson.[57]

Packed off to Boston in 1746, John Bowdoin returned to Northampton County in the fall of 1753.[58] Once back in Northampton County, John Bowdoin, under the patronage of Littleton Eyre, quickly took his place in county society and affairs. In January 1754, John married Grace Stringer, the daughter of Hillary Stringer, a magistrate, and his wife Elishe Harmonson Stringer, the younger sister of Bridget Harmanson Eyre. Littleton Eyre signed as security for the marriage license.[59] Near the end of the year, Littleton invited his 22-year-old protégé into a business partnership, establishing the firm of Bowdoin and Eyre, and the following year he welcomed him to the bench as a new justice of peace for the county.

Through the 1750s and early 1760s, the firm of Bowdoin and Eyre flourished, selling many varieties of goods to their neighbors that they had imported from Britain, New England, Madeira, and the Caribbean or that they had purchased from fellow merchants in Virginia. By the mid-1750s, Eyre operated a storehouse in Eastville, given to him on the death of his friend Kendall Harmanson, from which he sold the goods that the firm had imported.[60] From general household merchandise to specialized goods, they stocked the basic necessities as well as luxury items that had become fashionable. They sold stoneware jugs, rugs, saddles and bridles, powder and shot, bonnets, yards and ells of fabric of silk, cotton, and wool, hats, garters, shoes, buckles, tools of all kinds, packs of cards, horn books, psalters, common prayer books, bibles, quills, and quires of paper, some of these latter items possibly obtained by Eyre from the printing office in Williamsburg on his periodic visits to the capital when called to attend as a member of the House of Burgesses.[61]

Perhaps imported in one of their own ships that traded with the Caribbean colonies of Jamaica, Barbados, St. Kitts, Nevis, and Antigua, Eyre and Bowdoin supplied their neighbors with rum. In April 1755 they sued Elizabeth Laylor, an ordinary keeper, for payment of "1 hogshead and 118 gallons of rum charged" to her account on September 1, 1753.[62] The firm of Eyre and Bowdoin proved to be very effective in court when forced to recover debts from those who could not make their payments because they were such a commanding presence inside the courtroom. Sitting as magistrates on the raised bench, they knew exactly what the court docket was and were able to press their cases at opportune times when their opponents may have been unprepared or unrepresented by legal counsel. Time and again, the court order books record their stepping down from the bench when one of their cases came up before their fellow magistrates. The clerk marked them officially absent from their judicial duties. They may have stood alongside the public behind the bar in the courtroom as prominent

Fig. 24. Drawing of the mill on Eyreville Creek.

bystanders watching the proceedings, or they may have taken a more active role in the case—called as witnesses by their counsel with their account books and promissory notes in hand. Whatever happened, there appear to be few examples of a debt case brought by the firm of Bowdoin and Eyre against a defendant that were not resolved then and there in its favor by their colleagues on the bench. After the case was completed, they climbed the stairs of the magistrates' platform and resumed their places in the proceedings, which in the case of Littleton Eyre by this time was in the pedimented chief magistrate's chair in the center of the tribunal. It was a home court advantage that seldom failed and kept the credit side of the ledgers in the black.[63]

By the late 1750s or early 1760s, a third partner, Isaac Smith from Accomack County, joined the firm. It appears from later records that Smith assumed the task of book-keeper (the man responsible for the account books and ship manifests), keeping track in the neat hand of a trained clerk of all transactions relating to the expanding business of Bowdoin, Eyre, and Smith.[64] Severn Eyre had joined his father in the business by the early 1760s and took over much of the work of corresponding with business associates about the kind of goods that were in demand in Virginia,

looking after the consignment of cargos to ship's masters, and dealing with customs officials. In 1763 Severn wrote to Francis Newton and Thomas Gordon, English merchants in Madeira, about an invoice of items the firm shipped aboard the Liverpool-based snow *Hope*, captained by John Manex. In this bill of lading were "three hundred Bushells Indian Corn," which he wished them to receive and dispose of at a good price. In return, Eyre asked the merchants to ship him "one Pipe best London Wine, two Boxes Citrons, four neat Baskets for Ladies, & half dozen Nun Flowers [orchids] for caps." He wanted the wine to be "of the very best kind, and I would chuse it to be of a rich amber color."[65] In the early 1770s, Severn received permission from the county court to build a mill on his own land, which not only operated for the family's use but those of his neighbors and whose products found their way to Hungars Wharf where they were loaded aboard ships that increased the company's export sales (Fig. 24).[66]

Shipping news published in the *Virginia Gazette* in the late colonial period documents one part of Bowdoin, Eyre, and Smith's trade—commerce between the Caribbean islands and the Eastern Shore. The company purchased some of the commodities that would be shipped from plantations in the area. It paid Jacob Nottingham for 509 bushels of corn in 1768. Littleton Eyre received credit in Isaac Smith's accounts that same year for £213.5.0 for grain harvested from his own plantations, including 400 bushels of corn from Hungars, 1,164 bushels of oats from Town Fields, 322 bushels of wheat from the same land, and 1,330 bushels of oats from the home and mill farms. All were shipped out on their sloop, *Betsey and Esther*.[67]

At Hungars Wharf, laborers loaded the hold of one of their ships with peas, corn, oats, wheat, and other grains, building and coopering materials, which when fully laden would set sail on an excursion of several weeks that took it down the bay and out into the ocean. Sometimes the route varied, with the ship sailing eastward across the open waters of the Atlantic to Madeira or Lisbon where the crew traded grain for wine. The *Betsey and Esther*, first under the command of Captain John Wilkins and then, at the end of the colonial period, Captain Stephen Sampson, made three or four journeys a year. Much depended on seasonal variability in the weather, catching favorable winds and avoiding tropical storms. In addition, Bowdoin and Eyre tried to coordinate these voyages to match the harvesting and processing of crops in Virginia and the islands. A successful voyage would last two to two and a half months as Wilkins and Sampson brought the ship back to its landing at Hungars filled with barrels of rum, sugar, and other items such as chocolate and coffee desired by Virginia colonists. Most of this cargo was then offloaded to the warehouses owned by the company at the Ferry Land for later distribution and sale to customers on the Eastern Shore. On occasion, some barrels and crates from the voyage were transferred to a smaller sloop, the *Liberty*, captained by Eyre's slave mariner, Stephen Booker, which then sailed the Chesapeake to deliver its goods to wharves in Norfolk or landings along the James River and other riverine storehouses.

Port records from the district of Accomack published in the *Virginia Gazette* in 1768 provide a complete log of the

voyages made by the *Betsey and Esther* that year and suggest the range of ports and variety of goods exported from the Eastern Shore and brought back from the Caribbean and southern Europe:

> January 15: "Entered in the district of Accomack. Betsey and Esther, Stephen Sampson, from Madeira, with 10 hhds. and 16 quarter casks of wine."

> March 18: "Cleared in the district of Accomack. Betsey and Esther, Stephen Sampson, for Barbados, with 2690 bushels of corn, 15,000 shingles, and some livestock."

> May 31: "Entered in the district of Accomack. Betsey and Esther, Stephen Sampson, from Barbados, with 24 hhds. of rum, and 13 barrels of muscovado sugar."

> July 4: "Cleared in the district of Accomack. Betsey and Esther, Stephen Sampson, for Barbados, with 2600 bushels of corn, 366 bushels of oats, 40 bushels of peas, and 5000 shingles."

> September 20: "Entered in the district of Accomack. Betsey and Esther, Stephen Sampson, from Antigua, with 3 tierces and 12 barrels of brown sugar, 31 hhds. of rum, and 4 hhds. of molasses."

> October 10: "Cleared in the district of Accomack. Betsey and Esther, Stephen Sampson, for Lisbon, with 2500 bushels of corn, 400 bushels of oats, 30 bushels of pease, and 5000 shingles."[68]

Presumably, Sampson returned to the Eastern Shore early in the new year laden with wine and the cycle would begin again. But the new year brought increasing difficulties for merchants like Bowdoin, Eyre, and Smith in maintaining their trade connections because political tensions between Parliament and the American colonies had erupted once again with the enactment of a series of new measures aimed at levying an indirect tax on glass, lead, paints, paper, and tea, all of which had to be imported from Britain. Passed in

1767 and 1768 and known collectively as the Townshend Acts after Charles Townshend, the Chancellor of the Exchequer, this was but the latest effort by the British government to find ways of getting the colonists to help offset the enormous debt brought on by prosecution of the Seven Years' War.

Where the Stamp Act aroused immediate controversy because of the direct tax on paper that was used in all manner of business and government transactions, the Townshend Acts seemed to be less confrontational because they imposed indirect taxes on just a few imported items. However, over time these too drew opposition by many American merchants in Boston, New York, and Philadelphia, who put pressure on their English trading partners to work for their repeal. By 1769, with the urging of George Washington and George Mason, members of the House of Burgesses passed a resolution arguing once again that Parliament had no right to impose a tax on Virginians without their consent. Governor Botetourt dissolved the assembly, and the members of the House including Severn Eyre adjourned to the Raleigh Tavern on May 18 to form the Virginia Association, which declared that the acts had "the sole purpose of raising a revenue in America" and were "injurious to property and destructive to liberty." The burgesses and merchants who crafted the resolution hoped that it would "encourage industry and frugality" at home by developing domestic manufacturing to offset the loss of trade and income from those who agreed not to import a long list of items subject to the British taxes, though they recognized that certain exceptions were to be made for things that could not be readily produced in the colony. Leading the list of signatories was Speaker Peyton Randolph and Treasurer Robert Carter Nicholas, followed by more than 80 House members and local merchants including George Washington, Richard Henry Lee, Carter Braxton, Patrick Henry, John Blair, Jr., Patrick Henry, Thomas Jefferson, John Harmanson, and Severn Eyre.[69] Concerned about the efficacy of the non-importation agreement, the association met in June 1770 to renew its pledge and set up county committees to enforce the adopted measures. Once again Severn Eyre appended his signature, this time just below that of Thomas Jefferson.[70] However, it was ineffective as many merchants in America chose to ignore it and continued to trade as usual.

A few surviving letters from Severn Eyre's London partners from this period reflect the machinations made by English and American merchants to find compromises or ways around the prohibitions. Accused in Virginia of "aiding in forwarding the duties upon Americans, and also the Stamp duty," the London woolen drapers Mauduit, Wright & Co. wrote a letter to the *Virginia Gazette* in May 1769 denying such sentiments and claimed the opposite, that they "were the first people who began opposition to such duties" and had signed a petition to Parliament against the acts.[71] In June, the firm sought to reassure Bowdoin, Eyre, and Smith of their anti-tax sentiments. Unaware of the nonimportation agreement the Virginians had just signed, the London merchants then informed them that they were shipping a number of woolen goods that they believed would "meet your approbation."[72]

Even with Severn Eyre's signature on the nonimportation agreements, his associates debated the merits of following its strictures. In May 1770 John Bowdoin wrote to Isaac Smith about the situation. He observed that their two brothers, Preeson Bowdoin and Thorowgood Smith, who had formed a separate mercantile partnership, were in favor of trading with English merchants and intended to send "for a Cargo of goods, whether the revenue Acts are repealed or not as they say it answers no purpose for us not to import & other people to do it." Bowdoin believed that nonimportation "would never answer the purpose here in Virga. as the trade is so dispersed all over the Country & not one half of them join in the association," but he was not as willing as the brothers were to begin importing again until "the revenue Acts are repealed."[73]

Just a month earlier, pressure from English merchants led to the repeal in April 1770 of all the goods enumerated in the Townshend Acts except for tea. After that, the Virginia Association lost its resolve. In a July 1770 letter to Severn Eyre, London merchant Samuel Gist, a Bristol orphan who as young man made a fortune in Virginia in part by marrying the widow of a prosperous tobacco planter at Gould Hill in Hanover County before returning to England, hoped that the repeal would initiate "a thorough reconciliation" between the mother country and her American colonies and awaited new orders from his old customers.[74] In September he informed Eyre that he had shipped him in the *Two Sisters* "a cargoe of Goods that I hope will meet a ready & a Profitable Sale" and that "no time has been lost in getting them ready since we knew the resolutions of the Associations."[75] John Wilkins, a mariner from Norfolk, had been in England and met with Gist concerning the type of goods Bowdoin, Eyre, and Smith wished to import as well as negotiated some personal business on Eyre's behalf including the sale of some pieces of silver as well as the purchase of a stone roller for the garden at Eyre Hall.[76]

Although normal trade seem to have resumed by the early 1770s, the disruptions caused by the English insistence on imposing duties on American imports remained an unresolved issue. Severn Eyre died in January 1773, but the firm's old trade practices soon provoked another crisis. The English began to crack down on smuggling and started to enforce laws that had often been overlooked in the past, such as the prohibition of trade with foreign merchants in ports not under English jurisdiction. In the spring of 1775, merchants in Virginia were warned by the Royal Navy that lax shipping regulations would no longer be tolerated.[77] Bowdoin, Eyre, and Smith got caught up in these contentious issues when two of its ships, the *Betsey and Esther* and the *Liberty*, were seized by the *Magdalen*, a Royal Navy vessel, and libeled in the vice-admiralty court in the

capitol in Williamsburg for alleged violations of the trade acts including a stop at St. Eustatius, a Dutch island in the Caribbean. Despite George Wythe's spirited defense of the case, John Randolph, the attorney general, judge of the court, and an ardent Tory, ruled against the firm on April 12, 1775 and the two ships were condemned and most of the cargo forfeited.[78]

However, before the ships could be sold at public auction, armed conflict broke out on April 19 at Lexington and Concord in Massachusetts between English troops that had been sent out from Boston to seize powder and arms in those towns. In Williamsburg, Governor Dunmore had plotted a similar scheme, and, early on the morning of April 21, enlisted the captain of the *Magdalen*, the same ship that had seized the *Betsey* and *Liberty*, to take a contingent of armed marines under the cover of darkness and remove 15 barrels of gunpower stored in the magazine in the capital. They were successful and carried them off to their mooring at Burwell's Landing on the James River where they loaded the powder aboard the *Liberty* and sailed downriver into the open waters of Hampton Roads to keep it from falling into the hands of angry colonists who had stormed the city after they had heard of the theft.

The Royal Navy held on to both of the Eyre, Bowdoin, and Smith ships, using them in armed raids that summer, harassing towns and plantations in Hampton Roads. On September 2, a huge storm swept through the area and the *Liberty* was cast adrift on the Back River in Hampton. The inhabitants of the city plundered the "King's stores" on the wrecked ship and then set her on fire.[79] In December 1775, the Royal Navy dispatched the *Betsey* to Boston with an American prisoner on board as well as a supply of corn and potatoes intended for the British troops stationed there. Before it reached port, an American privateer captured the *Betsey* off the coast of Massachusetts. The following spring, the ship was libeled and sold at auction. Before it was sold, Preeson Bowdoin heard word of its fate and in May 1776 wrote to George Washington in Cambridge to claim his rightful ownership of it and ask the general to look into the matter. Washington's response has been lost, but the sale occurred three weeks later.[80] It remains unknown whether Bowdoin ever recovered his property.

In early October 1775, John Bowdoin, the merchant who had entered into partnership with Littleton Eyre in 1754 and had welcomed Severn Eyre into the business in the 1760s, died, effectively ending the partnership of Bowdoin, Eyre, and Smith—and leaving only Isaac Smith to sort out the interwoven finances of two closely knit merchant families.[81] Severn Eyre left six young children when he died in 1773, but none were old enough to take up the mantle to revive the family's commercial fortunes or assume the political leadership necessary to steer them through the calamitous times of the Revolution.

NOTES

1. Northampton County Court Order Book, No. 20, 1732–1742, 51, June 12, 1733.

2. *Virginia Gazette* [PD], July 7, 1768, 2:2.

3. Northampton County Court Order Book, No. 20, 1732–1742, 10, June 17, 1732.

4. It is possible that Littleton Eyre may have been sent to the College of William and Mary when his father was still alive. Unfortunately, the college records are too spotty to verify if this was the case. By the time he became the ward of Gertrude Littleton Harmanson, he was about 18 and may have been considered too old for enrollment. Gertrude Littleton Harmanson's nephew Southey Littleton attended William and Mary in 1703, when he was around 11 years old. When Southey's father Nathaniel Littleton II wrote his will that year, he directed that his wife was to keep his son "at the Colledge 4 years or longer." In 1712 Southey Littleton married Mary Eyre, the daughter of Daniel Eyre I. James Handley Marshall, *Abstracts of Wills & Administrations of Northampton County, Virginia, 1632–1802* (Camden, Maine: Picton Press, 1994), 170.

5. George Harmanson had a long distinguished public career serving on the county court and the House of Burgesses, and as head of the county militia at the rank of lieutenant colonel. *Virginia Magazine of History and Biography* 48, no. 2 (April 1940): 148.

6. Jean Mihalyka, *Marriages, Northampton County, Virginia, 1661–1854* (Bowie, Md.: Heritage Books, 1991), 35, 50.

7. George Harmanson to Littleton and Bridget Eyre, April 9, 1735, Eyre Hall Family Papers, Virginia Historical Society, Richmond.

8. Lynda R. Heaton, "Littleton Waller Tazewell's Sketch of His Own Family 1823: Transcribed and Edited" (master's thesis, College of William and Mary, 1967), 51.

9. Northampton County Wills & Inventories, No. 18, 1733–1740, 285-86, September 11, 1732.

10. Notice of J. Manby, customs collector for the Port of Accomack, March 14, 1764, Eyre Hall Family Papers.

11. "An Act for vesting seven hundred acres of land, with the appurtenances, lying on Cherristone's Creek, in the parish of Hungar's and the county of Northampton, in Littleton Eyre, Gent. in fee-simple, October 1754," in William Waller Hening, *The Statutes at Large, being a Collection of all the Laws of Virginia* (New York, Philadelphia, and Richmond, 1819-23), 6:443-46.

12. Robert Dinwiddie to James Abercromby, February 18, 1755, in R. A. Brock, ed., *The Official Records of Robert Dinwiddie, Lieutenant-Governor of the Colony of Virginia, 1751–1758*, (Richmond: Virginia Historical Society, 1883), 1:507.

13. John C. Van Horne and George Reese, eds., *The Letter Book of James Abercromby, Colonial Agent, 1751–1773* (Richmond: Virginia State Library and Archives, 1991), 140, 143.

14. Will of Littleton Eyre, May 7, 1768, Northampton County Wills & Inventories, No. 24, 1766–1772, 174-75.

15. In 1768 Eyre paid Thomas Nelson, secretary of the colony, £15 for rent of the land: Estate of Littleton Eyre in account with Bowdoin, Eyre & Smith, 1768-80, April 11, 1781, Northampton County Wills & Inventories, No. 26, 1777–1783, 404.

16. John B. Bell, *Northampton County, Virginia, Tithables, 1720–1769* (Bowie, Md.: Heritage Books, 1993), 271, 287, 303, 319, 323, 336, 356.

17. In his will, Littleton Eyre gave his grandson Preeson Bowdoin a young "Negro boy George to wait on him." He had previously done the same for his son-in-law, also named Preeson, when he had married his daughter Sarah Eyre on February 19, 1759. At that time he received "a negro boy Esau." Will of Littleton Eyre, May 7, 1768, Northampton County Wills & Inventories, No. 24, 1766–1772, 174-75.

18. In 1739 Littleton Eyre served as a churchwarden. Jean Mihalyka, ed., *Loose Papers and Sundry Court Cases, Northampton County, Virginia*, vol. 2, *1732 to 1744/5* (Bowie, Md.: Hickory House, 1997), March 1739.

19. Frank Walczyk, ed., *Northampton County Orders, 1753–1758* (Coram, N.Y.: Peter's Row, 2005), 139, December 9, 1755.

20. Walczyk, *Northampton County Orders, 1753–1758*, 82, 85, 92, 95, 99, 102, 113, 116, 122, 127, 130, 137.

21. Robert Dinwiddie to Littleton Eyre, February 1, 1755, in Brock, *Official Records of Robert Dinwiddie*, 1:482-83.

22. On the meeting dates of the House of Burgesses in 1755, see H. R. McIlwaine, ed., *Journals of the House of Burgesses, 1752–1758* (Richmond: Virginia State Library, 1909).

23. Gail Walczyk, ed., *Northampton County Orders, 1748–1751* (Coram, N.Y.: Peter's Row, 2005), 52, November 15, 1749.

24. "An Act to vest eighty seven acres of land, appropriated for a glebe in the parish of Hungars . . . to be sold," February 1745, in Hening, *Statutes at Large*, 5:390-91.

25. "An Act for appointing several new ferries," February 1745, in Hening, *Statutes at Large*, 5:364. The act set the cost for ferriage "from York, Hampton, and Norfolk towns, to the land of Littleton Eyre, on Hungars River. . . . The price for a man passing singly, twenty shillings, for a horse the same; for a man and horse, or if there be more, and for each, fifteen shillings." A later act set additional rates for coaches, chariots, wagons, and carts, and hogsheads of tobacco, October 1748. Hening, *Statutes at Large*, 6:19-20.

26. J. P. Kennedy, ed., *Journals of the House of Burgesses, 1766–1769* (Richmond: Virginia State Library, 1906), 21, November 6, 1766; 60, December 7, 1766; 97, March 7, 1767; and 103, March 30, 1767. Perhaps because of the threat to the ferry monopoly by others, Severn Eyre kept a brief and perhaps not complete account of the traffic between Hungars and Norfolk and Yorktown between November 1766 and February 1767. During that time, fees amounted to nearly £50. Severn Eyre Miscellany Book 1762-1768, Eyre Hall, Northampton County, Virginia.

27. Littleton Eyre to George William Fairfax, September 23, 1757, George William Fairfax Letters and Documents, vol. 1, 1742–1761, 6, Fairfax of Cameron MSS, Colonial Records, Library of Virginia, Richmond.

28. *The Virginia Historical Register* 3 (1850): 144–45.

29. Bursar Book 1745–1770, 1–2, 9, 28, Office of the Bursar Records, Special Collections, Swem Library, College of William and Mary, Williamsburg.

30. Lyon G. Tyler, "Early Courses and Professors at William and Mary College," *William and Mary Quarterly*, 1st ser., 14, no. 2 (October 1905): 72.

31. *Catalogue of William and Mary College, in the State of Virginia, 1855* (Williamsburg: J. Hervey Ewing, 1855), 20–22; Kennedy, *Journals of the House of Burgesses, 1766–1769*, 3, 79; J. P. Kennedy, ed., *Journals of the House of Burgesses, 1770–1772* (Richmond: Virginia State Library, 1906), 3, 113.

32. Walcyzk, *Northampton County Orders, 1753–1758*, 253, February 14, 1758; Jean Mihalyka, ed., *Loose Papers and Sundry Court Cases, Northampton County, Virginia*, vol. 3, *April 1744 to July 1761* (Bowie, Md.: Hickory House, 2005), Packet 48, Churchwarden Presentments, March 1758.

33. Northampton County Deeds, etc., No. 19, 1750–1763, 418–19, June 12, 1759.

34. On the merchants of Norfolk including John Taylor, see Thomas Costa, "Economic Development and Political Authority: Norfolk, Virginia, Merchant-Magistrates, 1736–1800" (Ph.D. diss., College of William and Mary, 1991), 65–67.

35. Hungars Parish Vestry Book, 1758–1782, 186, Northampton County Clerk's Office, Eastville, Virginia.

36. Severn Eyre Miscellany Book 1762–1768, 42–47, June 15–August 3, 1762.

37. L. H. Butterfield, ed., *The Adams Papers: Diary and Autobiography of John Adams*, vol. 1, *1755–1770* (Cambridge, Mass.: Harvard University Press, 1961), 364.

38. Hungars Parish Vestry Book, 1758–1782, May 22, 1762.

39. Severn Eyre Miscellany Book 1762–1768, 4, 31.

40. Northampton County Court Order Book 1765–1771, 31–32, February 11, 1766.

41. Kennedy, *Journals of the House of Burgesses, 1766–1769*, 268, 274, 288, 312; Kennedy, *Journals of the House of Burgesses, 1770–1772*, 38, 59, 90, 169, 172, 295.

42. Kennedy, *Journals of the House of Burgesses, 1770–1772*, 301.

43. *Virginia Gazette* [PD], January 28, 1773, 2:3.

44. *Virginia Gazette* [PD], January 28, 1773, 2:3.

45. *Virginia Gazette* [PD], June 24, 1773, 3:3.

46. *Virginia Gazette* [PD], February 18, 1773, 2:3.

47. *Boston Gazette*, April 12, 1773.

48. Partial ownership was a common means of allowing merchants to divide their liabilities in case ships and their cargoes were damaged, destroyed, captured, or lost at sea.

49. After Drummond died in 1751, his widow Katherine and his partner Littleton Eyre advertised the sale of another larger ship of 90 tons that was riding anchor in Cherrystone Creek in Northampton County. *Virginia Gazette* [H], October 31, 1751, 3:2.

50. Entries and Clearances, Port of Accomack, 1748–1753, Naval Office Lists, 5/1445/004, Colonial Office, Public Records Office, London, microfilm, John D. Rockefeller Jr. Library, Colonial Williamsburg.

51. Entries and Clearances, Port of Accomack, 1748–1753, Naval Office Lists.

52. William Lightfoot Account Book, 1747–1764, 93, June 24, 1754, Lightfoot Papers, Special Collections, John D. Rockefeller Jr. Library, Colonial Williamsburg.

53. Letter from Littleton Eyre to George William Fairfax, September 20, 1757, George William Fairfax Letters and Documents, vol. 1, 1742–1761, 6.

54. It not entirely clear from Washington's accounts if these shipments went to Washington at Mount Vernon or to the estate of Daniel Parke Custis in New Kent County. Custis's widow Martha married George Washington in January 1759, a couple of years after the death of Custis. W. W. Abbot, ed., *The Papers of George Washington*, Colonial Series, vol. 6, *4 September 1758–26 December 1760* (Charlottesville: University Press of Virginia, 1988), 266–70.

55. Marsha Hamilton, *Social and Economic Networks in Early Massachusetts: Atlantic Connections* (University Park: The Pennsylvania State University Press, 2009), 94–95.

56. Andrew Hamilton is now best known as the lawyer who successfully defended the newspaper publisher Peter Zenger of New York who was accused of libel brought by the governor of that colony in 1733 for printing articles in his paper accusing the government of malfeasance. The case is considered an important milestone in establishing a free press in the American colonies. Will of Peter Bowdoin, in Marshall, *Abstracts of Wills & Administrations of Northampton County, Virginia, 1632–1802*, 318–19.

57. William Allen became an important patron of the painter Benjamin West.

58. Frank and Gail Walczyk, eds., *Northampton County Orders, 1751–1753* (Coram, N.Y.: Peter's Row, 2005), 50–51, June 10, 1752; Mihalyka, *Loose Papers and Sundry Court Cases, April 1744 to July 1761*, Packet 41, October 1753.

59. Mihalyka, *Marriages, Northampton County, Virginia, 1661–1854*, 12.

60. The storehouse is mentioned in the will of Littleton Eyre, May 7, 1768.

61. For purchases from the printing office in Williamsburg see *Virginia Gazette* Journals 1750–1752, July 28, 1750, August 3, 1750, October 9, 1750, March 12, 1751, May 16, 1751, July 27, 1751, April 14, 1752, and *Virginia Gazette* Journals 1764–1766, May 3, 1765, August 31, 1765, John D. Rockefeller Jr. Library, Colonial Williamsburg; Mihalyka, *Loose Papers and Sundry Court Cases, April 1744 to July 1761*, Packet 43, May–July 1743; Packet 43, February 1755; Packet 43, March 1755; Packet 46, September 1756; Packet 48, November 1757; Packet 50, September 1759.

62. Mihalyka, *Loose Papers and Sundry Court Cases, April 1744 to July 1761*, Packet 45, April 1756.

63. See, for example, Walcyzk, *Northampton County Orders, 1753–1758*, 90, February 12, 1755; 94, March 11, 1755; 101, April 9, 1755; 120, August 13, 1755; 161, April 13, 1756; 207, March 8, 1757; and 247, December 14, 1757.

64. See, for example, Isaac Smith to Severn Eyre, May 7, 1770, Eyre Hall Family Papers.

65. Letter from Severn Eyre to Messrs. Newton and Gordon, merchants, Madeira, May 7, 1763, Business Records #38611, Library of Virginia, Richmond. For a study of the Madeira wine trade in early America, see David Hancock, *Oceans of Wine: Madeira and the Emergence of American Trade and Taste* (New Haven: Yale University Press, 2009).

66. Northampton County Minute Book, 1771–1777, 108, December 8, 1772.

67. Estate of Littleton Eyre in account with Bowdoin, Eyre, & Smith, 1768–80, April 11, 1781, Northampton County Wills & Inventories, No. 26, 1777–1783, 404, 406.

68. *Virginia Gazette* [PD], March 10, 1768, 3:1; May 26, 1768, 2:2; June 23, 1768, 2:3; September 8, 1768, 2:2; October 27, 1768, 4:2; and November 17, 1768, 2:2.

69. *Virginia Gazette* [PD], May 25, 1769, 1:1–2.

70. Julian P. Boyd, ed., *The Papers of Thomas Jefferson*, vol. 1, *1760–1776* (Princeton: Princeton University Press, 1950), 43–48. See also Glenn C. Smith, "An Era of Non-Importation Associations," *William and Mary Quarterly*, 2nd ser., 20, no. 1 (January 1940): 84–98.

71. *Virginia Gazette* [PD], September 7, 1769, 3:1.

72. The goods that Mauduit, Wright & Co. shipped to Eyre, Bowdoin, and Smith included "serge duffels, German serge, and broad cloths," items that were on the Virginia Association's nonimportation list. Letter from Mauduit, Wright, & Co. to Bowdoin, Eyre, and Smith, June 15, 1769, Eyre Hall Family Papers.

73. John Bowdoin to Isaac Smith, May 19, 1770, Eyre Hall Family Papers.

74. Samuel Gist to Severn Eyre, July 21, 1770, Eyre Hall Family Papers.

75. Many of the goods shipped by Gist in the *Two Sisters* ended up in Williamsburg. In late November, merchant John Carter advertised "Just Imported in the Two Sisters, Capt. Taylor, from London, . . . A large assortment of Goods for the Season" including "a variety of glassware, and Queen's china &c. &c." Samuel Gist to Severn Eyre, September 9, 1770, Eyre Hall Family Papers; *Virginia Gazette* [R], November 29, 1770, 3:1.

76. John Wilkins to Severn Eyre, December 18, 1770, Eyre Hall Family Papers.

77. *Virginia Gazette* [P], March 3, 1775, 2:3.

78. The documents in the case are reproduced in George Reese, ed., "The Court of Vice-Admiralty in Virginia and Some Cases of 1770–1775," *Virginia Magazine of History and Biography* 88, no. 3 (July 1980): 320–32.

79. William Bell Clark, ed., *Naval Documents of the American Revolution* (Washington, D.C.: U.S. Government Printing Office, 1964), 1:1296.

80. Preeson Bowdoin to George Washington, May 6, 1776. Washington letter to Bowdoin of May 10, 1776 has not been found. Philander D. Chase, ed., *The Papers of George Washington*, Revolutionary War Series, vol. 4, *1 April 1776–15 June 1776* (Charlottesville: University Press of Virginia, 1991), 218, 259.

81. The *Virginia Gazette* noted that Bowdoin had died after a painful illness of six weeks. *Virginia Gazette* [Pi], October 19, 1775, 3:3.

WORKING THE LAND

SAM FLORER

The Eyre family's landholdings, and therefore their wealth and influence, steadily grew from the time Thomas Eyre settled on Virginia's Eastern Shore in the 1640s to the ascendance of Littleton Eyre, culminating in the construction of Eyre Hall in 1759. As noted in the first two chapters of the family history, they accomplished their rise through luck, hard work, and strategic marriages with well-connected Eastern Shore planter and merchant families. Littleton Eyre's success as a large plantation owner corresponded with his political and social power within Northampton County. Littleton's sons and grandsons maintained their family's influence through the management of these lands and their harvests. By the late 1850s, the Eyres adjusted their approaches to meet changing economic and agricultural conditions, yet still based their wealth and power on the land. The family's reliance on the labor of enslaved men, women, and children remained a constant throughout these years. Not only was their labor necessary for the land to be profitable, but they themselves, as human chattel, were a valuable commodity. Although the Eyres added shipping and trade to their portfolio of business investments, the land and agricultural practices that depended upon slave labor remained the backbone of their economic success. This essay sheds light on the operation of those landholdings and the lives of the marginalized people whom the Eyres held in bondage who worked the fields for their benefit.

Landholdings

Before he turned 30, Littleton Eyre owned four separate plantations totaling over 1,300 acres. Littleton's considerable inheritance did not satisfy his desire for land, and he soon began expanding the plantations he inherited from his father and in-laws. The most significant of Littleton's acquisitions, both in acreage and for the future direction of the family, occurred in 1754 with the purchase of 700 acres along Cherrystone Creek on the bayside. This became the nucleus for the Eyre Hall plantation, where Littleton would move the family in 1759. By the time Littleton died in 1768, he had increased his holdings to 4,850 acres, making him one of the largest landowners on all of the Eastern Shore and representing the high-water mark of the Eyre family's properties (Fig. 25). There is no definitive answer as to why Littleton embarked on this land acquisition program. However, the more land he owned, and the more wealth he produced by working it, the more his social and political influence in the community grew.

In contrast to his father's driving ambition to acquire as much property as possible, Littleton's heir, Severn, actually slightly reduced the size of the family's holdings.[1] Severn's only major addition was the lease of approximately 500 acres of prime farmland from the Virginia government, known as Townfields or the Secretary's Land.[2] After these changes, the Eyre family operated a total of approximately 4,000 acres of land at the following plantations: 1,670 acres at Eyre Hall, 914 acres at Hungars, 620 acres at Broad Creek, 315 acres at Seaside, and 500 acres at Townfields (Fig. 26).

These numerous lands proved bountiful, and the family relied on their successful cultivation as the cornerstone of their wealth and influence. In line with late eighteenth-century regional trends, corn and oats made up the bulk of the family's agricultural output. A comparison of recorded yields of oats and corn from the years 1768, 1773, 1774, and 1776 reveals an average of roughly 913 bushels produced at the Hungars estate, 997 bushels at the "home" farm at Eyre Hall, and 1,989 bushels from Townfields, these numbers representing a roughly even split between corn and oats.[3] Trade in tobacco rarely appeared in the family's business records, reflecting the exhaustion of the Eastern Shore's soil due to decades of heavy tobacco cultivation. However, small amounts here and there indicate the Eyres still grew the once ubiquitous cash crop.[4] The family also sold small amounts of wheat, peas, flax seed, and sawn lumber—the latter commodity made possible by the operation of a mill on a creek adjacent to their Eyre Hall land, known as Eyreville Creek by later generations.[5] In addition, they raised considerable numbers of hogs, cattle, and sheep. Littleton's 1769 estate inventory lists 170 hogs, 166 cattle, and 208 sheep.[6] Like most large landowners of the region, diversification played a crucial role in the Eyres' agricultural success.

Name	Approximate number of acres owned at time of inheritance	Approximate number of acres owned at time of death
Thomas (d. 1657)	Unknown	200
Thomas II (d. 1715)	533 (from stepfather)	1,133
Severn (d. 1728)	400 (from Isaac Foxcroft)	633
Littleton (d. 1768)	1,343 (half from in-laws)	4,850
Severn (d. 1773)	4,850	4,036
William (d. 1808)	1,230	1,565
William L. (d. 1852)	1,565	777
John (d. 1855)	3,119	1,255

Fig. 25. Eyre land ownership.

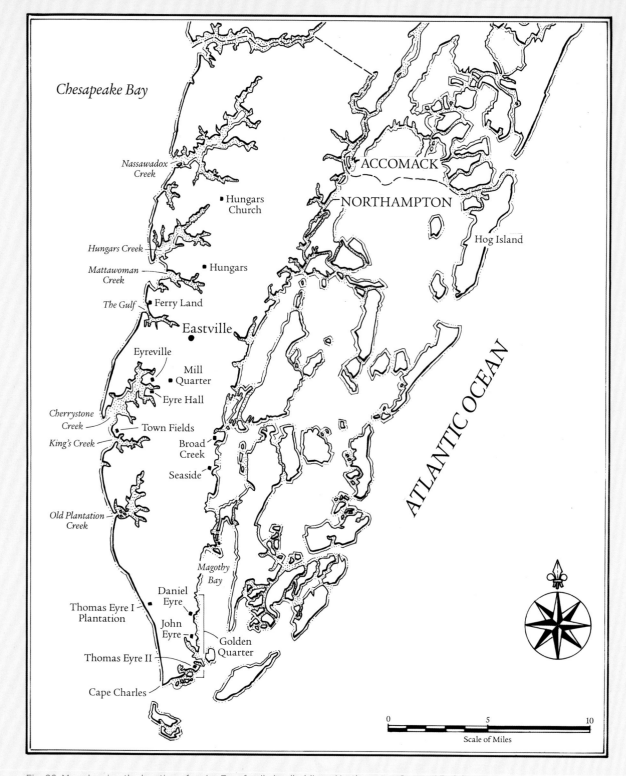

Fig. 26. Map showing the location of major Eyre family landholdings, Northampton County, Virginia.

Working the Land in the Late Colonial Period

As members of Virginia's landed gentry class, the Eyres built their estates on the backs of enslaved laborers, a practice that had become commonplace in Northampton County by the beginning of the eighteenth century. As the Eyres acquired more land, they also acquired more bondsmen either through inheritance, marriage, natural increase, or purchase (Fig. 27). By 1727 the first Severn Eyre, Littleton's father, had ten enslaved people listed in the county tithable list.[7] However, it is important to note that tithables in the

Slaveholder	Most slaves owned at one time	Names of known enslaved people
Thomas (d. 1657)	Unknown	Unknown
Thomas II (d. 1715)	2	James, Daniell[1]
Thomas III (d. 1719)	8	Jeffry Senr negro man, Henry, Stephen, Mulbrey, Hannah very old negro woman, Jonny, Sarah Junr, Moll[2]
John Eyre (d. 1719)	13	Anniday, George, Samboe, Frank, Woman and Child, Sarah, Grace, Esther, James, Ben, Betty[3]
Severn (d. 1728)	22	James, Sue, Mingo, Zacharyah, Eoronio, Sis, Sam, Marlborough, Mingo, George, Hannah, Jonathan, Ben, Pug, Sub, Zachariah, Judie, Jude, James, Mathews, John, Metkis, Peg, Lin, Little James, Miney, Esau, Jacob, Eli, Stephen, Benjamin, Sitt, Indea, Bridget, Sarah, Betty, Susse, Tom[4]
Littleton (d. 1768)	76	Harman Johnson, James, James, Minny, Esau, Betty, Sunter, Jack, Peter, Mingo, Legro, Santo, Hannah, Jenny, Charles, Luke, Tom, Betty, Minny, Sarah, Cleary, Eliz, Youth, Mils, Ely, Pete, Stephen, Sunton, Clare, Sam, App, Liverpool, Harry, Adam, Will, Hanable, Toney, Mary, Rachal, Cate, Rose, Scip, Betty, Grace, Sarah, Judith, Claire, Dick, Hope, Leah, Esther, Charles, Tom, Bidey, Stephen, Daniel, Peter, Gundy, Sarah, Amey, Judith, Comfort, Taby, Lucey, Prisciller, Isaac, Jacob, David, Left, Ezekiel, Joe, Simon, Ameriler, Tamer, Abigail, Abraham, Legro, Chocolate, Sarah, Luke, Luke, Grace, Jane, Riah, Elisha, Heziah, Siss, Hannah, Ricah, Patience, Jamie, Clara, Jennie, Precilla, Bedi, Eli, Billy, Peter, Luke, Minnie, Abel, Hope, George, Jacob, Isaac, Sam, Lazerus, Jacob, Simon, David, Lesnbe, Jonathan, James, Pegg, Henry, Solomon, Tom, Charles, Stephen, Judith, Comfort, Tabby, Lucy, Tom, Laroon, Abigail, Amy, Mary, Lydia, Betty, Candice, Southy, James, Adam, Phebe, and Ephraim[5]
Severn (d. 1773)	163	Tom the Elder, Luke the elder, Ben, Isaac, Luke little, Tom the younger, Gundy, Beedy, Jonathan, Laroon, Grace, Elisha, Abel, Nin, Hesiah, Grace Junr, Daphne, Tamer, Nanny, Adah, Bridget, Uriah, Clary, George, Sukey, Spencer, Dion, Amorella, Sam, Hannah, Rica, Betty, Tamer, Jane, Esther, Powel, Sarah, Pleasant, Hannah, Billy, George, Betty, Lukes, Jacob, Tabby, Annis, Lucy, Elzy, Bridget, Southy, Abigail, Sarah, Mingo's wife, Rose, Leah, Luke, Agnes, Abraham, Mingo, Stephen Booker, Dick, Abel, Lub, Left, Simon, Jacob; at Mill quarter: James, Amorellas, Leah, Clary, Sarah, Harry, Dick, Leah, Legro, Jacob, Abraham, Esau, Ezekiel, Judah; at Hungars: Leah Hungars, Minny, Ladis, Abel, Clary, Comfort, Ephraim, Mandy, Levin, George, Nim, Phillis, Abigail, Peg, Ben, Ciss, Rachel, Tabby, Jane, Solomon, Ryca, Mary, Jemmy, Dinah, Elijah, Legro, Rachel, Ladis, Betty, Sarah's, Peter, Ezekiel, Stephen, Charles, Peter, Hope, Harry, Jacob, Daniel, Peter Hungars, Peter Gova, Peter little, James Peter's, Ciss, Hannah, Patience, Lucy, Betty, Beck, Frank, Kate, China, Esther, John, Amy, Mary, Ledah, Betty, Nanny, Letty, Luke, Abner, York, Chocolate, Sunter, Cato, Patience, Priscilla, Kate, Esther, Bob, Shadrack, Allice, Judah Peter's Wife, Phebe, Dillah, Ebby, Cloe, Sam, Priscilla, Joe, Salt, Jenny old, Candis, Sunter, Roses, Maria, Daniel[6]
Severn (d. 1786)	59	Stephen Booker, Dick, Abel, Sub, Left, Simon, Jacob, Leah, Clary, Harry, Dick, Leah, Lagro, Jacob, Abraham, Esau, Ezekiel, Judah, Leah, Minny, Abel, Sam, Judah, Clary, Ladis, Comfort, Ephraim, Manday, Levin, George, Nim, Phillis, Jack, Abigail, Peg, Esau, Ben, James, Ciss, Ezekiel, Rachel, Tabby, Jean, Solomon, Rica, Mary, James, Elijah, Legro, Rachel, Lity, Betty, Peter, Peg, Sarah, Steven, Appy, Adah, Frank[7]
Littleton (d. 1789)	64	Peter, Judith, Ebby, Dilly, Sam, Cloe, Tom, Sarah, John, Betty, Frank, Beck, Cate, China, Esther, Clear, Betsy, Esther, Robert, Shadrack, Elishe, Abby, Sidah, Harry, Patience, Polly, Hannah, Violet, Peggy, Peter, Ciss, Lucy, Charles, York, Chocolate, Cate, Sunter, Patience, Hannah, Jacob, Peter, Amy, Mary, Betty, Candis, Letty, Luke, Abner, Priscilla, Joe, Sall, Jack, Jenny, Daniel, Sunter, Maria, Daniel, Priscilla, Cate, Isaac, Tony, Phebe, Luke, Jacob[8]
William (d. 1808)	32** (** excluding children under 12)	York, Chocolate, Cate, Sunter, Patience, Hannah, Jacob, Peter, Amy, Mary, Betty, Candis, Letty, Abner, Priscilla, Joe, Sall, Jack, Daniel, Sunter, Maria, Priscilla, Cate, Isaac, Tony, Phebe, Luke, Jacob, Dinah, *Daniel, *Lewis, *Jenny and child, *Luke, *Abraham[9]
William L. (d. 1852)	55** (** excluding children under 12)	George, Carter, Tom, George, Peter, Tom, Esau, Able, Coster, Levin, Rickey, Billy, Nim, Henry, Sam, Abel Booker, Jacob, William, Charles an infant, Lucy, Maria, Mary, Clara, Daphne, Amy, Betsy, Rosy, Priscilla, together with six infant children whose names are not known[10]
John (d. 1855)	90	†Luke, †Larodu, †Sam, †Jacob, †Spencer, †Edy, †Rob, †Julia and her 3 children, #Jack Crawley or Cortright, #Severn, *Billy, *Jonathan, *Jim, *John, *Mingo, *Nin Carter, *Bill, *Esau, Nat, Nancy, Eliza[11]
		* Escaped or carried off by the British in the War of 1812 † Sold to John Nivison, Norfolk, 1797 # Escaped by whaleboat, 1832

Fig. 27. Table showing the known names of enslaved people of the Eyre family from the early eighteenth to the mid-nineteenth century.

1720s did not include anyone under the age of 16, which meant enslaved children were not included in the survey.[8] Many of these names match a list from Severn's 1728 estate inventory that includes 22 men and women.[9] The latter list's inclusion of "Negro's of John Matthews" indicates the Eyres' long-standing participation in the common practice of renting enslaved people, usually to assist with the planting or harvesting of crops.

Littleton's spectacular growth of the family's fortunes in the mid-1700s corresponded with a considerable increase in the number of people the family enslaved. His 1769 inventory contains the names of 76 individuals, making him one of the largest slave owners in Northampton County.[10] Littleton's son, Severn, inherited these people upon his father's death and quickly added to the family's

ownership of human chattel. The 1782 property tax lists indicate that Margaret Eyre, Severn's widow, owned 178 enslaved people, the largest number in the family's history. In fact, Margaret was by far the largest slaveholder in Northampton County that year; the next largest was Littleton Savage, who enslaved 99 people.[11] For the most part, it is hard to trace where these people lived or worked. No plats or maps from the period depict slave housing on Eyre land, and the surviving records specify where only a handful of enslaved people worked.[12] A few references noted familial connections, such as "Sarah, Mingo's wife" and "Rachel and Child Jane."[13] Slavery's lifetime of service, as well as its commodification of the human body, is demonstrated by the court's classification of longtime Eyre slave Legro as "superannuated."[14]

While the vast majority of the Eyres' enslaved people toiled in support of the family's agricultural pursuits, an estate the size of theirs necessitated a diverse workforce. To tend to the personal needs of the Eyres, at least four enslaved people—Rose, Sarah, Centre, and Morear—worked inside the Eyre Hall mansion. Another record involves a slave named Will, who was paid £1.14.9 in October of 1774 "for Oyl," demonstrating ways enslaved people personally profited from their own labor by making and selling goods on the side. That same year, William Wood, the Eyres' overseer, purchased "a negroe Blacksmith boy," underscoring the skilled labor many enslaved people possessed and the various types of enslaved tradesmen upon which slave owners relied.[15] The fact that only fragments of these enslaved people's lives have survived, while reams of papers inform us about the day-to-day minutiae of the Eyres, represents another inequity caused by the most unequal of all institutions and helps to conceal the harsh realities that they faced.

In addition to enslaved Black people, the Eyres employed white workers and managers to help operate their various estates. Tithable records for Severn Eyre from the 1720s intermittently list the names of white men who worked for the Eyres and lived on their various properties.[16] These yearly lists indicate he employed one white man, Edmund Joynes, in 1741, but that number jumps to nine in 1743, including men with notable Eastern Shore last names such as Clegg, Evans, and Scarburgh. By the 1760s, white laborers and tenants no longer appear under Littleton's tithables, only the names of enslaved people.[17] It seems likely that he acquired enough enslaved laborers to make hiring large numbers of white wage laborers no longer necessary.

Even though the Eyres did not regularly employ large numbers of white laborers after the 1740s, they continued to rely upon white men to help manage their many Northampton County properties. Isaac Smith's accounts from the 1760s through the 1770s report numerous payments to local artisans for work including blacksmithing, shingling, and carpentry. He paid others for agricultural jobs including mowing and pasturing horses. During this period only two men received yearly wages, William Wood and John Phillips. Of the two, Wood seems to have served as the family's principal overseer from 1773 to at least 1781. This timeline aligns with Severn's death and the coming of age of his eldest son, Littleton. Wood's importance can be surmised through his management of the

Eyres' various accounts and his purchase of expensive items on behalf of the family, such as horses and enslaved people. In return, his yearly wages during the period ranged from £90 to £137, a substantial sum. In contrast, John Phillips earned only £18.15 a year. Perhaps Phillips worked under Wood as a junior overseer. An enslaved labor force of over 70, with five separate farms, would require the attention of more than one white man to oversee their work.[18]

Farming in the Antebellum Period

The Eyres did not radically change what they grew on their land from the eighteenth to the nineteenth centuries—the two main crops were corn and oats.[19] This generalization applied to Eyre Hall, under the ownership of John Eyre, and Eyreville next door, run by his nephew William L. Eyre. John produced 4,000 bushels of corn and 1,800 bushels of oats in 1850. William L. reported growing 2,500 bushels of corn and 800 bushels of oats the same year.[20] Other agricultural products, such as peas and potatoes, numbered less than 100 bushels combined for both men. Both John and William L. owned a fair amount of livestock, but much less than what the family possessed in the 1770s. Instead of several hundred head of cattle, hogs, and sheep, the two men combined owned approximately 45 cattle, 70 sheep, and 180 swine.[21] These numbers reflect the shrinking lands the family owned, meaning less available pasturage to support large herds of animals. For a number of decades John had also rented much of his land to tenant farmers. This reliance on rental income might explain why the 1850 agricultural census reports John with only 885 acres of land, when tax records from the same year indicate he owned approximately 1,300 acres. In addition, census records list over 600 acres of that 885 acres as unimproved, indicating John was not actively using over two-thirds of his reported farmland.[22]

Corresponding with their reduced landholdings, John and William L. held fewer people in bondage than their predecessors. Regardless, they still enslaved many more men, women, and children than the average Northampton County slave owner.[23] According to the 1850 Federal Census Slave Schedule, John owned 50 enslaved people, while his nephew owned 36. This record proves especially somber, as it reveals that out of the 86 people they owned, 30 were children under the age of ten.[24] Between 1854 and 1860, women enslaved by the Eyres, including Rose, Polly, and Eliza, gave birth to at least 17 children.[25]

Records do not provide much information about who directly managed the Eyres' nineteenth-century enslaved population. William L. employed Shepherd Roberts as an overseer in at least 1850, when he appears in census records.[26] It is unclear how deep of a relationship Roberts had with the family, as the 1860 census lists him working for neighbor John T. W. Custis.[27] John does not have any white men listed under his household in census or tax records from the same period and neither does Severn, William L.'s son and the inheritor of all Eyre lands upon John's death in 1855. Using white tenants

to fulfill overseer duties could explain the lack of a plantation manager for both men.

From the 1720s to the 1850s, the Eyres relied on land, and the enslaved people who worked that land, as the foundation of their wealth and influence. Reaching the peak of their powers by the 1760s and 1770s, the family's vast estates provided the stability needed to retain political and social power throughout the changing economic and political landscapes in the first half of the nineteenth century. That would change dramatically not long after Severn Eyre came into this inheritance.

NOTES

1. Will of Severn Eyre, March 15, 1769, Northampton County Wills & Inventories, No. 25, 1772–1777, 136–38.
2. Will of Severn Eyre, 136–38; Ralph T. Whitelaw, *Virginia's Eastern Shore: A History of Northampton and Accomack Counties* (Richmond: Virginia Historical Society, 1951), 1:174.
3. Estate of Severn Eyre in account with Bowdoin, Eyre & Smith, 1773–81, April 11, 1781, Northampton County Wills & Inventories, No. 26, 1777–1783, 407–21; Estate of Severn Eyre in account with Bowdoin, Eyre & Smith, 1782–87, September 11, 1787, Northampton County Wills etc., No. 27, 1783–1788, 495–500.
4. Estate of Severn Eyre, 407–21; Return of the Collection of Taxes, Northampton County Deeds, etc., No. 22, 1785–1794, 130–31, 233–34.
5. Estate of Severn Eyre, 407–21.
6. Inventory of the estate of Littleton Eyre, October 14, 1769, Northampton County Wills & Inventories, No. 24, 1766–1772, 224–26.
7. John B. Bell, *Northampton County, Virginia, Tithables, 1720–1769* (Bowie, Md.: Heritage Books, 1993), 127.

8. William Waller Hening, *The Statutes at Large, being a Collection of all the Laws of Virginia* (New York, Richmond, and Philadelphia, 1819–23), 4:133.
9. Inventory of the estate of Severn Eyre (d. 1728), August 14, 1728, Northampton County Wills, Deeds, etc., No. 26, 1725–1733, 154.
10. Inventory of the estate of Littleton Eyre, 224–26.
11. Northampton County Personal Property Tax List, 1782.
12. A Judah, Leah, and Peter all have Hungars, a main Eyre plantation, after their names, while a Jacob has Mill Quarter, another property occasionally mentioned, after his name; from Division of Severn Eyre's slaves, May 14, 1782, Northampton County Wills & Inventories, No. 26, 1777–1783, 542–44.
13. Division of Severn Eyre's slaves, 543; Inventory of the estate of Severn Eyre (d. 1773), February 27, 1774, Northampton County Wills & Inventories, No. 25, 1775–1777, 395.
14. Division of Severn Eyre's slaves, 543.
15. Inventory of the estate of Severn Eyre (d. 1773), 395, 409, 414.
16. Bell, *Tithables*, 14–127.
17. Bell, *Tithables*, 323, 356, 383, 391.

18. Inventory of the estate of Severn Eyre (d. 1773), 410, 411, 413.
19. *Farmers' Register* 3, no. 4 (August 1835): 233.
20. Seventh U.S. Census, Agricultural Schedule, 1850, Northampton County, Virginia.
21. Seventh U.S. Census, Agricultural Schedule, 1850, Northampton County, Virginia.
22. Agricultural Schedule, 1850; Northampton County Land Tax Lists, 1826–1850.
23. For more details about slavery in Northampton County during the antebellum period, see Kirk Mariner, *Slave and Free on Virginia's Eastern Shore: From the Revolution to the Civil War* (Onancock, Va.: Miona Publications, 2014), 81–110.
24. Seventh U.S. Census, Slave Schedule, 1850, Northampton County, Virginia, Severn Eyre.
25. Leslie Anderson Morales, ed., *Virginia Slave Births Index: 1853–1865* (Westminster, Md.: Heritage Books, 2007), 2:202–3.
26. Seventh U.S. Census, Population Schedule, 1850, Northampton County, Virginia, Eastville District.
27. Eighth U.S. Census, Population Schedule, 1860, Northampton County, Virginia, Eastville District.

NOTES FOR FIG. 27

1. Will of Thomas Eyre, January 23, 1714, Northampton County Wills, Deeds, etc., 1711–1718, 104.
2. Inventory of the estate of Thomas Eyre, October 28, 1719, Northampton County Wills, etc., No. 15, 1717–1725, 73–76.
3. Will of John Eyre, April 21, 1719, Northampton County Deeds, Wills, etc., 1718–1725, 24–25; Inventory of the estate of John Eyre, August 12, 1719, Northampton County Deeds, Wills, etc., 1718–1725, 56–58.
4. John B. Bell, *Northampton County, Virginia, Tithables, 1720–1769* (Bowie, Md.: Heritage Books, 1993), 3, 15, 26, 55, 77, 106, 127; Inventory of the estate of Severn Eyre (d. 1728), August 14, 1728, Northampton County Wills, Deeds, etc., No. 26, 1725–1733, 151–54.
5. Bell, *Tithables*, 271, 287, 303, 323, 336, 356, 383;

Inventory of the estate of Littleton Eyre, October 14, 1769, Northampton County Wills & Inventories, No. 24, 1766–1772, 224–26.
6. Division of Severn Eyre's slaves, May 14, 1782, Northampton County Wills & Inventories, No. 26, 1777–1783, 542–44.
7. Inventory of the estate of Severn Eyre (d. 1786), 1787, Northampton County Wills & In[ventories], No. 28, 1788–1792, 42–45.
8. Division of Littleton Eyre's slaves, July 12, 1791, Northampton County Wills & In[ventories], No. 28, 1788–1792, 291–92.
9. Division of Littleton Eyre's slaves, 291–92; Will of William Eyre, December 18, 1807, Northampton County Wills & Inven'ys [Inventories], No. 33, 1808–1813, 53–55; "Definitive List of Slaves and Property: Inventory of property carried off by the

British forces, 1827–28," 20, Records of Boundary and Claims Commissions and Arbitrations, 1716–1994, Record Group 76, National Archives, Washington, D.C.
10. Affidavit of William Nottingham Sr., 4 October 1832, Governor's Office, Letters Received, John Floyd, Record Group 3, Library of Virginia, Richmond; William L. Eyre and etc. to Taylor and all trustees, Northampton County Deeds, etc., No. 29, 1828–1834, 325–27.
11. Deed of sale between John Eyre and John Nivison, November 4, 1797, Tazewell Family Papers, Box 2, Folder 4, Library of Virginia, Richmond; "Definitive List of Slaves and Property: Inventory of property carried off by the British forces, 1827–28," 20; Affidavit of William Nottingham, Sr.; Will of John Eyre, 24; *Morning News* (Wilmington, Del.), December 17, 1884, 5.

The Bounty of Eyre Hall

FROM WORKING PLANTATION TO SUMMER RETREAT IN THE LONG NINETEENTH CENTURY

CARL R. LOUNSBURY

LONGEVITY IN AN AGE OF UNCERTAINTY

DURING THE FIRST 30 YEARS OF ITS EXISTENCE, EYRE Hall had three owners: Littleton Eyre, the builder, who lived there between its construction in 1759 and his death in 1768; his son Severn Eyre, who suffered from chronic ill health and died in 1773 at the age 37; and Severn's first-born son Littleton, named after his grandfather, who did not inherit the property until his 21st birthday in 1782, but who, like his father, died at a young age in 1789. This pattern of rapid turnover of ownership was not unusual, but a common-place in the colonial era when lifespans were decidedly short. Although the first Littleton Eyre may have established Eyre Hall as the family seat, there was little guarantee that it would continue. Disruptions in family life—whether through failures in succession from one generation to the next or from external events such as economic setbacks or wars—remained strong deterrents to such continuity.

The prospects of Eyre Hall remaining the family home at the end of the eighteenth century were far from propitious,

despite the large number of children that Severn Eyre left behind when he died. However, it succeeded in remaining so, primarily thanks to the healthy constitutions of a few individuals. In the 230 years since 1789, Eyre Hall has had only four owners, whose lifespans have defied actuarial odds in a remarkable stretch of longevity that have had a profound impact on how those successive proprietors perceived and treated their birthright. Breaking with the Eyre tendency to die relatively young, John Eyre, Severn's third son, inherited the Eyre Hall estate at the age of 21 on the death of his older brother Littleton, and oversaw its affairs for the next 66 years until his death in 1855. However, he died childless and was succeeded by another Severn Eyre, the grandson of his younger brother, William. Like his great-uncle, this Severn came into possession of the property in his early twenties and proceeded to live a very long time, dying in 1914 at the age of 82.

These two owners, whose lifetimes spanned the history of the American republic from the federalist politics of the Washington administration to the progressive era of Woodrow Wilson, faced and weathered the challenges to

Fig. 28. Passage of Eyre Hall looking south, ca. 1895.

their social and economic status, which suffered tribulations wrought by the rise of Jacksonian democracy, the Civil War, the abolition of slavery, and several depressions. Their inherited wealth gave them the means to adjust their sources of investments and accommodate the impact of new technologies such as steamships and railroads, which reduced the isolation of the Eastern Shore and opened it to new markets and agricultural practices. After John and his wife Ann made substantial alterations in the first quarter of the nineteenth century to make the house more comfortable and fashionable, including the introduction of new furnishings and the expansion of the garden, few changes to the fabric of the house and its contents occurred over the next century.

In the 1880s Severn Eyre and his young family left Eyre Hall and settled in Baltimore, returning to the place during the summers and for holiday retreats. By the early twentieth century, in the twilight of Severn's tenure, the place began to be seen as a nostalgic exemplar of an earlier age, a storehouse of family objects, legends, and traditions. Most of John and Ann's furniture, ceramics, books, and garden remained intact and in use (Fig. 28). Preservation and survival rather than expansion and change became the dominant attitude toward Eyre Hall at the end of the long nineteenth century. Those perspectives would continue to influence the stewardship of the Baldwin family, who oversaw its management in the twentieth and early twenty-first centuries.

SORTING OUT: LIFE AT
EYRE HALL, 1773–1789

When Severn Eyre died in Norfolk in January 1773, he left a family composed of six children (four boys and two girls) ranging in age from 12 to less than a year old. His widow Margaret, age 33, had her hands full as the new chatelaine of Eyre Hall. She shared her second-floor bedchamber with William, who was a baby, along with his sister Sarah, who was not quite three.[1] To help her manage a young household, Margaret relied upon the help of her husband's business partners John Bowdoin and Isaac Smith, who kept track of the tangled financial and material assets that linked the income and expenditure of the firm and the family at Eyre Hall. She could also draw upon the medical and business advice of her two brothers in Norfolk, Dr. James Taylor and John Taylor, who were merchants.

Severn left Margaret a wealthy widow, an executrix who could draw on the resources produced by livestock and crops raised on an estate spread across four working plantations, which employed overseers, tenants, and scores of slaves. The equitable dispersal of these resources rather than their consolidation was Severn's intention. In his will written in 1769 and twice amended by codicils prior to his death in order to account for the birth of his two youngest children, Severn intended to divide his estate among his three oldest sons, Littleton, Severn, and John, with cash legacies to his daughters. Severn devised to Littleton the Eyre Hall property with the mill quarter amounting to 1,570½ acres; his namesake Severn received the Hungars plantation and other lands that totaled 869½ acres; and his third son John was given the Broad Creek and Seaside plantations totaling 915 acres. Severn sold his business partner John Bowdoin the 486-acre Ferry Land property on Hungars River. Except for four body and domestic servants willed to his wife Margaret, Severn specified that the rest of his slaves (which numbered more than 160) were to be divided equally between Littleton,

Severn, and John as well as all his household goods and silver not specifically reserved for his wife. Margaret received £10,000 from his estate, as well as an annual stipend to manage the household until Littleton reached his majority. He left £2,000 for his eldest daughter Margaret (Peggy) and later added a £1,500 legacy to his younger daughter Sarah (Sally), after she was born. Finally, in his last mortal hours, Severn bequeathed to his new son William the houses and lot he owned in Norfolk.[2]

Had all of his children lived much longer than they did and managed their own inheritance for more than a decade (only one son and one daughter lived as long as their father), then the eighteenth-century apogee of Eyre power and influence would have splintered and the domestic and decorative objects of that age would have been dispersed across many different households, growing more fragmented as each new generation subdivided its heirlooms. Yet, that was not to be, and no one could have predicted such an outcome in 1773 or even nine years later when Margaret relinquished her responsibilities to her first-born son, Littleton, who turned 21 and took legal possession of Eyre Hall. In 1782, before the estate was divided up among her children, Margaret Eyre held in their name 3,163 acres of land in four parcels valued at £1,414.7.6 for tax purposes, in addition to a mill worth £25. The personal property tax lists recorded 178 slaves in her possession, 47 horses, and 173 cattle.[3]

Guided by John Bowdoin (until his death in late 1775), Isaac Smith, and Dr. James Taylor, who were appointed executors of the estate along with Margaret, we catch a more detailed glimpse of family life and plantation management at Eyre Hall than at any other time in its long history. Isaac Smith's meticulous accounts from the late 1760s through the middle of the 1780s document the income and the expenses of the family in an unparalleled level of detail. We see the income produced by the Eyre slaves tending and harvesting the crops from the home farm (Eyre Hall),

Hungars, Seaside, and the rented land at Townfields. Every year, the enslaved laborers raised and reaped from these fields hundreds of bushels of oats, corn, wheat, flax seed, and peas as well as some tobacco, the first three of which were the principal crops shipped to overseas markets from Hungars Wharf. Those who worked on the Eyre estate also shipped beef, pork, ham, and bacon to foreign and domestic customers, as well as planks and shingles cut and sawn during winter months. They tended livestock including lambs, cattle, and hogs for consumption on the estate as well as for sale to neighbors. Additional income derived from renting land to neighbors, houses in Norfolk, and a share of the profits in a rope walk in which Severn had invested in Norfolk. The Eyres on occasion hired out their slaves; Stephen Booker, the mariner, worked for the partnership of Bowdoin, Eyre, and Smith for a number of years in the early 1770s for which Severn was paid £30 per annum. In 1773 and 1774, a slave named Judith was hired by Southy Goffigon of Northampton County for £3 per year.[4]

On the debit side of the ledger, the accounts record payments to maintain the farming operations and cover a variety of family expenses. White overseers were hired to manage farm operations on the various plantations. What could not be repaired by skilled slaves required the attention of local blacksmiths, coopers, and carpenters who made or mended cart wheels, harnesses, tools, baskets, barrels, and hogsheads. Each year, the estate paid white craftsmen to mow fields, tar buildings, and repair ships. Household expenses included the repair of a silver punch ladle in 1773, probably by a local silversmith, William Snead, who had a shop and store at Bridgetown near Hungars Church. Snead later made a pair of silver shoe buckles for Peggy Eyre in 1779. A decade earlier, cabinetmaker James Wilkins turned banisters and fabricated a bedstead to accommodate the expanding household.[5]

Food, medicine, clothing, and education account for a substantial portion of household expenses. Although the plantation provided nearly all the meat, milk, cheese, grains, legumes, and vegetables that graced the dining room table, the Eyres enhanced the variety and taste of their meals with imported foodstuffs and drinks including wine, rum, molasses, coffee, tea, as well as sugar and spices such as nutmeg, cinnamon, and pepper, nearly all of which were purchased from Norfolk merchants such as Eilbeck and Ross, Thorowgood Smith, Matthew Phripp, Paul Loyall, and Margaret's two brothers. These general merchants also sold the family ducks, turkeys, and firkins of butter. Norfolk was furthermore the source for medicine and medical attention, as Dr. James Taylor played an important part in overseeing the health of his sister's children. Not only had he attended Severn Eyre in his last illness, but he shipped boxes of medicine to Eyre Hall over the years. Beyond the usual nostrums prescribed by doctors, the Eyres took the unusual step of having the two oldest boys, Littleton and Severn, inoculated in 1774 against smallpox by the leading advocate in the region, Dr. Henry Stevenson of Baltimore.[6]

Smith's accounts are filled with references to clothing and the purchase of imported textiles like linen, velvet, and alamode. At a cost of £10.10.0, Paul Loyall supplied the family with 70 yards of the latter material, a lightweight glossy silk fabric that was used for Severn Eyre's funeral in Norfolk. Merchants also sold them miscellaneous "cloth" and thread in addition to manufactured items such as shoes, hats, bonnets, and gloves. The Eyres turned to local tailors to fashion vests, jackets, coats, and britches. In 1773 William Cary received £1.10.0 for making two suits of clothes for the boys. The following year Hart the tailor fabricated a new vest for Severn, and in 1775 was paid for unspecified "children's clothes." An additional tailoring bill from Hart in 1776 brought the cost of his labor at his work bench to more than £6, or three times the price that the Eyres paid for a card table from master cabinetmaker Anthony Hay of Williamsburg. Given the growth of the children over these years, new pairs of shoes were in great demand; by the early 1770s Littleton and Severn seemed in need of new ones almost yearly. There also must have been constant attention to patching, altering, and the refitting of older clothing and the making of new pieces within the household. No women's or girls' garments are enumerated in the accounts, suggesting that these items were sewn by seamstresses at home from imported materials. From Norfolk, Dr. Taylor shipped imported calico for Peggy and a pair of stays. Outside some imports of ozenbrigs and "rough cloth," the accounts are silent on the importation of coarse fabrics that would be used to make clothing for the enslaved population. Their absence suggests that many of those who worked for the Eyres had the never-ending task of processing, weaving, spinning, and sewing homegrown materials to keep a large workforce clothed.[7]

Like most members of the Virginia gentry, the Eyres understood the social and political value of refined manners and academic education. Preparation for success in business, politics, matrimony, and society began at home with the education of the rising generation in the conventions of polite behavior and genteel ways exercised in conversation and deportment in the parlor and at the dining room table. Margaret Eyre no doubt instructed her children in the protocols for various social occasions that allowed them to successfully negotiate the intricacies of such customs among their peers.[8] She insured that her daughters were proficient with needle and thread, versed in the art of serving tea, efficacious in the management of domestic affairs, and perhaps accomplished in voice or with a musical instrument. In the early 1770s, the Eyres possessed a guitar and would eventually own a number of instruments and sheet music that brought family, relatives, and friends together in musical entertainments. Virginians loved dancing, which was learned at home but also taught through formal instruction. Margaret Eyre paid for dancing lessons for Littleton in 1774 when he was 13 and probably the other children when they reached the same age. That instruction was put to good use when Littleton

and Severn attended two balls in 1779 accompanied by a chaperon.[9]

Formal education also began at home. Because of their social standing and wealth, the Eyres certainly could afford to hire tutors who may have resided with the family or lived nearby and taught their young children and others in the area to read, write, and cipher before the older boys went off to a grammar school. The Smith accounts from this period mention a number of names of teachers hired by the family but do not reveal whether they were in residence at Eyre Hall at any time. Except for the two older boys, Littleton and Severn, it is not clear what sort of formal instruction the two girls, Peggy and Sally, and the two younger boys, John and William, received during the 1770s and early 1780s. When young, John may have attended a local school, as he later recalled that "when a school-boy it was my habit to rise early and prepare my lessons. I took a cold breakfast because I had not time to wait for the family meal. Dinner I carried along with me to be eaten, cold, of course, at the "old field school," and returning at evening, was too tired to do more than get a slice of cold bread and glass of milk, and hurry off to bed."[10]

In 1773 the estate paid Isaac Morris £6.15.0 "for schooling three children," but just which three they were is not clear. Matthew Donovan, who may have been a tutor in Northampton County gentry households before his death in 1776, appears associated with the Eyres as early as the late 1760s when he served as one of the witnesses to Severn Eyre's will in 1769. Though the specific years of his service as a teacher are not given, later accounts indicate that he taught Littleton for 13 months and Severn for two years and was paid £10 per year per child. Donovan's debits to the estate suggest the possibility that he may have been a private tutor, who certainly instructed them in the next stages of their education, perhaps introducing them to Latin, history, geography, and rhetoric in preparation for their future studies in grammar school.[11]

Around 1774 or 1775, Littleton Eyre traveled north to attend school in Delaware, most likely the Wilmington Academy, a grammar school that had begun to attract gentry from the region as well as from Maryland, Virginia, and other southern colonies. His uncle Preeson Bowdoin, who had lived in Philadelphia for a number of years, had probably drawn the young man's attention to the school. Bowdoin's son, Preeson, Jr., may have also attended the school. Supported by the leading gentlemen of the town, the grammar school was housed in a two-story stone building erected on Market Street a few years earlier. The school attracted more than a hundred students by the early 1770s. Robert Patterson served as one of its principals in the early years and, by the time of the Revolution, he was training his pupils in military tactics beside their regular curriculum in moral and natural philosophy.[12] It was a none-too-subtle reminder that the Revolution was making Wilmington a difficult place to study, given that it was exposed to the maneuvers of the British and American armies.

Littleton may have wished to stay longer, but the war forced the closure of the school and he returned home by 1776. Smith's ledger shows that in 1777 the family paid a tutor, William Vere, to help supplement his interrupted grammar school education.[13] In the fall of 1778, at the age of 17, Littleton began college at his father's alma mater, William and Mary. Tagging along with him was his younger brother Severn, age 14, who entered the college's grammar school. The two boys were apparently fitted out with new suits by their mother, were given "pocket money," and were ferried across the bay to Yorktown and on to Williamsburg. A surviving book in the library at Eyre Hall marks Littleton's entrance into college life. On the flyleaf of each of the four volumes of *The History of the Arts and Science of the Ancients* is inscribed "William Littleton Eyre, August 17th domini 1778, William and Mary College." Both boys may have boarded outside the college during their years in Williamsburg. The following year, 1779, Dr. Taylor paid for his nephew

Littleton's tuition, room, board, and pocket money. Littleton made the most of his two years at William and Mary and was admitted as a member of the newly organized scholastic society, Phi Beta Kappa, before he left in 1780.[14]

The two years that Littleton and Severn were in Williamsburg together were momentous ones that offered many distractions outside the classrooms of the college building. Although some students, such as James Monroe, had left school to serve in the ranks of Washington's army, the college remained open as the city had not suffered the ravages of the war that swept across distant battlefields. Even so, the capital was a hothouse of activity associated with its prosecution as legislators met in sessions to debate the funding and support of the war and the exercise of sovereign powers under a newly established state constitution. Patrick Henry, followed by Thomas Jefferson, resided in the Governor's Palace as they tried to assert the administrative authority of the new state government despite the very weak powers prescribed to the office by the constitution. It was an ideal place for Littleton to observe the operations of a nascent state government first hand, to hear and perhaps participate in debates about the authority of its judicial, legislative, and administrative powers. For a budding politician, it was as good an education as the one he absorbed on the college grounds. At the end of his time in Williamsburg, the state government decamped from the city. In April 1780, state officials packed their papers and moved the capital to Richmond, in part to avoid the threat of British forces capable of sailing up the James and capturing the town.

After two years of grammar school, Severn Eyre returned to William and Mary for the fall term of 1780. At age 16, he was set to begin his college studies. Dr. Taylor paid his tuition and his accommodations off campus with Mrs. Newton. This town seemed deserted with the disappearance of the government, but the lull was a prelude to the whirlwind of war that placed Williamsburg near the center of its ultimate resolution on the battlefield at Yorktown in October 1781. That spring Lord Cornwallis and his British army marched into Virginia from North Carolina and in April ironically threatened the new capital of Richmond before turning east. Whatever instruction had been going on at the college ceased in the late spring as it shuttered its doors. In June, Cornwallis's army camped in Williamsburg before moving on to Portsmouth after which it established defensive positions at Yorktown. That strategy failed spectacularly when British forces capitulated on October 19 after a three-week siege by Washington's army and his French allies under General Rochambeau. Following the surrender, the French wintered in Williamsburg. French officers quartered in the President's House at the college and accidentally set fire to it, leaving it charred and roofless, but reparable. Somehow, William and Mary officials managed to work around the damages wrought by the climax of the Revolution and opened its doors to students once again. Smith's accounts are ambiguous as to whether Severn Eyre ever returned to finish his collegiate studies at William and Mary.[15]

Apparently the war had had some impact on Eyre Hall. When British ships entered the bay in the early 1780s, troops raided plantations where they seized crops and livestock and encouraged slaves to quit their masters, following the practice devised by Governor Dunmore at the beginning of war. Besides the disruption of trade, some unspecified privations had diminished the profitability of the plantation. John Eyre recalled a few years later that "the late unhappy war considerably injured" the estate, which sustained "heavy losses."[16]

In March 1782 Littleton Eyre turned 21 and took up his inheritance of Eyre Hall. A change in legal ownership did little immediately to alter any of the family dynamics or living arrangements at the hall, which had been presided over by his mother Margaret, and still housed his five younger siblings. Isaac Smith's detailed accounts of the household tail off soon thereafter, which makes it impossible to trace

the material wellbeing of the occupants or the state of affairs on the various Eyre plantations still held in trust until the other sons reached their majority. No doubt Littleton worked to restore the fortunes of the plantation and sought to re-establish or open new markets for its produce. With worn-out fields and a depressed tobacco market following the war, Littleton may have decided to cease the cultivation of what little tobacco had been produced previously on his lands.

What can be traced is the path that Littleton took into public affairs, following in his father's and grandfather's footsteps. He was first elected by the citizens of Northampton County to be one of their representatives in the Virginia House of Delegates in 1784, at the age of 23. They returned him to that position in subsequent elections in 1786 and 1787. Besides his public duties in Richmond, he was also appointed to serve as a magistrate on the county court in Eastville in 1785, which he dutifully attended each month over the next three years.

The high point in his short-lived career was his election as one of two county delegates that gathered with 168 others in Richmond in June 1788 to debate the merits of ratifying the new constitution of the United States, which had been drawn up in Philadelphia the previous year. Representing Accomack County was his brother-in-law George Parker, who had married his sister Peggy two years earlier, and his uncle, Dr. James Taylor, who served as a delegate from Norfolk. The new state capitol designed by Thomas Jefferson was still under construction so the representatives convened in the Richmond Academy on Broad Street. The academy was later replaced by a theater, which burned in 1811 with a tragic loss of life, and the site is now occupied by the Monumental Church that was erected to commemorate the disaster. Although he did not take a prominent role in the debates, Littleton believed that the document had strengthened the national government; however, like many other Federalists at the convention, such as James Madison,

George Wythe, and Edmund Randolph, he did not feel that it needed to be amended with a bill of rights before it was ratified. Patrick Henry strenuously opposed that position. In the end, Littleton supported its adoption, which passed by a relatively close vote on June 27. Madison later introduced a bill of rights in the first congressional session when it convened the following year.[17]

If politics and estate management commanded the attention of Littleton Eyre, his brother Severn was drawn toward medicine, perhaps influenced by his uncle James Taylor of Norfolk. Although Taylor, like many American physicians, had been educated in Edinburgh, Severn decided to begin his medical studies in London and, after spending some time with his uncle in Norfolk, departed the city in June 1785 on a five-week voyage across the Atlantic. After landing in Liverpool, he traveled to London where, in early August, he called on tobacco merchant Samuel Gist, whom he described as "an old acquaintance of my father and grandfather's." Gist, in fact, was one of the principal London merchants who had carried on an extensive trade with the firm of Bowdoin, Eyre, and Smith in the 1760s and early 1770s. Young Severn asked Gist if he would advance him money on a £400 bill of credit from General Thomas Nelson that he possessed. He was shocked when his father's old trading partner turned down his request.[18] What Severn had not been aware of was the poor state of credit among many merchants on both sides of the Atlantic—a postwar depression made many American merchants' creditworthiness more dubious, just as many English merchants who had been deeply invested in trade with America suffered bankruptcies in the war's aftermath. Gist's unwelcome response would not have come as a surprise had Severn been more aware of business matters, but the hard feeling that it engendered made his entrance into English society all the more difficult as he then had to scrimp and borrow money to establish his life as a medical student in the metropolis.

By the middle of August he had paid his 40 guineas entrance fees to study at Guy's and St Thomas's Hospitals, located on the south side of London Bridge in the borough of Southwark (Fig. 29). In October he found convenient lodgings in a house at 1 Canterbury Square just off Tooley Street only 100 yards east of the hospitals. His first months were filled with lectures on chemistry, anatomy, surgery, and the practice of "physick" and "materia medica" (history of pharmacy). Severn also learned the rudiments of his profession through clinical rounds in which students observed approaches to the treatment of "ye worse cases of ye hospital."[19] He found the routine exhausting, but fulfilling.

By December, he had discovered that being a good physician meant more than mastering the texts he was assigned and studying his lecture notes. He wrote to Littleton that "you cannot conceive that there is much pleasure in studying intricacies, for there are few facts in which all physicians agree, this science still remaining in obscurity, each medical man endeavouring to support his particular hypothesis & every one laboring to add something out of the common tract & of course I must endeavor to be acquainted with each & thereon erect my own." As much as he wished to see his brother John come visit him in London, he thought that if their mother did allow him to come to Britain, John should plan to "enter on ye study of physick not to [spend] 3 years at healing with ye pestle, but to repair directly to Edinburgh [where Severn hoped to continue his medical studies the following year] when 3 winters will make him master of his profession and gain him adept" knowledge of the practice of medicine. Afterward, Severn mused that he and John would return to America and practice their profession together, if not in Northampton County then in Norfolk where there was greater opportunity.[20]

Although Severn felt overwhelmed by his studies, complaining to Littleton that "Saturday eveng. & Sunday is the only leisure time to crawl out of this lonesome [house], which convenience compels me to put up with," he did concede that "there are comforts even here" and that he had "two good rooms" in his rooming house, where he could "order what I please for dinner as there are no other boarders in the house." He took advantage of being in the great metropolis, which offered the 22-year-old, country-raised colonial eye-opening spectacles and pleasures that proved too tempting to pass up. Early on, he had "lost every sense of shame & virtue, mostly by the insinuation of the abandoned rakes of this town." He visited Vauxhall Gardens, where he observed "Musick & fine women in abundance," and declared that "the sight of so many desirable women did by no means convey such delectable feelings as 'tis nature to suppose a young man, just arrived from a country where there are no desirable prostitutes & after five weeks confinement at sea, would enjoy, but on the contrary was sensibly affected to behold women every way calculated to render the married state happy." On New Year's Day 1786, Severn noted that he "had company with a couple of lovely Scottish girls, drank tea & spent ye eveng., waited on them home."[21]

Severn seemed transfixed by the scale of the city and the contrast between wealth and poverty, spectacle and squalor. On a trip to Newgate Prison to visit a friend, he found it "impossible for human creatures to exist in such filth as is, for want of conveniences and the numbers indiscriminately bundled together." On the Lord Mayor's Day in early November, he watched a parade of members of the different trade guilds filled "with colours, musick, & a great number of men fantastically dressed; next three men in such armour as was worn some hundred years ago." He observed "big-bellied Justices who all proceed to their different halls to glut themselves" and in the same evening witnessed the coach of the prime minister, William Pitt the Younger, demolished by a mob angered by an unpopular tax. Pitt escaped to the Guildhall where he was escorted home by an armed guard. In the spring, Severn's cousin Preeson Bowdoin arrived in London. Bowdoin had been traveling on the continent, and the two walked around the city catching up on news of family and friends. One day in late March, they came upon Thomas Jefferson, the American minister to France who was in London to help John Adams negotiate a trade treaty. Preeson, who had met Jefferson previously, introduced him to Severn and the three chatted briefly before moving on.[22]

Severn attended Covent Garden and Drury Lane Theatres on several occasions, and at the latter one night in April 1786 he sat in the pit where the space he was "squeezed in . . . scarcely admit a ribit to turn, was taken off my legs & after every exertion to prevent my ribs from being broke was carried up about 150 steps & ushered into ye pitt gallerys attended by an immeasurable mob," though he observed that the "whole boxes . . . were lined with people of rank." In the crush of the crowd on leaving the theater, he saw a woman lying on the floor whom someone had told him was dead. Even so, when he took a stroll one evening, he "acknowledged the superiority of this country to ours in even the most trivial respects."[23]

Although he was deeply engaged in his studies and exploring his new surroundings in London, Severn was often homesick and wrote to Littleton of how his thoughts frequently turned to Eyre Hall, where there was "the card table, gallantry, a pair of good horses . . . & ye luxuries of ye table engrossed my whole attention." He begged his brother to "write me a long letter, mention every[thing], ye most minute circumstances of family concerns, whether Mama has recovered from ye Asthmas wh. was so troublesome, whether Margt. has yet got a protector, tell her 'tis almost time, whether Sally still continues in Norfolk; how Billy is situated for schooling &c. lastly how you spend your time. I know that if you only have a comp[anion] you are satisfied, but when you'll find one eql. to little Kendl. or Duff I am at a loss to determine.... Have you arranged ye plantn. in ye order you wished [?]."[24] Perhaps alluding to the difficulty Littleton may have faced in re-establishing Eyre Hall's profitability, Severn wrote that if he were in need money for "ye benefit of brothers & sisters," Littleton should sell a few acres of land and "strip Hungars" [Severn's plantation] of its resources since his older brother had the power to "make use of the plantan. as your own; 'twould give me [satisfaction] that anything on wch will contribute to the benefit yr family, is at their service.... I know that a good plantation & negroes are not to be despised."[25]

Unfortunately, his musings about his studies, extra-curricular pursuits, and thoughts of home took a darker turn. The stress of balancing education and pleasure appears to have caught up with him, and he wrote to Littleton in April 1786 admitting that he had "lost my health." In another letter to his brother on May 9, he acknowledged that his plan to spend the summer in France and the winter in Edinburgh had to be postponed as he could now "scarcely get to ye hospital & back again," declaring that in "all events I must endeavor to recover strength & intermix pleasure with study." In the early summer he traveled to Brighthelmstone [Brighton] in an effort to restore his health at the seaside village. By mid-July, he had returned to London where Charles Steuart, a Scots merchant who had lived in Norfolk before the Revolution and was an acquaintance of his uncle, Dr. James Taylor, found him "emaciated, with all the appearance of being far gone in a consumption." Severn claimed he was "better & getting strength" and was determined to travel to Bristol, where he intended to fully recover. He made it to Bristol, but his illness worsened, and he died in a boarding house there on August 9. Severn was buried in the port

city three days later. Afterward, Steuart wrote to Dr. Taylor about the circumstances of his nephew's death and offered his condolences, observing that Severn was "a very amiable young man, of the most correct principles and honourable sentiments." After Taylor received the news in November, he wrote to his sister, Margaret Eyre, informing her of Severn's death and offering her what consolation he could, especially since "it is the first shock of the kind you have ever experienced."[26]

It would not be the last. Littleton, the first born, died unmarried less than three years later, on May 7, 1789, at the age of 28. The cause of his death is not known. He was buried in the graveyard at Eyre Hall near the double grave of his grandparents, the first owners of the plantation. Even as the family was recovering from the loss of Littleton, a trunk filled with Severn's clothing and other effects arrived from Bristol in the fall of 1789, a stark reminder of the earlier loss.[27]

EYRE HALL IN THE AGE OF JOHN EYRE, 1789–1855

The fortunes of Eyre Hall fell unexpectedly to the third son, John, who turned 21 on May 2, 1789, five days before Littleton died. In his will, which was drawn up in 1787, Littleton devised to John "the plantation whereon I now live with all the land adjoining it, containing by estimation fifteen hundred acres and upward."[28] Any thought that John may have entertained earlier about joining his brother Severn in the medical profession had long vanished, and his destiny was reshaped once again by his sudden inheritance of the Eyre Hall plantation. As the new head of the family, he was also expected to take Littleton's public role in local and state politics: positions on the Northampton County court in Eastville and the General Assembly in Richmond. A man with a retiring disposition not prone to seeking the limelight, John grew slowly into a respected public figure with a measured temperament and sound judgment. However, those qualities proved in the long arc of his life to be out of place in a changing public arena where deference to an elite social order was beginning to fray and where a more rough-and-tumble kind of public discourse emerged, culminating in the rise of Jacksonian democracy where voting rights were expanded to include all adult white males regardless of property qualifications. If John never achieved the success in the political realm that his predecessors had, his long tenure as the steward of Eyre Hall was considered to be something of a golden era: a period in which, through his wise investments, he restored (and even increased) its prosperity after the disruptions of the Revolutionary period and kept a firm hand on its management for many decades. John Eyre's marriage to the spirited Ann Upshur in 1800 also initiated an effervescence of genteel hospitality that led one chronicler to write, more than half a century later, that under their welcoming conviviality the "distinguished homestead was in its zenith." The house, its furnishings, and the garden were substantially improved by the couple who regularly hosted relatives and guests and took pleasure in their company.[29]

The golden era got off to an embarrassing start only weeks after Littleton's burial. The change in ownership of Eyre Hall and John's coming of age led to a lawsuit submitted that summer in the Northampton County chancery court. George Parker and his wife Margaret "Peggy" Eyre Parker and her younger sister Sarah "Sally" Eyre, age 19, who was represented by her mother Margaret Eyre, "her next Friend," brought a bill of complaint against their two surviving brothers, John Eyre and William Eyre. Because William was described as "an Infant under the age of twenty one years [he was 17]," he was represented by his older brother John, who was his legal guardian. The two sisters complained that they had not received the full amount of their legacies that had been stipulated in their father's will. According to the terms of the will, Severn Eyre left Peggy £2,000 that she was to receive either when her brother Littleton turned 21 years of age on March 5, 1772 or when she married, whichever event occurred first. Peggy married George Parker, a neighbor and aspiring lawyer, on October 12, 1786, just a few weeks before the family received the sad news of the death of their brother Severn in England. Sally was to receive £1,500 under the same terms, according to one of the codicils of her father's will. Though unmarried, she too should have received her inheritance on her oldest brother's birthday seven years previously.[30]

The two sisters and their mother acknowledged—and Isaac Smith's detailed accounts show—that £1,074 divided equally had been paid to Peggy and her sister Sally from Severn Eyre's estate in November 1786, shortly after Peggy was married. However, the suit noted that this was far short of the full amount that was due to both of them. The plaintiffs contended that John and William, as the inheritors of their father's estate on the death of their two older brothers, should be responsible for disbursing the remaining money due from their respective estates along with the interest that had accrued dating back seven years. John Eyre responded on behalf of his brother for the defense by acknowledging the legitimacy of the legacies in their father's will, but arguing that they did "not think it consonant to the principles of Justice" if they were burdened by "the payment of any Interest arising" from the unfulfilled payments: the disruptions and "many capital losses" caused by the war made it impossible to meet the demands of the plaintiffs without unduly diminishing the value of the estate, which, he asserted, was never the intention of their father.

On August 12, 1789, the justices decided that both John and his brother would be liable for the remainder of the two legacies and that the sisters were "entitled to two and a half percent only on the respective legacies devised to them by their father . . . from the time they became due until the day of the judgement." Peggy was granted the sum of £1,800, which included £337 in interest, and her sister Sally received £1,200, of which £237 was interest.[31] It was a strong rebuke of the two young men who had or were about to assume control of the Eyre family property, now divided into two portions.[32] This subdivision of their father's land and slaves would continue until it was consolidated once again into single ownership when John died in 1855 and his grandnephew, William's grandson, Severn Eyre, took control.

Although this family squabble was settled in public, Eyre Hall remained home to three of the four remaining siblings and their mother Margaret through most of the 1790s. John was now the owner of the estate, but was unmarried. After her marriage, Peggy had settled at Kendall Grove near Eastville with her husband George Parker. Younger brother William continued to live at Eyre Hall until he came into his majority in 1793, and probably did not move out until after he married the 16-year-old Grace Duncombe Taylor of Norfolk in 1796.[33] The following year, John and William bought several tracts of the Kendall estate across the creek north of Eyre Hall, and by 1800 William and Grace had established their residence in a new brick house on the property that they now called Eyreville.[34] Younger sister Sally also resided at Eyre Hall until her marriage to Dr. James Lyon of Carlisle, Pennsylvania, in July 1799. They settled on land near Eastville not far from Kendall Grove and the Hungars plantation owned by William. Three months earlier, in April 1799, the oldest sister, Peggy Parker, died at the age of 33, and was buried at Eyre Hall next to the grave of her third child, George, who had died in 1796 when he was five.

Ann Upshur's marriage to John Eyre on February 24, 1800 ushered in a new era at Eyre Hall. Ann was from a large and prominent Eastern Shore family who lived at Warwick, a brick house on a long narrow peninsula known as Upshur Neck on the seaside in neighboring Accomack County. Born on October 4, 1780, she was the eldest of three children of Abel Upshur II and his wife Elizabeth Gore Upshur. Her two younger siblings were Elizabeth, or "Betsy," who was two and a half years younger, and Arthur, who was born in 1789, a few months before their father died in 1790. Their mother remarried in 1792. Her new spouse was John Upshur, a second cousin to her first husband. John lived at Brownsville, a seaside property only a few miles south of Warwick in Northampton County.[35] That union was short-lived as Elizabeth Upshur died in early 1794. Even before that tragic event, Ann and her sister had been sent north to Philadelphia to attend a boarding school run by a couple named Fullerton. A year after their mother's death, Ann wrote to her stepfather: although she and her sister Betsy were still grieving over their "fatal misfortune," she hoped that her mother "had gone to a better world." She was deeply grateful to have him "to protect our orphan situation & inexperienced youth," and was comforted to know that "we are not destitute when we have a friend like you." She encouraged him to come see them in Philadelphia in the near future, as "it would cheer your mind from melancholy reflections which are incident to the country." Written with a maturity not evident in many 15-year-olds, Ann also dutifully reported their expenses and explained that some of the bills that they had incurred at the boarding house were due to the fact that Mrs. Fullerton had raised the rates "on all the young ladies." Her letter reveals how difficult it must have been for the two young sisters, but their sadness appears to have been partially leavened by the enjoyment they took in the friends that they had made in the city, which included the Cunninghams and their Teackle relatives.[36] It was there that Ann and Elizabeth's interest in music blossomed.

By the late 1790s, Ann and Elizabeth Upshur had finished their studies in Philadelphia and returned to the Eastern Shore. Like all young people of the period, they probably paid extensive visits to the homes of relatives or close friends of their family, where parties and other entertainments allowed them to meet eligible suitors. A few may have been newcomers to the region, but many were probably familiar from the years of intermingling and marital ties that now stretched back several generations, binding a small circle of gentry families who presided over the social and political affairs of the region.

Just such circumstances brought John Eyre and Ann Upshur together in the summer of 1798, when they met at the home of Colonel Custis Kendall and his wife Susanna Gore Kendall. Custis Kendall was in the process of selling his old plantation just north of Eyre Hall to William Eyre and was now living in a house located a few miles south of Brownsville, Ann's stepfather's plantation. Mrs. Kendall may have been a relative of Ann and Elizabeth's on their mother's side of the family. Unfortunately, Ann had fractured her leg in an accident while there and was thus confined at the Kendalls for several weeks while it mended. John Eyre visited them while Ann was recovering and was apparently infatuated by her charm. John had just turned 30 and Ann was not quite 18, but their age gap was immaterial. Years later, Ann's sister Elizabeth believed this encounter was probably "the beginnings of Mr. Eyre's attachment" as the two young women "experienced the grateful . . . attention from that family as well as from others." On June 16, 1798, John Eyre wrote coyly to Elizabeth at Colonel Kendall's house that "the Family at Eyre Hall, much interested in Miss Ann Upshur's salutation, have sent this to enquire how she is. They at the same time beg leave to offer their services, in any way in which they can be acceptable—If they have any article which can alleviate her sufferings it will give them great pleasure to furnish it, there being nothing within their power which they would not do to make her confinement tolerable." He added that "if Books of entertainment will be acceptable they shall be sent."[37]

Wooed by the promise of books and other gifts, Ann was clearly impressed by John's solicitous manner, and their newfound friendship turned serious. A year and a half later they were wed. Ann's sister Elizabeth soon followed suit, marrying Littleton Dennis Teackle three months later, on May 27, 1800. Before they turned 20, both women had made advantageous marriages to wealthy men from prominent interconnected families. Born in 1777, Teackle was from a prosperous family from northern Accomack County and was related on his mother's side to the Upshur family. He was probably familiar with the two Upshur sisters by the time they were in Philadelphia. He had lived in Philadelphia with his family in the 1780s but returned to Accomack the following decade. At the time of his marriage to Elizabeth Upshur, Littleton was shifting his budding business interests northward across the state line; he purchased land on the Manokin River on the western edge of Princess Anne, the seat of Somerset County, where his uncle, John Dennis, a member of the United States House of Representatives, established his home at neighboring Beckford.

In 1802 Littleton and Elizabeth Teackle began construction on a ten-acre estate of an ambitious five-part, two-story brick house, the first masonry dwelling in Princess Anne. Known as the Teackle Mansion, the house would not be finished until 1819, when the two flanking wings were completed along with many outbuildings. The entire ensemble contained more than two dozen rooms, including an interior marble-laid bath and underground cistern, and was by far the most opulent dwelling in the region. The mansion, furnishings, and gardens were sustained by Teackle's diverse mercantile portfolio, which extended to banking, shipping and importing foreign goods, supplying the United States Navy with timber, and operating one of the earliest steam-powered gristmills in the region. Yet, the success of Teackle's schemes fluctuated wildly, buoyed by economic prosperity and brought low by war, recession, and acts of God such as fires and hurricanes.[38]

The grandeur of her sister's mansion in Princess Anne may have been a spur to Ann and her new husband John to make improvements at Eyre Hall. The mansion, garden, and many of the service structures were now 50 years old and needed repairs or replacement to make them more fashionable. Although John's mother Margaret remained in residence until her death in 1812, the exodus of all John's siblings from Eyre Hall meant that the couple could remodel a nearly empty house. John and Ann made substantial changes to the house and grounds. The garden was expanded and a new brick-and-wood fence was erected to enclose it and the graveyard. An avid gardener, Ann prevailed upon her husband in 1819 to erect "a green house for my amusement, and gratification," a hobby that she also shared with her sister Elizabeth. The two shared cuttings and plants from their gardens.[39]

Hand in hand with home improvements, Ann and John sought to restock their home with the most fashionable accessories in order to entertain on a lavish scale. Ann's propensity for entertaining, coupled with John's "decided and lively taste for the embellishments of life," prompted a wholesale refurbishing of the house.[40] The preponderance of objects dating from the first quarter of the nineteenth century in the catalogue of this book testify to the lengths to which the couple went to make this a well-appointed home.

Gardening and music were two of the passions of Ann Eyre's life that were among the crowning achievements of the hospitable hosts of Eyre Hall in the early nineteenth century. Strolling among the parterres in the garden or examining the subtropical fruit trees and flowers that flourished in the greenhouse were pursuits matched by the musical entertainments inside the house. The entrance passage was filled with great joy as family and friends gathered around the piano to listen to stirring marches celebrating the prowess of the new country, or joined in the singing of popular songs from romantic English and American ballads played on Ann's piano and accompanied on fiddle, flute, or guitar by the more accomplished of those assembled around the room. Ann's collection of popular songs began when she was in Philadelphia and continued to grow over the decades.

Off to the east side of the stair passage, the smaller ground-floor room contained a well-stocked library that John Eyre had organized and expanded with collections of contemporary poetry, novels, and histories that visitors could take out of the bookcase and read during leisurely moments in the room or take outside and leaf through while sitting on a bench in one of the porches that radiated off the passage, where they could catch breezes or admire the blooms of the garden. The books that John and Ann accumulated, which were later augmented by the many volumes acquired by their nephew William L. Eyre of Eyreville, reflected the popular tastes of the period; the library was by no means that of a professional or a scholar, but one that had appeal to a broad range of interests.

Ann and John Eyre opened their house to their wide network of kin, neighbors, and wealthy and well-connected visitors from across the state and region. With no children of their own, they welcomed many relatives who came for long visits, which promised good conversation, splendid meals, and polite and lighthearted entertainments. A visitor from King and Queen County, Virginia, who traveled to Eyre Hall in 1825, recounted that their "style of living reminded him of what he had read of the luxury of the Nabobs of India—strawberries, raspberries and such things in February."[41] Above all others, they reveled in the company of their nephews and nieces who lived nearby and were frequent guests at Eyre Hall. These included Emily's older sister, Sally Taylor Eyre from Eyreville, and her cousins, William Eyre Lyon and Margaret Alice Lyon, and Severn Eyre Parker and his younger sister Sally B. Parker from Kendall Grove. Ann Eyre's death in the summer of 1829, a few months short of her 49th birthday, diminished much of the sparkle that radiated from the place. A younger relative, Mary Upshur, writing under the pseudonym Fanny Fielding, was too young to have known her kinswoman personally, but did get to know the house a number of years later and became acquainted with and taken by John's genteel manner late in his long life. The author wrote admiringly that "Mrs. Eyre is said to have been one of the most gifted ladies of her day;

talented, highly educated, witty and fluent in conversation, and moreover an exquisite musician, so that with qualities of heart commensurate with these endowments, it is not strange she should have been the centre of a brilliant and admiring circle. To the county gentry of both sexes, during her life and after, Eyre Hall was a most attractive place of resort, and strangers visiting the 'shore' considered their mission but half performed unless they had been entertained here."[42] Ann's brother Arthur Upshur had inscribed on her tomb in the Eyre Hall graveyard similar sentiments concerning the woman who had "freely extended hospitality of the delightful mansion over which she presided." Those who knew her "were well acquainted with the benignity of her disposition, her sympathies with the sorrowing and distressed and the vivid brilliancy of her well tutored, refined and classical mind."

John was 61 when his wife died and would live another quarter century before blindness and the frailties of old age overtook him in 1855 (Fig. 30). By the time of Ann's death he had been retired from active public life for more than a decade, preferring to step aside and let a younger generation take up the responsibilities of serving in local and state government. Conservative by temperament, John started his public career in 1794 when, at the age of 26, he was elected as a member of the Federalist party to represent the Eastern Shore counties of Northampton and Accomack in the Senate of Virginia, one of 19 members of the upper chamber of the General Assembly. Apparently, John was not

an outspoken politician and was seldom in the forefront of Senate deliberations. As one observer noted, "like Washington, [who] took little part in debate, he also, like Washington, exercised influence due to his sound judgment and weight of character."[43] John supported proposals that strengthened the powers of the national government, which had been enhanced by the new United States constitution that his brother Littleton had voted to ratify in 1788. John was duly returned to the Senate for five more terms, finally stepping down after the 1801 session. The growing strength of the Democratic-Republican party in Virginia—reflected at the national level by the election of Thomas Jefferson to the presidency in 1800—may have made the thrust and parry of Senate debate less attractive for a diffident individual such as John.[44] His recent marriage may have also made the annual trek and sessions in Richmond less appealing.

Rather than withdrawing entirely from politics, John took a seat on the Northampton County magistrates' bench in 1801 and remained an active participant in administrative and judicial affairs in his community well into the 1810s. He may have felt more comfortable dealing with individuals whom he had known his entire life and took great interest in improving the county's infrastructure of roads, bridges, and public buildings in Eastville. During this time, the clerk's office was repaired; the courthouse fittings were renewed and the windows glazed with iron sash bars; and, in 1816, a new, one-story, one-room, brick debtors' prison was constructed.[45] After previously having served as an overseer of the poor, in 1802 John served on a committee of magistrates to manage the construction of a poor house to alleviate the problems of the most destitute in the community.[46] His brother William sold the county a parcel of land partitioned off from the family's Hungars plantation to erect a brick structure to house the poor as well as a workhouse for able-bodied indigents.[47] John's work on the bench during these years was said to have been performed "with uprightness, firmness, and ability, as well as with the most scrupulous diligence and exactness," attributes similar to those expressed of his father and grandfather when they occupied similar positions.[48]

On July 4, 1808 more than two dozen leading members of the Federalist party on the Eastern Shore gathered in Drummond Town (now Accomac) in Accomack County to celebrate Independence Day. Turning from celebration to politics, they contemplated the next national elections and unanimously agreed to support John Eyre as a candidate for the House of Representatives in opposition to the Democratic-Republican incumbent, Burwell Bassett of New Kent County. The following day, Colonel John Cropper, Jr. of Bowman's Folly, a distinguished Revolutionary War officer, wrote to Eyre letting him know what had transpired and sending him a list of those who had endorsed his candidacy.[49]

The twelfth congressional district had been held recently by the Federalists including Thomas Evans (1797–1801), who was among the subscribers to pledge their support at the Drummond Town meeting, followed by John Stratton (1801–1803), who had lived at Elkington near Eastville. Stratton's death in 1804 allowed Bassett the opportunity to take the open seat in the 1805 elections for the opposition. He had run unopposed in 1807, so the Federalists were determined to nominate someone who had political experience from the Eastern Shore. Eyre knew his opponent Burwell Bassett well as they had served together in the Virginia Senate in the 1790s. Bassett, a nephew of Martha Dandridge Custis Washington, was a few years older than John, but had a long political career and commanded a large following among landowners in his native New Kent County and surrounding counties of the lower peninsula. Flattered by this unsolicited endorsement from respected men of his party, Eyre allowed himself to be drafted as its candidate. Less than two weeks after he had received Cropper's letter, news of John's candidacy appeared in a Norfolk newspaper and spread to others in the region.[50]

During this period Virginians did not hold their congressional elections in the fall of a presidential election year but in the following spring after the new congress had convened. Voting took place at the county seats during court days, so it was spread out over a few weeks. There was very little active electioneering involved at this time. A well-placed endorsement or editorial in a newspaper, many of which had strong affiliations with one party or another, was about as much print as was devoted to congressional or state races. When there were no strong issues to divide the two parties, the strength of personal reputations translated into votes. Incumbents had a natural advantage over challengers. Furthermore, in a district that extended from the Eastern Shore through counties in the lower peninsula and cities such as Williamsburg and Hampton, there were far more eligible voters on the western shore. In the first decade of the nineteenth century, many of those landowners moved away from the advocacy of a strong national government that they had avowed in previous years. Only the Eastern Shore remained strongly anti-Jeffersonian in sentiment.[51] The election results returned in the spring of 1809 overwhelmingly favored Bassett, who won with more than 57 percent of the vote. While Eyre dominated the polls in Accomack and Northampton Counties, he was drubbed in the far more populous lower peninsula.[52]

Despite his defeat in 1809, John ran against Bassett three more times, in 1811, 1815, and 1817. The 1811 election produced the same results as John carried the Eastern Shore but lost badly on the lower peninsula. John sat out the 1813 election. The 1815 elections came at the end of the war with Great Britain in which the Chesapeake had been the scene of major battles including the sacking of Washington in August 1814, which culminated in the burning of the capitol and president's house. Throughout the war, the Eastern Shore of Virginia had been subjected to raids by British troops who carried off crops and livestock and enticed a number of slaves to leave their masters.[53] The poor showing of American forces in the Chesapeake was only redeemed by the defense of Fort McHenry in Baltimore Harbor. John Eyre's Federalist Party made a strong showing in the 1815 election, but still fell short by less than 5 percent of the vote. Two years later, in the fourth matchup, the results were a rout. Because of their lukewarm support for the war, especially in New England, the Federalist party collapsed. John Eyre was soundly defeated. After this miserable showing, John conceded what had been evident from his first campaign eight years previously: the peculiar conservatism espoused by Eastern Shore Federalists had lost all credibility in other parts of eastern Virginia. Recognizing the futility of running against the anti-Federalist headwinds that swept over eastern Virginia, John retired from active politics and his appearances in the public arena thereafter were few and most often ceremonial.

John was much more successful as a businessman. For more than 60 years, he increased the value of his estate through a strategic shifting of his assets. In the early nineteenth century, the agricultural underpinnings of Virginia's economy were in sharp decline. Evident on most farms in the Tidewater, but to a lesser extent on the Eastern Shore, the sustained planting of tobacco for more than a century and a half had exhausted the fertility of the soil. The shift away from tobacco meant that many planters had more slaves than were needed to tend less labor-intensive crops. Crop prices declined, land values plummeted, and many migrated in search of better prospects. Some sought relief by selling out and moving to fresh lands beyond the mountains in Kentucky and Tennessee or the southwest territories of Alabama, Mississippi, and farther west. Others found that the demand for bondsmen in these new regions provided an outlet for their surfeit of slaves and were willing to put them up for sale to meet the demand in these new settlements.

Although large planters on the Eastern Shore were never as wedded to the production of tobacco in the second half of the eighteenth century as those in counties along the James and Rappahannock Rivers and Piedmont had been, some such as the Eyres found themselves with far more slaves than they needed. Although the personal property tax for Northampton County listed 178 slaves in Margaret Eyre's possession in 1782, by the time that John Eyre and his younger brother took control of the family's fortunes and divided between them the slaves that had been owned by their two brothers in 1789 that number had been reduced. From the late 1780s through the 1810s, the Eyres sold some slaves and willed others, especially children, to friends and family members.[54] A few were given their freedom. Finally, some slaves took flight from their bondage. In 1814, eight slaves from Eyre Hall and six from Eyreville either slipped away or were taken by British raiding parties when the British fleet sailed into the Chesapeake in force.[55] From the 1820s to the early 1840s John Eyre and his nephew William L. Eyre, who reached his majority in 1827, each owned on average between 20 and 30 slaves above the age of 12, along with numerous younger children not enumerated as tithables on the annual property tax lists. Even though the size of their enslaved workforce was far smaller than it had been in the late colonial period, John and William L. Eyre still retained their position as two of the largest slave owners in Northampton County. During this time, many planters in Northampton County decided to free some of their slaves to reduce the costs of feeding, clothing, and housing their workforce. The annual personal property tax rolls listed several hundred free Black people living in the county.[56] Some of them occupied land owned by the Eyres. In 1820 Jim Weeks was listed on the rolls as a free Black man, presumably superannuated, who lived "tax free" at John Eyre's mill. His son Billy was also a free man living there with his father. Others on John Eyre's land included Edmond Sample, George Stevens, John Weeks, and Eli Weeks. Daniel Pool and Daniel Riddix were free Black men residing on William Eyre's estate Eyreville.[57] These manumissions were not acts of moral uprightness, but calculated decisions to cast off those who were no longer useful to the Eyres. They were acts of repudiation rather than redemption.

The increasing number of free Black people in the county became a source of grave concern among the planters following Nat Turner's Rebellion, which occurred in Southampton County in August 1831 when slaves led by Turner killed more than 50 whites over a few days before the local militia retaliated, killing more than a hundred slaves and free Blacks over the next few days and adding to the carnage by trying and hanging more than 50 implicated in the event following its bloody suppression. Spooked by the events in Southampton, the leading citizens of Northampton County formed a committee and signed a petition to the state legislature requesting permission to remove the "free colored population" of the county to Liberia. Led by John Eyre, Judge Abel P. Upshur, Severn Parker, and others, they felt isolated on the Eastern Shore, "cut off from prompt assistance from other parts of the state" should free Black people make common cause with their enslaved brethren. The committee agreed to raise money to undertake the task, in conjunction with the American Colonization Society, of transporting the county's 1,834 free Blacks to Africa.[58] Nothing came of the petition for this wholesale deportation, but planters such as John Eyre and his nephew William L. Eyre became increasingly apprehensive about their hold on their chattel laborers and did all they could to maintain their control. They had good reason to worry. In July 1832, a group of 18 slaves from a number of plantations including a few from Eyre Hall and Eyreville escaped in a whaleboat from the Bowdoin wharf on Hungars Creek and sailed to New York City. Rather than letting it stand, both men supported the dispatch of a slave catcher to the metropolis to get their slaves returned. Three years later, more than 150 white leaders met at the courthouse in Eastville as they reacted to a series of anti-slavery societies in the northern states calling for the immediate emancipation of slaves. The group elected John Eyre the chair of the meeting, and he appointed Judge Upshur, Severn Parker, William L. Savage, and others to draw up a rejoinder to this threat. With no moral qualms about the rectitude of their position, they dug in their heels to defend the institution against perceived internal and external threats. The committee declared that "our slaves are our property" and the institution of slavery was protected by the United States constitution. They demanded that the private anti-slavery societies be prevented from agitating for such a goal.[59] Eyre and his compatriots stood firmly against any further assault upon the system that maintained their livelihood.

Even with a smaller labor force, John Eyre could sustain his farm operations because he leased much of his arable farmland to tenants. Although he continued to raise corn and oats on his home plantation fields (for which he needed his own laborers), he entered into a number of leases with neighboring farmers to grow crops on out-parcels and other lands in his possession. His laborers maintained the buildings on these leased lands and also manured them with the lime of oyster shells and Magothy Bay beans, a local ground cover that improved crop yields. The tenants were responsible for the upkeep of the fencing and their own labor to bring in their crops. In return for the use of the land, the tenants shared half of the harvest with their landlord. Enriched soil produced more bushels and barrels of oats and corn, which put more money into the pockets of Eyre and his tenants.

Tenant farming only worked on the Eastern Shore—unlike in the rest of Virginia—because, by the early nineteenth century, there were far more people on the peninsula than there was land for them to farm profitably. Curious to discover why this system of farming thrived here whereas the rest of the state remained steeped in the agricultural doldrums, the editor of the *Farmers' Register*, Edmund Ruffin, a prominent advocate of improving southern agricultural practices by promoting crop rotation, calcareous manures, and soil conservation, traveled to the Eastern Shore in the summer of 1835. What Ruffin discovered in his discussions with farmers in Northampton County was that its population was unusually rooted to the land. There was little out-migration compared to the rest of the state. He found that "the people of the Eastern Shore only, of all the inhabitants of Virginia, as a community, feel that they are *at home*—that they and their children are to live and die where they were born, and have to make the best of their situation." They were "attached to the place of their nativity, and seldom think of emigrating to the far west, or even to the 'Western Shore' (as they call all Virginia except their own narrow streak of land)." This attitude meant that "there are far too many for the land," with the result, Ruffin observed, that "the average price of land in Northampton, is three times as high as that of the average of the lands in Prince George and Surry, which border the James River."[60]

Given that land here retained its value, unlike in most areas of Virginia during this period, Ruffin asserted that "large landholders may, if it is desired, derive their entire income, with ease and with sufficient profit, from tenants." The agricultural reformer singled out John Eyre as one of the principal beneficiaries of the system. He noted that Eyre "has long had a large proportion of his lands . . . in the hands of tenants." Although the terms for renting the land were negotiated each year, the owner of Eyre Hall told the editor that "he had never denied the continuation of the possession" except to one person. One of his tenants had "held the same farm for 35 years, paying half the product as rent, and in that time increased the landlord's share from less than 40 barrels of corn, to more than 100. He did this in part by clearings, and by using the means of manure which the location offered, and which the landlord aided in and though not in his obligation, to his own profit as well as his tenants. Another of his farms was held 28 years by one tenant, who then died, and was succeeded by his son." Ruffin concluded that "such cases would seem to show that there is more attachment to rented land on the Eastern Shore, than is felt on our side of the Chesapeake for freehold inheritances on which the owners were born, and on which perhaps several generations of their ancestors were buried."[61]

Buoyed by his inherited assets and flush with the money that accrued to him as a landlord, John Eyre began to invest money in real estate and took on the role of banker in this rural society. While most of his affairs focused on the Eastern Shore, his reach extended throughout the Chesapeake. With his many Taylor connections, he maintained real estate interests in Norfolk. He also speculated in land development in the new capital of Washington. Just how early he decided to invest in the city is unknown, but his commitment was substantial; indeed, he purchased dozens of lots throughout Major L'Enfant's gridded plan, from squares in the area along the Tiber and the Mall to Judiciary Square and the capitol. As late as 1830 he still owned nearly 40 lots that he wished to sell "on reasonable terms."[62]

At home, the Northampton County deed books from the 1790s through the 1840s are filled with nearly 120 mortgage transactions with county residents. John loaned money with interest to his neighbors when they sought to purchase land, slaves, and livestock or construct new houses and improve their farm buildings, wharves, and even ships. He also took mortgages on properties when his neighbors were short of cash. Occasionally, he was a speculator, using his liquidity to purchase farms or parcels of land at foreclosure sales at bargain prices and then selling them in more propitious times. When necessary, he resorted to the court to recover his investment when the mortgagees defaulted on their loans.

Banking and real estate ventures were part of John's effort to look out for the financial wellbeing of his extended family. On several occasions he saved his siblings and in-laws from financial embarrassment. Among those who suffered reversals was his brother-in-law, Dr. James Lyon, in 1809. At the time, Dr. Lyon was in his early fifties and had been in partnership with Dr. Edward Evans for a number of years, ministering to the needs of families and friends in the area. Their 1804–8 account book lists calls made at Eyre Hall, Eyreville, Kendall Grove, and other plantations, as well as the poor house, where they treated a variety of ailments, dressed wounds, administered purges, and prescribed pills and elixirs to its inmates. The doctors took care of slaves that fell ill or were injured by accidents.[63] Lyon and Evans had a busy practice but the accounts end in 1808, and, the following year, Dr. Lyon found himself in need of a lot of money. In November 1809, he mortgaged a large variety of expensive household goods to his mother-in-law Margaret Taylor Eyre for $1,500. The items included many silver pieces, a set of blue-and-white table china, mahogany tea and dining tables, a sideboard, secretary and bookcase, four bedsteads, and a fortepiano. Some of these items may have been given to Sally by her mother when she had married Lyon in 1799, or may have been purchased by the couple in subsequent years. Along with these status items, Lyon added all his livestock.[64] At the same time, he also signed a mortgage with John Eyre offering up 16 of his slaves as collateral.[65] These mortgages were to be paid back in two years, but it is not clear if that happened. Unhappily, Dr. Lyon died in November 1811 just as the mortgages were coming due, and John and Sally Lyon became executors of the estate. Four months later, Margaret Taylor Eyre died at the age of 73. Tragically, her daughter Sally died a year and a half later, in October 1813. These three estates were entangled and John Eyre was left with sorting them out.[66]

John and his wife also assumed responsibility for the two Lyon children, Margaret Alice 11, and William Eyre 10, who were orphaned and now became their wards. The obligation was not new, for a similar circumstance had transpired a few years earlier. John's younger brother William, the master of Eyreville, died in 1808 followed shortly by his wife Grace early the following year. John became guardian to their three surviving children. Fortunately, William and

Grace's deaths did not leave a web of debt as had befallen the Lyon heirs.

As the paterfamilias of the next generation of Eyres, John invested portions of their inheritance, including the legacies left them on the death of their grandmother Margaret Taylor Eyre, in real estate, buying and selling on their behalf to increase the value of their estates. When John relinquished his guardianship of William and Margaret Lyon in 1824, he paid his nephew $26,381 and his niece $19,593. William Lyon died two years later, at age 23, but his sister Margaret received another payment totaling $17,282 from her guardian in 1831, probably made to coincide with her marriage that year to William Eyre Taylor of Norfolk.[67] It is not clear if some of the silver and other status goods that Sally and James Lyon had mortgaged eventually came back into the possession of their daughter, or whether they may have remained in the hands of their guardian to cover her parents' debts.

Yet another case of John Eyre coming to the rescue of his extended family occurred in the late 1820s, when he bailed out his high-flying brother-in-law, Littleton Dennis Teackle, whose finances were often precarious, running from boom to bust. Littleton and his wife, Elizabeth Upshur Teackle, had temporarily lost title to the Teackle Mansion in Princess Anne, Maryland, in 1812 when his business interests took a downturn. After recovering their financial foothold, they finished the mansion, but further setbacks in the 1820s forced a lawsuit by his creditors, which meant that he lost possession of the property again. In 1828 John Eyre stepped in and purchased the property, which was sold by a United States marshal to settle Teackle's debts. As a sign of affection for his niece, who had spent many long visits at Eyre Hall over the years, and as a legal maneuver to keep the property away from the unsteady hands of his brother-in-law, Eyre transferred title to the property to Elizabeth Anne Upshur Teackle in 1831. Ever thankful for her uncle's generosity, Elizabeth finally sold the estate in 1839 when she married Aaron Quinby.[68]

For the last 20 years of his life, John continued to entertain at Eyre Hall. Music remained an essential part of those occasions. He purchased a Nunns & Clark piano around 1846, which must have been a delight on many occasions and remained a prominent feature in the parlor through the 1920s. John Marshall, a traveling musician who often came to instruct and entertain John's guests, died in 1848 while at Eyre Hall and was buried in the family graveyard in tribute to the warm affections in which he was held by the family.

John's benevolence extended beyond his family to the wider community where he was remembered for a number of kind gestures and charitable acts. After his death, one acquaintance extolled the variety and extent of his generosity: "Mr. Eyre was kind to the poor. When it happened that there was a local scarcity of bread stuffs, and corn sold in the county for six or seven dollars per barrel, he would dispose of his in small quantities to the poor for $3 per barrel, and would keep it on hand that he might supply the poor. . . . Church building committees always felt sure of liberal contribution to their enterprise. Whether Episcopal, Methodist, Baptist or Presbyterian, this Philanthropist invested in all the houses of worship on the 'Shore' if he was applied to."[69] How much of this was true is hard to measure, but other sources suggest that his largesse was indeed felt across the county. In 1851 John may have been one of the principal donors of the $1,550 necessary to alter and renovate Hungars Church, a structure that his grandfather oversaw the construction of more than a century earlier in 1742.[70] Two years later, John contributed $2,000 to the parish for the erection of a new rectory.[71] In appreciation of his gift, the vestry installed a stone plaque on the façade of the two-story brick dwelling inscribed "Presented to the Protestant Episcopal Church in Hungars Parish by John Eyre 1853."

John died on June 19, 1855 at the age of 87 and was buried at Eyre Hall next to his beloved wife Ann. In death, he sought through the provisions in his will to look after and help others whom he cherished. To the closest relatives of his wife's family, he bequeathed the hundreds of acres of land in Accomack County that came to him with Ann's marriage, in the knowledge that the parcel would improve their livelihood and would hardly be missed by the primary heir to his fortune. To Margaret Alice Lyon Taylor, the niece whom he looked after when she was orphaned, John gave many cherished household objects including the portrait of his father "taken by Benjamin West," his pews in Hungars Church and Christ Church in Eastville, as well as $50,000. A man of his time and place—who was as wedded to the prejudices of racial slavery and defended it as strongly as any southern planter—John did not reward freedom to his aged house slaves Nat and Nancy, but did give them a retirement home on the Eyre Hall estate and an acre of land associated with it for their own cultivation. They were also dismissed from having "to perform any service" in the future. The remainder of his estate passed to his closest heir, Severn Eyre, his grandnephew.[72]

THE EYRES AT EYREVILLE, 1800–1855

For more than 50 years the cadet branch of the Eyre family lived at Eyreville, the estate just north of Eyre Hall. Purchased from the Kendall family in the late 1790s, William and Grace Taylor Eyre demolished earlier dwellings near the peninsular point of the property on the north side of Eyreville Creek that divided it from Eyre Hall. In their place, they constructed in 1800 a two-story brick dwelling house laid in Flemish bond, which survives as the back section of a much-expanded house. However, little original interior fabric remains. William's son, William L. Eyre, expanded the house in the 1830s, more than doubling its size with a two-story brick addition to the south (Fig. 31). The front

Fig. 31. Eyreville (and floorplan, see opposite). The original section was built by William Eyre in 1800. The front section was added by his son William L. Eyre in 1839. The front porch dates to the mid-twentieth century.

façade was laid in Flemish bond while the sides were in 1:3 bond. Stone lintels (now removed) capped the window openings. The enlarged dwelling had an entrance porch (the present is a much later replacement) that sheltered an arched doorway with transom and sidelights that opened into a wide passageway with an arched opening at the end of the passage that led to the original section of the house. There were two large reception rooms on either side of the front passage that featured stone chimneypieces. As large as Eyre Hall and ornately finished, William L. Eyre's expanded house formed the core of the Eyreville plantation.

William and Grace Eyre lived at Eyreville for only a decade. During this time William figures little in public records other than selling some land from their Hungars

plantation to the county to establish a poor house and serving as an overseer of the poor for a short while.[73] He probably focused his attention on managing his farm operations at his Hungars and Eyreville plantations. About 30 slaves that he had inherited at the death of his older brothers worked these two farms.[74] William failed to live as long as his father, dying at the age of 36 in 1808. His widow Grace survived him by only a few months, dying at the age of 29. Three of their six children had not survived past their first birthdays, and their oldest, Sarah, died at the age of 17 in 1815. In 1809 Uncle John and Aunt Ann became the guardians of Sarah and her younger siblings Emily Ann 4, and William L. 3, who both lived into adulthood and married. Presumably at their parents' death, the children came to Eyre Hall to live, and

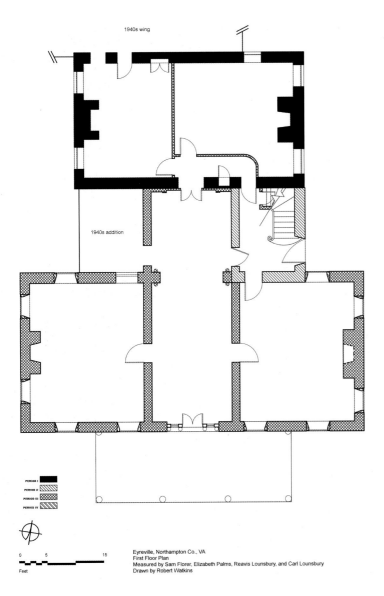

Carlisle Bank, was for many years on the board of trustees of the college. Like his brother, George found his marriage partner in Northampton County when in 1815 he wed Anna G. Savage of Cugley plantation across Cherrystone Creek from Eyre Hall.[75] George Lyon may have visited Eyre Hall to see his Lyon niece and nephew, and spoken with John Eyre or William about the college.

William spent only a year at Dickinson before he moved on to Hampden-Sydney outside the town of Farmville in Prince Edward County, Virginia. His time there was just as brief, and he apparently made so little impression that he appeared in the school's alumni records as "Robert Eyre 1824–25." Four inscribed books in the Eyre Hall library place him on the campus during the year. Restless or bored with his collegiate experience, William L. Eyre moved from the rural solitude of Hampden-Sydney to Charlottesville in the fall of 1825, where he started his third college in as many years, Thomas Jefferson's newly opened University of Virginia. When Eyre arrived, the finishing touches were still being made to the architecture of the grounds, which was laid out in a U-shape with two long arms with five, two-story professors' pavilions designed in variations on the classical orders interspersed with one-story student rooms fronted by a colonnade that linked the ensemble together (Fig. 32). Dominating the Academical Village was the massive, unfinished Pantheon-inspired domed library, which closed the upper end of the sloping grounds.

As magnificent and unusual as the setting of the new university, Jefferson's high-minded expectations of student conduct and lax rules of discipline jeopardized his pedagogical experiment from the very moment the first students stepped onto the grounds in March 1825. Rather than end the semester in the late spring and allow for a summer sabbatical, Jefferson and the board of visitors decided to continue through the end of the year so that many of the students, who came quite unprepared, but whose parents could afford the steep tuition, could begin to

Eyreville may have been rented or simply shuttered for 15 years until William L. Eyre returned from college and took up residence there in the mid-1820s.

Nothing is known of William L. Eyre's childhood or early education. John Eyre looked after his nephew's estate, keeping track of the expenses of his young ward when he went to receive more formal education, perhaps at an academy, before he enrolled at Dickinson College in Carlisle, Pennsylvania, in 1823, when he was 17 years old. The choice of Dickinson probably stemmed from the ties that the Lyon family had with the town and the college. Dr. James Lyon was a native of the city, and he had a number of siblings who still lived there. His younger half-brother George Armstrong Lyon, a lawyer and president of the

meet the expectations of the European professors and two native ones that Jefferson had hired. The sons of wealthy merchants, professionals, and planters, the students chafed at the restrictions placed on them against drinking and carousing as well as the exclusion of personal body servants to take care of their daily needs. Resentment flared into infractions against many of the rules; some took out their aggression on the enslaved workers hired by the university and a few were punished. The heat of the summer did nothing to quell the rising insubordination.[76]

William L. Eyre stepped into a tinderbox of student insolence. No sooner had he arrived in late September, with the semester dragging on now for more than six months, than he became caught up in a major altercation with the professors. On September 30, students hurled a bottle of urine and a deck of playing cards through the window of one of the professors' pavilions. The following night, more than a dozen students donned masks and gathered in the center of the grounds where they taunted their professors. In the midst of the brazen crowd of drunken students stood William Eyre, braying loudly "Damn the European Professors."[77] When professors George Tucker, a friend of John Eyre, and John Emmet came out to quell the ruckus, they were attacked by the students who hurled bricks and sticks at them. Because they were masked, the professors could not identify the miscreants in the dark, and the next day some of them threatened to resign because of the aggressive assault.[78]

Two days later, in an effort to restore equilibrium on campus, tease out and punish the culprits, and lay down more stringent rules of behavior, an ailing Thomas Jefferson, the rector of the university, accompanied by members of the board of visitors including James Madison, met with the students in the Rotunda. Shaken by the incident, he declared it "the most painful event of his life," and overcome by emotion and tears sat down unable to speak further. Brought low by this heartbreaking scene, the students eventually broke their vow of silence and named the ringleaders of the riot, including Jefferson's grandnephew Wilson Miles Cary and William Eyre.[79] After being unmasked by his fellow students, William told the authorities that he had indeed donned a mask and spoken ill of the European professors but denied that he had been drinking and declared that he was not in the party who threw sticks. When asked why he joined in, he meekly rejoined that "he did it for fun without any evil design."[80] Perhaps before he even set foot in a classroom, William L. Eyre was banished from the university for five years, one of four students who were expelled for their immature impetuosity.

After his ignominious banishment from Charlottesville, William L. Eyre returned home, the gloss of collegiate education forever tarnished. Back on the Eastern Shore, William turned 21 in 1827 and took up the management of his estate at Eyreville. His uncle John Eyre formally ended his guardianship and paid William $12,286 from the profits he had garnered in running the estate during the previous 15 years.[81] With money in hand, William set out to find a wife to help him run his estate. He only had to travel across Cherrystone Creek to Cugley plantation on Savage's Neck to court Mary Burton Savage, one of the daughters of Thomas and Margaret Savage, whom he had probably known for some time. She was the younger sister of Anna Lyon who had married George Lyon of Carlisle. In March 1828 they were married. Their first son, John, named after his uncle, was born at the end of the year but died the following summer and was buried at Cugley. Two years later, on August 15, 1831, a second son was born. They named him Severn after William's grandfather. It appears that there were no other children, so, as an only child, Severn had the full attention of his parents and eventually their understanding that he would become heir to his great-uncle's estate across the creek.

From the late 1820s and through the rest of his life, William L. Eyre's chief interests at Eyreville were twofold. The first was scientific farming—that is, using new methods to improve the yield of his worn-out fields through crop rotation, ground cover, manures, and other enrichments, adopting new plowing methods, and developing practices that would enhance the breed of his draft animals and livestock. He was one of the first subscribers on the Eastern Shore to Edmund Ruffin's *Farmers' Register*, which was the mouthpiece of agricultural improvement in the state. In 1834 he wrote to Ruffin that, "fully sensible of the necessity of doing something to improve the condition of my own farm, I determined to alter the mode of cultivation heretofore pursued, to attend particularly to manuring, and to cultivate *less land*." He sought the agronomist's approval of his use of crushed oyster shells on his fields to increase the fertility of the sandy soil.[82] Drawn to the Eastern Shore by Eyre's experiments, Ruffin visited his plantation in the summer of 1835 and praised what he saw, stating the Eyreville "exhibits a high state of improvement, and of productiveness that is

rare in this county—and which he has principally produced himself, and within the few years which he has been in possession. The land, however, though much impoverished, was originally among the best, which of course gave the greater facility to profit, by the application of putrescent manures. Mr. E. has also abundant means to use calcareous and marine manures, and has availed of them to some extent, but not so much as might have been expected."[83]

William L. Eyre's second passion was horses, specifically breeding them for racing. His interest came naturally in a family that had prints of some of the most famous mid-eighteenth-century English thoroughbreds framed and hanging on the walls of Eyre Hall. The county's personal property tax lists in the late 1820s and 1830s document Eyre's ownership of studhorses.[84] In 1835, the same year that Edmund Ruffin visited Eyreville, William began to keep a studbook, to record the breeding of his blooded stock. Horse breeding was a rich man's endeavor, and horse racing was the most glamorous and competitive of all sporting events in the antebellum era—where gentlemen could win and most certainly lose money on the outcome of head-to-head matchups. And so, it seems, a neophyte such as William L. Eyre fell prey to the temptations of the turf. As early as 1832, William, "being indebted to various persons," was forced to mortgage Eyreville, his slaves, and household goods in order to raise money to cover those debts. Coming to his rescue were his brothers-in-law Thomas L. Savage and William L. Savage, as well as William Eyre Taylor of Norfolk, the husband of his cousin Margaret Alice Lyon Taylor, who provided him with the money.[85] In order to repay them, William was forced to sell some of his assets. In 1834 he parted with Hungars, the 526-acre plantation that had been in the family since the first Severn Eyre had been given it by Isaac Foxcroft in 1693. William L. Savage purchased it for $6,000.[86] The following year, he sold 217½ acres of land attached to his Eyreville estate for $5,000.[87]

Fig. 33. The steamboat *Louisiana*, sketch by Alfred Waud.

Although there are no personal records to track the worsening of William's solvency, it is clear from personal property and land tax records that the Eyreville estate was diminished in prosperity compared to Eyre Hall from the late 1830s through the 1840s. Where once the taxes paid on each estate were roughly equal, by the late 1840s John was assessed seven times the annual amount for personal property that his nephew was. To help protect Mary Eyre and afford her a modicum of relief, Uncle John Eyre stepped in to protect some assets. In 1839 he set up a trust with her brother William L. Savage and purchased a slave named Richard from her husband for $750, for Mary's "separate use and control." In 1843 John bought a coach horse for her from Peter Bowdoin for her "separate use and advantage." The same year William mortgaged "all his plate and all his books at Eyreville along with a saddle, bridle, gold watch, and two guns" to William S. Floyd for cash.[88]

William's financial woes came to a head in 1850 when he was sued by three of his creditors for loans long overdue. On May 29, the master of Eyreville "was committed to the jail of said County charged in execution by virtue of a capias ad satisfaciendum" obtained by three of William's creditors. The small one-room brick debtors' prison in Eastville, which had been erected under the direction of John Eyre when he was one of the county magistrates in 1816, now welcomed his disgraced nephew metaphorically until he signed papers turning over his entire estate to the county to be sold at public auction in order to pay off his creditors. On the first day of the August court session, notice was posted on the courthouse door of the public sale of Eyreville at auction in ten days' time. As he had done so many times in the past, the 82-year-old John Eyre stepped forward to rescue a member of the family. With the highest and perhaps only bid of the auction, John paid $1,000 for the real and personal estate of his ruined nephew.[89]

It is hard to know what John felt about his spendthrift heir. The following year, he did make sure that much of

William's personal estate including, ironically, many of its horses, were entrusted to Mary Eyre's estate intended for her own use and not liable to her husband's debts. John also sold off 326 acres of Eyre Hall land, perhaps to cover further liabilities that might arise when William became the master of Eyre Hall. However, William L. Eyre did not survive his ancient uncle, dying July 11, 1852 at the age of 45, the cause of death unknown. His son Severn Eyre, who would turn 21 the following month, would be the new heir, perhaps to the relief of his great-uncle.

EYRE HALL IN THE AGE OF SEVERN EYRE, 1855–1914

Severn Eyre grew up and prospered in the steam age. In 1843 Severn's father wrote to his brother-in-law in Philadelphia, William L. Savage, noting the young boy was recovering "from a very sore foot occasioned by poisoned oak, also a bite on his arm," but was looking forward to a trip that he would take with his mother, Mary Savage Eyre, to visit her brother in a few days. They would travel by water from the Eastern Shore to Baltimore and there catch a train to Philadelphia. William L. Eyre also described the busy season of visitors that had made Eyreville a lively placed filled with cousins who had arrived by train and steamship from as far away as Carlisle and Washington. He also mentioned how Mary and Severn would meet up with "Uncle [John] Eyre" in Baltimore along with other relatives and neighbors before heading north. He mused that "all the world and his Wife are going to Baltimore on Thursday."[90] By this time, steam packet boats called at Hungars and other Northampton

Fig. 34. Nassau
Hall, Princeton
University, 1837.

sites and maintained frequent connections to Baltimore, Washington, and Norfolk that made possible such carefully planned visits (Fig. 33).

By the late 1840s, Severn had become quite familiar with steamship and railway timetables. When he was 14, Severn took a steamer to Baltimore and caught the train to Philadelphia and then a branch line to Burlington, New Jersey, to attend the newly established Oakwood School on the outskirts of that town, where William Savage's in-laws, the Chaunceys, lived.[91] Perhaps Savage had recommended this Presbyterian prep school to the Eyres. Severn's academic progress there allowed him to enroll in the fall of 1846 at Princeton, and over the next four years his journeys from Eyreville to New Jersey were made easier by the steamships that plied the Chesapeake and the fact that Baltimore had also become a major hub in the expanding network of railroads.

Unlike his father, Severn took his collegiate studies at Princeton, or the College of New Jersey as it was known then, seriously. Since its founding in the middle of the eighteenth century as a Presbyterian school, the college had attracted many southerners. James Madison graduated in the class of 1771 (Fig. 34). When Severn enrolled in 1846, half of the 20 members in his freshman class were from the South.[92] Like his namesake 90 years earlier, Severn brought his body servant with him to Princeton.[93] By the time of his senior year in 1850, 103 out of the 235 students at Princeton came from the South, including 16 from Virginia. Severn became good friends with Archibald Stirling, Jr. of Baltimore, who was in the class behind him.[94] Perhaps in a summer recess or on his way to or from Princeton, Severn paid a visit to his classmate in Baltimore, who no doubt introduced him to his younger sister Margaret. He would soon become a familiar guest in the Stirling household.

Severn graduated from Princeton with an A.B. degree in the spring of 1850, perhaps returning home to learn of his father's very public humiliation.[95] If so, it did not deter him from continuing his education and perhaps may have been a spur to escape any domestic awkwardness. He spent the following year pursuing legal studies at the University of Virginia, perhaps as a conscious effort to redeem the family's name at that institution.[96] He finished his legal education at

Harvard in 1852, where he received an LL.B. degree on July 21, 1852.[97] The pursuit of a legal education may not have derived solely from any inherent propensity for the subject, but may have been seen by Severn as a practical course of training for a profession that would allow him to pursue the means of making a lucrative living in the wake of his father's economic calamities. If Severn had proudly walked across the stage that day to receive his diploma, the necessity that may have driven him toward that achievement had been obviated ten days earlier when his father died at Eyreville. Less than a month from his 21st birthday, Severn Eyre had suddenly become heir to his great-uncle John's sizeable Eyre Hall estate.

On completion of his education at Harvard, Severn Eyre may have returned to Eyreville to look after his mother and put his estate in as much order as possible. He may have used his newly acquired legal knowledge in straightening out his father's finances. In June 1853, he probably returned to his alma mater at Princeton where he and others received an honorary A.M. degree at the annual commencement.[98] But foremost on his mind during this period was spending time in Baltimore courting the sister of his Princeton classmate. The eldest daughter of Archibald and Elizabeth Walsh Stirling, Margaret Yates Stirling was born in 1833 and grew up in a large and well-connected Presbyterian family.[99] Her father had a long career at the Savings Bank of Baltimore, which culminated in his being made its president in the early 1850s. A number of her siblings became prominent professionals in their fields. Severn successfully won Margaret's hand, and on April 24, 1854 they were married in Baltimore.[100] A strategic and loving marriage filled with promise tragically ended nine months later when Margaret Stirling Eyre died on January 25, 1855.[101] The cause of this tragedy was not identified in the brief newspaper announcement, but, given the timing of her death, it is quite possible that she died in childbirth along with the baby.

Five months after the death of his young bride, Severn's uncle John died at Eyre Hall in June. How Severn reacted to these turbulent events is unknown.[102] From tax records, it appears that the widower Severn and his widowed mother Mary vacated Eyreville and took up residence at Eyre Hall within the year. One of the first things that he did on inheriting the property was to get an injunction in the Northampton County circuit court to prevent the sheriff from assessing a tax on the estate that was valued at $105,384 in personal property and $18,089 in real estate. (This conservative estimate of the estate at $123,446 would be the equivalent of $3,638,650 in 2020.) This tax on the collateral inheritance of an estate had been passed by an act of the Virginia General Assembly in 1854, and Severn sued in higher courts to have it declared unconstitutional. "Eyre v. Jacob, sheriff" reached the Supreme Court of Appeals of Virginia and was heard by justices in Richmond during the April 1858 term, which by a split decision upheld the constitutionality of the law, meaning that Severn was required to pay the taxes on the estate.[103]

Perhaps disconsolate over the death of his wife, eager to lose himself among the diversions of his class, and in need of getting away from the Eastern Shore, Severn, now flush with cash despite having to pay taxes on his great-uncle's estate, did what other Eyres had done before him, including his uncle John, and decided to invest in a spa. In this case, in 1855 he purchased stock in the White Sulphur Springs Company in Greenbrier County in the Alleghany Mountains, which was reaching the height of fashion among the elite from all parts of the East Coast.[104] With his investment Severn became owner of a one-story frame dwelling nestled with others into the hillside in a group designated South Carolina Row. Just how often Severn made his long journey to the mountains is not recorded, but, as a wealthy 24-year-old widower from an old Virginia family, his presence at the resort would have been noted among the fashionable habitués who flocked to the springs for its therapeutic and social attractions.

On June 27, 1860, the United States census taker listed Severn Eyre, 28, as a farmer, living at Eyre Hall with his mother Mary Eyre. The enumerator estimated that Severn's real estate was valued at $70,000 and his personal property at $50,000. Though unnamed, 90 slaves lived on his lands at Eyre Hall and Eyreville and ranged in age from 90 years to three months. Thirteen were over the age of 60, and 15 were under the age of 12. There were 44 males and 46 females. Besides space in domestic outbuildings such as kitchens, the Eyre slaves lived in ten houses on the estates.[105] Except for one right behind the kitchen, the location of these structures at Eyre Hall is not precisely known, but presumably they stood on the fringes of the fields east of the main house. Some may have been near the overseer's house south of the main entrance drive. That same year, the county tax records noted that Severn owned 1,079 acres at Eyre Hall, 600¾ acres at Eyreville, and one acre near Eastville. Although the 1860 personal property tax list does not exist, the one for the following year recorded Severn as the owner of four pleasure carriages, 24 horses and mules, 43 cattle, 80 hogs, and 90 sheep. He owned 1,000 ounces of silver plate, $800 of household and kitchen furniture, and $4,000 in bonds, securities, and cash.[106]

By any measure, Severn Eyre was one of the wealthiest men in Northampton County when Virginia seceded from the Union in 1861. Unlike earlier generations of Eyres, he chose to play no political role in local or state affairs. On his return to the Eastern Shore in the mid-1850s, he did not enter the public arena like many earlier generations of Eyres, nor did he become embroiled in the hot disputes that were tearing the country apart. Although the Eastern Shore had many supporters of the secessionist cause—and, as a large slaveholder, Severn might have been attached to such political sentiments—he chose not to side with the hotheaded enthusiasts. Instead, he remained loyal to the Union, but perhaps not with a wholehearted passion. Although Accomack County remained a stronghold of

Unionism, Northampton County had more Confederate sympathizers, and troops were raised in the region to fight for the Southern cause. Those who had enlisted in the Confederate army largely withdrew across the bay after a federal army under General Henry Lockwood invaded the Eastern Shore of Virginia from Maryland in November 1861 and pacified the two counties with little trouble. It was a strategic move made by the national government to prevent food and other materiel from being shipped from the Eastern Shore to other parts of Virginia.[107] It also kept Washington from being completely outflanked from the east and did much to alleviate the secessionist pressures among the slaveholders in Maryland to push the state out of the Union into an alliance with its Southern brethren.

Although the county courts continued to function under local officials and the occupation was relatively benign, there were some minor raids, smuggling, and other civil disturbances including the destruction of a lighthouse on Smith Island just off the southern tip of the peninsula by some Confederate sympathizers. In August 1863, the citizens of Northampton County were assessed $20,000 to pay for the damage. A large number of Northampton citizens were exempted from the tax but 200 were not, Severn Eyre among them. Many of these men postponed their payment, but Eyre promptly paid the $304 he was assessed. However, he became outraged when President Lincoln decided to suspend the collection of the levy because of their prevarications. Severn wanted restitution and traveled to Washington to see Abraham Lincoln. On March 2, 1864 he went to the White House but was unable to obtain an audience with the president. Furious at not seeing him, he wrote a letter to the president the next day asking him to have the federal officers who had collected the money return his portion. He justified his actions by declaring his loyalty to the Union and noted that he had "never voted for secession, or been in any way connected with it, and had in no shape or form violated any law of the

Govt, after the occupation of the place by the Federal Govt, and had gained the execration of a few people by my Union sentiment.... Being a law abiding citizen I paid my tax as soon as the bill was presented to me.... I cannot think you could have intended your order should affect loyal men in this way." He complained that he had "been made poor by the war" and hoped that a note from the president to the Treasury department would be a welcome "act of justice to an unfortunate individual who is a sufferer by the war & much in want of the money."[108] There is no evidence that Lincoln responded directly or heeded Eyre's request.

Severn Eyre's relative wealth did suffer because of the Civil War, although perhaps not as precipitously as his letter to Lincoln implied. That said, the effects of the occupation on the last years of servile labor in Northampton County are not well documented, and little is known about its end at Eyre Hall and Eyreville in the final years of the war. Because Accomack and Northampton Counties were occupied by federal troops, the freedom granted to slaves in areas held by secessionists in Lincoln's Emancipation Proclamation—published in September 1862 and in effect at the beginning of 1863—did not extend to the Eastern Shore. Here, in areas still loyal to the Union, slavery was left untouched.

Even though the legal status of slavery remained intact, federal occupation did speed its decline. In 1862 and 1863, the county courts became increasingly quiet on issues relating to slavery. They dropped the sanctioning of slave patrols to regulate the movement of bondsmen and also ceased granting exemptions to slaveholders who wished to have their older slaves taken off the personal property tax lists.[109] This relaxation of oversight and the presence of federal troops provided the impetus for many slaves to leave their masters. In 1861 and 1862, the number of slaves above the age of 12 and not exempted because of age on Severn Eyre's plantations remained steady at 42 and 44, approximately what it had been in the last years before the war. However, by 1863, the last year that slaves were

enumerated in personal property lists for the county, the number of slaves had dropped to 36.[110] Clearly, some stayed to work the fields but others fled. Across the county, some left their masters to seek employment with the occupying forces as laborers or used their skills as watermen for the military. By the fall of 1863, recruitment of Blacks into the Union army with the promise of freedom at the end of their enlistment drew many into service. Even at this late date, the federal officials offered to pay slaveholders $300 for each slave who had enlisted, provided the slaveholders could prove their loyalty to the Union.[111] We do not know how servitude ended on Severn Eyre's plantations or what happened to those who had been enslaved on them. Did the slow trickle evident in 1863 of people making the best of a chaotic situation and taking their chances in fleeing turn into a torrent as the death knell of the Confederacy rang ever louder in the spring of 1865? Who remained and why, and what happened to those who left and where did they go? How did these former bondsmen restructure their lives in the postwar period?

Even if the end of slavery at Eyre Hall and Eyreville has left no record, the effects of the war on Severn Eyre's personal property can be measured in the decline in livestock and the reduction in the value of household goods. As the number of laborers decreased during the war, so too did the number of horses and mules needed to work the fields and haul goods. From 24 in 1861 their number was reduced to nine in 1864. The reduction of pleasure carriages from four to two over those years diminished the need for these animals. The number of cattle fell from 43 to 30, and the number of hogs dropped from 80 to 25, since there were fewer mouths to feed. The value of Severn's household and kitchen furniture decreased from $800 in 1861 to $300 in 1864, and the amount of silver during these three years diminished by half from 1,000 to 500 troy ounces. Despite the obvious setbacks, Severn was never forced to sell land to make ends meet and retained a healthy portfolio of bonds, liquidities, and other

Fig. 35. Severn and Margaret Parker Eyre with her mother, Ann Floyd Parker, 1865, Fort Monroe, Virginia.

investments. He probably was not a man who had traded in his cash for Confederate bank notes.[112] He must have tucked away those assets in Baltimore, perhaps at the Savings Bank.

Although the war had a deleterious effect on Severn Eyre's economic livelihood, it may have helped him focus on his future and the need to find a suitable marriage partner. The restrictions on travel across the bay meant that Severn had to look closer to home to find a wife, or perhaps to Baltimore, where he maintained many friendships, yet the uncertainty of the times probably made him reluctant to leave Eyre Hall for stretches of time. Like his father, Severn did not have to look too far to find his next wife. Born in 1840, Margaret Shepherd Parker was the oldest daughter of John Stratton Parker and his wife Ann Floyd Parker of Old Castle, a plantation on Cherrystone Creek just to the north of Eyreville Neck. Though nine years older, Severn had probably known her since she was a child as they grew up on neighboring plantations and the Parkers were distant cousins of the Eyres. John Parker's father Jacob, who had bequeathed the Old Castle plantation to his son on his death in 1829, was a half-brother of George Parker who had married Severn's great-aunt Peggy Eyre in 1786. When Severn became interested in Maggie Parker is unknown, but they married on January 19, 1865. He was 33 years old and had been a widower for ten years, and she had just turned 24 the previous November.

After the wedding, Severn and Maggie, accompanied by her mother, Ann Parker, caught a steam packet from Cherrystone Creek to Old Point Comfort where they enjoyed the pleasures of the Hygeia Hotel in the shadow of the ramparts of Fort Monroe. The Hygeia had been a celebrated watering place for the beau monde for many decades as it was known for its moderate summer temperature with salubrious sea breezes, baths, fine dining, and many entertainments.[113] Steamship connections from Washington, Baltimore, and other parts of the Chesapeake and from northern cities by way of Hampton Roads made the resort a convenient destination. While there, Severn and Margaret arranged to have their photograph taken by the Kimberly Brothers studio, which had flourished photographing the many Union officers who had been stationed there through the war (Fig. 35).

From the late 1860s through the early 1880s, Severn and Margaret called Eyre Hall their home. The absence of accounts and personal papers from this period obscures the efforts Severn made to come to terms with farming a large plantation in the absence of slave labor. It is not known what happened to the freedmen who remained in the area in the years following the Civil War, or the inducements or arrangements Eyre made to entice any of them or others to work the fields of Eyre Hall and Eyreville. Severn did sell an acre of land in 1868 to the trustees of the African Methodist Episcopal Church for $100 so that the congregation could have title to the property where "Hayman Chapel" stood.[114] Perhaps this church was established by freedmen who had been bondsmen of the Eyre estates. In 1867, there were two Black men who voted in an election in the same district as Eyre Hall whose names were Dennis Eyre and Jay Eyres. Were they former slaves who tried making a living in the region after the war?[115]

The 1870 census provides a snapshot of life at Eyre Hall five years after the war. Listed as the head of the household at Eyre Hall was Severn, 39, farmer, and his wife Maggie, 29, whose occupation was "keeping house." Severn's mother Mary had died in 1866, so there were no other family members living with them. Severn had a personal estate valued at $80,000, which was only $5,000 less than it had been in the 1860 census. Given that his personal property had previously included many slaves, his standing in 1870 suggests that he had other resources to weather the substantial loss that came with emancipation. His real estate was valued at $50,000—a drop of $20,000 from ten years earlier—which could be attributed to a general depression in the value of land following the war in Northampton County.[116]

Listed immediately after Severn and Maggie and enumerated as part of the same family by the census taker, but living in a different dwelling, were nine individuals whose race was identified as Black: Bob Eyre, male, 70, gardener; Cantis Eyre, female, 65, domestic servant; Nelly Eyre, female, 60, domestic servant; Nat Jarvis, male, 30, laborer; Nat Smith, male, 40, laborer; Bridgett Smith, female, 30, laborer; Caesar Smith, male, 30, laborer; Lessard Smith, male, 14, laborer; and Peggie Wilkins, female, 22, laborer. Just what familial relationship these people had to one another is not clear. Were they former Eyre slaves? Those with Eyre surnames probably were, but the status of the others is uncertain. Just below this family group, the census taker listed five other families who occupied three houses, all of which could have been on Eyre Hall property. All of those listed were African Americans.[117] Given that some of these individuals had jobs such as "domestic servant" and "hostler," it seems likely that they worked for the Eyres in the house and kitchen and in the stable taking care of the horses and the carriages, which now numbered seven in the personal property tax list.[118] Others listed as laborers may have worked the fields or possibly in the grist- and sawmill that Severn owned nearby. Did they occupy former slave quarters that may have been upgraded since the war, or did they live in new buildings dispersed across the estate?

The 1870 agricultural and industry schedules of the United States census provide a little more detail on the scale of Severn's farm and business operations. According to the former, he had 250 improved acres under plow or pasture and 400 acres of woodland. That year his fields produced 300 bushels of wheat, 3,000 bushels of corn, and 900 bushels of oats. The farm was valued at $20,000, including more than $200 in farm equipment. Livestock included 6 horses, 11 mules, 12 milk cows and 30 "other cattle," 10 oxen, and 25 sheep. No swine were listed, but, based on the county property lists for 1870, Severn owned 50 hogs.[119] Severn Eyre also operated a steam-powered grist- and saw mill, perhaps located between the Eyreville and Eyre Hall boundary near the county road (now U.S. Route 13). He had $7,500 invested in the operation and employed seven men at the mill, who sawed lumber whose yearly value was $3,300 and ground corn and wheat into flour valued at $700 per annum.[120] Farming and milling kept money coming to the estate for the next decade, but it was by no means reaping huge profits during this time. By the early 1880s, Severn was ready to make a break from farm life for a variety of reasons.

Having children reshaped the trajectory of Severn and Maggie's life. In May 1871, Maggie gave birth to a son whom they named William Littleton Eyre, after Severn's father. In November of the following year a daughter, Grace, was born, perhaps named after Severn's grandmother. Both children were born in Baltimore rather than at Eyre Hall, perhaps as a precaution because the city would have provided accessible medical attention if there were any complications in childbirth.[121] A third child, Mary, was born in April 1875 at home at Eyre Hall, in the southwest bedroom on the second floor. She was probably named after Severn's mother.

Although Eyre Hall was their home in the 1870s, business, school, holidays, and activities pulled Severn and Maggie and their three young children increasingly away from the farm. During this decade, Severn probably depended on his in-laws, John and Ann Parker, to look after

Fig. 36. Grace, William, and Mary Eyre, ca. 1880.

his farm and mill operations in his absence. The Parkers had moved to Eyreville during this time. In March 1879, one of Maggie's younger sisters, Lucy, married the hotel magnate C. C. Willard of Washington at Eyreville.[122] Willard was the proprietor of the Ebbitt House, a popular hotel with the military in the postbellum era; he also owned, with his family, the eponymous Willard Hotel on Pennsylvania Avenue near the White House that attracted the political and social elite. Because of his association with the Eyres, Willard was said to have provided jobs in his hotels for a number of African Americans from Northampton County for many years.[123] Another sister, Nannie Parker, never married and became very close to her nieces and their offspring.

Friends and family in Norfolk, Washington, and Baltimore—combined with the convenience of steamship connections—made it possible for Severn and his young family to travel extensively throughout the region. In the absence of letters, diaries, and other personal papers, the collection of photographs of William, Grace, and Mary document their visits to these and other cities from the mid-1870s through the early 1890s (Fig. 36). With the onset of respiratory problems in his teens like many of his ancestors,

Fig. 37. William at St. Paul's School, Concord, New Hampshire, late 1880s.

William enrolled in the exclusive, Episcopal-affiliated St. Paul's School in Concord, New Hampshire, where the cooler climate was seen as a respite from the heat and humidity of southern boarding schools. While at St. Paul's, W. G. C. Kimball took William's photograph as well as those of his classmates and their activities and societies (Fig. 37).[124]

Business, education, and polite society drew the Eyres to Baltimore on a permanent basis in the early 1880s. They first moved into a townhouse at 103 West Monument Street in the old fashionable part of town, but after a few years relocated one block farther west at 223 West Monument, now the site of the Maryland Center for History and Culture. Almost immediately, the Eyres shed the slow pace and solitude of country life for the larger and busier stage of urban life. William, Grace, and Mary needed good tutors and schools as well as the social activities that would integrate them with their peers: the children whose fathers comprised the professional and business leaders of the city. William was packed off to boarding school by the end of the decade, and Grace and Mary were educated at home and developed local friendships. Severn and Maggie were welcomed into this circle of families and enjoyed an array of entertainments that regularly filled the pages of the *Sun*. They were the beau monde of Baltimore, whose social events, philanthropic good works, and marital alliances were recorded in the newspaper and a formal guide to the city's elite families. The *Social Register* acted as a checklist noting marriages, deaths, new debutantes, club memberships, college alumni, and overseas trips made by these families.[125] They socialized at their private clubs, worshiped in the same churches, and sent their children to the same schools, camps, riding stables, and music teachers. They even took vacations together or met regularly at the best resorts. In the winter of 1884, Severn and Maggie spent nearly two months at the Hygeia Hotel at Old Point Comfort, which had grown even larger since their visit in 1865.

Severn and Maggie filled their social calendars with afternoon teas, dinners, receptions, musical events, weddings, and charitable balls. During the winter season one year, the *Sun* highlighted "the brilliant reception at the house of Mr. Enoch Pratt," which was "attended by a large number of ladies and gentlemen" and that "Mrs. Pratt was assisted in receiving guests by Mrs. Severn Eyre."[126] The Eyres and the Pratts were fast friends, and, at another reception celebrating the opening of a branch

of the Pratt Free Library, the couple were again assisted by Mrs. Eyre.[127] Every year there were rounds of parties celebrating a new crop of debutantes, a role that Grace and Mary dutifully fulfilled in the 1890s. In "the news of the fashionable world," the *Sun* reported on December 11, 1891 that "Mrs. Severn Eyre, 223 West Monument Street, gave a reception from 7 to 10 last night, followed by a supper, in honor of her debutante daughter, Miss Grace Eyre." It was no small affair—guests included a score of debutantes, their parents, and a host of young men numbering more than 50 people.[128] Four years later, it was Mary's turn to shine as one of "this season's rosebuds." In December 1895, newspapers noted that "Mr. Robert E. Lee, son of the late Gen. W. H. F. Lee of Fairfax County, Va., was in Baltimore . . . and was the guest of Mr. and Mrs. Severn Eyre . . . at a tea given in honor of their debutante daughter, Miss Mary Eyre."[129] Although the daughter of an old Unionist did not land the son of a Confederate general, Mary did find her lifelong match during the whirl of debutante parties in DeCourcy Wright, the son of Judge D. Giraud Wright of Baltimore. So these extravagant seasons of balls and dinners served to solidify the bonds of those families inscribed in the *Social Register*.

Severn regularly attended dinners for gentlemen of his acquaintance and social standing, especially members of the Maryland Club including Dr. William DeCourcy, Judge D. Giraud Wright, and Enoch Pratt. Sometimes these were held in homes and at other times in private clubs or hotels.[130] In the late 1880s and 1890s, he was a sponsor and regular attendee of the annual banquets of the Princeton alumni where "songs of old Nassau—rang in the Lyceum Parlors," followed by lectures from distinguished professors including, one year, Woodrow Wilson, who chose to speak about the role of athletics at the school. As one reporter observed of these yearly banquets, the heart of the gathering was for "followers of the orange and the black . . . to eat and to drink, and to tell stories of days gone by."[131]

In between the cigars, champagne, and tureens of turtle soup at these male social gatherings, Severn solidified his business connections with entrepreneurs, lawyers, bankers, and industrialists. In those conversations, he became convinced that sound investments in stocks returned greater yields than all the bushels of corn grown in his fields on the Eastern Shore. He realized that there was little money to be made in the old cash-crop economy and put his money in railroads, steamships, and other industrial enterprises that drove the postwar economy of America. The Old Bay Line ran a daily service between Baltimore and Norfolk. Railroads in these two important cities connected the Chesapeake to major cities on the East Coast and inland to entrepôts on the Ohio and Mississippi Rivers. In 1884 a new rail line, the New York, Philadelphia and Norfolk Railroad, opened, which ran from a junction at King's Creek just below Princess Anne in Somerset County, Maryland, to the ferry terminal at the new town of Cape Charles on the bay in lower Northampton County. Passengers continuing through could catch the train ferry to Norfolk. Not only did it connect inhabitants of the region to major cities, it transformed the economy of the Eastern Shore. With a rail line running down the spine of the peninsula, an outlet was provided for truck farmers and watermen to ship their produce to urban markets (Fig. 38). The old agricultural patterns that had sustained Eyre Hall were changing.

Severn was elected to the board of directors of a number of these companies that were transforming the economy of the region. Not only was Enoch Pratt a good friend, but he was also a fellow board member of the Old Bay Line.[132] For nearly a dozen years from the 1880s through the early 1890s, Severn Eyre and his Baltimore friends spent two or three days in early May attending the annual meetings of steamship and railroad companies. Stockholders of the Old Bay Line gathered at the company office in Baltimore to review the books and set agendas for the coming year. Some were also on the board of the Seaboard & Roanoke Railroad and would embark on one of the Bay Line steamers in the evening for a trip to Portsmouth to attend the annual meeting of the railroad company the following day. Occasionally, a similar meeting of the Roanoke and Tar River Railroad might be scheduled for the day after. In 1887 Severn was re-elected president of that rail line. He also held stock in and was on the board of the Carolina Central Railroad and would sometimes attend its annual meeting in Wilmington a few days after his meetings in Portsmouth and Norfolk, after which he would catch an Old Bay Line steamer back to Baltimore, or sometimes stop off on the Eastern Shore to visit Eyre Hall.[133]

In the late fall of 1889, Severn Eyre applied for a passport for himself and his three children. Together with Maggie, the family boarded an ocean liner sometime thereafter and

spent many months traveling in Europe, especially in the south of France where the dry air of the Mediterranean climate was thought to be beneficial to young William, who had left St. Paul's School but remained in fragile health due to a pulmonary disease. The family no doubt enjoyed the sights and their time together, and William's conditions may have improved from the travel. After their return to America, William took a job with the Baker-Whiteley Coal Company in the city, a firm responsible for moving coal from the mines of Pennsylvania to the docks of Baltimore Harbor. Although William showed a "marked business capacity" with Baker-Whiteley, his health failed and he traveled once more to find respite. This time he went to Thomasville, Georgia, with its "dry warm atmosphere," a place which doctors recommended for patients suffering from acute pulmonary problems due largely to its vast, longleaf pine forests that were thought to be therapeutic.[134] In early 1893 he returned to Baltimore, but succumbed to his illness as his family "stood hopeless, helpless, and heartless in the presence of the unequal conflict." William, "their pride and joy, the object upon which rested so many hopes . . . the only son and only brother" died at home on April 30, 1893.[135] His death occurred a month before his 22nd birthday. After the funeral service was "read over his remains" at the house, his casket strewn with flowers was escorted by relatives and friends to the dock where the steamer *Virginia* transported it across the bay to the Eastern Shore. William, the last male Eyre heir, was laid to rest in the family burial ground at Eyre Hall.[136]

One of the pallbearers at William's funeral was a cousin from Norfolk, Robert Barraud Taylor, Jr., the great-grandson of Sarah Eyre and Dr. James Lyon. The Taylors continued to be close to Severn. His cousin Margaret Lyon Taylor, Robert's grandmother, had inherited the West portrait of Severn Eyre, as well as other items from John Eyre when he died in 1855. On occasion, the Taylors would visit the Eyres in Baltimore, so Robert and his younger brother Richard Baker Taylor had developed friendships with Severn's three children, William, Grace, and Mary.[137] Some three years after William's death, Richard and Grace became romantically involved. Richard had studied at the University of Virginia and turned to the law as a career, like so many in his family. He was in Baltimore for Christmas 1896, and, on November 17, 1897, several newspapers reported that "a wedding of interest to society in both Baltimore and Norfolk took place today at noon in Grace Church, when Miss Grace T. Eyre, daughter of Mr. Severn Eyre of Baltimore, was married to Mr. Richard B. Taylor of Norfolk."[138] Following the wedding the couple made their home in Norfolk, and on September 6, 1898 their first and only child, Margaret Eyre Taylor, was born (Fig. 39). Sadly, the marriage was not a good match and the two drifted apart in the following decade.

Fig. 41. Severn Eyre,
Margaret Parker Eyre,
and Nannie Parker, north
porch, Eyre Hall, 1890s.

Not to be upstaged by her older sister, Mary Eyre announced her engagement to William Henry DeCourcy Wright in October 1897, a month before Margaret's wedding. Wright was the only child of Judge David Giraud Wright of Baltimore, "who is well known in this city" and was a fellow member of the Maryland Club with Severn Eyre, and of his wife Louisa Wigfall Wright.[139] They were married on April 14, 1898 at the Eyres' townhouse at 223 West Monument Street (Fig. 40).[140] A son, DeCourcy Eyre Wright, was born in January 1899. Their daughter, Grace Eyre Wright, was born in April 1915, and named after her aunt Grace.

Now that their two daughters were married and had young children to look after, Severn and Maggie journeyed to Eyre Hall by themselves in the summer of 1899 to relax, enjoy the garden, and take care of immediate needs on the farm (Fig. 41). However, their solitude was disrupted at the beginning of September when Maggie fell ill. Within a week she was in a critical condition, and, despite the presence of doctors from Norfolk and Baltimore who had been called in for consultation, she did not recover. At age 58, Maggie died at Eyre Hall on September 14, with Severn and their two daughters in attendance. She was buried in the family graveyard next to her son William. Because she "was well known in Baltimore society," her illness and death received a lot of press coverage. The obituaries reflected the usual pieties, spoke of her esteemed Virginia lineage and that of her husband, and the charm of their "beautiful country home," which was described as a "noted place of horticultural interest."[141]

After Maggie's death, Severn withdrew from active engagement in the companies in which he had invested over the previous 20 years. In the new century, he fell into a peripatetic routine wherein he spent the winter and spring months in Baltimore; he then traveled to the Greenbrier for the summer season, where he would reside in his cottage on South Carolina Row; afterward he made the trip across the bay to Eyre Hall for a few months before returning to Baltimore.[142] While at Eyre Hall, he looked after the harvesting of his corn crop and began to divest surplus land that he had owned for years. After his father-in-law, John S. Parker, died in 1889, he purchased his old plantation, Old Castle, at public auction. He held onto it for a while and then began to sell off parcels of it at the end of the century. In 1909 he reduced the size of his Eyre Hall holdings by selling 315 acres on its southern edge.[143] He also began selling land that bordered the Eyreville estate that had been in his family for many years.[144] This reduction of landholdings culminated in 1904 with the selling of Eyreville, his birthplace, to a consortium of investors from Worcester County, Maryland, for $21,500.[145] The new owners turned Eyreville into a truck farm, where vegetables and fruits were grown for export by rail and steamship to urban markets. The process was transforming much of the Eastern Shore and making a few farmers prosperous again. After a turnover in ownership, in 1942 Eyreville came into the possession of Guy L. Webster, who thoroughly renovated the house and made several additions. Webster owned and operated the Webster Canning Company of Cheriton, which was one of the largest independent vegetable packers in the country.

In 1904 Severn moved out of the townhouse on West Monument Street and lived for a couple of years with his daughter Mary and her husband DeCourcy Wright on Park

Fig. 42. The Maryland
Club, Baltimore.

Avenue. Now in his seventies, old age caught up with him. In the winter of 1907, his daughter Grace came up from Norfolk to look after him.[146] In March he fell critically ill in Washington, where he convalesced for several weeks. After that, he took up residence in an apartment on Read Street, "where he kept a retinue of old family servants," but "most of his waking hours" were spent in conversation and dining at the Maryland Club, "where he had a great many friends," who in their prime had been the power brokers of the city and state (Fig. 42). At the end of the day, "he would be assisted by his negro 'body servant,' who would return for him at 11 or 12 o'clock at night" and walk him home to his Read Street apartment, which was a block south of the club.[147]

In 1910 Severn suffered a grievous blow with the death of his eldest daughter, Grace Eyre Taylor. Estranged from her husband, Grace had been visiting her sister Mary and her family when she died at their home on Park Avenue on September 4.[148] She was 37. Once again the Eyre family members boarded a steamship for the trip across the bay that brought Grace's remains home to Eyre Hall to be buried next to those of her brother William in the graveyard. After her mother's death, 12-year-old Margaret Eyre Taylor came to live with her aunt and uncle in Baltimore until she married in the late 1920s.

One last honor was bestowed on Severn Eyre. On March 20, 1913, he was invited to the White House in Washington to meet the new president, Woodrow Wilson. A newspaper

noted that as an alumnus (from the class of 1850) of the college that had served as the springboard for Wilson's meteoric rise in politics, Severn was "one of the oldest living Princeton graduates."[149] What did they talk about? Did they recall the time some 18 years earlier when they met in Baltimore's Lyceum at the uproarious alumni banquet? Or perhaps they spontaneously recalled the words from *Carmina Princetonia* and sang in praise of "Old Nassau." Given the president's dour personality, it doesn't seem likely!

Severn decided to spend most of the summer of 1914 at Eyre Hall. He especially enjoyed sitting in a rocking chair in the shade of one of the porches where he could catch a breeze that wafted through the wide passage of the house (Fig. 43). On Thursday afternoon, July 9, he was in his accustomed place when he was suddenly taken ill and died "before any aid could be rendered him." Unlike so many in his family—from his children to his more distant ancestors, who died young from consumption and other painful respiratory illnesses—Severn's death was unusual in that it came quickly to a man nearing his 83rd birthday, an age that had only been surpassed by his great-uncle John Eyre, from whom he had inherited the estate nearly 60 years earlier. As soon as they heard the news, DeCourcy and Mary Eyre Wright, still grieving over the death of their 14-year-old son Eyre Wright a few weeks earlier in a tragic car accident near Annapolis, caught a steamer across the bay to preside over the burial. Their niece Margaret Eyre Taylor probably came with them to bid farewell to her grandfather. The funeral took place on Sunday July 12 at Eyre Hall, where Severn was laid to rest in a grave between his wife and mother.[150]

After 125 years in the hands of two men, the Eyre Hall estate passed to two women on the death of Severn Eyre—his daughter Mary Eyre Wright and his granddaughter and her niece Margaret Eyre Taylor. Except for a bequest of $10,000 to Nannie F. Parker, his wife's sister, and $3,000 to John Nelson, the African American valet who looked after him for many years, Severn left the residue of his vast real and personal

Fig. 43. Severn Eyre on the porch at Eyre Hall.

property to his daughter and granddaughter in equal shares. With this inheritance, they would guide the destiny of Eyre Hall in the twentieth century. They both inherited from Severn healthy constitutions that enabled them to live into their eighties. Had they not lived and passed on this inheritance to their children according to the terms of his will, Severn's contingency was to turn over the entire estate to the Hospital for Consumptives of Maryland, known as the Eudowood Sanatorium, in Towson, an institution that had been established in 1894 to fight tuberculosis and other respiratory diseases that had been such a scourge in the lives and fortunes of the Eyre family for generations.[151]

NOTES

1. This sleeping arrangement is evident in the 1774 inventory made after Severn's death. Noted in the bedchamber that included Margaret's furniture and her other personal possessions were two children's beds, bolsters, and pillows. Inventory of the estate of Severn Eyre, February 27, 1774, Northampton County Wills & Inventories, No. 25, 1772–1777, 390.

2. Will of Severn Eyre, March 15, 1769, Northampton County Wills & Inventories, No. 25, 1772–1777, 136–38.

3. Northampton County Land Tax, 1782, Margaret Eyre.

4. Estate of Severn Eyre in account with Bowdoin, Eyre & Smith, 1773–81, April 11, 1781, Northampton County Wills & Inventories, No. 26, 1777–1783, 415–20, entries for 1773 and 1774.

5. Estate of Littleton Eyre in account with Bowdoin, Eyre & Smith, 1768–80, April 11, 1781, Northampton County Wills & Inventories, No. 26, 1777–1783, 405, entry for December 1769.

6. Accompanied by a retainer, Littleton, 13, and Severn, 10, probably traveled to Baltimore for the procedure. Estate of Severn Eyre in account with Bowdoin, Eyre & Smith, 1773–81, *passim*; on the inoculation, 414; Estate of Severn Eyre in account with Bowdoin, Eyre & Smith, 1782–87, September 11, 1787, Northampton County Wills etc., No. 27, 1783–1788, *passim*. In 1771 Dr. Stevenson claimed that he had only lost 17 patients out of the thousands that he had inoculated. *Pennsylvania Gazette*, 3:2, March 14, 1771.

7. Estate of Severn Eyre in account with Bowdoin, Eyre & Smith, 1773–81, *passim*; Estate of Severn Eyre in account with Bowdoin, Eyre & Smith, 1782–87, *passim*.

8. On the emergence of genteel society in colonial America, see Cary Carson, *Face Value: The Consumer Revolution and the Colonizing of America* (Charlottesville: University of Virginia Press, 2017).

9. Estate of Severn Eyre in account with Bowdoin, Eyre & Smith, 1773–81, 409, 412.

10. Quoted in Fanny Fielding [pseud.], "Southern Homesteads. Eyre Hall," *The Land We Love* 3, no. 6 (October 1867): 508.

11. Estate of Severn Eyre in account with Bowdoin, Eyre & Smith, 1773–81, 408; Estate of Severn Eyre in account with Bowdoin, Eyre & Smith, 1782–87, 497.

12. Elizabeth Montgomery, *Reminiscences of Wilmington* (Philadelphia: T. K. Collins, 1851), 293–94; Lyman P. Powell, *History of Education in Delaware* (Washington, D.C.: Government Printing Office, 1893), 45; "Memoirs of Thomas Gilpin," *Pennsylvania Magazine of History and Biography* 49, no. 4 (1925): 318–19.

13. Estate of Severn Eyre in account with Bowdoin, Eyre & Smith, 1773–81, 411, 414.

14. Estate of Severn Eyre in account with Bowdoin, Eyre & Smith, 1773–81, 411–13.

15. Estate of Severn Eyre in account with Bowdoin, Eyre & Smith, 1782–87, 495.

16. "Parker & wife & Sally Eyre vs. John Eyre & William Eyre," August 12, 1789, Northampton County Court of Chancery Records, Clerk's Office, Eastville.

17. Katherine E. Harbury, "Littleton Eyre (1761–1789)," *Dictionary of Virginia Biography* (Richmond: Library of Virginia, 1998–, published 2016), http://www.lva.virginia.gov/public/dvb/bio.asp?b=Eyre_Littleton_1761-1789, accessed April 30, 2020.

18. Alton Brooks Parker Barnes, *A Young Virginian in Old London: Severn Eyre, Student of Physic* (Olney, Va.: Lee Howard Co., 1989).

19. Severn Eyre to Littleton Eyre, October 16, 1785, Eyre Hall Family Papers, Virginia Historical Society, Richmond.

20. Severn Eyre to Littleton Eyre, October 16, 1785, December 4, 1785, and February 20, 1786, Eyre Hall Family Papers.

21. Barnes, *Young Virginian in Old London*; Severn Eyre to Littleton Eyre, August 15, 1785, and October 18, 1785, Eyre Hall Family Papers.

22. Barnes, *Young Virginian in Old London*.

23. Barnes, *Young Virginian in Old London*.

24. Severn Eyre to Littleton Eyre, February 20, 1786, Eyre Hall Family Papers. In his letter, Severn mentioned "little Kendl. or Duff," who were two young men, George Kendall and Edward Duff, who had been romantically linked to Peggy Eyre. Both had died in the previous two years. It was said that George Kendall had left land to his fiancé Peggy Eyre in his will. A few years after his death, she and her husband, George Parker, decided to name their home Kendall Grove in gratitude and honor of his memory. Ralph T. Whitelaw, *Virginia's Eastern Shore: A History of Northampton and Accomack Counties* (Richmond: Virginia Historical Society, 1951), 1:311–12.

25. Barnes, *Young Virginian in Old London*; Severn Eyre to Littleton Eyre, February 20, 1786, Eyre Hall Family Papers.

26. Barnes, *Young Virginian in Old London*; Charles Steuart to Dr. James Taylor, August 25, 1786, and Dr. James Taylor to Margaret Taylor Eyre, November 20, 1786, Eyre Hall Family Papers.

27. John Lean of Bristol to Dr. James Taylor, November 18, 1789; "Inventory of the Effects of

Mr. Severn Eyre Deceased taken 12 August 1786," Eyre Hall Family Papers.

28. Will of Littleton Eyre, May 21, 1787, which was proved in court on June 9, 1789, Northampton County Wills & In[ventories], No. 28, 1788–1792, 135–36.

29. On John Eyre's character see his obituary by George Tucker, *Daily National Intelligencer* (Washington), July 1855. On Eyre Hall in the era of John and Ann Eyre, see Fielding, "Southern Homesteads. Eyre Hall," 507–9.

30. "Parker & wife & Sally Eyre vs. John Eyre & William Eyre," August 12, 1789, Northampton County Court of Chancery Records; Estate of Severn Eyre in account with Bowdoin, Eyre & Smith, 1782–87, 498, November 6, 1786.

31. "Parker & wife & Sally Eyre vs. John Eyre & William Eyre," August 12, 1789, October 13, 1789, Northampton County Court of Chancery Records.

32. Northampton County Wills & In[ventories], No. 28, 1788–1792, 291–92, September 3, 1789.

33. Grace Duncombe Taylor (1780–1809) was the daughter of John and Sarah Barraud Taylor of Norfolk. Her older sister Ann Nancy Taylor (778–1861) married James Preston, who served as governor of Virginia from 1816 to 1819. Her older brother was Robert Barraud Taylor (1774–1834), a lawyer, politician, and later a judge. During the War of 1812 he commanded the American troops that repulsed the British invaders at the Battle of Craney Island in June 1813, which prevented the enemy from taking Norfolk and seizing its naval base. In 1831, Judge Taylor's son, William Eyre Taylor, married Margaret Alice Lyon, the daughter of Dr. John and Sarah Eyre Lyon and niece of John and Ann Taylor of Eyre Hall. In 1897, their grandson Richard B. Taylor married Grace Eyre, the daughter of Severn Eyre of Eyre Hall.

34 Northampton County Deeds, etc., No. 23, 1794–1800, 257, 291–92, 300, and 492, September 11, 1796, August 8, 1797, September 11, 1797, and July 8, 1799.

35. John Andrew Upshur, *Upshur Family in Virginia* (Richmond, Va.: The Dietz Press, 1955), 131.

36. Ann Upshur to John Upshur, April 10, 1795, Upshur Family Papers, Special Collections, Swem Library, William and Mary, Williamsburg.

37. John Eyre letter to Elizabeth Eyre, June 16, 1798 with a note at the bottom by Elizabeth Upshur Teackle dated October 1, 1829, a little more than three months after Ann's death. Papers of the Quinby Family 1759(1800–1898)1968, Box 1, Folder 1, Albert and Shirley Small Special Collections Library, University of Virginia Library, Charlottesville.

38. Paul Baker Touart, *Somerset: An Architectural History* (Annapolis: Maryland Historical Trust, 1990), 62, 77–83, 342–44.

39. Quote from letter of Ann Eyre to Mr. McHenry of Baltimore, April 20, 1819, original in Clements Library, University of Michigan, transcribed by Furlong Baldwin, 1986, Eyre Hall, Northampton County, Virginia. On Elizabeth Upshur Teackle's passion for gardening and providing cuttings for her sister's garden at Eyre Hall, see Touart, *Somerset*, 343.

40. The quote is from George Tucker's obituary for John Eyre published in *Daily National Intelligencer* (Washington), July 2, 1855.

41. Unidentified newspaper clipping, Eyre Hall.

42. Fielding, "Southern Homesteads. Eyre Hall," 505.

43. *Daily National Intelligencer* (Washington), July 2, 1855.

44. For a study of state and national politics in Virginia in this period, see Norman K. Risjord, "The Virginia Federalists," *The Journal of Southern History* 33 (1967): 486–517.

45. Northampton County Order Book, No. 34, 1801–1807, 40, August 10, 1801; Northampton County Order Book, No. 35, 1808–1816, 358, September 13, 1808; and Northampton County Order Book, No. 36, 1816–1822, 28–29, May 13, 1816.

46. Northampton County Order Book, No. 34, 1801–1807, 79, 83–84, January 11, 1802, February 8, 1802.

47. Northampton County Deeds, etc., No. 24, 1800–1805, 296–97, October 9, 1803; Whitelaw, *Virginia's Eastern Shore*, 326–27.

48. *Daily National Intelligencer* (Washington), July 2, 1855.

49. John Cropper Jr. to John Eyre, July 5, 1808, Eyre Hall.

50. *North American and Mercantile Daily Advertiser* (Baltimore), July 16, 1808, 3.

51. Risjord, "The Virginia Federalists," 505–9.

52. *Universal Gazette* (Philadelphia), April 13, 1809, 3.

53. Whitelaw, *Virginia's Eastern Shore*, 297.

54. Some documented examples include the following three. In his will of 1785 Severn Eyre gave two of his friends their choice of his "negro boys under the age of eighteen." In 1789 John Eyre sold "one Negro girl named Hannah" to Antony de Donjeux for £25. In 1797 John Eyre sold to John Nivison of Norfolk 11 enslaved individuals: 5 men, 3 women, and 3 children. Their names were Luke, Laradu, Sam, Jacob, Spencer, Edy, Rob, and Julia and her three children. Northampton County Wills, etc., No. 27, 1783–1788, 432, April 20, 1785; Northampton County Deeds, etc., No. 22, 1785–1794, 331; Deed of sale between John Eyre and John Nivison, November 4, 1797, Tazewell Family Papers, Box 2, Folder 4, Library of Virginia, Richmond.

55. "Definitive List of Slaves and Property: Inventory of property carried off by the British forces, 1827–28," 60, Records of Boundary and Claims Commissions and Arbitrations, 1716–1994, Record Group 76, National Archives, Washington, D.C.

56. For slave ownership statistics and the rising number of free Black people, see the Northampton County Personal Property Tax Lists, 1789–1860.

57. Northampton County Personal Property Tax List, 1820.

58. *Richmond Enquirer*, November 11, 1831, 2.

59. *Richmond Enquirer*, September 18, 1835, 2.

60. Edmund Ruffin, "Notes of a Hasty View of the Soil and Agriculture of Part of the County of Northampton," *Farmers' Register* 3, no. 4 (August 1835): 236.

61. Ruffin, "Notes," 239.

62. *National Intelligencer* (Washington), April 5, 1830.

63. Journal of Lyon and Evans, 1804–1808, Eyre Hall.

64. Northampton County Deeds, etc., No. 25, 1805–1815, 477–78, November 15, 1809.

65. Northampton County Deeds, etc., No. 25, 1805–1815, 478–79, November 15, 1809.

66. David R. Scott, *Abstract of Wills and Administrations, Northampton County, Virginia, 1800–1854* (Camden, Maine: Picton Press, 2008), 243; Will of Margaret Eyre, October 30, 1809, Northampton County Wills & Inven'ys [Inventories], 1808–1813, No. 33, 286–87.

67. William Eyre Lyon died in Providence, Rhode Island, on May 31, 1826. He was 23 years old. He was buried in the North Burial Ground in Providence. *Newport Mercury*, June 3, 1826; *Narragansett Historical Register* 4, no. 4 (April 1886): 288–89; Northampton County Deeds, etc., No. 28, 1824–1828, 111; Northampton County Deed Book, No. 29, 1828–1834, 250.

68. Touart, *Somerset*, 344.

69. Unidentified newspaper clipping, Eyre Hall.

70. *Journal of the Fifty-Seventh Annual Convention of the Protestant Episcopal Church in Virginia, held in St. Paul's Church, Richmond, on the 19th, 20th, 21st and 22nd of May, 1852* (Washington, D.C.: John T. Towers, 1852), 58.

71. *Sun* (Baltimore), August 29, 1853, 1.

72. Will of John Eyre, February 21, 1855, Northampton County Wills, No. 39, 1854–1897, 22–25.

73. Northampton County Order Book, No. 34, 1801–1807, 20, April 14, 1801; Northampton County Deeds, etc., 1800–1805, 296–97.

74. Between 1795 and 1810, the personal property tax lists recorded William Eyre as owning between 22 and 32 slaves over the age of 16. In 1802, he petitioned the court to release him from paying taxes on three of his slaves, Peter, Amey, and Leah, "by reason of age and infirmity." Northampton County Personal Property Tax Lists, 1795–1810; Northampton County Order Book, No. 34, 1801–1807, 79, January 11, 1802.

75. William Henry Egle, *Pennsylvania Genealogies: Chiefly Scotch-Irish and German* (Harrisburg, Pa., 1886), 390–91; *Catalogue of Officers and Students of Dickinson College, May 1823* (Carlisle, Pa.: Fleming & Geddes, 1823).

76. Alan Taylor, *Thomas Jefferson's Education* (New York: W. W. Norton & Company, 2019), 258–69.

77. Minutes of the General Faculty, vol. 1, 24, April 12, 1825–December 2, 1826, October 5, 1825, Albert and Shirley Small Special Collections Library, University of Virginia Library, Charlottesville.

78. Ironically, George Tucker later got to know William's uncle John Eyre quite well during long sojourns spent together at White Sulphur Springs spa in Fauquier County. He wrote his obituary in the leading Washington newspaper in 1855.

79. Taylor, *Thomas Jefferson's Education*, 272–74.

80. Minutes of the General Faculty, vol. 1, 24, October 5, 1825.

81. Northampton County Deeds, etc., No. 28, 1824–1828, 356.

82. *Farmers' Register* 1, no. 12 (May 1834): 731.

83. *Farmers' Register* 3, no. 4 (August 1835): 239.

84. Northampton County Personal Property Tax Lists, 1827, 1828, 1834.

85. Northampton County Deeds, etc., No. 29, 1828–1834, 325–27, September 17, 1832.

86. Northampton County Deeds, etc., No. 30, 1834–1838, 54–56.

87. Northampton County Deeds, etc., No. 30, 1834–1838, 120.

88. Northampton County Deeds, etc., 1838–1842, 109; Northampton County Deeds, 1842–1846, 23, 111.

89. Northampton County Deeds, etc., No. 33, 1846–1850, 474–76, August 23, 1850.

90. William L. Eyre to William L. Savage, September 3, 1843, Eyre Hall.

91. This boarding school, opened by Enoch Wines in 1844, attracted many students because of its rigorous studies. The Eyres may have been drawn to the place since the Reverend Shepard K. Kollock was the pastor of the Presbyterian Church in Burlington. He was the younger brother of Henry Kollock whose *Sermons on Various Subjects* had been given to Mary by William the Christmas before they were married. *American Journal of Education* 22 (September 1860): 14–15.

92. *Catalogue of the Officers and Students of the College of New Jersey, 1846–47* (Princeton: John T. Robinson, 1847), 16.

93. DeCourcy McIntosh email to author, May 27, 2020.

94. *Catalogue of the Officers and Students of the College of New Jersey, 1849–50* (Princeton: John T. Robinson, 1850), 8, 11, 17.

95. *General Catalogue of Princeton University, 1746–1906* (Princeton: Princeton University, 1908), 179.

96. University of Virginia, *Alumni Bulletin*, 3rd ser., 7, no. 5 (October 1914): 677.

97. Harvard University, *Order of Exercises for Commencement: July 21, 1852* (Cambridge: Harvard University, 1852); *Quinquennial Catalogue of the Officers and Graduates of Harvard University, 1636–1895* (Cambridge: Harvard University, 1895), 309.

98. *Trenton State Gazette*, June 30, 1853.

99. A number of her siblings became successful professionals in their respective fields: Archibald, Jr., a lawyer and district attorney in the city; Robert, a doctor; and Yates, an admiral in the United States navy.

100. Baltimore County Marriage Cards, 1851–March 1, 1885, issue bk LSN 1851–1865, 166, Maryland State Archives Reel No. 23.14.

101. *Sun* (Baltimore), January 26, 1855, 2:4; *Maryland Genealogical Society Bulletin* 34 (1993): 386.

102. Although nothing is known about how Severn Eyre took the death of his wife, there is some evidence that the Stirling family, especially Archibald Stirling, Jr., Severn's Princeton classmate, kept the memory of his deceased younger sister alive. His son, Archibald Stirling III, named one of his children after his great-aunt. Margaret Eyre Stirling was born in 1888 and in 1911 married Willard Augustine Baldwin of Baltimore. Baldwin was a distant relative of Henry duPont Baldwin who in 1928 married Margaret Eyre Taylor, the granddaughter of Severn Eyre. Henry duPont Baldwin, *Genealogy of the Baldwin Family* (Baltimore: privately printed, 1961).

103. "Eyre v. Jacob, Sheriff," in Peachy R. Grattan, *Reports of Cases Decided in the Supreme Court of Appeals of Virginia*, vol. XIV, *April 1867 to October 1, 1858* (Richmond: J. H. O'Bannon, 1889), 526–33.

104. William Alexander MacCorkle, *The White Sulphur Springs* (New York: Neale Publishing Company, 1916), 56–57.

105. Eighth U.S. Census, Population Schedule, 1860, Northampton County, Virginia, Eastville District; Eighth U.S. Census, Slave Schedule, 1860, Northampton County, Virginia, Severn Eyre.

106. Northampton County Land Tax List, 1860; Northampton County Personal Property Tax List, 1861, Severn Eyre.

107. Susie Ames, "The Federal Policy Toward the Eastern Shore of Virginia in 1861," *Virginia Magazine of History and Biography* 69, no. 4 (October 1961): 432–59.

108. Severn Eyre to Abraham Lincoln, March 3, 1864, Abraham Lincoln Papers Series 1: General Correspondence, 1833–1911, Library of Congress, Washington, D.C.

109. Kirk Mariner, *Slave and Free on Virginia's Eastern Shore* (Onancock, Va.: Miona Publications, 2014), 208–9.

110. Northampton County Personal Property Tax List, 1861, 1862, and 1863, Severn Eyre.

111. Mariner, *Slave and Free*, 209–10.

112. Northampton County Personal Property Tax List, 1861, 1862, 1863, and 1864, Severn Eyre.

113. *The Hygeia Hotel, Old Point Comfort, Va.* (New York: Leve & Alden, ca. 1886).

114. Northampton County Deeds, etc., No. 37, 1867–1871, 207.

115. "List of Colored Electors Voting in the 2nd District, Northampton County, State of Virginia, at Elections held October 22, 1867," Military Rule Election Records of the Virginia Secretary of the Commonwealth, 1867, Box 26, Folder 1, Library of Virginia, Charlottesville. Thanks to Sam Florer for bringing this reference to my attention.

116. Ninth U.S. Census, Population Schedule, 1870, Northampton County, Virginia, Eastville District.

117. Ninth U.S. Census, Population Schedule, 1870, Northampton County, Virginia, Eastville District.

118. Northampton County Personal Property Tax List, 1870, Severn Eyre.

119. Ninth U.S. Census, Agricultural Schedule, 1870, Northampton County, Virginia; Northampton County Personal Property Tax List, 1870, Severn Eyre.

120. Ninth U.S. Census, Industry Schedule, 1870, Northampton County, Virginia, Eyre, Duval & Co.

121. The dates and places of birth for the Eyre children are listed in Severn Eyre's passport application of October 17, 1889: U.S. Passport Applications 1795–1925, Roll 341, 16 October 1889–30 November 1889, National Archives and Records Administration, Washington, D.C.; on the birth of Mary Eyre at Eyre Hall, DeCourcy McIntosh email to author, May 27, 2020.

122. *The Churchman* 39 (March 22, 1879): 13.

123. Furlong Baldwin conversation with the author, October 27, 2017.

124. An online exhibit of early images by Kimball and other photographers of St. Paul's students and their activities can be found in "Formmates and Friends: The Early Cabinet Card Portraits of St. Paul's School," Ohrstrom Digital Library, St. Paul's School, http://www.ohrstromblog.com/spsarchives/archives/category/formmates_and_friends, accessed July 2020.

125. For a list of the families inscribed in the who's who of Baltimore blue bloods at the beginning of the twentieth century, see *Social Register, Baltimore, 1902* 16, no. 6 (New York: Social Register Association, November 1901).

126. *Sun* (Baltimore), January 19, 1887, 1.

127. *Sun* (Baltimore), November 6, 1888, supplement, 2.

128. *Sun* (Baltimore), December 11, 1891, supplement, 4.

129. *Sun* (Baltimore), October 26, 1895, 9; *Alexandria Gazette*, December 9, 1895.

130. *Sun* (Baltimore), May 23, 1883, 4; Robert Brugger, *The Maryland Club: A History of Food and Friendship in Baltimore, 1857–1997* (Baltimore: The Maryland Club, 1998).

131. *Sun* (Baltimore), February 8, 1895, 8.

132. *Virginian-Pilot* (Norfolk), May 8, 1889, 1.

133. *Sun* (Baltimore), May 6, 1884, 4; May 5, 1885, 2; May 4, 1886, 4; May 4, 1887, 4; *Charlotte Home and Democrat*, May 15, 1885.

134. See Charles Fayette Taylor, *A Concise Presentation of the Modern Methods of Treating a Disease* (Philadelphia: The Medical World, 1887), 367.

135. Unidentified newspaper clipping in the possession of Eyre descendant DeCourcy McIntosh, New York City; also *Sun* (Baltimore), May 2, 1893, 8.

136. Quote from a second unidentified newspaper clipping in the possession of DeCourcy McIntosh, New York City.

137. See, for example, *Sun* (Baltimore), December 14, 1887, 4.

138. *Sun* (Baltimore), December 26, 1896, 10; November 4, 1897, 10; *Richmond Dispatch*, November 18, 1897.

139. *Democratic Advocate* (Westminster, Md.), October 2, 1897.

140. *Sun* (Baltimore), April 15, 1898.

141. *Sun* (Baltimore), September 13, 1899, 7; September 14, 1899, 8; September 15, 1899, 7; September 16, 1899, 12; *Peninsula Enterprise* (Accomac, Va.), September 23, 1899.

142. *Virginian-Pilot* (Norfolk), February 25, 1900, 14; *Evening Star* (Washington), June 23, 1900; *Sun* (Baltimore), August 2, 1900, 10.

143. Whitelaw, *Virginia's Eastern Shore*, 191.

144. Northampton County Deeds, etc., No. 45, 1890–1892, 181, 199, 207; Northampton County Deeds, etc., No. 46, 1892–1893, 463; Northampton County Deeds, etc., No. 48, 1895–1897, 172; Northampton County Deeds, etc., No. 50, 1898–1899, 119; Northampton County Deeds, etc., No. 51, 1899–1900, 34.

145. *Peninsula Enterprise* (Accomac, Va.), July 30, 1904.

146. *Virginian-Pilot* (Norfolk), January 4, 1907, 5.

147. *Sun* (Baltimore), July 1914, exact date unknown, from a clipping in possession of Eyre descendant DeCourcy McIntosh, New York City.

148. *Sun* (Baltimore), September 7, 1910.

149. *Washington Times*, March 20, 1914, 14; *Sun* (Baltimore), February 8, 1895, 8.

150. Descriptions and quotes about the death of Severn Eyre are from two unidentified newspaper clippings in the possession of DeCourcy McIntosh, New York City.

151. Will of Severn Eyre, August 25, 1910, Northampton County Wills, No. 40, 1897–1920, 279.

ESCAPING ENSLAVEMENT BY WHALEBOAT, 1832

ALEXANDRA ROSENBERG

Fig. 44. The bayside of Northampton County has many creeks that in the antebellum period contained docks and wharves such as the one owned by Peter Bowdoin at Hungars Wharf.

Fig. 45. Detail of a map of New York, 1832, showing the Whitehall slip at the end of Whitehall Street next to Battery Park at the southern tip of Manhattan.

In July 1832, 17 enslaved people and one free Black man boarded a whaleboat stolen from Northampton County resident Peter S. Bowdoin and put into action their dreams of escaping enslavement.[1] The getaway was cleverly conceived and executed by individuals who used their knowledge of Virginia's waterways, the maritime economy, and the material culture of the bay to hide themselves in plain sight (Fig. 44).[2] Their escape, however, was not without precedent. Led by Isaac, who had failed in a similar attempt two years earlier, the other 17 involved in the scheme fled from several plantations in the area, crowded into Mr. Bowdoin's whaleboat, rigged the sails stolen from Eyre Hall on Cherrystone Creek, and navigated the stolen vessel out of Hungars Creek into the Chesapeake Bay. Rounding the tip of the Eastern Shore, they sailed up the Atlantic coast and reached New York City, where they docked their vessel at White Hall slip adjoining the Battery on the East River (Fig. 45).[3] Its weary members sought safety and anonymity among the transient population of mariners, stevedores, and others who worked and lived in the streets and alleys of Lower Manhattan (Fig. 46).

Once alerted to the enormity of this daring escape, but already well aware of the likely destination of its participants, Northampton leaders including John Eyre hired two different slave catchers to

apprehend those who had fled to freedom. The process dragged on for many months, in part due to the resistance of New York's African American community, the cholera epidemic that had ravaged the city, a court case, and the efforts of abolitionists to help these desperate individuals.[4]

Many of those who took the risk of sailing to freedom clearly had experience as watermen and were quite capable of navigating their small craft down the bay and up the coast. The presence of Black mariners sailing in these waters was commonplace in the colonial

Fig. 46. *South Street from Maiden Lane, New York*, ca. 1827, painting by William I. Bennett.

and antebellum periods. In the late colonial period, Peter Bowdoin's grandfather and John Eyre's father had been business partners in an extensive maritime trade. Their firm, Bowdoin, Eyre, and Smith, had entrusted a number of their bondsmen with transporting and delivering goods in the Caribbean and throughout the Chesapeake.[5] Severn Eyre had hired out his capable mariner, Stephen Booker, to the firm in order to transport cargo in a sloop with three other enslaved men around the bay and its major rivers in the 1770s. However, by the time of the whaleboat incident, attitudes about the free movement of the enslaved in Virginia had changed substantially.

Less than a year earlier, the state experienced the bloody uprising and suppression of Nat Turner's rebellion in Southampton County in August 1831. It was one of the largest and deadliest acts of resistance executed by enslaved laborers in the country.[6] The fear of further uprisings stirred white leaders to further tighten the restrictions already placed on both enslaved and free Black people. Among the petitions submitted to the Virginia legislators by Northampton County citizens in December 1831, one addressed their concern for loosely supervised Black watermen. It sought to halt the hiring out of enslaved labor to out-of-state oystermen. The residents of Northampton County who signed this petition believed that outside oystermen "devoted themselves to the work of 'universal emancipation,'" and that their presence in local waters would only provide free and enslaved Black people with exposure to abolitionist ideologies.[7]

Although the land routes taken by enslaved people to freedom are well known, the bold escape by whaleboat suggests that Virginia's waterways provided a much different and less familiar means of escape. The Chesapeake Bay—its tributaries, marshlands, and islands—has played a major role in shaping the social and economic life of Virginia's Eastern Shore since its earliest settlement. Among the occupations recorded in the 1860 United States Census for Northampton County, eight different jobs fell under the category of "Maritime Occupations." These jobs included sailor, fisherman, mariner, waterman, lighthouse keeper, sea captain, and ship's carpenter.[8] Although listed for free individuals, these occupations were also filled by enslaved people as well. For example, former governor Littleton Waller Tazewell noted in his accounts for his Old Plantation Creek estate that he "paid the negros for oysters clams & terrapins $6.10" on December 14, 1851.[9] This entry alludes to the presence of skilled Black watermen in the antebellum period who took advantage of the natural abundance of aquatic life to make their living on the water, or to supplement their income and diet.

Both free and enslaved laborers played important roles in the water-based economic system that flourished on the Eastern Shore. So common was the presence of Black watermen in the Chesapeake Bay that Frederick Douglass chose to flee enslavement on Maryland's Eastern Shore by water, just three years after the 1832 whaleboat escape. Douglass claimed that those who escaped by water "were less liable to be suspected as runaways; [they] hoped to be regarded as fishermen; whereas, if [they] . . . [had] take[n] the land route, [they] [w]ould [have] be[en] subjected to interruptions of almost every kind. Any one having a white face, and being so disposed, could [have] stop[ped][them], and subject[ed] [them] to examination."[10]

Although the 18 who sailed for freedom from Northampton County did not leave behind written records regarding the planning and execution of their escape, Frederick Douglass did. His comments reflected the perceived advantages of choosing a maritime-based route north, rather than a more established overland route. The whaleboat escapees' decision to organize their flight when they did may have been motivated by talk they overheard among local planters and merchants concerning an effort to deport many of their free kin.

The African colonization movement arose during a period when Virginia was suffering an agricultural downturn. As noted in Chapter 3, many slave owners on the Eastern Shore had manumitted some of their enslaved laborers when the cost of maintaining them in servitude proved unsustainable. Scores stayed in the county and lived on the margins, no longer enslaved, but not truly free. By the 1830s, Northampton County had a large number of free Black people, which troubled many of its white citizens. In another petition submitted to the General Assembly in December 1831, nearly 100 white citizens of Northampton County sought "to remove free people of color from their county." They argued that their status as free people of color "exposes them to distrust & suspicion" and proposed several measures to curtail their disruptive presence, foremost of which was the idea "that all free persons of colour should be promptly removed from this county," and perhaps be "sent to Liberia in Africa."[11]

Northampton County had a free Black population living near Eastville that was sizable enough to unsettle its white residents. Jack Cortwright, one of the whaleboat crewmen who was captured in New York, denied the assertion made by slave catcher Edward R. Waddey in the New York Circuit Court that he was the property of John Eyre. He claimed instead that he was a free man, not a slave, and that his "mother was a free woman, named Susan Cortwright, who lived . . . at her own house at Eastville," and that his father was also a free man named Sailor Jim, who had worked at sea.[12] Jack clearly had close ties to the free Black population in Eastville, and is evidence that free Black people who made their living at sea freely commingled with its enslaved and free Black residents.

Many white residents of Northampton County saw free Blacks, like Jack and his mother, Susan, as a threat to the social order. It is possible that his enslavement after he was caught and brought back to Northampton County was a political statement made to scare free Black people into going along with the colonization movement's goals in order to maintain their freedom elsewhere, or risk being re-enslaved. Slaveholders clearly wanted to eliminate the liminal spaces occupied by the free Blacks living in their county by proposing their complete removal and relocation to Liberia. When faced with the realization that they might be forced to move to an unfamiliar country—cut off from family and kinship ties made and maintained on the Eastern Shore—individuals like Jack might have felt very motivated to attempt such an escape.

The motives for leaving an increasingly hostile environment were strong, and the voyage to freedom by way of the bay and high seas was dramatic. Unfortunately, there is no documentation describing how those involved planned for the getaway and kept it a secret, or even noting the length of their voyage. As a result, it is impossible to know if, when, or where they stopped their boat in order to rest, replenish, and acquire food, water, and any other necessary supplies.

Similarly, there is no written record of anyone who might have helped them on their quest for freedom.[13] Their successful arrival in New York City indicates that some of those onboard the whaleboat had experience in skilled sailing, and intimately knew the waters, winds, tides, and general geography of the bay and Atlantic coast.[14]

The owner of the whaleboat, Peter S. Bowdoin, owned the "ferry franchise at Hungars Wharf," which had previously been operated by the Eyre family until the early 1770s.[15] It seems likely that those who purloined the vessel were familiar with its operation and, among the variety of craft that may have been associated with Bowdoin's waterborne businesses, knew that the whaleboat best fit their requirements for size and seaworthiness. Unfortunately, it was not described in any of the court records other than its value, which was $150. Modern scholars of later nineteenth-century New England whaling have observed a smaller vessel used for these purposes was "a double-ended, light, open boat with a length . . . between twenty-seven and thirty-one feet and a beam of slightly more than one-fifth the length. It was pulled with oars and sailed" and was designed to be operated by approximately six people.[16] But were these late nineteenth-century New England whaleboats related in any way to the one that was owned by Peter S. Bowdoin decades earlier in the Chesapeake?

Whaling in the Chesapeake has a history dating back to at least the late seventeenth century. Small-scale whaling enterprises played an important part in the lives of Eastern Shore residents heretofore little noticed. Eyre family records show a connection with whaling in the early eighteenth century. The 1719 inventory of Thomas Eyre III's estate listed four different objects related to whaling: "80 lbs whale bone @ 12d pr," "4 old Casks pr whale bone & an old Joynt," "3 Whale Lances & 2 harpoons Iron," and "One Whale boat & oares."[17] The "whale bone" might possibly refer to baleen, which was used in corsetry. However, it might also simply refer to the bones of whales, which are most often seen in museums today as intricately decorated scrimshaw; whale bones also provided an alternative to ivory-handled products, such as dining utensils. Although nowhere near the flourishing industry it became in New England, the presence of a whaleboat, lances, harpoons, and barrels of bone suggests that some Virginia Shore residents had pursued the smaller whales that swam in the bay.

So, Peter Bowdoin's possession of a whale boat in 1832 should not be surprising. What is more difficult to discern are the boat's attributes. Some light might be shed on its form based on another such whaleboat that was involved in a theft during the Revolution. In July 1779, three enslaved laborers belonging to Isaac Smith—the old business partner of Severn Eyre and John Bowdoin—stole a whaleboat that Smith described as a large vessel "calculated for 9 oars, of the whale-boat construction, her inside painted red, and has a white bottom, her frame cedar and mulberry, and her foremast step of oak and painted red." Valued at more than £100, it was "a very long boat." Smith noted that the three men who stole the boat "took off one sail, but may have more," and that it was "probable they may change the color of the paint" to mask its appearance in order to avoid detection.[18]

The size of Smith's stolen whaleboat seems to be most similar to descriptions of the ships used during the American Revolution to conduct raids on the Long Island sound. "Some were thirty-two feet long, and impelled by from eight to twenty oars, and would shoot ahead of an ordinary boat with great velocity, and leave their pursuers far behind."[19] In fact, Smith believed that those who purloined his whaleboat were intending to use it "to plunder, the boat being well calculated for that purpose. It is supposed they lurk frequently about the straits and islands up the Bay; Hunger River, and Pocomoke, are the probable places for them to rendezvous."[20] If Bowdoin owned one of these long whaleboats, then it could have accommodated the 18 individuals who stole it from his landing in 1832.

One can only speculate as to the hardships faced by the escapees while on the water; no written documents detail the conditions they faced. However, what is known is that, once the whaleboat and its passengers reached New York City, it was not long before state-appointed slave catchers began scouring the city for them. Although the escapees had successfully reached a free state, under the Fugitive Slave Act of 1793 slave catchers were legally permitted to cross state lines to recover the enslaved laborers. Two slave catchers were hired to conduct a search and capture those who remained in New York City. Ultimately, a total of 14 of the 18 who fled to freedom are known to have been apprehended by the two slave catchers. William S. Floyd captured five escapees and encountered a sixth during his time in the city.[21] Edward R. Waddey, the second slave catcher, submitted a petition to the Northampton County government in 1838, claiming that he was never reimbursed for the expenses he accumulated during his mission. In it, he listed the names of the nine escapees he had captured and those who claimed their ownership.[22] This document provides incredible insight into the lengths and expenses that enslavers were willing to go to in order to reclaim their bondsmen; but also attests to the extensive use made by friends of the fugitives in New York of the state's judicial system to mitigate the federal laws in the name of abolition and other subterfuge employed to protect escapees from recapture and re-enslavement.[23]

Fourteen of the 18 escapees were captured and brought back to Northampton County where they were publicly punished in order to discourage others from doing the like (Fig. 47). Some were probably sold to people beyond the Eastern Shore. One asylum-seeker remained for a time in a New York City jail with a $10,000 bail, where he had been placed to protect him from being captured by William S. Floyd. When returned to Northampton County, Jack Cortwright was enslaved by John Eyre after failing to have his hereditary status as a free man legally recognized in the New York Supreme Court. The fate of the remaining three escapees is unknown. They were never recorded as having returned to Northampton County, so it is possible they had cheated the odds and found their freedom.[24]

Four of the nine escapees listed in Edward Waddey's petition were tried at an oyer and terminer court by the Northampton County magistrates on November 9, 1833. None of the four men were charged with running away but with larceny for the theft of Peter Bowdoin's whaleboat. Caleb, enslaved to Polly Nottingham, pled not guilty.[25] Of the four brought before the court, Caleb was the only one who was assigned legal counsel.[26] Perhaps Polly Nottingham valued Caleb enough to pay the $5 required for him to have legal representation. It paid off as Caleb was the only escapee who was acquitted.[27]

George, enslaved to the heirs of John E. Nottingham, was accused of the same crime, and pled not guilty. George was found guilty of larceny, but the court recommended and granted benefit of clergy, which was a degree of clemency for first-time offenders or those who showed contrition for their crime.[28] Jack Cortwright, alias Cooler, also pled not guilty, and was given benefit of clergy. The punishment for both George and Jack was to "be burnt on the left hand by the jailor according to law and moreover receive two lashes on [their] bare back[s] to be well laid at the common whipping post."[29] And, as noted earlier, Jack also lost all claims of his status as a free man.

Isaac, who was enslaved to Southy Spady, found himself in troubling circumstances. He had already been granted benefit of

Escapees	Enslavers
Jack Cortwright (born free, then enslaved)	John Eyre, Eyre Hall
Severn	John Eyre, Eyre Hall
Carter	William L. Eyre, Eyreville
George	Heirs of John E. Nottingham
Tom	Unknown
Joe	Charles B. Stockley
Michael	Abel Scott
Caleb	Polly Nottingham
Charles	George F. Wilkins
Ben	George F. Wilkins
Ben	Margaret Williams Southy
Black	George T. Outten
Isaac	Southy Spady
James "Jim"	Southy Spady
Ben	James Segar
Henry	Lucy Stratton
Southey	Ann Tyson
Ann	William Thomas

Fig. 47. List of those who escaped on the whaleboat, July 1832.

clergy for his involvement in an unsuccessful water-based escape in 1830, and was therefore unable to receive it again. Fellow fugitive Caleb testified against him. Isaac pled not guilty to larceny, but was found guilty and sentenced "to be hanged by the neck until dead." He was valued at $500—the sum to be given to Southy Spady as compensation for his death.[30] Isaac was set to hang on January 10, 1834; however, his sentence was changed one day prior to his execution and he was sold south.[31] Being sold south was not a physical death sentence for Isaac, but it was a social death.[32]

The fate of the other ten individuals brought back to Northampton County is unknown. Like Isaac, some of them may have been ostracized and put up for sale by their enslavers. Another water-based escape occurred in 1849, where "17 likely young negro men, belonging to several persons living above Eastville, went off in one of the large sailing lighters" but were captured when their boat was forced to land near Chincoteague. Former governor Littleton Tazewell, who also owned plantations in Northampton County, speculated that the captured men would "be sent over to Norfolk for sale" and told his son that, "altho' they can't be kept on the Eastern Shore," he would "have no objection to owning them, if they can be got low."[33] Tazewell's explanation of the results of this later escape suggests that fugitives from slavery were considered too much of a risk to be kept on the Eastern Shore, and had to be sold elsewhere.

Overall, this account of the stolen whaleboat emphasizes the fraught position of enslaved and free Black people living on the

Virginia Eastern Shore during the early nineteenth century. In a world where one's social status as a slave was legally defined, hereditary, and for life, the 17 men and one woman who boarded Bowdoin's whaleboat gambled their chances for breaking that degraded fate on a daring scheme. They planned and executed their escape through careful coordination. The fugitives belonged to 13 different claimants whose homes and properties stretched from the bayside to the seaside, and from Old Plantation Creek in the south to Hungars Creek in the north (Fig. 48). Some of them labored for families who had many enslaved Black workers—one such being that of John Eyre, who had 29 bondsmen at Eyre Hall in 1830.[34] Others fled from widows who may have had only one or two enslaved laborers. Yet others may have been rented out by their owners to supplement their income. Regardless, all who fled successfully kept their dangerous plans close to their chests so as not to attract unwanted attention. They overcame the restrictions placed on them by their enslavement by embracing what the natural landscape had to offer them—water routes to freedom. Their actions are a testament to their resourcefulness, cunning, and resilience when faced with the suffocating tensions exacerbated by the shock of Nat Turner's Rebellion of a few months earlier. Their actions speak to their desire for freedom. Their experiences, thoughts, and feelings were not recorded; however, Frederick Douglass, who made his way to freedom in a similar way, spoke passionately of the meaning of the Chesapeake Bay to those enslaved who knew it so well:

"Our house stood within a few rods of the Chesapeake Bay, whose broad bosom was ever white with sails from every quarter of the habitable globe. Those beautiful vessels, robed in purest white, so delightful to the eyes of freemen, were to me so many shrouded ghosts, to terrify and torment me with thoughts of my wretched condition. . . . The sight of these always affected me powerfully. My thoughts would compel utterance; and there, with no audience but the Almighty, I would pour out my soul's complaint, in my rude way, with an apostrophe to the moving multitude of ships: –

'You are loosed from your moorings, and are free; I am fast in my chains, and am a slave! You move merrily before the gentle gale, and I sadly before the bloody whip! You are freedom's swift-winged angels, that fly round the world; I am confined in bands of iron! O that I were free! O, that I were on one of your gallant decks, and under your protecting wing! Alas! betwixt me and you, the turbid waters roll. Go on, go on. O that I could also go! Could I but swim! If I could fly! O,

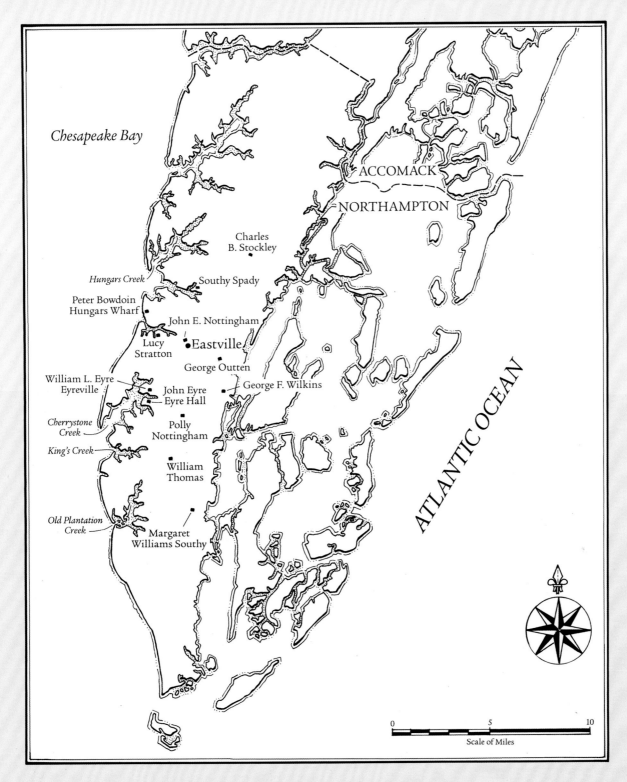

Fig. 48. Detailed map of Northampton County showing the location of some of the slave owners who had an enslaved person escape on Peter Bowdoin's whaleboat, July 1832.

why was I born a man, of whom to make a brute! The glad ship is gone; she hides in the dim distance. I am left in the hottest hell of unending slavery. O God, save me! God, deliver me! Let me be free! Is there any God? Why am I a slave? I will run away. I will not stand it. Get caught, or get clear, I'll try it. I had as well die with ague as the fever. I have only one life to lose. I had as well be killed running as die standing. Only think of it; one hundred miles straight north, and I am free! Try it? Yes! God helping me, I will. It cannot be that I shall live and die a slave. I will take to the water. This very bay shall bear me into freedom.'"[35]

NOTES

1. "The Commonwealth of Virginia v. Ben and others, Slaves, &c., Peter S. Bowdoin Dep.," October 4, 1832, Governor's Office, Letters Received, John Floyd, Record Group 3, Library of Virginia, Richmond; Affidavit of William Nottingham, Sr., Northampton County, Virginia, October 4, 1832, Governor's Office, Letters Received, John Floyd, Record Group 3, Library of Virginia, Richmond; whaleboat trial at oyer and terminer court, November 9, 1833, Northampton County Court Order Book, No. 39, 1831–1836, 249–52, 282; Kirk Mariner, *Slave and Free on Virginia's Eastern Shore* (Onancock, Va.: Miona Publications, 2014), 138.

2. Edward R. Waddey, "Petition to the General Assembly of Virginia Requesting the Sum of $1,745," petition 11683807, January 1, 1838, Race & Slavery Petitions Project, University Libraries of University of North Carolina at Greensboro from Library of Virginia Legislative Petitions Repository; Kirk Mariner, *Free Blacks of Northampton County, Virginia 1782–1864: A List from Local Sources* (Onancock, Va.: Miona Publications, 2017); see "Jack Cartwright," "Jack Cooler," and "Jack Cortwright" in Mariner, *Slave and Free*, 138–41; Northampton County Court Order Book, No. 39, 1831–1836, 249–52, 282.

3. Mariner, *Slave and Free*, 138.

4. "Case of Slavery," *New York Spectator*, November 25, 1833; Charles E. Rosenberg, *The Cholera Years: The United States in 1832, 1849, and 1866* (Chicago: University of Chicago Press, 1987), 34–45; Mariner, *Slave and Free*, 140; "The Commonwealth of Virginia v. Ben and others, Slaves, &c."

5. George Reese, "The Court of Vice-Admiralty in Virginia and Some Cases of 1770–1775," *Virginia Magazine of History and Biography* 88, no. 3 (1980): 301–37.

6. Randolph Ferguson Scully, *Religion and the Making of Nat Turner's Virginia: Baptist Community and Conflict, 1740–1840* (Charlottesville: University of Virginia Press, 2008), 1.

7. Jersey Bell et al., "on Behalf of Fifty-eight residents of Northampton County, Va.": "Petition to Cease Hiring-Out of Enslaved Workers to Out-of-State Oystermen," petition 11683120, December 6, 1831, Race & Slavery Petitions Project.

8. Eighth U.S. Census, Population Schedule (for free individuals), 1860, Northampton County, Virginia.

9. Accounts for New Quarter, Old Plantation, December 14, 1851, Tazewell Family Papers, Box 11, Folder 8, Library of Virginia, Richmond.

10. Frederick Douglass, *Narrative of the Life of Frederick Douglass: An American Slave* (New York: Barnes & Noble Classics, 2003), 78.

11. William Collins et al., "on Behalf of Ninety-Six Citizens of Northampton County, Va.": "Petition to remove local free blacks to Liberia," petition 11683101, December 6, 1831, Race & Slavery Petitions Project; "Petition to Remove Free Slaves, Northampton Co.," *Richmond Enquirer*, November 11, 1831.

12. "Case of Slavery," *New York Spectator*, November 25, 1833; Mariner, *Slave and Free*, 140–141.

13. "The Commonwealth of Virginia v. Ben and others, Slaves, &c."; Affidavit of William Nottingham, Sr.; Northampton County Court Order Book, No. 39, 1831–1836, 249–52, 282; Mariner, *Slave and Free*, 138.

14. Philip D. Curtin, Grace S. Brush, and George W. Fisher, *Discovering the Chesapeake: The History of an Ecosystem* (Baltimore: The Johns Hopkins University Press, 2001), 16–17. During the summer months, the Chesapeake Bay region experiences winds coming up from the south. These southerly winds will push any vessel with sails up the Atlantic seaboard with relative ease, provided there are no dangerous storms during this typically rainy, hot and humid hurricane season.

15. Mariner, *Slave and Free*, 138.

16. Willits D. Ansel, Walter Ansel, and Evelyn Ansel, *The Whaleboat: A Study of Design, Construction, and Use from 1850 to 2014*, 3rd ed. (Mystic, Conn.: Mystic Seaport, Inc., 2014), 1, 13.

17. Inventory of the estate of Thomas Eyre, October 28, 1719, Northampton County Wills, etc., No. 15, 1717–1725, 73–76.

18. *The Maryland Journal, and the Baltimore Advertiser*, July 27, 1779.

19. Ansel, Ansel, and Ansel, *The Whaleboat*, 14, referencing David Steel, *Elements and Practices of Naval Architecture* (London: C. Whittingham, 1805), pl. 31.

20. *The Maryland Journal, and the Baltimore Advertiser*, July 27, 1779.

21. Mariner, *Slave and Free*, 138–41; Waddey, "Petition to the General Assembly."

22. Waddey, "Petition to the General Assembly." Waddey claims to have brought back Ann, enslaved to William Thomas; Ben, enslaved to John Segar; Ben, enslaved to George Wilkins; Caleb, enslaved to Polly Nottingham; George, enslaved to the estate of John E. Nottingham; Henry, enslaved to Lucy Walton; Isaac and Jim, both enslaved to Southy Spady; and Jack Cooler, enslaved to John Eyre.

23. Mariner, *Slave and Free*, 140; Waddey, "Petition to the General Assembly." Waddey made several trips to New York City while searching for the rest of the fugitives from slavery. At one point, he was even thrown in jail for his efforts.

24. Mariner, *Slave and Free*, 138–41; Waddey, "Petition to the General Assembly"; "Case of Slavery," *New York Spectator*, November 25, 1833.

25. Northampton County Court Order Book, No. 39, 1831–1836, 249.

26. In 1792 slaves were given the right to court-appointed legal counsel, with a fee of $5 to be paid by the master. A. L. Higginbotham, Jr. and Anne F. Jacobs, "The Law Only as an Enemy: The Legitimization of Racial Powerlessness through the Colonial and Antebellum Criminal Laws of Virginia," *North Carolina Law Review* 70, no. 4 (1992): 1011–12.

27. Northampton County Court Order Book, No. 39, 1831–1836, 249.

28. "Benefit of clergy originated in medieval England as a means of sparing those who had mastered the ability to read. . . . In a 1732 act the Virginia legislature extended benefit of clergy to women, blacks, and Indians . . . . Benefit of clergy was abolished for free persons in 1796 but continued to apply to slaves for certain offenses until 1848." Higginbotham and Jacobs, "The Law Only as an Enemy," 1009–11.

29. Northampton County Court Order Book, No. 39, 1831–1836, 250, 282.

30. Northampton County Court Order Book, No. 39, 1831–1836, 250–52.

31. Mariner, *Slave and Free*, 141.

32. Orlando Patterson, *Slavery and Social Death: A Comparative Study* (Cambridge, Mass.: Harvard University Press, 2018), 5. Patterson states that "[t]he condition of slavery did not absolve or erase the prospect of death. Slavery was not a pardon; it was, peculiarly, a conditional commutation. The execution was suspended only as long as the slave acquiesced in his powerlessness. The master was essentially a ransomer. What he bought or acquired was the slave's life, and restraints on the master's capacity wantonly to destroy his slave did not undermine his claim on that life. Because the slave had no socially recognized existence outside his master, he became a social nonperson." By selling Isaac south, away from any family, friends or other kinship and social networks that he may have established for himself throughout his life, Southy Spady used his power to not give Isaac a physical death, but a social one, which was psychologically and emotionally damaging.

33. Littleton Tazewell to John Tazewell, October 5, 1849, Tazewell Family Papers, Box 9, Folder 1.

34. "John Eyre, Hungars Parish," Fifth U.S. Census, Population Schedule 1830, Northampton County, Virginia.

35. Frederick Douglass, *Narrative of the Life*, 63–64.

HEALTH RETREATS AND PLEASURE GROUNDS

ROBERT WATKINS

In June 1762, Severn Eyre embarked on a journey from Williamsburg to the thermal springs in the sparsely settled western mountains of Virginia. After 244 miles and two weeks of travel, he arrived at his destination, only to be ill for nearly the entire two weeks of his stay. But neither the arduousness of the journey nor his miserable experience at the health retreat diminished his faith in the healing virtues of mineral springs.[1] In fact, Severn continued to travel to find more salubrious climes to restore his health in the years to come. His trip to the springs was but the first documented example of the importance that the Eyres placed on health-related travel over the next century and a half. Poor health and early death plagued the family over many generations, threatening and occasionally disrupting the orderly transfer of wealth and status from one generation to the next. However, their wealth was also something

they used in search of health. Many of the family's health retreats were in earnest pursuit of cures, but the liberty to travel so extensively was limited only to wealthy and well-connected families. The Eyres' visits to fashionable resorts reveal the interrelationship of wellbeing and sociability. They frequented springs and resorts to take the waters but also to reinforce their status and to enjoy the company of the elite with whom they mixed in the baths and ballrooms.

Thomas Eyre I died at a relatively young age with three children under the age of ten, but his widow's astute marriages ensured the future prosperity of their descendants. More than half a century later, Thomas's great-great grandson, Severn Eyre, was the first Eyre to visit the springs in western Virginia. At the age of only 27, he traveled to the Hot Springs, a newly established thermal

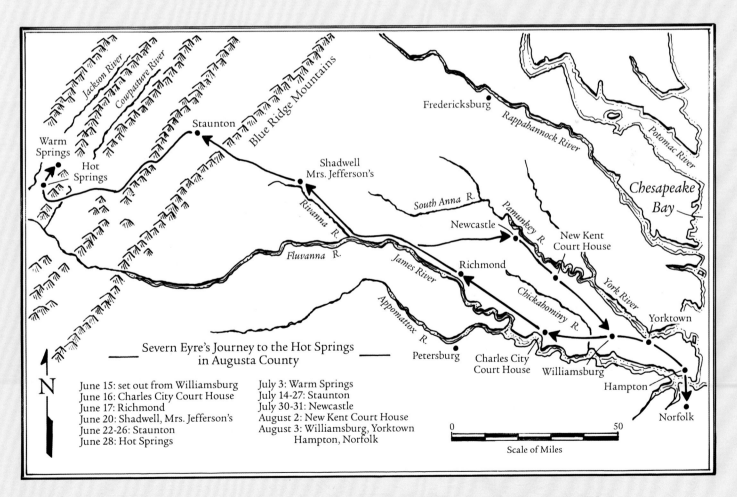

Fig. 49. Map of the route taken by Severn Eyre from Williamsburg to the Hot Springs, and his return to Norfolk, June–August 1762.

Fig. 50. View of Fauquier White Sulphur Springs, 1857, from John J. Moorman, *The Virginia Springs*.

bath located in what was then Augusta County. Though the Hot Springs would later develop into an eminent resort community, the springs were only a remote and primitive outpost in 1762.

An unhealthy constitution likely compelled Severn to make the arduous trek from the Tidewater to the mountains in search of a cure. He recorded his journey, noting the stops and the hosts as he made his way westward (Fig. 49). He took a southern route up the lower peninsula through Charles City County before stopping in Richmond and at Staunton in the Shenandoah Valley. On his return, he took a more northerly route south of the Rappahannock River to New Kent County. In total, he logged 594 miles over his nearly two-month journey that ended in Norfolk, his wife's hometown.[2]

While Severn's journey to the springs was seemingly necessitated by poor health, he made the most of the great distance and visited many people on his journey across Virginia. He noted in his itinerary his accommodations in private dwellings and taverns along the way, including that of Thomas Jefferson's widowed mother Jane at Shadwell on the Rivanna River—in the shadow of the mountain where her son would build Monticello. Severn maintained an active social life along his health pilgrimage, akin to the deliberately social health treatments that would later characterize Virginia's resort springs in the nineteenth century.

Situated in the eastern Appalachians and Blue Ridge Mountains, the Virginia springs first attracted health-seeking visitors in the mid-eighteenth century. Nearly two thousand men and women traveled to Berkeley Springs, Warm Springs, and Hot Springs each year in the middle of the century.[3] Severn arrived at the springs four years before the first hotel was constructed. His accommodations at the

Hot Springs likely resembled those at Berkeley Springs in 1761, which consisted of "nothing but about 40 miserable Hutts and the Baths are done round with Boughs of Trees."[4]

Given his long journey across the Virginia mountains to the Hot Springs, Severn's two weeks there appear to have provided him with little relief. In addition to bathing at the Hot Springs, Severn filled his days of treatment with trips to the nearby Warm Springs and Jackson's River. The unique mineral compositions and temperatures of each spring offered different remedies for his symptoms. He complained of being "sick" or even "very sick" on six of his days there and of it raining on five days.[5] His illness may have resulted from both travel fatigue and his acclimations to the mineral spring water. Some visitors reacted poorly to the spring water and became ill after bathing; after a visit to the Warm Springs in 1813, Matilda Palmer wrote that "I was not improved by my excursion, I have been sick almost constantly since I came home and my cough is worse than it ever has been."[6] Either his illness or his treatment suppressed his appetite. In a July 8 entry, Severn lamented that "since the fourth instant nothing but bread to eat with some butter."[7] After 14 days of mixed health, his sojourn to the springs concluded, but his chronic illness continued to plague him on his journey home. In Staunton on July 18, he recorded that he "took a Vomit in the Morning – sick of a Fever in the Evening."[8]

Severn suffered from poor pulmonary health his entire life and died in 1773, at the age of 37. His two eldest sons, Littleton and Severn, died in their twenties. Severn had traveled to London in 1785 to study medicine, but his health failed him and he died of consumption the following year in Bristol, where he had traveled in search of a cure.[9]

Fig. 51. View of White Sulphur Springs, West Virginia, later known as the Greenbrier, 1857, from John J. Moorman, *The Virginia Springs*.

Fig. 52. Plan of White Sulphur Springs, West Virginia, 1859, from John J. Moorman, *The Virginia Springs*. Severn Eyre's cottage on South Carolina Row is No. 18 encircled on this map.

The third son, John Eyre, the unexpected inheritor of Eyre Hall, had a much more robust constitution, living to the age of 87. Still, despite his good health, John was drawn to curative resorts. In 1837 he became one of the board members of the Fauquier White Sulphur Springs Company near Warrenton along with other distinguished leaders from across the state including George Tucker, professor at the University of Virginia.[10] John invested in the company and lent his name to advertisements in newspapers attesting to the water's curative powers.[11] His involvement with the Fauquier White Sulphur Springs represented the start of a new and markedly different engagement with health spas from his family's earlier curative pursuits.

The luxurious resort bore little resemblance to the mineral springs John's father had visited 75 years earlier (Fig. 50). While the elder Severn Eyre experienced difficult travel and accommodations at the springs in 1762, numerous fashionable hotels had opened throughout the Virginia mountains in subsequent decades, establishing some of the region's most exclusive resort areas. John traveled to the spa to relax, take the waters, and engage in conversation with prominent Virginians, many like himself from old families, who gathered there during the season. Among them were members of the Tazewell family, who owned plantations on the Eastern Shore, and who are known to have visited the Fauquier Springs numerous times in the 1830s and 1840s.[12] George Tucker, who had taught at the University of Virginia, later recalled that he "had

seen him [John Eyre] at the crowded watering place admired by all for the blended dignity and amenity of his manners."[13] Besides good company, John found the waters beneficial to his health, writing to his nephew in 1843 that he felt "much improved by his trip there."[14]

Improved westward transportation advanced the development of mineral springs resorts in the Virginia mountains. Beginning in the 1810s and '20s, the springs resorts attracted wealthy summer travelers not only from Virginia but from across the South. Visitors continued to trek to the springs seeking cures for ailments, as recommended by physicians or by word-of-mouth. Like the Warm

1830, either John, a new widower, or his nephew, William L. Eyre of Eyreville, visited Saratoga Springs, New York's most prominent spa resort, which also was the mecca for horse racing in the North.[17] William had a keen interest in raising thoroughbreds and in horse racing so may well have made a pilgrimage to Saratoga that year.

A quarter century later, John Eyre's grandnephew and inheritor of Eyre Hall, Severn Eyre, made a substantial investment in a fashionable springs resort. In 1855, he purchased $10,000 worth of stock in the White Sulphur Springs Company at Greenbrier at a time when it was improving its grounds by building a large brick building as the centerpiece of the spa, which had one of the largest dining rooms anywhere in the country (Fig. 51). Even given the new hotel building's vast capacity, Severn's investments guaranteed his family ownership of an elegant private cottage on the resort grounds (Fig. 52).[18] He became owner of a one-story frame dwelling nestled into the hillside, with a deep front porch supported by a series of Doric columns that was designated "Cottage 18" and later known as "Cottage C" in South Carolina Row (Fig. 53). The well-appointed Greek Revival cottage publicly identified the Eyres as preeminent guests at Virginia's largest and most distinguished resort and ensured the family could visit whenever they wished. After the Civil War, other Virginia springs resorts lost visitors as new resorts developed in the Southeast, but White Sulphur Springs (later renamed the Greenbrier) emerged as a leading spa destination.

Severn and his family visited the resort together in the 1870s and '80s, and he continued to visit the Greenbrier after the deaths of his son William Littleton Eyre in 1893 and his wife Margaret in 1899. Washington and Baltimore newspapers announced Severn's arrival at the resort on several occasions during the summer of 1900.[19] Whereas it took his namesake Severn Eyre two weeks on horseback to reach the Hot Springs in 1762, the later Severn took the train multiple times a season to the mountain resort in the late nineteenth century.

The Eyres also went to other resorts. Severn and his wife, Margaret, visited Old Point Comfort in 1865 for their honeymoon. The couple visited again in 1884 and stayed for more than two months at the fashionable Hygeia Hotel, along with several other Baltimoreans, to "seek the refuge of a seaside sanitarium." The hotel attracted visitors not only for the adjacent beaches and sea air but for its promise of a lively and well-regarded social scene (Fig. 54). From

and Hot Springs Severn Eyre had visited in 1762, each spring had its own individual mineral composition and therefore offered differentiated treatments. Beyond the spring water, the resorts provided a health refuge by virtue of their fresh air, cooler mountain climates, and relief from the heat and sickness of muggy and miasmatic summers.

The resorts boasted voguish architecture and carefully landscaped grounds modeled on British resorts, and, in addition to health treatments, they also offered antebellum visitors an arena for socializing and entertainment. The resort at Fauquier White Sulphur Springs flourished during the heyday of mineral springs tourism in Virginia and competed against numerous established resorts. For southern visitors and investors, each resort had a distinct reputation: Fauquier White Sulphur Springs was exceptionally fashionable and social, while the Hot Springs continued to attract primarily health-seeking guests.[15]

Over the course of a season, members of the southern gentry would visit the numerous Virginia springs resorts in a circuit. The associated costs of travel, accommodations, and leisure time prohibited all but the wealthiest and most prominent members of southern plantation society from completing the itinerary. The financial barriers to the Virginia springs generated an assumption of camaraderie among the elite guests. Spa travelers demonstrated their refinement through public socializing, including nightly dancing and paying and receiving visits in private cottages. John Eyre invested in one of Virginia's most fashionable resorts, "better calculated to promote the comfort and please the taste of visitors, than are to be found at any other watering-place in the State," thus confirming the Eyre family's place as leaders among southern gentry.[16]

The Eyre family continued to participate in spa travel and its associated genteel rituals throughout the nineteenth century. In

Fig. 54. The Hygeia Hotel in front of Fort Monroe, Old Point Comfort, Virginia, 1862, painting by Edward Sachse.

the beginning of that year the hotel could boast one of the largest dining rooms in the country, as well as a new ballroom—a fact noted by the Baltimore *Sun* in March 1884, which also remarked on the recent arrival of such notables as former president Ulysses S. Grant and his family, who were there for a brief holiday.[20]

Severn and Margaret's son, William, traveled even more extensively for his health. Like several of his forbearers, William suffered from a lifelong illness and died at the age of 22. His obituary bemoaned his illnesses at length and described his travels before his death.[21] In 1890–91, William visited resorts in the south of France with his parents and two sisters in an effort to improve his health. Shortly before he died, he traveled to Thomasville, Georgia, a resort town extolled for the effects of its fresh pine air on pulmonary ailments.[22]

In the era before modern medicine, the promise of the curative properties associated with dry salubrious breezes and the healing benefits of mineral springs lured those who could afford to travel. Members of the Eyre family who were chronically ill—such as Severn Eyre in the late colonial period and his great-great-grandson William L. Eyre in the 1890s—sought to alleviate their suffering by traveling to distant places. Those blessed with good constitutions—such as John Eyre in the antebellum period and his grandnephew Severn Eyre in the second half of the nineteenth century—traveled extensively within Virginia, along the Eastern Seaboard, and abroad on journeys to improve their wellbeing and to enjoy the restorative pleasure of leisurely pastimes among genteel society in pleasant surroundings.

NOTES

1. Severn Eyre Miscellany Book 1762–1768, June 28–July 13, 1762, Eyre Hall, Northampton County, Virginia.
2. Severn Eyre Miscellany Book 1762–1768, August 3, 1762.
3. Carl Bridenbaugh, "Baths and Watering Places of Colonial Virginia," *William and Mary Quarterly*, 3rd ser., 3, no. 2 (April 1946): 163.
4. Robert Boyd to Henry Bouquet, October 28, 1762, in *The Papers of Henry Bouquet*, ed. Louis M. Waddell (Harrisburg: Pennsylvania Historical and Museum Commission, 1994), 6:125–26.
5. Severn Eyre Miscellany Book 1762–1768, July 8–12, 1762.
6. Matilda Palmer to Septimia Randolph, October 2, 1833, Randolph-Meikleham Family Papers, 1792–1882, Accession #4726-a, Albert and Shirley Small Special Collections Library, University of Virginia Library, Charlottesville.
7. Severn Eyre Miscellany Book 1762–1768, July 8, 1762.
8. Severn Eyre Miscellany Book 1762–1768, July 18, 1762.

9. Severn Eyre to Littleton Eyre, April 1786, quoted in Alton Brooks Parker Barnes, *A Young Virginian in Old London: Severn Eyre, Student of Physic* (Olney, Va.: Lee Howard Co., 1989).
10. *Globe* (Washington), September 23, 1837; *Daily National Intelligencer* (Washington), August 1, 1838.
11. "Fauquier White Sulphur Springs," *Globe* (Washington), September 23, 1837.
12. Among the Tazewell Family Papers are numerous letters mailed to John Tazewell at Fauquier White Sulphur Springs in the 1830s and '40s. See, for example, Hugh Blair Grigsby to John N. Tazewell, August 8, 1831 and August 15, 1831, Tazewell Family Papers, Box 6, Folder 12, Library of Virginia, Richmond, and W. R. Taylor to John N. Tazewell, September 4, 1838, Box 7, Folder 13.
13. *Daily National Intelligencer* (Washington), July 2, 1855.
14. William L. Eyre to William L. Savage, September 3, 1843, Eyre Hall.
15. Charlene M. Boyer Lewis, *Ladies and Gentlemen on Display: Planter Society at the Virginia Springs 1790–1860* (Charlottesville: University Press of Virginia, 2001), 50.

16. William Burke, *The Mineral Springs of Western Virginia* (New York: Wiley and Putnam, 1846), 380.
17. Letter from John Upshur to William Upshur, August 24, 1830, Upshur Family Papers, Special Collections, Swem Library, College of William and Mary, Williamsburg.
18. William Alexander MacCorkle, *The White Sulphur Springs* (New York: Neale Publishing Company, 1916), 56–57. For images of the cottages in South Carolina Row, see 130, 136.
19. *Evening Star* (Washington), June 23, 1900; *Sun* (Baltimore), August 2, 1900; *Sun* (Baltimore), August 18, 1900.
20. "Old Point Comfort Virginia's Famous Watering Place in Winter," *Sun* (Baltimore), March 7, 1884, 1. On the charms of the Hygeia see Harrison Phoebus, *Hygeia Hotel, Old Point Comfort, Virginia* (New York: Leve & Alder Printing Co., n.d.).
21. *Sun* (Baltimore), May 2, 1893, 8.
22. The town's webpage gives an overview of its history as a popular resort area. "Our History," City of Thomasville, https://thomasville.org/our-history, accessed May 15, 2020.

HOOFPRINTS

On January 1, 1927, Margaret Eyre Taylor dressed in her finest riding clothes and had her photograph taken mounted on one of Eyre Hall's stable of horses before she rode around the estate that she had inherited on the death of her grandfather Severn Eyre in 1914 (Fig. 55). As a young girl who came down from Baltimore to visit her grandfather in the summers when he was in residence, she may have developed a love of horses that seems to have descended in the Eyre family over many generations. Old Severn had been a judge at races in Norfolk's Campostella racetrack in earlier years and was often called upon to judge these animals at county fairs in Baltimore and agricultural gatherings on the Eastern Shore such as the Keller Fair.[1] His father before him, William L. Eyre, was so enamored with breeding and racing thoroughbreds that his excesses in this sport of southern gentlemen landed him in a debtors' prison in Eastville before he was bailed out by his great-uncle John Eyre. John, too, was a keen horseman and breeder, but he did not let his enthusiasm get the better of his judgment as it did his spendthrift nephew's.

Horses were part of Margaret's heritage. When she walked through her grandfather's house in those early years of the twentieth century, she saw evidence of that heritage on full display. In the paneled front passage hung a series of 1753 British racing prints in their original frames (Fig. 56). Upstairs there were additional nineteenth-century horse prints testifying to the family's long interest in the sport of horse racing. She may have leafed through William L. Eyre's studbook that recounted the breeding of some of the finest racehorses in the region. Or, her grandfather may have regaled her with the fanciful story of how one of the family horses, Morningstar, won the large silver bowl that had been in the family for two centuries and lapped champagne from it after winning the race (see Cat. 64).

Venturing outside and down the steps of the south porch, Margaret may have glimpsed a solid shaped stone that served as a mounting block for those who arrived at Eyre Hall on a horse or provided a convenient step for those climbing into a carriage or phaeton. The mounting block sits in quiet testament to the immeasurable horse traffic on the estate. It has not served its purpose in many decades—not since Margaret Eyre Taylor wandered around the grounds during those summer months in the first decades of the twentieth century. In 1940, after she had made Eyre Hall her home, the stable burned, as did the great barn nearby—an event remembered by her son Furlong Baldwin as an eight-year-old boy. Horses still had a presence at Eyre Hall in those Great Depression years as they served more mundane purposes: along with the mules that were kept on the farm, they were used for plowing the fields and for pulling carts and wagons. Following the war, tractors began to replace animals, lessening the need for work horses and mules. With that, the symbiotic relationship between the Eyre family and horses that had been so integral to their lives came to an end.

That relationship had begun three centuries earlier, when the first Eyre settled on the Eastern Shore. In the 1650s surgeon Thomas Eyre I may have depended on a horse to make his rounds among his patients by following narrow horse paths that preceded the establishment of permanent roads. The first British horses to reach North America—six mares and one stallion—did so at Jamestown in 1609. The Jamestown settler's plans to use them as work horses, riding horses, and eventually breeding horses came to naught in the 'Starving Time' of that winter, during which these seven horses instead became food. When Sir Thomas Dale arrived to take charge

Fig. 55. Margaret Eyre Taylor, January 1, 1927.

of the fledgling colony in 1611, he brought 17 British horses, and the Virginia Company encouraged the importation and breeding of horses to aid in getting around and working on the nascent tobacco plantations.[2] While the initial accumulation of horses in Virginia was gradual, "by 1649, approximately two hundred horses lived in Virginia, and by the end of the century, enough horses populated the colony to cause the authorities to no longer encourage their importation."[3] Horses made their Eastern Shore debut when Argall Yeardley imported a horse purchased from George Ludlow of York County in 1642, and a small shipment of horses arrived from New England in 1645.[4] Documents from the second half of the century increasingly refer to "horse paths" and the "horse bridges," which would have been instrumental for navigating the web of creeks cutting into the Eastern Shore's topography.[5]

With this network of paths expanding and an increase in public infrastructure—the Virginia Assembly had ordered the first public roads on the Eastern Shore in 1657—riding horses was becoming more ingrained in Eastern Shore life.[6] Furthering the opportunity for horses to reach the peninsula, the General Assembly authorized the first franchise for a ferry across the Chesapeake Bay in 1705. In that year, the legislature listed a ferry route "from the Port of Northampton to the port of York" and another "from the Port of Northampton to the port of Hampton," listing the fare for both as fifteen shillings for a man and "for a man and horse thirty shillings."[7] In the 1740s, Littleton Eyre entered into the ferrying business with routes "from York, Hampton, and Norfolk towns," to his land on Hungars Creek and "from thence to either of the aforesaid places." Because of the importance of horses in transporting people and

goods from the Eastern Shore to these towns, the same piece of legislation also authorized "the courts of the several counties wherein such ferries shall be kept" to "appoint proper boats to be kept at the said ferries, for the convenient transportation of coaches, wagons, and other wheeled carriages."[8]

While the early colonists brought with them this need for work animals, they also brought the English horseman's mindset and fostered what came to be known as a distinctly Virginian love of horses. Historians have long noted the growing appreciation of horsemanship among the rising gentry class of tobacco planters and merchants, and the development of breeding and racing horses as a popular pastime. They have explored how horses were a natural component in fashioning the Virginia gentleman's identity. "Competition was a major factor shaping the character of face-to-face relationships among the colony's gentlemen," and "[i]n large part, the goal of the competition within the gentry group was to improve social position by increasing wealth." In addition, the horse itself was a visible, living asset. "Possession of one of these animals had become a social necessity," and "[o]wning even a slow-footed saddle horse made the common planter more of a man in his own eyes as well as in those of his neighbors." Riding horseback physically—and symbolically—elevated any rider above those traveling afoot.[9]

Naturally, men pitted their animals against one another in races to prove their skills in improving the breed as well as their own prowess in the saddle. The age-old English practice of pitting two or more running animals together in a test of speed at racecourses in Newmarket and Ascot, and the eventual founding of the Jockey

Club, proclaimed racing's popularity among the gentry. Between the 1680s and 1720s, the first stallions from North Africa and the Middle East—coveted for their build, endurance, and temperament—arrived in England. Their arrival spurred a breeding frenzy, with aristocratic horsemen scrambling to have one of these three stallions cover their native English mares. This phenomenon led to a "new kind of English racehorse," and these horses "grew taller and stronger, ran faster, and became even better looking with a dish face, arched neck, and high-set flourish of a tail."[10] These highly esteemed horses became known and formally recognized as thoroughbreds.

Discerning horsemen in Virginia followed the exploits of these new breeds with great enthusiasm, and the Eyre Hall prints celebrated their exploits. One of the first men to import these Arabian-blooded horses into Virginia was Samuel Gist of Gould Hill plantation in Hanover County who set the trends of importing and breeding thoroughbreds in the colony around mid-century.[11] Gist later returned to his native England and set up in London as a tobacco importer whose customers included both Littleton and Severn Eyre. Perhaps letters between these merchants also touched on matters of the turf.

Colonists had been racing their own "Virginia horses" long before the new breed began to dominate, especially in shorter, quarter-mile straightaway races called quarter races. Usually only two horses and their riders raced in these sprints, and they often ran multiple heats.[12] These shorter straight paths suited the then-forested terrain of mainland Virginia, though oval racetracks were just

beginning to come into fashion in England and would later become common in the racecourses that became popular in America. In these early days, quarter horse racetracks were rather ephemeral, for all that the racers and spectators required was the open space—typically near a church or courthouse.[13] Saturday afternoons had become the favorite time for racing at well-known tracks in Williamsburg, Surry, and Henrico as well as "on nameless country roads or convenient pastures."[14] The Eastern Shore was no exception. Northampton County had a reputable quarter racing track called Smith's Field laid near Hungars Parish Church not far from Littleton Eyre's residence before he moved to Eyre Hall in the late 1750s. Races were customarily held at Smith's Field during the fall.[15] The Eyres would not have had to leave Eyre Hall to take in a race, for there was a quarter racetrack on the property's flat fields, as Furlong Baldwin remembers from family lore.

Competitive races were always a rich man's game. It took money to breed and raise the best thoroughbred horses and to house, feed, and take care of these prized possessions. For some like William L. Eyre, the desire to be an important player pushed them to financial disaster. Like all gentry families, the Eyres had many enslaved African American men and boys serving as stable hands, groomsmen, and coachmen, and these people would have come to play increasingly prominent roles in caring for horses beginning in the 1820s (Fig. 57). This was the era of the studbook, American jockey clubs, and widespread American thoroughbred breeding, fostering a need for more specialized and focused care for these financially expensive

Fig. 58. Cover and pages from William L. Eyre's Stud Book,
Eyreville, 1835–1864. The cover is cut from a burlap flour sack.

creatures. Not only did enslaved and free young Black men continue to care for family horses like those of the Eyres, but they also became esteemed trainers. Though it was not uncommon for Virginia planters to ride their own horses in seventeenth- and eighteenth-century races, by the antebellum years jockeys were overwhelmingly enslaved or free Black men and boys. Unfortunately, the surviving records from Eyre Hall and Eyreville do not indicate whether, and if so which, enslaved persons tended or perhaps even raced horses there, but this was almost undoubtedly the case.[16]

No matter when the Eyres or their enslaved horse handlers started racing horses themselves, the material culture of Eyre Hall is bound up in horses—they not only served as necessary draft animals that labored in the fields and transported goods to awaiting Eyre family ships at Hungars Wharf, they also pulled the carriages in which the Eyres traveled to services at Hungars Church, and they became prized possessions to test against their neighbors and all comers at Smith's Field or on impromptu courses.

The first mention of any studhorse at Eyre Hall lies in John Eyre's 1798 personal property tax record, which lists one studhorse. John Eyre's stallion almost certainly stood stud at Eyre Hall, and maybe brought in a bit of extra income from covering fees, though whether or not any fellow horse owners brought their mares to breed remains a mystery. According to his tax records, John Eyre kept one studhorse at Eyre Hall until 1807, excepting two years, and over time he gradually lowered the rate of covering, perhaps indicating diminishing success in breeding his studhorse. General breeding,

though, occurred during this period at Eyre Hall; indeed, one visitor to Eyreville wrote to her mother in 1852, "[T]here is a beautiful little colt at Eyre Hall . . . named Leila."[17]

It is John Eyre's nephew, William L. Eyre of Eyreville, who stands out as the greatest horse enthusiast in Eyre family history. Definitely striving to be an improving gentleman farmer in his adult life, William kept horses at Eyreville, where he enslaved 30 people, primarily for agricultural work, and some of these enslaved men almost certainly tended the horses. William L. Eyre had grown up in a culture and family saturated in both utilitarian and recreational horses. He had almost certainly grown up attending races into his adult life, perhaps at the Richmond, Petersburg, Norfolk, Washington City, or Baltimore Jockey Clubs. Though it is feasible that he did, there is no record of Eyre holding a jockey club membership in his life, but he probably at least kept up with the race results and recaps that jockey clubs published in newspapers everywhere.

One historian has observed that men like William L. Eyre ran modest breeding operations. She noted that such planters owned "a few Virginia mares and an imported English stallion or two. Less prosperous breeders enjoyed the pastime too, but their broodmares had to work on the farm as well as produce young horses."[18] William's efforts fit this description. In 1826 he purchased a gray mare named Betsey Springer from Thomas D. Johnson of Baltimore. Though he could not definitively prove her thoroughbred pedigree, William himself was convinced of it and declared her ten years later to be "the most celebrated mare ever on the E. Shore of Va." who was

Fig. 59. William R. Johnson, "the Napoleon of the Turf."

"ever put to racing in harness or under saddle."[19] Decades later, in 1890, the Eastern Shore's *Peninsula Enterprise* broadcast that another "Betsy Springer" would be competing in a Fourth of July trotting race at Belle Haven racetrack, perhaps confirming Eyre's boasts that Betsey Springer had gained Eastern Shore fame.[20] The county's personal property tax lists in the later 1820s and 1830s document Eyre as being in possession of a small handful of studhorses.[21]

In 1835, the same year that Edmund Ruffin visited Eyreville, William began to keep a studbook to record the breeding of his blooded stock. Between the lines of this studbook, we see William trying to assert himself as a gentleman farmer by accumulating a handful of "blooded" horses among his estate and by associating with other horsemen of the day (Fig. 58). As his correspondence with the *Farmers' Register* indicates, Eyre was eager to share his experience with experts in the field. In 1837, he proudly wrote to the editor of the *American Turf Register and Sporting Magazine,* "I have lately gone into the rearing of such stock."[22]

William meticulously recorded in the studbook his connections with influential people in the antebellum breeding and racing world. Many of the horse owners with whom he did equine business were local to the Eastern Shore, such as Thomas Henry Bayley of Mount Custis in Accomack County. However, he did become involved with some more renowned figures in the racing world, most notably William Ransom Johnson, known by his sobriquet "the Napoleon of the turf" (Fig. 59). At one time, Johnson had owned Sir Archy, one of the most celebrated racehorses of the early 1810s, many of whose progeny dominated the field for decades to come. From his Oakland plantation in Chesterfield County, Virginia, Johnson arranged races from New York to North Carolina and was keen to improve the

pedigree, setting out his stallions to breed with mares from good blood lines. Eyre got caught up in this passion and boasted to the editor of *American Turf* that among the best that had been bred at Eyreville were Cherryton in 1836 and Henrietta Temple in 1837. Siring these two horses were two of Johnson's reputed stallions, Agrippa and Sidi Hamet, both of whom had lineage that could be traced back to Sir Archy. Eyre also did business with another well-known figure in the Virginian horse network, Hugh Campbell of King and Queen County, Virginia.[23] He purchased a dam named Circassian from Campbell, and this mare also could trace her lineage back to one of Sir Archy's offspring.[24] Eyre bred Circassian with a stallion owned by another big name in mid-Atlantic racing, James Bowdoin Kendall. Kendall was originally from Northampton County himself and a descendant of Custis Kendall. Having moved to Baltimore sometime in the 1820s, Kendall became the proprietor of a local track, which came to be known as the Kendall Race Course. He even advertised for contractors to build a trackside dining room, testifying to an era when races were becoming more formally social events with longer round tracks, grandstands, and jockey clubs. Kendall often appeared in newspaper accounts of races throughout the 1830s and 1840s as he entered a great many horses in races alongside giants like William Ransom Johnson. William L. Eyre's shared Eyreville roots surely helped facilitate a business relationship with Kendall, and the association undoubtedly gave an added gleam to his studbook in his eyes.

Only one record of William L. Eyre entering a horse in a formal race survives, though he very well could have participated in others. According to the *American Turf Register*, William entered an unnamed blooded mare—she could have been Circassian, Henrietta Temple, or even the then-aging Betsey Springer—to the "Eastern Shore, Virginia, Atlantic Course" to run one-mile heats for $200.[25] Who rode William's mare and the results of the race are unclear, but his fondness for the races is not in doubt.

The renowned late seventeenth-century silver "Morningstar" bowl, which now sits on the dining room table, holds pride of place in the modern narrative of horses at Eyre Hall. Though the particulars of the story are admittedly vague and the event unlikely, the fact that Eyres past and present have kept this anecdote alive in family memory is significant. By telling and retelling this story, they have and continue to participate in a tradition that historian Fairfax

Fig. 60. Curtilage with the fields beyond, Eyre Hall.

Harrison has called the "Equine F.F.V. [First Families of Virginia]." A horse blithely gulping champagne out of a large silver bowl is a sensational image. The Morningstar story evokes notions of high society, and some might find it strangely charming, ridiculous, or perhaps both. Just how involved the eighteenth-century Eyres were in horse racing remains elusive, but they certainly were familiar with the culture. The collection of six 1753 English racing prints by Henry Roberts that once hung in the passageway testifies to an equine state of mind. By showcasing these hand-colored prints of some of England's most esteemed thoroughbreds—with their pedigrees written in fine script in the margins—the Eyres participated in the greater English racing world. Merely looking around the property today, taking in the wide-open fields that border the road leading to the house, the Eyres had a perfect tract of land for quarter racing (Fig. 60). Though the hoofprints are long gone, their traces remain as visible as ever in the stories, prints, and photographs of Eyre Hall.

NOTES

1. James E. Mears, "Horse Racing on the Shore: The Keller Fair – Part I," in *The Shore Line* (Onancock: Eastern Shore of Virginia Historical Society, 1970), accessed July 2020 via the Eastern Shore of Virginia Historical Society online blog *History Between the Waters*, http://esvhs.blogspot.com/2014/10/horse-racing-on-shore-keller-fair-part-i.html. This column for the Eastern Shore of Virginia Historical Society's *The Shore Line* reports Mears's own research and personal recollections of fairgrounds—particularly concerning Eastern Shore horse racing—on the Eastern Shore at the turn of the twentieth century.

2. Fairfax Harrison, *The Equine F.F.Vs: A Study of the Evidence for the English Horses Imported into Virginia before the Revolution* (Richmond, Va.: Old Dominion Press, 1928), 35–36; Virginia C. Johnson and Barbara Crookshanks, *Virginia Horse Racing: Triumphs of the Turf* (Charleston, S.C.: The History Press, 2008), 15–17; Julie A. Campbell, *The Horse in Virginia: An Illustrated History* (Charlottesville and London: University of Virginia Press, 2010), 11–13.

3. Campbell, *Horse in Virginia*, 13.

4. Jennings Cropper Wise, *Ye Kingdome of Accawmacke; or, The Eastern Shore of Virginia in the Seventeenth Century* (Richmond, Va.: The Bell Book and Stationery Company, 1911), 307. According to Wise's study of surviving Eastern Shore inventories, there are no records of horse ownership on the Eastern Shore prior to Yeardley's 1642 purchase.

5. Ralph T. Whitelaw, *Virginia's Eastern Shore: A History of Northampton and Accomack Counties* (Richmond: Virginia Historical Society, 1951), 1:264, 365, 508. These pages are just a few on which Whitelaw includes direct quotes from the seventeenth-century Eastern Shore referencing horse paths and bridges.

6. Wise, *Ye Kingdome of Accawmacke*, 291.

7. Whitelaw, *Virginia's Eastern Shore*, 1:39.

8. William Waller Hening, *The Statutes at Large, being a Collection of all the Laws of Virginia* (New York, Richmond, and Philadelphia, 1819–23), 3:470–73; Hening, *Statutes at Large*, 5:364–65.

9. T. H. Breen, "Horses and Gentlemen: The Cultural Significance of Gambling among the Gentry of Virginia," *William and Mary Quarterly* 34, no. 2 (1977): 243–47. See also Jane Carson, *Colonial Virginians at Play* (Williamsburg: Colonial Williamsburg Foundation and University Press of Virginia, 1965); Cary Carson, *Face Value: The Consumer Revolution and the Colonizing of America* (Charlottesville: University of Virginia Press, 2017); Rhys Isaac, *The Transformation of Virginia, 1740–1790* (Chapel Hill: University of North Carolina Press, 1982); Kathleen M. Brown, *Good Wives, Nasty Wenches, and Anxious Patriarchs: Gender, Race, and Power in Colonial Virginia* (Chapel Hill: University of North Carolina Press, 1996).

10. Campbell, *Horse in Virginia*, 22–23.

11. Campbell, *Horse in Virginia*, 25; Harold B. Gill, "A Sport Only for Gentlemen" *Colonial Williamsburg Journal* 20, no. 1 (Autumn 1997): 49–53; John Eisenberg, "Off to the Races," *Smithsonian Magazine*, August 2004, https://www.smithsonianmag.com/history/off-to-the-races-2266179/, accessed October 2020. See Campbell and Gill for a more thorough who's who of early Virginia horse breeding. For instance, John Tayloe II and John Tayloe III made a significant name for their family in thoroughbred breeding and racing.

12. For details on how the "Virginia Horse" developed from Spanish and English horses crossbreeding, see Campbell, *Horse in Virginia*, 3–17.

13. Gill, "A Sport Only for Gentlemen."

14. Breen, "Horses and Gentlemen," 251.

15. Carson, *Colonial Virginians at Play*, 109.

16. Edward Hotaling, *The Great Black Jockeys: The Lives and Times of the Men Who Dominated America's First National Sport* (New York: Prima Publishing, 1999); Jessica Dallow, "Antebellum Sports Illustrated: Representing African Americans in Edward Troye's Equine Paintings," *Nineteenth-Century Art Worldwide* 12, no. 2 (Autumn 2013), http://www.19thc-artworldwide.org/autumn13/dallow-on-edward-troye-s-equine-paintings, accessed July 2020.

17. Maria L. Savage to "Mother" Lauretta [?], March 3, 1852, Garrett Family Papers, Box 1, Folder 5, 1786–1928, Special Collections, Swem Library, College of William and Mary, Williamsburg. Transcribed by Elizabeth Palms.

18. Campbell, *Horse in Virginia*, 43.

19. William L. Eyre Stud Book, 1835–1864, 5, 7, Eyre Hall, Northampton County, Virginia.

20. *Peninsula Enterprise* (Accomack, Va.), June 21, 1890.

21. Northampton County Personal Property Tax Lists, 1827, 1828, 1834.

22. *American Turf Register and Sporting Magazine* 8 (April 1, 1837): 384.

23. *The American Stud Book* (New York: The Jockey Club, 1873), 162, 197, 237, 272, 287, 299, 300, 549.

24. William L. Eyre Stud Book, 1835–1864, 3, 4; *American Turf Register and Sporting Magazine* 8 (April 1, 1837): 384.

25. "Races Omitted in the Calendar for 1840," *American Turf Register and Sporting Magazine* 12 (September 1841): 527.

Eyre Hall in the Twentieth Century: "I'm Home"

GEORGE W. McDANIEL

*"I would never want it to get burned down because
it's historic and my ancestors worked there,
and I have a lot of love for that."*

ANTHONY FOEMAN

"All around was family."

HELEN BURTON

"At Eyre Hall, I didn't feel a sense of segregation."

ROBERT CURTIS, JR.

*"I remember everybody on the farm looking out
for us and being incredibly kind and caring."*

EYRE BALDWIN

*"That same place that's so beautiful encompasses
both a legacy and a reality in the nation that
are ugly, violent, and unacceptable."*

MOLLY BALDWIN

I T WAS A WONDERFUL WEDDING AT GRACE AND St. Peter's Church in Baltimore. After the reception, the couple departed, motoring through the South and, on their way back, taking the two-hour ferry ride from Norfolk to Virginia's Eastern Shore. This was new country to the groom, who was from Kentucky, though his family had deep roots in Delaware. It was farm country, isolated, with mostly dirt roads covered by oyster shells. After disembarking the ferry, they drove a short distance, turned down a long allée lined with trees, and arrived at the bride's family farm house, a place ancient but not well kept. To the groom's surprise, his wife declared, "I'm home." She meant it.[1]

What was this home? As has been described, it was named Eyre Hall and had been in the family of the bride, Margaret Eyre Taylor Baldwin, since the mid-eighteenth century (see Fig. 8). In the antebellum era, it had been owned by her grandfather, Severn Eyre, who on his death in 1914 left it in equal, undivided shares to his daughter, Mary Eyre Wright, and his granddaughter, Margaret Eyre Taylor. Margaret was the daughter of Severn's older daughter, Grace Eyre Taylor, who had married a member of the prominent Taylor family of Norfolk. With Grace's death in 1910,

151

Margaret, her only child, inherited her mother's share at age 12. (Upon her death in 1979, Margaret Eyre Taylor Baldwin joined her mother Grace and other Eyre family relatives in the graveyard of Eyre Hall.)

A well-respected Baltimore lawyer, William Henry DeCourcy Wright served as trustee of the two sisters' shares in the estate and managed Eyre Hall long distance, coming down by boat once a month to check on things. Mary Eyre Wright chose not to live at Eyre Hall, preferring their home on Cathedral Street in Baltimore and their farm in Baltimore County. As a result, Eyre Hall was hardly operable for most of the year and began to decline. However, accompanied by her aunt Mary's daughter, Grace Wright, Margaret Taylor frequented Eyre Hall on sojourns throughout her youth (Fig. 61). They loved their time together at Eyre Hall, and, despite a 16-year age gap and different parentage, became like sisters. In fact, after her mother's death in 1910, Margaret Taylor became the ward of DeCourcy and Mary Wright and lived with them and Grace.[2]

On the subject of Eyre Hall and Margaret Taylor, Grace's son DeCourcy Wright McIntosh observed, "Cousin Marg is a round peg in a round hole." Perhaps her devotion to the property was because she had known Severn Eyre, who was characterized in his 1914 obituary in Norfolk's *Virginian-Pilot* as the "wealthiest man in Northampton County with an estate valued at $750,000," the equivalent of over $19 million dollars in 2020. Severn was the last of the family to carry the surname of Eyre, which "had been conspicuous in Northampton County for two hundred years." Margaret had adored him, spending parts of her girlhood summers with him at Eyre Hall (Fig. 62). It was Severn Eyre's bequest to Margaret that helped fund Eyre Hall's upkeep and renovation during her ownership from the 1930s into the 1960s, because farming in the twentieth century could not sustain its myriad expenses.[3]

On April 10, 1928, Margaret married Henry duPont Baldwin. His father's family had been tobacco farmers in Anne Arundel County, and his mother a child of the duPont family from Wilmington, Delaware, who had moved to Kentucky. Henry had been reared in Kentucky and graduated from the Massachusetts Institute of Technology in engineering. Soon after their marriage, they fulfilled Margaret's dream and moved to Eyre Hall. As a result, DeCourcy Wright, as trustee, divided the estate, giving Margaret the house and about 300 acres around it, and his wife, Mary Wright, the balance of 700 acres of farmland or more (Fig. 63).

Mary Wright's daughter Grace had married David Gregg McIntosh. Upon her demise, Grace's share was inherited by her son DeCourcy (Dick) McIntosh and his sister Anne Lowe McIntosh. Through a series of arrangements, Dick and his sister traded their land with Margaret's son, Furlong Baldwin. Dick put his approximately 325 acres under a conservation easement and sold them in the early 2000s for a hunting preserve. As a result of those arrangements with Furlong Baldwin, the peninsula of Eyre Hall returned to one ownership, its land consisting of all that in and around the main house, but also extending to Cherrystone Creek and to Route 13, bounded on the south by Eyre Hall Creek and on the north by Eyreville Creek.[4]

From 1931 onward, Henry and Margaret Baldwin lived at Eyre Hall full time. Gradually, they began to modernize the eighteenth-century house, renovate its historical features, and make modest improvements to the landscape, replacing dead or lost trees along the entry lane with cedars and crepe myrtles, which can still be seen today. Their son Henry Furlong Baldwin, named after his paternal grandfather, was born in 1932, shortly after their move to Eyre Hall (Fig. 64). As he recalls, the changes she made were substantial but at the same time subtle, and they took place over time: "You didn't wake one day, and notice great change, but instead you woke up five years later and realized it was different from five years before. It was her home. It was the way she wanted it. She just didn't want sudden change, and I don't blame her."

Fig. 62. Margaret Eyre Taylor at Eyre Hall, early 1910s.

Fig. 61. Margaret Eyre Taylor playing the Nunns & Clark square piano (see Cat. 137) in the parlor at Eyre Hall, ca. 1925. Her cousin Grace Eyre Wright stands next to her.

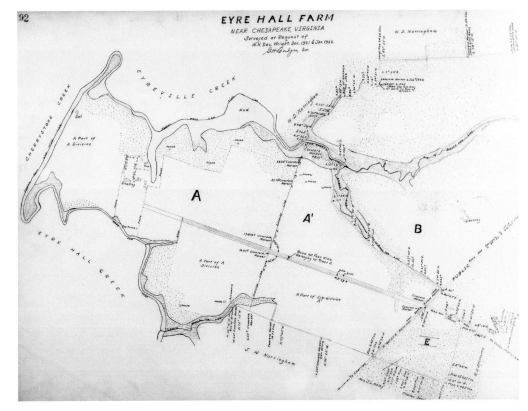

Fig. 63. Plat showing the proposed division of the Eyre Hall estate between Mary Eyre Wright and her niece Margaret Eyre Taylor, 1922.

The Baldwins rented the land for truck farming, producing broccoli, cabbage, and other winter crops, and tomatoes, sweet potatoes, white potatoes, and beans in warm weather. Migrants harvested the crops as they moved northwards with the seasons. According to Furlong, the farmland was rich, so it was used to raise crops, rather than cattle. "You don't waste good farmland raising cattle. Out West, you could have 100 acres per cow, but not here." They did raise domestic animals like horses and mules for farm work, cows for milk, hogs for meat, and chickens for both meat and eggs.[5]

Using his engineering skills, Henry Baldwin capitalized on the bounty of the Chesapeake by building a packing plant for clams and oysters on the point at the juncture of the Cherrystone Creek and its tributary, Eyre Hall Creek. Watermen would bring in their catch, and the plant processed and shipped clams and oysters, whole or shucked. Critical to operations was the 4:00 p.m. train, leaving Cape Charles, bound for Boston. As Furlong Baldwin recalls, everything had to make that train. Clams and oysters were shipped in the baggage car. If not going to points further north, they were switched in Philadelphia to the Broadway train and sold in the wholesale market in Chicago about five o'clock the next morning. If the oysters and clams were shucked, they were in gallon cans and potato barrels packed with ice, or if raw, left in their shells, loose, in burlap bags. In Eyre Hall's kitchen today is a 1934 ad from *Town & Country* for Cherrystone Clams, Henry Baldwin's brand. His packing

terrapins to swim out. Terrapins sent to "fancy restaurants and clubs" were a modest financial success until a hurricane smashed the pen, releasing all the terrapins, which enjoyed their new-found freedom by swimming about the creeks and marsh.[8]

Furlong remembers eight or nine abandoned tenant houses, now demolished, that dotted Eyre Hall's landscape. In the absence of local stone, the bricks from their chimneys were gathered, cleaned, and broken by African American workers, who on rainy days sat in the woodsheds at Eyre Hall, breaking them into smaller pieces for reuse. They then rolled the brick chips into the garden paths at Eyre Hall, using the eighteenth-century English roller with an axle through it, which still resides by the side of the garden wall. Today, the garden paths remain and are swept of dirt and sand, but as Furlong recalls, "During Mother's time, they were pale pink in color, due to the brick. Pretty elegant."[9]

Furlong recalled that the location of antebellum slave quarters was near the "little branch off Eyreville Creek." During his youth, only the locust posts upon which they stood remained, forming "little rectangular boxes" outlining the locations and sizes of the dwelling houses. When the "magnificent barn" burned in 1940, its flames consumed two carriages dating from the late 1800s. The barn had oak stalls with wrought iron between each stall so horses "couldn't bite each other across the wall." After World War II, tractors arrived, and mules gradually disappeared, as did much manual farm labor. Mules had been used not only in the fields but to pull mowers to cut Eyre Hall's acres of grass. In the fields big rigs were used, consisting of eight mules abreast to pull a "six- or eight-bottom plow," which unearthed a wide swath. Before the war, Furlong Baldwin remembers, about 95 percent of the farm work was done by horses or mules, requiring stables, corn cribs, equipment sheds, and other buildings on Eyre Hall's landscape. When a friend offered Henry Baldwin a job in his factory manufacturing airplane parts in Baltimore, he

plant, Cherrystone Seafoods, was located on Cherrystone Creek. There is also an advertisement for the Pump Room in Chicago, declaring "These oysters slept in Cherrystone Creek last night."[6]

Nothing was wasted. Oyster shells were used for road construction, there being no local stone available for gravel. What is now the four-lane U.S. Route 13 was then a two-lane dirt road, covered with oyster shells from the packing plants along the creeks. According to Furlong Baldwin, oyster shells were preferred since they were more durable than clam shells, which after having been steamed became brittle and broke into powder. A frequent scene was the mule carts and trucks filled with oyster shells, leaving the packing plant to supply shells for the construction of state roads and farm lanes.[7]

Although the packing plant was not a major financial success, it did provide income for the Baldwins and the many plant workers and watermen. To supplement income, Henry Baldwin devised a pen in which to raise terrapins for the market. Built of tall upright boards sunk into the creek bottom, the pen was located near the packing plant at the mouth of Eyre Hall Creek. Spaces between the uprights allowed water to pass through but were too small to allow took the position and never returned to live at Eyre Hall. In 1962 he and Margaret formally separated, though they never divorced.[10]

While they lived at Eyre Hall, "being in the social circuit" was not of great interest to Henry and Margaret Baldwin, their son remembers. They were not golfers or tennis players, nor did they belong to country clubs. As her son explains, Margaret did belong to a ladies' club, but it was not "her thing." When young, she had horses at Eyre Hall, for she loved to ride, but being near the water and the marsh, the flies and mosquitoes were so worrisome that she eventually gave up riding.[11]

In the years before mass media, the Baldwins and Eyre Hall's African American residents did enjoy good conversations, offering entertainment to family and friends and reminiscing about those who had passed on or were rarely seen. Drawing from the local lode of story nuggets, Furlong Baldwin became an excellent raconteur, opening a window into family life and social relationships. A telling example revolves around the butler Severn Weeks, who lived in the house, now torn down, located behind the kitchen. He lived there with the cook William Frazier and the housemaid named Lena in the 1930s and '40s (Fig. 65). According to Baldwin, Severn Weeks was the "dance king of Northampton County." In the absence of Furlong's parents, he would not simply serve food to Furlong and his sister Mary, but dance while doing so—the Turkey Trot, the Strut, the Big Apple, Cotton-Eyed Joe, and the Suzy Q.[12]

Above all, Weeks loved to sail. Furlong's father had a 65-foot bugeye, a traditional Chesapeake Bay work boat, which he had converted to a cruising vessel. Furlong, his father, and friends would sail to Oxford, St. Michael's, or Annapolis, or over to Hampton or Norfolk. The Eyre Hall cook, William Frazier, who was quite stout, was terrified of the water and refused to go out in the boat, so the cooking fell to Severn Weeks. On the boat's stove, Severn would fry chicken and bake biscuits, and they would eat below. While

Fig. 65. Eyre Hall cook William Frazier and Furlong Baldwin, ca. 1942.

they dined, Severn would sail the boat in his starched white coat and black trousers.

As was often the case, when they pulled into port, girls would come out in a rowboat and ask Mr. Baldwin if Severn Weeks could come ashore. "Pick him up at nine," Mr. Baldwin would reply. Severn would put on his light brown dancing shoes, and off he'd go. Being only six or seven, Furlong would be asleep by then. About six in the morning, Furlong would awaken and Severn would be returning, after having danced all night. He'd show Furlong the small trophies he'd won. "He was a piece of work," Furlong concluded. "Starched white coat. Black trousers. Sailing that bugeye up the Bay. He loved it."[13]

"In essence, I grew up at Eyre Hall," Furlong recalls. "It was the Depression, and though we had a home in Baltimore, we spent every vacation and so much time here. Since my older sister wouldn't play with me, I learned to play by myself and would leave the breakfast table with many things to do. At that time we only had mules and no tractors, so I learned to harness mules and drive carts and how to crab pot. I'd play games in the woods. I never put a bridle on a 'mule': she was a 'cavalry horse.' Though she would only walk, I was independent and would imagine. Each creek had a freshwater spring to explore, and an exciting thing was to go and try to shoot a cottonmouth water moccasin with a 22 rifle. I used outhouses at my friends' homes. You would use a red corncob, and a white one to see if you were clean. If not, you'd get another red one. The big thing I loved was catching fatback fish, or menhaden. I'd feed everybody on the farm. My maternal grandfather taught me too. When here, he fished practically every day. He would go duck shooting in the morning and fishing in the afternoon in the winter, two creeks up, catching croaker, perch, and gray trout. People used to say to me, 'You went to Princeton.' I replied, 'Fifty percent of my education came from growing up at Eyre Hall.'[14]

"Mother's favorite room was what grown-ups called the parlor, off the front hall, which we used when we had guests or put up Christmas trees. Even though no one warned, 'Don't do it,' we children didn't go in there but maybe twelve times a year. It was very formal. Mother loved it, and we would sit in those starched chairs during holidays. Listening to my mother, I learned about the history of Eyre Hall. I did happen to live in a bigger house than my friends did, but I didn't think about it. Mother never poured our history into me. I realized that this place was pretty and loved it and have been absorbing its history for 70 years by osmosis. There was no epiphany; it just sort of slid in. Also, I would never forget. As for our family's history, we've lived here for eight generations and on the Eastern Shore for eleven. We came in 1624. My ambition is to live until 2024 because I want to have a party, celebrating our 400 years of being here. That's my goal.

"The china and silver in the dining room are important (see Cat. 75). The seventeenth-century silver punch bowl is now one-of-a kind in America, but, among all the silver pieces, what says it all—continuity and change at Eyre Hall—are the eighteenth-century silver pitcher and the twentieth-century one Mother received as a wedding present, standing next to one another. As for the china, since Washington died in 1799, the brown sepia pattern represents a memorial to him from 1800 and has been in this dining room at least since my mother's lifetime. Since this was her home, Mother would say, 'Let's use the brown china. It's Christmas.' Our family and friends would eat on it. Finally, someone said, 'Peggy, do you know what you're doing?' Our regular china was the Canton. All our dogs ate table scraps. We'd scrape them onto the Canton platters and put them down for the dogs. Daddy had a pointer that lived to be 19, and the slightly smaller Canton platter was his. Nobody thought it was special, and then all of a sudden, you realized it was."[15]

Growing up in a farm environment on the Eastern Shore, Furlong remembers an Eyre Hall "soundscape" far different from the one heard today in much of America. There were no honking horns and only rarely sirens. Trains whistled at every road crossing, so, depending on the direction of prevailing winds, one could hear the trains and know their locations as they chugged across the Shore in accordance with their schedules. Especially in warm weather with the windows open in the house at night, one could hear the trucks on Route 13, shifting gears up or down as they approached Cheriton, two miles south, and Eastville, three miles north. "You knew exactly what was going on." If lucky, one could hear the fog horns and clanging bells of the Bay's ferry boats, since the bridge and tunnel connecting the Eastern Shore to Norfolk were not built until the early 1960s, making the Eastern Shore much more isolated than it is today, and ferries essential.[16]

While there were always seagulls crying or laughing as they circled about, shore birds in abundance arrived in the spring, along with cardinals, bluebirds, chickadees, hummingbirds, woodpeckers, and more, their colors flashing against the sky and their calls filling the air. The presence of birds distinguished the seasons' cycles, one example being the arrival and departure of ducks and geese.

During warm weather one heard the loud rat-a-tat-tat-tat of woodpeckers sharpening their bills on the soft brick of Eyre Hall's orangerie and dovecote. Added to that were the rhythms of insects like June bugs and cicadas and frogs like peepers and bullfrogs. They were "just country sounds," Furlong explains, "simply wonderful."[17] They were the same sounds heard by his ancestors and by African Americans over the course of their 400 years on Virginia's Eastern Shore and by Native Americans for millennia.

Trains and buses also connected Eyre Hall's residents to the wider world. Passenger trains would not stop at every station, but, if requested in advance, they would stop at the crossing near Eyre Hall. Such trips illustrated the times, an example being a bus trip Furlong made from Baltimore to Eyre Hall when he was under 12. At Salisbury, two hours from Eyre Hall, he had to change onto the bus bound for Cape Charles, and ask the driver to drop him off at Eyre Hall's entrance. "Nobody thought that was unusual or that somebody was going to kidnap you."

Another trip introduced him to race relations in the wider world. While every town on the Eastern Shore had eating or sitting areas, water fountains, and restrooms marked "White" or "Colored," Furlong had not registered what segregation really meant until he was ten, when a bus trip taught him. Put on a bus in Baltimore by his mother and being shy, he wanted to sit by himself, so he kept passing seats and going back and back until he found an empty row. "A nice Black man said to me, 'Young man, you don't really belong back here. I suggest you move forward.' I didn't know what it was about until I was older. I wanted to be Black. Heck, they were eating biscuits and fried chicken out of paper bags. But he'd said, 'Young man, I don't . . .' And I said, 'Oh, all right.' So up I went and sat next to a person already there, a white person. But it was the gentlest thing. It wasn't mean or hostile or angry. I never said anything to anybody about it, but as I got older, I realized that was my first introduction to Jim Crow. I hadn't had a clue. Later, when I was 13 or 14, all of a sudden,

I realized what was going on. But at the time, segregation meant nothing to me. I would have gotten on the bus and sat with our people at Eyre Hall. Why not? I was brought up in the world, but I didn't understand the hostility of the world. I kind of understood the world, but if you were Pinky or Georgie, why wouldn't I have sat with you?"[18]

Later, when a junior at Princeton in the 1950s, Furlong used that introduction to Jim Crow to good benefit. This time, he was on a bus riding with his lacrosse team from Princeton to Durham to play Duke. The athletic trainer was an African American, Bobby Sinker, whom Furlong adored. When they stopped for lunch in a small Virginia town, someone asked Sinker if he was going to get lunch. "No, I'm not hungry," came the reply. Furlong was the only one who understood what was going on, so he asked Sinker what he wanted since he was going to get lunch and bring it back to the bus and eat there. "We had this nice lunch on the bus. He was my friend. That's why I had been confused at ten years old on that bus in Baltimore by that gentle reminder that I didn't belong there. Very strange. I guess I understood the Black and white part, but I didn't understand the animosity part of it. These were my friends. I lived with these people every day, and I didn't understand it."[19]

When growing up in the 1930s and before World War II, Furlong recalls that workers outdoors were paid $5.50 a week until after World War II, and indoor workers double at $2 a day or $11 a week. Each of the outdoor workers had their own house and a small tract of land for a garden and hog pen. After the war, farming changed because mules and mule teams were no longer needed, and tractors came into use. With tractors, one did not need as much farm labor, so the African American population at Eyre Hall diminished. To make ends meet, the Baldwins leased a lot of land for truck farming, with most of the work on the garden and grounds done by African American residents. "They would go home and eat their lunch or sit in the woods and eat. We'd cook a huge pan of cornbread and take it to them." Living with

African American families close by brought opportunities for what writer Bryan Stevenson calls "proximity learning,"[20] which taught Furlong uncomfortable lessons: "I didn't understand it, and then I did understand it. I knew we had more than they did, but when I first understood it was when, in the late '30s or early '40s, a man with 14 children came up on Christmas Eve, when it was already dark, and asked my father, 'Can I borrow $5 to make Christmas?' What did they get? One orange and one peppermint stick? Then it occurred to me, because in the other room was a train set and a wagon and a football. That's when it really registered. I remember that so vividly, 'Can I borrow $5?' Fourteen kids, at 6 o'clock at night on Christmas Eve. There were tough times here. There really were."[21]

After World War II, the landscape changed considerably. The large barn had burned and not been replaced; abandoned tenant houses, probably former slave houses, were pulled down and bricks in their chimneys used for the garden; and, later, the small dwelling behind the kitchen was demolished. Even before the war, a large extended family consisting of Lawrence Bagwell and his sister Pinky Bagwell Foeman and her husband William and their many children had taken up residence and begun working. Lawrence Bagwell became the farm's overseer in the 1940s and '50s and lived in the brick overseer's house, constructed in 1798 (see Fig. 136). According to his grandniece, Joyce Ramassar, Lawrence cultivated a large garden near the house. In warm weather vegetables and fruit like tomatoes, beans, strawberries, and cantaloupes fed the family fresh from the garden, or, if suitable, were preserved for the winter. In cold weather, turnips, broccoli, collards, and other vegetables sustained the family. An orchard supplied apples, pears, and figs. What his family did not consume, Lawrence would take to markets in Eastville and other nearby towns to sell.[22]

After Lawrence's death and then Margaret Baldwin's in 1979, the house was restored and enlarged by Furlong's sister, Mary Eyre, and her husband, David W. K. Peacock, who made it their home. Mary Eyre had graduated from Vassar College in 1950 and forged a distinguished career in the Central Intelligence Agency for 30 years. Upon her retirement, Eyre Hall exerted its pull, so she and her husband chose the house for their residence. Both Mary and Georgia Curtis, the remarkable woman described in the Scrapbook of Recollections, were born in 1929; upon Mary's return, they became close and enjoyed simply "talking to one another." Mary died in 2015 and is buried at Forest Lake, New Jersey, her husband's family retreat.[23]

Near the brick house was the home of Lawrence Bagwell's sister, Pinky Bagwell Foeman, and her husband William. There they raised many of their nine children, the first child Bertha being born in 1909 and the last, Georgia, in 1929. Four of those children—Ben, Dorsey, Georgia, and Daisy—continued working at Eyre Hall and occupied the tenant houses whose locations around the fields on either side of the entrance lane are shown on the site map (Fig. 66). As the map indicates, the homes of Lawrence Bagwell, of his sister Pinky Foeman, of their sister Lizzie Press, and of Pinky's four children transformed Eyre Hall into a community of one extended family.[24]

In the twentieth century the strength of that family—in fact, the entire Eyre Hall community—was tested when hurricanes swept the coast. The Baldwin family could have felt no obligations, but did, and offered their sturdier house as refuge to the African American families. As if in an unspoken contract, the elders assumed responsibility and exerted authority. Beginning in the 1940s onwards and perhaps earlier, African Americans like Pinky Foeman and later her daughter Georgia Curtis had keys to the main house. From the Baldwins and African Americans alike, there was not one mention of something being broken or stolen. The elders were in charge.

Hurricanes illuminated the faith of Pinky Foeman for all in the African American community to see. According to her grandchildren, she viewed hurricanes not as a danger

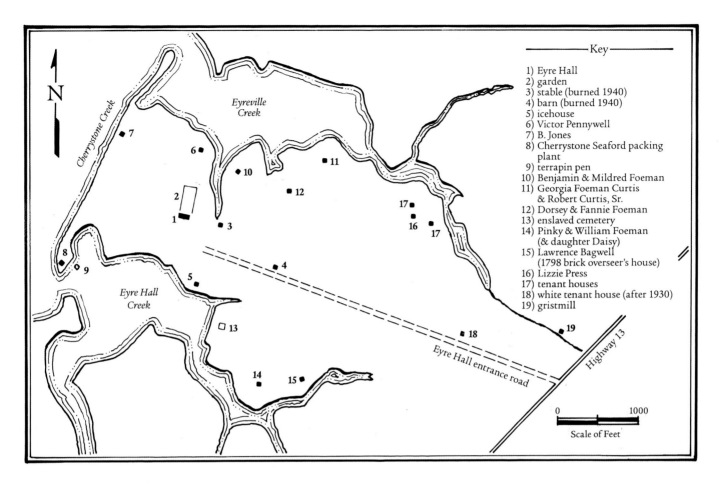

Fig. 66. Map of Eyre Hall in the mid-twentieth century showing dwellings, work buildings, and other features with the names of those who occupied the tenant houses.

Key
1) Eyre Hall
2) garden
3) stable (burned 1940)
4) barn (burned 1940)
5) icehouse
6) Victor Pennywell
7) B. Jones
8) Cherrystone Seaford packing plant
9) terrapin pen
10) Benjamin & Mildred Foeman
11) Georgia Foeman Curtis & Robert Curtis, Sr.
12) Dorsey & Fannie Foeman
13) enslaved cemetery
14) Pinky & William Foeman (& daughter Daisy)
15) Lawrence Bagwell (1798 brick overseer's house)
16) Lizzie Press
17) tenant houses
18) white tenant house (after 1930)
19) gristmill

to be feared but rather as an expression of God's will to which she answered. While everyone else retreated to the main house with her blessing, she declared, according to her granddaughter, Joyce Ramassar: "'No, I'm not going anywhere. If the Lord wants to take me, then He will take me, whether I am in the big house or my house.' We'd get upset and try to persuade her to leave since we didn't want her to be by herself, to no avail. So her daughter, my Aunt Daisy, who lived with her, would stay. Pinky had her rocking chair and so strong was her faith, she wouldn't move from there, and would sit in front of the window and watch everything."[25]

With the demise of horse-and-mule farming and the development of more mechanized agriculture, canning factories grew in towns nearby. Increasingly, many farms in the 1950s and '60s, including Eyre Hall, leased land for truck farming, growing tomatoes, cucumbers, and other vegetables picked by migrants. In the early 1940s, an entrepreneur, Guy L. Webster, who purchased and renovated

Eyreville across Eyreville Creek, had a large canning factory in nearby Cheriton (Fig. 67). One of Pinky's son and Eyre Hall resident, Ben Foeman, worked a second job at the factory (Fig. 68). Webster also rented land at Eyre Hall for many years until he sold his factory, which then closed. As Pinky's children and grandchildren became adults in the last half of the twentieth century, Eyre Hall could no longer provide steady work, and better opportunities beckoned elsewhere, so they left. This diaspora is described in their oral history interviews in the Scrapbook of Recollections.[26]

Today, Eyre Hall's fields continue to be leased and grow wheat, corn, and soybeans. Over the course of two years, each is grown separately and sold to feed the large broiler industry on the Eastern Shore. However, for the first time in probably four centuries, no African American families live on the Eyre Hall estate. Not that they have all left the area; indeed, several families, like those of Helen Burton and Anthony Foeman, featured in the Scrapbook of Recollections, own homes in nearby towns. For all these

African Americans as well for Furlong and his children and granddaughter, their memories of Eyre Hall in the twentieth century give us informative glimpses so we might see Eyre Hall not simply as a historic site but as a home, where real people lived out real lives in real places.

For example, Helen Burton, a granddaughter of Pinky Foeman, explains "Eyre Hall is home because I was raised there and had cousins, uncles, aunts, and grandmother there. When I was maybe four, I remember my dad, Benjamin Foeman, taking me to the big house to my grandma, Pinky, and she'd take care of me. Or, he'd show me the garden, where I used to go with Molly and Eyre, Furlong's two kids, and play hide and go seek and all of that. We'd go all through the house, and they showed us all the different colored rooms. My dad rode us all on the back of the tractor. My dad was the caretaker, responsible for the grass and the garden and whitewashing the fences. All around was family.

"My mom and dad always told me if you're going to do something, do it right, and don't start something you can't finish. Mother taught us like this: If we were doing something wrong, she was going to show us how to do it right. So now, whenever I go to work, I'm going to give them a day's work and make sure I get it right. It comes from the older ones and how they raised us."[27]

A great-grandson of Pinky Foeman, Anthony Foeman offers yet another twentieth-century perspective (Fig. 69). He considers "Eyre Hall my home because I was born there, August 24, 1964, delivered by the midwife, Miss Hannah Wise, who charged $5. As a boy, we used to play hide and go seek in the garden by the big house and run through the woods all the time. Me and my brother had a trail that we would go to my grandfather's brother's house, Ben Foeman, and we'd go down there and play with those kids because there were so many at our house: 13 of us grandkids, my grandparents, and their four kids—my mother Deloris and her three sisters, Melba, Mildred, and Carol. Me and my brother used to hunt deer, rabbit, and squirrels. My grandfather taught us how to fish, and we'd catch 'hardheads' [croaker] and 'fatbacks' [menhaden], plus plenty of crabs, sharks, eels, speckled trout, and flounder. We'd put food on the table.

"My grandfather was not the kind of person that would be angry with anyone. He would take the shirt off his back and give it to you if you was white, Black, purple, or yellow. My grandfather looked at everyone the same. There wasn't none of this, 'Just because you have this much money or just because you have a fancy car and all that.' My grandfather treated them just as well as he would treat

Fig. 69. Anthony
Foeman, 2019.

anyone. All he ever taught me was to respect people like he wanted to be respected. I mean if they ask you something and you didn't know, then you didn't know, but if you knew, you told the truth.[28]

"I graduated from Northampton High School in 1982 and went into the military, and when I came home, I saw my grandfather Dorsey Foeman was getting old, and it didn't feel right. He raised me. So I left the Army in 1987, was hired by Mr. Furlong, and that made me the ninth generation in my family to work on Eyre Hall. When my grandfather Dorsey was living, Mr. Furlong would come around to his house on Sundays and sit on the porch with him and discuss what needed to be done the next week. Eyre Hall, I know every inch of it. Today I live not far away, and here, I've got fresh air and don't have to worry about walking over the top of people trying to get somewhere. There's not smog or a bunch of shooting. I can go outside and not worry about a drive-by. Whenever my grandchild comes, I can let her go outside and play and don't have to watch her. When I go to Eyre Hall, I feel a whole lot better. I may remember my grandfather Dorsey and go places where we used to sit and talk, like down at the waterfront. Sometimes I can be riding the tractor and think about the times with him, and maybe shed a couple of tears."[29]

According to Joyce Curtis Ramassar, another grand-daughter of Pinky Foeman, who grew up at Eyre Hall in the twentieth century: "When I think of Eyre Hall, what comes to mind are your roots. We were fortunate to have our whole family here; the generations of my grandmother Pinky with her brother, Uncle Lawrence, her sister Lizzie, and my grand-

mother's children— Uncle Dorsey, Uncle Ben, Aunt Daisy, and my mother, Georgia Foeman Curtis. Having my whole family here, how lucky can you be? Growing up together with cousins, uncles, aunts, and grandmother, that is what was special about Eyre Hall (Fig. 70). We roamed wherever we wanted to. We swam in the creek and built homemade boats and floated them there. We walked through the garden. My father built a treehouse in the yard. When fields were empty after Webster had finished all the summer crops, we'd use the field for baseball. Webster, a good man, would sit out there and watch us play—all my cousins, my mom, and uncles.

"Whatever happened in the seventeenth century, that is not part of the time period I know about. I didn't even know I was living on a plantation, because my definition of a plantation was quite different from living here. To me, it was a place where you had people centered in one location who didn't have the freedom to say what they thought. I don't know anybody on this farm that didn't say what they thought. Even to the owners of this farm, they were very outspoken. Mrs. Baldwin had a way of treating everyone as if they were people, and that's why I couldn't get in my head about when I found out this place had been a plantation.

"Regarding discrimination, my mother didn't play. 'You don't have the right to discriminate against any race because if you cut yourself and drain all your blood, there's no way that you're going to drain one race separate from the other because you will have too many involved. You can't say you are one thing or the other or that you don't like this group because they are white, because your father's grandfather, who raised him, was from Scotland and married a Nigerian. And your father's mother was a Cherokee, who died giving birth to him.'"[30]

When asked about growing up during the era of seg-regation in the twentieth century, Joyce's brother Robert Curtis, Jr., his wife Paulette Curtis, and cousin Helen Burton reflected on life at Eyre Hall and the limited opportunities

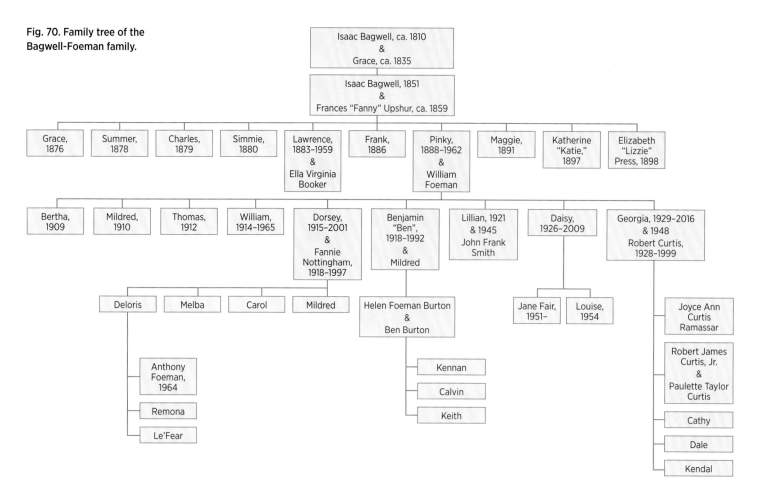

Fig. 70. Family tree of the Bagwell-Foeman family.

Isaac Bagwell, ca. 1810 & Grace, ca. 1835

Isaac Bagwell, 1851 & Frances "Fanny" Upshur, ca. 1859

Grace, 1876 | Summer, 1878 | Charles, 1879 | Simmie, 1880 | Lawrence, 1883–1959 & Ella Virginia Booker | Frank, 1886 | Pinky, 1888–1962 & William Foeman | Maggie, 1891 | Katherine "Katie," 1897 | Elizabeth "Lizzie" Press, 1898

Bertha, 1909 | Mildred, 1910 | Thomas, 1912 | William, 1914–1965 | Dorsey, 1915–2001 & Fannie Nottingham, 1918–1997 | Benjamin "Ben", 1918–1992 & Mildred | Lillian, 1921 & 1945 John Frank Smith | Daisy, 1926–2009 | Georgia, 1929–2016 & 1948 Robert Curtis, 1928–1999

Deloris | Melba | Carol | Mildred

Helen Foeman Burton & Ben Burton

Jane Fair, 1951– | Louise, 1954

Joyce Ann Curtis Ramassar

Anthony Foeman, 1964

Robert James Curtis, Jr. & Paulette Taylor Curtis

Remona

Kennan

Le'Fear

Calvin

Cathy

Keith

Dale

Kendal

---

available in a rural, segregated community, where for so many African Americans getting a good job and moving ahead meant leaving the Eastern Shore (Fig. 71). However, there were nuances. As Robert Curtis, Jr. remembered: "Going to school sometimes, Black kids would look at me because they'd think I was different from them because my hair was always curled, since my dad is half Cherokee."

A newcomer from New Jersey to the community after her marriage in 1976, Paulette recalled: "My first encounter with segregation was when I went to a doctor's office in Cape Charles, which had a sign to the right that said 'whites' and a sign to the left that said 'blacks.' I asked my husband, 'What does this mean? I've never seen this before.' He said, 'We have to sit on the Black side, and the whites go there.' They even had a water fountain for the Blacks and the whites. That was my first encounter with segregation. It really did bother me." But Eyre Hall seemed different.

As her husband explained, "When Eyre Baldwin, Furlong's son, would come and sit at our table and eat just like he was home. He would sit there and ask my mom Georgia, 'What's this? This is good.' Mama would say, 'This is biscuit, navy beans, and neck bones.' He said 'Well, I don't know what it is, but it's good.' His sister Molly would also come around. She would never eat, but they always came in our house, and we never felt different about that. Whenever they took us up there, Furlong and them would tell them to give us lunch, something to drink, or whatever we wanted. I felt more comfortable at Eyre Hall than we did when we went out in the streets because everybody was so friendly back there."[31]

According to Robert Curtis, Jr., "One time we had a big party right down at the Eyre Hall house. Mrs. Baldwin, Furlong, Helen's mother, and all of us were there, and folks about my age were there. I used to play guitar, and my cousin had his drums, plus other guitars down there. Helen's oldest brother, who was my age, was there. We had a big party until about 12 or 1 o'clock that night." Robert does not recall how they got the party going. "We asked, 'Could this happen?' It was in the long hallway of the house. Right there. We cranked it up and played. We had electric guitars and drums. Played some of everything. I will never forget that. Dancing and everything. Mrs. Baldwin was there, and Furlong too. All

of my family was there. I think they got together and said, 'Let's all of us get this together. Everybody on the farm. We just get in here and show you the things we do,' so that's what happened. That was about 1963 or '64, when I was about 13 or 14." Helen remembers "Y'all having the party. We tried to go, but my mama said, 'You're too young.' My older sisters and brothers went and brought back food, snacks, and stuff for me and said it was fun, but we were too small."[32]

Robert Curtis, Jr. elucidates his background. "I was born on Eyre Hall, perhaps at my grandmother Pinky's house before it burned down. It was one of the old houses, like two rooms downstairs and two rooms upstairs. My mother, Georgia Foeman Curtis, moved us perhaps to Delaware, where we stayed for two or three years, and when we came back to Eyre Hall, we built a new house, which is still standing. To catch the school bus, we had to walk about a mile and a quarter because not too many people had cars (Fig. 72). Beginning when I was about five or six, my mother took me to the big house, where she would be cooking and doing things. While she taught me a lot, I learned a lot on my own by going around the farm and looking at plants, flowers, and the beautiful parts of the house. Everybody was family that lived on Eyre Hall."

According to Paulette Curtis, his wife, they lived for a while with Robert's mother Georgia Curtis, at Eyre Hall. "She taught me how to do the silver and brass and would take me to work with her at Eyre Hall." The values of integrity and hard work that she absorbed as a youth seemed to merge with those of the African American families of Eyre Hall. "My father was a perfectionist, and I took after him. So too was my mother-in-law, Georgia Curtis. For example, she taught me how to polish silver or brass so it sparkles like brand new. It was so beautiful to see and something to be proud of. I also whitewashed fences along with other families and am still polishing silver and brass. I had to get used to country living, for there was no such thing as plumbing; I had to get used to pumping water, lifting pots to take your bath, and washing clothes by hand on the little scrub board. A lot of work. But I love the fresh air, the greenery of the trees, and hearing the birds in the mornings. It's really a beautiful place to be."[33]

Dick McIntosh, an Eyre descendant and Furlong Baldwin's cousin, often visited Eyre Hall when growing up and remembers: "Race relations at Eyre Hall were peaceful. I don't remember any upsets or unpleasantness. We were fond of the African Americans who worked there and knew we were dependent upon them, just as they, I imagine, knew they were dependent upon us. We accepted a kind of interdependence. Since Furlong was 11 years older than I and would have his friends down working on the farm, the Black children were my playmates. That's the way it was. In fact, when Furlong had parties there like weddings, he always invited the Black families to come. We'd all dance and have a good time. It was an extension of our having grown up there. We knew the different characteristics of each person, and they knew ours. Perhaps that was because everybody, Black or white, had enough freedom at Eyre Hall for their personality to emerge and to express themselves and be themselves. Why? We all felt an attachment to the place. Perhaps it was also due to Margaret Baldwin, because she was happy and not a controlling person."[34]

Fig. 73. Eyre Baldwin, 1970s.

Fig. 74. Molly Baldwin, Daisy Foeman, and Georgia Foeman Curtis dancing in the Eyre Hall kitchen, 1980s.

The memories of Eyre Baldwin, Furlong's son, evoke a lively site. According to Eyre: "My earliest memories of Eyre Hall are of a lot of laughter, a lot of love. We'd go to the creek, sail, or spend time in the gardens. I remember everybody on the farm looking out for us and being incredibly caring. As a child, you just knew it was natural and honest. I grew up in Baltimore when my parents were together, and we would come down for vacations (Fig. 73). Probably around 1975 or 1976, I started spending summers here with my grandmother and came on weekends and holidays from boarding school. I became pretty entrenched in the community and in Eyre Hall. As a teenager, I worked on farms that supplied canning companies and in seafood houses in nearby Oyster and Cheriton. I probably understood Eyre Hall's history when I was 14 or 15, because I knew what was here, how my grandmother did things, and that the things we used, whether it was the silver or the china, were hers. There would be long conversations about portraits, silver, china, and antiques at the table. You would have to be a fool not to hear something that was going to stick. So much was still intact. I appreciated that."[35]

The memories of Molly Baldwin, Furlong's daughter, add different colors to the portrait: "I was born in 1959 in Baltimore, grew up there until I was about 16, and in the summers, came to Eyre Hall. It was home. I'd spend a lot of time with Georgie and Daisy, following them around and hanging out with them. All of their children plus Dorsey's and Ben's, we all played for hours in the garden and in the water. It was beautiful. As I got into pre-teens, I was separated from them. That was hard. I didn't understand it. I was a little kid, and all of a sudden because they were African American and I was white and I lived in this house and they lived in smaller houses on the farm, we were separated."

Molly spoke of how her father "ingrained in me, not drilled directly: 'You're given a lot of opportunity and privilege—and to whom much is given, much is expected'" (Fig. 74). She observed, "There are things about Eyre Hall that are extraordinary. There're beautiful parts of its history and not-beautiful parts. It's physically and geographically beautiful. The garden was and is extraordinary. I was born into a lot of privilege and had opportunities that most people in the world don't have, and take seriously the commitment to give back. But I don't do it just because of that. While the house is extraordinary, to me it stands for things in the United States that are not good, that are unacceptable: the history of slavery, the history and the tragic reality of racism in our nation today, even in the country where lots of people have come from other countries to work for no money or hardly any money. So I have mixed feelings about the place—not the people—and take seriously my responsibility as a white woman to understand the privilege I come from and to be respectful. My father and mother and the way I was raised obviously gave me enough strength to follow my own calling. As a result, in some small way I hope I can help the world to be more fair and just."[36]

Interpreting what Eyre Hall has meant over the decades, Furlong Baldwin reasoned: "Had I not been successful in banking, I would have still fought to keep Eyre Hall. It would have gotten shabbier and shabbier. My real push has been to be successful enough that I'm able to pass it along to my granddaughter with the means to run it. Beyond that, I have no idea. If I hadn't been successful and we needed a new tractor, that wouldn't have been possible. I would have been in tears, but it wouldn't have been possible. As for my mother and father sustaining Eyre Hall by truck farming, there wasn't any money in it. We rented most of it out and farmed a little bit ourselves, but it wasn't enough to live on. Nor did the seafood packing plant or terrapin venture produce enough income. Fortunately, Mother had a little income thanks to Severn Eyre. As they say in that good old southern way, we went three generations and lived off somebody's brightness."[37]

Furlong further observed, "Despite what the books say, you can go home again. After I divorced in 1973, I came home 45 weekends a year. This is where I want to be. What I gave up was a perfectly normal social life in Baltimore, but it wasn't what interested me. I sure didn't want to be the extra man at a dinner party Saturday night." When asked about Eyre Hall's attraction, he explained: "If you didn't love Eyre Hall, you would hate it. There ain't an in-between.

My joy and my hobby is this place. It used to be when I was working and got here on a Saturday, the lawnmower was broken. The next Saturday, the water pump didn't work. The next Saturday, the roof blew off. It's a killer, but I love it. I want to leave it in the best shape I can and hope my successors get as much pleasure out of it as I do. People come and say very nice things about it, but it's my home. Though a little bigger than most, I like it the way you want your home to be."

And he concluded: "Eyre Hall has changed and is very demanding. In the '30s everything was cheaper. I look at buildings and remember those 80 years ago because I remember when those boards were there, 80 years ago. Eyre Hall's like me—my boards are coming off, too. . . . If you didn't love it, Eyre Hall would break your back. This is my beach house. This is my golf club. This is my whatever. I don't want that. I want this. I'm home."[38]

Like his mother before him, Furlong Baldwin means it.

NOTES

1. Furlong Baldwin fourth interview with Elaine Eff, September 28, 2007.
2. Dick McIntosh interview with George McDaniel, February 12, 2020.
3. Dick McIntosh interview with George McDaniel, February 12, 2020; *Virginian-Pilot* (Norfolk), July 10, 1914, 11.
4. Dick McIntosh interview with George McDaniel, February 12, 2020.
5. Furlong Baldwin second walking tour with Elaine Eff, September 28, 2007.
6. Furlong Baldwin fourth interview with Elaine Eff, September 28, 2007.
7. Furlong Baldwin fourth interview with Elaine Eff, September 28, 2007; Furlong Baldwin second walking tour with Elaine Eff, September 28, 2007.
8. Furlong Baldwin fourth interview with Elaine Eff, September 28, 2007; Furlong Baldwin second walking tour with Elaine Eff, September 28, 2007.
9. Furlong Baldwin fourth interview with Elaine Eff, September 28, 2007; Furlong Baldwin second walking tour with Elaine Eff, September 28, 2007.
10. Furlong Baldwin second walking tour with Elaine Eff, September 28, 2007; Furlong Baldwin fifth interview with Elaine Eff, September 28, 2007.
11. Furlong Baldwin fourth interview with Elaine Eff, September 28, 2007.
12. Furlong Baldwin fifth interview with Elaine Eff, September 28, 2007.
13. Furlong Baldwin fifth interview with Elaine Eff, September 28, 2007.
14. Furlong Baldwin interview with George McDaniel, May 11, 2019.
15. Furlong Baldwin interview with George McDaniel, May 11, 2019.
16. Furlong Baldwin fourth interview with Elaine Eff, September 28, 2007.
17. Furlong Baldwin fourth interview with Elaine Eff, September 28, 2007.
18. Furlong Baldwin fourth interview with Elaine Eff, September 28, 2007.
19. Furlong Baldwin fourth interview with Elaine Eff, September 28, 2007.
20. Bryan Stevenson, *Just Mercy: A Story of Justice and Redemption* (New York: One World Press, 2015), 50.
21. Furlong Baldwin second part of second interview with George McDaniel, May 13, 2019.
22. Joyce Curtis Ramassar interview with George McDaniel, July 30, 2019.
23. Joyce Curtis Ramassar interview with George McDaniel, July 30, 2019; Mary Peacock obituary, *Washington Post*, September 13, 2015.
24. Joyce Curtis Ramassar interview with George McDaniel, July 30, 2019.
25. Joyce Curtis Ramassar interview with George McDaniel, July 30, 2019.
26. Joyce Curtis Ramassar interview with George McDaniel, July 30, 2019; Furlong Baldwin third part of second interview with George McDaniel, May 13, 2019.
27. Robert Curtis, Jr., Paulette Curtis, and Helen Burton first interview with George McDaniel, May 12, 2019.
28. Anthony Foeman second interview with George McDaniel, May 12, 2019.
29. Anthony Foeman second interview with George McDaniel, May 12, 2019.
30. Joyce Curtis Ramassar interview with George McDaniel, July 30, 2019.
31. Robert Curtis, Jr., Paulette Curtis, and Helen Burton interview with George McDaniel, May 12, 2019.
32. Robert Curtis, Jr., Paulette Curtis, and Helen Burton interview with George McDaniel, May 12, 2019.
33. Robert Curtis, Jr., Paulette Curtis, and Helen Burton interview with George McDaniel, May 12, 2019.
34. Dick McIntosh interview with George McDaniel, February 12, 2020.
35. Eyre Baldwin interview with George McDaniel, May 13, 2019.
36. Molly Baldwin second interview with George McDaniel, July 31, 2019.
37. Furlong Baldwin first part of second interview with George McDaniel, May 13, 2019.
38. Furlong Baldwin first part of second interview with George McDaniel, May 13, 2019.

A SCRAPBOOK OF RECOLLECTIONS BY THOSE WHO CALLED EYRE HALL "HOME"

GEORGE W. McDANIEL

"What was important and what was not" is a quotation from my oral history interview with Joyce Curtis Ramassar, at least the fourth generation of an African American family who lived and worked at Eyre Hall. She was reflecting upon her childhood there and on Eyre Hall's early garden because, as a young woman, she found it a place where she could think about things and find clarity in decision-making. She was not alone in this, for the garden has meant many things to many people over the span of three centuries. It has been a place of thought, a place of play, a place of work, a place of imagination, and a place of beauty. Different people at different times have perceived it in different ways; indeed, the garden—like Eyre Hall itself and other historic sites—carries myriad meanings, depending on one's point of view.[1]

In addition to documents, objects, and even buildings and landscapes, there are, fortunately, oral histories in the twentieth and twenty-first centuries that provide answers to questions we wish we could have asked people of previous ages. These commentaries breathe more life into Eyre Hall and allow us to better understand multiple perspectives, like those of the garden. As Lonnie Bunch, historian and secretary of the Smithsonian Institution, has observed, this is critical because too many people of the past have been relegated to anonymity or been omitted completely, especially African Americans. By recording oral histories and using many other forms of evidence, historians may remedy that situation and give more people both personal and collective identity and voice.

This Scrapbook therefore builds on the foundation established by earlier chapters, and, by using oral histories and recent photographs, seeks to give identity to a wider range of people at Eyre Hall and to the places they knew. It adds to, rather than replaces, the picture created by other essays. These snapshots were not taken by professional photographers, but are family pictures, which descendants have kept and kindly shared with this project since they too have wanted to contribute to Eyre Hall's history. As Robert Stanton, former director of the National Park Service, pointed out, quoting African American historian Carter G. Woodson, "they won't know unless you tell them."[2] The Eyre Hall contributors wanted to share their snapshots so that readers could see the faces and demeanor of their elders and of themselves in ways that would not have been possible for their ancestors in earlier centuries.

These studies of Eyre Hall will not, of course, "wrap up" Eyre Hall's history, but it is hoped that they will open up its past and prompt more research and interpretation in the years to come by scholars, students, and family members alike. Eyre Hall is a gold mine of history, especially since its courthouse records from the seventeenth century to the present remain intact, having not been damaged by hurricanes or burned during the wars that swept the area. Though altered, its main house, as has been described, remains substantially intact, as does its garden and several outbuildings. The house is filled with historical artifacts, each with a story to tell, some told here by people who touched them. As for archaeology, nothing deeper than a plow has disturbed most of its earth, so the entire site awaits excavation in accordance with a strategic plan. Oral history informants abound, and their varied accounts show how much there is to explore. As a result, Eyre Hall stands as a living and learning laboratory for generations to come.

From Baldwin family members as well as from African Americans associated with Eyre Hall, one common sentiment expressed about Eyre Hall in the twentieth century was that it was a homeplace. Abundant stories were told to illustrate this. To test their veracity, I asked Joyce Ramassar, a straight-talking African American born on the property, how that feeling could be, since her family and relatives had labored for years in a house and on land they never owned. Without hesitation, she explained: "When my mother passed away in August 2016, I stayed here until September, taking some of her personal things back to my house. There's something that registered in my mind: my mother is buried here. She is where she wanted to be. I tried to get her to move to Florida with me, and she said, 'No. I don't want to live in Florida. This is my home.' After that, there was not a year that I did not come back home here because I considered this to be home. I would come here two or three times a year, and it always felt like home. My mother is buried here. Over there is my birthplace, a part of me. The house that my mother and father built by tearing down old boards from another house and that my uncles and aunts all worked together on is still there. We were raised in that place. No matter what happens to it, Eyre Hall will always be my homeplace. Home is not ownership of a place. Home is where the love is, where you feel loved in the house. I could live in a teepee as long as there was love—that's the most important thing, not the size of the house or the shape of the house or the look or the value. It's the people that live in the house that makes the home."[3]

Joyce and other African American descendants of those who lived and worked at Eyre Hall spoke genuinely of their life there. Amidst the wider world of racial prejudice, their elders guarded them against prejudice and taught them values of respect, hard work, dignity, and tolerance. Within their own households, they did not put up with bigotry. Pushing this issue further, I frankly asked whether she was "Uncle Tomming" me, a white interviewer. She replied: "Furlong [Baldwin, the current owner of Eyre Hall] tells me, 'One thing about you, Joyce, you are very open and don't sugarcoat anything.' Nobody can force me to say things that I do not believe in because my mother taught us: 'Don't live this fake, phony life because it will find you out. Just be truthful about things. Tell it the way it is, and you will be able to live with yourself.' Being able to live with myself is important to me. When I see people, I see them for who they are. It doesn't matter whether they are white, brown, yellow, or red. The character of the person is what matters to me, not the color of their skin."[4]

None of this is to sugarcoat the history of Eyre Hall. As Molly Baldwin explains: "There are things about Eyre Hall that are extraordinary. There are beautiful parts of its history and not beautiful parts. It's physically and geographically beautiful. The garden was and is extraordinary. While the house is extraordinary, it stands for things in the United States that are not good, that are unacceptable: the history of slavery and the history and the tragic reality of racism in our nation today. That's the complexity of Eyre Hall."[5]

"Complexity" Eyre Hall has indeed, enough to be puzzled over by scholars, students, and family members for years to come. Hence the need for the site to be preserved, studied, lived in, and opened periodically for research, education, and tours. This sharing of history is critical, for Eyre Hall is like a film that frame by frame allows us to see ourselves as Americans from our worst to our best. It thereby helps us, as Lonnie Bunch has urged, to "remember not just what we want to remember, but what we need to remember."[6]

NOTES
1. Lonnie Bunch, *A Fool's Errand: Creating the National Museum of African American History and Culture in the Age of Bush, Obama, and Trump* (Washington, D.C.: Smithsonian Books, 2019), 4–10.
2. Robert Stanton, "Curating Black America," The Marion Thompson Wright Lecture Series, Rutgers University at Newark, N.J., February 21, 2015.
3. Joyce Curtis Ramassar interview with George McDaniel, July 30, 2019.
4. Joyce Curtis Ramassar interview with George McDaniel, July 30, 2019.
5. Molly Baldwin second interview with George McDaniel, July 31, 2019.
6. Bunch, *Fool's Errand*, 4–10.

Margaret Baldwin: "An Extraordinary Lady"

Born in 1898, Margaret Eyre Taylor Baldwin was the granddaughter of Severn Eyre and, due to her mother's death in 1910, inherited her mother's half of Eyre Hall when her grandfather died in 1914. Married to Henry duPont Baldwin in 1928, they made Eyre Hall their home in the early 1930s and raised two children there, Mary and Furlong (Fig. 75).

Furlong Baldwin:

"Mother may have been the last real lady on earth by the old-fashioned definition. She didn't stand on a soapbox and give speeches. She grew up in Virginia and Baltimore, went to private schools, and was a combination of Virginia and Maryland—not that one was more enlightened than the other—in her actions and wonderful voice. She would sit up straight and was elegant-looking, and though I'm prejudiced, I'm not the only person who said that. Her charm was that she was non-judgmental. She was unbelievable! Someone would say something critical about someone, and Mother would say, 'Well, they didn't do anything to me,' and ended the conversation.

"Due to his alcoholism, my mother and father separated in 1962, and, for the rest of their lives, lived apart. Mother loved my friends and my children's friends. Three or four times in the summer, we would have eight or nine people here, and Mother sat at the dining table and presided. That was the best thing that ever happened to us. It was Mother who was the hostess, and Mother who did this, that, and the other. She was an extraordinary lady. Gossip wasn't her thing. I remember when Blacks first started going to the Episcopal Church, all the members of her bridge club in Baltimore, started in 1917, were saying, 'Oh, dreadful, dreadful, dreadful!' Mother simply said, "How can you be a strong church person and have a reaction to that?" Controversy wasn't her thing. 'You're a Christian. How can you object?'"[1]

As Baldwin explained, "Here on the Eastern Shore, my parents did have some friends. My father had a sailboat, so sometimes we would go across the Bay and visit somebody, but the network was here. They would have guests for dinner and play bridge, but there was not much social life. It was all connected to Christ Church, the Episcopal Church in Eastville. I don't think they knew any Baptists.

Fig. 75. Christmas at Eyre Hall, 1936. Left to right: Lucille Dandalet, Polly Baldwin, Furlong Baldwin, age 4, Mary Baldwin, age 7, Henry Baldwin, and Margaret Taylor Baldwin.

"Mother gave up a lot of things so my sister and I could go to school wherever we wanted to. I remember going to her and saying I really wanted to go to Princeton, and she said, 'Well, all right.' Whether that meant she didn't paint a room or get a new dress, I'll never know. She just said, 'All right.' She was something else.

"She was a loner. When her relationship with my father became really bad, she would come down here in the summer and stay by herself. In her sixties, we would get Daisy Foeman, her maid at Eyre Hall, to spend the night with her. I'd visit weekends, and she was perfectly happy. She was home. We had no concerns about security, being so far in the country. I still leave my keys in the car, so I don't lose them. Someone will say, 'Can I borrow your truck? Where are the keys?' 'In the ignition.'[2]

"When my mother broke her hip and had surgery in the hospital in Baltimore, I came to see her that evening. My son Eyre and his best friend were up in the bed with her, so much did they love her. They called her 'Mama B.' His friends loved her. She loved them. It was that non-judgmental thing. She was an independent, gentle soul. She lived here in the summer, and after I got divorced in 1973, I started coming down every single weekend. I'd see a light on when I got here, and she would be reading or be in bed by then. She'd been perfectly happy during the week. She might get a friend to come. Dealing with people, I never heard her raise her voice. She was the last lady. Just a lovely voice, slightly Virginian, soft."[3]

Joyce Ramassar:

According to Joyce Ramassar, who grew up at Eyre Hall, daughter of Georgia Foeman Curtis and granddaughter of Pinky Foeman, "Ms. Baldwin was a graceful lady. You would not have a reason to say a mean word to her. She was the sweetest lady, a beautiful lady, and was very respectful. What do I remember about her? I used to come and help her when she would get dressed up to have dinner. One day she asked me to help her fasten the back of her bra. While I was trying to hook it, she said, 'I can see you back there laughing.' And I was.

"She gave me a special gift. When she came back from Baltimore one weekend, she had this bra that had an underwire in it. She said, 'You're going to need to wear this type of bra.' She had bought me one. I'll never forget that.

"She was a real lady, and I don't know anybody on this farm that wouldn't say the same thing. Nobody had bad words to say about her. My mother Georgia truly loved her, and even went to Baltimore and took care of her when she was sick. Mrs. Baldwin had a very special attachment to my mother. She had a way of treating everybody like they were people, and that's why I couldn't get in my head when I found out that this place had been a plantation, because we didn't grow up with that idea. With a plantation, you think about materialistic things, but we were not materialistic. We were happy with what we had, and we were a happy bunch of children on this farm."[4]

Dick McIntosh:

A cousin and frequent visitor to Eyre Hall, Dick McIntosh remembers, "Our family used to call her 'Cousin Marg' since we were closely related (see Fig. 75). She taught me a lot about Eyre Hall because, as a youth, I used to drive down with her, and she'd relate its history. Once there, she'd tell me who this was, and that was. She was sophisticated enough to know that the contents were 'good,' and we knew they represented the materialistic side of the family's history, but no one went on and on about it.

"This was a time before a lot of research had been done into the architecture of the house and its antiques. One day a group of interns arrived from Colonial Williamsburg, surveying wood graining and marbleizing. Cousin Marg told them Eyre Hall didn't have any, but welcomed them inside to look around. To her amusement, they found almost every baseboard was marbleized, the back side of every closet door wood grained.

"Another example was when my mother and Cousin Marg were touring Georgian plantation houses on the James River. As the guides were pointing out this distinctive feature or that, Cousin Marg, to the surprise of the guides, could be heard to say in her matter-of-fact, Virginia way, 'Oh, we have that at Eyre Hall,' or 'That reminds me of Eyre Hall.' She was simply comparing that house to her own and leaving many wondering what and where was this place called 'Eyre Hall.'

"She was never swollen with pride about Eyre Hall. 'This is just the way it is,' was her attitude. She knew the contents were good, but never thought of it as a museum. It was never, 'Don't touch that.' I remember the barrel organ in the front hall fascinated me as a child. I didn't know how rare it was and used to play it again and again until I broke the handle. Cousin Marg was dismayed but didn't react as if I'd destroyed a crown jewel. She simply took the handle and had it fixed.

"She was also a fine conversationalist. When her daughter Mary and son Furlong would bring friends down, she loved to entertain them and had a good sense of humor."[5]

Robert Curtis, Jr. and Paulette Curtis:

Robert Curtis, Jr., son of Robert and Georgia Curtis, Sr., and his cousin Helen Burton, daughter of Ben Foeman, were both grandchildren of Pinky Foeman and grew up at Eyre Hall. Paulette Curtis, Robert's wife, grew up in New Jersey. As adults, all lived near Eyre Hall and continued to work there occasionally. Paulette recalled, "When Ms. Baldwin died,

we attended her funeral at Eyre Hall. It wasn't that many people—just some of her church people around in Eastville and her family and my mother- and father-in-law, Georgia and Robert Curtis. They had her laid away really nice. Now I hadn't really gotten to know her, but I remember when she would come down from Baltimore, she would have a little doggy, Honeybunch, in the car."

As Robert remembers, Margaret Baldwin "was a very nice lady towards me when I was young. One night I stayed with her because my aunt Daisy, who often stayed in the house when she was alone, was sick. I had to stay all night and was no more than 12. She was strong-minded. I see where Furlong takes after her because she was very straight. She managed things, handled business, and knew what needed to be done to take care of the farm, the house, and all the situations."

According to Paulette, "I can remember when they would have dinner parties, and my mother-in-law Georgia Curtis and her sister Daisy Foeman would be in the kitchen cooking. I can still hear Mrs. Baldwin when they needed some more food, ringing this little bell. When I cleaned the silver and brass at Eyre Hall, I cleaned that little bell, and when I hear its sound, I think of Mrs. Baldwin. I think too of Daisy, who would have her little apron and little hat on and go see what Mrs. Baldwin needed in the dining room."[6]

Eyre Baldwin:

Born in 1962, Eyre Baldwin, the son of Furlong Baldwin, loved his grandmother deeply. Part of that stemmed from his firm belief that his "grandmother was completely unjudgmental, and that was the beauty of this home and this farm, of the people who lived and worked here. We were friends. There was respect. I don't know how she came by that. It may have been her Christian values. If that's what her Book said, that's how she lived her life. That's why many people liked Eyre Hall. It was an easy, warm place to be."[7]

NOTES

1. Furlong Baldwin interview with George McDaniel, May 11, 2019.
2. Furlong Baldwin fifth part of second interview with George McDaniel, May 13, 2019.
3. Furlong Baldwin fourth part of second interview with George McDaniel, May 13, 2019.
4. Joyce Ramassar interview with George McDaniel, July 30, 2019.
5. Dick McIntosh interview with George McDaniel, February 12, 2020.
6. Robert Curtis, Jr. second interview with George McDaniel, May 12, 2019.
7. Eyre Baldwin interview with George McDaniel, May 13, 2019.

Pinky Bagwell Foeman: "The Strongest Woman I Ever Knew"

Born in 1888, Pinky Bagwell Foeman was the daughter of Isaac Bagwell, born ca. 1851, and Fannie Upshur Bagwell, born ca. 1859, who were married in 1875 (see Fig. 70). She was the seventh of ten children. While the U.S. Censuses of 1880 and 1900 record their birthplace as Virginia, their status before 1860 and whether they were at Eyre Hall or its vicinity are not known. Since many family records and photographs were destroyed when her house burned down, her family's roots require further investigation. After the Baldwins came to Eyre Hall, Pinky and two of her siblings, her older brother Lawrence and youngest sister Lizzie, came to live at Eyre Hall. Replacing William Frazier, who died in 1945, Pinky became the cook at Eyre Hall. She and her husband, William Foeman, who according to family lore was a seaman from Barbados, were married in 1908 and had nine children (Fig. 76). Four stayed at Eyre Hall: Georgia and Daisy working in the main house, and Dorsey and Ben on the farm and in the garden.[1]

Pinky was a force to be reckoned with. Her religious faith and sense of integrity were rock solid, giving her an inner strength that permeated everything she did, enabling her to face unflinchingly the ups and downs of life as well as her own death. She set high standards for herself, her family, and those with whom she worked. Among her high standards were those for good food, because according to all accounts—ranging from the Baldwins to her children and grandchildren—she was an outstanding cook. She made everything from scratch, and, although she could read, she used no cookbook or recipes, memorizing the preparation of each dish. At the Baldwins and at home, she cooked over a wood stove with minimal controls. Since she intuitively added a "pinch of this and a pinch of that," her senses of taste, smell, hearing, touch, and sight must have rivalled those of any celebrity chef. While Pinky was an artist in the kitchen, she was more. She stood for time-tested values and passed those on to her descendants and others, who carry them with them today, as these recollections attest.

Joyce Ramassar:

Georgia Foeman Curtis's daughter Joyce Ramassar was a granddaughter who loved Pinky deeply and recalled that her grandchildren called Pinky "Big Mama." According to Joyce, "From what I was told, Pinky's mother came here from New Orleans, and her mother was from Mali, which I found out through Ancestry. com. My grandmother never said where she was born, nor did my Aunt Katie, Aunt Elizabeth, or Uncle Lawrence, or how they got here. They never talked about that, so I really don't know. Pinky's mother's mother spoke French, and I assume that's because she came from a French-speaking place. Pinky told me her mother was French Creole.

"They were distinguished-looking people because my Uncle Lawrence, Aunt Lizzie, and Pinky had gray eyes with a bluish tint. My grandmother was a dark-skinned lady and had beautiful eyes that were between gray and blue. In her house Pinky had a big oval picture of her mother, and when that house burned down with that picture and valuable documents like Bibles and birth certificates, it brought my mother to tears. I always talked with my mother about that beautiful picture, the only one I ever saw of her grandmother. She was the most stunningly beautiful woman. She had this long brown hair that came down to her waist.

"Even though she didn't attend church often, Pinky was a very religious person, reading the Bible all the time and picking verses from the Scriptures, which she would quote whenever teaching about life. She went to her husband's church, the African Baptist Church in Cheriton. He was William Foeman and a deacon in the church, in whose graveyard both he and Pinky are buried. He too was very religious, loved his children, and was strict. They had four boys and four girls, and you did not defy him. My mother said he was a very good papa.

"He didn't have a lot of friends because he had an accent since his home was in Barbados. My mom said he was not talkative to strangers. He never worked at Eyre Hall. In fact, my grandmother met him in Baltimore when she was living with her sister and he was working as a seaman. He would go back to sea, and they finally started to talk, and got together over time, and married in 1908 in

Northampton County. All the sons of William Foeman and Pinky were Foemans because the father's name was Foeman, and Foeman is not spelled the way they spell it here in America. It's F-o-e-m-a-n. That's how I found out that my grandfather was from Barbados. There's 'Foemans' from Barbados, and there's 'Formans' in America.[2]

"Pinky believed there was a heaven and a hell and said that when you come to your last day in life, you better make a choice because you are either going one place or the other. She said that's what the Bible says, and if the Bible says it, so be it. You're not going to live a perfect life, but you have to make sure that you get forgiven because when you pass out of this world, you are going one place or the other. Make sure your soul is right with God. She always taught us that."[3]

As Joyce recalled, "Pinky was the best cook. Many times I would sit in the kitchen at Eyre Hall and watch her and learn. She'd always break off something and give it to me. She had a hearty laugh and was a joy to be with. She was very neat, always particular about how she dressed and looked—a lovely lady, the light of my life until she died. Some grandchildren said she spoiled me. When I was born, I only weighed 2 pounds, 9 ounces, so Pinky told my parents, 'Let me take care of her.' She used to make my baby food, strain it through cheesecloth, and put it in jars. By the time I was about three years old, Mother said you would never have known I weighed 2 pounds, 9 ounces (Fig. 77).

"Pinky was a straightforward, honest lady. She said what she meant and she meant what she said. She demanded respect from not just her grandchildren or her children but from everybody. I remember just about everybody that came in contact with her always called her Miss Pinky. I know that wasn't the norm, but I know when the insurance man came, he would always ask me for Miss Pinky.

"Pinky taught us to respect people as you would want them to respect you. She was strict. Her laughter was one thing, while her voice had a growl. When she spoke, she was commanding. To everybody, including her adult children, when she had something to say, she said it. She did not mince words at all. She was a no-nonsense person. You could either like it or not, but she was straight up. If you did not want to hear her opinion, it was best not to ask. She was exactly the same with everyone.

"For fun and on holidays, everybody got together, and Pinky did all the cooking with help from my mom and aunt. She had a big phonograph, the wind-up type, and used to play a lot of records on it, both religious and secular. She had a lot of jazz music and religious music. Where she got them, I don't know, but she had a huge collection and enjoyed listening to it.

"She and Mrs. Baldwin got along great. In fact, she used to come and spend the night in the big house because it got to a point when her husband wasn't here, Mrs. Baldwin was by herself. I used to walk with my grandmother, and we would sit on the steps. Mrs. Baldwin would drive down from Baltimore, and when she got here, she would take me home, and my grandmother would stay at the house with Mrs. Baldwin until morning.

"I can't remember her having fear of anything, even up to the time she died. I was 11 and remember she went into a coma. They took her to the hospital and she never came out of it. I remember going to see her. She had complete peace on her face. She was the strongest woman I ever knew."[4]

NOTES

1. The Northampton County, Virginia, marriage records note that on August 18, 1875. Isaac Bagwell, a Black male, age 25, married Fanny Upshur, a single, Black female, age 20. Isaac was born in 1851 in Northampton County, Virginia. His father was named Isaac and his mother was named Grace. Fanny was also born in Northampton County. Her father was Caleb Upshur and mother Sarah Bayly. The tenth U.S. Census Population Schedule for 1880 lists Isaac and Fanny living in the Eastville District of Northampton County. Isaac's occupation is given as coachman. By this time, they had three children: Grace 4, Sumner 2, and Charles 1. The 12th U.S. Census Population Schedule for 1900 tracks the growth of the family who were still living in the Eastville District. Isaac's occupation is listed as butler. Children still at home included daughter Sammie 18, Lawrence 16, Frank 14, Pinky 10, Maggie 9, Katie 3, and Lizzie 1.

2. Joyce Ramassar interview with George McDaniel, July 30, 2019. According to the Northampton County marriage records, William Foeman married Pinky Bagwell on October 14, 1908. The 15th U.S. Census Population Schedule for 1930 records William and Pinky Foeman living with eight of their nine children (Bertha, the eldest, had either married or moved away) in the Capeville District of Northampton County. They apparently did not move to Eyre Hall until the mid- to late 1930s at the earliest.

3. Joyce Ramassar and Louise Hayman interview with George McDaniel, July 30, 2019.

4. Joyce Ramassar interview with George McDaniel, July 30, 2019.

Georgia Foeman Curtis: "Power of Example"

Born in 1929, the daughter of Pinky and William Foeman, Georgia Foeman Curtis lived her entire life at Eyre Hall, working as a cook and housekeeper and dying in 2016. Urged in her old age to join her daughter in Florida, she refused, saying that Eyre Hall, despite everything, was home. She married Robert Curtis, Sr., who worked at the U.S. Navy base in Norfolk. From the mountains of North Carolina, he was of mixed African American, Scottish, and Native American heritage. They raised their children at Eyre Hall. Like her mother, she was a person of strong values, spoke her mind about prejudice and phoniness, loved her children, and was close to them, especially as they matured. Her home was a welcoming place for her family and friends, though there was no doubt as to who was in charge.

Georgia is remembered for performing many tasks and doing them well. She believed in education and in helping others, including teaching people to read. She felt called to help others, in response no doubt to her deeply felt religious beliefs, instilled by her parents. As her children attest, that calling encompassed not just her home and church, but her community. It also extended to Margaret Baldwin, and in immeasurable ways Georgia helped her as age took its toll, including going to Baltimore to care for her. According to both Furlong Baldwin and Georgia's children, the two clearly grew to love one another. To many today, a cross-racial relationship of that type may seem hard to believe, but, over the course of their lifetime at Eyre Hall, the two ladies had come to know one another well and had worked it out. Their relationship is an illuminating detail, but only one in the larger portrait of Georgia Curtis, a portrait more completely painted by the following stories from different people who knew and respected her and perhaps a portrait evocative of other African American women who sought to make a way out of no way.[1]

Dick McIntosh:

An Eyre descendant who visited Eyre Hall frequently, Dick McIntosh paints a clear detail in the larger portrait of Georgia Curtis. As he recalls, "Georgia was extraordinary. She was beautiful, tall, bright, and no matter the occasion, elegant (Fig. 78). In 1998, when my daughter got married at Eyre Hall, there were just a few people invited, mostly

Fig. 76. Pinky Foeman at Eyre Hall.

family. I'd forgotten we hadn't invited Georgia, so I sent word for her to please come. A short while later she arrived, elegant and wearing a hat at just the perfect angle. As one admiring Eyre family member remarked, 'That's what happens when you give Georgia as much as 10 minutes to get dressed.'

"She was extremely loyal to Eyre Hall. The tragedy perhaps is that despite her gifts, because of race, she was not positioned to go further."[2]

Robert Curtis, Jr.:

The son of Georgia Curtis, Robert Curtis, Jr., adds to the portrait by sketching both his parents and Georgia's talents and values. "My parents, Robert and Georgia Curtis, lived in a house maybe not even a quarter of a mile from Furlong's house. I could walk from my house to his in about five minutes. My father came from North Carolina. My mother met him maybe at a party or picnic, and then he started coming down to Eyre Hall, and they started dating together like that. That's how it was. He worked at Eyre Hall for a very short time, maybe no more than about six months or a year, and then he went across to Norfolk and got a job there at the naval base. He would come home on the weekends.

"My mother was very much a lady. She was talented. She could cook, she could paint, she could draw, whatever. She also helped everybody out. When she got a car, she would stop at everybody's houses, ask if

Fig. 77. Georgia Foeman Curtis and Robert Curtis and their daughter Joyce, ca. 1948.

Fig. 78. Georgia Curtis, left, her sister Daisy, center, and their aunt Lizzie Bagwell Press, right.

Fig. 79. The Curtis family. Left to right: daughter Joyce Curtis Ramassar, Robert Curtis Sr., Georgia Foeman Curtis, and Robert Curtis, Jr.

they wanted to go to the stores. She was also quick to catch on to anything, and after my grandmother Pinky died she took over the cooking. Mother always did her jobs right, and though she could do stuff like the brass and silver real good, she didn't want to because there was so much of it. If she did it, she knew she was going to have to do it right, but she was doing so many other things in the big house and in her own."[3]

Joyce Curtis Ramassar:
The daughter of Georgia and Robert Curtis, Joyce contributes to the portrait by recalling how Georgia, as a mother and as a person, believed in and acted on the values of her elders, especially her mother Pinky. Of special importance was their mixed racial heritage, which Georgia saw as a firm reason for why prejudice against skin color should have "no room in your life." By telling us of the many facets of Georgia's life, Joyce's sketches enable us to see Georgia as a more complete person.

"My mother shaped my life because she was much like her mother, Pinky Foeman (Fig. 79). She raised her children to respect everybody. When we were children, there's one thing that she taught us: 'Prejudice, you have no room for it in your life,' explaining that 'you have a father who was raised by his Scottish grandfather, and your dad's grandmother is from the Cherokee Reservation in North Carolina. If you have prejudice, you're going to be arguing with yourself. No matter whether you like it or not, you can't remove the blood that runs through your veins.' She taught us: 'Respect people for who they are.' If you run into somebody that you think you cannot get along with, avoid them. You cannot curse. Or use foul language. In her house you could not say even the little words we didn't even consider to be curse words.

"My mother was a brilliant woman and did a lot of work for people who could not read and even worked with one of the societies that taught people to read. She did taxes for people that couldn't understand them and wouldn't charge them. If anybody had legal papers they didn't understand, they would come to her. Sometimes I would say, 'Mom, why do you do all of this stuff, and you don't charge them?' She said, 'It's not about charging people for everything in life. You don't depend on people to give you rewards. You get them from God Himself. I don't worry about that type of thing.' She also taught us: 'Get your education.' As much as my mother hated to see us children go, she never would hold us back, telling us: 'I would rather see you fulfill your dreams in life than stay here and not.' There was no talking back at her house. Once she said something, that was it. You didn't question it.

"Until I became an adult and married, I did not get along with my mother because I had my own ideas about life and she had hers. When I had matured enough to have a good relationship with her, I would come home every year, and we would talk for hours. She would tell me so many things, and that is when I started to understand who my mother was. As teenagers, we are a little rebellious, but I'm glad that she was there to give me instructions. She was a person that you could talk to because she would listen to you talk. She would give you a chance to say what you had to say and then give you her opinion. She would tell you: 'Don't ask my opinion if you don't want to hear what I have to say.' She was very strict about that.

"When Mrs. Baldwin became elderly and ill, Mother left Eyre Hall and went to Baltimore to take care of her. My mother truly loved Mrs. Baldwin, and Mrs. Baldwin loved Mother.

"I loved my mother and my father. When my father passed away, I thought that was the most hurtful thing that ever happened, but when Mother passed away, there was no comparison to the grief I felt. I loved my father but my mother, I miss her still: her presence, her voice, the conversations, and her cooking. When she passed away in August, I stayed here here until September, taking some of her personal things back to my house, and something registered in my mind. My mother is buried here. She is where she wanted to be. I tried to get her to move to Florida with me. She said, 'No. I don't want to live in Florida. This is my home.'"[4]

Molly Baldwin:

Furlong Baldwin's daughter Molly lives in Baltimore and is an active leader in social justice, with a special focus on prison reform and immigrant rights. She reflects on Georgia as a person and on the influence Georgia had on her. "In looking back on my youth, I think of the impact particularly of Georgie, as I used to call her. It's funny because when I was little, it wasn't that she sat me on a stool and told me things. It was her power of example. Until she died, we had what I believe was an extraordinary and, for me, a very special relationship. When I used to go see her, I spent a lot of time talking to her about the world and what was fair.

"That gift is extraordinary, and it came to me from all those things at Eyre Hall. I think that sets the foundation of how I approach my work and life. I can't remember as a kid what Georgie and I talked about. I remember following her around, sitting in the kitchen at Eyre Hall, and how Daisy used to sing songs over and over. We also used to sing a song about Daisy with Daisy. I have a terrible voice. I don't know how Georgie put up with it.

"As I became an adult, I would talk to Georgie about the world, about justice, about racism. She clearly understood we lived in a racist world, but believed in humanity and in justice. She had a picture of Martin Luther King in her living room, and where I sat, I always looked at that picture. She knew about the work I did, so we would talk about that. She would listen, and that was an extraordinary gift.

"When I was pretty young, I think Georgie understood I had a calling. I just started working with young people. I couldn't figure out what else I could do. As a kid, I don't know I understood that. In a way it gave me a confidence that other people don't have and enabled me to use that calling responsibly, not because I felt guilty or thought it was a nice thing to do, but because I couldn't help myself. It took my father and me a long time to come to peace with our differences, but he's really been supportive. Between opportunity and sense of self, I just had enough of whatever to be able to follow a calling. I'm blessed in many ways because I've been able to see the world from all different perspectives. I can't be other than who I am, but somewhere I think I learned about empathy and passion. Georgie was the one who understood.

"Why didn't Georgie leave Eyre Hall and the Eastern Shore? That's a good question. For her, it was clear: Eyre Hall was home. She loved it. She grew up there. She lived there. She raised her children there, and it was her home. There wasn't even a discussion. A few weeks before she died, I went to see her at the nursing home. I felt really lucky. While she might get confused, she knew who I was. She looked at me and said, 'I just want to go home.' I remember her looking at me, going, 'I just want to go home.' That's the complexity of Eyre Hall."[5]

NOTES
1. Molly Baldwin second interview with George McDaniel, July 31, 2019.
2. Dick McIntosh interview with George McDaniel, February 12, 2020.
3. Robert Curtis, Jr., Paulette Curtis, and Helen Burton first interview with George McDaniel, May 12, 2019.
4. Joyce Curtis Ramassar interview with George McDaniel, July 30, 2019.
5. Molly Baldwin second interview with George McDaniel, July 31, 2019.

Different People: "Stay on the High Ground"

The First Generation of Owners, Managers, and Workers at Eyre Hall

After Severn Eyre died in 1914, there were no year-round residents in the main house at Eyre Hall for almost 15 years. As noted earlier, Eyre Hall had been inherited by Severn's daughter Mary Eyre Wright and his granddaughter Margaret Eyre Taylor and was managed by Mary Wright's husband, William Henry DeCourcy Wright, who lived in Baltimore. Not until the estate was divided between the two heirs and Margaret had married Henry duPont Baldwin in 1928 did Eyre Hall become a permanent home again.[1]

Margaret Baldwin and her husband renovated the house and tried to make a living from the estate. By the late 1930s, Lawrence Bagwell, the brother of Pinky Bagwell Foeman, worked as foreman, and, as that generation aged, a second generation assumed responsibility in a gradual and uneven sequence, all the while learning from the values and skills of their predecessors. The following is an account of individuals, not previously sketched, who were closely associated with Eyre Hall from the 1930s through the end of the twentieth century.

Henry duPont Baldwin (1898–1974) was an MIT engineering graduate, related to the well-known duPont family of Delaware. He met his wife Margaret Eyre Taylor in Baltimore, where she was living at the time. When he and Margaret modernized the old house in the 1930s and made other improvements to the estate, he ensured good architects were hired and reliable infrastructure installed. He loved to sail and passed on his skills to his son Furlong and daughter Mary. Though never divorced, he and his wife separated in 1962.[2]

Lawrence Bagwell (ca. 1883–1959) was the son of Isaac and Fannie Upshur Bagwell, who were born in 1851 and 1859 respectively, presumably in Northampton County. Although the exact year of his birth is unknown, census reports illuminate the arc of his life. For example, the 1900 census shows Lawrence, age 15, as living with his parents and working as an "oysterman" with his younger brother Frank, age 14, also identified as an "oysterman," while his sister "Pinky," age 11, was "at school." The 1910 census identifies him as a "Farmer," age 22, living with his mother Fannie, age 48, a widow,

employed as a "Cook" for an unidentified "Private Family." It shows that, by age 22, Lawrence had assumed responsibility as "head of the household." In the late 1910s, Lawrence worked as a farm laborer for William L. Rippon, a truck farmer. The 1920 census identified him, age 34, as a "Laborer" on a "Farm" with two sisters, four nieces, and two nephews living with him. In 1923, at age 37, he married Ella Virginia Booker. The 1930 census showed him living by himself (his wife Ella Virginia Booker having predeceased him) on Eyre Hall Road as a "General Farmer," while another 1930 census described him as a "Truck Farmer." His 1959 death certificate listed his occupation as "laborer, landscape gardener" and his cause of death as "heart disease." He was buried in the African Baptist Church Cemetery in Cheriton near Eyre Hall.[3]

Living along "Eyre Hall Road" in 1930, Lawrence may have come to work at Eyre Hall in the 1920s and rose to be the foreman of Eyre Hall farm perhaps in the 1930s, and definitely by the 1940s. He held the position until his death in 1959, when he was succeeded by his nephew, Dorsey Foeman, whom he had trained. As his grandniece Joyce Ramassar recalls, "Uncle Lawrence kept everything going when nobody else was here. The Baldwins knew they didn't have to worry, because Uncle Lawrence and Uncle Dorsey were very dedicated. They were good at what they did, and the Baldwins had a lot of respect for the work they did (Fig. 80)."[4]

The story by Furlong Baldwin about how Lawrence got his name suggests that Lawrence's parents were connected to Eyre Hall, at least by the early 1880s. Furlong's maternal grandmother, Grace Eyre Taylor (1872–1910), was said to be "a great favorite" among the African Americans at Eyre Hall. When Fannie Upshur Bagwell had a son in 1883, she brought him in her arms to Grace and said, "Name this child." Grace thought and thought; at age 11, the only men she knew were her father Severn and her brother Littleton, but she was reading *Little Women*, one of whose main characters was Theodore 'Laurie' Laurence. "That's where Lawrence got his name, from Laurie in *Little Women*."[5]

Dick McIntosh recalls that Lawrence Bagwell was farm manager and lived in the old brick overseer's house built in 1798. "Lawrence was debonair. I remember him riding the big mower to

Fig. 80. Lawrence Bagwell, long-time farm manager of Eyre Hall.

Fig. 81. Dorsey Foeman succeeded Lawrence Bagwell as manager of the Eyre Hall farm.

Fig. 82. Ben Foeman, Dorsey's younger brother, worked in the garden and as a farm manager at Eyre Hall.

cut grass, pulled by a pair of mules. Lawrence stood upright on the mower, managing the mules with the reins, bare footed, wearing leather riding leggings and puttees my grandfather had given him. He had style."

Bagwell was a well-known figure in Northampton County. As McIntosh recounts, "Everybody in the county knew him. When my mother was a girl, she'd been invited to a party and went to a shop in Cape Charles because she needed a dress. Having no cash with her and buying on credit, she was asked, "Who will vouch for you?" She answered, 'Lawrence Bagwell.' Responded the shop owner, 'That's fine.'"[6]

The Second Generation of Owners, Managers, and Workers

Dorsey Foeman (1915–2001), the third son of William and Pinky Bagwell Foeman, learned from his uncle and assumed the role of foreman of Eyre Hall upon Lawrence's death in 1959 (Fig. 81). Dick McIntosh said, "Dorsey Foeman was the strongest person I ever saw. He was good-looking, but, unlike his uncle, was not so much a ladies' man and stayed close to his family and Eyre Hall." According

to his nephew Robert Curtis, Jr., Uncle Dorsey was "real good in gardening." He could plant anything from watermelons to corn. "Anything you would look at, he could grow in his garden."[7]

Dorsey Foeman helped raise Furlong along with his own grandson Anthony Foeman, instilling in both important values and skills. As Anthony remembers, "My grandfather was the one that practically raised Furlong. That's what he used to tell me. Much of what Furlong learned probably came from my grandfather, by him coming home on weekends and talking to my grandfather. He taught Furlong how to start chainsaws and work equipment and how to go fishing. He taught him how to not always argue about things that weren't worth it. My grandfather would say, 'Don't worry if something falls through. You can pick it up and make it on the next round.' Things like that. 'You respect others like you want to be respected.' I guess he taught him to be a better man. My grandfather taught me about the values of life and how to respect and that, if something happens, don't worry about it, 'You can always overcome the bad doings.' My grandfather is probably the reason that I work so hard today.

"He worked full time at Eyre Hall while his wife Fanny worked at the Holly Farms chicken-processing plant, now Tyson's. He'd cut

Fig. 83. Daisy Foeman and her younger sister Georgia Curtis on the left.

firewood, plant the vegetable garden for Mr. Furlong, and run errands for them. My grandfather taught me that when you weed a garden, you don't take the hoe and just chop the top of the grass off. You have to get the root. If you don't get the root, when you go back out days later, the weed will be coming back. That's a lesson in life. When cutting the grass with a mower, he taught me to make sure you don't cut your foot. Stay away from the cutter blade, and if it clogs up, cut it off before you get underneath and take the grass out. He taught me how to prune a tree by cutting the limb back to the solid piece of the tree. That way you don't have a bare nub hanging out. Inside the house, he taught me how to wax the floors and do it right. First, the floor is dry and don't put the wax on too thick, just lightly. We put the floor wax on by hand, which was butcher's wax. After it dries, you use the electric buffer to get the excess wax off and then finish with a towel under the buffer. Applying that wax took a lot of knee work, but thanks to the finishing towel, the floors shone.

"My grandfather Dorsey's sisters, Aunt Georgia and Aunt Daisy, cleaned inside the house and did the furniture. To polish silver, my grandfather always used lukewarm water. He put the polish on a cloth, rubbed it on the silver until the cloth would turn grayish black, and that's how you know you're getting all the tarnish off. Then you rinse it with lukewarm water. If the silver had teeny beads or ridges, you gently scrubbed them with a soft toothbrush, put it in the water, and off comes the tarnish, so it looks brand new, just as silver as it should. Brass was almost the same, but you had to be careful on a door, dresser, or windowsill and not get the varnish on the wood. The knobs on doors and especially the little ones on dressers were the most difficult. My grandfather did it right, and that's what he taught me."[8]

Benjamin Foeman (1918–1992), the younger brother of Dorsey Foeman, served as farm foreman and was especially skilled in the garden (Fig. 82). As Joyce Ramassar recalls, "Uncle Ben, as we called him, helped manage Eyre Hall and was the gardener. Many of those plants he would graft. For example, Mrs. Baldwin would want him to do something special with a rose bush, so he'd take a limb off one rose bush and tie it on another one, and the rose would change so you would see new and beautiful colors. She always depended on him to do the garden because he was good at it."[9]

According to his daughter Helen Burton, "my father and Uncle Dorsey were the caretakers of Eyre Hall, cutting all the grass, doing everything in the garden, and basically anything they needed done to the big house. My dad was a good man and loved all his nine kids. He had two jobs, working at Eyre Hall during the day and at Webster's canning factory in Cheriton at night. He was dedicated to Eyre Hall and was close to Mrs. Baldwin. The Baldwins gave all of them lifetime rights there. Until a couple of years before he passed, he was still cutting wood, trimming trees, growing his own garden, and doing whatever he could to provide for his family. That wasn't easy, but he just went on and on like that. He learned how to do a whole lot of different things. For example, he loved cutting the lawn. Whenever he cut the grass, it was like nobody but him."[10]

Robert Curtis, Jr. remembered well his uncle's dedication, skills, and positive attitude. "When it snowed down there, he could clean the roads so good we could get out. For us, Uncle Ben would make a way." He marveled at Ben's gardening skills. "He could take flowers or a bush, move it fast, and plant it so quickly. Sometimes the Baldwins would ask, 'Where did you get this from? We didn't buy these from the store,' but Uncle Ben knew how to take two different-colored flowers and put them together, so they would grow together. As for how he learned about gardening, God gave him that gift."[11]

Daisy Foeman (1926–2009), the daughter of Pinky and older sister of Georgia Foeman Curtis, grew up on Eyre Hall and continued to live there, working as housekeeper and server for the Baldwins and residing with her mother (Fig. 83). She too had strong values, which she passed on to her daughter Jane Foeman Fair. Her special gift for humor was widely appreciated. As her niece Joyce Curtis Ramassar remembers, "Daisy could have been the greatest comedian you ever would have seen. I remember her sitting in a chair against the wall in the dining room, and her job was to watch people during Garden Week. Furlong, my mother, and I were in the kitchen. This lady came through. Daisy said that she said, 'Oh, you're here to watch the silver?' Daisy answered, 'No. I'm here to watch you, and make sure the silver stays here!' Furlong couldn't stop laughing. Crazy laughing. He said, 'Do you know what Daisy just told that lady?' It was true too."[12]

"Daisy was not a good cook, so they never let her touch the food, but she would serve it, help out during Garden Week, and help Mother with cleaning silver and doing housework. Furlong enjoyed my family because they would tell a lot of jokes and laugh like crazy."[13]

According to Dick McIntosh, "Daisy was very sweet and funny. She and her sister Georgia, though different, were quite a pair. As a child, I could hear them joking and laughing while they did the housework. They loved one another."[14]

Mary Eyre Baldwin Peacock (1929–2015), Furlong Baldwin's sister, worked for 30 years for the U.S. Central Intelligence Agency, before retiring and returning to Eyre Hall with her husband, David Peacock. Joyce Ramassar observed, "As far as this big house being a home [to Mary], I don't know if it was. She was very smart, very educated. After she'd grown, she was never here much. She would come down every once in a while. When Mary moved back to the farm and lived in the brick house where my uncle Lawrence had lived, she became closer to Furlong and my mom. She would come to my mother's house and talk, which was different, because when she was younger my mom didn't like her attitude.

"Her personality was different from Furlong's. He was almost like an only child because Mary was always gone, so he had a great attachment to the people that lived on the farm. Education was tops with Mary, and she was very generous because she helped my aunt Mildred's daughter get into college and paid for it. Mildred's daughter became a lawyer. Mary was a no-nonsense person."[15]

Dick McIntosh (b. 1942) is the son of Grace Wright McIntosh and a cousin of the Baldwins (see Fig. 8). Visiting Eyre Hall often as a youth, Dick loved it, and, though he has sold his share of Eyre Hall's land, he remains close to the place and to the Baldwin family. Since Dick and Joyce Ramassar are fairly close in age, she has clear memories of his visits to Eyre Hall. "One day, all the family was going sailing. My grandmother Pinky and I were here. He told a lie and said he was sick, so couldn't go. He was up in the green room. About 15 minutes after they left, he came downstairs to the kitchen where we were, and said to me, 'I really want to learn how to dance. Can you teach me how to dance?' At that time, the cha-cha was a big thing. My grandmother said, 'You're sick.' She had a heavy voice. 'You're supposed to be sick, and now you want to dance?' He said, 'Well, I was just wondering if she could teach me how to dance.' My grandmother said, 'I'll tell you what, she's not teaching you how to dance! You're going back to bed because you're sick.'

"A couple of times he would say, 'Can you just teach me a few steps of how to dance?' My grandmother knew he was persistent, and sometimes I stayed here in the big house with my grandmother until it was time to go at night. I remember one night Dick was driving us home. My grandmother lived right around the corner there, and as he was turning onto my grandmother's lane, she said, 'Where are you going?' He said, "I'm going to take you home." She said, 'Not before you take my granddaughter home.' My grandmother Pinky, she was a stickler. She was strict."[16]

Years later, as Dick recalls, at the wedding reception at Eyre Hall when Furlong's son Eyre was getting married, Joyce and he took to the dance floor. "Joyce asked, 'Do you remember? It was me who taught you how to dance.' I answered, 'I do indeed.'"[17]

Furlong Baldwin (b. 1932) became the owner of Eyre Hall after his mother's death in 1979. After graduating from Princeton and serving in the U.S. Marine Corps, he forged a career in banking, eventually retiring as CEO, president, and chairman of the Mercantile Bankshares Corporation and Mercantile-Safe Deposit & Trust Company of Maryland. An avid student of history, he has supported both educational and historical organizations such as Johns Hopkins University, the Virginia Historical Society, the Colonial Williamsburg Foundation, and the Maryland Center for History and Culture, which named its research library after him in recognition of his interest and leadership.

According to Joyce Ramassar, "Furlong was very close to my uncle Dorsey, and I used to see them sitting on Uncle Dorsey's porch, talking. He'd come to my mom's house and talk to her. Furlong and Daisy liked to get together a lot because Daisy was always kidding around and telling jokes. I think he missed out on that from his childhood. I don't think he really had a companion, somebody that he could really talk to during his childhood other than his mother. The fact that his father and mother broke up probably made a difference in his life.

"He's a very upfront person. He tells you what he thinks, and he doesn't get angry with you if you tell him what you think. He would listen and wouldn't whitewash anything. He would tell you the way it was—almost like a father would talk to you. When I would come home during the summertime, I would talk to him about my job and going forward. I talked to him about 401(k)s and stuff like that because we had a lot of investments and stuff on the job. He would give me the best advice he could. We always talked about family. He would talk about his mother. He missed his mother a great deal. Those are the types of conversations we would have."[18]

Reflecting on his legacy, Furlong Baldwin says, "I'd like to be remembered in the only way which is honorable and decent, and that is: Whatever job I had to do, I did it the best I could. I say to people, 'In warfare, the critical thing is to have the high ground. The enemy can take it away from you, but in your personal life, you are born on your high ground. Only you can lose it.' Your high ground is the moral high ground. Unlike in warfare, only you can lose your personal high ground by doing something stupid or something that's not right or just being lazy. I'd like to think I kept the high ground, which was in my power to do, and that I lived my life that way. I'd like to see that in my children, and I do. I hope someday my granddaughter will understand this. You have a lot of choices, but if you stay on the high ground, it works out. It works out."

"I've also been lucky. I was born into this situation at Eyre Hall. Why me? I don't know. I've had an interesting career. I didn't do one thing to earn the privilege of being the interim caretaker of Eyre Hall. That's all I really am. I'm now one of ten people who has been its caretaker. I'm the luckiest person I know, and I mean it. I like to think I could honorably say that I put more back in than I took out. I don't know how else to pay for that luck. End of subject."[19]

NOTES

1. Dick McIntosh interview with George McDaniel, February 12, 2020.
2. Furlong Baldwin personal communication with George McDaniel at Eyre Hall, August 1, 2019.
3. 12th U.S. Census, 1900, Northampton County, Virginia, Capeville District; 13th U.S. Census, 1910, Northampton County, Virginia, Capeville District, Bayside Road; 14th U.S. Census, 1920 Northampton County, Virginia, Capeville District; 15th U.S. Census, 1930, Northampton County, Virginia, Eastville District; World War I Draft Registration Card, September 12, 1918, Lawrence Bagwell, born September 1884, residence, Chesapeake, Northampton County, Virginia, farm laborer, employer: William. L. Rippon, truck farmer, relative Simmie Bagwell; Northampton County, Virginia, Marriage Records, September 5, 1923, Lawrence Bagwell male, Black, age 37, father: Isaac Bagwell, mother Fanny Bagwell, spouse: Ella Virginia Booker; Northampton County, Virginia, Death Certificate, October 23, 1959. Lawrence Bagwell, died Northampton County, Virginia, heart disease, father: Isaac Bagwell, mother: Fannie Upshur, spouse: Ella Virginia Booker (decd.), buried African Baptist Cemetery, Cheriton, occupation: laborer, landscape gardener, date of birth December 25, 1888, informant: Elizabeth Press, Eastville, Virginia.
4. Joyce Curtis Ramassar interview with George McDaniel, July 30, 2019.
5. Furlong Baldwin fifth interview with Elaine Eff, September 28, 2007.
6. Dick McIntosh interview with George McDaniel, February 12, 2020.
7. Dick McIntosh interview with George McDaniel, February 12, 2020; Robert Curtis, Jr., Paulette Curtis, and Helen Burton first interview with George McDaniel, May 12, 2019.
8. Anthony Foeman second interview with George McDaniel, May 12, 2019.
9. Joyce Curtis Ramassar interview with George McDaniel, July 30, 2019.
10. Robert Curtis, Jr., Paulette Curtis, and Helen Burton first interview with George McDaniel, May 12, 2019.
11. Robert Curtis, Jr., Paulette Curtis, and Helen Burton first interview with George McDaniel, May 12, 2019.
12. Joyce Curtis Ramassar interview with George McDaniel, July 30, 2019.
13. Joyce Curtis Ramassar interview with George McDaniel, July 30, 2019.
14. Dick McIntosh interview with George McDaniel, February 12, 2020.
15. Joyce Curtis Ramassar and Louise Hayman interview with George McDaniel, July 30, 2019.
16. Joyce Curtis Ramassar interview with George McDaniel, July 30, 2019.
17. Dick McIntosh interview with George McDaniel, February 12, 2020.
18. Joyce Curtis Ramassar interview with George McDaniel, July 30, 2019; Joyce Curtis Ramassar and Louise Hayman interview with George McDaniel, July 30, 2019.
19. Furlong Baldwin sixth interview with Elaine Eff, September 28, 2007.

Foodways: "She Used No Recipes"

Whether in the big house or tenant houses, what made food at Eyre Hall memorable was not so much the types of food served but rather the quality of the cooking and the feeling of togetherness that meals nurtured. The food served here also reflected both the mixture of global cultures and the continuation of traditions. Regrettably, it is not known how the talented cook Pinky Foeman learned to cook, but she probably learned from her mother, Frances Bagwell, and other relatives, cooking fare traditional to the Eastern Shore. Like many southerners, white or Black, they were not culinary adventurers and valued what was local, fresh, and homemade.[1] Family lore notes that she cooked for a famous hotel in Baltimore and won at least one award before she became the cook at Eyre Hall.

After the cook William Frazier died in 1945, Pinky Foeman assumed his job. Since her marriage to William Foeman in 1908, she had been cooking for her own family. As her grandchildren recall with pride, she cooked everything from scratch and used no recipe book. Preferring what she knew, she cooked only over a wood stove, both at Eyre Hall and in her own home. It was only after her death in 1962 that Eyre Hall "modernized" to a gas stove, which her daughter Georgia used, taking Pinky's place. Wood stoves had no dials, timers, or thermometers as modern stoves do, yet cooks like Pinky knew well how to operate them and mastered the culinary art.

In all of the recorded recollections of Eyre Hall, no cookbooks or recipes are credited. Instead, Margaret Baldwin and her son Furlong celebrated the skills of cooks William Frazier, Pinky Foeman, and Georgia Curtis, who had learned the art from their elders and probably by experimenting on their own. Attuning all their senses, they assessed how the food should look, smell, taste, feel, or even sound both as they were preparing the dish and when it was finished. No doubt they would have agreed with Brendan Walsh, dean at the Culinary Institute of America, who believed that a great home cook is one who "puts all the senses on high alert." They probably would have also agreed with the master chef Jacques Pépin, who explained that to be a great cook one must not only love to cook but love to eat—indeed, we know that Pinky and her daughter Georgia both enjoyed the pleasure their food gave as well as the rituals accompanying a meal, both at the Baldwins' or in their own homes.[2]

Rituals made meals more than mere consumption. Examples abound: Mrs. Baldwin serving as a wonderful hostess and conversationalist at the head of Eyre Hall's dining room table; Pinky lining her grandchildren up along the stairs in her house to watch her as she cooked over her wood stove; her daughter Georgia having set times for meals for family to gather round; Pinky's son Dorsey cooking at the start of each day a big breakfast of pancakes, eggs, bacon, sausage, and more for his family. According to Marcie Cohen Ferris in *The Edible South*, such rituals in southern homes, whether Black or white, were repeated again and again as they were thought to be *worth* repeating. Across Eyre Hall, as culinary historian Michael Twitty has explained, dinner tables served "as a place where people used food to tell themselves who they are, to tell others who they are, and to tell stories about where they've been." As both historians concluded, eating good food and telling stories around the dinner table provided enjoyable ways to share both food and culture. Such was the case in traditional societies whether in Europe or Africa.[3]

One of the reasons the food was so good was that almost all the ingredients were fresh. There was no freezer, no refined flour, no cheap manufactured convenience foods. Most food was what was on hand, whether from the garden, henhouse, smokehouse, farm, woods, sky, or Chesapeake Bay. Just as food writer Nathalie Dupree favors "high quality, fresh, local, and seasonal ingredients," so too did Pinky and Georgia. Furlong Baldwin attests to this, recalling that Pinky's cooking was so tasty that his friends would "almost weep" over her deviled crabs.

When a hog was killed, his family ate pork for such a long time he got sick of eating pork chops and, when grown, refused it until one day he tasted them again and thought to himself, "Umm, that's pretty good."

While we may celebrate the bounty of food, we should also remember that it was not equally available, especially to African American tenants. However, the experiences of food—from its acquisition like hog killing, fishing, hunting, or gardening to its cooking and to the valuing of a meal as family time—show how food provided creative ways of self-expression and served to connect people both within and across racial lines. It may also illuminate how they made this place into their home.[4]

Furlong Baldwin:

"We used to have hot bread three times a day: biscuits, muffins, and rolls. William, Pinky, and then Georgia just turned it out automatically. I asked, 'Georgie, how did you learn it?' 'Watching Mama.' That's how she cooked. Everything she made was from scratch, using no artificial or boxed products, canned food, or anything like that. She taught me how to make yeast rolls, and to this day I make them.

"Pinky could make the best cornbread and fried chicken. She used a lot of different spices, and that's what made it so delicious. She could make the best cake. Her favorite, a caramel cake, had this caramel topping on it that was absolutely delicious. The thing that amazed me was the contrast between what they were eating at home and how they would cook the most beautiful meals here. At home, they didn't have much.

"When I was a little boy, hog killing was like planning for D-Day. We'd have a dozen hogs, and each of the families would bring a dozen. I would help with making sausage and chopping up the lard and all that. We used it all. We'd have hams, shoulders, jowls, bacon, sausage, scrapple which I love, and lard. All our sausage was smoked, plus the bacon, hams, jowls, and shoulder, so they would last. What you couldn't smoke, you had to eat. Since there was no freezer, for about two months we ate so much damn fresh pork."

Eyre Hall's dining room is a place Furlong associates with good meals and good times: "We were lucky. You're in the country, and fortunately had a cook. In my lifetime, there were only three: William Frazier, Pinky Bagwell Foeman, and the last cook, Georgia Foeman Curtis. I could bring any number of my friends down here, and there would be crabs and fried chicken. When my children, Molly and Eyre, were growing up, we would have crabs, fried chicken, and all those good things. Mother loved doing for them. We would show up Friday night after work, and Georgie was cooking, and we'd eat for two days. We would sail, water ski, and eat, so this dining room holds fun memories. It wasn't a place for contention.

"When we were little, we ate in the children's dining room, which was also the playroom, and now the den. Finally, you got up to having breakfast and lunch in the dining room. When you got to dinner, and I don't know at what age, it was a big deal. My sister Mary

was older, but we ate breakfast and lunch in that little back room. I think that's the way a lot of people were raised. We ate the same meal, just in the children's room. Mother took a dim view of such a thing as a hotdog.

"My first dinners in the dining room were the same things my parents had been eating: fried chicken, fish, and veal, whatever we had at hand. I didn't know what salmon was. As for special occasions, I don't remember trumpets blaring, but we had our own vegetable garden, so local vegetables were our fare, plus figs, raspberries, strawberries, cantaloupe, and watermelon.[5]

"Living on a farm had its advantages. We raised sheep, so once a month we'd kill a lamb, and have lamb chops, lamb stew, and a leg of lamb once a week, because it had four legs. We had plenty of pork—ham, bacon, pork chops, tenderloin—once a day for three weeks. Chickens were abundant, so lots of fried chicken. There were always fresh vegetables. During the tomato season, we'd have fresh tomatoes for breakfast, tomato salad for lunch, and stewed tomatoes for dinner. Nobody thought it was boring. We had fresh cornbread with it. All southern and local. One time my father tried to persuade me to eat hog's brains. I had to stop at brains. Couldn't go there.

"The Bay served us well. We'd probably have soft crabs once every two weeks. They used those little spider crabs. I remember one lady came with a friend of mine, and she stopped at 14 crabs. I asked, 'Why did you stop?' She replied, 'I don't know. I guess it's time for dessert.'

"Crabmeat salad was a regular part of lunch. Pinky and Georgie's specialty was their deviled crabs. Pinky and Georgie made very good deviled clam dip for which they would grind up the clams. For oyster stew, they added a lot of fresh oysters from the Bay, plus plenty of milk and butter. But the crab and the clam thing, people would rant and rave about those. Mother had soup every night for dinner. I eat soups all the time—summer, winter, hot soups, cold. Since I've lived alone, if I eat nothing else for dinner at home, it'll be soup. For dessert, we'd have things like rhubarb and prune whip, gingerbread, pudding, boiled custard, baked custard, and rice pudding—things you hardly have at home any more. All prepared using a wood stove.

"During the summers, we'd make ice cream, adding fresh strawberries, peaches, raspberries, or whatever we had from the gardens and orchards. Herbs came from our garden. You didn't go to a store and buy, for example, bay, because we had four huge bay bushes in the garden. We'd just strip off what we needed and use it. Thinking of bay, I remember the barbers used to use a bay-scented thing when they cut your hair. They even combed your hair with it. Afterwards, I'd see my grandfather, and he'd say, 'Damn boy, you smell some kind of sweet.'

"When Mother was still living and my children came down, she and Georgie would just lay on the food. My children, Eyre and Molly, never asked for anything special because it was fried chicken, hot cakes, biscuits, spoon bread, and grits bread. When I was growing up, we never had 'store-bought bread.' I discovered it in sandwiches at school. Instead, we had hot bread three times a day. It's a miracle all of us didn't weigh 5,000 pounds. I was going to say 'Mother got away with it,' but she had one helping of everything, and that was it, plus one piece of candy a day. With Mother, it was regular sit-down meals, three times a day. My children liked that you could wear a bathing suit or polo shirt for breakfast or lunch, but at dinner, coat and tie. When my children asked friends to visit, they'd say, 'Bring a coat and tie for dinner.' Mother always changed for dinner. It wasn't until after she died that we stopped that.[6]

"If I were to imagine that our dining table at Eyre Hall could talk, it would tell you it's never seen pizza being served as part of a meal. We didn't know what pizza was. My mother never had a piece of pizza. Not that she would turn her nose up at it. She just didn't know what it was. She wouldn't slide into a pizza joint. Now recently, we've come down here late some nights, driving down from Baltimore, and eaten a little pizza in the kitchen. But not in the dining room. Light the candles and have pizza? The gods would rattle and roar."[7]

Joyce Ramassar:
"When she wasn't working at the big house, Pinky kept her grandchildren. In her house were stairs down into the kitchen. When she was cooking, she would line us up on those steps down to the kitchen, and we'd watch her cook. You could hear a pin drop. She didn't have to say anything. We just knew. You are going to sit here. You're going to be quiet and not make noise.

"She had this wood stove that had a hutch on top of it and an oven. On one side, it had the place where you put all the wood. She made biscuits and yeast rolls from scratch, also cornbread, never thick, but thin. To control heat and temperature, there was a groove

in the middle of the stove, and she would pull it out and turn it either to the left or the right or in the middle."

A talented person, Pinky could do just about anything. "Gardening was one of her favorite things. She got a lot of joy out of being outside and planting and was very particular. She had no weeds and got us to help pull them, so her garden looked very professional. Around her pump were the herbs she cherished. Her garden was on the left-hand side of the house, and she was always planting vegetables there. She used to go back in the woods, give me a basket, and we picked different leaves and the bark off trees. She would boil the bark and make tea. I thought it was strange, but it was good once she made it. There was saffron in the back of the house, which she used a lot of. She lived a very simple life.

"Before Eyre Hall, my grandmother had temporarily lived in Baltimore and cooked for a fine hotel, Mother said, where she won a cooking award. She used a lot of different spices, and that's what made her food so delicious. She could make the best cake. Her favorite, a caramel cake, had this caramel topping on it that was absolutely delicious. Everything she cooked was on a wood stove and made from scratch, using no artificial preparations, boxed products, canned food, or anything like that. She taught me how to make yeast rolls, and to this day I still make them."

Joyce spoke of her mother's hard work and attitude toward meals: "As an adult, when I would come home to Eyre Hall, my mother Georgia would get up at 5 in the morning and be in the kitchen cooking. I'd be in bed because I'm on vacation, coming to see her. I could hear her in there, beating pots and stuff like that. I'd go in the kitchen and she'd be cooking, and we would sit there and talk for hours while she was cooking. She always made breakfast. I said, 'Mom, you don't have to do that.' 'Nope. Nope. This is what I do.'

"She had set times for these meals. You just didn't eat whenever you wanted to. It was like that when we were kids. We always had to sit at the table together. You could not sit in another room and eat. Everybody had to eat together. No questions asked. For breakfast she finished by 9 o'clock. She made lunch every day, and she made dinner at 5:30 and expected you to be there at those times. Even when I was there on vacation as an adult, if I wasn't there to eat at her set time, she would say 'I fixed the food. You know where it is.' This is the time she expected us as a family to be together."[8]

Anthony Foeman:

"I lived with my grandfather Dorsey, Pinky's son, who taught me how to raise chickens and hogs. Me and my brother used to name hogs and named one Susie. She was the best because we used to ride her back, like she was a horse. When my grandfather killed Susie, me and my brother said we wasn't going to eat none of Susie. So he said, 'It was either you eat Susie, or you get nothing to eat.'

"When he killed Susie, we all got up at 4 o'clock that morning. My grandfather had this big cast-iron black pot, where we had to put firewood underneath it to start the boiling. My grandfather's brother, Ben, would come with the rifle and shoot the hog in the middle of his forehead. We'd drag him out and put him inside that big scalding pot of water. They had these little wooden scrapers, which had what looked like an iron bell, and we used them to get the hair off the pig. Then you'd hang the pig, slit him open, and take out all the guts. Everybody had a part in it. My grandma would be in the kitchen, getting the stuff set up to make sausages, because she would grind it up right there. After she'd made sausages, she'd make chitlins. We would have ham, pork chop, hog maw, and hog jowl. We ate almost every piece of the hog.

"My grandfather would take the hams to the smokehouse behind the big house. He'd put the hams and sides inside of the salt bed, salt them, and later light the hickory wood, and hang the hams and sides up. That's where we cut our bacon off. The smokehouse still stands today. If you go in there, you can smell the smoke, and we used to love it. I would be at my grandfather's house, maybe a quarter of a mile away, and you could smell that pig being smoked.

That was the best smell in the world, so you had no choice but to eat Susie.[9]

"My grandfather Dorsey was a breakfast man. We'd get up in the morning, get our bath, brush our teeth, and every morning he would have cooked us breakfast: pancakes, sausage, bacon, and eggs, almost everything he'd raised. He'd take us out to the end of the road to go to school. All 13 grandkids in that one six-room house, plus my grandparents' four daughters. Seven in one room, and my mom, her sister, my sister in another room. Me and my brother used to sleep with my grandfather. He'd snore! We would nudge him and then he'd quit for a little bit, and we'd get our chance to sleep.

"We'd eat lunch at school, but my grandmother used to make homemade biscuits and would have dinner for everybody, about 17 of us. We only had a small table, so we used to sit at the tables in the dining room and kitchen or hold the plates in our laps in the living room. Everybody was piled up, but it wasn't like everybody would eat at the same time because some wanted to eat now and some later. Since I always wanted to get hot biscuits off the pan, I wanted to be first."[10]

Robert Curtis, Jr.:

"My mother Georgia would bring home leftovers from the Baldwins' dinners because it was a lot of food that she cooked—homemade biscuits, sweet potatoes, green beans, and a lot of ham. At home she also used to cook so much, like homemade biscuits and ham with this honey taste to it. She knew how to bake bread and make it in a certain shape. She could just cook! It came from her mother Pinky."[11]

NOTES

1. Marcie Cohen Ferris, *The Edible South: The Power of Food and the Making of an American Region* (Chapel Hill: University of North Carolina Press, 2014), 3, 324–27, 333.

2. Brendan Walsh quoted by Judy Hevrdejs in "The Sounds of Cooking," Food and Dining Section, *Chicago Tribune*, May 31, 2014, https://www.chicagotribune.com/dining/ct-xpm-2014-05-31-sc-food- 0530-sounds-20140531-story.html, accessed July 2020; "Home and Away," Jacques Pépin interviewed by Anthony Bourdain, *YouTube*, November 19, 2015, https://www.youtube.com/ watch?v=U3QYai6bv5M&list=PL2F405F2DE0A7C782& index=31, accessed October 2020.

3. Ferris, *Edible South*, 322; Michael Twitty, *The Cooking Gene: A Journey through African American Culinary History in the Old South* (New York: Amistad, 2017), 150.

4. Ferris, *Edible South*, 325; Furlong Baldwin fourth interview with Elaine Eff, September 28, 2019.

5. Furlong Baldwin interview with George McDaniel, May 11, 2019.

6. Furlong Baldwin fourth interview with Elaine Eff, September 28, 2019.

7. Furlong Baldwin interview with George McDaniel, May 11, 2019.

8. Joyce Curtis Ramassar interview with George McDaniel, July 30, 2019.

9. Anthony Foeman first interview with George McDaniel, May 12, 2019.

10. Anthony Foeman second interview with George McDaniel, May 12, 2019.

11. Robert Curtis, Jr., Paulette Curtis, and Helen Burton first interview with George McDaniel, May 12, 2019. Though no written records survive, Pinky did pass her knowledge to her daughter Georgia, who passed it to her children and other relatives who now live across the nation.

The Future of Eyre Hall: "Eyre Hall Needs to Be Lived In"

What will happen to Eyre Hall? Should it remain in the home of the same family that has owned it for centuries? Should it become a historic site, owned and operated by a non-profit organization and open to the public? Why is Eyre Hall significant? How can it contribute to the future? The list of questions could go on, and they have been asked and received much thought and discussion. Most do agree that Eyre Hall warrants a place in the future of the state and nation, not because a famous person lived there or a significant moment in our nation's history happened there, but because its continuity in ownership and operations and its abundance of evidence allow us to see America as it evolved over time. We can see what has changed and what has stayed the same. We can connect with real people at the real places where they lived. Few if any historic sites today can still claim ownership by the same family since the 1750s. It is fortunate that the family has retained a wonderful collection of artifacts and documents. Fortunate, too, that their ancestors chose not to destroy the integrity of the place in the late nineteenth and early twentieth century when there was money to do so. Of course, they made some modern improvements since the main house has been continually lived in, but nothing drastic. Since nothing deeper than a plow has disturbed most of its earth, archaeological sites abound. And since the Northampton County court records have survived unbroken from the early seventeenth century onwards, historians may continue to investigate questions of Eyre Hall's past and how it illustrates the nation's.

No one connected to Eyre Hall wants to see the property developed. All recommend it remain a home and not become a museum. Fortunately, the current owner, Furlong Baldwin, has established an endowment to fund the myriad expenses an historic place generates, but has also given freedom to his heir to sell the property, protected by preservation and conservation easements. African American descendants too have their thoughts. The following excerpts articulate the variety of opinions that coalesce into a general consensus.

Furlong Baldwin:

"Has my family ever considered selling Eyre Hall? Not even a subject of conversation! I would never consider selling it. Nor did my mother. It never occurred to her. As for the future of the house's contents: thanks to my will, the furniture, the family portraits, the silver, and other furnishings belong to the house. In fact, all of the collection is in a trust of its own. My only grandchild, Gracie, my son Eyre's daughter, will inherit the property. When she turns 40, if she wants to sell it, it's her option. It would kill me, but you can't rule from the grave. I can take you through this county and show you houses whose owners said, 'I'm not going to let my children sell my house.' And with time, the houses eventually fell to the ground.

"For three generations, nobody contributed to Eyre Hall's upkeep, but I was lucky to be able to put something back in and have maintained Eyre Hall because I love it. There will be enough for my granddaughter Gracie to maintain it, thanks to an endowment, so my hope is that Eyre Hall goes on. But what can I do about it? I'll be out there in the graveyard. I may talk to her out there. I've got a conservation easement on the land and a preservation easement on the house. They restrict what can be done right down to the color of the paneling or the preservation of the wallpaper. A new owner wouldn't have much wiggle room."[1]

Anthony Foeman:

"Since Eyre Hall was a slave plantation and my ancestors were slaves there and bad things happened, I was asked 'why not burn it down?' That's not the solution. I feel as though Eyre Hall is part of me, and I'm part of Eyre Hall. I'll always be part of Eyre Hall, no matter what. Burn it down? No, that would never cross my mind. I would never want it to get burned down because it's historic and my ancestors worked there and I have a lot of love for that, and that's why I love the Baldwins the way I do. They are like family.

"I would like Eyre Hall to survive into the future because I want my children and my grandchildren to know about it: how important it is to our family, how much work we put in there, and how to just always respect everyone around there because they will respect you the same. What I would like them to know about my ancestors is that we should still try to keep searching and finding out more and more about them and how they respected the people that owned Eyre Hall as we do now. Respect is the number one thing in my mind. You should always respect, no matter what, and that's what I would like for them to know."[2]

Joyce Curtis Ramassar:
Contemplating Eyre Hall's future, Joyce concluded, "It's a memorable place, and what I would not want to see is commercialization. Too many properties with a lot of memories of people who were born and lived there have been wiped out by commercial properties and turned into malls and housing. Once you do that, there're no memories left of that place because there's nothing identifiable to the people born and raised there. What I would like to see is something to identify the people that lived here, like a lane with the name of the person that lived on that lane.

"It might not be important to other people, but it will be important to the last generation that lived here. My grandmother Pinky and her brother, Uncle Lawrence, her son Uncle Dorsey, and all the rest of them are the last ones we have any personal attachment to. Each one of them had a lane going directly to their house, so naming those lanes for them would mean something for generations to come. We have grandchildren, and they may want to come and see one day, when I'm gone, where 'my grandmother' was born. They can come here and see their great-grandmother Georgia's name on the lane, not mine. They would know exactly its location, and that would mean something to them.

"Eyre Hall should remain a part of history. This house should be open to the public to see, because young people these days have no idea what happened before the 1900s. There are so many people in the United States that don't know what an historical house looks like. There's nothing I would change. Otherwise, it would not carry the history that actually determined what this house was in the first place. I don't care whether you are African American, white American, or whatever American. White Americans cannot erase how they—not all white Americans— treated slaves. They can't erase that. It's always going to be there, whether they talk about it or don't. Since my great-grandmother was born on a Cherokee reservation, I wanted to see exactly how she lived, so I took my kids there. That's history, and you cannot erase it."[3]

Molly Baldwin:
"I would hope that Eyre Hall could be a place to tell the truth. It could be a place of reconciliation, a safe place to have the most difficult conversations we need to have in the country so that we can move forward. Why Eyre Hall? What does Eyre Hall offer? I know Eyre Hall is a place that's beautiful, with a historic building and gardens. Could you create a place that has both a beautiful and a painful legacy and be a place of healing and reconciliation? I hope so."[4]

Eyre Baldwin:
"One of my biggest fears about Eyre Hall is that it becomes too sterile and becomes a museum. It is a home. It isn't just a house. Grace may stay away for years, but if she comes home every once in a while, I hope she will raise the windows, have her friends hanging out the windows, and that they use the property the way we did."[5]

Grace Baldwin:
"When I was growing up here, my friends loved Eyre Hall. They still do. It's filled with memories. Every year we gave tours during Garden Week and were assigned rooms to explain the history of, say the front hall or blue room. When I was about 11, what I liked most in the 'yellow room' was the dresser. It had a little secret compartment I'd show. People loved it!

As I think about its future, Eyre Hall needs to be lived in. It was a source of happiness for my childhood memories. It should not be tiptoed around in. It needs to stay intact and stay as a home."[6]

NOTES
1. Furlong Baldwin interview with George McDaniel, May 11, 2019.
2. Anthony Foeman third interview with George McDaniel, May 12, 2019.
3. Joyce Curtis Ramassar and Louise Hayman interview with George McDaniel, July 30, 2019.
4. Molly Baldwin second interview with George McDaniel, July 31, 2019.
5. Eyre Baldwin and Grace Baldwin interview with George McDaniel, July 30, 2019.
6. Eyre Baldwin and Grace Baldwin interview with George McDaniel, July 30, 2019.

ARCHITECTURE

The Architecture of the House

CARL R. LOUNSBURY

THE COMPLETION OF THE TWO-STORY FRAME mansion house at Eyre Hall in 1759 signaled Littleton Eyre's arrival at the pinnacle of gentry society on the Eastern Shore of Virginia. Though not the grandest house erected in Northampton County—that achievement belonged to John Custis's extraordinary three-story brick house, Arlington, built on Old Plantation Creek as early as 1675—Eyre Hall was nonetheless a trend-setter in a way that the over-the-top scale of Arlington would never be. Although it was only 40 feet square, it nevertheless matched the aspirations and the pocket books of the area's late colonial planter-merchant class that was by no means as wealthy as the great tobacco planters of the James and Rappahannock River plantations, who erected larger, two-story brick dwellings that have long been regarded as the epitome of early Virginia architecture. Not only was Eyre's house a costly undertaking—with its elegant suite of decorated rooms, imported English brass mortise locks and hinges, and paperhangings—but its square-shaped side-passage plan and two-story pedimented portico, which was an eye-catching innovation for contemporaries who caught sight of it as they sailed up

Cherrystone Creek, set the precedent for elite housing in the region for the next 50 years.

DESIGN

At first glance, Eyre Hall looks not unlike most old houses on the Eastern Shore—a large boxy wooden section with an enfilade of additions strung out to one side (Fig. 84). Its gambrel or Dutch roof, one of the first in the region, afforded more space for second-floor rooms than a one-story gable-roof house did.[1] The form became popular among the Eastern Shore builders over the next half century. Even its beaded weatherboard siding and scalloped wooden shingles are materials that covered most well-built Chesapeake dwellings in the late colonial period. But the common cladding and present elongated arrangement of Eyre Hall masks the sophistication of the original plan and its decorative ornamentation, which stood well outside local building traditions. Eyre Hall was inspired by classical design principles, and its decorative elements derived directly from the architectural

189

Fig. 84. South façade of Eyre Hall with early nineteenth-century housekeeper's wing to the right.

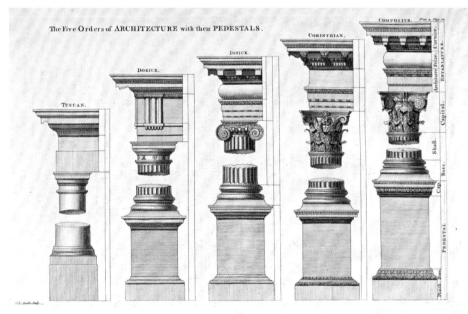

The Five Orders of ARCHITECTURE with their PEDESTALS.

TUSCAN.   DORICK.   IONICK.   CORINTHIAN.   COMPOSITE.

Fig. 85. The five classical orders of ancient architecture: Tuscan, Doric, Ionic, Corinthian, and Composite. Isaac Ware, *A Complete Body of Architecture* (London, 1756).

vocabulary of the ancient world. This design aesthetic had gained currency in the Chesapeake in the late seventeenth century and was based on English interpretations of Renaissance ideas shaped by the authoritative precedents of Roman architecture, whose ruins were measured and design intentions revealed and codified in publications that outlined the relationship and configuration of those elements comprising the five orders of classical architecture (Fig. 85). Early modern architects discovered that the essence of Roman architecture was its modular system. The constituent parts of each order—base, plinth, column, capital, and entablature—were calibrated on some proportion of the diameter of the column, which was the module. Ornamental details and measurements varied with the different orders, from the smaller and simplest Tuscan and Doric orders, to the more intricate Ionic and Corinthian orders, to the largest and most florid known as the Composite order.

The rules of classical design stressed the importance of proportion: that all elements of a building should be related to one another in terms of their size and scaled in relationship to the whole. Classical rules dictated that the height of the Doric cornice should be twice the width of its column. This relationship might be modified up or down depending on the height of the column or, when there was no column, to the height of a wall or other feature. But such adjustments needed to be carefully modulated since, as one English architectural publicist noted, "there is a proportion from which if we vary too much we lose all elegance." There was "a certain degree of proportion within which all that is beautiful is confined."[2]

A corollary to these rules of proportion was the idea that classical architecture should reflect a hierarchy of prominence appropriate for a particular element, façade, or space compared to others. To reflect its importance, the main façade of a building, for example, would be more embellished than the rear or side elevations. Public rooms received the best materials and were more decoratively ornamented than private or service rooms. In tall buildings, the story or floor level that contained the most importance spaces generally had the largest apertures. The windows at Eyre Hall reflect relational proportioning (see Fig. 84). Those on the main floor with the public rooms are proportional within themselves, that is twice as tall as wide, but their size was relative to their position on the façade. By comparison, the second-floor windows lighting the more private bedchambers are only one and a half times as tall as their widths, and the height of the cellar openings only three-quarters of their width.

Just as integral to classical design as proportion and hierarchy was symmetry. Like proportion, symmetry was an aesthetic ideal based on the comparative relationship of constituent parts in terms of size, position, and quantity. The notion of symmetry governed the relationship of one building to another or one element to another in terms of balance, wherein various parts of a feature or space reflect a mirror image on either side of an imaginary center line. This principle of equipoise applied to plan as well as elevation. Thus a door might be placed in the center of a façade and windows of the same scale placed equidistant from the centerline of the doorway. At Eyre Hall, the fireplace walls in the two ground-floor rooms are fully paneled and have doors to closets on one side and to a shared vestibule on the other and arranged the same distance from the middle of the hearth opening (see Fig. 96). Symmetry also governed the layout of the gardens and the arrangement of buildings within the curtilage of the Eyre Hall landscape. The real achievement of colonial builders was their skill at integrating the functional aspects of a building with the classical precepts that emphasized proportion, hierarchy, and symmetry.[3]

The Eyre Hall that Bridget and Littleton Eyre moved into in 1759 successfully joined these rules of classical design with the more prosaic aspects of devising circulation spaces and creating sources for heat, light, and air in the house through the arrangement of its public rooms and service spaces in a way that matched the needs and expectations of the family. Unfortunately, nothing is known about who was responsible for its design and construction. No person has been identified as the contractor; no names of joiners, carpenters, bricklayers, plasterers, painters, or any other craftsmen or laborers have come to light. This is not unusual, as very few houses preserve their original construction documents—contracts with specifications, building accounts, or any ancillary drawings—that might have revealed the builder and the identities of the craftsmen responsible for their execution.

In the absence of such records, we can speculate about the source of the original design ideas. Based on evidence from other gentry houses built during this period, we can also envision a plausible scenario of how the process developed from the initial conceptualization of the project to the final coat of paint. The client sometimes served as

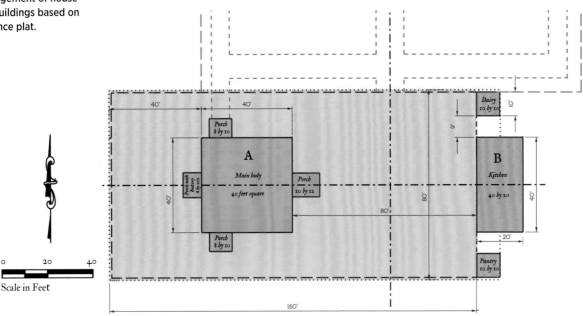

his own general contractor, responsible for overseeing the gathering of materials and labor necessary and developing the plan and finishes of a project in consultation with skilled craftsmen in face-to-face conversations on the job site. In such cases, documents were few except accounts kept by the client in order to keep track of costs and payments. At other times, the client turned over the supervision to a contractor or undertaker (as the position was called in the eighteenth century).[4] In the late colonial period, there were a handful of these men in the Chesapeake knowledgeable in the new classical language of architectural design who also commanded a large labor force of skilled craftsmen capable of executing large commissions such as a gentry house like Eyre Hall, and had the financial wherewithal and managerial skills to oversee a major construction project.[5] In consultation with the client, the builder devised the plan and the details of ornamentation and finishes and oversaw the work of craftsmen and laborers on the site. The source for the plan or for a specific feature such as a chimneypiece might derive from a standing structure or a much-admired feature well known to the client and builder. Design was rarely static, and often improvisational. Ideas were freely discussed on the work site as the two conversed and may have sketched schemes on the back of a piece of woodwork. Gentry clients also became involved in the building process by using their enslaved laborers to saw timber, excavate

foundations, and haul materials as well as carry out other jobs that required specialized skills. It seems highly likely that Littleton Eyre may have employed such men at Eyre Hall.

Even in the absence of documentary evidence that would put names to the design and craftsmanship, we can trace their intentions in the landscape and fabric of Eyre Hall. The orientation of Eyre Hall on its site and the ornamentation of the spaces inside reveal the impact of classical design ideals. The arrangement of the rooms of the house reflects the transformation of English urban plan type to a rural situation unbound by restrictions on plot size or orientation and integration into a streetscape. Although informed by English fashion, the function and relationship of those spaces responded to the social needs and expectations of colonial planters rather than a metropolitan culture.

SITE PLAN

Standing more than 500 yards east of the shoreline of Cherrystone Creek on flat land surrounded by fields and woods along Eyreville Creek to the north and Eyre Hall Creek to the south, the mansion house at Eyre Hall is approached today from the east by a mile-long tree-lined lane with agricultural fields on either side. A fence running

Fig. 87. West pedimented
portico, partially rebuilt
ca. 1806–7.

Fig. 88. Digital reconstruction
of the second capitol,
Williamsburg, 1751–53.

north to south encloses the eastern edge of the curtilage. At its south end, the fence turns 90 degrees and runs westward to another fence parallel to the first, which defines the western edge of the house lot. It encloses a grove of trees and lanes that turn northward and run alongside the sprawling house. Although there are several doors on the south side of the house, the one beneath a raised one-story porch at the west end of the projecting two-story gambrel-roofed section suggests that this is the primary entrance to the dwelling. And so it has been for the past 200 years. But, originally, it was not the main entrance to the house, and the principal approach to Littleton Eyre's mansion was by water, not land.

When devised in the late 1750s, the orientation of the house and the arrangement of its garden, service buildings, and other features followed a rational hierarchical order. The Eyre Hall site may not have been devoid of earlier cultural features, which, if so, probably determined where the new house would be built. In the late seventeenth century, when the land was owned by William Kendall, a tanning house operated somewhere on the property. In 1685 he gave the land to his daughter Mary and her husband Hancock Lee, noting that it was where they were then living. So it is quite possible, but not proven, that they built a brick house on the site which later became Severn Eyre's kitchen. If so, and this 40-by-20-foot structure was their dwelling house and had survived, then it helped define where Severn Eyre

chose to build his new mansion house.[6] As a significant but subservient service building, it would stand in a formal relationship with the main house (Fig. 86).

What is evident is that the mansion house and associated buildings and spaces were originally oriented from west to east—that is the most formal and elaborate spaces of this ensemble faced the west and the subservient spaces associated with the kitchen, services, stables, barns, sheds, and accommodations for enslaved workers were arranged behind the house to the east. The west gambrel-side of the house was the principal façade dominated by its tall front porch facing Cherrystone Creek (Fig. 87). Supported by a double tier of columns or square posts (the originals were replaced in 1807), the central pedimented portico—measuring 11½ feet in width and 8 feet in depth—was a relatively new feature in colonial Virginia architecture and appeared in such prominent buildings as the second capitol

in Williamsburg, which had only been completed in the early 1750s. Littleton Eyre, who sat as a member of the House of Burgesses in the new building, may have been deeply impressed by it (Fig. 88). Few, if any other dwellings in the colony, had such a prominent feature this early.

With impassable roads and meandering horse trails, most travelers arrived at Eyre Hall by water in the colonial period, not the long lane to the east. Littleton Eyre laid out his house and grounds to reflect this riparian orientation. The prominent porch acted as a signpost for those approaching the house. This was made even clearer by a fence that enclosed a west forecourt or yard located 40 feet from the west wall of the house with a west gate centered on the portico.[7] On the ground floor of the porch, a large, eight-paneled door led into the entrance hall that stretched the length of the house, which also had exterior doorways at each end on its north and south walls. The north doorway of the transverse passage gave access to an enclosed formal garden, and the south doorway provided a secondary entrance to the house for those who arrived by land.

On the east side of Littleton's house, an enclosed, one-story vestibule located between the two internal chimney stacks projected outward 8 feet on center from the east façade, a match in length and width to the portico on the opposite side of the house. A door on the east side of the vestibule opened into a service courtyard (Fig. 89). Opposite this doorway, some 80 feet east of the east wall of the main house, was the west wall of Littleton's brick kitchen with its central doorway. The main house and kitchen were perfectly aligned. The two ends of the 40-foot-long kitchen lined up with the two ends of the east wall of the main house. The vestibule, which did not originally have a projecting pedimented porch, provided access from the house to the kitchen and other service buildings.

PLAN

The arrangement of the rooms in Eyre Hall contained within the original 40-foot-square, gambrel-roofed section of the house derived from an older English urban form known as a side-passage plan (Fig. 90). The west side of the house is composed of a wide cross or transverse passage divided into two visually distinct sections with an open-string staircase in the north end that ascended from the back of the passage along the partition wall before it turned at right angles near the midway point where the upper flight rose westward back across the passage to the second-floor rooms. The east or

FIRST FLOOR PLAN

SCALE - 1/4"=1'-0"

■ PERIOD I
▨ PERIOD II
▨ PERIOD III
□ PERIOD IV

Fig. 90. Ground-floor plan with later additions to the east.

back side of the dwelling contains two rooms of unequal size, which are heated by separate internal chimneys on the east gable end. The prototype for the plan emerged in London and other English cities in the late seventeenth century as a way of housing a broad class of urban dwellers in rowhouses, which contained multiple connected units with a similar layout of rooms compressed into a rectangular configuration with narrow frontages. Although there were many variations in these plans, the direct ancestor of the Eyre Hall side-passage plan consisted of a narrow passage with doorways that provide entrance into the house from the street at one end and to the back of the lot at the other. A staircase to the upper floors was located either on the blind-faced party wall or against an internal front-to-back partition wall that separated the passage from one or two flanking rooms that contained chimneys on the other party wall. Nicholas Barbon, a speculative builder, erected hundreds of such rowhouses in the new streets and squares in the west end of London in the last quarter of the seventeenth century (Fig. 91). Individual houses in these rows had a frontage from 20 to 30 feet and a depth of 35 to 50 feet.[8] The plan was intended for the middling sort; the poorer folk and artisans of London lived in dwellings with much narrower frontages and different internal arrangements.[9]

No building schemes of rows on Barbon's scale ever appeared in Boston, New York, or Philadelphia in the early eighteenth century, but the side-passage rowhouse plan— more often constructed singularly or as a modest row of two or three units—did appear by the 1750s before it eventually became a fixture in urban development in some growing American seaport cities such as Baltimore by the beginning of the nineteenth century.[10] With a modest population of no more than 2,000 people in the mid-eighteenth century, there was little demand for rowhouses in Williamsburg. Even so, at least two brick rowhouses, one a duplex and another composed of six units, were built during the time that Littleton Eyre was a member of the House of Burgesses (1742–1761) and a regular visitor to the capital. More pertinent to the Eyre Hall design was the construction of about a half dozen side-passage houses during this time. A number of these, including the Orrell House, William Lightfoot House, Seymour Powell House, and the Tayloe House, were built as timber-framed, gambrel-roof dwellings. All of them, as well as the two-story brick Palmer House built next to the capitol in the mid-1750s, were either square in plan or shaped like a boxy rectangle whose street façades were longer than their double-pile depth.

Fig. 92.
Tayloe House,
Williamsburg.

These Williamsburg houses had shed the narrow proportions of the urban rowhouse plan and stood independently as single dwellings sitting on their own lots. All had a side passage containing the stair to the second-story chambers with two heated rooms flanking the passage. A single, internal gable-end chimney provided heat for these public rooms, which contained angled corner fireplaces. In the absence of contiguous party walls, the houses had gable-end windows that provided light for the passage and additional light for the two rooms. Though the staircase in most of these houses rose at the back of the passage, two of them are arranged in a manner that was similar to the Eyre Hall staircase. The Orrell House measures 28 feet square and has a 9-foot-wide passage. The staircase rises toward the center of the house along the exterior wall near the front entrance. Halfway up, it turns at right angles and the upper flight cuts across the passage to land near the center of the house on the second floor. The Tayloe House, built sometime in the 1750s by John Tayloe II of Mount Airy, a member of the governor's council and a very wealthy planter and industrialist from the Northern Neck, is a much grander affair, with a fully paneled front room and raised paneled wainscoting in the passage and rear ground-floor

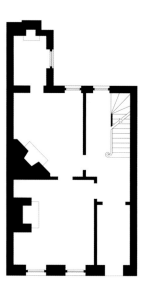

Fig. 91. Side-passage rowhouse plan, London, late seventeenth century.

room. Sitting on a back street, the gambrel-roof house is 36 feet wide by 30 feet deep, with a 12-foot-wide passage (Fig. 92). As at Eyre Hall, the passage has one-story porches at the front entrance (rebuilt) and a later one at the back. Despite its size, the heated rooms share an internal chimney. The open-string staircase rises along the partition wall just beyond the doorway to the large parlor room on the street front. At the landing, the upper flight returns free of the outer wall. On the upper floor, the stairwell is bound by a wall on one side only, the other three sides being protected where necessary by the balustrade. This arrangement produced a spatial continuity between the two floors rarely found in colonial domestic architecture.

The fully paneled parlor of the Tayloe House and the dramatic arrangement of the staircase in the wainscoted passage certainly demonstrated how fashionable flourishes could enhance the form of the best of these town-house plans. It seems likely that Eyre may have visited Tayloe's house on a social occasion and seen the wide passage being used as more than a circulation space—filled as it was with seating furniture, tables, and a marble shelf with wrought-iron brackets that made the space habitable, especially in the summer, when it could be cooled by cross breezes. Ever since Virginians began to erect houses with wide stair passages, they used them as Tayloe did in Williamsburg, as a place to sit and dine in the summer time. William Fairfax observed this function in 1735, when he noted they "have a large Porch before the Door & generally another behind the House, in one of which or [in the] Hall & passage they always sit & frequently dine & sup," with the only drawback in the era before widespread use of screen doors being "the musquitoes . . . [that] are very troublesome."[11]

None of these Williamsburg houses served as the precedent for the Eyre Hall plan, but they do illustrate the fact that dwellings with gambrel roofs and side-passage plans had become a common type by mid-century. If Littleton Eyre were looking for design inspiration for his new mansion house, Williamsburg dwellings provided not only a variety of types and decorative treatments, but showed him how the elite socialized in them—how the architectural finishes of rooms could be fashioned to impress guests. In conversations with his fellow burgesses, he may have also learned who were the best craftsmen and contractors in the region, those who knew how to translate impressions into bricks and mortar.

THE MANSION HOUSE, 1759

The rural setting of Eyre Hall released the side-passage plan as it had developed in Williamsburg from the last vestiges of its urban origins. With no street front to respect, the house could be oriented in a different manner, and so it was with the two-story pedimented portico on the west gambrel-side that gave the building a balanced façade and broad proportions and the heightened aspect of a two-story house. The Eyre Hall design diverged from the Williamsburg models by turning the side-passage plan into a transverse or cross-passage plan. The main entrance into the house was not at one of the two ends of the passage but near its center in the gambrel-end wall beneath the pedimented portico (see Fig. 87). A tall, eight-panel door opened into the center of a space that looked like a formal entrance hall, very much after the fashion of grander English houses of the period. At 40 by 40 feet, the footprint of Littleton's mansion house was one and

a half times larger than Tayloe's Williamsburg residence, the largest of the capital's side-passage houses. This extra size allowed Eyre Hall to accommodate two separate chimneys to heat the larger entertaining rooms and main bedchambers. Having two chimneys freed the fireplaces from their corner positions in a shared stack arrangement and allowed them to be placed in a more formal position as the centerpieces on the back walls of the four principal rooms. The added space also made it possible to expand the width of the passage, making them feel more like a room rather than just an elongated corridor.

The novel, two-story pedimented portico of the west façade announced from the outside the principal entrance through which guests entered into a well-appointed, fully paneled space.[12] Although the passage extended the length of the house, it was designed to read and function as two very distinctive spaces of different widths divided visually by a graceful 10-foot-wide and 4-foot-deep elliptical archway at the center point, stretching from a 2-foot-wide projecting buffet on the west gambrel-end wall to an enclosed closet of equal dimensions projecting from the east partition wall. The front west door opened into the northwest corner of a fully paneled room measuring 15 feet in width and 20 feet in length from the west passage door to the face of the arch opening. This entrance hall is given further monumentality by two Ionic pilasters rising from plinths in the east and west corners of the south entrance wall, which are mirrored by a pair of matching pilasters on the stub walls of the arched opening at the north end of the room (Fig. 93). All four walls are sheathed in a double tier of raised panels divided at the chairboard level by a molded surbase. All the woodwork in this and all the other ground-floor rooms was finished with a coat of tan-colored paint. The base retains in places fragments of its original imitation-marble paint scheme.[13] The room is crowned with a full classical Ionic entablature; the cornice features undercut modillions; the frieze is cushioned; and there is a double architrave beneath. A fluted

Fig. 93. Entrance
hall, Eyre Hall,
looking south.

Fig. 94.
Staircase.

keystone accentuates the center of the north arch and is matched by an identical one that is centered over the eight-panel south doorway. The edge-grain heart-pine floorboards in this room, as well as all the others on the ground floor, measure between 4 and 5 inches in width and are secured by a series of wooden dowels drilled in their sides and secret nailed. Everything in the room—from the complex double moldings of the stiles and rails of the paneling to the entasis of the fluted pilasters—exemplifies the fidelity to academic classicism. This woodwork is an impressive introduction to the house, equal in workmanship to that found in the best mid-century gentry houses in Virginia.

Measuring 20 feet in width, the north space of the passage beyond the arch is wider than the entry and contains the open-string staircase that rises southward in the northeast corner of the east partition wall just south of the door into the library or office (Fig. 94). Because the east partition wall is 5 feet deeper than it is in the entry hall, the staircase

Fig. 95. Arch that encloses the upper flight of the stair, view looking north.

does not jut out into the north passage space. The staircase ascends along the east wall before it turns at a landing at right angles, where the upper flight rises westward within the spandrels of the arched opening. The plaster soffit of the arch hides the stringer and the underside of the treads and risers of the stair as it ascends to the second-floor landing. The decorative features of the lower flight are typical of the period. The molded and twisted handrail rises from a curtail step at the bottom and is supported by a series of turned, column-and-urn balusters rather than a newel post. There are three balusters on each tread to support the railing, which is ramped where it meets the wall of the landing, which is part of the spandrel of the enclosed space above the arched opening.

Like the hall, this extension of the cross passage reads less like a circulation space and more like a room and seems to have functioned as such when first built. The space measures 16 feet from the west outer wall to the paneled area beneath

the stair stringer and is 14 feet from the matching, eight-panel door on the north wall to the north face of the stub walls supporting the arch opening. There are two windows in this space, one on the west wall and another on the north wall just east of the north doorway, which provides light for the staircase. The east, north, and west walls have raised panel wainscoting that sits on a marbleized base and stands 3½ feet in height and is capped by a molded surbase. The walls above are plastered and may have been papered early if not originally. Littleton's 1769 inventory included "a parcel of stampt Paper for hangings," which may have been used in this space.[14] If so it was replaced by a bluish paper around 1810 and finally by the present colorful French scenic paper. These walls are capped by a dentilated Doric cornice. The cornice returns where the stair ascends on the east wall.

The south wall of the north passage consists of two paneled stub walls that support the spring of the arch (Fig. 95). The east one next to the staircase contains a low

Fig. 96. Parlor
looking east.

paneled door that opens into a closet, which now contains a staircase to the cellar. The west stub wall is the side of a buffet, a storage closet that has a pair of panel doors above the chairboard level on the west face of the area beneath the impost of the arch. These double doors are secured by side hinges and, when opened, reveal four curved shelves flanked by fluted pilasters (see Cat. 71). These buffet shelves displayed Littleton and Bridget Eyre's collection of porcelain, silver, and stemware when the house was first built, and they indicate that the north room probably served as the place where the family took their meals before the dining room was built about a decade later.

A doorway in the center of the east wall of the south entry hall opens into the largest room on the ground floor, the principal entertaining room known as the parlor. The door is on center with the fireplace of the internal chimney at the east end of the room. The room is nearly square. From the partition wall to the fireplace wall, the room is 19 feet in length and is 20 feet from north to south. Two south-facing windows illuminate the room. Befitting its high status, the walls of the parlor are fully paneled, with a double tier of raised panels divided at the surbase. Like the entry hall, the room is enhanced by a pair of fluted pilasters that sit on a plain plinth on the west entrance wall flanking the doorway and on the east fireplace wall framing the later neoclassical chimneypiece (Fig. 96). The room is capped by a Doric cornice very similar to the one in the north stair passage. The dentils in the parlor are larger than those in the passage. As in the entry hall, the cornice breaks out above the pilasters.

Two doorways with raised eight-panel doors flank the outer sides of the two fireplace pilasters. The one on the south side opens into a small storage closet, which is lit by a window on the east gambrel-end wall. This aperture retains its original pair of nine-light sashes with 1¼-inch-wide muntins, the only ones to survive on the ground floor. Original shelving survives on the fireplace wall on the north side of the closet and on the south wall opposite it.

The north doorway on the fireplace wall of the parlor leads to an enclosed vestibule, a space that measures 10 feet square and extends out from the east wall of the main block approximately 8 feet as a one-story gabled roof enclosure (now extended by a pedimented porch). The space is lit on the south side and may have had a matching aperture on the north side originally, but was altered a few years later to provide access through a short passage to the dining room addition (Fig. 97). The vestibule has an eight-paneled outer door on the east gable end that provided access to the kitchen and service buildings across a courtyard to the east. The walls of the vestibule are plastered above raised-panel wainscoting. In the northwest and southwest corners of the vestibule below the wainscoting are a pair of single doors that open into a storage space built into the area between the vestibule walls and the masonry sides of the two chimneys.

The vestibule not only offered external access to work spaces to the east, but also provided internal communication between the parlor and the last room in the original 40-foot-square house—the smaller library/office-chamber in the northeast corner. It measures 19 feet across the east fireplace wall and 14 feet from fireplace wall to the east partition wall with its door to the north stair passage. Two windows overlooking the garden are on the north wall. The room is modestly finished compared to the other spaces on the ground floor. It has a raised panel dado 3½ feet in height with plaster walls above except for the central section of the fireplace wall, which is fully paneled from the base to the cornice (Fig. 98). The cornice, which rings the room, is small

Fig. 97. East vestibule looking northeast.

Fig. 98. Library/ chamber looking southeast.

and unembellished. As in the parlor, the mantel is an early nineteenth-century replacement.

Although the function of this space during Littleton and Bridget's time is uncertain, it may have been used in the same manner as when their son occupied the house between 1768 and 1773. According to the list of items in Severn's estate inventory of 1774, the space probably served as his office and bedchamber as it contained a variety of personal possessions such as his silver-mounted fowling pieces, sword, razor, money scales, violin, looking glass, and 300 volumes of books as well as a bed, dressing chest, easy chair, and candlesticks and stand.[15]

Although the second floor was a private space with chambers, dressing rooms, and storage rooms, it is well finished with much the same trim and details found on the ground floor. All the floorboards on this floor are made with tight, edge-grained heart pine measuring between 4 and 5

inches in width, doweled and secret nailed. The hardware on nearly all the raised, eight-panel doors—except the one to the enclosed garret door and the closet doors in the east chambers—are mortise locks and hinges. Such top-of-the-line British hardware is rarely seen in such profusion in public and private spaces in gentry houses in the Chesapeake. All the door and window openings are trimmed with double architraves.

The second-floor plan mirrors the layout of the ground floor except the circulation space is confined to the center section of the west half around the stair landing (Fig. 99). This corridor provides access to all the storage and bedrooms on the floor and to the enclosed staircase to the garret. There are no windows in this space. Before a glazed door was installed in the nineteenth century in the doorway leading to the second-floor porch of the west portico, transoms above the bedroom and storage-room doors

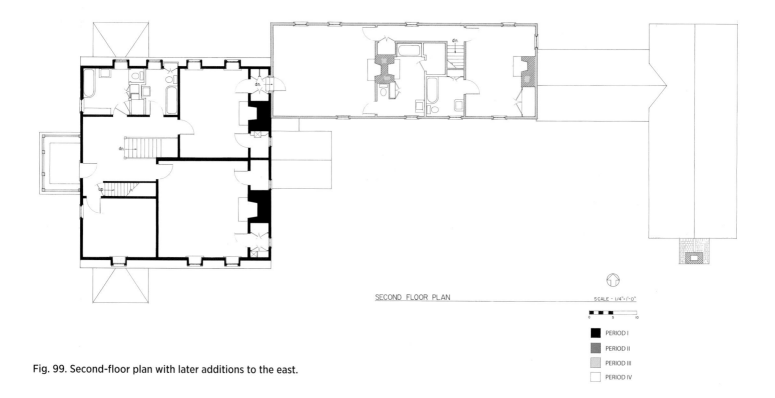

SCALE - 1/4"=1'-0"

0   5   10

■ PERIOD I
▨ PERIOD II
▦ PERIOD III
☐ PERIOD IV

Fig. 99. Second-floor plan with later additions to the east.

provided its only natural light. Like all the rooms on this floor, the passage walls are finished with a 3½-foot-high, raised paneled dado with simpler molded stiles and rails than found in the wainscoting below stairs (Fig. 100).

The plan of the second floor is divided into quadrants. The two on the eastern side contained the two large heated bedchambers, mirroring the size and arrangement of partitions of the parlor and library below. Over the parlor in the southeast corner is the main chamber measuring approximately 19 feet square. Entrance into the room is from the northwest corner. The room is lit by two windows on the south wall. Both are framed with window seats since they are contained within the area between the inner wall and the sloping roof frame of the lower part of the gambrel roof. A raised panel dado covers the lower walls with plaster above and a small cornice. The east fireplace wall has a fully paneled overmantel above the simple double architrave that frames the opening of the firebox (Fig. 101). At the back is a cast-iron fireback. Slightly taller than it is wide, the fireback is embossed with the name of its maker, "B. Grymes," and the date it was cast, "Novr 5th 1758" (see Cat. 150). Two doors on either side of the fireplace open into storage closets. Each closet is lit by a small window in the east gambrel-end wall. The second-best chamber in the northeast corner over the

Fig. 100. Second-floor stair landing and corridor.

Fig. 101. Second-floor southeast bedchamber looking east.

Fig. 102. Second-floor northeast bedchamber looking east.

library/office-chamber below measures 18 feet in depth and 14 feet from the door on the west partition wall to the fireplace wall. The layout and trim originally matched the larger chamber with two flanking closets on either side of the paneled fireplace (Fig. 102).

The western half of the second floor responds to the ground-floor partitions that form the side-passage spaces. However, the northwest quadrant of the upper floor is subdivided into a pair of unheated rooms, each 9½ feet square, in the northeast corner of the house over the stair passage. Early on, these two small rooms served as storage and domestic work spaces but, even so, had the same paneled dado as elsewhere. Each room was lit by a window with a seat on the north wall, reflecting the fact that the north façade of the house has four bays of openings whereas the south side only has three on each floor. In the southwest corner of the second floor is a small unheated chamber located over the entrance hall, which measures 15 feet in width and is 12 feet deep. It has a window seat in the south wall above the south doorway. Access to the room was through a doorway in the northwest corner just beyond the enclosed staircase to the garret.

The garret contains two unheated rooms. The enclosed staircase rises in one flight from west to east and alights at a small landing with a batten door on the left that leads into the west room and another batten door directly ahead that opens into the east room. Because of the slope of the gambrel roof, the east room is 20 feet in width north to south and 19 feet east to west and is lit by two small eight-light sash windows with their original wide muntins on the east gambrel end. The walls are covered by a rough coat of plaster and whitewashed. The floorboards range in width from 5½ to 11 inches and are butted together and face nailed with clasp nails. A peg rail runs along three sides of the room. The smaller west room is slightly longer—at 20 feet—but is only 13 feet wide, since the staircase encroaches upon the space on the south side. The room is finished in the same manner as the east one but only has a single, eight-light window in the center of the west gambrel end. There is much graffiti in this room along the south and west walls, much of which is illegible except for William Eyre's name, dates from the 1790s, and a phrase declaring his everlasting love for a young woman, perhaps his future wife Grace Taylor. More graffiti appears on the walls above the lower steps of the garret stair—mainly early nineteenth-century dates and initials, the rest of it mostly indecipherable.

THE DINING ROOM ADDITION, EARLY 1770s

The Virginia gentry took pride in their hospitality. They enjoyed welcoming neighbors as well as visitors into their houses, where formal entertainments culminated in the host sharing the bounty of his larder and cellar in a sumptuous meal at his dining table. In the last years of the Revolution, the Marquis de Chastellux, an aide to the French general Rochambeau, observed that "Virginians have the reputation . . . of living nobly in their houses, and of being hospitable; they give strangers not only a willing, but a liberal reception." Generously received and invited to share in their largesse, the marquis perceptibly diagnosed the social dynamics that shaped the plan of their houses, which he declared to be "spacious and ornamented, but their apartments are not commodious . . . for being in general ignorant of the comfort of reading and writing, they want nothing in their whole house but a bed, a dining-room, and a drawing room for company. The chief magnificence of the Virginians consists in furniture, linen, and plate . . . and [they] content themselves with a well-stored cellar and a handsome buffet."[16]

There is no evidence that Chastellux visited Eyre Hall in his travels across Virginia, but his description of the core elements of the planter's house—the parlor, sparse bedchambers with few writing desks, but entertaining rooms well provided with furniture, table linens, and silver service pieces displayed in buffets along with queensware and Chinese punch bowls with a cellar filled with casks of wine—could easily have been taken from Severn Eyre's 1774 inventory of the goods and spaces in Eyre Hall including a dining room, which had been added to the northeast corner of the house sometime before his death. Although the rooms were not designated in the inventory, the route the enumerators took as they walked through the house can be followed, and the items listed in them provide the best evidence of how Severn and Margaret Eyre furnished the house and its new one-story, dining room wing.

In the early 1770s, guests who visited Eyre Hall when Severn and Margaret Eyre presided over its affairs would have been greeted in the paneled entry hall. The Eyres positioned 18 "passage chairs" around the perimeter of the room, with some perhaps spilling over beyond the arch into the north stair passage. They may have also arranged for a large leather couch in the room for more comfortable seating, perhaps as an enticement for conversations during the warm months when the doors at the north and south ends of the passage

Fig. 103. Dining room.

would be opened to catch cross breezes. A tea table allowed for refreshments to be served in the space. Some of the serving bowls and other equipage associated with tea and other libations may have been displayed in the buffet on the west wall beneath the arch. A glass lanthorn, which provided some light to the space in the evenings, probably hung from the fluted keystone on the south face of the arch in the center of the room.

What probably garnered the attention of visitors were the 40 framed copperplate engravings that were arranged in tiers on the upper section of the raised panel wainscoting between the surbase and entablature. The images displayed on the walls were a microcosm of the Eyres' view of their place in the world. Prints of ancient Roman ruins whose architectural vocabulary was reflected in the woodwork of the room underscored the owner's appreciation of the role of classicism in shaping contemporary education, aesthetics, and politics. The English landscape prints of the seats of English nobility expressed the affinity between those country

estates and the fine houses and gardens of Virginia gentry such as the Eyres. They spoke of the natural political and social order of society in which the occupants of Eyre Hall took their rightful place as partners in the British American empire. Finally, a series of small sporting prints of English racehorses revealed the family's same strong passion for the turf as felt by many of their English peers.[17]

When the door on the south wall of the entry hall opened into the parlor, guests beheld a room richly furnished with the best furniture in the house suitable for formal and fashionable entertainments. A dozen mahogany chairs were arrayed around the room, as well as two mahogany armchairs. The two most expensive mahogany tables were in the room, along with a mahogany sideboard, and two mahogany card tables. Two gilt pier glasses hung on the fully paneled walls, and above the fireplace on the east wall hung a gilt chimney mirror. The furniture could be arranged in a variety of ways to accommodate a few intimates or a dozen or more guests for card games, conversations, formal and informal entertainments, and the consumption of fashionable beverages such as tea, coffee, or chocolate, or enjoying a glass of wine or punch. The mirrors enhanced the reflected light of candles and the fire in the hearth during an evening's gathering.[18]

In the rituals of hospitality in colonial Virginia, the high moment occurred in the afternoon when the host and his guests sat down for a formal meal. When Littleton and Bridget Eyre first moved into the house, that meal took place in the north end of the passage during summer months and perhaps in the parlor when it was cooler. Spaces that served many purposes were not unusual in gentry houses during that time and remained quite common long afterward in more modest houses. However, by the time that Severn and Margaret inherited the house in the late 1760s, they probably felt the need to have a dedicated dining room and so undertook the construction of a large, 24-by-20-foot heated room off the northeast end of the house (Fig. 103). It was the most logical place to construct a wing since it could be accessed with little disturbance to the original arrangement of the house through a small extension off to the north side of the east vestibule. The new wing projected northward 8 feet beyond the plane of the north wall of the original house (see Fig. 90). Two windows on the north side of the new dining room afforded views into the garden. A large fireplace on the east gable-end wall provided warmth on cooler days. Finally, the dining room was located closer to the kitchen; the steps from the east door of the vestibule led to the kitchen about 70 feet away.

Another solution that had little impact on the arrangement of the original house but proved advantageous to the function of the dining room and the parlor were a pair of buffets constructed in the north and south walls of the vestibule. The double-door closets on these walls inserted above the surbase over the original storage spaces below provided a generous place to display the plate, ceramics, and stemware of the new dining room and parlor. All the specialized tablewares and accoutrements used during the meal were stored when not in use in these new buffets. Their paneled doors nearly match those below, except that moldings of the stiles and rails are simpler than those below, which corresponded to the more complex pattern of the original woodwork throughout the house. The simpler moldings also appear on the dado in the three-foot long passage connecting the dining room to the vestibule.

The architectural trim of the dining room was modest. Unlike the rest of the house, the dining room was not paneled originally, but had a base and plastered walls. Severn may have considered the raised full paneling that his father installed in the late 1750s a little old-fashioned as many new houses were furnished with "modern wainscoting," which consisted of a dado of flush sheathed boards. Was it papered instead? Evidence from other houses in the Chesapeake suggest that dining rooms of the late colonial period were wallpapered, so it is possible that Severn and Margaret chose to cover their new room in this fashion.[19] If so, evidence for it disappeared when the room was substantially repaired in the 1930s renovations. What did hang on the walls were three large looking glasses, valued slightly less than the gilt pier glasses in the parlor. The original chimneypiece was replaced in the 1930s or perhaps earlier. Even so, the room was spacious and provided a logical route through the public spaces of the house.

Severn and Margaret furnished the dining room with two mahogany tables (not as valuable as the two in the parlor) and a dozen walnut chairs. In addition to the dining furniture, the space contained a cherry case and 14 bottles, a plate warmer, and a clock. The presence of a mahogany desk and book case reflected the fact that the dining room sometimes served as an office to conduct business after the women had left the table.[20]

Fig. 104. Brownsville, Northampton County, built in 1806.

Fig. 105. Brownsville, stair passage.

THE ARCHITECTURAL IMPACT OF EYRE HALL

Novel in its time, the plan of Eyre Hall influenced many planters and merchants on the Eastern Shore who constructed dwellings that replicated its form in varying degrees of fidelity through the first quarter of the nineteenth century. The most superficial resemblance was to the many double-pile, gambrel-roofed and gable-roofed, side-passage and cross-passage houses, which appeared by the 1770s and continued to be built well into the 1820s and 1830s.[21] Besides the boxy form of Eyre Hall, these buildings also exemplify the pattern of adding dining rooms or other spaces offset against the heated fireplace wall opposite the passage, which created over time a telescoping effect when these one-story wings were strung out with additional connecting rooms including kitchens often placed at the far end. A few of the side-passage houses such as Brownsville, a well-appointed brick structure erected by John Upshur in 1806 at a cost of $10,000, had additional features indebted to the Eyre Hall design (Fig. 104). Upshur, the stepfather of Ann Upshur Eyre, seems to have been inspired by Eyre Hall's staircase design. The open-string stair with curtail step rises in one corner of the paneled dado passage and turns at right angles back across the width of the hall. The undercarriage was encased within a graceful arch whose architrave has a scrolled keystone at its midpoint (Fig. 105).

Thomas Littleton Savage also knew Eyre Hall very well as a friend of the family who provided the security for the marriage of Margaret Eyre to George Parker in 1786 and was

a witness to Littleton Eyre's will in 1787.[22] So impressed was he with the design that he chose to faithfully copy it after he married Mary Savage. In 1791, the couple built Elkington near Eastville (Fig. 106).[23] The two-story frame house is slightly smaller than Eyre Hall, measuring 36 feet square rather than 40, but in all other respects replicated its plan (Fig. 108). The transverse-passage arrangement features a two-story pedimented portico on the west gable end whose central doorway provided access into a wide passage with doors that opened onto one-story porches at each end of the passage. The staircase is configured in the same fashion as at Eyre Hall, except that the arch enclosing the soffit of the upper flight of the stair is skewed rather than symmetrical (Fig. 107). The passage is also papered like its prototype with French wallpaper, but here it is printed with lively hunting scenes. On the east side of the house, there is the same enclosed vestibule as at Eyre Hall that gives access on

Fig. 106. Elkington,
Northampton County,
built in 1792.

Fig. 107. Elkington, stair passage looking south.

Fig. 108. Elkington, ground-floor plan.

one side to the door to the dining room, which is offset on its north side 8 feet from the plane of the north wall of the main block. The only difference in the arrangement between Eyre Hall and Elkington is that, at the latter, an enclosed staircase descends through the west end of the dining room from the chamber above and lands in the vestibule, making the dining room feel less spacious.

Not restricted to the Eastern Shore, the cross-passage plan appeared in both urban and rural locations throughout Virginia and Maryland in the late eighteenth and early nineteenth centuries. Among the most refined is the two-story brick dwelling erected at an intersection in Norfolk by

merchant Moses Myers in 1793. The front entrance is treated more formally than at Eyre Hall or other Northampton County houses as the modillion cornice returns on the gable entrance façade, creating a pseudo-pediment with a D-window in the gable tympanum. Measuring 42 feet across the front gable end and 36 feet deep, the house has a 13-foot-wide transverse passage with staircase on the partition wall. In Hanover County, the Tinsley family built a smaller rustic interpretation of the form at Totomoi plantation around 1800. The 32-foot-square plan features a two-story pedimented portico, which sheltered the main entrance into the cross passage on the west gable end of the frame house.

EARLY NINETEENTH–CENTURY IMPROVEMENTS: "A GENEROUS HOSPITALITY REIGNED IN HIS HOME"[24]

In the first quarter of the nineteenth century, John and Ann Eyre made substantial improvements to Eyre Hall, though they did not change the plan of the original house. They modernized some of the architectural features and raised and expanded the east wing to accommodate more service spaces and bedchambers. Their handiwork transformed the house inside and out through the use of more delicately proportioned neoclassical details that mitigated the beefiness of the original Georgian features. The aesthetic difference between the two styles is most evident on the inside with the neoclassical mantels installed in the two ground-floor rooms of the old house. In the parlor, craftsmen reworked the old firebox and faced it with fine-veined light gray marble slabs. They installed a well-proportioned neoclassical chimneypiece (Fig. 109). The carved entablature is supported by flanking three-quarter engaged fluted columns that taper from a central band in both an upward and downward direction. The column bases sit on a low plinth. The capitals are decorated with embossed anthemion flowers. The three-part frieze of the chimneypiece—featuring delicate gouge work, reeding, beading, bead-and-reel carving—has two outer panels with

classical swags and stylized anthemions framing a central panel with swags attached to a ribbed urn with delicate bellflowers. Like the classical figures in the frieze above the columns, much of this decoration may be composition ornament rather than carved wood.

In contrast to the neoclassical finesse of the parlor mantel, the one in the smaller library is an exercise in abstraction (Fig. 110). The chimneypiece and the facing of the firebox are composed of finely grained dark gray marble. The stylized post-and-lintel construction of the chimneypiece eschews the delicacy of the neoclassical and is a precursor of the bolder and less fastidious forms of the Greek Revival that would dominate American architecture in the coming decades. The original library mantel may have been replaced when the one in the parlor was done, but it is possible that it may postdate it by a decade or more since it is evident that John and Ann continued to tinker with the house as they added new furnishings and made other changes to Eyre Hall through the 1820s.

A substantial but subtle alteration to the house occurred when workmen replaced the window sash. They removed nearly all the old sash with their wide glazing bars and installed new ones with fashionable thinner muntins, giving the apertures a more transparent appearance. In place of the tan woodwork of the colonial period, the Eyres had the entertaining rooms painted a bluish green and the doors grained.[25] They also papered the northern half of the

Fig. 111. South porch.

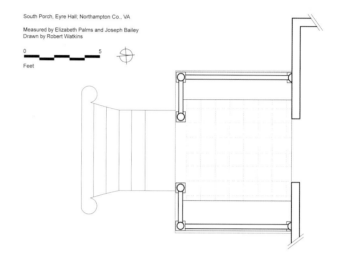

Fig. 112. South porch, paving and plan.

South Porch, Eyre Hall; Northampton Co., VA

Measured by Elizabeth Palms and Joseph Bailey
Drawn by Robert Watkins

0   5
Feet

passage with a bluish paper around 1810 or slightly later. In 1817 they replaced that wallpaper with a stunning French scenic paper, "Les Rives du Bosphore" (see Fig. 123).

On the outside, the Eyres repaired or entirely replaced the three original open porches on the north, west, and south side and added an open porch to the east vestibule between August 1805 and January 1807 when they expanded the east wing.[26] Although they retained the original half-arched base of the west pedimented portico, masons rebuilt the solid bases of the north and south porches, finishing them in 1:5 bond (Fig. 111). They preserved the Flemish bond beneath the projecting part of the east vestibule but added brick foundations for a 5-by-10-foot open porch added to the east end. All the porches were fitted with new stone steps, variegated paving stones, and their platforms were railed in with built-in benches on each side (Fig. 112). Their roofs were supported by attenuated neoclassical Doric columns that must have been far less ponderous than their colonial predecessors. This work preserved the pedimented portico capping the second-story west porch, but the north and south porches received hipped roofs.

The most noticeable improvement to the house during this building campaign was the expansion of the east wing. The one-story, dining room wing added to the northeast corner of the house by the early 1770s was raised to two full stories and integrated structurally and visually with the construction of a housekeeper's apartment to the east (Fig. 113). This apartment extended nearly 33 feet, enlarging the east wing to 57 by 20 feet, and bringing it into closer proximity to the kitchen. The expanded service wing interrupted the earlier visual relationship between the garden layout and the service yard, blocking the north–south axis that flowed from one to the other. In an era that placed increasing emphasis on improving integrated service spaces, this aesthetic rupture could be overlooked given the benefit of having more storage space in a room dedicated to that function immediately east of the old dining room. The room probably had shelves, drawers, and presses in which to keep many of the necessities and accoutrements that were required to entertain on a grand scale. It may have been at this time that the Eyres introduced a call-bell system throughout parts of the house. Crank handles

Fig. 113.
East wing.

located near a fireplace or some other convenient place in public and private rooms connected to a system of wires that were embedded in wall cavities until they exited at some exterior locations where they were connected to brass bells that would ring to summon servants to different designated rooms. All evidence of that system has disappeared, except for a couple of bells that had survived and been remounted on the south eaves of the east wing, which, if there originally, would have been within earshot of the old kitchen.

The new east wing had a passage that ran lengthwise along the south face, which was lit by a window on either side of a central double door. Some of the old molded English stone porch steps were reused to provide access to this doorway from the south courtyard. Inside the doorway, the corridor turned right to a door to the housekeeper's room and left to the storage room and further along to a doorway at the end that opened into the dining room. A pair of arches flank the south exterior door and define a small vestibule in front of a steep staircase on the north side that rises in a straight run to the second floor (Fig. 114). The upper story of the east wing contained three new heated bedchambers—two over the new service wing and another to the west over the dining room, all of which were connected by a short corridor in the center of the addition running along the north wall overlooking the garden. These

Fig. 114. Corridor in east ground-floor wing.

Fig. 115. Late nineteenth-century view of the house.

modestly finished second-floor rooms more than doubled the number of heated bedchambers for guests and extended family members, which must have been filled constantly in a period that was famed for the hospitality of its generous and welcoming hosts.

POSTBELLUM SUMMER RETREAT

The improvements implemented by John and Ann Eyre in the first decades of the nineteenth century suited the needs of their successors, Severn and Margaret Eyre. Severn was a young widower when he inherited the house in 1855 from his great-uncle, and he made no changes until a number of years after he remarried in 1865. The end of slavery had a substantial impact on the service spaces and other domestic routines. At some time in the postbellum decades, Severn demolished the old kitchen and replaced it with a one-room kitchen attached to the east end of the east wing (see Fig. 125). It is not clear if this occurred before Severn, Margaret, and their three children, who were born in the first half of the 1870s, departed to live full time in Baltimore in the early 1880s, or after Eyre Hall became a summer retreat in the last

years of the century. Certainly by the turn of the century, Severn had added an open porch about 8 feet in width that ran the length of the east wing from the new one-story kitchen in the east to the dining room at the west end. The only other alteration made to the house was the construction of a small framed room for a toilet off the north side of the library, which was entered through the north closet door. By the end of the century, the livery of Eyre Hall had changed. Severn's workmen painted the weatherboards a dark color (perhaps a medium gray), which contrasted to the white trim of the porches, cornice, end boards, windows, and doors and the dark green of the louvered window shutters. They also covered the brick foundations of the house and porches with white paint (Fig. 115).

REHABILITATION AND MODERNIZATION, 1930s

The marriage of Severn Eyre's granddaughter Margaret Eyre Taylor to Henry duPont Baldwin in 1928 heralded the last major transformation of Eyre Hall. For more than 40 years it had been a comfortable, but increasingly old-fashioned country retreat. The house had become dowdy with few modern conveniences such as electricity, central heat, or running water, features that had become common in urban homes but still remained novelties in rural Virginia. The kitchen had an old wood-fired cook stove. Margaret Taylor Baldwin decided that she would restore the ancestral retreat and turn it into a home for modern living and the farm a place of renewed productivity.

In 1930 she hired Samuel and Victorine Homsey, architects from Boston who were related to her husband, to turn her dreams of renewal into a reality. The Homseys presented Margaret with a set of architectural drawings in April 1931 showing different schemes that explored ways in which to introduce bathrooms, closets, a new kitchen, and service spaces in the old house and new additions. One sketch showed the insertion of a large, three-part window as a replacement for the two original windows on the north wall of the dining room, moving the two windows in the old pantry and housekeeper's room and insertion of a doorway with a classical frontispiece in between these shifted openings to make the north wall of the east wing more symmetrical as well as provide access directly into the garden from this wing. Although she was eager to have modern systems in the house, Margaret consciously rejected designs that introduced new features that would substantially alter the appearance of the old house. The Homseys soon accepted her philosophy of preserving the old and making the new blend in with the historic character of the house.

An essential part of the new work included major structural repairs to the roof and cellar. In the garret, workmen installed wooden trusses with vertical iron rods to support the second-story girders; in the cellar, new bracing was introduced to support the first-floor framing, and some of the brickwork including jambs was rebuilt. An assessment of the structural integrity in the east wing found that the foundations supporting the late eighteenth-century dining room addition required substantial repairs. Workmen had to replace the failing foundation walls with new ones. They took up the old floorboards in order to replace the sills and a number of the sleepers, and then relaid them. This room, like nearly all the rest, had its original plaster removed and replaced. The Homseys designed a new neoclassical chimneypiece to enhance the fireplace.

In August 1932, the architects, who soon opened a branch of their practice in Wilmington, Delaware, devised a design that the owners approved, which featured four bathrooms on the second floor. In order to serve the two heated bedrooms in the old part of the house, two small bathrooms were created in the space taken up by the two old unheated storage spaces in the northwest corner (see Fig. 99). The partition between the two was shifted slightly to the east and the original wainscoting reused downstairs to enhance the dining room. The other two bathrooms were designed to fit into the space that had been the smaller central bedroom in the east wing, which would provide en suite accommodations for the large west bedroom over the dining room and the smaller east bedroom above the old housekeeper's room. All four bathrooms featured the latest in 1930s plumbing fixtures, in colors that matched the tiled walls in each of the different bathrooms—yellow, blue, purple, and green.

Given more leeway with the design for a new kitchen and service rooms east of the original east wing, the Homseys showed that they understood the early architectural vocabulary of the colonial period and were able to develop a design that in many ways replicated the pattern of the telescoped arrangement of some Eastern Shore houses, particularly Kendall Grove where the architects also adapted a number of details from its service wing. The 1932 design drawings of the service wing consisted of a relatively small, one-story kitchen in the same place against the east end of the housekeeper's wing where Severn Eyre's late nineteenth-century kitchen had been. The kitchen wing was connected at its east end by a 7½-foot-wide screened breezeway with

Fig. 116. New kitchen and service wing, ca. 1935.

steps on the south face that provided entrance into this new wing. The new kitchen measured 16 feet in length and 13 feet deep, with the sink on the north wall between two windows that overlooked the garden and a stove on the south side between two matching windows. The overall length of the kitchen and breezeway was 24 feet. On the east side of the breezeway was a one-story wing set at right angles measuring 43 feet in length from north to south and 17 feet in width. Whether the architects were aware or not, the footprint of the new service wing was located almost precisely on top of the site of the original brick kitchen, whose foundations must have turned up when the building was under construction. The northern part of the wing extended 5 feet north of the breezeway, and the southern part was dominated by a large exterior brick chimney laid in Flemish bond. The wing was divided into two levels—the floor in the northern half was the same height as the breezeway, which provided access to a servants' dining room, storage room, and small toilet. The southern part of the wing was entered at ground level from the west façade and contained a small bathroom at the north end, the remainder of the space being designed for storage and a furnace.

Under Mrs. Baldwin's direction, Samuel Homsey's design made the new kitchen and service wing appear to be a natural extension of the house in a way that fit the pattern of old Eastern Shore dwellings where service spaces and kitchens were connected to the main house (Fig. 116). By siting the new kitchen where the Victorian one had been and the service wing on the footprint of the original kitchen that had stood at right angles to the early east wing, the architects devised a solution that echoed earlier arrangements. They drew upon details found at Kendall Grove to anchor the new design in the local vernacular. The foundations of the kitchen and breezeway consisted of three low relieving arches that replicated those found on the porches and the connecting passageway to the service wing at Kendall Grove, which was built in the early nineteenth century and was the

home of the Parker family who had intermarried with the Eyres. They also borrowed from this neighboring house the use of flush-beaded sheathing boards for the exterior cladding of the new Eyre Hall service wing. In addition, they replicated another, more unusual detail from Kendall Grove. The windows in the new Eyre Hall kitchen appear to be double six-over-six-pane sashes, but in fact each of the apertures is composed of a single 12-pane sash that slides up into a wall cavity when opened.

The construction of the new kitchen service wing, the new bathrooms, the repair and upgrade of the dining room, and the installation of heating, plumbing, and electrical systems continued through 1934 and possibly into 1935. These were the last major changes made to the house—although Samuel and Victorine Homsey continued to provide designs for buildings and structures on the estate for the Baldwins through 1940, including the entrance gates to Eyre Hall from Route 13 inspired by the early nineteenth-century garden fence.

In 1990 Furlong Baldwin, who had inherited Eyre Hall from his mother on her death in 1979, was forced to undertake major repairs to the house after a tornado swept through the estate, uprooting many trees and toppling chimneys whose falling bricks crushed the 1930s east porch, the roof of the wing, and caused other damage throughout the house including water damage to the French wallpaper in the north passage. Besides repairing the structural damage and restoring the wallpaper, Baldwin decided to renovate the 1930s kitchen and service wing. He retained the

Norfolk firm of Hanbury, Evans, Newill, Vlattas to redesign the kitchen, enclose the breezeway to make it a breakfast room, and convert the north room of the service wing into an office and enlarge the adjoining bathroom. The firm also designed a small, one-story frame cottage for an office for Mr. Baldwin overlooking Eyreville Creek at the north end of the old paddock northeast of the house. This most recent work, and an ongoing schedule of regular and conscientious maintenance, has left the fabric of Eyre Hall in the best condition that it has been in for well over a century.

NOTES

1. Gambrel- or Dutch-roof houses first appeared in the Chesapeake region in the 1740s and express the growing importance that residents ascribed to the upper floors. The steep slope of the lower section of the two-part roof allowed for more headroom in upstairs chambers, which were also more likely to be heated than one-story, gable-roof houses. See Mark Wenger, "Town House & Country House: Eighteenth and Early Nineteenth Centuries," in *The Chesapeake House: Architectural Investigation by Colonial Williamsburg*, ed. Cary Carson and Carl R. Lounsbury (Chapel Hill: University of North Carolina Press, 2013), 131–32.

2. Isaac Ware, *A Complete Body of Architecture* (London: T. Osborne and J. Shipton, 1756), 132.

3. For a more detailed analysis of the emergence and application of classical design principles in regional building practices, see Carl R. Lounsbury, "The Design Process," in Carson and Lounsbury, *Chesapeake House*, 70–77.

4. For an overview of the construction process at the gentry level in the colonial period, see Barbara Burlison Mooney, *Prodigy Houses of Virginia: Architecture and the Native Elite* (Charlottesville: University of Virginia Press, 2008), 149–224.

5. For the rise of contractors for public building projects in colonial Virginia, see Dell Upton, *Holy Things and Profane: Anglican Parish Churches in Colonial Virginia* (Cambridge, Mass.: MIT Press, 1986), 23–34; Carl R. Lounsbury, *The Courthouses of Early Virginia: An Architectural History* (Charlottesville: University of Virginia Press, 2005), 168–215.

6. Ralph T. Whitelaw, *Virginia's Eastern Shore: A History of Northampton and Accomack Counties* (Richmond: Virginia Historical Society, 1951), 1:189. For further speculation on the origins of the brick building that was Eyre Hall's first kitchen, see the following section on the domestic service buildings.

7. This fence line and gate location were discovered by archaeologists in April 2019 and July 2020. Nicholas M. Luccketti and Anthony W. Smith, "Archaeological Testing of a 19th-Century Slave Quarter and the West Yard at Eyre Hall, Northampton County, Virginia," unpublished report, James River Institute for Archaeology, July 2020.

8. John Summerson, *Georgian London*, 3rd ed. (Cambridge, Mass.: MIT Press, 1978), 44–51; Dan Cruickshank and Neil Burton, *Life in the Georgian City* (New York: Viking, 1990), 51–60.

9. Peter Guillery, *The Small House in Eighteenth-Century London* (New Haven: Yale University Press, 2004), 60–77.

10. Bernard L. Herman, *Town House: Architecture and Material Life in the Early American City, 170–1830* (Chapel Hill: University of North Carolina Press, 2005), 1–32; Mary Ellen Hayward and Charles Belfoure, *The Baltimore Rowhouse* (New York: Princeton Architectural Press, 1999).

11. William Fairfax to Bryan Fairfax, July 14, 1735, Papers of the Fairfax Estate, British Museum, London, cited by Wenger in "Town House & Country House," 126.

12. For a detailed analysis of the fabric of Eyre Hall, see Michael Bourne, "A Description of Eyre Hall, Cheriton, Northampton County, Virginia," unpublished report undertaken as part of the project of recording the plans for the Historic American Buildings Survey, Library of Congress, Washington, D.C., December 2004.

13. Susan L. Buck, "Cross-Section Paint Microscopy Report: Eyre Hall: Passage, Parlor, and Library, Northampton County, Virginia," May 18, 2015, 28.

14. Inventory of the estate of Littleton Eyre, October 14, 1769, Northampton County Wills & Inventories Book, No. 24, 1766–1772, 224.

15. Inventory of the estate of Severn Eyre, February 27, 1774, Northampton County Wills & Inventories, No. 25, 1775–1777, 393.

16. Marquis de Chastellux, *Travels in North America, in the Years 1780, 1781, and 1782* (London, 1787; New York: White, Gallaher & White, 1827), 296–97. For the importance of buffets in gentry houses, see Betty Crowe Leviner, "Buffet or Bowfat? The Built-in Cupboard in the Eighteenth Century," *The Magazine Antiques* (May 1999): 754-61.

17. Inventory of the estate of Severn Eyre, 391; for a description of the prints see McKinney's discussion of the surviving prints in the catalogue section of this book.

18. Inventory of the estate of Severn Eyre, 391.

19. On wallpaper in dining rooms in the region, see Margaret Beck Pritchard, "Wallpaper," in Carson and Lounsbury, *Chesapeake House*, 388–89.

20. Inventory of the estate of Severn Eyre, 391–92.

21. Some of the more notable ones in Northampton include Ferry House, built in the late eighteenth century on land that had been associated with the Eyres and Bowdoins on Wilsonia Neck; Coventon in Eastville, built in the late 1790s with a cross-passage plan with gable entrance; Liberty Hall, a side-passage plan erected in the late 1810s; and Caserta, a frame house with an odd roof configuration.

22. The connection with Eyre Hall became stronger in the next generation. Mary Burton Savage, Thomas's daughter by his second wife, ended up marrying William L. Eyre in 1828. She and her son Severn Eyre moved into Eyre Hall after John Eyre died in 1855. Severn married Margaret Stratton Parker whose father, John S. Parker, is buried at Elkington. His sister was the mistress of Elkington for much of the nineteenth century after Thomas Savage sold the house to John Stratton, an ambitious young politician who served a term in the United States House of Representatives.

23. Michael J. Worthington and Jane I. Seiter, "The Tree-Ring Dating of Elkington, Eastville, Virginia," unpublished report, Oxford Tree-Ring Laboratory, December 2019.

24. From the epitaph on John Eyre's gravestone.

25. Buck, "Cross-Section Paint Microscopy Report," 31–32.

26. The precise date of this work is documented in two insurance policies taken out by John Eyre with the Mutual Assurance Society of Virginia. In the 1805 policy, the plan of the house shows and describes a one-story wing on the northeast corner of the house. The 1807 policy indicates that the wing had been "altered from one to two stories" and expanded to 57 feet in length by 20 feet in width. Mutual Assurance Society of Virginia, policy no. 604, August 25, 1805, and policy no. 1186, January 22, 1807.

ARCHITECTURAL
HARDWARE

Old houses tell stories, from their outward appearance down to the smallest details. Even pieces of hardware, handmade with hammer and anvil or casting and file, can reveal much about the people who bought and used them. This is especially true for large eighteenth-century houses, complex in their arrangement and finish. Littleton Eyre's use of fittings, including fine English hardware, offers a striking example.

In the half century before the American Revolution, Virginia's grandees put architecture to work not just to show off their wealth and rank, but to create arenas designed for use by ladies and gentlemen who knew society's rules of etiquette and practiced its acknowledged good manners. Some buildings they built at public expense for public use—courthouses, churches, and the capitol at Williamsburg.[1] They gave no less attention to architectural decorum when they constructed or remodeled their own houses. Everything from plan, ornament, and paint colors to the choice and placement of locks and hinges served to choreograph the movement and activities of household residents as well as their genteel guests.

By mid-century proper gentry houses came with several best rooms, including a circulation passage or lobby, a primary reception room, an area for formal dining, and a first-floor bedchamber. Additional refined bedchambers were housed upstairs.[2] When planning his upscale house in 1759, Littleton Eyre chose to assemble those spaces in an economical package, a form described now as a side-passage plan with a pair of lower rooms opening off one side of the entry.[3] Condensed though it was, by building on a large scale below a generous gambrel roof, he made room for all the requisite accommodations, an unusually broad passage with a handsome parlor and a library/office-chamber alongside. As Carl Lounsbury suggests in his description of the house, formal dining was initially located at the rear of the passage, beyond a wooden archway that cleverly contains the upper run of the stair.[4]

Choices of finish animated the different character of domestic spaces, illustrated at Eyre Hall by the variety of original woodwork from the entrance and parlor to the most modest bedchamber. Respectability required plastered or paneled walls, sizable sash windows, paneled doors, and at least a few Roman moldings, all answering to the term "neat." Neatness also favored the *absence* of rude finishes, such as doors fitted with heavy strap hinges and unpainted wooden locks. Many Eastern Shore officeholders below

Littleton Eyre's rank built houses partially or entirely finished in this manner. But builders of Eyre's standing often indulged themselves with richer finishes, each in his own way. It was in those choices that one now sees expressions of personality as well as purse.

Owners chose degrees of elaboration and refinement in woodwork, paint colors, and quality of hardware to unify the appearance of interiors as a whole as well as to differentiate the succession of spaces through which family and guests moved. Originally, hardware and paint at Eyre Hall served as unifiers, while woodwork created the architectural gradations that marked the relative importance of different rooms. Originally, painted woodwork on the ground floor was uniformly tan, combined with gray marbled bases.[5]

Everywhere, the hardware was exceptionally fine (Fig. 117). Its quality throughout the house stands out when compared with that in gentry houses built elsewhere in Virginia. Peyton Randolph's townhouse in Williamsburg (1754–55), William Randolph's Wilton outside Richmond (1750–53), and Fielding Lewis's Kenmore (1772), just to take three contemporary examples, all mixed and matched polished brass and older-style iron hardware with various paint schemes, wallpaper, and woodwork of various qualities.

Littleton Eyre, on the other hand, favored consistency and uniformity when it came to picking out paint colors and ordering hardware. In 1759 there were many ways to hinge and lock doors. Carpenters could hang a door leaf on strips of leather, cheap staples, iron straps turning on pintles, dovetails in butterfly shapes, H and HL hinges, and hidden mortise hinges. At mid-century, when Eyre's London factor probably shipped the hardware order for the Virginian's new house, English hardware manufacturers still offered many top-of-the-line products, which only later lost their cachet when the Industrial Revolution made available a wider range of hardware and metal ornament at competitive prices. Eyre didn't skimp; he bought the best and installed it throughout the house regardless.

Refined eighteenth-century taste called for hiding the means of attachment. In the most dignified spaces doors fitted with HL hinges had the stationary arm hidden behind the architrave; the active one was then set into the face of the leaf and painted over, leaving only

Fig. 117. Escutcheon and handle, and lock plate, on first-floor passage door.

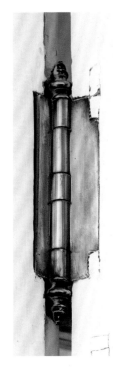

Fig. 118. Northeast chamber closet door. Raised, eight-panel door with HL hinges, one arm beneath architrave, mortise lock and brass escutcheon.

Fig. 119. Mortise hinge.

the outline, screws, nails, and washers visible. Eyre did just this on closet doors in his upstairs chambers (Fig. 118). A superior choice was to employ mortise hinges, with the one arm set and wedged into the edge of the leaf and the other hidden below, facing the doorframe. These cost more and required more skill to install; it made sense to restrict them to genteel spaces.

Brass was favored over iron because display was valued more than durability. The knuckles of brass barrels wore down more rapidly than ferrous metal. Because the working part of a hinge could not be hidden, the eye was diverted by threading decorative finials to the ends of the smooth-filed barrels, each ornament a miniature essay in classical shapes (Fig. 119). Wealthy gentlemen positioned brass mortise hinges strategically where they would be seen and appreciated. For example, builders of William Pasteur's Williamsburg house (ca. 1770) restricted their use to a pair of doors in the single best room. Thomas Jefferson acquired eight pairs, probably for his first Monticello; he later reused them only in his bedroom and on passage doors opening into the two-story hall when he rebuilt the house in 1796–1809. The spendthrift William Byrd III was more promiscuous; his brass hinges ran all the way from the first to the third floors in the grandly conceived Westover of 1751.[6]

Eyre Hall is more modest than Westover in scale and finish. But Eyre matched Byrd in his use of brass mortise hinges; he bought more than a dozen sets. Such hardware, hinges as well as locks, were sized for doors of different dimensions. Eyre's mortise hinges in three sizes ranged from 6 to 7 inches high on exterior doors and 5 inches

on the interior ones, all slightly larger than Byrd's selection. American customers almost always ordered such specialized hardware from Britain, so the long Atlantic crossing made exact matching difficult. Eyre's builders mounted the rear and right entry doors on the largest hinges and the more prominent front and left doors on the intermediate size. At least one right-hand lock had to make do on a left-hand door, so it was mounted upside down, a common eighteenth-century Virginia expedient.

The twin appeals of luxury and high fashion can be seen in the splendid locks at Eyre Hall (Fig. 120). Seventeenth-century locks and latches in the English-speaking world, and much later on the continent, often deliberately exposed their ingenious and elaborately decorated inner mechanisms. Such folksy ornament eventually fell out of favor, and the mechanisms were hidden away inside cases, usually iron cases on doors in better houses. Builders who sought an even smarter appearance bought rim locks with cases of polished brass. Inventive British locksmiths further developed locks that were housed in brass cases that could be snapped onto iron plates screwed to the door leaf. The showoff quality of such locks—Byrd used them—was emphasized when they were mounted on the outer face of closet doors rather than more securely inside.

At Eyre Hall brass rim locks were replaced by a newfangled mortise lock that swept the high-end American market in the 1760s, later becoming the most common choice for nineteenth-century doors. With a date of 1759, Eyre Hall may have the earliest group of mortise locks in Virginia. By mid-century, English locksmiths had

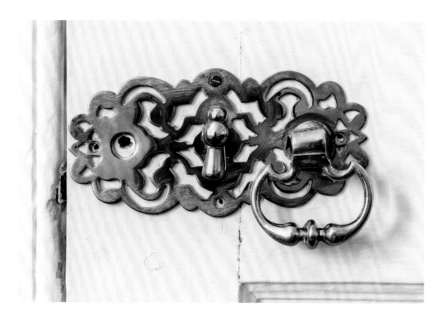

Fig. 120. Mortise lock escutcheon and handle on parlor door.

Fig. 121. Lock escutcheon and handle on closet door.

refined the workings of their products so that their cases could be slid into a mortise carefully chiseled into the edge of the leaf and covered by a metal plate. By turning a now-smaller key or the lock's handles, users easily threw the bolt in and out through the thin end plate to engage answering recesses in the doorjamb. The jamb mortises required only a flat strike plate, not the staple or box-shaped keeper that otherwise impaired the classical lines of the doorframe.

Eighteenth-century English mortise locks applied escutcheons to the face of doors around the keyholes and the handle spindles. Most pre-1790 escutcheons are neatly composed of an oval and circles linked by pierced arms. Escutcheons found in a few very elegant British buildings and occasionally in American houses have elaborately shaped and pierced baroque or chinoiserie plates reminiscent of Asian fretwork. Jefferson, not surprisingly, installed two versions of the highly elaborated escutcheons in prominent locations at Monticello, saving the conventional model for use elsewhere.[7] Littleton Eyre was the only other Virginia planter known to have purchased such opulent fittings. He fitted these heavily pierced escutcheons, richer even than Jefferson's best, on all the first- and second-floor room doors.[8]

Lock handles also came in different grades. Knobs were less expensive but required gripping rather than the graceful hand movements needed to operate stirrup-shaped handles. Like the brass finials on mortise hinges, the finest drop handles were careful Georgian design compositions, drawing on classical balusters and architectural beads for their shapes. The barrels were fastidiously composed in a way that deliberately prevented the handle from striking and marring the door. Usually a second, smaller handle was located on one side of the door to operate a night latch, not so useful on closets or any space seldom locked from inside. That this second handle was often present even when unusable indicates that locks were bought from stock, not bespoke.

However much Eyre admired superior hardware, cost still mattered. The most expensive fittings were not used wastefully in gentry houses; less expensive hardware was usually good enough for some upstairs bedchambers and always for service rooms and storage spaces. Eyre hung closet doors in his second-floor chambers on HL hinges, concealing them as best he could, just as William Byrd hung some of his third-floor doors on cheaper hinges. Closets were often fitted with rim (box) locks rather than mortise locks, an acceptable economy, closet interiors being less visible. Eyre did use mortise locks on closet doors upstairs, but he finished them with plainer escutcheons on both floors (Fig. 121).

The second-floor closet hardware shows that, while the upper bedchambers were predominantly private space, they were occupied by the Eyre family and therefore worthy of refinement. The same is true for respectable but plainer hardware found in the upstairs rooms over the east wing where grandson John Eyre enlarged the family's domestic space between 1805 and 1807.[9] All this attention paid to handsome hardware even in upstairs rooms contrasts with surface-mounted HL hinges for the plastered but plain attic rooms. Other strictly serviceable hardware fittings—strap hinges, for example, and wood- and iron-cased locks—remained in use for generations in kitchens, dairy, smokehouse, and agricultural buildings at Eyre Hall. The family's workers and overseers used similar locks and latches to secure the rooms they occupied in the house and in nearby outbuildings. Enslaved workers resorted to even more basic security devices in their own houses, age-old make-dos such as wooden bars and pegs wedged into doorframes.

Architecture makes physical and seemingly natural what its builders envision as their world in miniature. The location and finish of the rooms and workspaces that Littleton Eyre intended for members of his family and relegated to those who served them reflect how he wished his world to appear and operate, however much others resisted or supported his expectations.[10] Georgian brass escutcheons, shapely lock handles, and even pivoting keyhole covers brought art to the business of security in the plantation house. As in most Chesapeake slave owners' houses, every door at Eyre Hall could be locked against intruders or petty thieves, from the heavily paneled exterior openings to the smallest closet and cupboard.

As is commonly true of even the best-known Chesapeake houses of this era, correspondence and ledgers concerning design and construction are absent at Eyre Hall. Only rarely did owners explain their architectural preferences. George Washington, for example, observed that using mortise locks on exterior doors from his new reception hall would "make the room more uniform."[11] Robert Beverley, writing to his British agent in 1771, cited fashion as the measure of his taste. Because he wanted to fit up Blandfield "in a plain neat Manner," he would "willing consult the present Fashion for . . . that foolish Passion has made its Way, even into this remote Region."[12] Washington's and Beverley's letters notwithstanding, we know most about their aesthetic sensibilities from the houses they left behind. Likewise, Littleton Eyre's taste in this realm is read best in the building itself, from its imaginative floorplan to his choice of hardware fittings.

NOTES

1. Dell Upton, *Holy Things and Profane: Anglican Parish Churches in Colonial Virginia* (Cambridge, Mass.: MIT Press, 1986); Carl R. Lounsbury, *The Courthouses of Early Virginia* (Charlottesville: University of Virginia Press, 2005); Cary Carson, *Face Value: The Consumer Revolution and the Colonizing of America* (Charlottesville: University of Virginia Press, 2017). Other settings over which they held somewhat less visual control were taverns, horseraces, and cockfights, although, even there, gentry appearance was cultivated—as illustrated by the Eyre family's fine clothing, horses, and silver cockspurs.
2. Dell Upton, "Vernacular Domestic Architecture in Eighteenth-Century Virginia," in *Common Places*, ed. Dell Upton and John Michael Vlach (Athens: University of Georgia Press, 1986), 315–35.
3. Economical by being built with wooden, single-story walls and without pairs of rooms on both sides of the passage. The Tayloe House in Williamsburg is the closest parallel for an assertively accommodated gentry house using a side-passage plan ca. 1750s, and it lacks Eyre Hall's expansive spaces and level of finish. It too is frame-walled.
4. Stairs rise within the simpler rear of other gentry passages spanned by wooden arches, including at 1751–55 Carter's Grove and 1755–59 Gunston Hall, but not with their upper run so cleverly handled. Eyre Hall, Carter's Grove, and Gunston Hall are unusual in the enrichment of the entrance space with entablatures and pilasters on plinths, all omitted beyond the arches.
5. The paint has been most closely studied in first-floor spaces. Wallpapers were added to increase elaboration in the rear of the passage, the parlor closet, and possibly the first-floor chamber (now library). Those in the passage and closet were post-1810, but seemingly that in the passage predated the present scenic paper of 1817. Susan L. Buck, "Cross-Section Paint Microscopy Report: Eyre Hall Passage, Parlor, and Library, Northampton County, Virginia," May 18, 2015. A parcel of paper "for hanging," then loose and conceivably for the chamber or back passage, was listed in Littleton Eyre's 1769 inventory. Attic woodwork was unpainted but at some point was whitewashed.
6. The examples cited here reveal that polished brass was viewed as a handsome complement to woodwork independent of paint colors on the trim: tan at Eyre Hall and the Pasteur (Finnie) House, gray at Wilton, blue at Westover, off-white at Monticello, and natural-finish walnut at the Peyton Randolph House and his brother's Tazewell Hall. Door leaves could be handled with the same color, as they were at Eyre Hall and Wilton; painted darker; or faux-grained, as at Monticello.
7. Robert Self, "Restoration of Door Hardware at Monticello," *APT Bulletin* 35, no. 2/3 (2004): 7–15.
8. Examples surviving in widely dispersed buildings as well as shown in English hardware catalogues printed after Eyre Hall's era illustrate that, in spite of available variations, most Georgian brass fittings were closely reproduced as stock items. Matching hinges with clip-on brass plates and classical finials can be seen in houses on the north and south coasts of Jamaica as well as in Britain and the Chesapeake. For a lock escutcheon identical to the best at Eyre Hall but with plainer drop handles at Carshalton House, a building of country-house scale in Surrey, England, see Horace Field and Michael Bunney, *English Domestic Architecture of the XVII and XVIII Centuries* (Cleveland: J. H. Jansen, 1928), 115, 120.
9. Within Furlong Baldwin's memory, there were two brass servant bells mounted on springs high on the south wall of the east wing, where they could be heard by enslaved workers in the detached kitchen. Probably installed by John Eyre to be operated by wires coming from the parlor and dining room or a chamber, their pull locations have not yet been found.
10. More simply, as architectural historian Dell Upton says, "not every part of a house is used as it is meant to be." Upton, *American Architecture* (New York: Oxford University Press, 2020), 37.
11. George Washington to John Augustine Washington, July 29, 1787. John C. Fitzpatrick, ed., *The Writings of George Washington* (Washington, D.C.: U.S. Government Printing Office, 1939), 29:254.
12. Robert Beverley to Samuel Athawes, April 15, 1771, Robert Beverley Letter Book, 1761–93, Beverley Family Papers, Virginia Historical Society, Richmond.

WALLPAPER

MARGARET PRITCHARD

In 1817, Ann and John Eyre made the decision to install French scenic wallpaper in the rear portion of the passage of Eyre Hall, adding what is perhaps the most striking decorative feature of the house (Fig. 122). Since the rear passage and the library/chamber at Eyre Hall were the only locations in the original floor plan lacking floor-to-ceiling paneling, it is almost certain that wallpaper was used to define the more public space from the time the house was originally constructed. That notion is further corroborated by the inclusion of "a parcel of stampt Paper for hangings" in the 1769 inventory of Littleton Eyre.[1] This parcel, listed among other items typically found in storage areas, was likely excess paper from the passage installation. Additionally, paint conservator Susan Buck discovered a small fragment of an earlier blue paper trapped beneath the scenic pattern installed in 1817 that probably dated to the early nineteenth century.[2]

From the middle of the eighteenth century, Virginians were routinely incorporating the most up-to-date imported wallpaper patterns within defined architectural spaces, most notably in halls and passages. Numerous pre-Revolutionary orders and advertisements described papers as being suitable for passages, staircases, or entries, indicating that specific types of designs were called for in this location.[3] Initially, the most fashionable patterns for halls and entries were large-scaled architectural patterns that imitated carved stone ornamentation or applied stuccowork, elements often found in grand English halls. Monochromatic marble or stone columns, arches, and niches created a relationship between the exterior and the interior, providing wallpaper manufacturers with suitable designs that could be reproduced on paper.

While wallpapers replicating architectural motifs dominated passages and entrance halls throughout the eighteenth century, by the first decade of the nineteenth century the rigid and structured ordering of these elements gave way to a more open expression. The invention of the panorama in the 1790s by Irish painter Robert Barker provided a visual spectacle of distant landscapes that captivated audiences on both sides of the Atlantic. Paying visitors passed through a tunnel and staircase into the center of a circular room painted with a mural covering all 360 degrees of wall space, allowing viewers to imagine that they had been transported to an exotic land. The popularity of panoramas, combined with America's growing shift towards romanticism, laid the foundation for a robust market for scenic wallpapers in this country.

Two competing French firms dominated the market for scenic papers—Jean Zuber in Rixheim, Alsace, and Joseph Dufour, who moved his manufactory from Mâcon to Paris in 1808. Although business records for the Dufour firm no longer survive, export records from the Zuber manufactory document that significant quantities of scenic papers were shipped to numerous American ports, including Norfolk, Richmond, and Baltimore. In 1815, Baltimore auctioneer O. H. Neilson advertised, "French Hanging Papers Imported by Robert Elliott, viz:—several grand Turkish Views, Don Quixote, English Hunting and Gardening Scenes and views of the Monuments of Paris, &c. all of which will be so exhibited, that the spectator may behold connected all the parts of those grand representations of nature and of art."[4] It can be inferred from Neilson's advertisement, and subsequent advertisements in most American port cities, that retailers were importing their patterns from both Zuber and Dufour.

The fact that retailers were willing to stock such an extensive assortment of costly French scenic papers suggests that there was a ready market for them in the Chesapeake. Retailer S. P. Franklin's description of scenic papers as "Well Calculated for Halls and Passages" indicates that, by the first decades of the nineteenth century, naturalistic scenes had replaced architectural motifs as an effective vehicle for establishing a relationship between the interior and exterior.[5] Therefore, it is not surprising that Ann and John Eyre would have sought to replace an outdated wall treatment in the rear passage with a French scenic paper titled "Les Rives du Bosphore" (The Banks of the Bosphorus) that depicted Turkish architecture, landscape, and fashion. There was significant interest in the Ottoman Empire during the years prior to the introduction of this pattern because of the Russo-Turkish War (1806–12). Although Napoleon never declared war against the Turks, he eyed the strategically placed city of Constantinople (Istanbul) with the hope of negotiating with Russian tsar Alexander I to secure some portion of Turkish territory at the conclusion of the war.

Neilson and Norfolk upholsterer William Barron both advertised "Les Rives du Bosphore" in their inventories. While John Eyre could have purchased his paper from either retailer,

220 EYRE HALL

Fig. 122. View of wallpaper looking northeast in the stair passage at Eyre Hall.

his surviving correspondence indicates that he secured his set from William Gilmor, son of the wealthy Baltimore merchant Robert Gilmor, from whom he also may have purchased his suite of Baltimore painted furniture, also likely destined for the passage at Eyre Hall.[6] Eyre wrote, "Your letter accompanying the paper you so kindly procured for us was received some time since, the Paper recently suited the taste of Mrs. Eyre, & is generally admired. I have requested Mr. Smith to pay you the small balance you were good enough to advance to Mrs. E."[7] Although the specific amount that John Eyre paid Gilmor for his wallpaper is unknown, the price of scenic patterns generally ranged from $10 to $40, depending on the complexity of the design and the number of sheets required to form a continuous non-repeating panorama. Another advertisement placed by Barron noted: "Direct from Paris . . . Handsome view[s] of Land and Water Scenery, in the most admired parts of the world, at $20 a set, 30 breadths in a subject."[8] Although Barron did not specify the names of the individual patterns he stocked in this

advertisement, the fact that he mentioned that a 30-sheet pattern sold for $20 provides insight into the price range the Eyres likely paid for their 25-sheet set of "Les Rives du Bosphore."

The production of scenic panoramas was a labor-intensive undertaking. Once the designs were approved, separate woodblocks had to be carved for each element and color. "Les Rives du Bosphore" required a staggering 1,599 individual blocks to print the 70 different colors represented throughout the scenes (Fig. 123).[9] Each of the 13-foot breadths was approximately 19 to 20 inches wide. The sheets were printed so that the majority of the scene was confined to the lower third to half of the drop so that the horizon line could be viewed at eye level. The top half to two-thirds of the sheet contained enough sky to accommodate a variety of ceiling heights.

Dufour & Company made recommendations on the method for hanging their scenes. The brochure accompanying their first scenic paper, "Les Sauvages de la mer du Pacifique" (Savages of the Pacific Ocean, 1804), informed purchasers that the paper

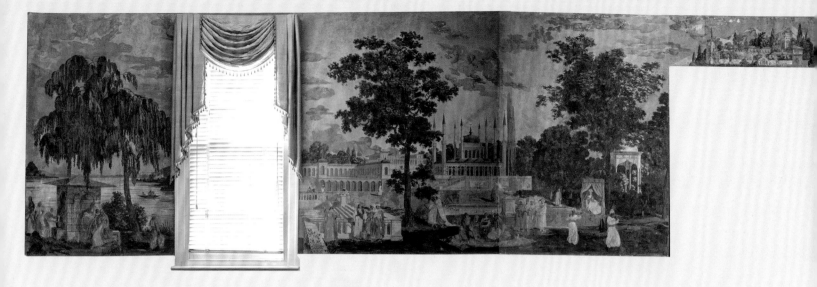

Fig. 123. Panoramic view of "Les Rives du Bosphore" as it wraps around the west, north, and east walls and the apertures and stairs of the north passage.

was designed so that "the two ends must join and form a kind of panorama designed to be cut into strips twenty inches wide so that they may be used singly or in groups of two, three, four, five, six, seven, eight, ten, or twelve strips or more, according to the desire of the owner or according to the arrangement of the interior which is to be decorated."[10] Naturalistic elements were incorporated within most of the sheets to aid in the transition between scenes when accommodating for doors and windows.

Fig. 124. Details from "Les Rives du Bosphore" over the library door on the east wall of the passage.

If hung according to Dufour's directions, the 25-sheet "Les Rives du Bosphore" would have been a perfect fit for the rear passage at Eyre Hall. However, the unknown craftsman who installed the paper recognized that he could achieve a more dramatic impact by varying the horizon line rather than hanging the paper in continuous, consecutive strips. He began the installation on the west wall of the rear passage by joining the sheets as recommended, carrying on in the traditional manner until he reached the exterior door leading into the garden on the adjacent north wall. Ordinarily, the cloudy sky, characteristic of Dufour's scenic papers, would have occupied the space over the door but, in this case, the paperhanger inserted a portion of another sheet illustrating buildings, creating the effect of a mountaintop village. The most ingenious placement, however, was his treatment of the stairway. Perhaps to balance the buildings he placed over the exterior door, he elevated the horizon line on the stairway wall by positioning another building over the doorway into the library (Fig. 124). Elevating the horizon line to the top third of the stairway wall created a blank space along the lower portion of the wall above the wainscot. In order to fill this space he spliced horizontal portions of other sheets depicting water scenes in such a way that it increased the appearance of the width of the river.

Dufour advised that, "[b]ecause of irregular spaces, and because it is impossible to plan in advance to meet the variations of rooms, it is the duty of the owners of the paper and of the paper-hangers to direct the placing of the decoration."[11] Fortunately, the paperhanger employed by John Eyre was given the liberty to exercise his creativity because, although initially imperceptible to the viewer, splicing the scenes in this manner created what may be the most successful known installation of "Les Rives du Bosphore."

NOTES

1. Inventory of the estate of Littleton Eyre, October 14, 1769, Northampton County Wills & Inventories, No. 24, 1766–1772, 224–26.
2. Susan L. Buck, "Cross-Section Paint Microscopy Report: Eyre Hall: Passage, Parlor, and Library, Northampton County, Virginia," May 18, 2015, 9.
3. Virginian Robert Carter ordered wallpapers for his Williamsburg House in 1762 that included one pattern "proper to hang a Passage & Staircase," Robert Carter to Thomas Blandon, February 16, 1762, Robert Carter Letterbook, 1761–1764, Colonial Williamsburg archives. In 1769, Nathaniel Lyttleton Savage, a resident of Virginia's Eastern Shore, received "8 pieces of paper hanging suitable for a passage," invoice of goods shipped to Nathaniel Lyttleton Savage, 1769. See Beatrix Rumford,

"Wallpaper in Williamsburg," unpublished report, Colonial Williamsburg Foundation.
4. *American Commercial Daily Advertiser* (Baltimore), October 27, 1815.
5. *Daily National Intelligencer* (Washington, D.C.), October 20, 1825, quoted in Catherine Lynn, *Wallpaper in America: From the Seventeenth Century to World War I* (New York: W. W. Norton, 1980), 229.
6. Robert Gilmor, Sr. moved to Maryland in 1767 and formed a successful merchant partnership with two gentlemen in Philadelphia. They specialized in foreign commerce. His wife, Mary Ann Smith Gilmor, was related to Ann Upshur Eyre. Mary Ann's mother was Ann Upshur Eyre's great aunt.
7. John Eyre to William Gilmor, October 31, 1817, Robert Gilmor Collection, MS 3198, Box 1, Folder 57,

H. Furlong Baldwin Library, Maryland Center for History and Culture, Baltimore.
8. *Norfolk (Va.) Herald*, May 14, 1819.
9. The initial date of issue of "Les Rives du Bosphore," the number of woodblocks and colors, and the most up-to-date and comprehensive work on Dufour wallpapers are found in Denys Prache and Véronique de Bruignac-La Hougue, *Joseph Dufour: Génie des papiers peints* (Paris: Mare & Martin, 2016).
10. The pamphlet accompanying "Les Sauvages de la mer du Pacifique" was translated and published in Nancy McClelland, *Historic Wall-Papers from their Inception to the Introduction of Machinery* (Philadelphia: J. B. Lippincott Company, 1924), 403.
11. McClelland, *Historic Wall-Papers*, 405.

Domestic Service Buildings

CARL R. LOUNSBURY

Gentry houses such as Eyre Hall did not stand alone but required a host of domestic service structures and housing for workers in order to make them function suitably as the seats of prosperous planters, merchants, and their families. Hospitality was one of the principal markers of gentility to which the proud owners of these houses aspired. By the eighteenth century, the genteel household required a host of status-defining accoutrements such as matching sets of porcelain, cutlery, linen, serving dishes, and lustrous silver tea services to stage refined formal entertainments for guests, relatives, and family members in well-appointed parlors and dining rooms. Many of the surviving domestic objects acquired by Bridget and Littleton Eyre and scores of others known only from contemporary documents testify to the effort expended by the builders of Eyre Hall to burnish their social position through their display and use.

Convivial conversations over tea and sumptuous meals around a generously provisioned table could not have happened without the labor of many hands, which set out the specialized implements, prepared and served food and drink, cleaned, polished, and stored items afterward in buffets, closets, drawers, boxes, and shelves in the house. In the seventeenth century, when there were far fewer specialized household goods, most of these chores occurred in the main house and many of them continued to be accommodated in multipurpose rooms in the smaller homes of farmers and laborers, but, on larger plantations, by the end of the century, they had been dispatched to outbuildings. Writing in 1705, Robert Beverley observed the trend among planters for consigning "all their Drudgeries of Cooking, Washing, Dairies, etc." to "[o]ffices detached from the Dwelling Houses, which by this means are kept more cool and sweet."[1] Not only did members of genteel society prefer to have the heat and smells of cooking removed from their entertaining rooms, but they also wished to reduce the presence of the slaves who performed these and other domestic duties.

The range of service buildings included kitchens, sculleries, laundries, wash houses, smokehouses, meat houses, dairies, coolers, pantries, henhouses, corncribs, woodsheds, stables, barns, and quarters where enslaved house servants lived. Slaves also slept in many of the work buildings, particularly in lofts in kitchens, stables, and coach houses. On many of the larger plantations in the Chesapeake, outbuildings were arranged in a formal relationship to the main house, sometimes flanking one or both sides or placed behind it. They were often grouped together or aligned in rows, but always in a subordinate relationship to the main dwelling house. Generally constructed of inferior materials and finished with fewer refinements, many service structures were highly specialized and their functions evident by their size, the presence or absence of chimneys, and in the placement of apertures. A few were painted, many were simply whitewashed or tarred, others had no coating whatsoever.

Although icehouses occasionally stood in work areas next to other outbuildings, many were located some distance away near a stream or pond, where it was more convenient to collect and store ice in square or conical pits that were generally lined with stone or brick for better insulation. The Eyres built an icehouse on the north bank of Eyre Hall Creek approximately 250 yards south-southeast of the domestic work yard (see Fig. 66). The superstructure that once covered the icehouse has long since disappeared, but the conical depression in the ground still defines it location.

THE KITCHEN

Eyre Hall once had a full complement of outbuildings, and the kitchen was the center around which the other structures were arranged. In 1867 Fanny Fielding, the pseudonym for the author and poet Mary Upshur who was related to the family, recalled the place had "the appearance of a village," with "its numerous outbuildings, for stables, carriage-house, barn, cow-house," and smaller service buildings arrayed east of the main house in a cluster around a brick kitchen "now ivy-crowned, which was once the home of the old, old Eyres."[2] If Fielding assumed that Littleton and Bridget Eyre lived in the building between the time they purchased the property in 1754 and when the main house

was completed in 1759, then she was mistaken. The Eyres remained in residence at their Old Town Neck plantation until they moved into the new house. However, she may have repeated contemporary stories that associated the old kitchen with the main dwelling house for those who lived on this property before Littleton Eyre took possession.

In the late seventeenth century, the land that was to become Eyre Hall belonged to William Kendall, who left it to his daughter Mary and her husband Hancock Lee. The Lees lived on the property for a few years in the 1680s, and they may have erected the brick building as their residence. If so, they enjoyed it for only a short time before they moved to Lee's estate at Ditchley across the bay in Northumberland County. Because the land was entailed for the next 70 years, it seems unlikely that any tenants would have undertaken the construction of a brick dwelling on land that was not their own, unless it was a close family member.[3]

Did the Lees build a brick house on the property before they departed, and could it have been converted into a kitchen sometime later and then survived until after the Civil War? Most evidence to substantiate that possibility disappeared a decade or two after Fanny Fielding described it. Severn Eyre demolished that kitchen and replaced it with a smaller wooden kitchen, which abutted the east end of the early nineteenth-century, two-story housekeeper's wing of the main house.

The end of slavery, coupled with the increasing use of cast-iron cook stoves, hastened the end of open-hearth cooking in detached buildings. Throughout the South in the late nineteenth century, the kitchen moved into the main house or an attached wing. Eyre's new one-story kitchen stood about 8 feet out from the south face of the housekeeper's wing. The new kitchen measured about 17 feet in length from east to west and approximately 19½ feet in width (Fig. 125). The kitchen had a window on the west wall and on the south wall and perhaps a matching one on the north side overlooking the garden. A door in the west end

painted cypress shingles, the one-story kitchen measured 40 feet in length (north to south) and 20 feet deep and stood aligned with the main house and its central door possibly centered on the east rear porch of the house (see Fig. 86). The kitchen had two internal gable-end brick chimneys.

Its size, materials, and two chimneys made John Eyre's kitchen an imposing centerpiece for his domestic service buildings. The building was far larger than most kitchens built in the colonial period, which lends additional credence to the idea that this was a recycled building, converted to new use when John's grandfather erected Eyre Hall in 1759. If it had been built as the principal dwelling on a 700-acre plantation by Hancock and Mary Lee in the 1680s, it would have been an ambitious undertaking in a colony where only a small handful of brick houses had been constructed. Most people lived in smaller wooden houses, often without masonry foundations. The 40-by-20-foot plan probably accommodated two rooms, perhaps an all-purpose hall and a smaller inner room or parlor with additional chambers on the second floor. Chimneys located on the gable ends of houses instead of a single massive one in the center buildings, which created lobby-entrance plans, had become fashionable in the third quarter of the seventeenth century for brick houses such as Page House (1662) in Middle Plantation and Bacon's Castle (1665) in Surry County.[5]

Whether newly built or converted, the brick kitchen served the family for more than a century. As noted earlier, the house and kitchen were sited in a formal relationship some 80 feet apart. In the two decades following his inheritance of the estate on the death of his older brother Littleton, John Eyre undertook improvements not only to the house and garden but the arrangement of the domestic workspaces. The 1796 insurance policy shows the kitchen flanked by two small outbuildings (see Fig. 86). A 10-foot-square wooden pantry stood 9 feet south of the kitchen, with its west side aligned with the west façade of the kitchen. In the colonial and early republican periods, a pantry was either a room or

of the kitchen led into the housekeeper's wing, and one on the gable end provided access to the smokehouse, servants' house, and dairy to the east. That late nineteenth-century kitchen in turn was replaced by a kitchen wing that was constructed in 1934 by Severn's granddaughter Margaret Taylor Baldwin and her husband Henry duPont Baldwin (see Fig. 116). The easternmost part of that addition stands almost entirely on the footprint of the old kitchen.

Without an archaeological survey of the site, the question of the kitchen's origins will remain unanswered. If Littleton Eyre erected the kitchen, the question arises as to why he built it so large and of brick. And if so, then why did he choose to construct his dwelling house of wood? In a colony where there was little natural building stone in the Tidewater, brick was the prestige material, so it would seem a little odd, though not unheard of, to reverse the use of these materials at Eyre Hall.[4] However, if it did precede the Eyres' ownership of the property in the 1750s, it might be one of the reasons why Littleton decided to erect his new house where he did, that is not far from a building that could be recycled as a kitchen.

Fortunately, evidence of the old kitchen appears in three insurance policies issued by the Mutual Assurance Society of Virginia to John Eyre in 1796, 1805, and 1807. A sketch on the earliest policy shows the kitchen located 80 feet east of the main house and approximately 56 feet from the newly built, one-story dining room wing that abuts the northeast corner of the original, two-story house. With brick walls and a building located near a kitchen or dining room that was used for the storage of provisions and kitchen implements. At Eyre Hall it may have served one of these purposes as well as being a meal house, a place where ground cereal grain was stored. On the north side of the kitchen, arranged in the same relationship as the pantry, was a 10-foot-square building described as the dairy—a vented space for the storage of milk, butter, and cheese. There were no other service buildings within 30 feet of the kitchen.

After John Eyre's marriage to Ann M. Upshur in 1800, the couple made additional improvements to the main house and outbuildings. The kitchen yard in the insurance policy dated August 1805 reflects the plan of the previous decade with the kitchen flanked by the pantry on the south and the dairy on the north. The policy indicated that there was an additional unnamed building at least 15 feet southeast of the pantry. What did change was the kitchen, which had grown in height with the addition of a second story made of wood built on top of the original brick walls. It must have provided additional storage and living space for the domestic slaves, whose numbers may have increased with Ann Eyre's residency. The appearance of many new furnishings along with ceramics, glass, and silver for the dining room and parlor suggests that entertaining at Eyre Hall probably increased significantly during this period. It may have been at this time—or certainly within the next ten or 15 years—that the Eyres installed a call-bell system that could be used to summon those who worked in the kitchen and its yard to the house. Two of those cast-metal bells have survived and were rehung in recent years on the south eaves of the east wing of the house.

Building continued apace over the next year and a half. In January 1807, a third insurance policy shows the east wing of the house raised to two full stories and extended an additional 33 feet eastward, leaving only a distance of 21½ feet between the end of the new housekeeper's rooms and the front of the old kitchen. If it was not a clerical error, then the position of the pantry and dairy were reversed, with the pantry now moved to the north of the kitchen and the dairy moved to the south. The present smokehouse appears on the policy sketch, not in its current position north of the dairy, but located a few feet behind the kitchen.

THE DAIRY

The oldest surviving outbuilding at Eyre Hall is the 10-foot-square framed dairy, which may be contemporaneous with the construction of the main house dating from the late 1750s, according to the dendrochronological evidence (Fig. 126).[6] Although the building was heavily repaired in the early twentieth century and moved around the kitchen yard two or three times since it was built, it is one of the earliest surviving dairies in the Chesapeake, with characteristic features that define it as a distinctive building type.[7]

The dairy sits on low brick pier foundations that feature v-shaped mortar joints, which indicates that the brickwork either dates to the first decades of the nineteenth century or was renewed sometime in the early twentieth century, perhaps when the present kitchen wing was added in the early 1930s. The building is covered with a low pyramidal roof surmounted at the apex by a decorative finial. The eaves of the building jut out 2½ feet from the wall plane, and the simple box cornice is coved below the facia and plastered. The deep eaves and coved plaster cornice are among the most distinguishable features of dairies erected in the Tidewater region in the late eighteenth and early nineteenth centuries. So, too, is the nearly 3-foot-tall band of vents at the top of the walls that extends around all four sides (Fig. 127). Vertical strigilated slats set about ½ inch apart fill the vents, which allowed heat to dissipate, protected against low raking sunlight, and kept out many larger animals tempted by the milk, cheese, and butter stored on the shelves inside. On the inside, each of the vents was fitted with a shutter or

Fig. 126. North elevation of the dairy. The dairy is the oldest surviving service building, dendro-dated 1759, the same date as the house. It is one of several structures of this type in the Chesapeake. The building has been moved at least three times around the service yard since its construction.

Fig. 127. The dairy from the southeast, with a series of strigilated slats beneath the deep cantilevered eaves of the pyramidal roof. The roof is an early twentieth-century reconstruction.

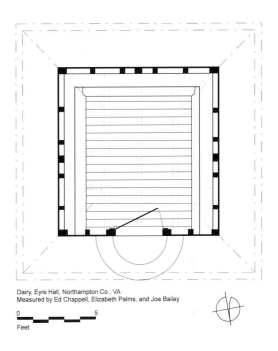

Dairy, Eyre Hall, Northampton Co., VA
Measured by Ed Chappell, Elizabeth Palms, and Joe Bailey

0   5

Feet

closing devise to help regulate the flow of air and protect against pests. The walls are covered by beaded weatherboards, which like the foundations and vents are smeared in coats of whitewash. On the north wall is a four-panel door dating from renovations made in the early 1930s, but is hung on original or early cross-garnet hinges. Two semicircular steps, the lower one of brick, the upper one a reused millstone, provide access to the raised floor.

On the inside most of the wall framing is original, consisting of hewn and pitsawn posts, studs, and down braces. Cripple studs are secured by wrought nails. Lath nail holes on the face of these wall-framing members indicate that the interior was originally sheathed with lath and plaster. The pyramidal framing—with a single king-post truss resting on the center of the three joists, which run in a north–south direction—was renewed in the 1930s with circular sawn material. Despite these major interventions, the dairy retains its double tier of shelves that extend around the east, south, and west walls (Fig. 128). The 1½-inch-thick shelves with molded nosing project out from the wall

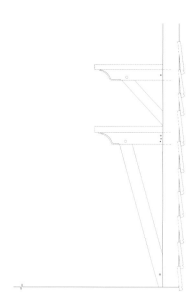

Fig. 128. Original
shelving for milk pans
and other implements.
Drawing of shelf framing.

nearly 1½ feet and are supported by brackets whose ends are chamfered. These are held in place by angle struts that are pegged into the brackets and toe-nailed into the face of the wall studs. The lower shelves stand 3 feet above the floorboards and the upper shelf 1½ feet above it.

THE SMOKEHOUSE

The construction of the smokehouse occurred in the same year that the east wing of the main house was expanded and raised to two full stories. The dendrochronological evidence is unambiguous, with the felling of two timbers dating to the winter of 1805 and a third to 1806. The January 1807 insurance policy shows that the building was located a few feet behind the back or east side of the old kitchen just north of center. At some point after that, it was moved to its present location where it is now aligned with the dairy, which stands 58 feet to the south.

Standing on a low brick foundation, the timber-framed building measures 12 feet 2½ inches square and is surmounted by a pyramidal roof with eaves that extend 1 foot 9 inches beyond the walls, which are sheathed by early if not original beaded weatherboards (Fig. 129). To allow smoke to escape, a series of slots have been cut in the cornice soffit, along with a series of smaller holes in the second weatherboard from the top. The wood finial at the apex of the roof is a replacement. The modern board-and-batten

door faces west and is secured by a pair of old H hinges rather than strap hinges. An iron security bar hangs from a hook on the unmolded north door jamb and threads into another hook lower down on the south jamb, where it could be secured with a padlock.

The interior of the smokehouse is well preserved and shows signs of generations of hams that were salted, hung on poles and hooks that extended from the plate to the apex of the roof, and cured from the smoke that rose from a 3½-foot-square brick-lined hearth in the center of the floor. Salting and fires have left a fuzzy texture and deep deposit of smoke blackening on the hewn and pit-sawn timbers (Fig. 130). As a measure of security and strength, three-inch-wide studs are set six to seven inches apart and mortised into the sills and plates. The studs are undercut on their outer face to create the slant for lapping the unfeathered weatherboards, done in the same manner as the framing of the contemporaneous expansion of the east wing of the main house. The north, east, and south walls have down braces extending from the six-inch-square corner posts and are set inside the plane of the studs.

The smokehouse retains its two original salting troughs, which are located on either side of the central hearth against the north and south walls. Each trough was fashioned from two hollowed-out logs that were fastened together. They measure 10 feet 11 inches in length, 2 feet 10 inches wide, 1 foot 6 inches high, and stand on three wooden runners on the thick plank floor.

Fig. 129. The smokehouse is dendro-dated to 1800. It originally stood behind the old kitchen but was moved to the north side of the old kitchen in 1807. The early brick hearth and salting troughs survive.

Smokehouse, Eyre Hall, Northampton Co., VA
Measured by Susan Kern, Jeff Klee
Elizabeth Palms, and Robert Watkins
Drawn by Robert Watkins

0   5
Feet

Fig. 130. Interior of the smokehouse showing the framing and smoke-blackened close studding of the walls with down braces and north salting trough.

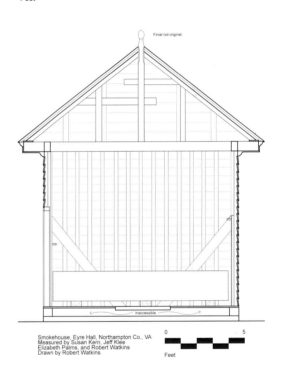

Final not original.

Inaccessible

Smokehouse, Eyre Hall, Northampton Co., VA
Measured by Susan Kern, Jeff Klee
Elizabeth Palms, and Robert Watkins
Drawn by Robert Watkins

0   5
Feet

THE DOMESTIC QUARTER

Until it was demolished in 1956, a one-and-a-half-story frame slave or servant quarter stood a few feet southeast of the smokehouse. A photograph from the early twentieth century, which depicts the herding of sheep and cattle from the front of the house to a fenced paddock east of the domestic service yard, captures a view of the building from the east (Fig. 131). Because the angle is so oblique, nothing can be made of the fenestration on the south front of the house, but the east gable end is visible. What can be seen is that the building had an interior brick chimney on the east gable end. The outer face of the lower part of the stack is exposed and sits flush with the weatherboards that cover the framing of the east wall. The upper part of the stack stepped in a few inches and was enclosed with weatherboards that run the full length of the wall up to the apex of the gable. The cap sticks out above the roof. Two small windows appear in the gable end to light the upper floor on either side of the stack. The front eaves of the building are not boxed. The feet of the rafters jutted out beyond the wall plane a few inches on the front and back walls as well as the east gable end.

The date of construction of this domestic quarter is uncertain. Two diachronic features from the photograph suggest that it may have been built in the middle decades of the nineteenth century, perhaps as early as the 1830s and as late as the 1850s. In the second quarter of the nineteenth century, many two-story houses in Virginia were constructed with internal end chimneys that had the lower base of their masonry exposed with the gable-end weatherboards set against their outer corners. Generally, the brickwork stepped in at the girt level that framed the second floor and weatherboards covered the upper outer face of the chimney. This unusual arrangement generally went out of fashion by the Civil War. If this feature suggests an antebellum date for the building of the quarter, then the unboxed overhanging eaves are more characteristic of a period running from the 1850s through the end of the nineteenth century. The one-and-a-half-story construction, too, tends to be more common around mid-century rather than earlier. So the question remains as to whether this structure was built as supplementary housing for slaves in the very late antebellum period—when the old kitchen with its second-story accommodations for domestic slaves was still standing—or sometime in the decade following the Civil War, when the Eyre family and any freedmen who remained at Eyre Hall had to adjust to new domestic arrangements. Was this house built to meet the demands of emancipated individuals willing to work for the family but with better domestic accommodations?

In the spring of 2019, archaeologists opened a series of test units in order to determine the size and construction of the quarter as well as recover artifacts that might determine its date of construction and shed light on those who occupied the building in the second half of the nineteenth and early twentieth century.[8] The building measured 24 feet in length and 20 feet deep and stood on low brick piers one brick thick (Fig. 132). The north wall of the quarter was in line with the north, gable-end wall of the old brick kitchen, which implies that the building was erected before the old kitchen was demolished after the late nineteenth century. The corner piers were L-shaped, and the longer south and north walls and the west gable wall had center piers. The east gable end with the brick chimney had foundation piers near or abutting the chimney base to support the interrupted sill. The handmade bricks were held together with lime mortar and may have been laid in an irregular English bond. Besides mature cut nails and window glass, the excavation yielded no further architectural debris—though it did recover some domestic artifacts associated with its inhabitants, primarily ceramics. These fragments consisted of whiteware (ca. 1820-60), ironstone (ca. 1840-1930), and porcelain, which was hard to date but likely consistent with the nineteenth-century occupation of the building.

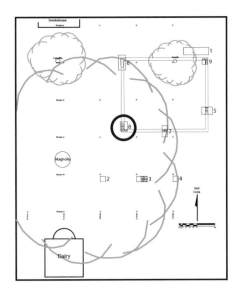

Fig. 132. Archaeological plan showing the location of the quarter, and the brick pier in the southwest corner of the building.

Although the date of its construction and the original occupants of this quarter are unknown, it is possible that it was erected around 1855 to fulfill one of the stipulations in John Eyre's will of that year. He wanted a house built for two superannuated slaves named Nat and Nancy. Nat had been the butler at Eyre Hall in John Eyre's later years, and Nancy was presumably Nat's wife. John also set aside an acre of land for their use in their retirement as well. The will noted that the land was to be "annexed to such house."[9] However, the excavated house stood in the middle of the kitchen service yard, so it is hard to argue that their home would have been positioned in such a busy location. It was more likely built in some distant corner of a field. If not built for Nat and Nancy, its early residents may have been the cook or indeed another butler. If the early occupants of the house are unknown, it is probable that members of the domestic staff hired by Margaret Baldwin lived here from the 1930s through the middle of the 1940s. During that time, William Frazier from North Carolina cooked for the Baldwin family, until he died suddenly in 1945; Severn Weeks served as a butler, and Lena, whose last name could not be recalled by Furlong Baldwin, was the maid. All three may have shared the house during their service at Eyre Hall.[10]

Furlong Baldwin, who pulled the house down in the mid-1950s, recalled that it had been unoccupied for many years and used in later years as storage. He described the plan of the house as having a central front door in the south wall facing the drive in front of the main house. There was one heated room on the ground floor. A short passage or vestibule in the southwest corner of the building provided access to a staircase, which ascended along the west gable end of the house to the heated second-floor room.

NOTES

1. Robert Beverley, *The History and Present State of Virginia*, ed. Louis B. Wright (London, 1705; Chapel Hill: University of North Carolina Press, 1947), 290.

2. Fanny Fielding [pseud.], "Southern Homesteads. Eyre Hall," *The Land We Love* 3, no. 6 (October 1867): 506.

3. On the pervasiveness of entail in the colonial period, see Holly Brewer, "Entailing Aristocracy in Colonial Virginia: 'Ancient Feudal Restraint' and Revolutionary Reform," *William and Mary Quarterly*, 3rd ser., 54 (April 1997): 307–46.

4. Elkington, a two-story frame house just west of Eastville with a plan identical to that as Eyre Hall, had a brick kitchen set at an angle to the dwelling when the property was insured in 1805.

Mutual Assurance Society of Virginia, policy no. 325, August 14, 1805.

5. For a discussion of the plans of emerging gentry houses in the late seventeenth century, see Cary Carson, "Plantation House: Seventeenth Century," in *The Chesapeake House: Architectural Investigation by Colonial Williamsburg*, ed. Cary Carson and Carl R. Lounsbury (Chapel Hill: University of North Carolina Press, 2013), 102–14. For plans of these houses, see pp. 22 and 111.

6. Daniel Miles and Michael Worthington, "The Tree-Ring Dating of Eyre Hall, Cheriton, Northampton County, Virginia," unpublished report, Oxford Dendrochronology Laboratory, April 2003.

7. As noted above, the dairy appears on the north side of the old kitchen in the 1796 and 1805

insurance policies, but is located on the south side in the 1807 one. In late nineteenth- and early twentieth-century photographs, the dairy appears to be situated further to the west along the south drive in front of the house than its present location.

8. Nicholas M. Luccketti and Anthony W. Smith, "Archaeological Testing of a 19th-Century Slave Quarter and the West Yard at Eyre Hall, Northampton County, Virginia," James River Institute for Archaeology, July 2020.

9. Will of John Eyre, February 21, 1855, Northampton County Wills, No. 39, 1854–1897, 24.

10. Furlong Baldwin interview with George McDaniel, May 11, 2019.

Home Farm

CARL R. LOUNSBURY

EYRE HALL IS A WORKING FARM. FOR SEVERAL centuries, the large fields bisected by the entrance road to the main house have been planted with a variety of crops tilled by hand and plowed by oxen, horses, and mules, which were replaced by tractors in the twentieth century. These fields were worked by slaves until emancipation, as well as white and Black tenant farmers in the years following the Civil War. Farm buildings associated with the raising, processing, and storage of tobacco, corn, wheat, oats, vegetables, and other crops raised in the Eyre Hall fields over the past four centuries have disappeared as mechanized farming and the renting of fields to neighboring farmers have all but eliminated the need to preserve such structures. As recently as 1940, a large barn stood in the southwest corner of the field north of the entrance lane, but burned that year along with an older stable located further to the west (see Fig. 66).

The oldest surviving farm buildings—consisting of a garage, stable, sheds, and smaller shelters for machinery and vehicles erected by the Baldwin family—date from the late 1930s through the early 1940s. Many of these buildings were designed by Victorine and Samuel Homsey, architects based in Wilmington, Delaware, to replace structures that had disappeared. They also designed new buildings such as a terrapin corral, an associated terrapin keeper's house, and a two-story seafood packing house on the edge of Eyre Hall Creek. Both were part of the efforts of the Baldwins to find new ways to turn the estate into profitable business ventures.

In 1934 the Homseys produced at least three different designs for estate cottages that ranged from modest two-room plans to larger ones with kitchen wings. It is not known whether the Baldwins approved and undertook the construction of any of these designs. However, they did begin to employ a number of African Americans in agricultural and domestic jobs who lived on the estate. Along the edges of the fields are about a half dozen tenant houses, most of which date from the mid- to late twentieth century, which replaced earlier tenant houses that were recalled by descendants of the Bagwell and Foeman families as being one- and two-story frame houses located in the same areas as their replacements. Some were built by the tenants themselves, such as the one that Robert Curtis built around 1950 for his family near Eyreville Creek.

Earlier buildings occupied by freedmen after the Civil War and by enslaved African Americans prior to that time had disappeared. According to the 1860 slave schedule of the U.S. census, there were ten slave quarters, which partially housed 90 enslaved workers located on the Eyre Hall and neighboring Eyreville plantation lands owned by

Fig. 133. Overseer's house
on Eyre Hall Creek.

Fig. 134. Plan of the overseer's house.

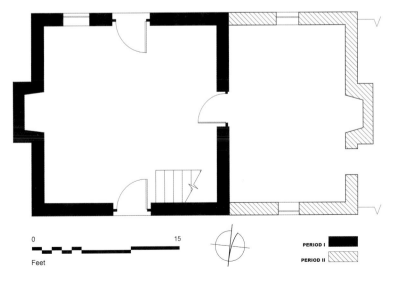

0   15
Feet

PERIOD I
PERIOD II

the last Severn Eyre.[1] A cursory archaeological field survey of the area just east of an inlet that defined the edge of the enclosed paddock used in the nineteenth and early twentieth centuries failed to reveal surface evidence of artifacts associated with quarters said to have been located on the western edge of the field north of the entrance lane.[2] Even so, Eyre Hall is ripe for future archaeological investigations for these and other sites that range in date from Native American occupation to the earliest European and African settlers in the colonial era.

THE OVERSEER'S HOUSE

The only early surviving building associated with the home farm at Eyre Hall is a one-story brick overseer's house standing at the southern edge of the fields that line the south side of the central entrance drive (Fig. 133). The house sits only a few yards from Eyre Hall Creek to the south. Originally measuring 20 feet square, the dwelling was heated by an exterior chimney on the east gable end and consisted of a single ground-floor room with a heated garret accessible by a staircase in the northwest corner (Fig. 134). The present staircase is a modern replacement. Two date bricks inscribed "1798" appear on the chimney and over the front door on the north façade, indicating that it was built during John Eyre's early tenure of the estate (Fig. 135).

Though modest in size, the fact that it was a brick structure indicated that it was intended for a person of some status, generally a white overseer who was employed by John Eyre to direct the work of the enslaved on the home plantation. The walls of the house were laid in Flemish bond with scribed joints with a double stepped watertable. Originally, the one-room house may have had only one window, which would have been opposite the chimney on the west gable end. Otherwise there were two central doors on the north and south walls which would have provided

some air circulation. The upper floor had at least one small square window on the north side of the chimney stack on the east gable. There may have been another in a similar position on the west gable, but, if so, it is now obscured by a later addition. The roof frame consists of pairs of common rafters, which are hewn and pit sawn and sit on board false plates at the eaves.

A very short time later, perhaps no more than a few years, a brick addition measuring 14 feet in length and 20 feet in width was constructed at the west end of the original house. An exterior chimney similar to the original was added to the west gable end of the addition. The walls were laid in Flemish bond with scribed mortar joints as the original section. The builders placed a small window (4½ feet by 2 feet) in the center of each of the north and south walls. The south window has a simple flat header-jack arch while the north has none. They may have also added a slightly larger window to the south wall of the original house just east of the doorway to provide light to the room when the one in the original west gable end was converted into a doorway connecting the two ground-floor rooms of the expanded house to form a hall and parlor plan. The addition may have also prompted the construction of a dormer window in the garret. The original section had a dormer added to the front and back slopes of the roof located over the two doorways below. The new west garret had a dormer on the southern roof slope overlooking the creek and was heated by a small fireplace in the west gable. A batten door hung on strap hinges provided access in the brick partition wall between the two garret rooms; the hooks on which the hinges were secured survive in place.

In the late nineteenth or early twentieth century, a frame addition was added to the west side of the house. In the middle of the twentieth century, the house was occupied

Fig. 136. Overseer's house, ca. 1960. African American farm manager, Lawrence Bagwell, lived here from the late 1930s until his death in 1959.

Fig. 137. Overseer's house with extension added in the early 1980s by Mary Baldwin Peacock, who lived there until her death in 2015.

by Lawrence and Lillian Bagwell, who were among the large family of African American tenants who worked and lived at Eyre Hall (Fig. 136). Lawrence served as overseer of the farm in the 1940s until his death in 1959 (see Fig. 80). In 1982 the frame house was rebuilt and the older brick sections upgraded when Mary Baldwin Peacock, Furlong Baldwin's sister, retired to Eyre Hall. She lived here until her death in 2015 (Fig. 137).

NOTES

1. For more details about the operation of the home quarter farm, see Part I, chapter 3, "The Bounty of Eyre Hall." For a study of slave houses on the Eastern Shore, see Doug Sandford, "An Overview of Slavery and Slave Houses in Northampton County, Virginia, 1860," unpublished paper, Virginia Slave Housing Project, University of Mary Washington, November 2017; see also *Vernacular Architecture Newsletter* 122 (Winter 2009): 1–8.

2. Surveys conducted by Nick Luccketti and Dave Hazard of the James River Institute of Archaeology in the spring of 2019 failed to reveal any concentration of artifact scatter in the area said to have been the location of a row of slave houses.

LANDSCAPE

Garden and Grounds

WILL RIELEY

IN THE MIDDLE OF THE EIGHTEENTH CENTURY, WHEN Littleton Eyre was planning his new demesne on the bayside of the Eastern Shore of Virginia, garden design and site planning for a complex of a main house, with its outbuildings, yard and garden, was highly conventional (Fig. 138). The yard gave a framework to the house and its immediate grounds and often included both a formal entrance and functional space for work associated with the house. The gardens were placed either within or adjacent to the yard.

Two sets of documents offer evidence that this arrangement of yard and "regular" garden ("regular" in the sense of "geometric," not "ordinary") was widespread geographically in eighteenth-century America. The first is a series of maps of North Carolina towns drawn by French cartographer Claude Joseph Sauthier[1] between 1768 and 1770. The second is the Warner and Hanna map of Baltimore from 1801.[2] These maps are unusual in that they show the scale and configuration of gardens in the towns they illustrate (Fig. 139).

The gardens of the late colonial and early federal periods in Virginia were typically formed on a simple armature—one with medieval roots. These gardens were rectangular, enclosed, with clear boundaries and simple geometric subdivisions. They were divided by internal paths, generally with 90-degree corners, giving the gardens a plan-view appearance of a window divided into panes. The internal subdivisions were often referred to as "quarters," "plats," or "squares" (even though they were often rectangles). These "squares" were frequently bounded by ornamental plants on their perimeter (often boxwood, yews, hollies, or flowers), surrounding medicinal plants, or "simples," and food crops in the interior. It was a pattern in evidence in America from the time of the seventeenth-century garden at Governor Berkeley's Green Spring.[3]

This pattern was widespread and culturally ingrained. In its most basic form, as at Bacon's Castle, it resembled a huge window sash with six panes, flat on the ground and aligned with the house. There were two major variations and several minor ones. The first major variation was whether the garden was centered on the primary access of the house, like Carter's Grove, King's Mill, and Brandon, or, alternatively, to one side or the other of the axis of the house, like Bacon's Castle, Prestwould, or Stratford Hall (Fig. 140). The second major variation was whether the gardens were flat or

Fig. 138. Aerial view of Eyre Hall and its garden
looking northeast.

Fig. 139. Detail from Warner and Hanna's map of
Baltimore, 1801, and detail from Sauthier's map of
Edenton, North Carolina, 1769.

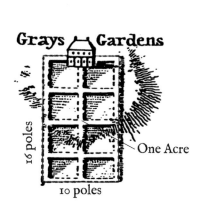

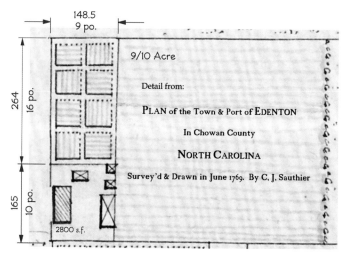

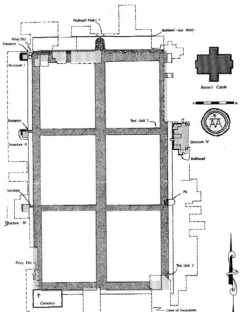

Fig. 140. Archaeological plan of the garden at Bacon's Castle, Surry County, Virginia. Plan by Nicholas Luccketti.

Fig. 141. The garden at the College of William and Mary, ca. 1740, a detail from the Bodleian Plate.

terraced. Terracing was utilized wherever there was sloping ground (and, in at least one case, where there wasn't).[4]

There are also examples closer to home for Littleton Eyre. Williamsburg, the center of political and cultural life in Virginia, had become an important focus of gardening activity by the early eighteenth century. Several important gardens were either in the town or easily accessible from it. As a member of the House of Burgesses from 1742 until 1761—the two decades prior to the construction of the house and garden at Eyre Hall—Eyre would have known these gardens well. His ownership of the only ferry connecting the Eastern Shore with towns near the capital made them even more accessible to him than to most of his neighbors on the shore.

Three of these were an easy walk from each other: the garden at the Governor's Palace built under the direction of Alexander Spotswood; the garden at the front of the College of William and Mary (possibly designed by London and Wise, "nurserymen to the King"); and the private garden of John Custis, correspondent of plantsmen John Bartram in Philadelphia and Peter Collinson in London. The garden at the front of William and Mary held an important place

in colonial Virginia (Fig. 141). The illustration on the so-called "Bodleian Plate" shows clipped yew or boxwood, or both, and broad, probably graveled, paths. The Bodleian Plate also shows the gardens of the Governor's Palace. They too boasted clipped evergreens and wide, graveled paths arranged with a strict symmetry.

Custis's principal seat was Arlington, located seven miles south of Eyre Hall, but he lived for a good portion of the year at his Williamsburg house, where he built a garden of distinction. Indeed, he credits himself with having "a garden inferior to few in Virginia."

The deep, rich soil and generally level terrain of Virginia's Eastern Shore provided little limitation to the configuration of the garden, nor did stones or rock outcrops impede the plows or hoes of planters and gardeners. The boundaries, shape, and extent of the garden were prescribed more by tradition than by the natural setting. Insurance documents from the late eighteenth century and early nineteenth century give us a good idea of what that organization was, and they form the basis for our understanding of how it changed over time.

THE YARD

As was typical of this era, at Eyre Hall the center of the domestic complex was the "yard" or "area" that enclosed a rectangle, in this case in the shape of a double square, 80 by 160 feet. This rectangle was laid out with its long side running almost exactly east–west (Fig. 142).[5] The house—a 40-foot square—was positioned 40 feet from the western edge of the yard and 20 feet from the north and south edges. This left 80 feet to the face of the kitchen, dairy, and pantry structures. The kitchen building was 20 by 40 feet and the dairy and pantry buildings were ten feet square. The perimeter was defined by a picket or paling fence. The 1796 insurance policy for Eyre Hall describes this fence thus: "paling with brick pillars instead of wood posts." Preliminary archaeological work by Nicholas Luccketti of the James River Institute of Archaeology verified the location of the north, west, and south walls. These locations revealed the remains of brick foundations which suggest a fence that has a brick wall in its lower half, and pales or pickets in its upper half, like the one in the background of this portrait of Anne Byrd Carter (Fig. 143).[6]

The fence in the painting above seems to have had wooden posts with turned finials on the tops of each, while the Eyre Hall insurance policy of 1796 clearly states that the fence has "brick pillars instead of wood posts." That description fits the fence that currently encloses the garden at Eyre Hall (Fig. 144). Family tradition holds that the existing garden fence was constructed by John and Anne Eyre at about the time of construction of the green-

Fig. 142. Littleton Eyre's Eyre Hall, ca. 1760.

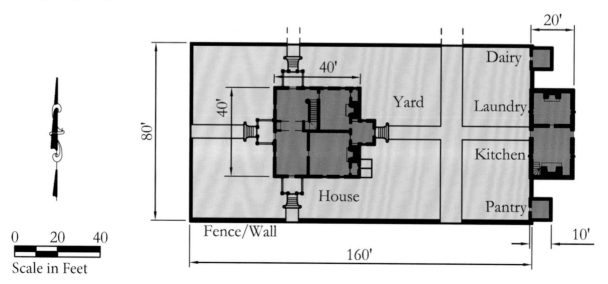

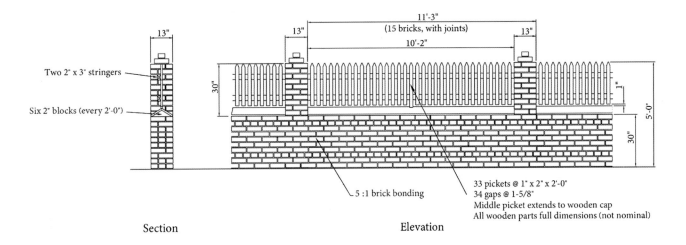

Two 2" x 3" stringers

Six 2" blocks (every 2'-0")

13"

30"

Section

11'-3"
(15 bricks, with joints)

13"

10'-2"

13"

1"

5'-0"

30"

5 :1 brick bonding

33 pickets @ 1" x 2" x 2'-0"
34 gaps @ 1-5/8"
Middle picket extends to wooden cap
All wooden parts full dimensions (not nominal)

Elevation

Fig. 144. Elevation and section of the current fence/wall
around the Eyre Hall garden.

house (1819). It is possible, if not likely, that this fence was patterned on the older yard fence, which would have still been extant at that time. Preliminary archaeological investigations by Luccketti have revealed remnants of the foundation for a wall on the line of this original wall/fence. The bricks are 8½ x 4 x 2½ inches, which would lay up with a half-inch mortar joint to 9 x 4½ x 3 inches (9-inch module in all three directions). The thickness of the wall, then, was 13 inches (8½-inch-length brick plus half-inch mortar joint plus 4-inch breadth of brick).

One certain difference between the existing garden wall and the original yard wall is that the former is laid in 1:5 bond, while the latter would have been laid in English or, more likely, Flemish bond like the foundation of the house. (In both the English and the Flemish bonds, header brick would alternate every course, while in the former, headers show every six courses vertically.) In both cases, the wall was 13 inches thick. The 13-inch-square piers of the existing fence/wall are 10 feet two inches apart, or 11 feet three inches on center (15 bricks with mortar joints).

In Virginia, the height of fences enclosing yards was set by regulation, first in the mid-seventeenth century, at 4½ feet and later, in 1748, at 5 feet.[7] This is the height of the current Eyre Hall garden fence (2½ feet of brick wall and 2½ feet of wooden pickets on a wooden base, between brick piers). This combination would have prevented entrance into the yard by small animals through the lower brick sections while still allowing air circulation through the upper sections.

Both laws and long tradition in Virginia had established that the function of fencing was to fence domestic animals *out* of yards, gardens, and cultivated agricultural crops. It was the responsibility of the owner to secure his property with fences of sufficient height and strength to keep free-ranging livestock out of these protected zones.[8] The reversal of these laws did not occur for nearly a century after Littleton Eyre built the Eyre Hall house, when the prevalence of field crops led to laws that required that animals be enclosed with fencing.

This highly ordered and geometric double-square fenced yard was subdividable into other squares and double squares. Between the east side of the house and the west side of the kitchen was an approximate 80-foot distance, the same as the distance from the north yard fence to the south yard fence, defining a square work yard between the house and the kitchen. On the west side of the house the fence was 40 feet from the house and 80 feet in length—creating an entry court in a 2:1 proportion. The north fence was 20 feet north of the house, and the south fence was 20 feet south of the house—in each case forming a corridor of 20 by 40 feet, another double square (Fig. 145).

Though hardly dispositive, the fact that the 2:1 yard abuts the kitchen, rather than enclosing it, suggests that the kitchen was already present when the house and its yard were appended to it. An incongruous combination of materials, in which the house is built of wood and the kitchen is constructed of brick, supports this conjecture. An

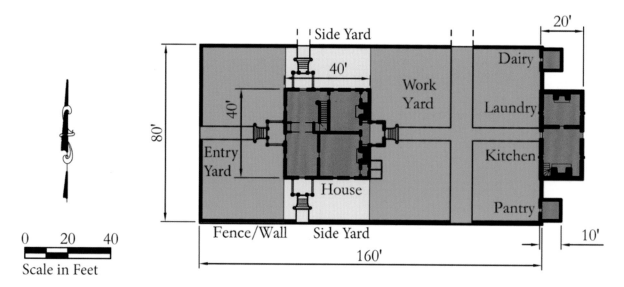

Fig. 145. Double square plan of Littleton Eyre's Eyre Hall yard, ca. 1760.

Side Yard

Dairy

Work Yard

Laundry

Kitchen

Entry Yard

House

Pantry

Fence/Wall   Side Yard

Scale in Feet

0   20   40

earlier brick house may have been remodeled to serve as the kitchen (and perhaps laundry, with quarters above) for the new wooden house built 80 feet to the west. This sequence of kitchen-first-house-after, while perfectly plausible, cannot be either verified or disproved because this kitchen building was demolished in the decade following the Civil War.

This rigidly symmetrical yard plan certainly was indicative of the desire to impose a deliberate and cogent order on unbridled nature. In the case of Littleton Eyre, it may also have marked the adoption of a methodical framework for his habitation that set him apart from his neighbors and was as clear a social marker as it was an aesthetic preference.

THE GARDEN

When visitors enter the garden adjacent to, and just north of, the Eyre Hall house, they are often first struck by the enchanting mixture of plants. Under an ancient yew or magnolia, they might encounter a bright display of beautifully configured modern annuals and perennials—carefully chosen, arranged, and planted under the direction of Furlong Baldwin's talented gardener, Laurie Klingel. Many historic gardens have been so simplified (because of the expense or fear of violating some historical imperative)

that it is a welcome surprise for visitors to come upon a garden whose history is respected, but not petrified, and in which each year reveals its own unique and jubilant display (Fig. 146).

After the visitors' initial encounter with this captivating composition of old and new plants, they may become aware of the enclosed regular rectangle of brick-and-picket fencing that defines the boundary of the garden; or they may make note of the smooth and worn paths in a "window-pane" pattern—a pattern whose history runs through medieval European gardens. It doesn't take long for them to see that this garden reveals multiple layers accumulated over succeeding decades and generations of ownership within one family.

A garden associated with an important mid-eighteenth-century house in Virginia was not an optional embellishment. The garden, like the yard, and a multitude of support buildings as noted in the earlier essay by Carl Lounsbury, was an essential and obligatory element of the manor house landscape. The garden linked with such a house was generally rectangular, its limits bounded by a fence or wall, and containing plants for nourishment, ornament, and medical application—the latter called "simples" at the time, and which today we would call medicinal herbs.[9] The garden of colonial Virginia was not a general area; nor was it

Fig. 146. A corner of the Eyre Hall garden in the spring.

an amorphous and unstructured composition reflective of the English landscape movement. It was a specific place with a clear and discrete boundary.

Royal English gardeners George London and Henry Wise translated and revised Jean de La Quintinie's *The Compleat Gard'ner* from its original French in 1699. In it, they advised that "a Garden must be well inclos'd with Walls, and not far distant from the House (Fig. 147)."[10] While this direction was written 60 years before the Eyre Hall house and garden were built, as garden writers Reginald Blomfield and Inigo Thomas noted, "Fashions travelled slowly in the eighteenth century, and many a formal garden in provincial towns and country places was laid out in the older style as late as the beginning of the nineteenth century."[11] If this were true of provincial towns in England, it was even more the case for rural plantations in the American South.

Fig. 147. Illustration from *The Compleat Gard'ner* showing squares and wide walks.

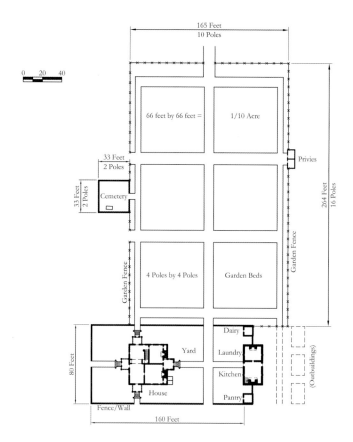

Fig. 148. Yard and
garden diagram,
ca. 1760.

So, the garden, following mid-eighteenth-century Virginia standards, would be enclosed by a wall or fence and was located relatively close to the house. Another typical characteristic of the garden in this era is that it would have 90-degree corners, or was "square," and was typically orthogonal with the house.[12]

When Littleton Eyre was completing his manor house, its messuages and appurtenances in 1759, this composition would certainly have included a garden. Not only was the garden an indispensable component of the manor house complex: the location of the graveyard suggests that the garden was in place before the burial of the cemetery's first occupant, Sarah Bowdoin, in 1760 (Fig. 148).[13]

This internment, marked with a low table monument, is orthogonal with the garden wall and would likely have been enclosed in a cemetery that was centered between the garden's second and third east–west walks. It is quite possible that the first six plats or squares of the garden were built in the first phase of the garden's development. This would have made the early garden 10 poles (165 feet) by 16 poles (264 feet), enclosing exactly one acre. In this case, the graveyard would have been centered on the western wall or fence of the garden. The coincidence of the eastern edge of

the graveyard with the western wall of the garden is a strong argument that the garden was built first, and that the graveyard was appended to it. Similar logic would suggest that the garden was added to the fenced yard that enclosed the house. The garden abuts the yard and has one side in common with it.

In the eighteenth century many Virginia plantation owners eschewed the tradition of burials in churchyards in favor of internment in their own family cemeteries, in or adjacent to their gardens. Philip Fithian recorded his host Robert Carter's preference in 1774: "He much dislikes the common method of making Burying Yards round Churches, & having them almost open to every Beast. . . . And that he would choose to be laid under a shady Tree where he might be undisturbed, & sleep in peace & obscurity—He told us that with his own hands he planted & is with great diligence raising a *Catalpa*-Tree at the Head of his Father who lies in his Garden."[14]

THE REGULAR GARDEN

While we do not have detailed documentation for the furnishing and planting of this garden in its early years, the conventionality of its layout lends it a predictability that narrows the possibilities substantially. To understand the size and proportion of the yard and garden, it is important to understand the units of measure employed at the time. When measuring relatively small areas of land adjacent to the house, the units employed would be very familiar to a modern-day American: feet, inches, and fractions of an inch. The tools for establishing required dimensions were the same as those used for the construction of the house itself. For longer and overall measurements, the ten-foot pole would be utilized. This tool was described in a late seventeenth-century manual:

The Garden at Eyre Hall

We shall begin therefore to measure the *Ground-plot*, to which Carpenters use a *Ten-Foot Rod* for expedition, which is a Rod about an Inch square, and ten foot long; being divided into ten equal parts, each part containing one foot.[15]

Indeed, the ten-foot rod or pole was so ubiquitous that it found its way into colloquial speech, as in "I wouldn't touch it with a ten-foot pole." When measurements were required more accurately than to the nearest foot, a two-foot folding rule was employed that was subdivided into inches and fractions of an inch. The measurements of the Eyre Hall yard almost all come out in even 10-foot increments, from the 40-foot house to the 10-foot dairy and pantry to the 80-by-160-foot overall measurement of the yard, to the 20-by-40-foot kitchen building. These 10-foot units of measurement work well in relation to the scale and dimensions of the buildings, but they do not align with land area measurements in acreage. For example, the yard is 12,800 square feet in area (80 feet by 160 feet). This results in an acreage of 0.293848. . . acres—hardly a round number.

The adjacent garden uses different units of measurement that evolved from ancient times in conjunction with land measurement and acreage. The base unit of length for such land measurement was the statute rod or pole of 16½ feet or 5½ yards. One square rod or pole equals one perch and there are 160 perches in an acre. Applied to the early Eyre Hall garden, if we begin with the western fence of the garden, which is aligned with the western wall of the house, and measure to the corresponding garden wall on the eastern boundary of the garden, we find the distance is very nearly 165 feet, or 10 poles. In looking at Henry Chandlee Forman's sketch plan of the garden from the 1970s, it is clear that the first six squares (all of a similar size) can be enclosed in a rectangle that measures 16 poles or 264 feet in the north–south direction (Fig. 149).[16]

This rectangle encloses an area of exactly one acre (165 x 264 feet = 43,560 square feet = one acre *or* 10 poles by 16 poles = 160 perches = one acre).[17] A typical one-acre lot in Williamsburg was also often 16 poles (264 feet) by 10 poles (165 feet).[18] The resulting 5:8 proportion is very close to the extreme-and-mean proportion of 1:1.618, also known as the Golden Ratio or Rectangle.

While the base unit of measurement for surveying land was the pole, by the time the Eyre Hall house and grounds were laid out in the eighteenth century, the actual *tool* for measuring distance was a metal chain, with links

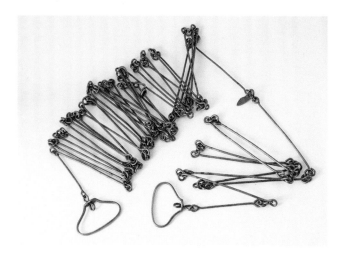

of 1/25th of a pole in length (0.66 feet or 7.92 inches). The English statute or "Gunter's" chain was 66 feet in length, composed of 100 links; however, in America a chain of half that length, 33 feet (50 links), was more prevalent. (Both Washington and Jefferson, for example, used a two-pole or 33-foot chain for their surveying). The chain also became a unit of measurement, so it was important to be aware of whether the Gunter's chain or the American two-pole chain was being utilized. Using a chain like the one pictured, the early garden was likely five (two-pole) chains by eight (two-pole) chains, enclosing exactly one acre. The six (probably original) garden squares measure 66 feet (four poles or two chains) on each side (Fig. 150).

Archaeologist Barbara Heath has documented the landscape development of two sites from Virginia's Northern Neck, Newman's Neck, and the Clifts during the period 1670 to 1730. She detailed the use of the statute rod (16½ feet) for larger measurements, and the builder's rod—or "geometrical" or builder's pole (10 feet)—for smaller divisions of land near the house.[19] It would be difficult to find a clearer example of this shift in tools and units of measurement than from the yard at Eyre Hall, measured into multiple units of the ten-foot builder's rod, and its garden, measured in units of the 16½-foot surveyor's rod or pole.

Because a garden of the rising gentry in Virginia was quite conventional, if we combine the traditional elements of the garden with remnants or documented aspects of the garden that we know, we are likely to come very close to the original configuration. We have noted that the original fence around the yard was probably composed of a low or

dwarf brick wall of 30 inches topped by another 30 inches of wooden palings or pickets supported by brick piers. The cemetery may have been enclosed by a similar fence. It is likely, however, that the garden fence would have been a paling fence, the most typical enclosure for a garden in Virginia at that time.

Though the most common fencing in Virginia in the mid-eighteenth century was unquestionably the Virginia fence or snake-rail fence, this rustic fencing was typically used to fence off field crops. It was generally regarded as too rustic to enclose a part of the manor house grounds, like the yard or the garden. A more appropriate fence would have been a paling fence, which would have occupied less space and given more protection against both wildlife and wandering livestock.

A paling fence was composed of vertical boards or split "pales" nailed or pegged to horizontal stringers which were in turn attached to vertical posts with one end buried in the ground. As noted previously, the minimum height of fencing for a landowner to be able to recover damages for losses inflicted by pillaging livestock was set initially by statute at 4½ feet, and raised in the mid-eighteenth century to 5 feet. This height was a minimum, and taller fences of 6, 8, or even 10 feet were sometimes employed around gardens.

In the early decades of the English settlement of Virginia, paling fences would have been constructed of split timber pales attached to rustic posts and stringers. When sawmills became available, it was more possible to have a fence of sawn boards attached to sawn stringers and posts—a more refined version of the paling fence. Often the tops of the boards would be sawn to the shape of an inverted V. Another common practice was cutting a single sloping angle off each board—an efficient if less elegant alternative.

Closely allied to the geometry of the enclosing fence is that of the garden walks or paths. The paths in regular gardens of the mid-eighteenth century were generally wide, smooth, and evenly graded. Like many aspects of

Fig. 151. The stone garden roller shipped by London merchant Samuel Gist to Severn Eyre.

Fig. 152. A roller in use. Illustration by William Pyne.

the garden, the width of the garden paths was practical as well as aesthetic. Wide paths allowed access to the garden beds by gardeners with carts and wheelbarrows; but, more importantly, they allowed visitors to the garden, including ladies in wide dresses, to walk comfortably through the garden.

Philip Fithian documented many strolls in the garden, often as an after-dinner amusement. He recounted one such visit during which the mistress of Nomini Hall joined him in the garden:

> When I had gone round two or three Platts Mrs. Carter entered and walked towards me. [20] I then immediately turn'd and met Her; I bowed—Remarked on the pleasantness of the Day—And began to ask her some questions upon a Row of small slips—To all which she made polite and full answers. As we walked along she would move the ground at the Root of some plant, or prop up with small sticks the bended *scions*—We took two whole turns through all the several Walks, and had such conversations as the *Place* and *Objects* naturally excited—And after Mrs. Carter had given some orders to the Gardiners (for there are two Negroes, Gardiners by Trade, who are constantly when the Weather will any how permit, working in it) we walked out into the *Area* viewed some Plumb-Trees, when we saw mr. Carter and Miss Prissy returning—We then repaired to the Slope before the front-Door where they dismounted—and we all went into the Dining Room. [21]

This short passage is rich in information about the garden. We learn, for example, that the garden is divided into "platts" or "squares" in the typical fashion. The fact that Mrs.

Carter herself is describing the contents of the garden and fussing over its details (e.g., propping up a "bended scion") suggests her direct charge, grasp, and hands-on approach to gardening matters. She answers Philip Fithian's questions with "polite and full answers." The garden has two full-time African American gardeners directed by Mrs. Carter. There is also, as stated elsewhere in the journal, a white, hired gardener who gives direction to the presumably enslaved gardeners and who works seasonally. Plum trees are in the "area" (or yard), rather than in the garden. There is a slope at the front of the house, suggesting that the house is on a raised earthen plinth.

The wide walks in gardens of this period were typically designed precisely and maintained meticulously. William Cobbett wrote in 1810: "As to the *art* of Laying-out, it would be to insult the understanding of an American Farmer to suppose him to stand in need of any instruction. A *chain*, or a *line*, and a *pole*, are all he can want for the purpose, and those he has always at hand. To form the walks and paths, is, in fact, to lay out the Garden." [22]

Thomas Hitt and James Meader advised in *The Modern Gardener* that "[p]articular care should be taken to keep the gravel walks constantly clear from weeds and litter, and *at least twice a week* let them be well rolled with a heavy roller." [23] In 1770, Littleton Eyre's son and heir, Severn, received correspondence about a garden roller he had ordered from a merchant in Norfolk. [24] This is likely the same stone roller that appeared in the inventory of February 1774, taken after his death. The roller was listed with "Spades, Rakes &c.," and valued at £2-10s-0d. [25] This garden roller would have been an important tool for the maintenance of the garden paths and the lawn areas. Hitt and Meader also averred that the gardener should "[l]et the grass walks and lawns be kept duly polled[26] and rolled. . . . Let the surface be gone over with a roll of stone or iron. This will make the bottom firm and smooth and bring it into proper order for mowing next month [March]."[27] Rolling the lawn tamped down the grass and seed and promoted growth and strong roots. Remarkably, this versatile and important garden tool, ordered in 1770 and inventoried in 1774, is still on the property at Eyre Hall, lying inconspicuously by the garden wall (Fig. 151). Its metal traces and handle are gone, but surviving examples and illustrations show its original configuration and use (Fig. 152).

The rolling stone was also used to keep the garden paths well compacted. Such paths in colonial Virginia were typically gravel, though marl, shell, crushed brick, and even cinders were occasionally used.[28] To this natural gravel or other aggregate was often added fine-particle material (clay or loam) in sufficient quantity to make the gravel "bind" or congeal into a hard and smooth surface. Periodic rolling was essential to maintain the desired smooth and uniform walking surface. A natural source of gravel was not present on the Eastern Shore, thus precluding its use in the Eyre Hall garden. Sand may have been added to the already sandy soil. According to the owner, Furlong Baldwin, there is evidence of brick dust having been used to surface the paths at some time—a plausible alternative.

Also among the garden tools in the inventory of Severn Eyre's estate are two items that give insights into how this garden was configured and maintained. One is a pair of garden shears. This tool indicates that many of the plants in the garden were sheared or pruned to precise, compact shapes. Plants that were often mentioned for this kind of shaping were boxwood and yews. If there was one tool that symbolized the English garden of the late seventeenth century, it would be the garden shears or hedge trimmer.

The second item is two "Water Potts." These would likely have been ceramic, not metal. Watering jars were commonly made of either clay pottery or metal. Existing examples tend to be metal, but this has more to do with the fact that clay pots are quite breakable—rather than the greater popularity of metal watering cans. Pottery watering jars were probably much more common, as they would have been less expensive and available locally from a potter. The three items were valued at 10 shillings, or about $85 in 2020 U.S. currency.

PLANTS

French and Dutch gardens of the early eighteenth century, as well as English gardens that were influenced by them, often divided the individual squares into highly ornamental designs of evergreens and flowering plants, called *parterres*. This motif was uncommon in America, where most of the squares were planted in a simple configuration of rows. One notable exception was Mount Vernon, where Benjamin Henry Latrobe reported in 1797: "For the first time since I left Germany I saw here a *parterre* stripped and trimmed with infinite care into the form of a richly flourished *fleur-de-lis*, the expiring groan, I hope, of our grandfather's pedantry."

According to garden historian Wesley Greene, "colonial Virginians had most of the vegetables with which the modern gardener is familiar. A few plants that were not found in the eighteenth-century garden are sweet corn, Brussels sprouts, and rutabaga. Asian vegetables, such as mustard greens, bok choy, and soybeans are also missing. On the other hand, the eighteenth-century gardener grew some vegetables that are seldom found in the modern garden, such as salsify, scorzonera, and cardoon."[29]

The planting areas around the inside perimeter of the fence were favorite locations for fruit trees—some of which were attached to the inside of the fence as *espaliers*. This same

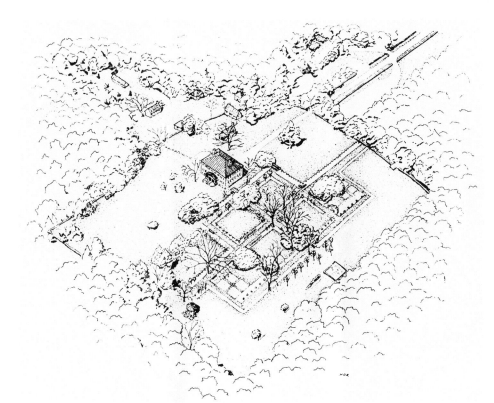

area was also often the site for flowers and flowering shrubs, including roses. The margin between the northernmost path and the north fence was a good location for the hotbeds, as they would have the fence to their north side and be open to the south.

Several feet adjacent to the paths, on the outside of the "squares," were often given to low plants that functioned as a border. Sometimes these were typical border plants like boxwood or yew; sometimes they were fruits, like figs, or berries; and sometimes they were flowers. Often, the corners of these squares were marked by box, yews, or hollies trimmed with shears into pyramidal or conical shapes. The squares closest to the house were more likely to contain flowers and/or evergreens. Squares closest to the house were also the most likely squares to be given over to lawn.

John Randolph's *A Treatise on Gardening, by a Citizen of Virginia* gives a window into the variety of plants grown in these gardens. This important pamphlet of gardening in Virginia was not originally dated, but the consensus among scholars is that the work was first published between 1760 and 1765—remarkably contemporary with the development of the Eyre Hall garden. The list of plants that Randolph featured gives a good indication of the focus of this adept

Virginia gardener. Randolph's book covers the cultivation techniques for 66 vegetables, 23 herbs and simples, eight fruits and eight ornamentals (including some simples). Clearly, his interest ran to comestible selections for his garden, as only 2 percent of the plants that he covered were solely ornamental.

Randolph's *Treatise on Gardening* revises the times of year for various work in the garden from those given by Philip Miller in his canonical English gardening manual—the model for Randolph's work—to ones more compatible with Tidewater Virginia. He also intersperses his own often contradictory observations. The treatise is particularly pertinent to the Eyre Hall garden because of its publication date—aligning nicely with Littleton Eyre's occupation—and its geographical proximity.

Other gardens contemporary with Eyre Hall, such as Richard Henry Lee's Chantilly and Lady Jean Skipwith's Prestwould, also offer clues to the shape, organization, and content of Littleton Eyre's garden at Eyre Hall. The basic armature of garden squares bordered by shrubs and flowers (and boxwood at several corners) with vegetables in the center is consistent with that found or described at other eighteenth-century gardens. In addition to the enclosing

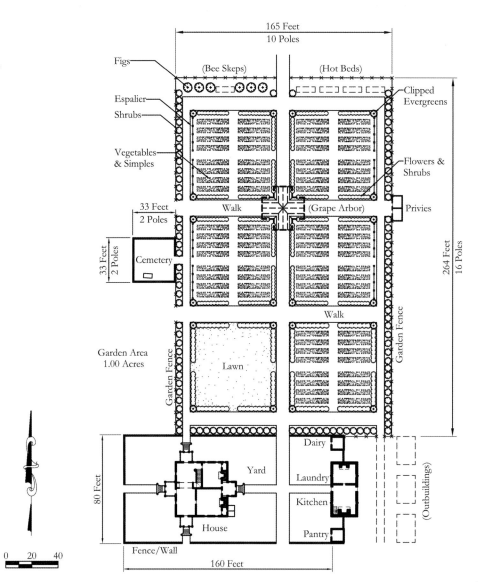

Fig. 155. Conjectural plan
of the garden at Eyre Hall,
ca. 1760.

165 Feet
10 Poles

Figs

(Bee Skeps)   (Hot Beds)

Espalier

Shrubs

Vegetables
& Simples

Clipped
Evergreens

Flowers &
Shrubs

33 Feet
2 Poles

Walk   (Grape Arbor)   Privies

33 Feet
2 Poles

Cemetery

264 Feet
16 Poles

Walk

Garden Area
1.00 Acres

Lawn

Garden Fence

Garden Fence

Dairy

Laundry

(Outbuildings)

Yard

Kitchen

80 Feet

Pantry

House

Fence/Wall

0   20   40

160 Feet

wall, drives, walks, and plantings, the Prestwould plan locates built structures in the garden including a green-house, an octagonal summerhouse, a bee house, two curved trellises or arbors and three arched arbors. In another parallel to Eyre Hall, a cemetery is located on the centerline of the garden (Fig. 153).

Littleton Eyre's garden, laid out before 1760, if typical of its form and period, would have contained some ornamental plants, but its focus would have been on vegetables and fruit for the table. And, while today, the ruin of the 1819 green-house is the only apparent evidence of a built structure in the garden, the mid-eighteenth-century garden would by necessity have had several structural elements inside its enclosing walls, most notably privies. Some of these structures such as trellises and arbors would have been both functional and ornamental. Trellises provided

sitting areas as well as support for espaliered fruits; arbors offered support for vines (especially grapevines) alongside their use as a shelter or shady and restful interlude during one's garden stroll. Smaller features might have included hotbeds or cold frames and bee skeps. The hotbeds would have contributed to a longer season for plants; the bee skeps would have housed the insects so necessary for pollination and a supply of honey.

These would have changed over time. When the green-house was constructed, hotbeds may have been removed (Fig. 154). When the garden evolved from a traditional flower, food, and "simples" garden to a purely ornamental one in the early twentieth century, structures for food crops, like trellises and arbors, would have been unnecessary. And, of course, indoor plumbing eventually made the privies obsolete.

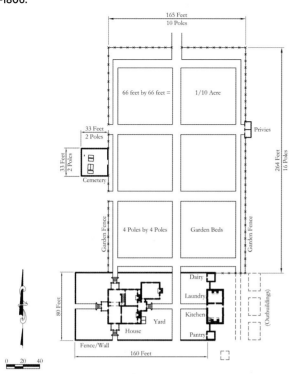

Fig. 156. John and Ann Eyre's Eyre Hall, 1796–1806.

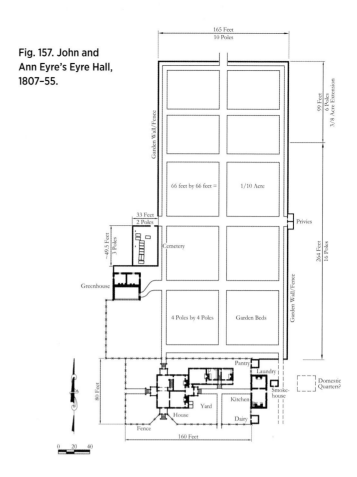

Fig. 157. John and Ann Eyre's Eyre Hall, 1807–55.

CONJECTURAL PLAN

The conjectural plan shows how all these elements may have been arranged in the yard and garden at Eyre Hall during the tenures of Littleton and Severn Eyre (1760–73), though we expect that it remained largely in this configuration until the dining room addition was created by Severn's son around 1806. This plan is a combination of elements that we may reasonably surmise from physical remains, like the fence/ wall and pathways, together with documentary information, like the insurance policies. This base of information may then be combined with historical elements of the "regular" garden that are so typical and universal that they may be assumed to create a plausible pastiche (Fig. 155).

CHRONOLOGICAL DIAGRAMS

The first major changes in the diagrams of the house, yard, and garden came in the early nineteenth century during the ownership of Severn Eyre. When his son, John,

inherited the property in 1789, the one-story dining room addition on the northeast corner of the house was already in place. Aside from further interments in the cemetery and the addition of one small building south of the old kitchen building, the basic geometry of the site plan remained the same (Fig. 156). A row of outbuildings is shown to the east of the kitchen building. These indicate only that supplementary support buildings are likely to have been constructed in this general area. The land east of the kitchen and the garden is a likely location for buildings like a barn, stable, carriage house, and woodsheds, along with the requisite paddocks.

In 1800, John married Ann M. Upshur. During the next half century, substantial expansion and reorientation of the site plan and the house took place. The addition east of the house was lengthened toward the kitchen, and the entire addition—including the earlier one that housed the dining room—was raised to a full two stories. A smokehouse was built to the east of the kitchen. The fence/wall design that enclosed the yard seems to have been the model for an expanded enclosure around the

Fig. 158. Severn Eyre's Eyre Hall, ca. 1890.

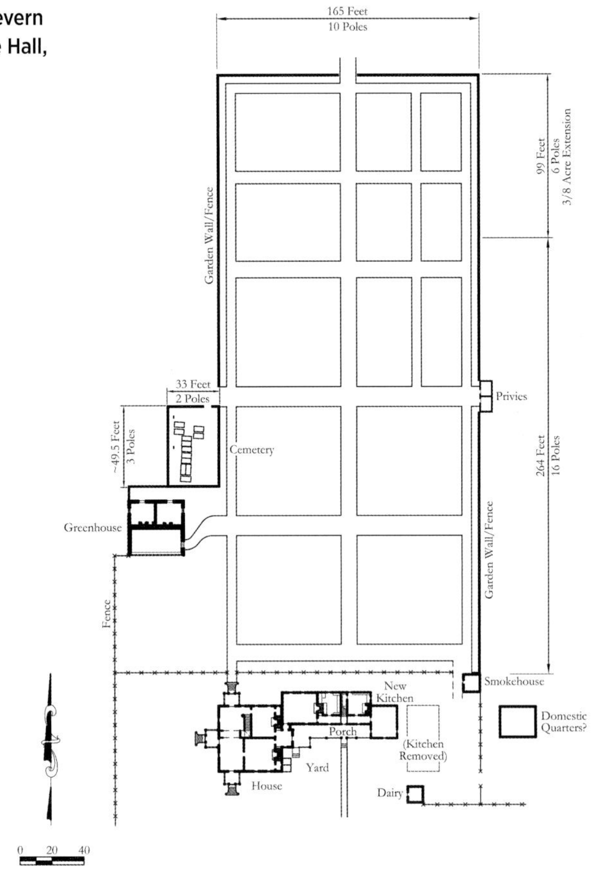

garden. Family oral history asserts that John and Ann enclosed the garden with the brick-and-picket fence/wall in the early nineteenth century. This is consistent with the 1:5 brick bonding on the wall and in the green-house that was constructed in 1819. During this half century the original brick-and-picket wall/fence that enclosed the yard was replaced with an ornate picket fence of tight spacing, in which the pickets alternate between tall and short pickets. Atop the posts are ornamental cast-iron finials. The area south of the new green-house was enclosed by a picket fence, and the western garden fence between the cemetery and the house was removed, effectively making the space south of the green-house a part of the garden (Fig. 157). It is possible, perhaps likely, that the domestic quarters building east of the kitchen was built before John Eyre's death in 1855. This brings the story of the Eyre Hall site up to the end of John Eyre's long life and to the eve of the Civil War, which would change its composition in both subtle and fundamental ways.

Finally, the cemetery was expanded to the north to accommodate John and Ann Eyre, below the largest and most ornate markers in the cemetery. After the Civil War, when the property passed to a later Severn Eyre and his wife Margaret, changes reflected the end of slavery and the shift in use from a working plantation to a summer retreat. By the late nineteenth century, large parts of the fence that enclosed the yard around the house had disappeared. The fence-lines marking the west, east, and south sides of this enclosure that was such an important part of the original site plan were either relocated or removed altogether (Fig. 158). The old kitchen, which may have been the oldest building on the site, was replaced by a small addition on the east end of the house. A porch was appended to the south side of the nineteenth-century additions to the house, completing a reorientation of the "front" of the house from the original west side, to the south.

In the garden, the geometric pattern remained largely intact, but the "regular" garden of "well-boxed" vegetables and fruits evolved into a large ornamental garden. One photograph of the garden from the turn of the twentieth century shows flowering shrubs, which would have been planted around the perimeter of the vegetable squares and kept in scale by pruning. In that view we see the squares with grass in lieu of vegetables and the lines of ornamentals having grown into large and naturalistic shapes—a transformation that was partly circumstantial and partly due to changing aesthetic norms (Fig. 159).

By the late nineteenth century, one change had a profound effect on the perception of the garden and grounds: during a snowstorm the glass that had covered the southern third of the green-house section of the roof collapsed, and the elegant little building that had been an important fixture in John and Ann Eyre's landscape fell into ruin. The transformation of the garden from a typical "regular garden" into an extensive ornamental one began in the decades after the Civil War and has continued until the present. Some of the early horticultural changes included introduction of more boxwood, both as edging and for ornaments

Fig. 159. Eyre Hall garden at the turn of the twentieth century.

Fig. 160.
Margaret Taylor
Baldwin's Eyre
Hall, ca. 1930s.

165 Feet
10 Poles

99 Feet
6 Poles
3/8 Acre Extension

Garden Wall/Fence

66 feet by 66 feet =

33 Feet
2 Poles

Privies

~49.5 Feet
3 Poles

Cemetery

1/10 Acre

264 Feet
16 Poles

Garden Wall/Fence

Greenhouse

4 Poles by 4 Poles

Garden Beds

Fence

Smokehouse

Domestic
Quarters?

House

Dairy

Fence

0   20   40

within some of the squares, and, later, the establishment of extensive plantings of crape myrtle and several magnolia trees which give the garden much of its present character and vertical scale.

Beginning about 1930, Margaret Taylor Baldwin, who had inherited the property from her grandfather, Severn Eyre, began a program of renovations, modernizations, and restorations that would extend to several decades (Fig. 160). Among the changes were the reinstitution of the picket fence on the line of the old yard fence south of the house, and the construction of a wing east of the house nearly on the foundation of the old kitchen building, which had been removed after the Civil War.

Furlong Baldwin inherited Eyre Hall from his mother in 1979. He made necessary repairs to the house, enclosed the breezeway connecting the eastern wing added by his mother, and stabilized the green-house or orangery. In addition, working with expert horticulturists Donna Hackman and more recently Laurie Klingel, Mr. Baldwin has kept the Eyre Hall garden vital and relevant to contemporary visitors (Fig. 161).

The difference between the trim and respectable garden of Littleton Eyre and the venerable landscape into which it has evolved is dramatic. The former was sunny, while the current version is mottled with shade. The organization of the early garden would have been apparent at a glance; that of its successor is more mysterious, though the remnants of its original layout are still discernable on the ground plane if you look for them. The early garden would have been dominated by comestible crops, while the current version is given over entirely to ornamental plantings.

Laurie Klingel's approach is to honor the historical integrity of the garden layout, by making replacements of boxwood, for example as close as possible to the locations of the originals. She avers that the garden borders are another matter entirely: "Here I exercise plenty of artistic license and do not subscribe to any one particular palette or historical interpretation. I use thousands of tulips, anemones, daffodils, camassias, and hyacinths to create a fluid rhythm throughout the garden—one that sparks the imagination and reminds us that the history of Eyre Hall is still happening."

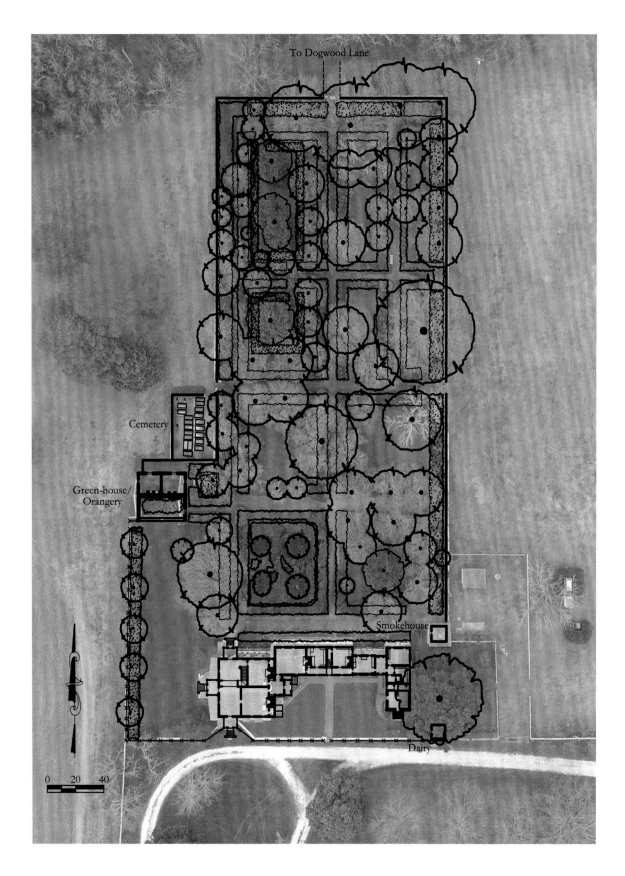

Fig. 161. Furlong
Baldwin's house and
garden, 2020.

To Dogwood Lane

Cemetery

Green-house/
Orangery

Smokehouse

Dairy

0   20   40

The garden at Eyre Hall has evolved in a continuum dictated by changes in the world around it, but still adheres to the fundamental appeal of living and working with plants for their spiritual uplift. Andrew Marvell's words, penned nearly a hundred years before the Eyre Hall garden was laid out, ring as true today as they did in the garden's earliest years (Fig. 162):

Fig. 162. Eyre Hall
garden, 2020.

What wond'rous life in this I lead!
Ripe Apples drop about my head;
The Luscious Clusters of the Vine
Upon my Mouth do crush their Wine;
The Nectaren, and curious Peach,
Into my hands themselves do reach;
Stumbling on Melons, as I pass,
Insnared with Flow'rs, I fall on Grass...

How could such sweet and wholesome Hours
Be reckon'd but with herbs and flow'rs![30]

NOTES

1. Sauthier was born in Strasbourg, France, near the border with Germany, in 1736. Stewart E. Dunaway, *Claude J. Sauthier and his Maps of North Carolina* (Morrisville, N.C.: Lulu Press), 8.
2. *Warner & Hanna's Plan of the City and Environs of Baltimore, 1891.* For a comprehensive description of many of the gardens illustrated on the Warren and Hanna plan, see Barbara Wells Sarudy, *Gardens and Gardening in the Chesapeake, 1700–1805* (Baltimore: Johns Hopkins University Press, 1998).
3. Green Spring, to which Virginia governor Sir William Berkeley retired in 1652, was located approximately four miles northwest of Jamestown.
4. At Brandon, archaeologist Nick Luccketti discovered that fill had been brought to the site to create the modest terracing exhibited in that garden.
5. This orientation is closer to a true east–west line than one generated from magnetic north in 1760. Magnetic north was 2½ degrees west of true north in 1760; magnetic declination in 2020 at Eyre Hall is about 11 degrees west of true north, while the layout of the house and yard are within a half degree of the true east–west. This suggests that the orientation to the true compass points, rather than magnetic ones, was intentional.
6. The location of the scene in the background has not been definitively established. The subject was the daughter of William Byrd II and Maria Taylor Byrd, of Westover, and wife of Charles Carter of Cleve. Anne Byrd Carter was a contemporary of Littleton Eyre.
7. William Waller Hening, *The Statutes at Large, being a Collection of all the Laws of Virginia* (New York, Richmond, and Philadelphia, 1819–23), 6:38–40.

8. Drew Addison Swanson, "Fighting over Fencing: Agricultural Reform and Antebellum Efforts to Close the Virginia Open Range," *Virginia Magazine of History and Biography* 117, no. 2 (January 2009): 105.
9. As Rudy Favretti pointed out in *Arnoldia* 31, no. 4 (July 1971), except for farmers who grew herbs to sell, like the Shakers, herbs were generally to be found in the garden with other plants, and not in a separate garden.
10. J. de La Quintinie, H. Wise, and G. London, *The Complete Gard'ner: or, Directions for cultivating and right ordering of fruit-gardens and kitchen-gardens . . .*, 4th ed. (London: Andrew Bell, 1704).
11. Reginald Blomfield and F. Inigo Thomas, *The Formal Garden in England* (London: Waterstone, 1985), 87.
12. A "square" during this era was a figure with square, or 90-degree, corners. What we call a "rectangle" might be called an "oblong square," while what we call a square might be referred to as "foursquare."
13. Sarah Bowdoin (1738–1760) was Littleton and Bridget Eyre's daughter, who had married Preeson Bowdoin in 1759, brother of Littleton's business partner John Bowdoin.
14. Hunter Dickinson Farish, ed., *Journal and Letters of Philip Vickers Fithian: A Plantation Tutor of the Old Dominion, 1773–1774* (Williamsburg: Colonial Williamsburg, 1943), 61, January 29, 1774.
15. Joseph Moxon, *Mechanick Exercises; or, The Doctrine of Handy-Works* (London: J. Moxon, 1693).
16. Henry Chandlee Forman, *The Virginia Eastern Shore and its British Origins: History, Gardens & Antiquities* (Easton, Md.: Eastern Shore Publishers, 1975).
17. 40 poles or 660 feet equals one furlong (⅛ mile).

A square furlong on each side encloses exactly 10 acres.
18. Several lots of this dimension and area are shown on the "Frenchman's Map."
19. Barbara J. Heath, "Dynamic Landscapes: The Emergence of Formal Spaces in Colonial Virginia," *Historical Archaeology* 50, no. 1 (2016): 27–44.
20. The rectangular subdivisions of the garden were called "squares," "oblongs," "parterres," or "platts." Fithian used the typical, if not universal, mid- to late eighteenth-century form of capitalization of nouns.
21. 'Area' is the yard surrounding the house. The garden typically abutted the yard or area. Farish, *Journal and Letters of Philip Vickers Fithian*.
22. William Cobbett, Esq., M.P., *The American Gardener* (Claremont, N.H.: Simeon Ide, 1810), 35.
23. Thomas Hitt and James Meader, *The Modern Gardener; or, Universal Kalendar* (London: Hawes Clarke and Collins, et al., 1771), 368.
24. John Wilkins Junr to Mr. Severn Eyre, December 18, 1770, Eyre Hall Family Papers, Virginia Historical Society, Richmond.
25. Equals about $250 in 2020 dollars. Inventory of the estate of Severn Eyre, February 27, 1774, Northampton County Wills & Inventories, No. 25, 1772–1777, 394.
26. In other words, cut or mown.
27. Hitt and Meader, *Modern Gardener*, 74.
28. Audrey Noel Hume, *Archaeology and the Colonial Gardener* (Williamsburg: Colonial Williamsburg Foundation, 1974), 15.
29. Wesley Greene, *Vegetable Gardening the Colonial Williamsburg Way* (New York: Rodale, 2011), ix.
30. Andrew Marvell, "The Garden," in *Miscellaneous Poems* (London: Robert Boulter, 1681).

GARDEN AND GROUNDS 259

Fig. 163. Eyre Hall
green-house east
façade.

Green-house

WILL RIELEY

WHEN VISITORS STROLL THROUGH THE garden at Eyre Hall, after enjoying the lovely juxtaposition of historic plants with modern ones in an early nineteenth-century framework, they often gravitate to the southwest corner of the garden where the stabilized brick ruin of a building stands (Fig. 163). This roughly 30-foot-square structure originally included, in its southern half, a green-house or orangery.[1] The northern half was further subdivided into two gardeners' workrooms, one of which contained the source of a remarkable system for circulating warm air through the base of the walls of the green-house to prevent the plants from freezing in the winter. As evidence has recently emerged, the significance of this structure in the history of American green-houses, orangeries, and conservatories has grown. Its construction date, and the Eyres' desire to stock it with interesting specimens, are apparent in a letter from Ann Eyre to John McHenry of April 1819:

> The presumptuous eastern shore woman again intrudes herself on the notice of Mr. McHenry in she fears rather a novel phase to his "mind's eye" when without ceremony, or any particular claims to his kindness she presents herself to him in the form of a beggar . . . my good husband is engaged in erecting a green house for my amusement, and gratification—and as we live, in

such a remote corner of the state—and do not extend our rambles in those directions, where the art of gardening is in its highest state of refinement—or where luxuries of this kind are to be met with—I do not even know what plants are most worthy to have a place in our little building—its scale is only 30- by 15- of course I shall not have room for a large collection—and should prefer only such as are most valuable—Mr. E. Wilson[2] informed me you have a handsome collection in your house—and now your bold beggars purpose is to ask of you cuttings or offsets from any plants you may have pruned or trimmed the approaching season—if you can oblige me without inconvenience.[3]

The recipient of this amiable request was John McHenry (1791–1822), of Baltimore.[4] He was the son of James McHenry, a surgeon who studied medicine under Benjamin Rush, served during the Revolution on the staffs of Washington and Lafayette, and was later appointed President Washington's secretary of war. He was the man for whom Fort McHenry was named. John McHenry's illustrious father had died three years before Ann's "presumptuous" missive was sent in 1819. By then, John would have inherited his father's country place, a mile west of the Baltimore courthouse.[5] His father had named the 92-acre estate "Fayetteville" in honor of the Marquis de Lafayette, for whom he had served as an aide during the Revolution and with whom he maintained a cordial friendship for the rest of his life.

We know that Fayetteville had a glass-house for raising plants because, in February 1805, James McHenry wrote of the duties of his servant, Ned: "He has the care of the cows, of the *Hot-house*, of the garden, of the Pidgeons, of the rabbits, of the guinea pigs, of the fowls, and, lately of a monkey."[6] It would not have been unusual for a physician like Dr. McHenry to have kept tender plants in a glass-house for medicinal uses as well as for diversion.

In addition to owning a place with a green- or hot-house, McHenry also leased a part of his property, adjacent to his own house, to one of the most prominent nursery operations in the region. In 1795, the year before Dr. James McHenry was appointed as Washington's secretary of war, he leased a portion of this property to English emigrant and nurseryman William Booth. Booth sold seeds, nursery stock, and green-house plants. He even sold some of the plants grown in Dr. McHenry's hot-house.[7] According to Edith Bevan, Booth's "five-acre nursery, located on what is now West Baltimore Street, adjoined the country seat of the Hon. James McHenry, from whom he rented the land for a term of 30 years."[8] Booth died in 1818, but the nursery enterprise continued in operation under the direction of Booth's widow, Margaret, for another ten years, during the ownership of John McHenry.

So, Ann Eyre's request for "cuttings or offsets" was directed to someone who was in an excellent position to oblige her with green-house plants, "only such as are most valuable."[9] In making this request to McHenry, she revealed important information about the structure in question. First, she referred to "our little building" as a "green house." In the early nineteenth century this designation had a far more specific meaning than modern usage would suggest.

Bernard McMahon (1775–1816) was a Philadelphia nurseryman who was entrusted by President Thomas Jefferson with the stewardship of the Lewis and Clark plant collection. A green-house, according to McMahon in 1806, was "a garden-building fronted with glass, serving as a winter residence, for tender plants from the warmer parts of the world, which require no more artificial heat, than what is *barely sufficient to keep off frost*."[10] As late as 1838, English horticulturist Charles McIntosh gave the same definition, stating that "The degree of heat required for green-houses is just sufficient to repel frost and to dispel damp."[11]

By contrast, a hot-house was heated to a minimum year-round temperature that would allow for the growing of truly tropical plants. This class of structure would require a more elaborate and extensive heating system than that for a green-house. A hot-house was often heated by a masonry or metal stove, or furnace, with masonry ducts to convey the warmth through the building, which was sometimes called a stove-house or simply a "stove." A hot-house usually had a glass roof to admit sunlight into the building, while a green-house's glazing was usually limited to the south wall—especially during and before the eighteenth century. Another important distinction between a green-house and a hot-house or stove is that the former was a decorative, often classical, garden structure, while the latter was much plainer and more utilitarian and was often sited in an inconspicuous location in or near the garden.

A green-house, then, would be suitable for growing citrus fruit, like lemons and oranges, as well as a mélange of gardenias, oleanders, geraniums, aloes, sedums, and many other plants that require cool winters but need protection from freezing ones. Later in the nineteenth century, when the term "greenhouse" (by then, generally without the hyphen or space) evolved to encompass almost any glass house for horticultural production, the word "orangery" came into wider use to designate an ornamental garden structure dedicated to growing citrus and other associated plants. This term was adapted from the French *orangerie*, which referred not only to the building for wintering the trees, but that part of the garden in which they were displayed during the warm months. So, while John and Ann Eyre and their contemporaries would have used the "green-house" appellation to describe this specific kind of edifice, "orangery" has a long period of use as well and is more specific and less prone to confusion with the broad modern definition of "greenhouse." Either designation, applied to the Eyre Hall plant house, with the caveats above, is correct.

The term "conservatory" is sometimes used interchangeably with the above expressions, but McMahon made a clear distinction. According to him, while the plants in a green-house or orangery were moved out of the structure and into the garden during the warm months, the plants in a conservatory were planted in the ground inside the structure. He wrote that "this structure is roofed as well as fronted with glasswork, and instead of taking out the plants in the summer, as in the Green-house, the whole of the glass-roof is taken off, and the plants are thus exposed to the open air; and at the approach of autumn frosts, the lights are again put on."[12] The Eyre Hall brick ruin, then, falls clearly within McMahon's early nineteenth-century definition of a green-house (or, a little later, an orangery), but *not* a hot-house or "stove," and *not* a conservatory.[13] This little building gives us a wonderful insight into a transitory and fleeting period in the history of green-house design in America.

In the early eighteenth century, Philip Miller provided a detailed design for a prototypical green-house that was very influential, not only in Great Britain, but also in its American colonies. He argued that the green-house should be topped with a second story, which would provide useful additional interior space.

Before 1740 a green-house had been constructed at the Westover plantation of William Byrd II (1674–1744) on the James River in Virginia.[14] Thomas Jefferson designed two versions of a green-house to be located between his main plantation street, Mulberry Row, and his vegetable garden at Monticello. The first, from 1776–78, was to be 24 by 35 feet

with five large south-facing windows. The second design, from more than 20 years later, was for a smaller building of 13 by 24 feet, with three 6-foot-wide windows. Miller also recommended that the green-house be bracketed by two hot-houses on the east and west ends of the structure. These wings would have more elaborate heating systems than would be required for the green-house, and their roofs were to be composed of glazed sashes or "lights."

Most of the green-houses in America were built on a straightforward plan—a one-story building with tall south-facing windows. They were designed both for ornament and for the function of protecting tender plants from freezing. By the beginning of the nineteenth century, when John Eyre had the green-house built for his wife, Ann, the fundamentals of green-house design were well established. The design of Eyre's green-house followed sound precedent based on centuries of experience, but this fetching little building also displayed its own inimitable qualities that made it unique.

That this green-house was still being enjoyed by John Eyre during the mid-nineteenth century, and that the customary citrus and geranium plants were still being cultivated, is documented in the following description from Fanny Fielding, who had known Eyre Hall before John Eyre's death in 1855:

> In the garden . . . stood the green-house . . . its inmates
> "laughing at the storm" in winter, and in summer
> blending their rich breath with the garden-flowers.
> Tall geraniums in their varied bloom mingled with the
> silver and gold of orange and lemon fruit and blossom,
> and such refined occupation as attention to these,
> alternating with similarly tasteful employments, made
> pleasant the old gentleman's [John Eyre's] solitary life.[15]

In his 1824 *Encyclopaedia of Gardening*, English garden writer John Claudius Loudon (1783–1843) noted that the green-house or orangery was historically located near the main house and that its façade corresponded architecturally

Fig. 164. Eyre Hall
house and immediate
surroundings, 2018.

with that of the principal residence.[16] The Eyre Hall green-house conforms to both conditions. It is sited orthogonally with the house: its north–south axis is at 90 degrees to the east–west axis of the house. It is 10 feet from the family graveyard to the north and adjacent to the garden to the east. The vertical angle of the green-house gable ends is very nearly the same as that of the upper section of the gambrel roof on the main house. The roofs were of the same wood shingle material. The similarity does not extend to the material of the walls, however. The green-house is brick, stuccoed or rendered to resemble coursed ashlar, while the house is frame with clapboard siding. This variation was conventional, however, as masonry walls were standard for green-houses—except for the glazed south façade. Bernard McMahon wrote that "the building ought to be of brick, or stone, having the front almost wholly of glass-work, ranging lengthwise east and west, and constructed on an ornamental plan."[17]

In looking carefully at the stabilized ruin of the Eyre Hall green-house, we find a close correlation between its design and the recommendations of McMahon in his canonical 1806 work, *The American Gardener's Calendar, Adapted to the Climates and Seasons of the United States* (Fig. 164). According to garden historian Peter Hatch, the *Calendar* was "the most comprehensive gardening book published in the United States in the first half of the nineteenth century."[18] Just as Jefferson would follow the *Calendar* meticulously in planting flowers and vegetables at Monticello, the designer and builder of the Eyre Hall green-house was almost certainly guided by McMahon's advice on green-house design and construction in a similarly methodical fashion. McMahon's *Calendar* was clearly the *vade mecum* for the Eyre Hall green-house.

Regarding the overall scale of the building, McMahon advised "as to its general dimensions . . . it may be from ten to fifty feet or more long, according to the number of plants which you intend it should contain; and its width

in the clear, from ten or fifteen to twenty feet, though for a middle sized house, fifteen or eighteen feet is sufficient."[19] The width of the building, then, is fixed between 10 and 20 feet. Ann Eyre described the width of the Eyre Hall green-house to John McHenry as 15 feet—squarely in the middle of this range. (The inside, or "clear," width of the green-house portion of the building is more nearly 14 feet 2 inches). The length of a green-house, according to McMahon, was more variable: 10 to 50 or more feet. At 30 feet, as described by Mrs. Eyre, or 28 feet 8 inches, clear, as built, this length is again in the middle of the range described by McMahon.

The standing brick walls of the ruin describe an almost square building bisected by a thick brick wall that extends from the ground to the peak of the gable.[20] The ridge of the gable runs east–west, parallel with the north and south façades of the building. The shadow of a partition wall and two fireplaces confirm that the northern portion of the building was further bisected into two rooms of nearly equal dimensions. Each of these rooms was accessed by exterior doors on the north wall of the structure. Windows lighting each of these rooms punctuate the eastern and western walls of the structure (Fig. 165).

These rooms, on the north side of the green-house, were consistent with Philip Miller's advice. "At the Back of the Green-house there may be erected an House for Tools, and many other Purposes; which will be extremely useful, and also prevent the Frost from entering the House that Way."[21] Such sheds on the north side of the green-house became common during the eighteenth century, not only for the storage of tools, but as workrooms and as a shelter for the

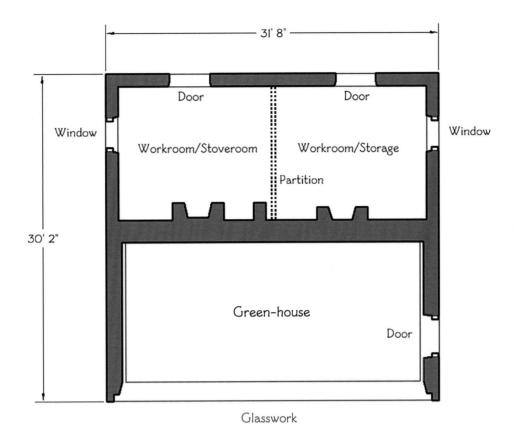

Fig. 165. Eyre Hall green-house ruin plan.

heating source that provided the modest heat required to prevent the tender plants from freezing, and a place to keep the fuel dry.[22]

One of the best descriptions of the value of rooms on the north side of a green-house comes a generation after the construction of the one at Eyre Hall, from Andrew Jackson Downing, landscape designer and enormously influential garden writer. He wrote of an ideal green-house for a two-acre property that was almost identical to his own green-house in Newburgh, New York, and which would have been built about the same time as the Eyre Hall green-house:

> This green-house is 14 feet wide by 40 feet long, and has a lean-to, or shed, at the rear, which affords cover for the furnace, with a place for fuel, and a long narrow apartment for a gardener's seed room, tool room, or work room, the latter being a place absolutely necessary in every residence of the size of a half-acre, if appropriated to ornamental purposes.[23]

As the garden at Eyre Hall had been enclosed, renovated, and perhaps expanded by the Eyres about a decade earlier than the construction of the green-house, these gardener's work and storage rooms would have been extremely useful appendages to that structure. This arrangement and dedication to specific uses is remarkably consistent with those prescribed by McMahon:

> Outside, at the back, should be erected a neat shed, the whole length of the house, completely walled in, to contain the fuel, garden-pots, &c, &c, and for the convenience of attending the fires and keeping them regularly burning; this shed will answer to defend the back wall of the stove from the cold air and frosts, to stow all garden utensils and tools in when out of use, in order to preserve them from the injuries of the weather.[24]

What is architecturally exceptional about the Eyre Hall green-house is that, rather than exhibiting a separate shed roof over a small addition to the back of the building, as was typical, a gable roof with a classical pediment was extended from the south wall of the green-house room to the north wall of the workrooms. The gable ends of the building, on the east and west sides of the building, slope in an angle of 6 inches of rise for each foot of run. The general arrangement can be seen in the two views of the digital model of the brick structure (Fig. 166).

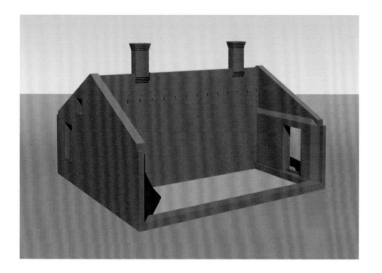 

Fig. 166. View from southwest of green-house room (left) and from northeast of workrooms (right).

Note that the wood-frame partition wall separating the two workrooms to the north is not shown on the illustration on the right. That partition, which bisects the masonry space, is clearly described by an obvious channel on the south wall where plaster is absent; but this partition is not otherwise visible in the current stabilized ruin. Physical evidence makes clear that these rooms had wooden floors over a ventilated space, plaster walls, and flat ceilings above. The ceiling height was a little more than 8 feet. The doors on the north wall and the chimneys above the roofline are aligned with each other, and they fall on the one-quarter and three-quarter marks as spaced from the east and west walls. This is not a casual or utilitarian relationship but an explicit architectural arrangement. One sees in the view from the northeast how the chimneys curve along the central wall, as they rise from the level of the first-floor ceiling to the ridge of the roof, to achieve these positions. When we add the floor in the first level, the partition wall framing, and the ceiling joists—all of these based on the surviving or photographic evidence and careful measurements—we begin to see the volume of the subdivision of space in the northern half of the building (Fig. 167).

While some questions remain about the specifics of the interior (for example, whether there was an interior door in the partition wall between the rooms), by adding the materials that we *do* know, we get a good idea of the appearance of the interior of these rooms (Fig. 168). These rooms seem to have been finished simply, but the plastered

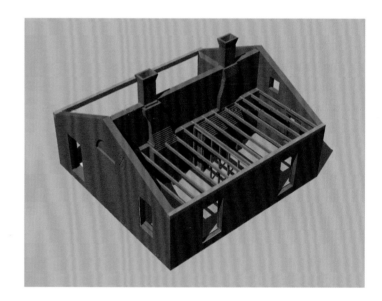

Fig. 167. View from northeast with assumed floor, wall framing, and ceiling joists.

walls, paneled doors, and wooden floors raise the level of finish of these rooms substantially above the rustic sheds behind green-houses described in contemporary literature.

"A pediment is said to lend a work so much dignity that for the sake of appearance not even the heavenly house of Jove was thought to be without one, although it never rained there." So wrote fifteenth-century Italian Renaissance architect Leon Battista Alberti. He then followed with explicit direction about the slope of the roof of a classical pediment.[25] "The section up to the vertex (that is, the ridge at the top) takes up no more than a fourth and not less than a fifth of the width of the façade."[26] In modern carpentry parlance,

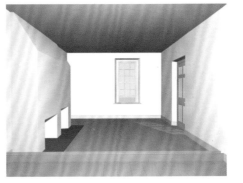
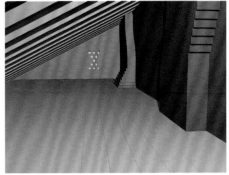

Fig. 168. Northeast workroom (left) and northwest workroom (right). Digital restoration. (Baseboard shows location of partition wall.)

Fig. 169. Digital model of loft above workrooms.

this means a roof should slope no more than 6 inches in one foot and no less than 4.8 inches in one foot. Or, in angular terms, it should incline 21.8 degrees to 26.6 degrees from the horizontal. Palladio, a century later, recommended a slope of 5⅓ inches per foot, or 24 degrees from the horizontal—very nearly the average of Alberti's limits.[27]

The slope of the Eyre Hall green-house is 6 in 12 or 26.6 degrees from the horizontal—consistent with Alberti's upper limit and a little steeper than the slope recommended by Palladio. A practical advantage to this angle is that it works well with the modular brick size used for the building, as its units will lay up to an even 2:1 horizontal to vertical ratio every three courses.[28]

In adding the floorboards to the loft above and the rafters that describe the aforementioned 6-in-12 slope, we may see the loft above the workrooms (Fig. 169). This loft space is lit by a small window on the western end wall and an unusual hourglass-shaped pattern of penetrations through the east wall. This space is only lofty enough for an adult to stand along its southern side, next to the wall, where it is a little less than 7 feet in height. Note that the corbelling of the brick in the chimneys makes them align with the north doors and the ridge of the roof outside. Various possible uses for this space have been posited over the years, from storage to sleeping quarters (which would mean a ladder or steep stairs connecting to the finished rooms below).

While both uses are possible, neither explains the purpose of the 11 openings in the hourglass shape. This pattern of openings seems incongruous with the small square window in the western end of this space. One use that would be consistent with the openings is a pigeon-loft or dovecote.

While dovecotes were sometimes separate buildings, many utilized the upper portions of buildings whose lower floors were dedicated to other uses and were therefore referred to as pigeon-lofts. As with the terms "green-house" and "orangery," some clarification of the "dovecote" term may be useful. Dovecotes were never home for what we call doves today. Dove was simply the old English word for pigeon.

The square window on the west side, hinged as a casement, would illuminate the space for tending pigeons, including the harvesting of squab. In addition, it is large enough to provide access by ladder and would offer a convenient portal to remove the litter, including the pigeon dung, periodically (typically annually during the winter). In this scenario, the operation would have been located on the opposite side of the structure from the house and garden. Entrance to elevated pigeon-lofts by means of an exterior ladder and small door or window was quite common (Fig. 170).

Another aspect of this symbiotic relationship between the green-house, workrooms, and possible pigeon-loft is that the two fireplaces and the furnace or stove that would provide heat to the green-house would also provide some heat in the coldest weather from the brick wall through which the flues from these heat sources run, heating the loft above the workrooms. It is not unreasonable to speculate that the loft space could have been divided, with the western room, lit by the window, serving as an upstairs space for the stove room, and the eastern room occupied by the pigeon-loft (Fig. 171).

In trying to understand how this structure looked from the outside, we have a significant aid in a photograph in the

Fig. 170. Nineteenth-century engraving of a pigeon-loft.

Fig. 171. Window frame in the western end of the loft.

Fig. 172. Photo of graveyard and north end of green-house building at Eyre Hall, ca. 1900.

Fig. 173. Semi-transparent overlay of digital model on photograph in Fig. 172.

Callahan Photograph Collection taken in 1890 depicting the north side of the green-house before the roof disappeared on that side.[29] By the time of this photograph, the building was showing signs of deterioration (Fig. 172). English ivy on the eastern half of the north wall obscured the eastern door, indicating that this door had not been used for access for some time. Because we know the distance from the eaves to the ridge of the roof, we can count the courses and determine the exposure of the shingles—7½ inches. We see the two-toned paneled door on the west end, hinged on the right or western side, swinging in. To measure distances on the drawing, we concluded that the most reliable method would be to align a digital model of the building over the photograph to produce a figure that could be scaled. The result was illuminating (Fig. 173).

Various elements in the model could be adjusted to align with the photograph. Because the digital model is scalable, we could measure elements shown in the photo that were no longer extant, such as the head height of the doors—a modest 6 feet 3 inches—and the height of the cornice—9¼ inches. The last measurement is important because a Tuscan cornice of that height would be in proportion to a full Tuscan order (column, architrave, frieze, and cornice) that extended from the sill-level to the top of the cornice of the green-house and workrooms.[30] This proportional exactness indicates a working knowledge of the classical orders. Thomas Savage pointed out that "Ann and John Eyre made subtle but fashionable changes to the house, including replacing a simple bolection fireplace molding in the parlor with a neoclassical chimneypiece featuring a

Fig. 174. View of the west end of
the green-house from Whitelaw's
Virginia's Eastern Shore, 1951.

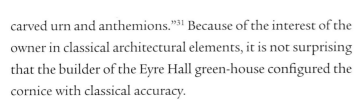

Fig. 175. North
and east sides of
digital model.

carved urn and anthemions."[31] Because of the interest of the owner in classical architectural elements, it is not surprising that the builder of the Eyre Hall green-house configured the cornice with classical accuracy.

Another important early photograph appeared in Ralph Whitelaw's *Virginia's Eastern Shore* (Fig. 174).[32] The photograph of the western side of the green-house taken before 1951 shows the shadow of the raking cornice, the lower chord of the pediment, and the shadow of the balustrade at the ridgeline of the building. At the chimneys, the stucco or rendering was omitted from the brick beneath in the sections where the wooden features had been lost. By this time, the roof was missing. With these photographs and the remaining information that could be measured or otherwise determined from the stabilized ruin, it was possible to construct a plausible representation of the northeastern side of the building, including its pedimented gable end (Fig. 175).

The shade and colors of the model were determined by the photos and by fragments of color on the surviving elements of the building.[33] The graveyard wall and garden plantings were omitted from this view to better show the details of the structure. The lunette window in the pediment would have been obstructed from the inside by the masonry wall that separated the green-house from the workrooms and loft. It was doubtless a dummy window, with stucco or rendering painted black behind the glass. A similar condition can be seen at the lunette window at Kendall Grove, a few miles to the north of Eyre Hall. (The Kendall Grove house

was built about five years before the Eyre Hall green-house.) This first-cut view gives a straightforward compilation of the known elements on these two sides of the building.

Turning to the south side of the structure, understanding its configuration requires not only looking at the physical remains and earlier photographs but also examining the oral history and the literature of the period. The sole room on the south half of the building is 14 feet 2 inches by 28 feet 8 inches (inside measurement). Its south wall is approximately 10 feet tall and its north wall about 18 feet tall. Perhaps because of a hypothetical illustration in Henry Chandlee Forman's *Virginia Eastern Shore and its British Origins*, the general assumption has been that the south wall was glazed and that the roof was shingled like the north side, as shown on the earlier photograph from 1890.[34] This roofing configuration is at odds with the recollection of current owner Furlong Baldwin's mother, Margaret Eyre Taylor Baldwin (1898–1979), who said that she had been told that the roof was glass and that it collapsed from the weight of snow. Ceiling joist pockets in the tall brick wall on the north side of this space, and termination of plaster at that height, indicate a flat ceiling about 13 feet above the floor. The flat ceiling would have precluded a glass roof—at least in that part of the room. If we look at the configuration of that ceiling, it would have been approximately 13 feet high for the northern two-thirds of the room and sloped down to the top of the south wall for the remaining one-third (Fig. 176).

This configuration would have left much of the interior volume in shadow. The angle of the sun at noon on

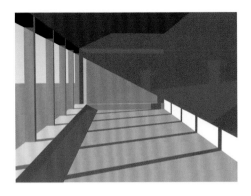

Fig. 176. Pattern of winter sun at noon on digital model—sloping ceiling enclosed.

Fig. 177. Pattern of winter sun at noon on digital model—sloping ceiling open.

Fig. 178. Hotbed as recommended by McMahon. Glass pieces overlap like shingles—as suggested for a green-house roof.

December 21 at Eyre Hall is 29¼ degrees above the horizon, which is illustrated in the digital model above. The relative shortness of the south wall would have severely limited the amount of sunlight that penetrated into the green-house. Only the lowest couple of feet of the tall back wall would receive any warming rays of the sun, and so this potential mass for storage of heat would have been largely unutilized in this configuration. Earlier green-houses at Mount Vernon, Mount Airy, and Wye House gained additional sunlight in the winter by using much taller glazed south walls.[35] The probable approach to addressing this issue by the designer and builder of the Eyre Hall green-house can be seen in McMahon's 1806 *American Gardener's Calendar*:

> Let one third of the front side of the roof, for the whole length of the house, be formed of glass-work, and the back wall raised, so as that a horizontal ceiling may be carried from the upper parts of these lights to it. . . . [Y]ou may carry the entire roof with a gentle slope from the front to the back wall, which must be made of a proper height for that purpose; one third or one half of such a roof may be made of glass-work; from the termination of which, carry the ceiling on a level to the back part of the house.[36]

If the flat ceiling section remained closed, but the sloping section that connects the south wall with the ceiling were opened to receive glasswork, it would create an overhead arrangement of one-third sloping glass and two-thirds flat ceiling, exactly as prescribed by McMahon. This configuration makes the shorter south wall perfectly practicable. The opening in the sloping portion of the roof extends the area of sunlight to a much larger portion of the

green-house and warms a much larger portion of the back wall (Fig. 177). In arranging the glasswork on the south wall and roof of the green-house, McMahon is, once again, explicit. He advises making the lights in the roof along the lines of those in a hotbed (what we would call a cold frame today). McMahon gives clear detailed instructions for constructing such a hotbed. The glass pieces would overlap like shingles. The individual sash may be opened for ventilation (Fig. 178).

For the vertical south wall, McMahon says, "As to the upright glasses, they are to be glazed in the ordinary way of house sashes." And of their limits: "[T]he bottom sashes must reach within a foot or eighteen inches of the floor of the house, and their tops reach within eight or ten inches of the ceiling . . . and it should have as much glass as possible, and a wide glass door, should be in the middle, both for ornament and entrance, and for moving in and out the plants; a small door at the end, for entrance in severe weather, will be found of considerable utility."[37] The Eyre Hall green-house has a single door in the east end of the building, just as prescribed by McMahon. As noted earlier, many of the plants may have been moved out of the green-house during the warm months of the year through the wide doorway in the middle of the building, as at Mount Vernon, where George Washington noted in his diary, on May 23, 1785, that the "sower [sour] Oranges were in the Area in front of the Green House."[38] These elements, added to the south and east façades, result in the following arrangement (Fig. 179).

The addition of lights, or glazed sash, in the sloping roof reconciles the flat ceiling indicated by the pockets in the tall

Fig. 179. South and east sides of digital model, with wall and roof lights.

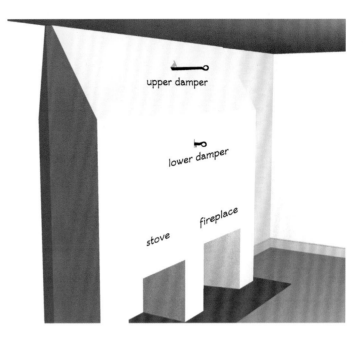

Fig. 180. Side-by-side arrangement in northwest workroom.

brick dividing wall with the family oral history passed on by Margaret Baldwin that the roof was glass and collapsed from a snow load. This illustration shows central doors as recommended by McMahon. The seven-bay spacing for the south windows aligns nicely with the ceiling joists—each window jamb falling under every other joist. The location of two fig trees, shown in an Historic American Buildings Survey photograph, aligns with the second and fifth window jambs, flanking the central door.[39] While glazed roofs were typical in *hot*-houses by the early nineteenth century, this building may represent the first *green-house* with roof lights constructed in America. It was a sensible way to add sunlight into the green-house without altering the eave and cornice line of the classical pediment. Though the addition of lights to the southern third of the room seems clearly to have come from McMahon, combining this technique with a classical pediment is ingenious and unique.

The heating system for this facility has been the focus of a good bit of head-scratching over the years. While we won't know for certain until some technological breakthrough makes the location of the flues and/or ducts within the walls apparent, we can make a reasonable conjecture. It may be that the simplest explanation is the closest to the mark. At first glance, there are two fireplaces in the northwest room and one in the northeast (Fig. 180). Upon closer inspection, it is clear that these two features in the northwest room are not the same. The western opening is indeed a fireplace,

with normal splayed firebox and smoke shelf. The second one, just to the east, has a lower head height and the sides of the box are square, not splayed. This would be the inlet for warm air to be conveyed into the walls of the adjacent green-house—the "stove" or "furnace."

While metal stoves or furnaces were in use by this time, McMahon eschewed their use in green-houses, advocating masonry as more reliable and safer for the plants. "Sometimes where a Green-house has been well-considered in these points, all is confounded by the introduction of a mettle [sic] stove and pipes, which never can be managed so as to give, when necessary, that gradual and well-regulated heat, which will protect the plants without injuring them."[40] It is possible that the stove had a metal face, to regulate the intake of air, but no attachment evidence is obvious, and most stoves of this and earlier periods did not utilize them.

When Furlong Baldwin had the brickwork of the green-house repaired and stabilized in 2010–11 by a team led by historic restoration mason Jack Peet, the duct that runs around the perimeter of the green-house room was opened. The masons uncovered a channel, duct, or flue that was clearly a part of the heating system for the green-house. Most hypocaust heating systems in hot-houses and green-houses utilized flues carrying smoke and heat from a fireplace or furnace through walls or under the floor to heat the structure indirectly, by warming the masonry which would, in turn, warm the interior of the space before

Fig. 181. Heating duct on south side of green-house room.

exiting through the chimney. In the Eyre Hall green-house, the 9-by-9-inch void around the base of the exterior wall was plastered smooth on the inside and revealed little or no buildup of soot (Fig. 181). Perhaps the system was never (or infrequently) operated. But possibly it was not designed to convey wood smoke, but rather warm air, heated by a cleaner-burning fuel, around the perimeter of the green-house. The duct was only one brick, turned on edge (as prescribed by McMahon), from the inside of the green-house, and about 13 inches from the outside.

Philip Miller cautioned that great care should be taken to ensure that smoke would not leak out of the flues and damage the plants.[41] From the time of John Evelyn, writers acknowledged the danger of smoke damaging plants in a green-house. McMahon declared that "the flues must also be furnished off with the best plaistering-mortar that can be made, in order to prevent any cracks through which the smoke might pass into the house, which cannot be too carefully guarded against, as it is extremely injurious to the plants."[42] The ducts at the Eyre Hall green-house are plastered just as McMahon recommended. Another suggestion to limit smoke damage was to use charcoal—cleaner burning than wood—as the fuel.[43] A similar effect could be obtained by using coals from a wood fire, which would give off less smoke, but substantial heat.

One logical interpretation of the configuration of the fireplaces, stove, and dampers in the Eyre Hall green-house is this:

1. A fire would be started in the fireplace of the northwest room. This would heat the flue and outlet of the western chimney stack. A fire would be built, or coals moved, to the stove from the adjacent fireplace. The lower damper would be open, allowing exhaust through the western chimney from the stove.

2. When the fire in the stove had become hot coals, the upper damper would be opened and the lower one closed, which would cause the draft of the western stack to pull air through the stove, through the loop in the green-house, and exit into the chimney at a higher elevation.

The eastern fireplace would operate as a conventional fireplace and chimney, except that the heat in the chimney would help to warm the tall wall separating the green-house from the workrooms. During cold nights, a gardener would need to sleep in the stove room to tend the fires, but in the climate of the Eastern Shore of Virginia this would be a rare occurrence. The goal, again, was to provide only enough heat to prevent the plants from freezing. McMahon advised that "[f]ires may also occasionally be used, and indeed are indispensable at times . . . even then you are to be very cautious, not to create *thereby* too strong a heat in the house, never above 40 or 45 degrees of Fahrenheit's thermometer; for this would cause your plants to push and get into a fresh state of vegetation, which would be extremely injurious to them during any of the winter months."[44]

The use of hot coals in the stove and infrequency of use probably account for the relative absence of soot in the ducts in the green-house. The following diagrams show the sequence described above. Purple shows the route of the smoke from the fireplaces; yellow, the fumes and warm air from the stove or furnace (Fig. 182). This view of the northern rooms indicates the three sources of heat for the building. On the left, the eastern fireplace warms the northeastern room and the chimney warms the interior wall that divides the green-house from the workrooms. On

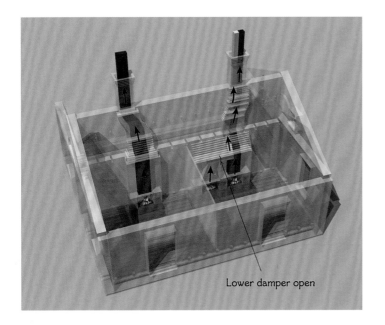

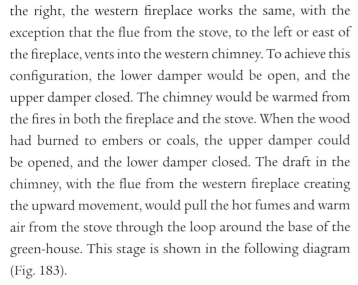

Fig. 182. First stage of heating green-house: lower damper open, upper damper closed. View from north.

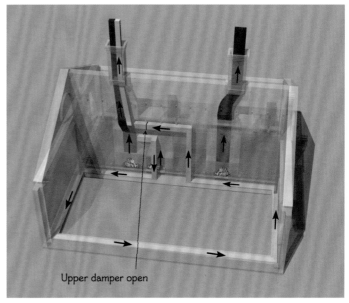

Fig. 183. Second stage: lower damper closed, upper damper open. View from south.

the right, the western fireplace works the same, with the exception that the flue from the stove, to the left or east of the fireplace, vents into the western chimney. To achieve this configuration, the lower damper would be open, and the upper damper closed. The chimney would be warmed from the fires in both the fireplace and the stove. When the wood had burned to embers or coals, the upper damper could be opened, and the lower damper closed. The draft in the chimney, with the flue from the western fireplace creating the upward movement, would pull the hot fumes and warm air from the stove through the loop around the base of the green-house. This stage is shown in the following diagram (Fig. 183).

The draft from the western chimney would pull the fumes and warm air from the stove, through the loop at floor-level in the green-house and into the chimney at the location of the upper damper. The dampers could be adjusted, not only to determine the route of the fumes from the stove, but also to regulate the amount of heat going through the loop. A gardener, skilled in the use of such a system, could manage the level of heat to keep the plants from freezing, but also prevent their damage from too much heat. Most writers about green-houses in the eighteenth and early nineteenth centuries recommended that the hot air ducts make several returns on the back wall. We do not

know the pattern of the ducts within the tall dividing wall; but considering the modest size of the building and the fact that this wall contains two chimneys that would have been warmed by fires, it is a reasonable conjecture that a simple loop system, like that shown, may have been utilized. Perhaps radar, X-ray, or some other remote sensing device will in the future solve the question of the exact route of the flues on the dividing wall.

McMahon observed that "a house constructed on this plan will very seldom require the assistance of fire-heat, which ought always to be used with great caution in a Green-house; [such a Green-house] will admit light, collect heat, and give health, beauty and vigour to all the plants."[45] He also advised that the green-house should stand in the pleasure ground and be constructed on an "ornamental plan." Some of the finishing touches of this structure confirm its adherence to this theme. Except for the space above the workrooms (the possible pigeon-loft), the interiors of the rooms were plastered. This finish survives in many places and has preserved the brick beneath it in many locations.

That the interior of the green-house was plastered is not surprising, as that finish is explicitly specified by McMahon and others who recommended that "the whole inside, both ceiling, wall and flues, be neatly finished off with good plaister and white-wash."[46] The storage/workrooms,

Fig. 184. Scored rendering on the west wall.

Fig. 185. Location of balustrade connection to chimneys.

however, were finished in a manner a cut above that for the typical utilitarian back-sheds described in the literature. It is apparent that the rooms had not only plastered walls and wooden floors but also paneled exterior doors (the photo of the north side of the green-house from the Callahan collection shows a flat-paneled door with two-toned paint). We don't know if the ceiling was plastered or if it had exposed ceiling joists. Since the walls were plastered and the ceiling joist spacing would accommodate a workable span for lath, it would be reasonable to suppose that the ceiling was plastered as well. There was a limit to the extravagance of these working spaces, however. There is no evidence of mantles, cornices or other ornamental interior woodwork, aside from the door and window architraves.

The outside finish was even more refined. Brick was widely regarded as a fine exterior material in early nineteenth century Virginia; however, the Eyres went for an even more upscale finish. From the seventeenth to the nineteenth century, masonry buildings (and occasionally wooden ones) were sometimes covered with exterior plaster, stucco, or *render*, which was troweled to a smooth surface and then scored with false mortar joints to give the appearance of ashlar. This brick green-house building was plastered on the inside and rendered and scored to resemble ashlar on the outside (Fig. 184). The only place to see the underlying brick would have been in the loft above the workrooms. The color of the render is a tannish gray, primarily from the color of the sand in the render or stucco. It is likely that

the original color was lighter before the lime in the surface material weathered.

Another embellishment to this building that is absent (and was absent as early as the late nineteenth century when the photograph from the north in the Callahan collection was taken) is its crowning element. Clearly visible today are shadows where posts of a balustrade that must have run along the ridge of the roof terminated at the chimneys (Fig. 185).

There are several possibilities for the form of the railing at the apex of the roof. The most obvious is a classical balustrade (considering the classical pediments at the gable ends of the roof). The difficulty with this approach is that the connection to the chimney is only 4 inches in width. A properly proportioned classical balustrade would have a terminal post (or uncut baluster) about 50 percent wider than that. Charles Bullfinch, Owen Biddle, and others have shown designs with Chinese railings along the ridge of buildings—sometimes between chimneys. While possible and plausible, there is no use of this kind of chinoiserie anywhere on the exterior of the Eyre Hall house. What *is* at the Eyre Hall house, on all four porches entering the oldest portion of the house, are slender balusters that incorporate miniature Tuscan columns (see Fig. 111). These porches are thought to have been remodeled by John Eyre in the early nineteenth century, only a decade or so before the construction of the green-house. A railing with this type of baluster, with its terminal posts, would fit very nicely within

Fig. 186. Digital reconstruction of Eyre Hall green-house/orangery

Fig. 187. Eyre Hall green-house/ orangery, stabilized 2010–11.

the 4-inch voids in the rendering at each of the chimneys and conform with familial precedent and a comfortable fit.

The railings were attached to both sides of the chimneys at the Eyre Hall green-house. This feature is completely consistent with the numerous admonitions in the literature of the era that the architecture of the green-house should be "constructed on an ornamental plan."[47] Its only function—apart from serving as a roost for birds—was aesthetic. When we add this admittedly conjectural crowning element and the scored rendering, we get a good idea of how this building may have appeared in or about 1820 (Fig. 186).

This little building is as charming as Ann Eyre's letter to John McHenry, but it is much more than an architectural confection. Nearly a hundred years before its construction, Richard Bradley remarked on the difficulty of balancing beauty and utility in this class of building:

> I cannot help taking Notice also, how much the
> Intent of such a Building ought to be regarded by the
> Architect; for hitherto I have not seen one *Green-house*
> in *England* which had the Beauty of a good Building,
> and good Convenience for the keeping of Plants at the
> same time.[48]

By combining the practical knowledge of McMahon and others with sound architectural and aesthetic judgment, the designer and builder of this addition to the Eyre Hall landscape managed to succeed in combining "Beauty" and "Convenience" just as Bradley said he should.

Derek Clifford observed that "only a good design makes a good ruin, and age cannot add distinction to what is maladroit or vulgar."[49] Part of the charm of the ruin of the Eyre Hall green-house is that it reveals the bones of a remarkably well-conceived and well-executed edifice. Its intrinsic beauty is exposed through the cycle of construction, use, deterioration, and, finally, thoughtful and respectful stabilization (Fig. 187).

Tantalizing questions linger, of course, some of which may be answered by archaeological investigations or technological devices that have not been employed yet (or perhaps invented yet). What is the relationship of this structure to the rest of the garden? Did the area south of the green-house function as the summer location for the plants protected in the winter by the green-house? What was the exact configuration of ducts or flues on the tall dividing wall that separated the green-house from the workrooms? What was the surface of the green-house floor?[50] The most important questions may rely on yet unidentified sources. How was this structure used by Ann and John Eyre and those that followed them? Who worked in those smoothly plastered workrooms? Were they enslaved or free, of African or European descent? How did they interact with this building and its owners? And who designed and built this singular structure?

The stabilized green-house ruin is a distinctive and evocative backdrop for the garden today. Absent the elegiac somberness that characterizes so many ruins, there is an engaging quality about this one that connects us with the "amusement and gratification" that Ann Eyre anticipated once it was filled with "the most valuable . . . cuttings and offsets." As the English poet William Cowper (1731–1800) wrote a few decades before its construction:

> Who loves a garden, loves a green-house too.
> Unconscious of a less propitious clime
> There blooms exotic beauty, warm and snug,
> While the winds whistle and the snows descend.
> The spiry myrtle with unwith'ring leaf
> Shines there and flourishes. The golden boast
> Of Portugal and western India there,
> The ruddier orange and the paler lime
> Peep through their polish'd foliage at the storm,
> And seem to smile at what they need not fear.[51]

NOTES

1. This term appears as "green-house," "green house," or "greenhouse" in various sources. "Green-house" is used here in line with eighteenth- and early nineteenth-century practice, and to differentiate structures of that type and era from the more general definition of "greenhouse" in recent times. The original forms are preserved in the period quotations.

2. Edward Hancock Custis Wilson (1794–1827), originally from the Eastern Shore of Maryland, owned land near Eyre Hall. He married the Eyres' neighbor Sally Stratton in 1818. Wilson was a member of the Virginia House of Delegates in 1817-18. He died at Clifton, his last home in Somerset County, Maryland.

3. Original letter in Clements Library, University of Michigan, transcription by Furlong Baldwin, 1986, Eyre Hall Family Papers, Virginia Historical Society, Richmond.

4. Baltimore was the nearest and most accessible large city to Virginia's Eastern Shore. Though it was 150 miles from Eyre Hall to Baltimore by the Chesapeake Bay—too far for the "Shore" to be considered under the cultural penumbra of that city—Baltimore was the third largest city in the United States with a population of 63,000 in 1820. Norfolk's population, by comparison, was 24,000 in that year.

5. John McHenry's older brother, Daniel, was killed in a fall from a horse in 1814.

6. Karen E. Robbins, *James McHenry: Forgotten Federalist* (Athens: University of Georgia Press, 2013), 258.

7. *Federal Intelligencer, and Baltimore Daily Gazette*, March 7, 1795.

8. Edith Rossiter Bevan, "Gardens and Gardening in Early Maryland," *Maryland Historical Magazine* 45, no. 4 (December 1950): 263.

9. J. C. Loudon (1783–1843) documented the care of numerous green-house plants in his book on the subject. John Claudius Loudon, *The Green-House Companion* (London: John Harding, 1824).

10. Bernard McMahon, *The American Gardener's Calendar, adapted to the Climates and Seasons of the United States* (Philadelphia: B. Graves, 1806), 78. The author's name was spelled "M'Mahon" on the original title pages.

11. Charles McIntosh, *Greenhouse, Hot House and Stove* (London: Wm. S. Orr & Co., 1838), 12.

12. Moveable glazed sash were often referred to as "lights." McMahon, *American Gardener's Calendar*, 82.

13. Charles Hind summed up these terms nicely in his review of Mary Woods and Arete Swartz Warren's *Glass Houses* (1988). "Orangery appears to be a Victorian word, and Vanbrugh and Hawksmoor's great orangery at Kensington Palace was called by contemporaries a green-house. What we now call a greenhouse was called a stove [or hot-house] until the early nineteenth century, and the conservatory, with its connotations of romance, is altogether a late term not in common use until the 1820s." *Garden History* 16, no. 2 (Autumn 1988): 202–4.

14. Andrew Faneuil, Boston merchant, often gets the credit for building the first American green-house in 1737, but Byrd's may have predated Faneuil's structure.

15. Fanny Fielding [pseud.], "Southern Homesteads. Eyre Hall," *The Land We Love* 3, no. 6 (October 1867): 507.

16. John Claudius Loudon, *Encyclopaedia of Gardening* (London: Longman, Hurst, Rees, Orme, Brown and Green, 1824), 570.

17. McMahon, *American Gardener's Calendar*, 79.

18. Peter J. Hatch, "Bernard McMahon, Pioneer American Gardener," in the facsimile edition of McMahon's *The American Gardener's Calendar* (Charlottesville, Va.: Thomas Jefferson Memorial Foundation, 1997).

19. McMahon, *The American Gardener's Calendar*, 79.

20. The earliest and largest section of the Eyre Hall main house is also square, 40 feet 3 inches on each side. The bisecting wall of the green-house is approximately 1 foot 11 inches in thickness from the ground floor up to the height of the ceiling joists on the northern half of the building. From that point up to the top of the gable, the wall is 1 foot 1 inch thick. The bonding of the brick is 1:5 bond, which is the same as the garden wall.

21. Philip Miller, *The Gardeners Dictionary*, 4th ed., vol. 2 (London: John and James Rivington, 1754), O 0 3.

22. The shed off the back of a green-house is sometimes referred to as a *bothy*.

23. Andrew Jackson Downing, *Horticulturist* 7 (November 1852): 527.

24. McMahon, *American Gardener's Calendar*, 90.

25. A Roman pediment would be more accurate, since pediments of ancient Greek temples were generally flatter than the range specified by Alberti.

26. Leon Battista Alberti, *On the Art of Building in Ten Books*, trans. Joseph Rykwert, Neil Leach, and Robert Tavernor (Cambridge: The MIT Press, 1988), 222.

27. Giacomo Leoni, *The Architecture of A. Palladio, in Four Books* (London: John Watts, 1715), 57.

28. The bricks are approximately 4 inches wide, 8½ inches long, and 2½ inches tall, which, with a half-inch mortar joint, lay up to a dimension of 9 inches for one course in length, two courses in breadth and three courses in height.

29. Callahan Photograph Collection, Eastern Shore Public Library, Accomac, Virginia.

30. Nine feet, three inches, according to Palladian proportions.

31. J. Thomas Savage, "Eyre Hall on Virginia's Eastern Shore," *The Magazine Antiques*, September 2009, https://www.themagazineantiques.com/article/eyre-hall-on-virginias-eastern-shore/, accessed October 2020.

32. Ralph T. Whitelaw, *Virginia's Eastern Shore: A History of Northampton and Accomack Counties* (Richmond: Virginia Historical Society, 1951), 1:197.

33. Paint remains on the window architrave contain both white and medium gray colors. Gray is the bottom or first layer. The photo from the Callahan collection shows the paneled doors as two-toned.

34. Henry Chandlee Forman, *The Virginia Eastern Shore and its British Origins: History, Gardens and Antiquities* (Easton, Md.: Eastern Shore Publishers' Associates, 1975).

35. In the summer months the sun would be much higher in the sky, meaning more shade inside. This was less of a concern for a true green-house or orangery, where the plants were taken outside in the summer.

36. McMahon, *American Gardener's Calendar*, 80. This approach is very similar to a design published in James Meader, *The Modern Gardener* (London, 1771), 438, which may have been the inspiration for McMahon's approach.

37. McMahon, *American Gardener's Calendar*, 79, 90.

38. *The Diaries of George Washington*, vol. 4, *1 September 1784–30 June 1786*, ed. Donald Jackson and Dorothy Twohig (Charlottesville: University Press of Virginia, 1978), 144.

39. HABS No. VA-809-E-3; NH-155, Prints and Photographs Division, Library of Congress, Washington, D.C.

40. McMahon, *American Gardener's Calendar*, 81.

41. Philip Miller, *Gardener's and Botanist's Dictionary* (London, 1733), under the entry for "Green-house."

42. McMahon, *American Gardener's Calendar*, 90.

43. Mary Woods and Arete Swartz Warren, *Glass Houses: A History of Greenhouses, Conservatories and Orangeries* (New York: Rizzoli, 1988), 29.

44. McMahon, *American Gardener's Calendar*, 159.

45. McMahon, *American Gardener's Calendar*, 80.

46. McMahon, *American Gardener's Calendar*, 81.

47. McMahon, *American Gardener's Calendar*, 79.

48. Richard Bradley, *The Gentleman and Gardener's Kalendar* (London: W. Mears, 1720), 87.

49. Derek Clifford, *A History of Garden Design*, rev. ed. (New York: Frederick A. Praeger, 1966), n. 6.

50. All eighteenth- and early nineteenth-century sources prescribe tile, stone, or brick flooring, but there is no obvious trace of any paving material still extant in the green-house.

51. William Cowper, "The Garden," in *The Task: A Poem, in Six Books* (London, 1784), 120.

Graveyard

CARL R. LOUNSBURY

NESTLED NORTH OF THE RUINS OF ANN EYRE'S green-house and adjacent to the west wall of the garden is a small rectangular enclosure that has been the burying place of the Eyre family since the 1760s (Fig. 188). The graveyard measures 33 feet from east to west and extends 46 feet from north to south. It shares the same low brick wall that encloses the back side of the green-house on the south side and the garden on the east. Entrance into the graveyard is through an iron gate at the northeast corner of the enclosure, which is near a double wooden gate in the west garden wall at the end of one of the cross paths.

The graveyard predates both the green-house and the present configuration of the formal garden, which was extended northward in the early nineteenth century when the present brick wall capped by pickets was built by John Eyre to enclose both spaces (see Fig. 144). Before then, the graveyard and garden were probably marked off by a wooden fence. The garden fence aligned with the west wall of the main house. A gate probably stood at the midway point of the west garden wall (see Fig. 155). It was at this center point that the Eyres decided to place their family graveyard as a paled-in appendage to the west side of the garden. The size of the enclosure was probably 33 feet square, or two poles in length by two poles in width. The position of the first

interment, which occurred a little more than a year after Littleton and Bridget Eyre had moved into their new house, matches closely where the center point of the original garden would have been located. John Eyre's extension of the garden northward by six poles (or 99 feet), and his enclosing it with a brick-and-picket wall, have obscured the earlier logic of its placement (see Fig. 157).

Arranged in an orderly fashion of two rows stretching from south to north, the graveyard contains 22 burials, which range in date from 1760 to 2015 (Fig. 189). The regularity of layout is enhanced by the general uniformity and color of the grave markers. All but three of them consist of large rectangular ledger stones laid flat on low brick sides a foot in height, though there are two taller chest tombstones with decorated stone sides (Fig. 190). Most of the stones measure about 6 feet in length (running east to west) and 3 feet in width and are approximately 5 inches in thickness and have beveled or molded edges. Three graves are marked by small upright headstones along the west and north walls, one of which [5] also has a footstone.

From the 1760s through the twentieth century, only one owner, Severn Eyre, who died and was buried in Norfolk in 1773, one of his sons and namesake, Severn (1764–1786), who died in Bristol, and a couple of married daughters— Sarah Eyre Lyon (1770–1813) and Mary Eyre Wright

Fig. 188. Eyre Hall graveyard looking south with ruins of green-house in background.

Fig. 189. Aerial view and plan of graveyard (north is to the right).

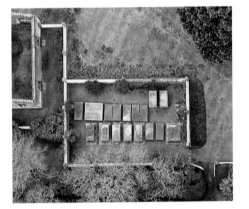

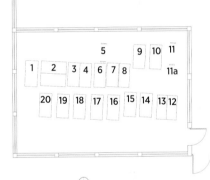

Key to the burials:

1. Sarah Eyre Bowdoin, 1739–1760
2. Littleton Eyre, 1710–1768, and Bridget Harmanson Eyre, 1715–1767
3. Margaret Taylor Eyre, 1739–1812
4. Littleton Eyre, 1761–1789
5. George Littleton Parker, 1791–1796
6. Margaret Eyre Parker, 1765–1799
7. William Eyre, 1772–1808
8. Grace Duncombe Taylor Eyre, 1780–1809
9. John Eyre, 1768–1855
10. Ann Upshur Eyre, 1780–1829
11. James Marshall, d. 1848
11a. Donald J. Trufant, 1931–2015
12. Lucie Dowling Taylor, 1911–1997
13. William Eyre Taylor, 1904–1987
14. William L. Eyre, 1806–1852
15. Mary Burton Savage Eyre, 1804–1866
16. Severn Eyre, 1831–1914
17. Margaret Parker Eyre, 1840–1899
18. William Littleton Eyre, 1871–1893
19. Grace Eyre Taylor, 1872–1910
20. Margaret Eyre Taylor Baldwin, 1898–1979

Fig. 190. View of graveyard looking north.

Fig. 191. Coat of arms of the Eyre family on the double slab graves of Bridget (d. 1767) and Littleton Eyre (d. 1768). Other inscriptions on the markers have worn away. The stone is a black Belgian marble that has faded to a light gray.

Fig. 192. Joined coat of arms of the Eyre and Bowdoin families on the grave of Sarah Eyre Bowdoin (d. 1760). Sarah's was the first burial in the graveyard.

(1875–1955)—were the only immediate members of the family either born or raised at Eyre Hall who are not buried in its graveyard. The earliest graves are those of the first generation to live at Eyre Hall. In the southwest corner is that of Sarah Eyre Bowdoin (d. 1760) [1], the daughter of the builder of Eyre Hall, Littleton Eyre (d. 1768) and his wife Bridget Harmanson Eyre (d. 1767) [2], who are buried beneath a double slab (Fig. 191). Sarah married Preeson Bowdoin, a neighbor and the brother of one of Littleton's business partners, and left a six-month-old son, also named Preeson, when she died in December 1760. Her grave is marked by the combined coat of arms of the Eyre and Bowdoin families, a none-too-subtle device to link the aspirations of the families together in commerce and dynastic ambitions even in the sorrows of death (Fig. 192). The west or top edge of her slab is aligned with the northeast corner of the green-house a few feet south on the other side of the wall. The inscriptions on her parents' graves have worn away, but evidence of the Eyre coat of arms is still distinguishable, one of the increasing means by which families on the make in America in the late colonial period asserted their distinguished British pedigree. It is highly likely that these gravestones were imported from England and placed over these first burials by Severn Eyre, the son of the builder, in tribute to his sister and parents, presumably in the short time between the death of his father in June 1768 and his own death in January 1773.

Because there is no natural stone in the Tidewater region of Virginia, colonists like the Eyres had to import nearly all their stone from England, whether for pavings, steps, chimneypieces, architectural dressings, or gravestones. Such costly burial markers remained the preserve of the wealthy, and few private graveyards or churchyards had such status symbols compared to more common impermanent materials. Paleontologist Marcus Key of Dickinson College suggests that Sarah Eyre Bowdoin and her parents' tombstones are made of black marble originating from quarries in Belgium, but were dressed in England, most likely by stone cutters in London. Although described as black marble because of their color when first polished or kept indoors, most fade to a nondescript gray when exposed to the weather. In fact, the stone is not marble but an organically rich limestone with abundant microfossils. Such stone was common in English graveyards and exported to the American colonies from the late seventeenth century until the end of the colonial period. Among the earliest in Virginia appear at Jamestown Church, including the so-called Knight's Tombstone, and those of Sarah Blair (d. 1713) and William Sherwood (d. 1678). At Bruton Church in Williamsburg, Colonel John Page's tombstone (d. 1692) is of the same material. John Carter's tombstone (d. 1670) in the chancel of Christ Church, Lancaster County, retains its black sheen that gives the stone its common name.

Following the Revolution, domestic quarries began to supply funerary stone for Virginians. The stones that mark graves at Eyre Hall from the nineteenth century appear to be fabricated from native gray limestones, four of which are signed by John D. Couper, one of the leading stone carvers of Norfolk. Couper was born in Norfolk in 1822. He carved his name or initials on the stone marker of William Eyre (d. 1808) [7], the youngest child of Severn Eyre and the builder of the earliest section of Eyreville. He also signed the gravestones of William L. Eyre (d. 1852) [14] and his wife Mary Burton Savage Eyre (d. 1866) [15]. Given that Couper did not begin his career as a stone carver until the 1840s, it appears that William Eyre's stone was a replacement erected long after his death, while the other two may have appeared shortly after their deaths, probably at the direction of their son Severn Eyre (d. 1914) [16]. This last Severn Eyre had been born at Eyreville and inherited Eyre Hall on the death of his great-uncle, John Eyre (d. 1855) [9]. If William Eyre [7] had not been originally buried at Eyreville and reinterred when it was clear that either his son or grandson would inherit Eyre Hall, then the Eyres considered Eyre Hall their permanent memorial place from the beginning of their occupancy of the plantation. Severn Eyre's choice of a ledger stone for these mid-nineteenth-century graves suggests a conservative mindset that chose the continuity of an old marker type over the novelty of new designs in funerary monuments that had grown popular during this period. If so, he was not alone, as a number of other ledger stones continued to appear in family cemeteries on the Eastern Shore through the Civil War.

The gravestones of John Eyre (d. 1855) [9], and his wife Ann Upshur Eyre (d. 1829) [10], stand apart from this pattern of ledger stone markers (Fig. 193). They are not aligned with the western row of graves, but are located more than 4 feet closer to the west wall of the graveyard. The pair are prominent chest tombs that stand more than 3 feet in height. Their white limestone side panels have fluted pilasters in their corners. Ann Eyre's tombstone features flush bead-and-buttwork panels with quarter-circle corners typical of a stylist detail popular in the early nineteenth century. The encomiums inscribed on Ann's gravestone were written by her brother Arthur Upshur, who died a year after his sister. The paneling of John Eyre's tombstone features deep panel channels with clipped corners as well.

There is only one marked child's grave. George Littleton Parker (d. 1796) [5] was the five-year-old son of Margaret Eyre Parker, who had married George Parker and lived at neighboring Kendall Grove. Young George's headstone is located next to the west wall, and his footstone is anchored only inches away from that of his mother's gravestone (d. 1799) [6]. The burial of infants or young children in the graveyard of their mother's family rather than at the home plantation of the father was not unusual. John Eyre (1828–1829), the older brother of the last Severn Eyre (1831–1914), was not buried at Eyreville, the home of his parents William L. and Mary Savage Eyre, but at Cugley, his mother's family plantation on Savage's Neck.

Two other headstones in the northwest corner of the graveyard indicate the burials of the only two non-family members. James Marshall (d. 1848) [11] was a traveling musician who spent much time at Eyre Hall entertaining family and friends in the second quarter of the nineteenth century. Marshall's stone was the fourth signed by Couper in the graveyard and may be the earliest dated commission that the stone carver had at Eyre Hall. To the east of the musician's grave is the headstone of Donald J. Trufant (d. 2015) [11a], a business colleague of Furlong Baldwin who had retired to the Eastern Shore.

CATALOGUE

Furniture

SUMPTER PRIDDY

Pier Table,
1825–35.
Cat. 22

EYRE HALL PRESENTS A SINGULAR OPPORTUNITY to pursue a range of unexplored subjects related to artisans and patronage in the colonial Tidewater. Well established in the region since the late seventeenth century, the Eyre family had rich agricultural lands and mercantile connections that maintained their prosperity. Their ownership of the property for nearly 300 years, and a wealth of family manuscripts, make it possible to document ties to the region's most accomplished cabinetmakers. These talented artisans—some linked by proximity, others through shared business or kinship—allowed the family to create a home filled with remarkable objects.

Eyre Hall's significance is attributable in no small part to the family's attentive respect for the past evident in their preservation of so many things associated with the house. The attic is filled to the rafters with obsolete pieces that no longer serve a purpose in the rooms below. They range from an early nineteenth-century "invalid rest," to a pair of carved rococo sofas that went out of style in Virginia five generations ago. These objects, when combined with the family's ever-respectful, almost reverential, mindset, present an opportunity to study a colonial Chesapeake family on a level that rarely occurs.[1]

The pattern that emerges for the acquisition of goods indicates that their choices of furniture, and the markets in which they acquired them, were as strongly shaped by business interests as by taste. In the colonial era, Hampton and Norfolk served as the destination for the Eyre family's ferry business, and a market for their grain, which was brokered by the Barraud family. Not surprisingly, this provided multiple opportunities to patronize Chesapeake artisans who served as the principal source for their household furniture during the colonial era.

One of the greatest surprises of this patronage of regional craftsmen was the degree to which family artisans contributed to their material needs—initially those in the Harmanson family of Northampton County. However,

by virtue of the convenient distance by water to Hampton Roads, the Eyre family logically looked to Norfolk brokers to market much of their agricultural produce—and sometimes used the proceeds to acquire furniture from local artisans. They patronized their talented kinsman, the joiner and carpenter Richard Taylor (1722-1784), as well as the Hampton cabinet- and chair-maker Edmund Allmand (1748-1795). Allmand had layered ties to the family. The ferry traversed the waters between Eyre Hall on the Eastern Shore and the dock at Ferry Point in Hampton. Allmand's shop stood adjacent to the dock.

As the Chesapeake's principal port, and the base of Virginia's fledgling navy, Norfolk was among the first victims of British military action at the beginning of the American Revolution. Sadly, the greatest damage was done by Revolutionary forces who set the city's waterfront warehouses afire with the hope of preventing the military stores along Norfolk's waterfront from falling into enemy hands. Much of the city fell into smoldering ruins.

The Eyre family's pattern of patronage changed dramatically after the war as they expanded their sphere northward towards Baltimore and Philadelphia. In many respects, the transition was both logical, and efficient. By 1776, Baltimore not only rivalled Norfolk in size, but had a thriving economy with a deep-water port.[2] The family was particularly drawn to the colorful surfaces and creative forms that emerged within Baltimore's community of artisans, where a growing population of Irish émigrés were strongly inclined toward designs in the ancient Grecian style. The Eyre family purchased a tremendous suite of "fancy" furniture as a refreshing alternative to the restrained mahogany furniture that had been the staple for the homes of most Virginia families.

After the War of 1812, the family occasionally purchased furniture in Philadelphia. Even if pieces from that city are few compared to those from Norfolk and Baltimore, transplanted Philadelphia cabinetmaker William Camp, who moved to Baltimore early in his career, nevertheless had a notable impact on the Maryland artisans from whom the family would purchase furnishings.[3]

* * *

1

Corner Cupboard or Bowfat

Attributed to a member of the Harmanson, Joyne, Brickhouse, or Kendall families
Northampton County, Virginia, 1775–90
Yellow pine throughout, with traces of the original blue paint
H. 74 in., W. 52½ in., D. 26 in.

In contrast to most Northampton County homes, only one of the furnishings at Eyre Hall originated on the Eastern Shore—a yellow pine corner cupboard or "bowfat" dating to about 1780, of which only the upper case survives.[4] Though only a fragment, it provides an excellent basis for discussing regional style, having arched upper "lights" and a distinctive row of dentils in the pronounced cornice that typify Eastern Shore cupboards.

The cupboard originally stood at Eyreville—the family planation adjoining Eyre Hall. In the late 1790s, William Eyre acquired the property with the help of his brother John, and in 1800 William built a two-story brick house. His son William L. Eyre would make a substantial addition to the front in 1839. The family sold the property in 1904, and brought the furniture to Eyre Hall at that time.

The cupboard opens a portal to a group of local artisans who were linked to the Eyre family by blood, marriage, and proximity. Among the candidates who are likely to have made the piece was the Northampton County cabinet- and chair-maker Harmanson Joyne (d. 1779), who had been closely involved in building for Custis Kendall at the end of his life. An audit of Joyne's estate reveals that Kendall still owed him £30 for overseeing various aspects of its construction. These included payments for "turning 80 bannisters for the Stair Case of the house," and £56 to family cabinet- and chair-maker John

Brickhouse for making "12 chair frames."[5] Certainly, they and other artisans within their circle had the talent to make the cupboard, included joiner James Harmanson (d. 1815), who, in 1813, received 5 shillings for making a coffin for the burial of local resident Bailey Scott.[6]

2
Chest of Drawers

Attributed to Richard Taylor I (1722–1784)
Norfolk, Virginia, 1750–65
Walnut primary, with yellow pine secondary; original plate brasses
H. 44 in., W. 42 in., D. 18 in.

As the prior piece suggests, prominent Tidewater families often included cabinetmakers and joiners within their bloodlines, and the Eyre family was no exception. The seemingly divergent careers were surprisingly common in eastern Virginia families, where primogeniture often destined elder sons to receive ancestral property—and encouraged younger ones to pursue the building trades to advance in other realms.[7] In looking back through the early ancestry for the Taylor branch of the family, there were at least two generations of talented furniture makers and housebuilders. Cousin Robert Barraud Taylor (1774–1834) of Norfolk was indeed an attorney, yet was the son of Norfolk joiner Robert Taylor (ca. 1745–ca. 1795) and grandson of Norfolk carpenter and joiner Richard Taylor I (1722–1784).[8]

Of the Norfolk artisans who potentially made the chest, it is the latter who stands out prominently. Richard Taylor I had a home, cabinet shop, and lumber business at the corner of Freemason and Duke of Cumberland Street in Norfolk.[9] The property descended to his son Robert Taylor, who married Lelia Barraud, and afterwards to grandson Robert Barraud Taylor—the Eyre family kinsman. Richard Taylor probably made the chest in the shop on that site. Just as the chest descended through family on the Eastern Shore, so the house descended through family in Norfolk.

The chest has many notable features, including the high quality of the pierced rococo brasses, full dust boards between the drawers, and a distinctive style of bracket foot—the latter being key to identifying Richard Taylor's work at a distance: the inner profile is dominated by a pronounced arc that curves inward at the base, and is resolved at the top with a projecting ogee flange. In the 1760s, when ogee feet came into fashion, Taylor adapted this inner profile to a new ogee design and continued to use it until the end of his life. A 1770s Petersburg china press signed by "Richard Taylor" has the same distinctive profile as the Eyre Hall chest—and is virtually identical to documented pieces subsequently made by his apprentice Thomas Sharrock.[10]

Richard Taylor I was renowned among his peers. An announcement in the *Virginia Gazette* in 1772 referred to him as "The Ingenious Richard Taylor" and offered for sale a billiard table that he had recently made, which was "as good as any on the Continent." MESDA researchers have also documented his sons Richard Taylor II (1745–1788) and Robert Taylor (ca. 1747–ca. 1795) as joiners. Richard I and II established an ancillary shop in Petersburg during the 1760s, and yet maintained their relationships with Norfolk—and moved back and forth between the two towns as required by business.[11] Richard's apprentice Thomas Sharrock eventually move to North Carolina, where he and his sons disseminated the Taylor family style southward as well.[12]

3
Side Chair

From a set that originally numbered 14
Attributed to Edmund Allmand (1745–1795)
Hampton, Virginia, 1765–80
Mahogany primary, with yellow pine blocking and slip seats
H. (overall) 33 in., W. (crest rail) 19⅝ in., W. (overall at feet) 17¾ in.,
D. (overall at feet) 19¾ in.

In the colonial period, the Eyre family sometimes relied upon artisans to whom they were linked through shared business pursuits. Among them was the Hampton "Cabinet and Chairmaker" Edmund Allmand (1745–1795). Allmand hailed from a family of shipbuilders and joiners whose forebears arrived during the seventeenth century. He apprenticed in 1760 to the Norfolk cabinetmaker John Selden, and, upon achieving his freedom in 1768, married Lucretia Braithwaite (b. 1752).[13] The couple followed dual traditions that were commonplace in Virginia artisan families: he opened a cabinet shop at the base of a pier at Ferry Point in Hampton, and she became proprietress of the Red House Tavern adjoining it.[14]

The pier at Ferry Point in Hampton was a principal hub for the ferries that traversed the waters between Norfolk and the Eastern Shore of Virginia. The Allmands' visibility brought them a constant flow of customers that included ship's captains, planters, and businessmen. In 1780, the couple's proximity to the pier, and their combined business acumen, helped Edmund to acquire a license from the Commonwealth of Virginia to personally *oversee* the ferries from Hampton to Norfolk and the Eastern Shore. The boat to "the Shore" landed at Hungars Creek and, through the years, the cabinetmaker earned the family's trust.

The Eyre family acquired a fine set of carved chairs from Edmund Allmand's shop, four of which have survived (Cat. 3). Each has a central "plateau" in the crest rail that is nearly 4½ inches wide, slightly arched across the top, and standing half an inch proud of the crest rail. Allmand carved an acanthus leaf in the upper center of the plateau, and an acanthus scroll at either end of the crest (Fig. 194).[15]

Fig. 194. Detail of the crest rail, Cat. 3. The creative design of the splat, combined with the acanthus leaf carved in the center of the crest, and the acanthus scrolls at either end, define one of the finest sets of straight-leg chairs from colonial Virginia.

Fig. 195. The cabinetmaker relied on a distinctive regional practice, by anchoring the base of the splat in an open mortise, cut into the inner face of the rear seat rail. He then filled the open mortise with a block, which is visible in the upper center of the rail. The corner braces of Cat. 3 are modern additions.

4
Armchair

In the manner of Edmund Allmand; possibly by Northampton County resident John Brickhouse
Eastern Shore of Virginia, 1770–80
Mahogany primary, with yellow pine slip seats
H. 38⅜ in., W. (arms) 25¼, W. (seat) 23¼ in., D. (at seat rails) 18½ in., D. (at floor) 22¼ in.

Two mahogany armchairs in an upstairs passage are the only ones to survive from a second set of chairs that are original to the home. The set clearly originate within Allmand's sphere, or among those who knew his designs. Nonetheless, the two armchairs differ enough in quality to indicate the hand of an artisan who greatly simplified the construction. The possibility exists that these hail from the workbench of the Eastern Shore cabinet- and chair-maker John Brickhouse, who is mentioned above, in the entry for the corner cupboard in Cat. 1, as having made "12 chair frames" for the family in 1779. If so, he appears to have relied upon the carved examples attributed to Edmund Allmand, yet simplified the design of the crest.[16]

Regardless of who made them, Edmund Allmand and his cabinetmaking son John Allmand (1765–1795) would both die in the yellow fever epidemic that swept Norfolk and much of the eastern seaboard in 1795, leaving the family to rely upon other artisans. They eventually turned to Allmand's finest apprentice, James Woodward (1769–1839), who would fill the void left in the lower Chesapeake community by their deaths.

Fig. 196. Detail of the rear seat rail, Cat. 4.

5
Card Table

Originally one of a pair
Attributed to the shop of Anthony Hay (d. 1770)
Williamsburg, Virginia, 1768
Mahogany primary, with secondary woods of ash (gate rail),
yellow pine (rear rail), and poplar (corner blocks)
H. 29½ in., W. 34½ in., D. 16 in.

This table epitomizes the classical reserve that often characterizes Virginian colonial furniture. It is attributed with confidence to the shop of the English-born Williamsburg cabinetmaker Anthony Hay who, about the time of its making, had expanded his business ventures by purchasing the Raleigh Tavern in Williamsburg.[17]

Isaac Smith, a business partner of Littleton Eyre, kept a record of expenses charged against Littleton Eyre's estate and entered the payment of £2.0.0 to "Anth^y Hay for a Card Table" on October 30, 1768, several months after Littleton Eyre's death.[18] Curiously, the piece does not appear in the 1769 inventory of his estate—suggesting it had not arrived by the time of his death. However, an appraisal taken after Severn's death in 1774 clearly mentions one card table valued at £2.0.0 and also a "pair of card tables" valued together at £6.0.0.[19] Although attributed to Hay, the tables almost certainly originate on the workbenches of other artisans with the shop, since Hay seems to have retired from bench work in 1767, when he purchased the Raleigh Tavern. Through the years, several master cabinetmakers oversaw production in the shop, included British émigré Benjamin Bucktrout (1744–1812), Norfolk-born Edmund Dickinson (ca. 1738–1778), and

William Kennedy, about whom little is presently known. Hay's enslaved cabinetmaker "Wiltshire" appears in Hay's estate inventory in 1771 and is presumed to have participated in their construction.[20]

A collateral descendant inherited one of the tables during the mid-twentieth century and recently donated it to Yale University Art Gallery.

Fig. 197. Detail of the drawer with a leg pulled back, Cat. 5.

6
Chest of Drawers

Probably Norfolk, Virginia, 1765–75
Mahogany and mahogany veneer primary, with secondary woods
of walnut (drawer sides) and yellow pine (dust boards, backboards,
drawer bottoms); original brasses
H. 38½ in., W. (case) 39⅜ in., D. (case) 20¼ in.

A simple yet sophisticated chest of drawers that differs
significantly from those made in the Taylor family workshops.
Nonetheless, the materials, the two-over-three graduated
drawers with cock-beaded edges, the full-depth dust boards,
and the cove base molding clearly indicate that it originates
either in Norfolk or one of the nearby towns of Hampton or
Suffolk. It is the only known piece from those towns in which
the design of the foot relies upon a straight inner profile, with a
tiny cove return at the top—a feature that generally appears on
provincial case pieces from Surry County.[21]

The maker went to considerable effort to make the case as
secure as possible from intrusion. In addition to incorporating
five locks into the design, he relied upon full dust boards that
run the depth of the case above and below each drawer, thus
making it possible to secure the contents. Chests with locks
and dust boards appeared frequently in prosperous southern
households with their steady stream of visitors.[22] The piece
logically descended through the entwined lines of the Cocke,
Barraud, and Taylor families, yet has no specific associations.

7
Basin Stand

Eastern Virginia, probably Norfolk, 1795–1810
Mahogany primary, with poplar drawer liners and a brass pull
H. 38½ in., W. 18 in., D. 16 in.

Functional pieces such as washstands often appear in Virginia
household inventories during the federal era, yet rarely survive
today. The stand's small scale and simple design nonetheless
represent a form that commonly appeared in Chesapeake
inventories during the late eighteenth and early nineteenth
centuries. The upper legs are square in section yet begin to
taper immediately below the drawer. The opening in the top
measures 7¾ inches in diameter, and receives a small bowl
commensurate in size with the piece.

8

Pair of Bedsteads

Attributed to James Woodward (1769–1839)
Norfolk, Virginia, ca. 1803
Mahogany posts and rails, with yellow pine slats
Carved and gilded eagle cornices attributed to Abraham DeRevere, New York and Norfolk, 1816–20
H. (posts) 92¾ in., H. (cornices with eagle finials) 13¾ in., H. (casters) 2 in., H. (overall, allowing for the cornice overlap at the top of the post) 96½ in., H. (cornices) 4½ in., H. (eagles) 9 in., W. (eagle wingspan) 19 in., D. (eagle carving) 5 in.

Edmund Allmand had a number of apprentices. His most accomplished was the Nansemond County native James Woodward (1769–1839), who settled in Norfolk. Woodward was among the most talented Norfolk artisans to survive the yellow fever epidemic of 1795, and had the business acumen that propelled him to the forefront of the artisan community.

A pair of exceptional bedsteads from Woodward's shop are among the finest pieces at Eyre Hall, yet are undocumented among Eyre accounts or correspondence. Nonetheless, they possibly found a route to the home through family ties to the Barraud family, possibly through Ann Blaws Barraud

(1784–1816) and her husband General John Hartwell Cocke (1780–1866) of Mount Pleasant, Surry County. About the time of their marriage in 1802, General Cocke placed an order with Woodward for a pair of bedsteads with turned softwood posts stained a red mahogany color, $30 for the pair. Woodward also made a single "mahogany tester bedstead, carved posts" for General and Mrs. Cocke of Bremo, for the substantial sum of $33—the destiny of which remains uncertain.

One must note, however, that the carved Woodward bedsteads at Eyre Hall have identical turnings to the stained examples documented for the Cocke family, and likely match the now missing carved bedstead identified on Woodward's receipt to General Cocke and Sarah Barraud. One must therefore wonder whether the carved Cocke bedstead that seems to have disappeared from Bremo went to Eyre Hall and was duplicated for the family by Woodward. The posts of the Eyre Hall bedsteads were shortened about 5 inches at the base in the nineteenth century.

Woodward's 1803 receipt to General Cocke raises other questions as well, for the cabinetmaker made no mention of the carved and gilded cornices with eagle finials—their wings outspread—that now crown the bedsteads. From the standpoint of scale and style, the eagle cornices seem considerably heavier than the delicately carved bedstead, and were likely added at a later date. The most logical candidate to have made them was the skilled New York carver and gilder Abraham DeRevere, who had layered connections to the Chesapeake and its artisans. In November 1816, he announced the opening of his Norfolk outlet in the "Fancy Furniture Store in Reilly's Buildings." He offered a remarkable range of goods for sale in the new establishment, among which one stands out: "Elegant Burnished Gilt Bed and Window Cornices." Equally significant for the Eyre Hall bedsteads, in October of 1820 DeRevere announced a move to a new Norfolk location "between the entrance to Mr. Woodward's Cabinet Ware-house and Mrs. Hastie's Boarding House." He then listed an exceptional inventory that included "a Handsome Assortment of Pier and Common Looking Glasses," a range of highly painted "Fancy Furniture," and "an assortment of French paper hangings."[23]

One suspects that DeRevere's move to a location beside Woodward's shop provided the impetus for the Eyre family to update the earlier bedsteads, by commissioning eagle cornices (Fig. 198). By simply entering the store, and meeting the gilder, the Eyre family also met the man who could provide pier and chimney glasses for the principal downstairs rooms. It appears that he soon made them on custom order, of the perfect scale for specific walls within the home (see Cat. 9).

DeRevere's carved wooden cornices have bold gadrooning that is ornamented with alternating stripes of gilding and cream-colored paint. To complete the design, he carved a total of six gilded American eagles—one for each visible side of the cornices. He was the only Norfolk artisan with the skill to produce the ensemble, and, by the time he was finished, he had elevated Woodward's bedsteads to an entirely new level. They are among the most impressive Virginia furnishings of the federal era to survive today.

Fig. 198. Detail of Cat. 8 showing one of six eagles carved for the bedsteads between 1816 and 1820 by Abraham DeRevere. H. (cornice) 4½ in., H. (eagle) 9 in., W. (eagle) 13¾ in., D. (eagle) 5 in.

9

Chimney Glass

Probably by Abraham DeRevere
New York or Norfolk, Virginia, 1816–20
Oil- and water-gilded surfaces on gesso and composition ornament, with poplar and white pine secondary
H. 27½ in., W. 66 in., D. 2⅝ in.

Only one other piece in the house can be attributed with some confidence to Abraham DeRevere—the chimney glass in the dining room. The form and the ornament are quintessentially New York in style, and represent a taste that reached the height of popularity between 1815 and 1820, when the gilder also had a shop in Norfolk. In light of DeRevere's New York training, and the Eyre family's associations with his ancillary shop in Norfolk, the attribution seems plausible.

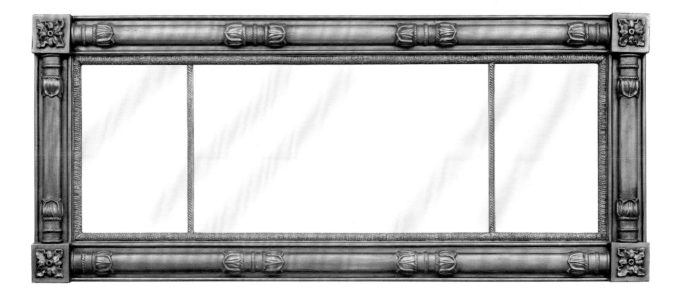

10

Pair of Pier Glasses

Probably Great Britain, 1790–1800
Oil- and water-gilded surfaces on gesso, with emblematic tablets of
reverse painting and gilding on glass; silvered mirror plate; white oak
and European pine secondary
H. 59½ in., W. (crest) 31½ in., D. 3 in.

A matching pair of looking glasses are among the finest
furnishings in the house, and reflect the family's progressive
tastes on the eve of the American Revolution. They originate in
Britain, and probably date to the 1790s, when the neoclassical
style was all the rage in London and Glasgow. When the pair
arrived, they likely displaced some of the old-fashioned looking
glasses that had been in the family since the 1720s and '30s—the
majority of which were moved upstairs to secondary spaces.[24]

The top of each mirror has a rectangular tablet of reverse-
painted glass with a diapered field, the latter with a central
vignette or "trophy" that consisted of a quiver crossed with a bow
and arrows. The emblem had ancient origins and layered classical
meanings—ranging from Cupid and love, to Diana the huntress—
that were widely recognized among Virginians such as the Eyres.

11

Sideboard

Attributed to Richard Lawson (1749–1803) or his circle, including William Patterson (1774–1816) and Robert Wilkinson (1774–1816)
Baltimore, 1790–1800
Mahogany, with mahogany and satinwood veneers and light and dark wood inlays; yellow pine secondary
H. 42¾ in., W. (overall at top) 72¾ in., D. (overall at top) 27 in.

This fine Baltimore sideboard relates to several depicted in
George Hepplewhite's influential design book, *Cabinet-Maker
and Upholsterer's Guide* (London, 1788). However, contrary to
most American precedents, the piece potentially predates the
publication. It represents a type that was likely introduced to
Baltimore by London-trained émigré cabinetmaker Richard
Lawson, who arrived in Baltimore in 1785—three years before
Mr. Hepplewhite went to press.

Lawson had learned his skills in the London workshop of
Seddon and Company, cabinetmakers to King George III, and
brought with him the newest of London style when he came to
Baltimore. One of the keys to his success was asking the well-
connected Maryland businessman John Bankson (1754–1814)
to join him in partnership—and then turning promotion
over to him. When Bankson retired in 1793, Lawson entered
a two-year partnership with Baltimore cabinetmaker Robert

Wilkinson (fl. 1793–1799). By the time it ended in 1795, the
style had filtered into broader circles. By 1797, when Lawson's
former apprentice William Patterson (1774–1816) went into
business on his own, bellflower designs from the shop were
beginning to inspire a new generation of Baltimore artisans
(Fig. 199).

Among the later designs that hailed from the group were
bellflower husks. There were numerous variants, of which
those on the sideboard became the Baltimore standard in the
early 1790s, when Lawson was still engaged in production. The
design likely originated at his bench, but otherwise within the
immediate circle of artisans with whom he worked.

Each of the husks has three, lozenge-shaped leaves. They
have pointed ends that converge at the top and splay at the
base. The bellflowers they make diminish in scale as they
descend the leg. Lawson's journeyman William Patterson

(b. 1774–d. 1816) relied on the design when he opened a shop of his own about 1800. The Eyre family sideboard originates either late in Lawson's career, or shortly afterwards, when Patterson, Wilkinson, Singleton, and others who had known the artisan, spread his influence throughout the Baltimore school.

The sideboard survives with virtually all of the original elements intact—except for the brasses. The drawer fronts have witness marks for the originals; these reflect an Adamesque design with rounded backplates that were nailed into place on either side, and held at the top with a single post that pierced

the upper center of the plate and continued through the drawer front. The post was then secured in place with a nut pendant ring: a progressive neoclassical style that originated in Robert Adam's circles during the 1770s. By the late 1780s, the single post was judged to be vulnerable. By 1790 it had given way to an improved bail or stirrup handle that was suspended between two posts. In short, the style of the original brasses underscores the case's comparatively early date, and strengthens its connection to London-trained cabinetmaker Richard Lawson, who introduced the neoclassical style to Baltimore during the 1780s.

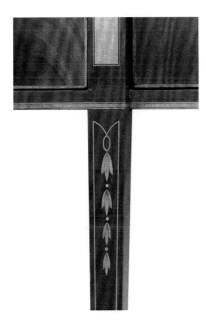

Fig. 199. Detail of Cat. 11 showing the bellflower husks on the legs of the sideboard.

Fig. 200. The refined scale of the dovetails of Cat. 11 reflects the high level of workmanship within Lawson's immediate circle.

12
Pair of Cutlery Cases

Probably London, 1785–95
Mahogany and mahogany veneer, with inlaid "shells" of stained and heat-shaded boxwood, exotic hardwood banding and shield-shaped escutcheons of fused silver plate; European conifer secondary
H. (overall) 15⅝ in., W. 8⅝ in., D. 12½ in.

Often known by Americans as "knife boxes" or "knife cases," these British examples reflect the same level of style that London-trained Richard Lawson brought to Maryland in the mid-1780s. British manufacturers who specialized in the form made it virtually impossible for small American cabinetmaking shops to compete on price.

The interior of each box contains 59 piercings for table and serving wares that include a dozen dinner knives and dinner forks, a dozen dessert knives and forks, a stuffing spoon, two marrow spoons, a carving knife and fork, and six table spoons. The interior of the lid sports a loosely interpreted bellflower and anthemion ornament (Fig. 201).

Fig. 201. Inside of one of the cutlery cases, Cat. 12.

13

Gentleman's Secretary

Attributed to Joseph Barry (1757–1838)
Philadelphia, 1795–1815
Mahogany and mahogany veneer primary, with light and dark wood inlays; yellow pine, poplar, and white pine secondary
H. (overall) 97½ in., H. (lower case) 46¾ in., W. (lower case, overall) 90⅞ in., W. (upper case) 92⅝ in., W. (upper case, overall, with cornice) 97⅛ in., D. (lower case) 24¼ in., D. (upper case, at cornice) 14½ in.

This is perhaps the most imposing case piece at Eyre Hall. It originated in the Philadelphia workshop of the renowned Irish-born cabinetmaker and furniture designer Joseph Barry (1757–1838).[25] He trained in London during the 1770s and arrived in Philadelphia in 1794, steeped in up-to-the-moment British design. The choice of turned feet, and the subtle application of figured oval veneer set flush into fields of cross-grained mahogany with mitered corners, are among the earliest examples of those features in an American context, and likely had a tremendous impact upon furniture styles in his adopted city. Although traditionally known as a library (or winged) bookcase, in 1793 the British designer Thomas Sheraton

seems to have introduced an entirely new name: "Gentleman's Secretary."[26]

The maker constructed the lower case as a single piece, the upper case in three separate sections, and the cornice as a separate unit. The vertical partitions of the interior have grooved sides for adjustable shelves. The writing drawer in the center has a hinged drawer that opens forward to create the writing surface; the fitted interior has drawers and pigeon holes (Fig. 202).[27]

For the secretary's façade, Barry selected figured mahogany veneer and relied upon a design of ovals set in mitered rectangular fields. The mullion arrangement reflects a design

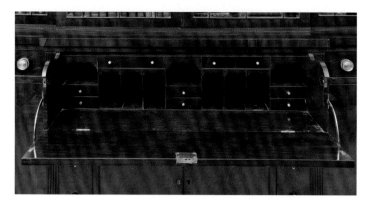

Fig. 202. Detail of the writing drawer, Cat. 13.

Fig. 203. Detail of the corner and cornice, Cat. 13.

Fig. 204. Detail of one of the legs, Cat. 13.

inspired by an engraving in the second edition of *The Cabinet-Makers' London Book of Prices*, published in 1793, the year before he arrived in America. Nonetheless, one suspects that the maker had mastered the design on his London workbench long before departing that city.[28] For the Eyre family to have acquired a piece of this stature from a British artisan who had recently arrived in America, underscores the family's adventurous sense of taste.[29]

The piece survives in pristine condition, with the original glass and hardware. Primary surfaces have never been abraded, and have a thin shellac finish applied in the twentieth century. The secondary surfaces are undisturbed, with superb oxidation.

14
Side Chair

From a set of four
Philadelphia, 1815–25
Mahogany primary, with mahogany veneer (crest rail and tablet of the medial rail); secondary woods of ash (front and rear seat rails) and poplar (slip seat frame)
H. 33 in., W. (seat) 17¾ in., D. (overall, at floor) 19¾ in.

The chair is one of four that survive from a larger set, and is contemporaneous with the Baltimore dining table. The form reflects a popular Philadelphia style, with a crest rail that is slightly bowed, and has a rolled border across the upper rear edge. The medial brace is the finest feature; it has a central tablet of figured mahogany within a cross-banded border, and is flanked at each end by a pierced, lyre-form scroll with a gadrooned surface. The details typify Philadelphia chair design of the classical era.

15

Banquet Table

Attributed to William Camp (1773–1822) or Edward Priestley (1778–1837)
Baltimore, 1805–15
Mahogany primary, with secondary woods of oak (gates) and white pine (inner rails); white pine cross brace beneath the top
H. 29 in., W. 56 in., L. (center drop-leaf section, overall, open) 72 in., L. (each D-end, overall, with the leaf raised) 45¾ in., L. (with the pair of D-ends assembled) 91½ in., L. (overall, with three sections extended) 13 ft. 10½ in.

Historically, the family's outlook towards dining was flexible, and it continues to be so today. Family and visitors start the day at a pine table in the breakfast room near the kitchen. It comfortably seats six. Larger gatherings take place in the dining room, where a three-part banquet table is adapted to the size of the gathering. The table is more substantial than most. It measures 56 inches in width, and to accommodate the scale has a plethora of legs. The center section has two drop leaves, and a total of eight legs; it resides most of the year in the passage with the leaves down, tucked against a wall near the garden door—convenient for a cool summer supper in a cross-breeze, but otherwise rarely used.[30]

As a rule, the dining room is furnished by the table's two D-ends, each having a single drop leaf, which generally remain together in the dining room throughout the year. When pulled together—as they generally are—they easily accommodate six for a meal, and potentially ten, especially when there are youngsters among the diners.

For large events, the drop-leaf center section is brought from the passage and placed in between the two D-ends. The resulting banquet table comfortably seats ten and potentially 14,

particularly when the latter includes children. Each D-end has a single drop leaf and adds another six legs—bringing the total to 20![31] When larger dinners are over, and the guests have left, the center is generally returned to the passage.[32]

Among the cabinetmakers likely to have made the table are William Camp (1773–1822) or his younger contemporary Edward Priestley (1778–1837). Camp trained in Philadelphia

Fig. 205. Table without the D-shaped ends, Cat. 15.

Fig. 206. Underside of the table, Cat. 15.

Fig. 207. End view of the table
with folded leaves, Cat. 15.

and arrived in the Baltimore in 1802. He found business so
brisk that over the next two decades he hired 53 apprentices.
Priestly offers an interesting contrast. Raised in Baltimore, he
had six apprentices during an equally long career—yet hired
journeymen as needed to meet the demands of business. Of
the hundred or more Baltimore cabinetmakers recorded from
the early nineteenth century, no others attained the same level
of production as these two, and many were associated at some
point or another.[33]

16
Dressing Glass

Great Britain, 1785–95
Mahogany and mahogany veneer, with light wood inlays
and brass hardware; oak secondary
H. 24 in., W. 19 in., D. 7¾ in.

17
Block–Front Dressing Glass

Attributed to Richard Lawson (1749–1803) and John Bankson (1754–1814)
Baltimore, 1785–92
Mahogany and mahogany veneer, with bone mounts, light wood stringing,
and pictorial inlays of boxwood; poplar and yellow pine secondary
H. 24¼ in., W. 16½ in., D. 7¼ in.

The family bedchambers had a number of dressing glasses, of which two inlaid examples with shield-shaped mirrors merit comparison. The first is British in origin (Cat. 16). It has canted corners with light wood ornament and includes a floral rosette trailed by five graduated bellflowers—and is typical of those imported in significant numbers all across federal America. The second piece (Cat. 17) is an exceptional American example, attributed with confidence to the partnership of two remarkable individuals. It is the product of British-born cabinetmaker Richard Lawson (1749–1803), who was employed early in life by the London firm of Seddon and Company, "Cabinetmakers to His Majesty the King." Shortly after leaving Britain in 1785, he settled in Maryland and went into partnership with the savvy Baltimore businessman John Bankson (1754–1814), who had ties to some of the state's wealthiest families. During their brief tenure together between 1785 and 1792, the men made and promoted exceptional furniture under the name of Bankson and Lawson, and became one of the most influential cabinetmaking firms in the Chesapeake. They assured their Baltimore clientele that "former customers in town, on the Eastern Shore of Maryland, and elsewhere . . . [would] be supplied at the shortest notice." They also advertised their furniture in Charleston newspapers.[34]

Bankson and Lawson made concerted efforts to incorporate original features into every piece. The distinctive combination of a block-and-cove drawer front with a shield-shaped mirror seems otherwise unprecedented. A reliance on bone for the delicate turnings of the ball finial, applied bosses, and drawer pulls provides a further contrast to the inlaid shell medallion. These convey the makers' subtle appreciation for detail and intricacy even in the smallest of furnishings. They constructed only one other piece of block-front furniture: a chest of four drawers that differed considerably in scale and proportion; the front had a closely related design, and yet was covered from side to side with exceptional veneers—and no appreciable inlay.

This Eyre family dressing glass is presently the sole piece from the shop with a confirmed history on the Eastern Shore of Virginia. Whether the Eyre family selected it from the cabinetmakers' Baltimore showroom, or placed an order for later delivery, remains unknown.[35] It stands in the master bedroom on the second floor, and has been there for generations.

18

Drop-Leaf Pedestal Breakfast or Library Table

Attributed to William Camp (1773–1822) or Edward Priestley (1778–1837)
Baltimore, 1815–25
Mahogany and mahogany veneer primary, with secondary woods of poplar (drawer and inner rail), oak ("fly" rails with 5-part barrel joints), and ash (stationary rails adjoining fly rails)
H. 29 in., L. (overall) 49 in., W. (leaves down) 25½ in.,
W. (leaves up) 58 in.

The table rests on the original brass paw feet on casters, and has the original ring pull on the drawer. The center of the turned pedestal is a bold, flattened cup that is flanked above and below by a bold cove and three torus moldings. The pedestal rests on four saber legs, having three reeds on the upper surface and ending in brass paw feet on casters.

The table survives in a fine state of preservation, with the original finish, all of the original hardware, and undisturbed secondary surfaces.

19
Tilt–Top Candlestand

Attributed to William Camp (1773–1822) or Edward Priestley (1778–1837)
Baltimore, 1815–35
Mahogany primary, with red oak secondary (pivot block)
H. 26¼ in., W. (top) 17 in., L. (top) 21⅛ in.

This classical candlestand typifies Baltimore examples of the form in the bold design of the urn and the crisp ring turnings of the column, and the rectangular top with rounded corners and reeded edges. The battens beneath the top rotate on pintles projecting outward from a red oak block, which is anchored to the top of the standard. When lowered, the top remains securely in place, until a brass latch below is released. The turned standard has a square tenon that projects upward through a block and is secured there by a wedge.

Each batten is secured to the top from below, with three screws that are countersunk about ⅛ inch into the lower surface of the battens. The heads of the screws were originally covered with mahogany-colored putty, most of which is now missing.

20
Dressing Table

Attributed to Edward Priestley (1778–1837)
Baltimore, 1825–35
Mahogany primary, with curl maple and mahogany veneers; poplar secondary; pressed glass knobs attributed to the Baltimore Flint Glass Works, 1831–34
H. (overall) 38 in., W. (overall) 43¹³⁄₁₆ in., D. (overall) 16⅞ in.

A lady's dressing table with superb choice of wood and lively details offers another perspective into Baltimore classical taste, and a significant contrast to the Finlay Brothers' painted surfaces. The juxtaposition of golden curl maple against crimson mahogany was a familiar one on furniture made from Baltimore northward to Maine in the classical era, but rarely appears in a southern rural context, and was an adventurous choice in an Eastern Shore home. The piece is especially notable for the up-to-the-minute pressed glass pulls. Pressed glass knobs are a rare survival in any southern context, and especially so when accompanied by documentation. These likely originated in William Baker's Baltimore Flint Glass Works (founded 1825) in the period 1831–34. Remarkably, the company's day book for these years survives, and an entry references knobs of a variety of diameters: 1 inch, 1¼ inch, 1½ inch, and 1¾ inches. It notes that some of the knobs had spindles to anchor them through the drawer front, while others did not. Among the designs they produced were "plain, ribbed, 1 ring, twist, solid," and "rib twist." Those on the dressing table are believed to represent the "ribbed" variety mentioned therein.[36]

21
Wardrobe

Attributed to Edward Priestley (1778–1837)
Baltimore, 1825–35
Mahogany and mahogany veneer, with white pine and poplar secondary
H. 81 in., W. (overall, at cornice) 61⅞ in., W. (case) 55½ in., D. (overall, at cornice) 23⅜ in., D. (case) 18¾ in.

A wardrobe in the yellow room upstairs is among the most successful of the form to originate in classical-era Baltimore. Its bold character, the subtle balance of figured wood contrasted to carved details, and the weight of the cornice versus the understated feet coalesce to reflect the maker's brilliant sense of design, as well as the Eyre family's aesthetic sensibilities—even when it came to functional pieces.

If the exterior of the case seems grand, the interior is purely practical. It has a vertical partition in the center, a pair of deep drawers on the lower right side, oval plate brasses having bail handles, and, in the space above them, four sliding "wardrobe" drawers with open fronts. Behind the door to the left is an open space for hanging clothes. Now having a modern brass bar, a closer look around the upper perimeter reveals a half dozen screw holes—evidence of the "cloak pins" that originally lined the upper perimeter of the space and were used for hanging clothes.

The piece is attributed with confidence to Edward Priestley. By the time he made it in the mid-1820s, his competitor William Camp (1773–1822) was not only dead, but the 22 workbenches from the shop had been dispersed at auction. With that, Edward Priestley quickly moved to the forefront of Baltimore's community of cabinetmakers and would remain there for another long decade.

FINLAY FURNITURE: TRANSITION FROM ROMAN TO GREEK

In contrast to their earlier preference for mahogany furniture, the Eyre family's taste underwent a notable change in the early nineteenth century. They moved away from classical Roman design and gravitated toward the substantial scale and sometimes colorful palette of ancient Grecian taste. That shift is apparent in a suite of furniture acquired during the 1820s or early 1830s from the Baltimore workshop of the renowned artisans John Finlay (b. Glasgow, ca. 1777–1844) and his brother Hugh (1781–1831). Purchases included a pair of pier tables; a set of klismos side chairs with wheel backs; and two hall benches with scrolled ends—all of which had woven cane seats. There was also a complementary suite of fancy Windsor [i.e. plank-bottom] furniture, with nearly identical ornamentation to the documented Finlay pieces. Each piece of seating furniture likely sported a down-filled cushion of colorful wool.

A brief survey of the Finlay brothers' history helps to place the Eyre family's tastes into a broader context. Older brother John seems to have led the way into the trade in 1799, when his name first appeared in the city directories as a "painter." In 1801, he advertised a shop and dwelling on Harrison Street, where he specialized in applying highly polished "jappan" finishes to decorative coaches for their better-off clients. It is possible that the Eyre family initially met the Finlays in the course of caring for the various vehicles that they are known to have owned between the 1780s and the 1840s, which included a coach, chariot, phaeton, and carriage.[37]

In 1803, the brothers placed a joint announcement in the Baltimore newspapers for their newly established "Fancy Furniture Manufactory" at 3 South Frederick Street, where they offered "All types of Fancy Furniture . . . of Various colors and patterns." The products included "TABLES . . . Jappaned [sic], Card, Pier, Tea, Dressing, Writing, Shaving and Corner, painted and gilt in the most fanciful manner." They ended with a postscript announcing that they "have for sale Two neat CARRIAGES."[38]

The Finlays reached a milestone in 1809 when architect Benjamin Latrobe hired them to ornament a suite of furniture for James and Dolly Madison at the President's House.[39] Latrobe's designs played a seminal role in reshaping American taste by steering interests away from reserved Roman classicism and toward the bolder forms and colorful surfaces of Grecian domestic design. The transition became evident in 1816, when the Finlay brothers specifically advertised "Fancy Grecian Chairs." At some point within the following few years, John and Ann Eyre purchased the Finlays' large suite of innovatively designed furniture for Eyre Hall.

The suite consisted of a pair of marble-top pier tables (Cat. 22 and Fig. 208); a set of distinctive "wheel-back" side chairs (Cat. 23); and several cane-bottom benches (Cat. 26 and Cat. 27). The Eyres also purchased a plank-bottom Windsor settee (Cat. 24) and a matching armchair (Cat. 25), with complementary designs—painted in subtle stripes of red and black to emulate rosewood. When the pieces arrived in Northampton County, the family placed them around the passage to share their up-to-the-minute purchases.[40]

The chairs have a distinctive roundel at each rear corner of the seat. Classical in origin, they provide sufficient mass to firmly anchor the steeply canted back. The outer surface of each roundel provides additional space for ornament, and here the makers added a red woolen ground and a polished brass rosette. The Eyre family placed the set around the walls of the passage, where they provided a worthy complement to the French scenic wallpapers.

The fancy Grecian benches have boldly turned legs with acanthus-leaf decoration and distinctive scrolled arms with rosettes. The workmen gilded meandering classical vines across the front of the rail (Fig. 209)—and highlighted the legs with acanthus leaves in colorful bronze powders.

The Finlay brothers rarely decorated Windsor furniture, yet made an exception at Eyre Hall, where a pair of plank-bottom Windsor settees and a pair of matching armchairs stand near the doorway to the garden. Typically, Windsor seating has plank bottoms and removable cushions because it is intended for occasional use out of doors—where it was potentially exposed to weather. Not surprisingly, the brothers modified their approach to the gilded detail by brushing extra layers of varnish to protect it and assure its durability when out of doors. Through the years, the layers have darkened substantially on the Windsors—concealing the gilding and dampening its impact for the viewer.

Fig. 209. Detail of painted decoration on the rail of Cat 27.

22
Pier Table

One of a pair
Attributed to John Finlay (ca. 1777–1844) and
Hugh Finlay (1781–1831)
Baltimore, 1825–35
Poplar, white pine, and soft maple with rosewood
graining and oil-gilded ornament; white marble top
H. (overall, with marble) 36½ in.; W. (overall, case) 40 in.,
D. (overall, case) 16⅛ in.; marble top ¾ × 41 × 19⅞ in.

Fig. 208. Detail of Cat. 22.

23
Fancy Side Chair

Attributed to John Finlay (1777–1844) and Hugh Finlay (1781–1831)
Baltimore, 1825–35
Poplar and soft maple with rosewood graining, oil-gilded ornament,
stamped brass appliqués on a red woolen ground, and a cane seat
H. 31⅛ in., W. (crest rail) 19¼ in.,
D. (at feet) 23⅛ in.

Fancy Windsor Settee

Attributed to John Finlay (1777–1844) and Hugh Finlay (1781–1831)
Baltimore, 1825–35
Poplar and soft maple with rosewood graining and oil-gilded ornament
H. 31¼ in., L. 66⅛ in., D. (at feet) 25½ in.

Fancy Windsor Armchair

Attributed to John Finlay (1777–1844) and
Hugh Finlay (1781–1831)
Baltimore, 1825–35
Poplar and soft maple, with painted, grained,
and oil-gilded surfaces
H. 30¾ in., W. 20½ in., D. 25½ in.

26
Fancy Windsor Curule Bench

Attributed to John Finlay (1777–1844) and Hugh Finlay (1781–1831)
Baltimore, 1825–35
Poplar and soft maple, with a painted and grained surface, and oil-gilded ornament
H. 27⅝ in., L. 70⅝ in., D. 20½ in.

27
Fancy Cane-Seated Bench with Scrolled Arms

Attributed to John Finlay (1777–1844) and Hugh Finlay (1781–1831)
Baltimore, 1825–35
Poplar and soft maple, with painted, grained, and oil-gilded ornament
H. 27⅝ in., L. 70⅝ in., D. 20½ in.

28

Set of Four Gilded Brackets
or Consoles

Possibly by John Finlay (1777–1844) and/or Hugh Finlay (1781–1831)
Baltimore, 1825–35
Water gilding with grey bole on gesso, with a wash of yellow bole on
the secondary areas of the back; the secondary wood is poplar
H. 15 in., W. (shelf) 12 in., D. (shelf) 7 in.

Among the other gilded furnishings in the house are four intriguing brackets that hang on the walls in the parlor and dining room. These were likely intended to support Argand lamps, and, although they are unrecorded in Eyre family accounts or correspondence, there were numerous opportunities to acquire them.

The brackets are ambitious in design, yet simple in execution. To carve the parallel flutes of the simple leafage, the artisan relied on two chisels, one an eighth of an inch wide and the other a quarter of an inch wide. He used these to carve flutes of alternating widths that cover literally every visible surface except for the shelves.

The identity of the maker remains something of a conundrum, for no others of the form are known. The Eyre family certainly had opportunities to buy brackets from carver and gilder Abraham DeRevere, whose shop adjoined James Woodward's during the late 1810s. However, the rudimentary

character of the details argues strongly against his being the source, and especially so when one compares them to the eagle cornices over the bedsteads.

Evidence for another potential maker derives from John and Hugh Finlay's early publicity. In 1810, the brothers revealed in the Baltimore newspapers that they had "on hand and continue to make . . . brackets for Lights, Busts and Time-pieces." They further noted that their inventory included "Plaster Figures for Mantle Ornaments and Candelabris [sic]."[41] Although no brackets are presently recorded from the brothers' shop, the rudimentary character of the carving of the Eyre Hall brackets parallels that which appears on other furniture from their shop. Furthermore, the brackets have a bold scale that suggests a style between 1825 and about 1835—when the brothers' business was at its height, and by which point DeRevere had long since left town.

29
Carved Tester Bedstead

One of a matching pair
Philadelphia, 1840–45
Mahogany and mahogany veneer on poplar
H. (posts) 91 in., W. (overall) 64 in., L. (overall) 81½ in.

The ebullient national mood that had helped to propel the economy forward through the mid-1830s took a sudden step backwards in the fall of 1837 with a worrisome downturn in business. By the end of the year, the country was headed into a devastating depression that caused Americans everywhere to suddenly take stock of finances. Americans' infatuation with brilliant color and contrasting woods immediately retreated, and by the end of the year the country was in a deep depression.

It took nearly a decade for the economy to recover, and, by the time it did, Americans had long since taken stock of their tastes—and made sobering adjustments. The Eyre family wouldn't venture into the market again for significant furniture purchases for nearly a decade. This time, they brought the principal bedrooms up to date—yet without relying on the contrasting veneers, colorful paint, or glistening hardware of the prior decades.

In the 1840s, John Eyre purchased a pair of Philadelphia bedsteads, each having enormous turned posts, a paneled headboard with an elaborately carved crest, and a simple wooden tester with a valance. He placed the pair together, in the large second-floor bedroom over the dining room in the east wing. According to family history, in the early twentieth century Severn Eyre slept in this bed and his servant slept in the other.

30
Bureau or Chest of Drawers with Mirror

One of a matching pair
Baltimore, 1835–45
Mahogany, mahogany veneer, and marble primary, with poplar, white pine, and mahogany secondary
H. (case) 40⅞ in., H. (overall, with mirror and glove boxes) 90¼ in., W. (case) 43¼ in., D. (case) 20¼ in.

A pair of equally substantial bureaus accompanied the bedsteads (Cat. 29). The surfaces were veneered and the only brasses were the tiny keyhole escutcheon discreetly placed near the top of each drawer front. The maker relied on two pairs of Ionic columns for ornament: those flanking the drawers on the front and, attached above, another pair to support the mirror, providing sufficient room for reflection. The piece stood on turned feet of substantial proportions, and had complementary finials flanking the mirror above.

* * *

The furniture of Eyre Hall can be understood—and best respected—when one avoids seeing the pieces as composing a "collection." The home and the things that fill it are different in many respects from the homes that most of us know today. At Eyre Hall, the early residents knew many of the cabinetmakers who made the furniture, but were also linked to them by blood, marriage, and/or entwined business relationships. Those were the things that help to shape a family's identity, define its legacy, and project its members toward the future. Knowing if an artisan or a builder has a family relationship to a planter for whom they work helps historians to view the planter's home, and the furnishings therein, from an entirely different perspective.

Today, builders sometimes construct houses for families that they have never met and, in some cases, never will. Yet in the eighteenth century, homes such as Eyre Hall, and the objects that filled them, were often a tangible expression of broader family talents. In Virginia, where traditions of primogeniture generally directed family inheritance toward elder sons, younger sons often became artisans.

Although English laws of primogeniture were ostensibly followed in colonial Virginia, the seemingly endless availability of land through most of the colonial period encouraged colonists to diverge from English traditions of inheritance. It was not unusual for the first son of an aristocratic family to inherit the lion's share of the parents' property, become a planter, and obtain a position of authority in the legislature, with the church, or in the court. A logical career choice for second and third sons in such families was to become a joiner who made furniture, a carpenter who constructed houses, or an "undertaker" who oversaw construction of larger public buildings. It was not unusual in such circumstances for an elder sibling who inherited property to help a younger one in the family secure lucrative contracts for building churches, courthouses, bridges, or other public works. When one looks at the broader context of Eyre Hall and its furnishings, these trades were followed among the Eyre kinsmen in the Harmanson and Taylor families, and had a measurable impact on the early furnishings of Eyre Hall.

NOTES

1. Among the few families the author could cite were the John Minson Galt and St. George Tucker families of Williamsburg. The former had furnishings that remained in the family home until 1978; at that point, a core group of objects was sold privately to Colonial Williamsburg, and the remainder dispersed at an onsite auction.

2. Baltimore had a population of about 500 residents in 1750, yet experienced 12-fold growth by 1775 when tax lists identified some 6,000 inhabitants.

3. Furniture from the shops of Quakers, who were generally abolitionists, seems to have held little appeal to the Eyre family, who were extensive slaveholders.

4. Most Eastern Shore cupboards were made in a single piece. Because this one is exceptionally

large, it may have been an exception, but, if not, may have lost the lower portion when stored on the damp earthen floor of an outbuilding.

5. Inventory of the estate of Harmanson Joyne, October 27, 1779, Northampton County Wills & Inventories, No. 26, 1777–1783, 351–56. Copy at MESDA, Winston-Salem, North Carolina.

6. "To cash paid James Harmanson for making coffin . . . 5 [shillings]," in Audit of the estate of Bailey Scott (d. 1813), Northampton County Wills, etc., No. 35, 1817–1822, 304; see also Will of James Harmanson, carpenter, November 3, 1815, Northampton County Wills, Inventories, etc., No. 34, 1813–1817, 240, which appoints brothers Henry and William Harmanson his heirs and executors. Copies at MESDA.

7. A number of Tidewater families had elder sons who inherited property and served in the legislature, and younger sons who became artisans. One can chart a half dozen cases in which the builders received lucrative commissions from the legislature or local governments to construct churches, courthouses, and bridges. The complementary traditions helped families to diversify their interests, as tobacco depleted their lands.

8. Richard Taylor's apprentice Thomas Sharrock (b. 1737; active 1762–1802 in Norfolk, Virginia, and Northampton County, North Carolina) made pieces during the 1760s and 1770s that are virtually identical to those of Richard Taylor II of Petersburg, and derive from the Taylor shop precedent. For more on Thomas Sharrock's

documented pieces, see John Bivins, Jr., *The Furniture of Coastal North Carolina, 1700–1820* (Chapel Hill: University of North Carolina Press for the Museum of Early Southern Decorative Arts, 1988), 502–3. Norfolk County, Virginia, Order Book 1755–1759, 55a, May 21, 1756.

9. Duke of Cumberland Street is now known as Duke Street.

10. The author strongly suspects that Taylor's Norfolk associate, cabinetmaker Hardress Waller, also relied upon the same foot profile for case pieces.

11. The reference to Richard Taylor's billiard table and character appears in the *Virginia Gazette* [PD], November 19, 1772.

12. A number of men in the Taylor family were "carpenters" and "joiners" in the mid-eighteenth century, yet outside apprentices were scarce. Aside from Thomas Sharrock (see note 8), only Samuel Lewelling and Theophilus Topping are documented—and neither of the latter continued in the trade.

13. For more on Selden, see Ronald Hurst and Jonathan Prown, *Southern Furniture 1680–1830: The Colonial Williamsburg Collection* (Williamsburg, Va.: Colonial Williamsburg Foundation, 1997), 110.

14. Allmand apprenticed to Selden on January 1, 1760, as cited in Elizabeth City County Deeds & Wills, Vol. E, 1758–1764, 109. The apprenticeship ended on September 22, 1768. Craftsman Database, MESDA, craftsman ID 447. Selden's workmanship is documented by a signed clothespress and chest of drawers made in 1775 for the Carter family of Shirley Plantation. See Wallace B. Gusler, *Furniture of Williamsburg and Eastern Virginia 1710–1790* (Richmond, Va.: Virginia Museum of Fine Arts in conjunction with the Colonial Williamsburg Foundation, 1979), 151–53, and Hurst and Prown, *Southern Furniture*, 110, 191, 389–93.

15. Through the years, the family relied upon the Baltimore furniture company of Potthast Brothers Inc. (1892–1975) to restore broken furniture in the house and replace pieces that were too badly damaged to repair. The company's origins date to 1892, when German immigrant brothers William, Vincent, John, and Theodore Potthast founded the company. It was the most prolific cabinetmaking shop in Baltimore during that era. One of the Allmand side chairs bears the Roman numeral "XIII" stamped inside the rear rail, signifying that the set originally contained at least 14 pieces.

16. Inventory of the estate of Harmanson Joyne, 351–56.

17. MESDA field researchers Frank Horton, Brad Rauschenberg, and Carolyn Weekley examined the table at Eyre Hall on March 11, 1975 and documented it in MESDA file S-4257.

18. Information about the 1768 purchase appears the following year in "Settlement of the Estate of Littleton Eyre, dec^d." It is notable that the document was not entered into record at Northampton County Court until April 1781: Estate of Littleton Eyre in account with Bowdoin, Eyre & Smith, 1768–80, April 11, 1781, Northampton County Wills & Inventories, No. 26, 1777–83, 404. It is possible that the family acquired the second table of the pair at a different time, though the date is unknown. The tables potentially embody London taste of the 1750s.

19. Inventory of the estate of Severn Eyre, February 27, 1774, Northampton County Wills & Inventories, No. 25, 1772–1777, 390–91.

20. Biographical information for master cabinetmaker Anthony Hay of Williamsburg, as well as the journeyman and enslaved artisans in his shop, can be found in Craftsman Database, MESDA, craftsman ID 15753. Further insights appear in Gusler, *Furniture of Williamsburg and Eastern Virginia*, 60–64. A brief discussion of the table can also be found in J. Thomas Savage, "Eyre Hall on Virginia's Eastern Shore," *The Magazine Antiques*, September 2009, 56–65.

21. Most Surry chests with the straight inner profile are more provincial in style and construction, and are typically made of walnut. This piece is potentially a precursor to those rural examples.

22. Wallace Gusler first observed a correlation between dust boards and security in *Furniture of Williamsburg and Eastern Virginia*, 83, 115, 152–59.

23. *American Beacon and Commercial Diary* (Norfolk), November 20, 1816; *Norfolk Herald*, October 11, 1820.

24. The concept of neoclassical pier glasses of this scale was rare in a colonial Virginia context, and examples of the form were likely not produced in America until the late 1780s and 1790s. It seems unlikely that these are the "2 Pier Gilt Glasses" that appeared in Severn Eyre's 1774 inventory accompanied by two mahogany tables, 12 mahogany chairs, two armchairs, and two card tables—furnishings meant to serve multiple functions and likely residing in the parlor.

25. A library bookcase of ca. 1810 bearing Barry's label exists in the collection of the Historic Savannah Foundation's Green-Meldrim House. Barry relied upon many of the same features for that piece, yet interpreted them through the lens of robust classical design.

26. By applying the name "Gentleman's Secretary," Sheraton conveyed a significant cultural shift that was taking place during the late eighteenth and early nineteenth centuries, in which designers, artisans, and consumers increasingly viewed specific furniture forms, and specific types of ornament, through the cultural lenses of gender and emotion, and inevitably applied names and/or adjectives that promoted those outlooks.

27. The projecting central bookcase with two doors is made as a single unit, flanked on either side by a smaller cabinet with a single door. The cornice is removable, and never had a parapet or finials above.

28. "Patterns for glazing bars for Bookcases, Cabinets, etc. designed by W. Casement," published in *The Cabinet-Makers' London Book of Prices*, 2nd ed. (London: London Society of Cabinet Makers, 1793), pl. 27.

29. Barry went back to London in 1811 so that he could again immerse himself within the city's forward-looking community of cabinetmakers. He returned to America with an expanded vocabulary of style that introduced Americans to robust classical design.

30. The table has a stationary leg on each corner and—on each side—two additional gate legs, which are needed to support the 56-inch-wide leaves.

31. The maker relied upon four iron hinges to support each leaf, instead of the usual three.

32. The table's tremendous scale presented an insurmountable challenge for on-site photography. Proper recording of the piece would have required moving the three sections to an enormous space, acquiring special lenses, and securing access to greater voltage than was available in the rural domestic context at the time.

33. The author is grateful to Alexandra Kirtley, Associate Curator of American Decorative Arts at the Philadelphia Museum of Art, for contributions to the paragraph. The table also has features in common with pieces attributed to Quaker cabinetmaker John Needles (1786–1878). A native of Talbot County, Maryland, he settled in Baltimore in 1809—which seems potentially late for the piece. He worked with Camp (1773–1822), before establishing a shop of his own.

34. For further information on Bankson and Lawson and their products, see Sumpter Priddy III, J. Michael Flanigan, and Gregory R. Weidman, "The Genesis of Neoclassical Style in Baltimore Furniture," in *American Furniture 2000*, ed. Luke Beckerdite (Hanover, N.H.: The University Press of New England for the Chipstone Foundation, 2000), 59–99.

35. *Maryland Journal and Baltimore Advertiser*, July 29, 1785.

36. See entries for March 14, 1834 in the 1831–34 daybook from William Baker's Baltimore Flint Glass Works, Maryland Center for History and Culture, MS 1546. The author is grateful to Arlene Palmer Schwind, former Curator of Glass and Ceramics at the H. F. DuPont – Winterthur Museum, for providing this citation.

37. The author is grateful to Carl Lounsbury for providing the citation to the Personal Property Tax Lists filed with Northampton County between 1780 and 1840.

38. *American, and Commercial Daily Advertiser* (Baltimore), March 5, 1803, 3:4.

39. Latrobe's Bank of Pennsylvania (1799) is often cited as the prominent structure that introduced Grecian details to an American audience. For more on Latrobe, see Alexandra Alevizatos Kirtley, Peggy Olley, and Jeffrey Cohen, *Classical Splendor: Painted Furniture for a Grand Philadelphia House* (Philadelphia: Philadelphia Museum of Art, 2017).

40. Alexandra Alevizatos Kirtley, "Benjamin Henry Latrobe and the Furniture of John and Hugh Finlay," *The Magazine Antiques*, December 2009, https://www.themagazineantiques.com/article/benjamin-henry-latrobe-and-the-furniture-of-john-and-hugh-finlay/. Among the Virginians who ordered Finlay furniture were the Skipwith Family of "Oak Hill" and "Prestwould" in Mecklenburg County, and the Mackall/Macgill family of Shepherdstown, Virginia (now West Virginia) and Georgetown, D.C.

41. *American, and Commercial Daily Advertiser* (Baltimore), December 16, 1810, 3:5; *Baltimore Evening Post*, January 1, 1811, 1:5. This advertisement appears to have been the brothers' sole publicity for brackets. However, they continued to make most of the forms mentioned throughout their careers.

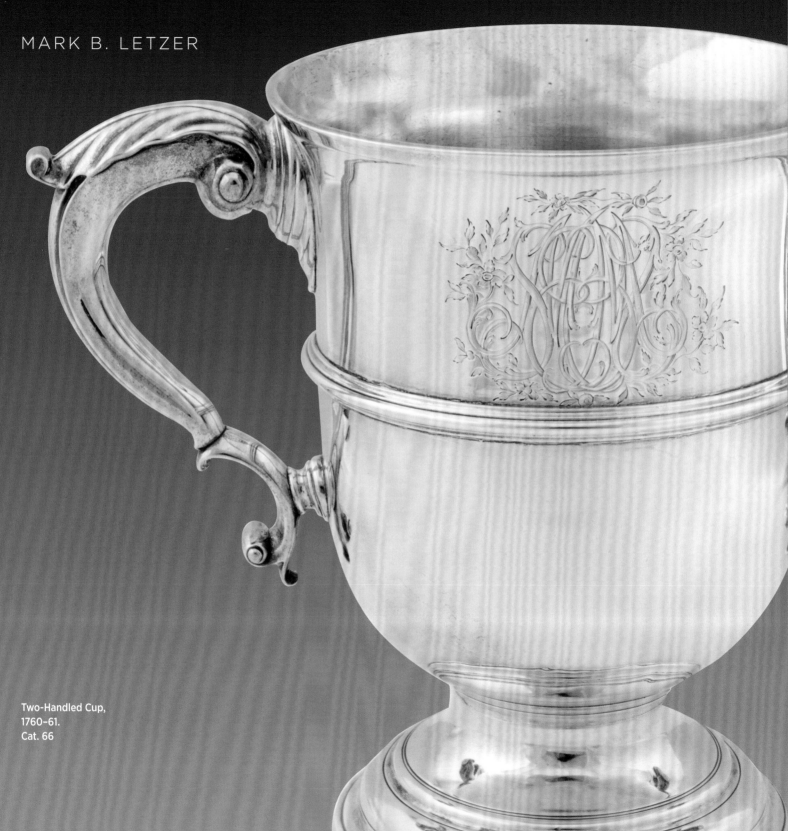

Silver

MARK B. LETZER

Two-Handled Cup,
1760–61.
Cat. 66

*"I will and bequeath unto my beloved kinsman Severn
Eyre . . . the silver punch bowl, sugar box ditto and the
silver cup thereto belonging, the new silver tankard,
twelve spoons ditto, two porringers ditto."*

WILL OF BRIDGET BOXCROFT, 1704[1]

S UCH IS THE FIRST MENTION OF THE EARLIEST
piece of silver associated with Eyre Hall. The so-called
"Morningstar" punch bowl cited in the bequest is
not only the oldest, but also the most significant
piece in this collection and one of the most important
to survive from colonial Virginia (see Cat. 64). Dating to
1692 and made during the reign of William and Mary,
non-ecclesiastical silver vessels of this size were very rare in
the colonies prior to the eighteenth century, especially in
the South.

Silver, also known as "plate" in the eighteenth century,
has been held in high esteem for millennia as a malleable
and recyclable metal—one of those luxury goods whose
ownership conferred status on those who could afford it,
distinguishing them from "those other sorts" who could
not. Silver has held this status-defining characteristic
from the very inception of its use (Fig. 210). A handsome
collection of plate was an enviable thing to possess in the
seventeenth and eighteenth centuries. In 1688, Virginia
planter William Fitzhugh wrote his agent in London
that "for now my buildings finished, my plantations well
settled . . . & being sufficiently stored with goods of all sorts,
I esteem it as well politic as reputable, to furnish my self with
an handsome Cupboard of plate which gives my present
use & credit, is a sure friend at a dead lift, without much
loss or is a certain position for a child after my decease."[2]
Silver signified wealth. During the colonial period, "specie"
or silver coins served as a ready source of metal other than

silver vessels that could be melted down to create new forms
or be converted into cash—before banks as we know them
today were in existence. Economics played a great role in the
colonial period with regard to silver. Wealthy Virginians and
other colonials with the means to do so ordered their plate
from factors or agents in London along with most of their
luxury items.

The domestic plate at Eyre Hall is typical of that
purchased by other wealthy families throughout the mid-
Atlantic area in the second half of the eighteenth century.
While there was little control when placing these orders
from factors in England, the only requirement was that the
pieces be in the latest fashion. There was great similarity
across the board from plantation to plantation regarding
the type and quality of the silver ordered to grace the table.
Factors had ready suppliers for the same types of objects.
London silversmiths specialized, with "large" workers
making items like coffeepots, baskets, epergnes, sugar
canisters, cream pots, and tea caddies, and "small" workers
items such as casters, salts, shoe buckles, and flat silver.
This specialization allowed individual tradesmen to focus
on their particular area of expertise and training. These
items were purchased by the factors and shipped to fill
orders from the American colonies. Silversmiths working
in the colonies also supplemented their own domestically
made wares with imported goods that could be added to
their stock inventory. Orders filled by factors often came
from the same sources. This is why silver manufactured by

Fig. 210. The silver items laid out on this eighteenth-century Williamsburg card table were all made in London in the seventeenth and eighteenth centuries. Card tables of this type had receptacles especially made for candlesticks, allowing card games to be played at night by candlelight. This particular assemblage points to the extreme wealth and social prominence of the Eyre family in the colonial period. Note the candlesticks placed in the receptacles along with the punch bowl flanked by two tankards and a pair of canns that belonged to Severn and Margaret Eyre.

individuals, or partnerships such as Thomas Whipham and Charles Wright, Daniel Smith and Robert Sharp, or indeed William Shaw and William Priest, turn up again and again in different collections dating from the eighteenth century in colonial America.[3]

A lot of the original silver at Shirley Plantation in Charles City County belonging to the Carter family is still on site. Very similar to Eyre Hall in content and function, many of the pieces throughout the house are marked by the same silversmith, suggesting that the factors at the time repeatedly patronized the same silversmiths to fulfill orders from America. Out of the 37 pieces of English silver still at Shirley Plantation, London silversmiths William Plummer and Edward and Robert Fennell appear as makers 20 times.[4]

Other plantations throughout colonial Virginia amassed large collections of silver as well. In 1774/75 John "Jackie"

Parke Custis acquired a large and impressive collection of silver with the help of his stepfather George Washington. All of this was in the neoclassical taste—a new style that emerged in architecture and the decorative arts in England and Europe in the 1760s as a response to the discoveries at Herculaneum and Pompeii. Unlike Washington, who ordered a lot of Sheffield plated objects, young Custis opted for the more costly sterling—perhaps influenced by his marriage that year to Eleanor Calvert.[5] Silver from the Randolph family, currently in the collection of the Colonial Williamsburg Foundation, has a salver not dissimilar to one at Eyre Hall bearing the Randolph crest.[6]

In southern colonial America, silver was not crafted locally until well into the eighteenth century. This was in contrast with the northern colonies, which had working silversmiths as early as the first quarter of the seventeenth century. This southern agrarian economy—unlike the more urban northern economy—precluded the settling of craftsmen in the South, as self-sufficient towns were not established as early as in the North. The plantation system was very different. Planters and burgesses in Virginia, as in the rest of the Chesapeake, would convene in towns like Williamsburg during meetings of the legislature. Some of these also had houses in these metropolitan areas. But before and even after these craftsmen settled here, planters and other consumers relied on their products from the mother country.[7]

The role of silver is especially interesting from a generational standpoint. As stated earlier, in southern colonial America most of the silver owned by the gentry was originally imported from England. This practice naturally evolved once the colonies attained independence from England after the American Revolution. The silver at Eyre Hall clearly follows this same path. The earliest pieces were made in England, but, immediately following the Revolution, the family began purchasing domestically produced silver. With few exceptions, the end of the

eighteenth century marked the end of imported English plate. After the Revolution, the Eyres still ordered English plate, but they increasingly turned to domestic markets in Norfolk, Baltimore, and Philadelphia to buy new pieces as well.

Family wills and inventories reveal that there was a vast amount of silver at Eyre Hall throughout the eighteenth century. The Eyres owned punch bowls, sugar boxes, silver cups, tankards, spoons, porringers, salt cellars, silver-hilted swords, dram cups, gilt canns, salvers, candlesticks, teapots, coffeepots, casters, butter boats, a punch strainer, sugar tongs, and a silver-mounted gun. All of these items touted their wealth, as well as being integral elements in entertaining friends and guests. The absence of diaries and letters from this period precludes our knowing how often and in what capacity the silver was used, but we can get some idea from the specialized cabinets known as buffets about where they may have been displayed. The house had a smaller footprint before the dining room addition was completed by Severn Eyre sometime before 1773. The original house comprised a central square block with a large passage on the west side that extended from one end to the other. It would likely have been used for many purposes including dining—in the north end, where the staircase is located. No doubt, the decorative buffet closet beneath the west end of the arched opening displayed the Eyre silver as well as other fashionable items such as ceramic punch bowls, tablewares, and stemware used for dining and entertaining.

After the addition of the dining room in the northeast corner, much of the silver and other decorative plate and dining implements were transferred to two new cupboards in the vestibule that led into the dining room. Severn Eyre's inventory from 1774 lists silver pieces, ceramics, and other items in these cupboards, and much of it was still on display in them as late as the middle of the nineteenth century.[8] This information is important, as sideboards traditionally used to display silver developed into the form more recognized today toward the end of the eighteenth century. The Eyres and others of their time would have most likely used hunt boards or placed the material directly on the table.

The bulk of the eighteenth-century silver surviving at Eyre Hall today can be documented from the earliest inventories. An inventory of the extant silver as well as the items that were historically part of this great house also shows a great quantity of pewter. This base metal was much less expensive and would have been used for all manner of household purposes, especially by the staff and for myriad kitchen needs. The first Severn Eyre's inventory of 1728 records a total of 159 pounds of pewter both old and new, indicating that it was heavily relied upon.[9] In the 1769 inventory of his son Littleton Eyre, the enumerators listed 59 pewter plates and 24 pewter dishes, as well as 14 pewter basins.[10]

Period wills and inventories are extremely important in tracking down precious items. Because of the intrinsic value of the material, silver objects were often singled out in wills as convertible wealth that might be passed to specific individuals. Because of the conscious act of transferring them from one individual to another, the line of ownership of silver pieces can be traced more easily than for nearly any other object. This is certainly evident in many surviving items at Eyre Hall. The silver punch bowl that was first mentioned in Bridget Foxcroft's will in 1704 shows up again and again through the generations (see Cat. 64).

In 1728, the first Severn Eyre devised his accumulated plate to his two sons, Littleton and Severn. His oldest son was given "my Silver punch bole & Silver Shugar box & my bigest Silver Tankard & one Silver [porringer] & half Dozen Silver Spoons & a Silver Cup belonging to the bole and one handmill," while his youngest was bequeathed "my next bigest Silver Tankard & one old one [Tankard] without a Lid & one Silver beeker one Small Silver Cup & one Silver porenger & Ye Remainder of my Silver Spoons & one hand mill."[11] Besides giving the punch bowl that he received from

his kinswoman, Bridget Foxcroft, to his eldest son, it is not clear what criteria were used to separate the silver between the two heirs. Unfortunately, young Severn died just a few years after his father, so his part of the estate reverted to his older brother Littleton. In turn, Littleton passed down the silver he inherited from his father—as well as what he accumulated along with his wife Bridget—to his only surviving child, Severn Eyre, on his death in 1768.

The second occupant of Eyre Hall, Severn Eyre only survived his father by five years, dying in 1773. In his will devised a few years earlier, Severn stipulated that his wife Margaret would receive some named pieces of silver and that his eldest son Littleton was to receive a "two quart Gilt Cup, the large silver Punch Bowl, 2 silver Candle Sticks, 1 Large Silver Salver, 1 Small do and tankard and one pint gilt cup." He then specified that "the rest of my Silver . . . I give to my Sons Severn and John equally to be divided."[12] When Littleton came into his majority in 1782, his younger brothers Severn and John divided the remainder equally between flat silver and hollowware (Fig. 211). However, neither got the largest and most impressive piece which was the large silver punch bowl. That had been reserved in Severn's will for his eldest son Littleton, who also inherited the Eyre Hall property. When Littleton's brother Severn died in London in 1786, he inherited his brother's plate, reuniting some pieces from their father's inventory in the hands of Littleton (Fig. 212).

When Littleton died prematurely in 1789, the large silver punch bowl and other plate in his possession passed to his brother John. In his will written two years earlier, Littleton stipulated that all his plate was to be divided equally between his two surviving brothers, John and William, "except the bowl and large cup with two handles," which he bequeathed to the oldest of his two siblings, John, who also inherited Eyre Hall from him.[13] This most important piece of silver was singled out in John Eyre's will of 1855. A widower with no children of his own, he bequeathed the large silver

Objects in Severn Eyre's 1774 inventory, with value given in shillings	Value in £	Recipients: ME = Margaret Eyre; LE = Littleton Eyre; SE = Severn Eyre; JE = John Eyre Source of bequest: w = from 1769 will; d = from 1782 division
2 dozen new tablespoons	30.0.0	1 dozen tablespoons ME-w; 1 dozen tablespoons SE-d
4 old tablespoons 60/, 1 new soup spoon 60/	6.0.0	4 tablespoons JE-d; 1 soup spoon SE-d
1 soup ladle 80/	4.0.0	JE-d
6 salts and spoons 240/	12.0.0	JE-d
1 pair candlesticks 200/	10.0.0	LE-w
2 sets of casters 400/	20.0.0	1 SE-d; 1 JE-d
1 pair butter boats 80/	4.0.0	1 SE-d; 1 JE-d
1 punch strainer 30/	1.10.0	JE-d
1 large waiter 240/, 1 large waiter 160/	20.0.0	1 ME-w; 1 LE-w
2 waiters 200/, 2 waiters 190/	19.10.0	1 ME-w; 1 LE-w; 1 SE-d; 1 JE-d
1 large two-handled mug	14.0.0	LE-w
1 coffeepot 300/, 1 tankard 280/	29.0.0	coffeepot JE-d; tankard LE-w
1 tankard 260/, 1 old tankard 100/	18.0.0	SE-d
1 pair canns 300/, 1 teapot 50/	25.0.0	1 cann ME-w; 1 cann LE-w; teapot SE-d
1 cross 200/, 2 tea tongs 50/	12.10.0	cross JE-d; 1 tong SE-d; 1 tong JE-d
1 punch ladle 5/, 16 teaspoons 80/	4.5.0	ladle JE-d; 1 dozen teaspoons ME-w; 4 teaspoons JE-d;
1 large punch bowl	30.0.0	LE-w
2 neat fowling pieces mounted with shot bag and flash &c.	16.0.0	SE-1787 inventory
	£275.15.0	

Margaret Eyre (1739–1812), wife	Littleton Eyre (1761–1789), son	Severn Eyre (1764–1786), son	John Eyre (1768–1855), son
1 dozen tablespoons-w	2 quart gilt cups-w	1 dozen new tablespoons, 15.0.0-d	4 old tablespoons 3.0.0-d
1 dozen teaspoons-w	large bowl-w	1 new soup spoon, 3.0.0-d	1 soup ladle 4.0.0; 1 salver 4.15.0; total: 8.15.0-d
1 salver-w	2 candlesticks-w	1 salver, 4.15.0-d	1 coffeepot 15.0.0; 1 cross 10.0.0; total: 25.0.0-d
1 small salver-w	1 large salver-w	2 tankards, 18.0.0-d	1 pair tea tongs 25/; 1 punch ladle 5/; total: 1.10.0-d
1 pint gilt cann-w	1 small salver-w	1 teapot, 10.0.0-d	6 salts and spoons 12.0.0; 1 set casters 10.0.0; total: 22.0.0-d
	1 tankard-w	1 pair tongs, 1.5.0-d	1 butter boat 2.0.0-d
	1 gilt pint cup-w	1 set casters, 10.0.0-d	1 punch strainer 1.10.0-d
	All the rest of silver not given to sons Severn and John equally divided-w	1 butter boat, 2.0.0-d	4 teaspoons 1.0.0-d
		Total value £64.0.0	Total value £64.15.0

Fig. 211. Division of Severn Eyre's plate between wife Margaret Eyre, and sons Littleton, Severn, and John Eyre based on his 1769 will and the 1782 division of his goods from his 1774 inventory.

1 silver-mounted gun	10.0.0
1 dozen new tablespoons	9.0.0
1 new soup spoon	2.0.0
1 silver salver	4.10.0
2 tankards	15.0.0
1 silver teapot	9.0.0
1 pair sugar tongs	0.18.0
1 set silver casters	9.0.0
1 butter boat	2.0.0
	£61.8.0

Fig. 212. 1787 estate inventory of Severn Eyre (d. 1786), who bequeathed all his plate to his brother Littleton Eyre.

Fig. 213. Silver objects dating from the late seventeenth century to the late nineteenth century on the sideboard in the dining room, Eyre Hall. Although the silver on this sideboard would not have been displayed this way in the period, it is indicative of how it is used today.

bowl and a small one to his niece Margaret A. Taylor, great-grandmother of the current owner, H. Furlong Baldwin.[14] Through the Taylor side of the family, the piece returned to Eyre Hall in the twentieth century.

The silver at Eyre Hall exemplifies common patterns of consumption. Because of Eyre Hall's relative isolation and the continuous ownership of the property by one family, the surviving pieces document their changing tastes as well as the evolution of new forms and styles over more than three centuries (Fig. 213). What had been English silver tastes in the

31

Tankard

John Bache
London, 1715–16
Silver
H. 8¼ in., W. 5½ in.

Fig. 214. Detail of the "GH" engraving, Cat. 31. Gertrude Harmanson, grandmother of Littleton Eyre, willed this tankard to her son Henry Harmanson in 1732.

colonial period began to change in the late eighteenth and early nineteenth century with the emergence of American centers of craftsmanship in nearby cities such as Norfolk, Baltimore, and Philadelphia that catered to an expanding consumer market. A number of items in the collection also highlight the growth of highly specialized implements and forms such as tea equipage that evolved to cater to more sophisticated forms of dining and entertaining.

A large tankard with the initials "GH" was owned by Gertrude Harmanson, Littleton Eyre's grandmother (Cat. 31 and Fig. 214). Marked by John Bache and dating to 1715/16, this piece is clearly mentioned in her will dating to 1732, according to which she had already given "unto my said son one large Silver tankard and six silver spoons . . . the Tankard & Spoons are thus GH."[15] This piece is clearly engraved "GH" on the bottom, along with the weight of 36 ounces. This tankard, like the punch bowl, is of Britannia standard, meaning that its silver content is 95 percent

to 5 percent copper or other alloys, unlike most of the collection of a sterling standard of 92.5 percent silver. This piece is no longer at Eyre Hall but still in the family.

Writing in the 1820s, Littleton Waller Tazewell, Gertrude Harmanson's great-grandson, remarked on her extraordinary reputation. He said that, following her husband's death, she had "managed all her estates herself, with as much industry and skill and attention as any man could have done—Mounted on horseback she rode from one end of the Eastern Shore to the other without any attendant visiting her different estates; and was reputed the best manager they had. During her widowhood she acquired by her own enterprize and exertion several landed estates and much property." He also noted that "part of the plate bequeathed by her will to [her] grandson Littleton Tazewell, and marked G. H., was still preserved in my family not many years ago, having been handed down to me from generation to generation since her death, now nearly a hundred years since. Other similar plate is I believe still preserved in the family of John Eyre esquire devised to him in like manner."[16]

Three other pieces in the collection also belonged originally to the Harmansons, as evidenced by their armorial device. A large pie-crust bordered salver used to serve alcoholic beverages marked by Robert Abercrombie and dating to 1746/47 is also engraved with the Harmanson arms and the initials "LBE" for Littleton and Bridget Harmanson Eyre (see Cat. 67). This salver is most likely the one in Severn Eyre's will dating to 1769. A privately owned salver close in size to this one and marked by Abercrombie dates to 1735/36 and is engraved with the crest of the Randolph family of Virginia. Originally belonging to Peyton Randolph, these salvers, along with another pair and a cup, are among the

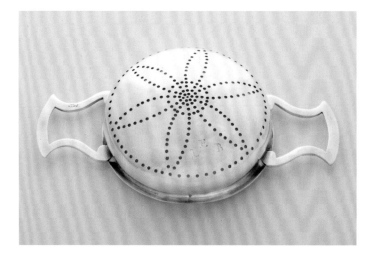

32

Punch Strainer

Unmarked
Probably London, ca. 1734
Silver
L. 6 in., W. 3⅜ in.

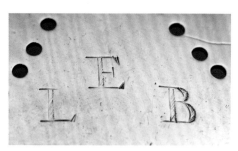

Fig. 215. Detail of the "LBE" engraving, Cat. 32.

dating to 1760/61 is engraved with Severn and Margaret Eyre's initials in a reversed cipher (see Cat. 66).

A sauce pan with a wooden handle engraved with the letter "E" also has a history of ownership in the house although no longer there. This piece is marked "S. L. Mitchell," but we have been unable to establish the identity of that silversmith. Sauce pans were used to heat and serve sauces at table. The wooden handle prevented the transmission of heat (Cat. 35). A covered sugar basin with a domed lid and marked thrice with the letter H (or a set of conjoined initials resembling the letter H) also has a family history, but the absence of any engraving makes it impossible to ascribe it to a particular individual (Cat. 36).

Lighting was an ever-present challenge in the eighteenth century, and candlesticks served as the only ready implement for that purpose. Although most households including Eyre Hall would have had candlesticks made of brass or other alloys, wealthy colonials also had examples made in silver. Intended to grace the dining table or the card table, the examples illustrated here were exuberant (Cat. 37). Marked by Francis Crump in 1763/64, they may be the pair bequeathed to Littleton Eyre by his father in 1769. With swirl decoration in true rococo taste, they are cast completely from a mold and remain the only pair in the house still extant from this period.

Pierced salts with cobalt-blue glass liners were also popular, and these examples are two of a total of at least six.

very few pieces documented to have been in Williamsburg in the eighteenth century.[17] A small punch strainer also has the initials "LBE" for Littleton and Bridget Eyre and, although unmarked, probably dates to ca. 1734 (Cat. 32 and Fig. 215). A set of three unmarked casters—which would have been used to dispense spices at table—similarly bears the crest of the Harmanson family and, like the strainer, are datable to ca. 1734. The largest one is still at Eyre Hall (Cat. 33 and Fig. 216), and a smaller pair are in the collection of MESDA, the Museum of Early Southern Decorative Arts.[18] Another pair of casters has no engraving at all; they are marked by Samuel Wood and date to 1741/42.

The next generation of silver dates to the marriage of Severn and Margaret Taylor Eyre. Three casters engraved "SME" in a mirror cipher also date to this period of occupancy (Cat. 34). They are marked by John Delmester and date to 1760/61. A handsome two-handled loving cup marked by Thomas Whipham and Charles Wright and also

33
Caster

Unmarked
Probably London, ca. 1734
Silver
H. 7 in.

Fig. 216. Detail of the
Harmanson crest, Cat. 33.

34
Set of Three Casters

John Delmester
London, 1760–61
Silver
H. 6⅝ in., H. 5½ in.

35
Sauce Pan

S. L. Mitchell
Probably American, ca. 1820
Silver and wood
L. 10 in., W. 4 in., H. 2¾ in.

36
Covered
Sugar Basin

Unidentified mark "H"
three times on base
American, ca. 1800
Silver
H. 8¾ in., W. 4 in.

37
Pair of Candlesticks

Francis Crump
London, 1763–64
Silver
H. 10⅝ in.

38
Pierced Salts with Cobalt Glass Liners

Maker's mark rubbed
London, 1770–71
Silver and glass
L. 3⅜ in., H. 1⁷⁄₁₆ in.

39
Soup Ladle

Maker's mark rubbed
London, 1793–94
Silver
L. 12½ in.

Two Pairs of Sauce Ladles

London, 1778–79
Silver
L. 7 in.

London, 1791–92 and 1807–8
Silver
L. 7 in.

The corrosive effect of salt on silver made it ideal to have a glass receptacle in which to place the condiment. The salts date to 1770/71, but the maker's mark is rubbed, making it impossible to read (Cat. 38). Archaeological activity under the porch has uncovered fragments of cobalt-blue liners, indicating that there were more of these originally.

The last of the eighteenth-century English silver still at Eyre Hall consists of four sauce ladles and a soup ladle. The soup ladle dates to 1793/94 and is engraved with the letter "E," with rubbed maker's mark. One pair of sauce ladles— also engraved with the letter "E"—dates to 1778/79; of the other two, one is marked "TB" and dates to 1807/8, while the other marked "CH" was made in 1791/92 (Cat. 39).

Sometimes, it is what is missing that is most surprising in a collection. The total absence of eighteenth-century cutlery and flat silver is intriguing. In the eighteenth century, knives and forks would have had silver pistol-grip handles and steel blades and tines. And silver spoons would certainly

40
Dessert Spoons

Charles Louis Boehme
Baltimore, ca. 1800
Silver
L. 7⅜ in.

41
Dessert Spoons

Hosea Wilson
Baltimore, 1815
Silver
L. 7⅜ in.

also have been present. But although cutlery is mentioned in the Eyre inventories throughout the eighteenth century, none of it remains—probably because these earlier forms of cutlery were gradually replaced by more modern styles.

The growth of Baltimore and Norfolk in the late eighteenth and early nineteenth century sparked the growth of local trades providing material that would be used in the great house. Undoubtedly, porcelain and other items made their way to Eyre Hall through these ports of entry. After the Revolution, silver was produced locally in both cities and appeared at roughly the same time. Although most of the Norfolk-made silver has a Taylor family origin, not all of it does. This indicates that the Eyres purchased silver in both port cities. John Eyre's inheritance of Eyre Hall marked the period of greatest accumulation for the house. Through several marriages with the Taylor family of Norfolk and visits to Baltimore, the silver at Eyre Hall includes pieces from both locations. John Eyre married Ann Upshur in 1800 and, over the next quarter century, the couple acquired silver in Baltimore along with furniture and other decorative arts.

The earliest Baltimore-made silver in the collection comprises a set of 13 tablespoons marked by Charles Louis Boehme and is engraved with the letter "E." Boehme

worked in Baltimore from 1799 to 1814 and was a very prolific silversmith (Cat. 40). There are only two other early Baltimore pieces from this period in the collection: two spoons marked by Hosea Wilson dating to 1815 and engraved with the letter "T," most likely for Taylor (Cat. 41). There are no other objects by early Baltimore silversmiths of the federal period still in the collection.

The most prolific nineteenth-century Baltimore silversmith was undoubtedly Samuel Kirk. Kirk arrived in Baltimore in 1815; in partnership with John Smith until 1820, he then struck out on his own. His firm was in business for the next 160 years. A tea service marked by Samuel Kirk and dating to 1824–29 comprises a teapot, cream pot, waste bowl, and sugar basin. They all have a finial of a Chinese man, reflecting the continuing taste for chinoiserie and fascination with the Orient that had been ever popular since the eighteenth century. The service is engraved with the initials "GTE" for Grace Eyre Taylor. It would have been engraved with her initials long after the period in which it was made, as she married in 1897 (Cat. 42). An unmarked nutmeg grater dating to the 1830s is engraved with the initials "MAT" (Cat. 43). Stylistically, it appears to resemble a Baltimore-made piece. Nutmeg was a very expensive spice,

42
Tea Service

Samuel Kirk and Son
Baltimore, 1824–29
Silver
Teapot H. 8 in., sugar basin H. 6 in., cream pot H. 6⅜ in.,
waste bowl H. 4⅞ in.

43
Nutmeg Grater

Unmarked
American, ca. 1830
Silver
L. 2⅞ in.

and having a silver implement solely for the purpose of grating was quite extravagant. A covered pitcher and stand—engraved "Robert Taylor Sr. to his Grandson W. L. Eyre—were also made in 1829 by Samuel Kirk. The decoration is a precursor to the popular allover repoussé-style decoration using ornate milled bands. Like the tea service described above, the pitcher is surmounted by a finial of a Chinese man (Cat. 44). William Eyre had married Mary Savage in 1828 and lived his entire life at Eyreville. Two small contemporary salvers marked by Samuel Kirk round out the earlier Baltimore material (Cat. 45).

John Eyre and William L. Eyre and their respective wives had Philadelphia connections, and the collection of surviving silver reflects that bond. Ann Upshur had been in boarding school in Philadelphia in the 1790s, and Mary Savage's brother lived in Philadelphia much of his life. Two footed salvers marked by Edward Lownes of Philadelphia date to around 1815 and are engraved with the initials "JA" (Cat. 46). Another pair of salvers engraved with the initials "JAE" for John and Ann Eyre and marked by silversmiths Joseph and Nathaniel Richardson predate the ones by Lownes; they date to ca. 1785 and are still in the family but not at Eyre Hall (Cat. 47 and Fig. 217). These were engraved at a later date as John and Ann did not marry until 1800. Other Philadelphia pieces in the collection are a basket marked by Bailey and Kitchen (active 1832–48) and engraved with the initials "WME" for William Littleton and Mary Savage Eyre and a four-piece coffee and tea service by Joseph Lownes engraved with the letter "E" and dating to ca. 1815 (Cat. 48 and Cat. 49). A swinging kettle marked by Bailey and Company of Philadelphia and dating to 1848–78

44
Pitcher and Stand

Samuel Kirk and Son
Baltimore, 1829
Silver
Pitcher H. 10¼ in., stand Dia. 8⅛ in.

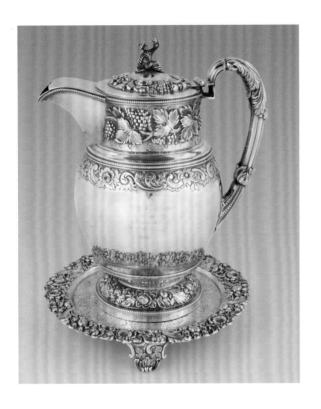

45
Salver

Samuel Kirk and Son
Baltimore, ca. 1925
Silver
Dia. 10³⁄₁₆ in.

46
Pair of Salvers

Edward Lownes
Philadelphia, ca. 1815
Silver
Dia. 8 in.

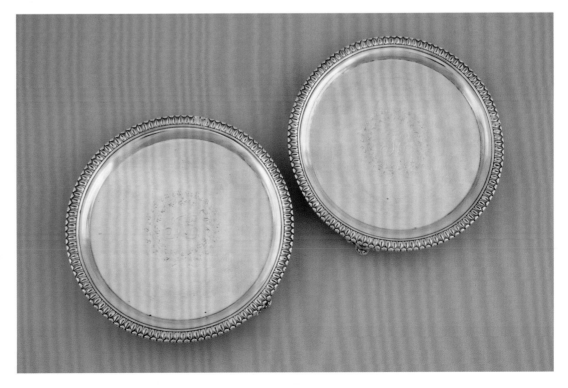

47
Salver

Joseph and Nathaniel Richardson
Philadelphia, ca. 1785
Silver
Diam. 9¼ in.

Fig. 217. Detail of "JAE"
monogram, Cat. 47.

is matched with the set by Samuel Kirk, obviously a later addition (Cat. 50). It is also engraved with the initials "GTE" for Grace Eyre Taylor.

Most of the existing flatware today at Eyre Hall is part of a large set of "King's pattern" dinner and dessert forks marked by F. Thibault of Philadelphia and dating to ca. 1810–36 (Cat. 51 and Fig. 218). The set comprises 17 table forks and 11 dessert forks all engraved with the letter "E." Eleven tablespoons marked Thibault & Brothers and dating ca. 1810–37 are also in the collection and are engraved with the initials "WME" for William L. Eyre and his wife Mary (Cat. 52).

Norfolk-made silver at Eyre Hall is almost exclusively flatware, with the exception of two beakers marked by Matthew Cluff (1780–1845) and engraved with the letter "T" (Cat. 53). Cluff worked in Norfolk as a silversmith, jeweler, and engraver from around 1802 to 1816.[19] A set of 11 tablespoons and a soup ladle marked by James Gaskins (1761–1827) are all engraved with the letter "E" (Cat. 54).

48
Basket

Bailey and Kitchen
Philadelphia, 1832–48
Silver
H. 9½ in. (top of handle), W. 11¼ in.

49
Tea Service

Joseph Lownes
Philadelphia, ca. 1815
Silver
Teapot H. 8½ in., W. 11 in., sugar basin H. 7½ in., cream pot H. 4¾ in., waste bowl H. 4⅜ in., Dia. 5½ in.

50
Teakettle, Stand, and Lamp

Bailey and Company
Philadelphia, 1848–78
Silver
H. 12¼ in., W. 9¾ in.

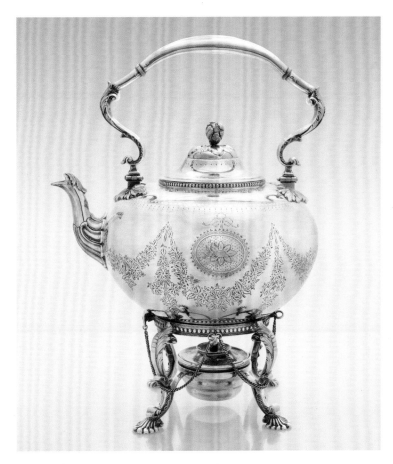

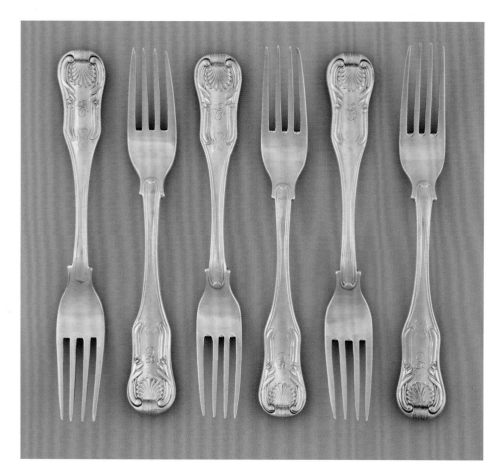

51
Table Forks

F. Thibault
Philadelphia, 1810–36
Silver
L. 8¾ in.

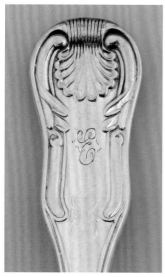

Fig. 218. Detail of the engraving, Cat. 51.

52
Tablespoons

Thibault & Brothers
Philadelphia, 1810–37
Silver
L. 9 in.

53
Pair of Beakers

Matthew Cluff
Norfolk, Virginia, 1802–16
Silver
H. 3⅜ in., W. 3¹⁄₁₆ in.

54
Tablespoons and Soup Ladle

James Gaskins
Norfolk, Virginia, 1770–76 or 1804–6
Silver
Tablespoons L. 8⅞ in., ladle L. 14¾ in.

Gaskins worked as a silversmith in Norfolk from 1770 to 1776 and again from 1804 to 1806.[20] Another ladle is marked by Joseph Clarico (1785–1828), as well as a teaspoon, and both are engraved with the letter "T" (Cat. 55 and Fig. 219). Clarico worked as a silversmith in Norfolk from 1813 to 1828.[21] The final piece of Norfolk silver is a small condiment ladle marked by George Ott (1770–1831) and engraved with the letter "T." Ott worked as a silversmith and jeweler in Norfolk from 1801 to 1830 (Cat. 56). He was in partnership with Matthew Cluff from 1802 to 1806.[22] The Eyres also owned a pair of sugar tongs marked by Cooke & White and engraved with the letter "E" (Cat. 57). Andrew White and William Cooke were in partnership as jewelers and watchmakers in Norfolk from 1829 to 1833.[23]

Among the earliest pieces of Virginia silver at Eyre Hall are spoons that were made by James Geddy (1731–1807), a silversmith working in Williamsburg in the 1770s (Cat. 58).[24] Eight teaspoons are engraved with the letter "E." These

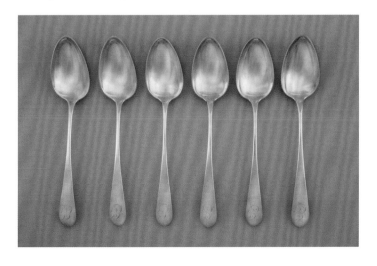

55
Soup Ladle and Teaspoons

Joseph Clarico
Norfolk, Virginia, 1813–28
Silver
Ladle L. 14 in., teaspoons L. 5⅝ in.

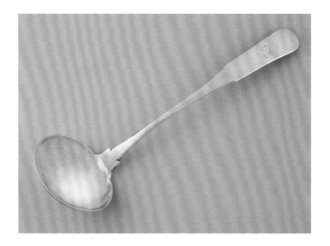

Fig. 219. Detail of the "T" engraving on the spoons, Cat. 55.

56
Condiment Ladle

George Ott
Norfolk, Virginia, 1801–30
Silver
L. 4⅝ in.

57
Sugar Tongs

William Cooke and Andrew White
Norfolk, Virginia, 1829–33
Silver
L. 6 in.

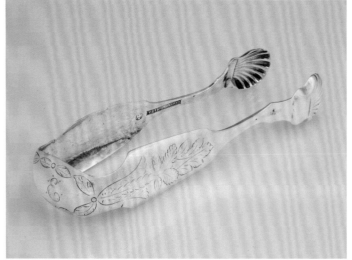

58
Teaspoons

John Geddy
Williamsburg, Virginia, 1760–70
Silver
L. 5⅜ in.

59
Galleried Tray

Goldsmiths & Silversmiths Company
London, 1880-98
Silver
L. 24 in., W. 17¼ in., H. 3¼ in.

could have been purchased by Severn on one of his many trips to Williamsburg to attend meetings of the House of Burgesses, though there is no documentation for them.

Although silver purchases declined greatly after the Civil War, they continued to persist into the twentieth century. A large galleried tray marked by the Goldsmiths & Silversmiths Company, 112 Regent Street London, dates to 1880-98 and is engraved with a large letter "E" (Cat. 59). There is a large fish platter of ca. 1894–1910 marked by silversmiths Jacobi & Jenkins of Baltimore and engraved with the initials "GET" for Grace Eyre Taylor (Cat. 60). Margaret Eyre Taylor Baldwin had her initials "MTE" engraved on a salver marked by Samuel Kirk & Son that dates to ca. 1925.

Margaret Parker Eyre appears in the Samuel Kirk order books as "Mrs. Severn Eyre" when she purchased a cast oval edge waiter in 1898. She is listed as living at 223 W. Monument Street in Baltimore.[25] Severn and Margaret undoubtedly purchased more silver from the Kirk shop, but the record books tend to be spotty. The Eyres had lived at this location since 1889, and, after Margaret's death in 1899, Severn remained at the address until 1903 or 1904. It

Fish Platter

Jacobi & Jenkins
Baltimore, ca. 1894–1910
Silver
L. 22 in., W. 10½ in.

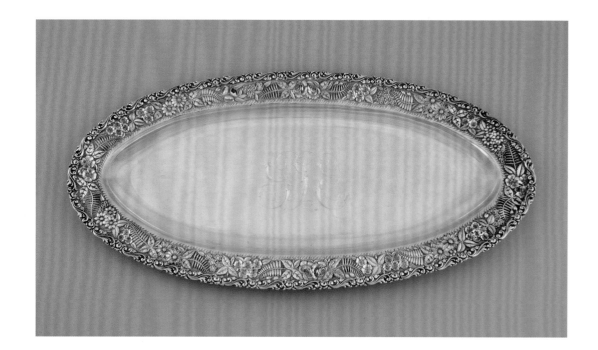

61

Footed Salver

William and Robert Peaston
London, 1759–60
Silver
Dia. 15¼ in.

is possible that this waiter was purchased to celebrate the birth of Margaret Eyre Taylor Baldwin. The whereabouts of the waiter are now unknown.

Perhaps unusually for a house with plenty of eighteenth-century material already in its cupboards, there are several pieces of eighteenth-century silver that seem to have been acquired at a much later point. A large salver dating to 1759/60 and marked by William and Robert Peaston was apparently given to Grace Eyre's husband Richard Baker Taylor by a gentleman who could not pay his legal bills (Cat. 61).[26] A set of four candlesticks marked by John Carter and dating to 1771/72 are also in this category (Cat. 62). They are still used at Eyre Hall today for entertaining. A rococo coffeepot marked by Daniel Smith and Robert Sharp dating to 1770/71 is engraved with the initials "GTE" for Grace Eyre Taylor, who obviously had the engraving done over a century after the pot's original manufacture (Cat. 63). The Eyres had very conservative values, and the surviving pieces are indicative of this. In the Colonial Revival period post-1876, it is not surprising that an item like this coffeepot would be embraced as a continuation of the original stylistic qualities of the material that had always been there.

62
Candlestick (One of Four)

John Carter
London, 1771–72
Silver
H. 12⅝ in.

63
Coffeepot

Daniel Smith and Robert Sharp
London, 1770–71
Silver
H. 13 in.

NOTES

1. Will of Bridget Foxcroft, January 13, 1704, Northampton County Orders, Wills, etc., No. 14, 1698–1710, 189.
2. John D. Davis, *English Silver at Williamsburg* (Williamsburg, Va.: Colonial Williamsburg Foundation, 1976), 2.
3. Private and public silver collections in Maryland and Virginia examined by the author.
4. Silver at Shirley Plantation. Inventory of the estate of Charles Hill Carter, Jr., 2004. Material provided to the author by Charles Carter, August 15, 2018.
5. Kathryn C. Buhler, *Mount Vernon Silver* (Mount Vernon, Va.: The Mount Vernon Ladies Association of the Union, 1957), 24.
6. Davis, *English Silver at Williamsburg*, 136.
7. Jennifer Goldsborough, *Silver in Maryland* (Baltimore: Maryland Center for History and Culture, 1983), 1.
8. Inventory of the estate of Severn Eyre (d. 1773), February 27, 1774, Northampton County Wills & Inventories, No. 25, 1772–1777, 392; Fanny

Fielding [pseud.], "Southern Homesteads. Eyre Hall," *The Land We Love* 3, no. 6 (October 1867): 508.
9. Inventory of the estate of Severn Eyre (d. 1728), August 14, 1728, Northampton County Wills, Deeds, etc., No. 26, 1725–1733, 151–54.
10. Inventory of the estate of Littleton Eyre, October 14, 1769, Northampton County Wills & Inventories, No. 24, 1766–1772, 225.
11. Will of Severn Eyre (d. 1728), February 28, 1728, Eyre Hall Family Papers, Virginia Historical Society, Richmond.
12. Will of Severn Eyre (d. 1773), March 15, 1769, Northampton County Wills & Inventories, No. 25, 1772–1777, 136.
13. Will of Littleton Eyre, May 21, 1787, Northampton County Wills & In[ventories], No. 28, 1788–1792, 135.
14. Will of John Eyre, February 21, 1855, Northampton County Wills, No. 39, 1854–1897, 22.
15. Will of Gertrude Harmanson, September 11,

1732, Northampton County Wills & Inventories, No. 18, 1733–1740, 285.
16. Lynda R. Heaton, "Littleton Waller Tazewell's Sketches of His Own Family 1823: Transcribed and Edited" (master's thesis, College of William and Mary, 1967), 52.
17. Davis, *English Silver at Williamsburg*, 132.
18. MESDA accession number 5794.5-6, Gift of DeCourcy E. McIntosh.
19. Catherine B. Hollan, *Virginia Silversmiths, Jewelers, Clock- and Watchmakers, 1607–1860: Their Lives and Marks* (McLean, Va.: Hollan Press, 2010), 155.
20. Hollan, *Virginia Silversmiths*, 306.
21. Hollan, *Virginia Silversmiths*, 148.
22. Hollan, *Virginia Silversmiths*, 580.
23. Hollan, *Virginia Silversmiths*, 171.
24. Hollan, *Virginia Silversmiths*, 318.
25. Samuel Kirk & Son, Inc. Papers, 1834–1979, MS 2720, H. Furlong Baldwin Library, Maryland Center for History and Culture, Baltimore.
26. Furlong Baldwin interview with the author, September 9, 2019.

64
"Morningstar" Punch Bowl

John Sutton
London, 1692–93
Silver
H. 6¼ in., W. 10¾ in.

One of the most spectacular and earliest silver punch bowls
with a Virginia history, the "Morningstar" bowl was won in a
horse race (according to family tradition), and was bequeathed
to Severn Eyre in 1704 by his relative Bridget Foxcroft. Although
it is unlikely that it was ever a prize in a race, it is extremely
important and one of only two non-ecclesiastical pieces of
seventeenth-century silver in Virginia.[1]

Dating to 1692, it is marked by London silversmith John
Sutton. Possessing a silver punch bowl of this size was indicative
of great wealth in the colonial era. Punch bowls—long popular as
a vessel in which to mix alcoholic beverages—were typically made
of tin-glazed earthenware such as delft and were imported from
England or Holland. Punch would have been made at table using
ingredients such as sugar, rinds of fruit, rum, and spices which
were available only to the well-off in this period.

65

Tankard

William Shaw and William Priest
London, 1754–55
Silver
H. 8½ in., W. 6¾ in.

Tankards were popular drinking vessels in both England and New England in the eighteenth century. This London example marked by William Shaw and William Priest is engraved with the crest of the Harmanson family and dates to 1754/55. Littleton Eyre married Bridget Harmanson in 1734, and this large piece likely came into their possession after their marriage. Lidded tankards were popular forms in England, but interestingly were rarely produced in the southern colonies and were much more popular in New England. They were especially effective in keeping insects and other vermin from entering a drinking vessel.

Fig. 220. Harmanson amorial, Cat. 65.

66
Two–Handled Cup

Thomas Whipham and Charles Wright
London, 1760–61
Silver
H. 8½ in., W. 11¾ in.

This exceptional "loving cup," marked by
London silversmiths Thomas Whipham
and Charles Wright in 1763/64, is
engraved with a spectacular reversed
mirror cipher or monogram with the
initials "SME" for Severn and Margaret
Taylor Eyre. This type of engraving was
very popular in the period, and it often
served as the only form of decoration—
as seen on this piece, as well as on the
pair of canns illustrated below (Cat. 68).
Severn and Margaret Eyre ordered several
pieces of silver in the 1760s for their
home at Eyre Hall. Two-handled cups of
this type were easily shared, especially for
communal toasts and other gatherings.

67
Salver

Robert Abercrombie
London, 1746–47
Silver
Di. 11⅛ in.

This handsome salver, marked by Robert
Abercrombie of London in 1746/47,
relies on the engraved armorial device of
the Harmanson family as its only form
of decoration. Salvers were used to serve
liquids and keep them from damaging
delicate tabletops. The pie-crust edge can
also be seen in furniture of the period.
Like the tankard illustrated above (cat.
65), it most likely came to Eyre Hall at a
later date, as Littleton Eyre and Bridget
Harmanson married in 1734.

68

Pair of Canns

Thomas Whipham and Charles Wright
London, 1762–63
Silver
H. 5 1/16 in., W. 5 in.

Canns or mugs were the drinking vessels of the eighteenth
century. Made from pewter or silver, they came in half pint,
pint, and quart sizes. They were the most common form of
silver drinking vessel in the eighteenth century. Canns were
usually made in pairs and were used by both men and women
to drink alcoholic beverages. This pair of canns was marked by
London silversmiths Thomas Whipham and Charles Wright in
1762/63 and engraved "SME," with a mirror cipher for Severn
and Margaret Taylor Eyre.

Fig. 221. Detail of the reversed cipher
"SME" monogram, Cat. 68.

Fig. 222. Detail of the
eagle thumbpiece, Cat. 69.

Fig. 223. Touchmark of
Nathaniel Morse, Cat. 69.

69

Tankard

Nathaniel Morse (1676–1748)
Boston, ca. 1715
Silver
H. 7¾ in., W. 8¾ in.

Of all the silver pieces extant at Eyre Hall today, perhaps none is more mysterious than the tankard marked by eighteenth-century Boston silversmith Nathaniel Morse. Of very large proportions, the tankard bears an eagle thumbpiece and no traceable engraving or armorial other than rubbed initials on the handle. Dating to ca. 1715, the tankard has no known association with the Eyre family; indeed, there is no information about its acquisition or whether it is one of the several tankards mentioned in family wills and inventories. It might have been acquired in trade or as repayment of a loan, as Morse appears to have had credit issues during his career. It is

unlikely we will ever know the origin of this particular piece.[2]

Not only is it highly unusual for such a piece to be found in a southern context, but the piece itself is also extremely rare. Morse apprenticed under Boston silversmith John Coney (1655–1722). He is known to have made only three other tankards that have been identified.[3] Two of them have identical cast thumbpieces. One is marked by Samuel Vernon (1683–1737) from Newport and is in the collection of the Metropolitan Museum of Art in New York, while the other is at the Museum of Fine Arts in Boston.

70

Cruet Set

William Abdy
London, 1784–85
Silver, glass
H. 10¼ in., W. 7½ in.

This cruet stand was marked by William Abdy of London
in 1784/85. Engraved with the letter "E," it is an example of
how English silver continued to be acquired by American
families even after the Revolution. Cruet stands were ingenious
contraptions that allowed many different condiments to be
grouped together and passed around the table. This extremely
elegant neoclassical example contrasts with the earlier rococo
casters in the collection.

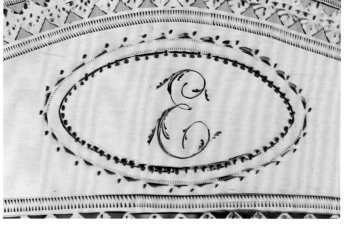

Fig. 224. Detail of the
cartouche "E," Cat. 70.

NOTES

1. James C. Kelly and Barbara Clark Smith,
   *Jamestown, Québec, Santa Fe: Three North American
   Beginnings* (Washington, D.C.: Smithsonian
   Institution, 2007), 88–89.

2. Frances Gruber Safford, "Colonial Silver in the
   American Wing," *The Metropolitan Museum of Art
   Bulletin* 41, no. 1 (1983): 31.

3. Patricia E. Kane, *Colonial Massachusetts Silversmiths
   and Jewelers* (New Haven: Yale University Press,
   1998), 704.

Ceramics

ROBERT HUNTER AND
ANGELIKA R. KUETTNER

Fig. 225. Punch Bowl,
1730–50.
Cat. 82

CERAMICS HAVE ALWAYS HELD A SPECIAL PLACE among the trappings of material life. Art critic Garth Clark maintains that, next to our underwear, ceramics are the most personal articles in our lives. Most of us experience that firsthand in our modern daily routines, relying upon fired clay objects for morning hygiene, the first sip of hot coffee, right through to serving the last meal of the day. For the ancestral residents of Eyre Hall, ceramics had much the same tactile engagement in household practices, from the chamber pots, tea bowls, and drinking cups, to the dessert plates and wash basins.

In addition to their aesthetic appeal, ceramics and their symbolic meanings have been studied in the context of colonial American history to understand social customs, fashion trends, and relative differences in economic and social status. The magnificent blue-and-white Chinese porcelain punch bowl, which has presided over Eyre Hall's family gatherings since the mid-1700s, was the ultimate eighteenth-century power object, evoking the formidable dragon of Asian mythology (Fig. 225). To this day, the Chinese dragon remains emblematic of the exotic Far East, good fortune, power, and nobility.

Archaeology reminds us that the vast majority of ceramics are destined for breakage and disposal. As the late archaeologist Ivor Noël Hume noted, only a few select ceramics will have that "keep me factor" and endure the passage of time.[1] As a consequence, to fully understand the acquisition, function, and ultimately the ownership of these ceramics, archaeological studies are likely to provide the best framework for viewing the significance of the ceramics history of the Eyre Hall household from the late seventeenth century until the present day. For the Chesapeake region, we can draw upon the pioneering studies in the Virginia Tidewater at Jamestown and Williamsburg and subsequently at nearly every great plantation home from Monticello to Mount Vernon for comparative data.[2]

CERAMICS IN THE SEVENTEENTH CENTURY

The ceramics assemblages from those earliest colonial sites reflect the cosmopolitan nature of seventeenth-century economies and trade networks. Households had access to English, Dutch, Portuguese, and Spanish tin-enameled wares, German and French stonewares, Italian slipwares, and English and Dutch coarse earthenware.[3] Even Chinese porcelains found their way to the wealthier Virginia households via both the English and Dutch trade routes. By the 1620s, coarse earthenware was being produced in Jamestown to augment the importation of European products.

The history of the Eyre family on the Eastern Shore of Virginia begins with Thomas Eyre I, who settled on land at the southernmost tip of Northampton County by the early 1640s and perhaps even earlier. We have a hint into the probable makeup of the ceramic types that the seventeenth-century Eyre family would have used from findings at ongoing archaeological excavations of a nearby property on Eyreville Neck.[4] Thought to be the oldest English settlement on the Eastern Shore and associated with Englishman John Howe, who came to Virginia in 1621, these excavations are in their preliminary stages. Archaeologists from the Virginia Department of Historic Resources (VDHR) have found on the property the remnants of a post-in-the-ground structure along with associated ceramics deposits. The composition of that rich ceramic assemblage mirrors those found in other early Chesapeake sites, including examples of coarse earthenware manufactured in Jamestown in the 1630s.

Little documentation exists of the actual ceramic world of the Eyre families for the first half of the eighteenth century. In the inventory of Thomas Eyre III (d. 1719) taken on October 28, 1719 we have the vaguest of entries listing a "parcel Dutch ware . . . 0. 5. 0," and a "parcel Earthen ware . . . 0. 3. 6."[5] The "Dutch ware" most likely would have been the blue-and-white delft manufactured by English potters, and the "parcel Earthen ware" may have included Staffordshire slipwares, a ceramic type also in common circulation in the period.

A decade later—on August 14, 1728—the inventory of the estate of Severn Eyre, Thomas III's older brother, offers slightly more specificity to the ceramics. The entry "9 pieces of blue & white Earthen ware . . . 4. 0" supports the presence of the ubiquitous English delft used throughout Anglo-America at this time, previously described as "Dutch ware" in Severn's father's estate. The listing of "1 Stone Jugg & Stone butter pot . . . 6. 6" refers to utilitarian items common for the storage of oils and foodstuffs and probably also of English origin, although, by that time, such objects were being produced in Yorktown, Virginia.[6] Likewise, the "1 Earthen Bason . . . 0. 6" might have been either of Yorktown or English manufacture.[7]

CERAMICS IN THE EYRE HALL HOUSEHOLD, 1759–1810

Members of the Eyre family were clearly active participants in what scholars have termed "the consumer revolution"— defined by the surge in interest for owning and displaying the latest and most fashionable goods.[8] By the middle of the eighteenth century, Anglo-American dining and drinking practices had evolved into highly regimented rituals within affluent households.[9] The Staffordshire ceramic industry responded to these formalized practices, introducing new ceramics types and forms and exporting them throughout the Anglo-American world.[10] Consumer competition for the up-to-the-minute styles in dinnerwares and tea services was at an all-time high.

Although a wide range of ceramic types—earthenware, stoneware, and porcelain—was introduced, in a myriad of colors and patterns, it was chinoiserie—the fascination with all things of Chinese design—that remained the single most influential aesthetic in ceramics. And while British imitations of Chinese ceramics were popular, Chinese porcelain remained the de facto choice for dining and tea or punch drinking for those elite households who could afford it.[11]

Information about the early ceramics at Eyre Hall derives from three sources. The first is the heirloom ceramics: those highly valued Chinese porcelains selected by successive generations of the Eyre family, some of which continue to be of service today (Cat. 71). The second is a collection of fragmentary vessels found in archaeological investigations under the flooring of the east porch vestibule of the original Eyre Hall house dating to post-1755. The large number of fairly complete mid- to late eighteenth-century ceramics that were found suggests an intentional disposal, perhaps a cupboard cleaning, most likely related to the architectural improvements made to the dining room and kitchen in the 1805–7 period.[12] Some of the more complete examples are shown in the cupboard (Cat. 72). The third and final source of information is the large body of comparative ceramic findings from archaeological and documentary research throughout the colonial Chesapeake—extensive resources that allow us to extrapolate about the overall nature and composition of the Eyre Hall households.

As a caveat, no information currently exists about the ceramics that would have been used by the enslaved residents of Eyre Hall. Generally, such information comes from archaeological excavations associated with the spaces used by enslaved families—kitchen, outbuilding garrets, and purpose-built slave quarters. Archaeology tells us that, while those families sometimes were permitted cast-offs from the main household, more often they were provided the cheapest ceramics available by their white masters.

The discussion that follows groups the ceramic evidence by functional category: Kitchen Food Storage and Preparation, Dining, Tea Drinking, and Punch Drinking. These categories reflect not only ceramic usage,

71
China Cupboard

This cupboard in the passage at Eyre Hall contains
surviving examples of Chinese porcelain including
dinnerwares and an assortment of eighteenth-century
punch bowls. These were items of conspicuous display,
being the most expensive of eighteenth-century ceramics
available to the Chesapeake consumer.

China and Glass Cupboard

Staged for display, this cupboard in Eyre Hall's east
vestibule contains ceramic and glass objects recovered from
underneath the north porch floor, which was excavated by
archaeologists from Colonial Williamsburg in 2000. The
top and bottom shelves have a variety of Chinese porcelain
tewares. The shelf second from the top has a miscellany of
eighteenth-century British earthenwares and stonewares.

but also were associated with specific behavior rituals, furniture forms, and even architectural choices in a given household.

KITCHEN FOOD STORAGE AND PREPARATION

The preparation, cooking, and storage of household foodstuffs relied on a variety of specialized ceramics forms, most of which were somewhat coarse earthenware and durable stoneware jars and jugs. In the absence of archaeological information, we have only the most limited suggestion of the utilitarian ceramics that were used at Eyre Hall. The 1769 inventory of Littleton Eyre lists "16 jugs with some Oils" and "4 earthenware porringers." These jugs were most like salt-glazed stoneware of British origin.[13] The slightly later inventory for Severn Eyre in 1774 specifically lists "11 stone Butter and Pickle Potts," also most likely of British origin.

DINING

In the eighteenth century, large ceramic dinner services were reserved for the affluent classes. The de facto choice for the American elite were services of Chinese export porcelain that could include upward of 250 to 350 pieces and were composed of dinner plates, supper plates, graduated serving dishes, soup tureens, and sauce tureens. As alternatives, and usually quite a bit more affordable, the Staffordshire industry began producing large dinner services in the mid-eighteenth century, first in white salt-glazed stoneware, and later refined earthenwares. The purchase of dinner services often corresponded to life events or economic shifts in households—marriage, architectural improvements, or a sudden influx of wealth, for example.[14] The acquisition of the four major services identified in the Eyre household seems to correspond to such events.

The 1769 inventory of Littleton Eyre, which is the first to record dining-related ceramics at Eyre Hall, lists "46 earthenware plates." If we can rely on the vagaries of the inventory process, those were earthenware dinner plates that were used in conjunction with 59 pewter plates and 24 pewter dishes. Unfortunately, there is no evidence to indicate whether these plates were English delft, white salt-glazed stoneware, or perhaps lead-glazed tortoise-type plates—all three coexisted at the time. There is certainly no mention of the more desirable "China," the code for Chinese porcelain. Of special interest, however, is the listing of the "6 Scallop Shells, & 4 pickle Do." Based on archaeological and inventory findings from Williamsburg, these were most likely highly fashionable English, soft-paste porcelain accoutrements: specialized items related to the mid-century interest in serving pickled "sweetmeats."[15]

The inventory for Severn Eyre taken in 1774 suggests that two sets of very fashionable dinnerware were acquired for the household after Littleton's death. The first is a group of blue-and-white Chinese porcelain and the second consists of the so-called "imari"-type decoration, having the addition of red enamel over the blue. The Chinese porcelain dinner service was a relatively small one, with only 31 individual objects listed: "1 china Tereen and Dish 50/ . . . 13 blue & white china plates . . . 22/6, 7 enamelled Do 15/ . . . 1 Dish 5/ . . . 4.12. 6."[16] The blue-and-white dish shown in Cat. 73 most likely represents the dish listed with the "china Tereen." Both types of decoration seem to have coexisted in most of the upper-level Chesapeake households of this period.

Also listed in the inventory is a set of "Queens china." "Queensware"—more commonly known today as creamware—was a product popularized by Josiah Wedgwood, who had made a special tea service for Britain's Queen Charlotte in 1767. The presence of both services is in keeping with the most fashionable Virginia households of the period.[17] The queensware service consisted of:

Dish

Jingdezhen, China, ca. 1760–70
Hard-paste porcelain
L. 17½ in.

74

Queensware Fragments

Fragments of queensware or cream-colored earthenware that had been used by the Eyres between 1770 and 1800 before being discarded and thrown in a rubbish pile beneath the east porch. Left to right: enameled decorated cup fragment, beaded edge saucer, and dinner plate.

13 Queen's china dishes.	.1.	2.	6
35 Queen's china Plates 12/6.	.0.	12.	6
2 fruit Dishes and 1 Butter boat 1/3.	.0.	1.	3[18]

Wedgwood's inexpensive, mass-produced creamware, perhaps the most studied British ceramic type of the eighteenth century, was an instant must-have acquisition for Chesapeake's upper classes.[19] It was the first truly modern consumer ceramic. Although initially marketed to the elite, it quickly turned into a product for the masses, ultimately becoming the cheapest ceramic type available, and it continued to be made in some form well into the nineteenth century. As a result, fragments of creamware—from the time of its introduction into the Chesapeake in 1769 until the nineteenth century—soon spread like a volcanic ash across a wide range of archaeological contexts.

Based on the valuations of the inventory taker, the Chinese porcelain was roughly four times more valuable or costly than the "queensware," a ratio that generally holds

Porcelain Service

Jingdezhen, China, ca. 1800–10
Hard-paste porcelain
H. of tureen 10¾ in.

Probably ordered around the time of the marriage of John Eyre to Ann Upshur in 1800. The porcelain service is decorated in sepia, brown, and gold with a faux gadroon and floral ribbon border that was popular at the time and is found on several services made for Philadelphia residents. A service bearing the initials of John and Rebecca Simms of Philadelphia was ordered by them around 1800 and bears the same border, but includes the tomb of George Washington as the central decorative motif of each piece. Each item in John and Ann Eyre's service bears an encircled script "E" that was probably originally gilt, but after many years of use now only reveals the iron red used as a base color for the gold lettering. The present owner of Eyre Hall, Furlong Baldwin, recalls many family dinners and special holiday meals in which the "brown china," as this service was known, graced the table of his family home.

Basket and Stand

Jingdezhen, China, ca. 1800–10
Hard-paste porcelain
H. 8⅜ in., L. 9 in.

This openwork basket and stand is part of the "brown china" service illustrated in Cat. 75. Referred to as a fruit or cake basket in the period, the form was often part of the dessert service and can be seen filled with berries in late eighteenth- and early nineteenth-century American still-life paintings.

Sauce Tureen and Stand

Jingdezhen, China, ca. 1800–10
Hard-paste porcelain
H. 5⅜ in.

Part of the Eyre family Chinese porcelain service illustrated in Cat. 75. The "E" monogram is repeated on the body, cover, and stand.

true for similar assessments for this period. Although the term "Queens china" implies a porcelain body, it was actually earthenware, prone to chipping, staining, and breakage. Unlike porcelain, creamware was a product destined to get "used up" and discarded. A single dinner plate in the so-called "Royal Shape" that was recovered in the archaeological investigations may be the sole surviving representative of the Eyre Hall queensware service (Cat. 74).

Not long after their marriage in 1800, John Eyre and Ann Upshur acquired a new Chinese porcelain dinner service; the couple's purchase coincided with extensive house renovations in 1806–7, which added a full second story and housekeeper's apartment to the earlier dining room (Cat. 75). This service had an extensive range of forms from sauceboats to covered tureens, and was custom-decorated in the neoclassical taste with orange and brown swags with

78
Oblong Dishes

Jingdezhen, China, ca. 1820
Hard-paste porcelain
L. 18 in.

These are just three dishes of an extensive
service of Chinese porcelain in the
"Canton" pattern, as it is often called
by collectors today. The blue-and-white
porcelain pattern was extremely popular,
and this particular service had many
pieces added in the nineteenth century.
According to family lore, these dishes
were used in the twentieth century as
receptacles for gathering table scraps that
were fed to the 19-year-old family dog.

the cipher "E" enameled on each piece. Pieces that survive
from that service include serving dishes, dinner and dessert
plates, covered tureens, covered vegetable dishes, openwork
baskets, and sauce tureens (Cat. 76 and Cat. 77).

John and Ann purchased another porcelain dinner
service probably after 1810 or so. Documented by
surviving examples, this service is an underglaze decorated
blue-and-white porcelain commonly referred to as Canton
ware, the most popular imported porcelain of the 1790s
to 1835 period.[20] A few dishes and plates from this service
are still used and displayed in the household (Cat. 78).
This ware was exported to American ports through
direct trade with China after the American Revolution.[21]
American merchants supplied upper-level households
from Portsmouth, New Hampshire, to Charleston, South
Carolina, and it could be found in nearly every home of
Virginia's gentry.[22]

One surviving creamware piece—an earthenware dish
with simple blue-line decoration that bears the transfer-
printed cipher "TLS"—offers surprising evidence of an
otherwise undocumented dinner service that came into the
Eyre family (Cat. 79 and Fig. 226). This English-made dish
would have been part of a much larger customized service

for Thomas Littleton Savage. We have little additional
information about the context for the dinner service, but at
the present time this dish is the only extant example from
a transfer-printed pearlware service made for a Virginia
family, which intermarried with the Eyres in the nineteenth
century.[23]

TEA DRINKING

Like many other social rituals of the period, the experience
of taking tea was a custom that spread from England to
her American colonies. Tea was introduced into English
society in the mid-seventeenth century, reached a pinnacle
of formalization in the mid-eighteenth century, and
subsequently declined as an elaborate ritual around the
turn of the nineteenth century. The exact date of the
introduction of tea to America remains somewhat cloudy.
Some have suggested that it may have first appeared in the
Dutch settlements of New Amsterdam as early as the mid-
seventeenth century. Most writers refer to the 1690s New
England advertisements for its sale in that region.

Silver teapots began to appear in 1690s inventories, a
time when some of the earliest British-made ceramic teapots

Large Dish

Staffordshire, England, ca. 1810
Lead-glazed earthenware
L. 14¾ in.

Although extensively spotted with food stains, this pearlware dish is an extremely important survival. In addition to a band of blue painted around the rim, the dish bears a transfer-printed cypher "TLS"—most likely for Thomas Littleton Savage—in serif block capital letters. It seems to be the only surviving example of a bespoke dinner service decorated with the initials. Archaeology reveals only a few rare examples of British ceramics transfer-printed with the initials of early Americans, including a creamware service owned by Philip and Ann Barraud of Williamsburg and Norfolk. To this day, the piece continues to grace the Eyre Hall dining table as a much-used and well-loved platter.

Fig. 226. Detail of the "TLS" cypher, Cat. 79.

also arrived in America. After 1720, teapots are found in archaeological assemblages throughout North America. The taking of tea, along with all its accoutrements, has been the subject of numerous social history studies.[24] One could ignore the ceramics and still see that tea drinking was an important activity for the Eyres in the eighteenth century by the presence in estate inventories of silver teapots, a "Mahoggony tea board," and a tea table. Corresponding archaeological evidence reinforces the important role of tea taking at Eyre Hall. The 1769 inventory of Littleton Eyre lists "7 Tea potts, 7 milk Do., 13 Coffee Cups and Saucers Earthen Sugar Dish, 20 tea cups and saucers." The 1774 inventory of Severn Eyre is much more specific and lists:

½ dozen large pint Cups and Saucers.	.1.	5.	0
10 Cups and 9 white china Saucers.	.0.	10.	0
12 Cups & Saucers 12/6 ½ Doz. large Do 10/.	.1.	2.	6
½ Dozen Coffee Cups 11 Saucers.[25]			

Archaeologists recovered a large number of Chinese porcelain tearwares, including 23 tea bowls, nine handled cups, and 40 saucers, representing almost a dozen different patterns. Some of the more complete examples of those tearwares are illustrated in Cat. 72. At least five of the patterns are standard blue-and-white chinoiserie, and at least another three are decorated in polychrome enamels.

In addition to the extensive evidence for Chinese porcelain tearwares, of special interest are two fragmentary

80

Teapot Fragments

Possibly Leeds Pottery, Yorkshire, or Staffordshire, England, ca. 1770–80
Lead-glazed earthenware

Intact examples of plain creamware teapots are today rare survivals above ground, but must have been much more prevalent in the period, based on archaeological evidence, newspaper advertisements, and trade catalogues. Closely matching the style of terminals illustrated in the pattern books printed by the Leeds Pottery, these fragments may be the product of that manufactory.

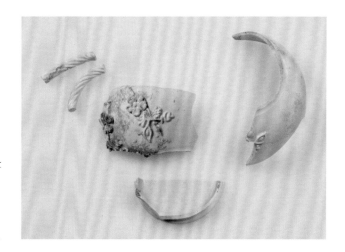

81

Teapot Fragments

Liverpool, England, ca. 1780
Lead-glazed earthenware

These fragments are from a creamware teapot that reflected the pro-Revolutionary stance of the Eyre family during the American Revolution. One side bears a transfer-printed portrait of Benjamin Franklin clad in his famous beaver-skin hat, above a banner with the words "BENJ: FRANKLIN / Born at Boston in New England / 07 Jan 1706 / L.L.D. / F.R.S." The transfer-printed decoration was derived from a French etching published in 1777 by Augustin de Saint-Aubin after an original drawing by Charles Nicolas Cochin the Younger. The etching was published in France and subsequently copied and published numerous times in the American colonies. The opposite side of the teapot is decorated with a transfer print of the trumpeting Angel of Fame riding on clouds, all within a late rococo cartouche that turns up on other creamware fragments found in American contexts. While punch bowls and straight-sided mugs printed with the same portrait of Franklin survive intact and have been found in archaeological contexts, this is the only example currently known of a teapot bearing the Franklin transfer print and the only creamware piece that includes the Franklin portrait with the Angel of Fame on the same object.

Fig. 227. Punch bowl, Liverpool, England, ca. 1780, lead-glazed earthenware, Dia. 9³⁄₁₆ in. This punch bowl bears the same transfer print of Benjamin Franklin as the teapot fragments seen in Cat. 81.

creamware teapots that were recovered from beneath the porch.[26]

The first is characterized by a globular body with applied floral sprigging and, most distinctively, an extruded rope-twist handle (Cat. 80). The type was made in the 1765–75 period by various manufacturers in Staffordshire and Yorkshire, but is most often associated with the Leeds Pottery. Although no mention is made of this specific vessel in the 1774 inventory, its existence confirms that fashionable "queensware" teawares were also used by the household in tandem with the dinnerware.

The second fragmentary creamware teapot is a highly important example of a previously undocumented form associated with the transfer print of an American historical figure (Cat. 81). Bearing the printed portrait of Benjamin Franklin, the teapot was produced during the time of the American Revolution by the British potters taking advantage of American consumers' fervor for patriotic objects.[27] While examples of Franklin's portrait are found on creamware punch bowls and tankards, the Eyre Hall teapot is the only example of this form to have this important American image (Fig. 227).

PUNCH DRINKING

The Virginia gentry are famously known to have enjoyed a variety of alcoholic drinks. Beer, fine imported wines, and champagnes filled their cellars, along with an array of distilled spirits. However, it was the concoction known as "punch" that was imbibed in huge quantities by the Virginia elite—so much so that a specific ceramics form was created. Punch seems to have been introduced into England from India around 1630 and consisted of various hot and cold mixtures of rum or brandy, fruit juices, sugar, and brandy.

Period prints, paintings, and other pictorial evidence indicate the everyday importance of punch. The punch bowl itself evokes images of eighteenth-century hospitality and conviviality better than any other single ceramic or glass object. It played an essential role in the ritual sharing of a strong alcoholic drink among the gentry and middling classes in Anglo-American society. Unlike tea, which could be enjoyed as a solitary experience, punch drinking was first and foremost a communal activity and generally restricted to masculine gatherings.

Business transactions, legal negotiations, gambling, singing, and general carousing were all acceptable behaviors.

The ownership of punch bowls was essential for an eighteenth-century gentleman—a key part of the household toolkit.[28] Peyton Randolph, a prominent citizen of Williamsburg, had "5 China Bowls" listed in his inventory of 1775 valued at £5. The 1771 inventory of Anthony Hay, owner of the Raleigh Tavern in Williamsburg, included among the tavern furnishings "16 China bowls" valued at roughly £1 apiece, a considerable sum relative to many of the tavern's furnishings.[29]

The Eyre family is distinguished by its ownership of perhaps early America's most important punch bowl—the 1692 silver "Morningstar" bowl made by John Sutton in London (see Cat. 64). The bowl remains a prominent fixture in the eighteenth-century inventories as "1 large silver Punch Bowl," which was valued at £30. Complementing this bowl, however, and perhaps used on a more practical basis, were a number of Chinese porcelain bowls that are listed in the eighteenth-century inventories and have survived to this day (see Cat. 71). The 1769 inventory of Littleton Eyre listed "3 China Punch Bowls."[30] No further information was given to associate the inventory list with the extant bowls. However, in the 1774 inventory of Severn Eyre, we see a hierarchy of values of four "china bowls" in the listing:

1 large china bowl 70/ 1 do 12/6.	.4. 2. 6
1 do 5/ 1 do 3/.	.0. 8. 0[31]

Multiple punch bowls, in varying capacities, were commonly listed in the inventories of wealthy Virginian

82

Punch Bowl

Jingdezhen, China, 1730–50
Hard-paste porcelain with underglaze blue decoration and overglaze red
enamels
Dia. 17½ in.

Massive Chinese punch bowl, lavishly decorated
in underglaze blue with a Chinese dragon
chasing pearls amidst billowing waves and coral.
In Chinese mythology, the dragon is usually
depicted as a creature that lives in the sea, as
shown here. Besides the underglaze blue, the
only other color that appears on the bowl is iron
red—used by the potter to highlight the dragon's
snarling mouth.

    The interior view of this large punch bowl
is illustrated in Fig. 225. The punch bowl was
the single most important ceramic object in
the households of Chesapeake's elite classes.
Chinese porcelain was the preferred material,
and most gentry households had several pieces
on hand. Not only did the expensive and highly
decorated bowls serve as objects of conspicuous
display, but the ritual drinking of the alcoholic
punch was integral to daily social interactions,
political debate, and economic transactions
throughout the eighteenth century.

83

Punch Bowls

A group of eighteenth-century Chinese
porcelain punch bowls that have survived
successive households at Eyre Hall. Dia. of
largest 9½ in. The so-called "imari"-decorated
red-and-blue bowls may be the examples
referenced in the 1774 inventory of Severn
Eyre. This type of decoration was often called
"burnt China" in colonial Chesapeake. The
other large bowl is decorated in the so-called
"Mandarin" style depicting Chinese figures in
an outdoor courtyard.

Punch Bowl

Jingdezhen, China, 1760–80
Hard-paste porcelain with overglaze polychrome enamels and gilding
Dia. 13⅝ in

consumers. Hosts needed to be well prepared for accommodating any number of guests, whether an intimate gathering of business acquaintances or a house full of family and friends. During his tenure at Mount Vernon, George Washington ordered punch bowls in as many as nine different sizes, from a half pint all the way up to two gallons.[32]

The Eyre households were well equipped to handle the most demanding punch drinkers. Without question, the large blue-and-white "dragon" bowl ranks as one of the most impressive surviving eighteenth-century punch bowls in an American domestic context (Cat. 82). British artist and satirist William Hogarth owned a similarly large bowl, not in Chinese porcelain but a blue-and-white delft imitation.[33] This bowl has cracks that were repaired with metal staples—not uncommon for such large and important household objects.[34] There are two other eighteenth-century punch bowls that have survived and are most likely indicated in the 1774 inventory (Cat. 83 and Cat. 84). The red-and-blue decorated bowls are often listed as "burnt" china in Chesapeake inventories and are not uncommon in archaeological contexts. The more elaborately decorated porcelain with Chinese figures and courtyard scenes are typically found only in heirloom collections.

NINETEENTH CENTURY AND BEYOND

In the nineteenth century, American consumers witnessed an explosion of ceramic wares from British ceramic manufacturers. With the advent of transfer-printing, an incredible range of decorated wares became available for rapidly changing tastes.[35] Full matching dinner services, tea and coffee wares, and even bathroom sets were produced in astonishingly large quantities and exported to nearly every corner of the world. Such services were easily within the price range of the expanding middle classes. Consumers had hundreds of patterns from which to choose, and archaeological evidence suggests that tablewares were continually replenished within many American households, owners seeking either to replace broken pieces or to acquire the latest styles as they became available.[36]

Unfortunately, for this period, there is virtually no information about what ceramics were purchased by John (d. 1855) or Severn (d. 1914), with the exception of several objects that have survived in the family. These include a wash basin and pitcher along with a toothbrush box and cover which were probably acquired in the 1830s (Cat. 85 and Cat. 86). This was a time when English manufacturers began to produce matching sets related to personal hygiene.

85

Wash Bowl and Pitcher

John & George Alcock (act. 1838–48)
Cobridge, Staffordshire, ca. 1830–40
Whiteware
H. 11⅛ in.

86

Toothbrush Box and Cover

John & William Ridgway (act. ca. 1814–30)
Shelton, Hanley, Staffordshire, ca. 1825–30
Whiteware
L. 12⅛ in.

The "India Temple" pattern made by John and William Ridgway of Staffordshire depicts a temple at the Chinese imperial summer palace, Bishu Shanzhuang ("Mountain Estate for Escaping the Heat").

Fig. 228. Detail of the mark identifying the India Temple pattern by John & William Ridgway on the bottom of the toothbrush box, Cat. 86.

Dish

William Taylor Copeland (1797–1868)
Staffordshire, England, ca. 1858
Whiteware
L. 13⅝ in.

This large serving dish would have been part of a much larger dinner service in excess of 125 pieces. The dish continues to be used for serving to this day.

The basin and pitcher are blue printed in the popular "Oriental" pattern, usually attributed to John and George Alcock of Staffordshire although reportedly produced by 19 different manufacturers.

The pattern name of the toothbrush box and cover, "India Temple," is printed on the bottom (Fig. 228). Made by Staffordshire potters John and William Ridgway in the 1820s and 1830s, the pattern shows the "Tower of the Supreme God," a temple at the summer palace of the Kangxi emperor (1654–1722) located some 100 miles north of Beijing in modern-day Chengde. These exotic Chinese landscapes were in huge demand by Western consumers, demonstrating the continued popularity of chinoiserie. Baltimore ceramics and glass merchant Matthew Smith (active 1803–32) ordered the India Temple pattern at least three times. On January 12, 1828, he wrote to his agents in Liverpool: "Herewith I hand an order for a few Articles. The India Temple pattern I want to match with what I have on hand and I wish Tureens and Covered Dishes. . . . This

I should like to receive as soon as practicable."[37] Smith is known to have supplied local consumers as well as other retail dealers, and, while no firm connection has been established with Eyre Hall, the possibility of one is intriguing.[38]

The final ceramic object of note from among the Eyre Hall heirlooms is a large earthenware dish printed in a purple arabesque design (Cat. 87). This particular shade of purple was very fashionable for American ceramic consumers on the eve of the America Civil War and has been found elsewhere in merchants' orders in Virginia.[39] Probably part of a very large dinner service, it serves as a reminder that, ultimately, successful ceramics are destined to be used and therefore potentially broken. The grounds of Eyre Hall are surely littered with the ceramics of the successive generations of families that have occupied the land. Archaeologists must await the opportunity to fully document the ceramics history of the property through the recovery of these discarded dishes.

NOTES

1. Ivor Noël Hume, *Early English Delftware from London and Virginia* (Williamsburg, Va.: Colonial Williamsburg Foundation, 1977), 14.
2. Ivor Noël Hume, *Pottery and Porcelain in Colonial Williamsburg's Archaeological* Collections (Williamsburg, Va.: Colonial Williamsburg Foundation, 1969), 31–33; Hume, *Excavations at Rosewell, Gloucester County, Virginia, 1957–1959* (Washington, D.C.: Smithsonian Institution, 1962); John C. Austin, ed., *British Delft at Williamsburg* (Williamsburg, Va.: Colonial Williamsburg Foundation in association with Jonathan Horne, 1994), especially the essay by Robert Hunter, "English Delft from Williamsburg's Archaeological Contexts," 24–29.

3. Beverly A. Straube, "European Ceramics in the New World: The Jamestown Example," in *Ceramics in America*, ed. Robert Hunter (Hanover, N.H.: University Press of New England for the Chipstone Foundation, 2001), 47–71; Martha W. McCartney, "George Thorpe's Inventory of 1624: Virginia's Earliest Known Appraisal," and Beverly Straube, "Photo Essay: Ceramics in Early Virginia," in *Ceramics in America*, ed. Robert Hunter (Hanover, N.H.: University Press of New England for the Chipstone Foundation, 2016), 3–32.

4. Report by Michael Clem, archaeologist, Eastern Region Preservation Office, Virginia Department of Historic Resources (DHR), https://www.dhr.virginia.gov/news/update-on-archaeology-at-eyreville-northampton-county/, March 5, 2020, accessed July 2020.

5. Inventory of the estate of Thomas Eyre, October 28, 1719, Northampton County Wills, etc., No. 15, 1717–1725, 75.

6. Norman F. Barka, Edward Ayres, and Christine Sheridan, *The "Poor Potter" of Yorktown: A Study of a Colonial Pottery Factory*, Vol. 3, *Ceramics*, Yorktown Research Series 5 (Denver: U.S. Department of the Interior, National Park Service, 1984), 352–56; Norman F. Barka, "Archaeology of a Colonial Pottery Factory: The Kilns and Ceramics of the 'Poor Potter' of Yorktown," in *Ceramics in America*, ed. Robert Hunter (Hanover, N.H.: University Press of New England for the Chipstone Foundation, 2004), 31–33, 44.

7. Inventory of the estate of Severn Eyre (d. 1728), August 14, 1728, Northampton County Wills, Deeds, etc., No. 26, 1725–1733, 151–52.

8. Cary Carson, *Face Value: The Consumer Revolution and the Colonizing of America* (Charlottesville: University of Virginia Press, 2017).

9. https://carnegiemuseums.org/magazine-archive/1996/sepoct/feat5.htm, accessed July 2020.

10. David Barker, "The Usual Classes of Useful Articles: Staffordshire Ceramics Reconsidered," in *Ceramics in America*, ed. Robert Hunter (Hanover, N.H.: University Press of New England for the Chipstone Foundation, 2001), 72–93.

11. Andrew David Madsen, "'All sorts of China Ware . . . Large, Noble and Rich Chinese Bowls': Eighteenth Century Chinese Export Porcelain of Virginia" (master's thesis, College of William and Mary, 1995); Andrew Madsen and Carolyn L. White, *Chinese Export Porcelain* (New York: Routledge, 2016).

12. Kelly Ladd and Mark Kostro, "Eyre Hall, Eastern Shore, Virginia, Archaeological Investigation," unpublished report, Department of Archaeological Research, Colonial Williamsburg Foundation, August 2001.

13. Janine E. Skerry and Suzanne Findlen Hood, *Salt-Glazed Stoneware in Early America* (Hanover, N.H.: Colonial Williamsburg Foundation in association with the University Press of New England, 2009).

14. Bernard Herman, "Multiple Materials, Multiple Meanings: The Fortunes of Thomas Mendenhall," *Winterthur Portfolio* 19, no. 1 (Spring 1984): 67–86.

15. Roderick Jellicoe with Robert Hunter, "English Porcelain in America: Evidence from Williamsburg," in *Ceramics in America*, ed. Robert Hunter (Hanover, N.H.: University Press of New England for the Chipstone Foundation, 2007), 165.

16. Inventory of the estate of Severn Eyre (d. 1773), February 27, 1774, Northampton County Wills & Inventories, No. 25, 1772–1777, 392.

17. Ann Smart Martin, "'Fashionable Sugar Dishes, Latest Fashion Ware': The Creamware Revolution in the Eighteenth-Century Chesapeake," in *Historical Archaeology of the Chesapeake*, ed. Paul A. Shackle and Barbara J. Little (Washington: Smithsonian Institution Press, 1984), 169–188; Martin, "To Supply the Real and Imaginary Necessities: The Retail Trade in Table and Teaware, Virginia and Maryland, c.1750–1810," final report to the National Endowment for the Humanities as part of "English Ceramics in America 1760–1860: Marketing, Prices, and Availability," Grant No. RO-21158-86, Department of Archaeological Research, Colonial Williamsburg Foundation, 1988.

18. Inventory of the estate of Severn Eyre (d. 1773), 392.

19. Susan Gray Detweiler, *George Washington's Chinaware* (New York: Harry N. Abrams, 1982).

20. https://apps.jefpat.maryland.gov/diagnostic/Post-Colonial%20Ceramics/Less%20Commonly%20Found/CantonPorcelain/index-cantonporcelain.html, accessed July 2020.

21. Jean McClure Mudge, *Chinese Export Porcelain for the American Trade, 1785–1835*, 2nd ed. (Newark: University of Delaware Press, 1962).

22. Leslie Warwick and Peter Warwick, "New Perspectives on Chinese Export Blue-and-White Canton Porcelain," in *Ceramics in America*, ed. Robert Hunter (Hanover, N.H.: University Press of New England for the Chipstone Foundation, 2012), 165.

23. The service may have belonged to Thomas Littleton Savage of Cugley (1760–1813). He was the father of Thomas Lyttleton Savage (1798–1855) and his sister Mary Burton Savage (1804–1866). Mary married William L. Eyre of Eyreville in 1828. Their son Severn Eyre inherited Eyre Hall in 1855. The creamware piece and perhaps others may have come into the family through this connection.

24. Rodris Roth, *Tea Drinking in 18th-Century America: Its Etiquette and Equipage*, United States National Museum Bulletin 225 (Washington, D.C.: Smithsonian Institution, 1961); Barbara Carson, "Determing the Growth and Distribution of Tea Drinking in Early America," in *Steeped in History: The Art of Tea*, ed. Beatrice Hogenegger (Los Angeles: Fowler Museum at UCLA, 2009), 158–71; Samantha M. Ligon, "The Fashionable Set: The Feasibility of Social Tea Drinking in 1774" (master's thesis, College of William and Mary, 1999).

25. Inventory of the estate of Severn Eyre (d. 1773), 392.

26. S. Robert Teitelman, Patricia A. Halfpenny, Ronald W. Fuchs, Wendell D. Garrett, and Robin Emmerson, *Success to America: Creamware for the American Market, Featuring the S. Robert Teitelman Collection at Winterthur* (Woodbridge, U.K.: Antiques Collectors' Club, 2010).

27. See Teitelman et al., *Success to America*; for a sampling of the numerous examples that survive above and below ground, see: http://www.benfranklin300.org/frankliniana/result.php?id=530&sec=0; Philadelphia Museum of Art, accession number 1940-16-139; and Colonial Williamsburg Foundation accession number 2008-91.

28. Eleanor Breen, "'One More Bowl and Then?': A Material Culture Analysis of Punch Bowls," *Journal of Middle Atlantic Archaeology* 28 (2012): 81–98.

29. Inventory and appraisement of the estate of Anthony Hay, February 2, 1771, York County Wills & Inventories 22, 1771–1783. Transcription available online, Colonial Williamsburg Foundation Digital Library, York County Project: https://research.colonialwilliamsburg.org/DigitalLibrary/view/index.cfm?doc=Probates\PB00010.xml&highlight=, accessed July 2020.

30. Inventory of the estate of Littleton Eyre, October 14, 1769, Northampton County Wills & Inventories, No. 24, 1766–1772, 225.

31. Inventory of the estate of Severn Eyre (d. 1773), 392.

32. Robert Hunter, "Hampton, Virginia," in *Ceramics in America*, ed. Robert Hunter (Hanover, N.H.: University Press of New England for the Chipstone Foundation, 2017), 48; Detweiler, *George Washington's Chinaware*.

33. Lars Tharp, *Hogarth's China: Hogarth's Paintings and Eighteenth-Century Ceramics* (London: Merrell Holberton, 1997), 49.

34. Angelika R. Kuettner, "Simply Riveting: Broken and Mended Ceramics," in *Ceramics in America*, ed. Robert Hunter (Hanover, N.H.: University Press of New England for the Chipstone Foundation, 2016), 122–40.

35. George L. Miller, Ann Smart Martin, and Nancy S. Dickinson, "Changing Consumption Patterns: English Ceramics and the American Market from 1770 to 1840," in *Everyday Life in the Early Republic*, ed. Catherine E. Hutchins (Winterthur, Del.: Henry Francis du Pont Winterthur Museum, 1994), 219–47; Patricia Samford, "Response to a Market: Dating English Underglaze Transfer-Printed Wares," *Historical Archaeology* 31, no. 2 (1997): 1–30.

36. Robert R. Hunter, "Ceramic Acquisition Patterns at Meadow Farm, 1810–1861" (master's thesis, College of William and Mary, 1987).

37. Cited in Roger Pomfret, "A Staffordshire Warehouse in Baltimore: The Letter Books of Matthew Smith 1802–32," *Northern Ceramic Society Journal* 26 (2010): 33–107, 100.

38. Many thanks to Ron Fuchs who provided this information from his upcoming publication, Ronald W. Fuchs II, "From Rehe, China to Staffordshire, England: The Voyage of a Chinese Image," *American Ceramic Circle Journal*, 2021 (in press).

39. Fuchs, "From Rehe, China to Staffordshire, England."

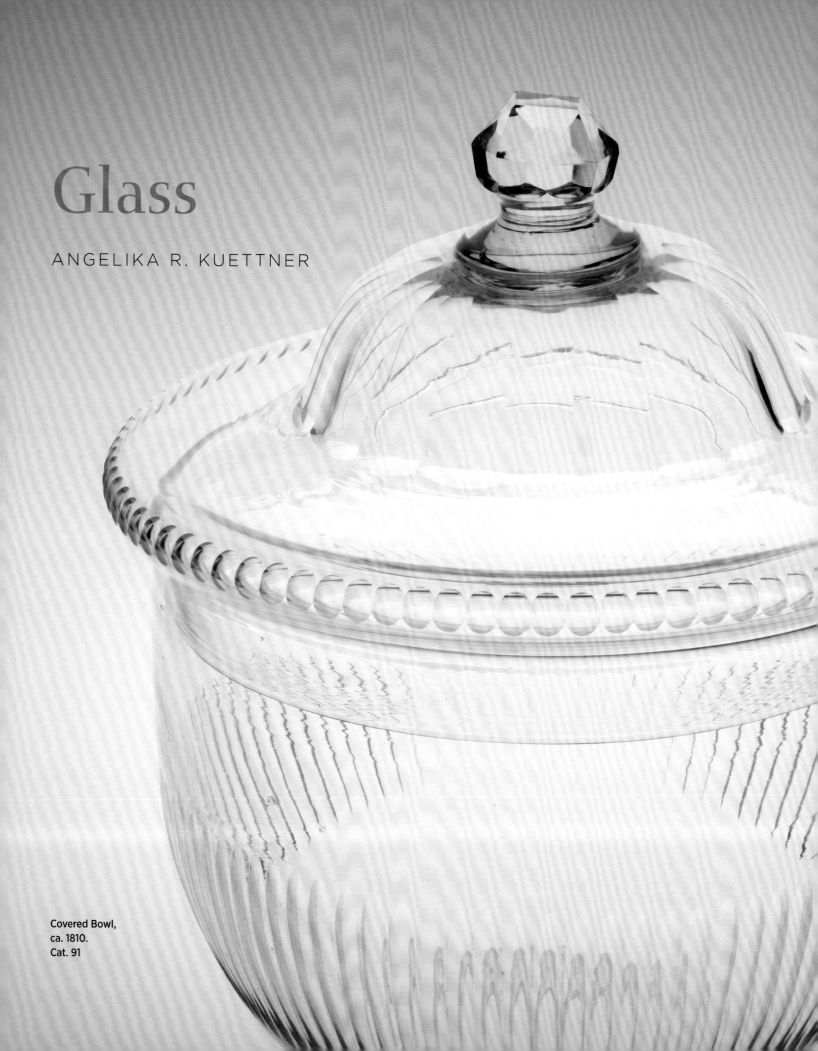

Glass

ANGELIKA R. KUETTNER

Covered Bowl,
ca. 1810.
Cat. 91

THE INTRINSICALLY FRAGILE NATURE OF GLASS often renders it "missing intact artifact" in any story of family succession. Even the most treasured glass object may meet its accidental demise with little hope of being restored to its original reflective or refractive glory. Those interested must frequently turn to the archaeological and documentary evidence to help unravel the tale of this delicate material. The story of glass survivals at Eyre Hall may be told in a similar fashion (Cat. 88). The surface archaeological finds from beneath the porch allude to a succession of glass styles used by the household throughout the eighteenth and into the early nineteenth century. Wine glasses with air or enamel twist, faceted, or button stems all paint a picture of the fashionable hospitality extended to inhabitants and visitors throughout the long eighteenth century. Chinese porcelain bowls and the family's prized silver bowl most likely held the punch from which enslaved individuals, servants, host, or hostess ladled the spirited concoction into the enamel- and air-twist glasses around the 1750s and '60s, the faceted glasses by the 1780s, and then the button-stem glasses around the turn of the nineteenth century.

Drinking vessels like wine glasses and bottles are the only glass objects seen in the earliest records predating the building and inhabiting of Eyre Hall. The early Eyre family inventories document the existence of household glass objects associated with drinking. The 1719 inventory of John Eyre's estate lists "3dz Glasses" and Thomas Eyre's probate notes "2 Glass bottles."[1] Severn Eyre's inventory records "46 glasses" at the time it was taken in 1728.[2] The

88

Glass Fragments

Glass fragments recovered from under the east porch vestibule, H. (tallest) 7⅛ in. From left to right: 1, 2: wine glasses, England, ca. 1770 and ca. 1760, colorless lead glass, the two reconstructed wine glasses representing two of five sets recovered from under the porch; 3: flask, Vista Alegre, Ílhavo, Portugal, ca. 1829, blown and molded colored (green) nonlead glass; 4, 5: salt cellar liners, London or Bristol, England, ca. 1770, cobalt-blue lead glass; 6: decanter, England, ca. 1770, colorless lead glass; 7: decanter, England, ca. 1765, colorless lead glass with wheel engraving reading "MADEIRA."

obvious choice for everyday genteel beverage consumption, these glasses were probably seen in use with the "1 Case wth 13 bottles" listed in the same document.[3] Case bottles were most often clear or green glass straight-sided rectangular bottles that outfitted a wooden bottle case sometimes raised on a stand. More due to the value placed on the case itself as a piece of furniture instead of its enclosed containers, bottle cases are known to survive in other Virginia households such as that of William Byrd III.[4]

By the 1760s, other glass forms for drinking begin to appear in the Eyre family documentary record. Littleton Eyre's inventory includes "a parcel of wines [sic], Beer & Tumbler Glasses."[5] Fragments recovered from under the porch vestibule included the broken bases of at least three styles of mid-eighteenth-century glass tumblers that may have been among the glasses listed in the probate. Tumblers may be likened to the Solo cups of the eighteenth century, and their utilitarian nature often precludes their survival above ground. Ceramic and glass retailers in America offered glass tumblers for sale throughout the eighteenth century. Norfolk retailers Balfour and Barraud advertised them by 1766, and it is possible that Littleton Eyre acquired his glassware from their shop.[6] Glass tumblers were also part of the shop inventory of John Lewis of Williamsburg at the start of 1770 and were probably available at other Williamsburg retailers earlier.[7]

The remains of an English glass decanter dating around 1765 and engraved "MADEIRA" (Cat. 88:7) further adds to the story of the genteel household. The wheel engraving—which included the name of the beverage within a cartouche suspended from an engraved chain—mimicked the appearance of fused silver plate, sterling silver, and enamel bottle tags popular at the time. Similar decanters with fine wheel engraving turn up archaeologically in other mid-eighteenth-century American contexts, including that of Henry Wetherburn's Tavern on Duke of Gloucester Street in Williamsburg, and Thomas Jefferson's home at Monticello.

Williamsburg and Norfolk newspapers advertised the importation and sale of such engraved objects to shop patrons surrounding both communities. These vessels, used to decant the beverages for which they were labeled, were offered for sale throughout early America.[8] The Madeira decanter fragments, the base of an undecorated glass decanter, and the neck and stopper of a possible third decanter seem to be the only remaining physical evidence of either the "4 decanters" listed in Littleton Eyre's 1769 inventory or the "5 decanters" recorded in Severn Eyre's probate.[9] Severn Eyre's "5 decanters" were subsequently divided between his sons Littleton, John, and Severn in 1782.[10] Often relegated to an inventory entry such as "a parcel of glass," these decanters were deemed important enough to mention and disperse in his will.

In addition to the various wine glasses and decanters that would have been found on the sideboard and dining tables or in the china closets at Eyre Hall, other glass objects such as salt cellars accompanied the silver and ceramics that graced the plantation's tables. Littleton Eyre's 1769 inventory included "2 glass salts" that can be traced down to Severn's 1774 inventory.[11] No extant examples to pair with those inventory references are known to survive in the present home, however; this may be because, by the late eighteenth century, the "2 glass salts" seem to have been superseded by pierced silver salt frames fitted with molded and cut cobalt-blue glass liners. The height of style in the last quarter of the eighteenth century, the 1770–71 English silver salts dress the Eyre Hall dining room sideboard to this day, but not all retain their original liners. Fragments of two of the original blue glass liners from the set of at least six, each bearing a six-point star pattern on its base, were recovered in the finds from under the porch, further speaking to the importation of fine British goods by the Eyre Hall household (Cat. 89). Although blue glass is advertised in early American newspapers, finding blue glass salt liners with histories of ownership in America is extremely rare.

89

Salt Cellar Frame with Two Liners

London, 1770–71 (for frame, see Cat. 38)
and London or Bristol, England, ca. 1770
(liners)
Silver and cobalt-blue lead glass

As is noted in the essay on ceramics, the inhabitants of Eyre Hall entered the 1800s with a bespoke Chinese porcelain service, each piece embellished with an "E" for the Eyre family name. The personalized ceramics did not grace the table alone, however. Glassware consisting of graduated jelly glasses in at least three sizes and custard cups with handles helped lay a sparkling dessert table and complement pieces from the sepia-decorated Chinese porcelain service including the openwork baskets and stands (Cat. 90). Similar in style to the decoration on the porcelain, each piece of blown and cut glass was engraved with a period feathered script "E." In a tantalizing reference, William Eyre's widow Grace delineated "all my glass marked E" in her 1809 will, in which she promised the fragile objects to her brother-in-law John.[12] The notation undoubtedly included the surviving 18 pieces of dessert glassware, but were there other pieces, as well? No other forms apart from the jelly and custard glasses survive, but in the late nineteenth or early twentieth century the family purchased new finger bowls also engraved with an "E" to supplement the ciphered dessert glasses passed down from Grace Eyre nearly one hundred years earlier. Other late eighteenth- or early nineteenth-century English cut-glass suites with Virginia histories include pieces bearing an engraved "N" for the John Nivison family in Norfolk, Virginia, relatives of the Eyre family through marriage.[13] However, very few sets of English cut glass survive intact, making Grace Eyre's will

reference and the 18 pieces from the original "E" ciphered suite even more significant.[14]

Grace Eyre's will also sheds light on a form often overlooked in period references, but a notable bequest among Chesapeake families beginning in the late eighteenth and early nineteenth centuries. Grace writes: "I give . . . my Sister Ann M. Upshur my two Glass Candle Shades."[15] Candle shades, often referred to as hurricane shades by collectors, were glass cylinders placed over candlesticks in order to shield a candle's flame from air movement, thus enabling the candles to burn more evenly and protecting surrounding objects from exposed flames and spattered wax. Several examples with Virginia histories survive in Colonial Williamsburg's collections (Fig. 229).[16] Unfortunately, the whereabouts of Grace Eyre's shades are unknown today. Perhaps they were discarded after the advent of gas or electric lighting. It may never be known if they, too, were engraved with an "E," like the other glass Grace bequeathed in her will. But the reference to the candle shades signifies the importance of the form as a valuable household object to Grace and her sister, and to other Virginia families in the period.

While the candle shades are documented in the paper record, but not in the material record, other early nineteenth-century forms survive in the material evidence, but are difficult to conjure from the documentary record. Recent research among experts identified glass flasks or

90

Dessert Vessels

From left to right: jelly glass, custard cup, jelly glass, custard cup, finger bowl or glass rinser

Colorless lead glass. Each piece is engraved with a feathered script "E" for the Eyre family. The glass rinser is a late nineteenth- or early twentieth-century addition to the dessert glass pieces noted in Grace Eyre's 1809 will.

pocket bottles recovered archaeologically at several sites in Williamsburg to be of Portuguese origin.[17] Similar fragments survive among the Eyre Hall archaeological finds. These blown and molded pale bluish-green glass flasks of elongated oval form bear distinctive cross-hatch diamond, leafy vine, and pseudo-diaper or star patterns. Products of the Vista Alegre glassworks in Ílhavo, the flasks and other glass objects were exported to America in the early nineteenth century when Portugal remained an ally of America during the Napoleonic Wars (see Cat. 88:3). The exact function of the bottles remains unclear; they most likely served various purposes, including holding alcoholic beverages (the prevalent function of the form in the eighteenth century), or dispensing scented waters (as recorded in the nineteenth century).[18]

In this brief examination of the glass survivals at Eyre Hall, objects associated with dining and drinking stand out as the most prevalent wares identified in the finds beneath the porch, intact above-ground survivals, and documentary references. An additional piece survives with a special family history, however. Although not listed in any of the inventories or noted in the wills, an important cut and engraved covered bowl has descended in the Eyre Hall household and retains pride of place among the family's prized glass (Cat. 91). The story it carries is one that speaks to the family's patriotic persuasion as much as the

Fig. 229. Candle shade, England, ca. 1790, H. 19½ in. The candle shade shown here with a silver candlestick descended in the Purdie family and was probably first owned by Dr. John Hyndman Purdie (1770–1845). It is similar to the form referenced in Grace Eyre's will and shows how the object was used to protect a candle flame from drafts.

fragments of the creamware teapot transfer printed with the portrait of Benjamin Franklin.[19] Between October 19 and 27, 1824, the Marquis de Lafayette visited Portsmouth and Norfolk, Virginia, during his fanfare return trip to the young United States. As close to a celebrity as one might be in the eighteenth or nineteenth century, Lafayette was greeted

91
Covered Bowl

Probably England or Ireland, ca. 1810
Colorless lead glass
H. 7½ in.

The covered bowl is shown here with its cover in place and propped next to the object. This is, perhaps, one of the most treasured objects in the Eyre household today.

by hosts of Virginians who traveled to the coast to catch a glimpse of the hero often referred to as "Washington's adopted son." Family tradition holds that the covered glass bowl was filled with mulberries from the Eyre Hall gardens and then the mulberries presented to Lafayette during his stay in Norfolk. Red mulberries were the most prevalent in Virginia at the time, but white mulberries were becoming equally abundant as the young nation encouraged domestic production of goods, since the white mulberries could be cultivated for silk production. White mulberries are typically in season on the Eastern Shore in late autumn, making the family story even more plausible.

The glassware evidence at Eyre Hall, like all of the objects that have descended in the household, tells an unprecedented story of use, disposal, dispersal, style, and—perhaps, most importantly—family.

NOTES

1. Inventory of the estate of John Eyre, August 12, 1719, Northampton County Deeds, Wills, etc., 1718–1725, 56–58; and Inventory of the estate of Thomas Eyre, October 28, 1719, Northampton County Wills, etc., No. 15, 1717–1725, 73–76.

2. Inventory of the estate of Severn Eyre (d. 1728), August 14, 1728, Northampton County Wills, Deeds, etc., No. 26, 1725–1733, 151–54.

3. Inventory of the estate of Severn Eyre (d. 1728), 151–54.

4. See Colonial Williamsburg accession number 1995-92 for the William Byrd III bottle case and stand with family history: https://emuseum.history.org/objects/3381/cellaret, accessed May 20, 2020.

5. Inventory of the estate of Littleton Eyre, October 14, 1769, Northampton County Wills & Inventories, No. 24, 1766–1772, 224–26.

6. See Balfour and Barraud advertisement in *Virginia Gazette* [P], July 25, 1766, 2.

7. *Virginia Gazette* [P], February 15, 1770, 3.

8. Philadelphia merchant Joseph Stansbury advertised for sale "pint and half pint decanters . . . labelled," *Pennsylvania Gazette*, January 18, 1770, 4. For further information, see Arlene Palmer, *Glass in Early America* (Winterthur, Del.: Winterthur Museum, 1993), 127.

9. Inventory of Severn Eyre (d. 1773), February 27, 1774, Northampton County Wills & Inventories, No. 25, 1772–1777, 393.

10. Division of Severn Eyre's will, May 14, 1782, Northampton County Wills & Inventories, No. 26, 1777–1783, 536–44.

11. Inventory of the estate of Littleton Eyre, 224–26.

12. Will of Grace D. Eyre, January 7, 1809, widow of William Eyre (d. 1808), Northampton County Wills & Inventories, No. 33, 1808–1813, 72–73.

13. See Colonial Williamsburg Foundation accession numbers 2008-53,1–2 and 2008-54 for a pair of rummers and a tumbler, all from a suite of English cut glass engraved with an "N" and of the same date as the Eyre family set of dessert glassware. The Nivison glasses descended from John Nivison to Littleton Waller Tazewell.

14. See Reino Liefkes, ed., *Glass* (London: Victoria and Albert Museum, 1997), 99–100.

15. Will of Grace D. Eyre, 72–73.

16. The collections of the Colonial Williamsburg Foundation include accession number 2016-95, which was passed down in the Purdie and Gwaltney families from its original owner, Dr. John Hyndman Purdie (1770–1845).

17. Glass expert Ian Simmonds has conducted extensive research on the archaeological fragments found in Williamsburg. See also Palmer, *Glass in Early America*, 375. And see Vasoc Valente, *O vidro em Portugal* (Porto: Portucalense Editora, 1950), 83.

18. Palmer, *Glass in Early America*, 364, 375.

19. See the essay on ceramics in this publication.

Paintings

LAURA PASS BARRY

Fig. 230. Family photographs in the parlor at Eyre Hall, 2020.

THE PAINTINGS AT EYRE HALL ARE EXTRAORDINARY documents of the plantation's extensive history, portraying multiple generations who lived at the property. They are rare survivors from one of the few Virginia collections remaining in private hands. The portraits record a variety of individuals—sons and daughters, husbands and wives, sisters and brothers, parents, grandparents, and cousins—putting a literal face to the names of numerous ancestors and relatives. Together with the wealth and breadth of other period consumer goods, they represent an astounding body of material that conveys and reinforces the Eyre family's wealth, status, and socioeconomic opportunity from the past 270 years.

From the eighteenth through the mid-nineteenth century, there was a demand for portraits. This was based on British precedent and the idea that your likeness conveyed a message about who you were, where you came from, or even, what you wished to be. From the beginning, British and European painters came to America in search of business opportunities. Over time, this was largely found in portraiture. Portraits represented financial accomplishment and social status for many of the nation's wealthiest citizens. By way of their extensive network of family and friends, Severn Eyre and his descendants were connected to members of the most powerful and influential families— the Mifflins, Teackles, and Chaunceys of Philadelphia; the Barrauds and Taylors of Norfolk; the Upshurs, Browns, Bowdoins, and Custises of the Eastern Shore; in addition to schoolmates, neighbors, and business associates like the Pages, Nelsons, Carters, and Tuckers—all of whom had their likenesses recorded. By way of reputation and reinforced through these varied relationships, the Eyres had access to some of the most notable artists working in the genre— Benjamin West, Thomas Sully, and James Peale to name a few—and they took full advantage.

The Eyre paintings represent a variety of forms from standard-format canvases to portrait miniatures. Each serves a particular purpose, whether it is the documentation of the homeowner or a token of affection. In some instances, the likenesses were created specifically for display in the house. In others, portraits of ancestors came to Eyre Hall in the early twentieth century at a time when Americans were keenly interested in preserving and celebrating their common past.

The catalogue entries start with the first-known painting of the family dynasty, that of Severn Eyre (1735–1773), son of the builder, and end with a portrait of Grace Woodward Eyre Baldwin (b. 1999), the next generation owner of Eyre Hall. In between are renderings of numerous individuals that played a role in the history of this plantation and/or the lives of its residents. Not represented are members of recent generations—Mary Eyre Wright (1875–1955) and her sister Grace Taylor Eyre Taylor (1872–1910); Margaret Eyre Taylor Baldwin (1898–1979); H. Furlong Baldwin (b. 1932) and his children. They, instead, appear in photographs, extending the tradition of family portraiture to the present (Fig. 230). As a collection, the likenesses at Eyre Hall are a celebration of a shared heritage and a tribute to a legacy of preserving and honoring the past.

Portrait of Severn Eyre (1735–1773)

Benjamin West (1738–1820)
Philadelphia, 1757–59
Oil on canvas
H. 49 in., W. 40¾ in.

When the death announcement for Severn Eyre (1735–1773) was published in the *Virginia Gazette*, he was described as a "Gentleman of Abilities, a warm Friend of his Country, and greatly esteemed."[1] Although his obituary was recorded nearly 15 years later, these characteristics were adeptly captured in the young man's painted portrait.

The painting was first documented in the 1855 will of Severn's son John Eyre (1768–1855) as "the portrait of my father Severn Eyre, taken by Benjamin West."[2] An early product of West, the portrayal was a statement of gentility, social and economic accomplishment for the family, coinciding with the construction of their stately plantation home. The Eyres' connection to the artist was most likely made through Littleton Eyre's (1710–1768) business partner John Bowdoin, whose younger brother Preeson apprenticed in Philadelphia before returning to Northampton County and marrying Severn's sister Sarah Eyre (1738–1760) in 1759. The arrangement, as stipulated in the will of Preeson's father, sent the boy to work with his great-uncle, merchant and chief justice William Allen.[3] Allen, along with his brother-in-law James Hamilton, were notable patrons of West, ultimately financing the artist's study trip to Italy in 1760.[4] Additionally, Lieutenant Governor Hamilton owned a notable painting collection in the colonies. He provided West with access to his "picture gallery" at Bush Hill and, in at least one instance, allowed the fledgling artist to copy a portrait.[5]

More than likely, West's commissions were made through familial and social connections.[6] In addition to the Bowdoins, the Eyres probably also learned about the artist through Severn's first cousin, Ann Eyre Mifflin Roberts. A surviving portrait of Ann's nephew Thomas Mifflin of Philadelphia, rendered by West between 1758 and 1759, is stylistically and compositionally like Severn's painting. Both likenesses portray a young male subject in an outdoor setting surrounded by symbols of popular sporting pursuits—Thomas with a hunting piece and fowl and Severn with his riding whip and dog.[7] It is undetermined whether the similarity between the two portraits was intentional or whether the artist was simply utilizing common artistic conventions.

The portrait of Severn most likely remained at Eyre Hall until its descent from John Eyre to his niece, Margaret Alice Lyon Taylor (1802–1888).[8] While family history suggests the painting stayed at the house from its commission onward, early photos from the 1890s omit the portrait and a 1922 reference to the painting's ownership cites Margaret's grandson, Robert Barraud Taylor III (1865–1935) of Norfolk as owner.[9] By the 1930s, a photograph in the Library of Congress collections show the portrait in its current location above the parlor mantle at Eyre Hall. By 1941, Margaret Eyre Taylor Baldwin (1898–1979) is noted as owner.[10] From the time of its commission to today, Severn's likeness remains a celebrated relic of early family history and is arguably the most revered object in the Eyre Hall collection.

Portrait of Severn Eyre (1735–1773)

Thomas Sully (1783–1872)
Philadelphia, 1850
Oil on canvas
H. 52 in., W. 43¾ in.

This likeness of Severn Eyre (1735–1773) by Thomas Sully resides in an adjacent room to the original from which it was copied. Family members retell the rationale of its commission as "a daughter who wanted a copy of the West portrait."[11] Duplicate canvases or copies were a common request by many eighteenth- and nineteenth-century descendants who desired an additional portrait of their loved one's likeness. At a time before the widespread use of photography, artists fulfilled this need, often decades after the original likeness was recorded. In 1850, the prominent Philadelphia portraitist Thomas Sully, who rendered other portraits of the Eyre family, painted a "Copy from an old picture" of "Mr. Ayers."[12] Measuring the same size, approximately 4 feet by 3 feet, there is no question this painting is the same portrait which hangs today at Eyre Hall.

Sully's accounts note the commission of the portrait for "Mr. Savage," most likely referring to William Littleton Savage of Philadelphia. By way of marriage, William was connected to the prominent Chauncey, Teackle, and Bancker families, all patrons of Sully.[13] His sister Mary Burton Savage's (1804–1866) husband was William Littleton Eyre (1806–1852), a grandson of Severn and a first cousin to Margaret Alice Lyon Taylor (1802–1888) who inherited the West portrait. A surviving letter supports a close relationship between the Savage siblings, confirming the possibility that Mary could have used her Philadelphia family connections for the duplicate painting.[14] She and her husband likely had a great interest in obtaining a canvas copy of the West if the two thought they were going to inherit Eyre Hall. But William Littleton predeceased his uncle John Eyre (1768–1855) two years after the commission of the painting, and ownership of the house passed to their son, Severn Eyre (1831–1914), along with the Sully copy. The portrait hence descended to Mary Eyre Wright (1875–1955), co-owner of the property and granddaughter of Mary Burton Savage, and later to Mary Wright's niece, Margaret Eyre Taylor Baldwin (1898-1979), mother of the current owner.[15]

Portrait Miniature of John Eyre (1768–1855)

Attributed to Lawrence Sully (1769–1804)
Norfolk, ca. 1795
Watercolor on ivory
H. 2½ in., W. 2³⁄₁₆ in.

A modern label on the reverse of this portrait identifies the subject as Severn Eyre (1735–1773). However, stylistic similarities to a miniature dated 1795 preclude the possibility of Severn being the sitter because he died two decades earlier. Another miniature with a strong familial resemblance to this subject is believed to represent Severn's youngest son William (1772–1808) (see Cat. 96), suggesting this likeness portrays a close family member. Of Severn's surviving sons, John (1768–1855) is the only candidate.[16] Comparison between the portrayals of William and John support this identification—the image of William, born four years later, appears younger than the likeness of his brother. Furthermore, a bust-length portrait of John (see Cat. 95), rendered by Thomas Sully in 1830 and depicting the subject nearly 35 years later, highlights a similar facial structure and features.

According to the family, the miniature of John was given to them by the same relative. Its modern, twentieth-century frame matches that of William's likeness and another depicting Ann Blaws Hansford Barraud (1760–1836) (see Cat. 97). Family records cite Mary Eyre Wright (1875–1955) as the owner of all three in 1926.[17] Given the mobility of portrait miniatures and the belief that these portraits left Eyre Hall, could they have descended through Margaret Alice Lyon Taylor, recipient of the West portrait, and her heirs who also relate to Ann Barraud?[18]

Portrait of John Eyre (1768–1855)

Thomas Sully (1783–1872)
Philadelphia, 1830
Oil on canvas
H. 41 in., W. 36 in.

This bust-length canvas of the builder's grandson, John Eyre (1768–1855), is proudly displayed in the parlor at Eyre Hall. Painted portraits continued to be popular through the first half of the nineteenth century, and this likeness of John reinforced his social status and power as the fourth owner of Eyre plantation. A reference in Thomas Sully's *Register of Portraits* documents the 1830 likeness: "Mr. Eyre of Virginia."[19] Handwritten notes recorded from the journal of the artist further elaborate the commission with the date that the portrait was started and completed.[20]

The fact that John's will directed that the portrait by West go to his niece, but contained no mention of his own likeness, suggests that the painting stayed at Eyre Hall after his death and was transferred to his grandnephew Severn Eyre (1831–1914) along with the house and its contents. But, an early Frick Art Reference Library record that documents the owner of the portrait as Robert Barraud Taylor III of Norfolk places doubt on this theory.[21] As the older brother and eldest child, Robert Barraud Taylor III (1865–1935) inherited a number of the Eyre family likenesses from his grandmother Margaret Alice Lyon Taylor (1802–1888). It seems more likely that the portrait of John left Eyre Hall and was later returned by way of Robert Taylor to the family of his sister-in-law, Grace Eyre Taylor (1872–1910), during their ownership of the property.[22]

Portrait Miniature of William Eyre (1772–1808)

Lawrence Sully (1769–1804)
Norfolk, 1795
Watercolor on ivory
H. 2 1/16 in., W. 1 3/4. in.

The identification of the subject of this portrait miniature as William Eyre (1772–1808) makes sense. Although it was once thought to represent William's son, William Littleton Eyre (1806–1852), a 1795 inscription confirms the object precedes William Littleton's birth. The initials 'L S' also appear on the likeness, indicating the artist as Lawrence Sully.

Arguably the lesser known sibling to his younger brother Thomas, Lawrence worked in Richmond and Norfolk, where he advertised himself as a "Miniature Painter (and Student of the Royal Academy, London)" who "would portray the ladies elegantly."[23] Between the years 1792 and 1804, he traveled between the two cities, rendering likenesses of members of the political and social elite, both male and female.

Lawrence's connection to the Eyres was most likely through their Norfolk relatives. William's mother, wife, and nephew were all members of the prominent Taylor family—daughters and son of the city's merchant and lawyer class. The miniature likeness of William, and that of his brother John, are rare documents of Severn Eyre's surviving male heirs.

Portrait Miniature of Ann Blaws Hansford Barraud (1760–1836)

Unidentified artist
Probably Norfolk, ca. 1790
Watercolor on ivory
H. 2⅝ in., W. 1¾ in.

This small likeness descended in the Taylor family along with portrait miniatures of brothers William and John Eyre (Cat. 96 and Cat. 94). Until recently, it was believed to portray Grace Duncombe Taylor Eyre (1780–1809), the wife of William. But comparison with two canvases in Colonial Williamsburg's collection confirm the identity of the sitter as Ann Blaws Hansford Barraud (1760–1836).

Ann Barraud was the daughter of Dr. Lewis and Ann Taylor Hansford and stepsister of Robert Taylor, the grandfather of William Eyre Taylor (1809–1870). She married Williamsburg physician Dr. Philip Barraud in 1783 and the couple lived there until 1799, when they relocated to Norfolk.[24] In addition to their Williamsburg home, numerous artifacts belonging to them survive today, including family portraits, furniture, silver, letters, archaeological fragments, and sheet music.[25]

The Barrauds had their likenesses recorded on several occasions. Ann sat for her portrait (Fig. 231) with Henry Benbridge around 1800 and again, nearly 30 years later, with William James Hubard. The survival of these paintings provides an extraordinary opportunity to document her physical attributes and discard any generic or formulaic conventions used by the artists. Ann's thick, dark, curly head of hair is especially distinguishable in both portraits as well as the miniature, representing a significant departure from the straight, light-colored hair of Ann's previously identified portrayal (see Cat. 98). The hairstyle and costume of this subject further place the miniature in the late 1780s or early 1790s, appropriate for a 30-year-old Ann.[26]

Fig. 231. Portrait of Ann Blaws Hansford Barraud attributed to Henry Benbridge, Norfolk, ca. 1800, oil on canvas, H. 35 in., W. 25 in.

98

Portrait Miniature; possibly Nancy Ritson Taylor (1775–1862)

Unidentified artist
Norfolk, 1785–1800
Watercolor on ivory
H. 1¹⁵⁄₁₆ in., W. 1⁹⁄₁₆ in.

Two surviving portraits help to refute the identification of this sitter as Ann Blaws Hansford Barraud (1760–1836) (see Cat. 97). Instead, the likeness possibly represents her niece Nancy Ritson Taylor as a young girl.[27] One of the first clues to this identity is the sitter's hair, a style that when worn down suggests a child. However, because the youth's costume was fashionable between the 1780s until the end of the eighteenth century, there are several possible subjects over the large span of time when the miniature was created.

A survey of females in the extended Eyre family surprisingly reveals very few candidates of the proper age as our portrait subject. It is tempting to attribute the likeness to one of Severn Eyre's daughters, as it was common for families to commission likenesses of multiple children. But Margaret "Peggy" Eyre Parker (1765–1799) is much too old, and her sister Sarah "Sally" Eyre Lyon (1770–1813), age ten in 1780, is only a viable option in the first few years of our date range. Margaret's daughter Sally Bagwell Parker (1789–after 1815) is also a possibility, but, much like her aunt and namesake, only fits into the end of our timeline. A third and fourth consideration is Ann Upshur Eyre (1780–1829), wife of Margaret and Sally's brother John, or Grace Duncombe Taylor Eyre (1780–1809), wife of their brother William. However, the history of the miniature's descent to William Eyre Taylor (1904–1987) before its gift to Eyre Hall suggests the subject portrays a direct ancestor.[28]

One possibility is Nancy Ritson Taylor (1775–1862), wife of Robert Barraud Taylor (1774–1834) and mother-in-law to Margaret Alice Lyon Taylor. Could the family's belief that the portrait depicts Ann Barraud simply be a case of mistaken identity by later generations, erroneously attributing the likeness to the wrong great-great-grandmother?[29] This sitter's youthful appearance is supported by Nancy's age as a young teenager in the mid- to late 1780s, dovetailing our subject's date range. The miniature furthermore resembles a privately owned canvas attributed to Nancy and once owned by William Eyre Taylor's father Robert Barraud Taylor III (1865–1935).[30] While the artist who created the miniature is likewise unknown, two possibilities are Henry Benbridge (1743–1812) or Pierre Henri (ca. 1760–1822), portrait artists who specialized in miniature painting and were documented as working in Norfolk.[31]

Portrait Miniature of Philip Barraud (1758–1783)

James Peale (1749–1831)
Philadelphia, 1794
Watercolor on ivory
H. 1⁹⁄₁₆ in., W. 1¼ in.

Eyre descendants believe this small watercolor depicts Norfolk physician Philip Barraud (1758–1783)—in part because it descended alongside another miniature thought to portray his wife, Ann Blaws Hansford Barraud (1760–1836).[32] But the differing size, date, and artist's hand confirm that the two likenesses were not meant to serve as a pendant pair. Instead, their connection was likely through their common ownership by direct descendant William Eyre Taylor (1904–1987).[33]

While the age of the male makes it possible that several Eyre family members could be the subject, the survival of two oil portraits of Philip Barraud strongly suggests he is the sitter. Barraud was painted on multiple occasions: first by artist William Dunlap in 1821 (Fig. 232) and later in the 1830s when William James Hubard copied his earlier likeness.[34] A similarity in facial features—the eyes, mouth, and nose as well as the hairline—between the three portraits supports this identification for the miniature.[35]

The artist of this portrayal is well known. The signature "JP" stands for James Peale, youngest brother of the celebrated artist Charles Willson Peale, who served for many years as the elder's studio assistant. In the early 1780s, James established his own reputation and, in 1786, decidedly focused his attention on portrait miniatures.[36] This likeness, dated 1794, was rendered in the middle of James's small-format painting career and is a charming example of the artist's work.

Fig. 232. Portrait of Philip Barraud attributed to William Dunlap, Norfolk, 1821, oil on canvas, H. 30⅜ in., W. 25 in.

100
Portrait of Sally Eyre Taylor (1832–1900)

Thomas Sully (1783–1872)
Philadelphia, 1835
Oil on canvas
H. 14 in., W. 12½ in.

Family descendants have always maintained this sitter's identity as young Sally Eyre Taylor (1832–1900), the daughter of William Eyre Taylor (1809–1870) and Margaret Alice Lyon Taylor (1802–1888). A reference in Charles Henry Hart's 1909 reprint of *Thomas Sully's Register of Portraits* confirms the attribution: "Miss Sally Taylor, daughter of William E. Taylor, Va."[37] However, the editor's speculation that there was "either an error in the Christian name or in the present identity of the subject," and his subsequent reidentification of the sitter as Fanny Taylor of Richmond, caused the record of the portrait's commission to be changed in later printed material. Twenty-two years later, when Edward Biddle and Mantle Fielding published their seminal work on the artist, the entry for the Taylor portrait mistakenly read "Miss Fanny Taylor."[38]

Records at the Frick Art Reference Library further complicate its history, with an erroneous citation that the painting was dated by Sully in 1830, two years prior to the subject's birth. The discrepancy was probably the result of a misreading of the painting's inscription, now indecipherable from age and discolored varnish. Nevertheless, the painting's small size, just 20 by 16 inches, corresponds to Hart's original description of the commission as "head" size, as well as the artist's definition of the standard-size formats he used.[39]

Like a few other family paintings, Sally's likeness descended through Robert Barraud Taylor (1865–1935), eldest brother of Richard Baker Taylor and his wife Grace Eyre Taylor (1872–1910), who, along with Grace's sister Mary Eyre Wright (1875–1955), were designated to inherit Eyre Hall from their father. Grace's premature death before her father meant that her part of the inheritance went to her daughter Margaret Eyre Taylor (1898–1979).

Portrait of Robert Barraud Taylor (1774–1834)

Cephas Thompson (1775–1856)
Norfolk, 1811–12
Oil on canvas
H. 27½ in., W. 22¼ in.

Marriages between prominent families aligned economic interests and ensured the continuity of social and political power through subsequent generations. They were the natural product of the interactions among upper-class men and women and the communities in which they lived. The union of Margaret Alice Lyon (1802–1888) and William Eyre Taylor (1809–1870) not only reconnected the Eyres and Taylors (the spouses' grandparents were first cousins), but it reinforced familial ties within a larger network of people who were related to one another. In this instance, Margaret and William's nuptials brought the Eyres together with the subject of this portrait, Robert Barraud Taylor (1774–1834).

A politician, jurist, and military commander, Taylor was described by his contemporaries as attracting "universal attention" with his "voice, action, [and] eloquence." His noted oratory skills undoubtedly aided him in his election to the Virginia House of Delegates in 1798 and 1799, and later as Norfolk representative in the state constitutional convention.[40] Further, this distinguished reputation was probably also what earned him the position of brigadier-general in the War of 1812, during which he was responsible for commanding troops at Norfolk.[41]

This likeness is one of two canvases of Taylor made by Cephas Thompson, a New England portraitist who wintered in Virginia. The artist's arrival was advertised in the local newspaper in January 1812: "C Thompson Portrait Painter respectfully informs the inhabitants of Norfolk for the better arrangement of business, his Room, no 10 Talbot Row, will be open for visitors on Saturdays only, which will be entirely devoted to their accommodation."[42] His surviving memorandum book additionally lists dozens of portrait commissions, including those of Robert Barraud Taylor and his wife.[43]

At an unknown date, a subsequent copy of the painting was made by the artist. While several other portraits were noted by Thompson as "copies," there is no such notation to explain the presence of two Robert Barraud Taylor paintings or to help differentiate which was the original likeness. An entry in the Frick Art Reference Library documents one of the portraits,

most likely the Eyre example, in the collection of Robert Barraud Taylor III (1865–1935) (who was also the owner of the Sally Eyre Taylor and John Eyre paintings and the West portrait of Severn Eyre).[44] However, updates to the citation by Mrs. Nellie Taylor, a distant cousin of Robert III, note the portrait's subsequent transfer to the College of William and Mary and its later acquisition by the Virginia Museum of History and Culture.[45] Is it possible that archivists at the Frick confused the later correspondence and assumed the portraits were one and the same?

Portraits of Margaret Shepherd Parker Eyre (1840–1899) and Severn Eyre (1831–1914)

Attributed to Louis Mathieu Didier Guillaume (1816-1892)
Probably Richmond, ca. 1855 and 1865
Pastel on wove paper
H. 22¼ in., W. 14¾. in.; H. 22¼ in., W. 14¾ in.

Family members suggest the male portrait portrays Severn Eyre (1831-1914), who inherited Eyre Hall from his great-uncle John (1768-1855) in 1855 and lived at the house until his death. The likeness certainly represents a 30-something-year-old, and the sitter's hairstyle and shirt collar support the idea that the portrait was made in the 1860s.

Descendants disagree, however, as to the identity of the woman. Severn married twice, first to Margaret Yates Stirling (1833-1855) in 1854, and second to Margaret Shepherd Parker (1840-1899) in 1865. Because the latter relationship yielded three heirs—William Littleton Eyre (1871-1893), Grace Eyre Taylor (1872-1910), and Mary Eyre Wright (1875-1955)—Margaret Parker has been the presumptive subject. Indeed,

the painting's long-time presence at Eyre Hall alongside its companion highly suggests it documents the second marriage and a surviving photograph of Margaret Parker confirms this identification (Fig. 233). A remaining mystery, however, surrounds the sitter's hairstyle and clothing, which dates earlier than her male counterpart—anywhere from the 1840s through the mid-1850s—a period prior to Margaret Parker and Severn's nuptials.[46]

The artist who created these drawings was likely Louis Mathieu Didier Guillaume, a Frenchman who lived in Richmond and worked "as a fashionable portraitist" in the late 1850s and '60s.[47] Like other artists of this period, Guillaume used photographs in the creation of his compositions.[48] Could this account for the difference in date between Margaret and Severn's likenesses? Did Severn commission a companion work of himself to accompany an existing portrayal of Margaret? This could easily be done by supplying the artist with a photograph and would account for the slight variations in the background of the portraits. It is possible the works were then placed into their current matching frames to celebrate the couple's engagement or marriage.

Fig. 233.
Photograph
of Margaret
Shepherd
Parker, ca. 1865.

104

Portrait of Grace Woodward Eyre Baldwin (b. 1999)

Stephen J. Griffin (b. 1954)
Easton, Maryland, 2010
Oil on canvas
H. 31½ in., W. 25½ in.

This charming likeness portrays Grace Woodward Eyre Baldwin (b. 1999), the granddaughter of H. Furlong Baldwin (b. 1932). She was 11 years old when the artist rendered her in front of the ruins of the property's early nineteenth-century greenhouse, celebrated as among the oldest in the state.

The portraitist was Stephen J. Griffin, a celebrated artist from nearby Easton, Maryland. Griffin is best known today for his landscapes of the Chesapeake Bay and New England boat scenes, but his background and course of study was in portraiture. Early training with Cedric and Joanette Egeli, husband and wife team of the noted Egeli family of painters, inspired Griffin and helped to shape his impressionist style.[49] His painterly approach to Grace's likeness is especially apparent in his choice of color and lighting effects. This portrait of the next generation heir currently hangs in an upstairs bedchamber where it is much admired.

1. *Virginia Gazette*, February 18, 1773, 2:3.

2. Will of John Eyre, February 21, 1855, Northampton County Wills, No. 39, 1854–1897, 22–25.

3. Will of Peter Bowdoin, December 20, 1744, Northampton County Wills & Inventories, No. 19, 1740–1750, 234. Preeson Bowdoin's grandmother, Elizabeth Brown Preeson, was a sister of Anne Brown Preeson Hamilton, the mother-in-law of William Allen. See R. Winder Johnson, compiler, *The Ancestry of Rosalie Morris Johnson* (Philadelphia: Ferris & Leach, 1905), 5.

4. West sailed to Italy in spring 1760 with William Allen's son, John, and his friend Joseph Shippen. William Allen wrote to agents in London and Leghorn (Livorno) requesting letters of credit and recommendations for the boys and "Mr. West, a young ingenious painter of this city, who is desirous to improve himself in that science, by visiting Florence and Rome." Robert C. Alberts, *Benjamin West: A Biography* (Boston: Houghton Mifflin, 1978), 27. West never returned to the colonies, later traveling to London where he lived for the remainder of his life.

5. Alberts, *Benjamin West*, 25. Hamilton purportedly allowed West to copy a portrait of St. Ignatius. Years, later when the artist was in Italy, both Hamilton and Allen commissioned West to copy a number of paintings. *The World of Benjamin West* (Allentown, Pa.: Allentown Art Museum, 1962), 20.

6. It is important to note that West's reputation in American art, specifically his influence on the development of historical painting, was not widespread until years after he left the American colonies, thus his name recognition would not have been widespread at this time.

7. Today the portrait of Thomas Mifflin is owned by Drexel University.

8. Will of John Eyre.

9. The ca. 1890s photograph of the parlor at Eyre Hall does not show the portrait, and it is unlikely it hung in the library given the Frick Art Reference Library (FARL) citation for the painting. See entry for "Severn Eyre" at https://arcade.nyarc.org/search~S6. Owner listed in 1922 as collection of "Robert Barraud Taylor, Norfolk, Va." and later "Mrs. Henry duP. Baldwin."

10. Photograph taken by Frances Benjamin Johnston ca. 1935, www.loc.gov/item/2017891019.

11. Furlong Baldwin conversation with the author, September 23, 2018. According to Baldwin, a now unlocated letter explained that John Eyre's younger sister wanted a copy of the West portrait. Because Sarah "Sally" Eyre Lyon died in 1813, this may have been a factor in her daughter inheriting the original West from John Eyre in 1855. It is uncertain why it took nearly 100 years for the commission to occur.

12. Painting is listed as no. 55. See Charles Henry Hart, "Thomas Sully's Register of Portraits, 1801–1871," *Pennsylvania Magazine of History and Biography* 32, no. 4 (1908): 400. No doubt "Ayers" was a phonetic spelling of Eyre. The surname was similarly misspelled in John Adam's August 22, 1770 encounter with Severn: "Rode to Cambridge in Company with Coll. Severn Ayers and Mr. Hewitt from Virginia." L. H. Butterfield,

ed., *The Adams Papers: Diary and Autobiography of John Adams*, vol. 1, *1755–1770* (Cambridge, Mass.: Harvard University Press, 1961), 364.

13. Edward Biddle and Mantle Fielding, *The Life and Works of Thomas Sully (1783–1872)* (Lancaster, Pa.: Wickersham Press, 1921), 92–93, 120–21, 294–95.

14. Letter from William L. Eyre to William L. Savage, September 3, 1843, Eyre Hall Family Papers, Virginia Historical Society, Richmond. An 1851 deed from John Eyre to his niece Mary further underscores the relationship of William Littleton Savage to the Eyres. As lawyer and sibling, Savage assisted with the legal conveyance of a horse from the uncle. Deed between John Eyre and Mary B. Eyre, January 3, 1851, Northampton County Deeds, etc., No. 34, 1850–1856, 37–38.

15. FARL entry for portrait can be found at www.digitalcollection.frick.org. Owner listed as collection of "Mrs. W. H. DeCourcy Wright, Baltimore, great-great-grand-daughter of Severn Eyre." Photograph taken by Frances Benjamin Johnston ca. 1935, https://www.loc.gov/pictures/item/2017891022. The portrait was relocated to Baltimore, most likely when the family's primary residence shifted north. It returned to Eyre Hall during Henry and Margaret Baldwin's occupancy. H. Furlong Baldwin conversation with the author, August 30, 2020.

16. Severn's two eldest sons were dead by the 1790s. Littleton, the eldest, died in 1789, and Severn in 1786 in London.

17. Photocopied catalogue cards of three miniatures found among family notes, now located at the Swem Library, College of William and Mary, Williamsburg, n.d. All three works have the same twentieth-century distressed black cove profile with gold fillet. Ownership of objects cited in 1924 by Mrs. William H. DeCourcy Wright. FARL entry for portrait miniature of John Eyre can be found at www.digitalcollection.frick.org. The same owner is listed for 1926 and further described as "great-great-granddaughter of the subject."

18. Margaret Alice Lyon Taylor's son Robert Barraud Taylor II (1838–1895) married Lelia Ann Baker, the granddaughter of Ann Barraud.

19. Hart, "Thomas Sully's Register of Portraits," 61.

20. Handwritten notes under the heading of "Account of Pictures painted by Thomas Sully" appear in the back of the *Journal of Thomas Sully's Activities, May 1792, 1793, 1799–December 1846*, typescript copy in the New York Public Library. They record that the painting was begun on August 3 and finished on September 30. The price was $75.

21. FARL entry for portrait can be found at www.digitalcollection.frick.org.

22. The West, the canvas portraits of John Eyre, Sally Eyre Taylor, and Robert Barraud Taylor, the miniatures of John Eyre, William Eyre, and Ann Barraud were all once owned by Robert Barraud Taylor III (1865–1935). It appears that most of these likenesses were given by Robert Taylor to the family—either to his sister-in-law Grace Taylor Eyre Taylor (1872–1910) or her sister Mary Eyre Wright (1875–1955) or his niece Margaret Eyre Taylor Baldwin (1898–1979)—prior to his death in 1935.

23. *Virginia Gazette* (Richmond), September 26, 1792; *Norfolk Herald*, June 6, 1795.

24. The couple moved to Norfolk when Philip accepted a position as superintendent of the U.S. Marine Hospital.

25. The Barrauds' Williamsburg home on Francis Street still stands today and is maintained by the Colonial Williamsburg Foundation along with several family portraits, a tea table, silver goblets, archaeological fragments, and Philip's walking stick. Bound volumes of Ann's piano music and family letters can be found in Special Collections, Swem Library, College of William and Mary.

26. The "chemise à la reine" or "gaulle" style was made popular by Marie Antoinette in the early 1780s before it was quickly adopted in England and America. The fashion was characterized by loose, unstructured dress, belted around the waist, and large hedgehog or teased hair.

27. Nancy Ritson Taylor's father-in-law Robert Taylor (1749–1826) was a step-brother to Ann Barraud. After the death of his father, Robert's mother remarried Ann's father, Dr. Lewis Hansford.

28. William Eyre Taylor (1904–1987) was the son of Robert Barraud Taylor III (1865–1935).

29. Nancy Ritson Taylor and Ann Blaws Hansford Barraud were grandmothers to Robert Barraud Taylor II and Lelia Baker Taylor, the grandparents of William Eyre Taylor who donated the miniature to H. Furlong Baldwin.

30. The canvas of Nancy Ritson Taylor is dated 1801 and is presumably still owned by a member of the Taylor family. See FARL entry for portrait at www.digitalcollection.frick.org.

31. Although he appears intermittently in Philadelphia records throughout this period, there is a lot that remains unknown about the life and whereabouts of Henry Benbridge between 1791 and the time he is recorded in Norfolk in 1801. Quite possibly, he was either living in Virginia or visited before this. Similarly, Pierre Henri is itinerant during this period and is documented in Richmond in addition to other cities along the southern East Coast between 1789 and 1820. Another research angle worth further pursuit is a ca. 1770 miniature of Joseph Prentis (1754–1809) in Colonial Williamsburg's collection. Although the artist is not identified, the likeness shares the distinctive brown background of the Eyre Hall miniature and the subjects are tangentially related. Prentis's wife, Margaret Bowdoin, was the daughter of Severn Eyre's business partner and a cousin to Nancy Ritson Taylor by way of her marriage. See eMuseum.history.org for more information.

32. The portrait miniature of Ann Barraud has since been attributed to another relative. See Cat. 98.

33. Philip Barraud (1758–1783) was the grandfather of Lelia Ann Baker who married Robert Barraud Taylor II (1838–1895). Robert Taylor's grandmother was Nancy Ritson Taylor (1775–1862), possible subject of the female likeness. The two miniatures descended to Lelia and Robert Barraud Taylor's grandson William Eyre Taylor (1904–1987) before coming to Eyre Hall.

34. The two bust-length canvases of Dr. Philip Barraud reside in Colonial Williamsburg's

collection: a portrait by William Dunlap from 1821 and a likeness attributed to William James Hubard dated 1833–36. See eMuseum.history.org for more information.

35. Complicating the matter is a privately owned miniature containing an engraved inscription: "Dr Philip Barraud of Norfolk, Va., 1758–1830." While costume details and hairstyle suggest it was rendered ca. 1800—the same date range as the miniature of Ann Blaws Hansford Barraud (1760–1836)—its identification as Philip and its association with Ann have yet to be determined. Barraud Family research file, Department of Collections, Colonial Williamsburg Foundation.

36. For more information on James Peale, see an entry on the artist in John Caldwell and Oswaldo Rodriguez Roque, *American Paintings in the Metropolitan Museum of Art* (New York: The Metropolitan Museum of Art, 1994), 1:135–36.

37. Hart, "Thomas Sully's Register of Portraits," entry no. 1667.

38. Biddle and Fielding, *Life and Works of Thomas Sully*, entry no. 1760.

39. Hart, "Thomas Sully's Register of Portraits," entry no. 1667; Biddle and Fielding, *Life and Works of Thomas Sully*, 81.

40. For a more complete description of Robert Barraud Taylor, see Hugh Blair Grigsby, *Discourse of the Life and Character of the Hon. Littleton Waller Tazewell* (Norfolk, Va.: J. D. Ghiselin, Jr., 1860).

41. Stuart L. Butler, "Defending Norfolk: An Early Battle with the British in 1813 Saves a Thriving American Port," *Prologue*, Spring 2013, https://www.archives.gov/files/publications/prologue/2013/spring/norfolk.pdf, accessed July 2020.

42. *Norfolk Herald*, January 1, 1812.

43. Thompson's "Memorandum of Portraits" includes the artist's commissions in Norfolk, Richmond, Alexandria, and other cities. His Norfolk paintings were rendered between the years 1811 and 1812. See *Cephas Thompson's Memorandum of Portraits* (Northampton, Mass.: privately printed by Madeleine Thompson Edmunds, 1965) for a facsimile of the "Memorandum." Further information can be found in Deborah L. Sisum, "'A Most Favorable and Striking Resemblance': The Virginia Portraits of Cephas Thompson," *Journal of Early Southern Decorative Arts* 23, no. 1 (Summer 1997): 1–101. The location of the the artist's oil portrait of Nancy Ritson Taylor (Mrs. Robert Barraud Taylor) is currently unknown.

44. FARL entry for portrait can be found at www.digitalcollection.frick.org.

45. Mrs. Nellie Taylor was a descendant of Robert Barraud Taylor I's brother Archibald Taylor. According to their website, the Virginia Museum of History and Culture acquired their copy of the Robert Barraud Taylor portrait in 1986.

46. The author appreciates the assistance of her colleague Neal Hurst, associate curator of costume and textiles at Colonial Williamsburg, for his thoughts on dating the hairstyle and costume for this and many of the Eyre Hall portraits.

47. Guillaume is best known for his equestrian portraits of Confederate leaders and the famous scene of Lee's surrender which currently hangs at the Appomattox Court House. He came to the United States purportedly at the urging of William Cabell Rives, who, as the American minister to France and president of the Historical and Philosophical Society of Virginia, commissioned a copy of a portrait from him. Guillaume settled in Richmond in 1857 and remained there for 14 years until relocating to Washington, D.C. in 1871. For more information, see "Chapter 2: 1838–1861," in *The Virginia Historical Society: An Anniversary Narrative of its First Century and a Half*, special issue, *The Virginia Magazine of History and Biography* 90, no. 1 (January 1982): 21–42. As an interesting connection, Guillaume also painted portraits of Daniel Cary Barraud (1790–1867) and his family. Daniel was a son of Philip and Ann Barraud; his daughter Courtney Cordelia Barraud Hanson was first cousins with Lelia Ann Baker Taylor whose son married the daughter of Severn and Margaret Parker Eyre.

48. There is an interesting pair of letters that survive between Guillaume and Mary Anna Custis Lee about the use of photographs in his studio. Transcribed by Colin Woodward, April 18, 2017, from photostats in the Henry Woodhouse Collection, Jessie Ball duPont Library, Stratford Hall. Lee Family Digital Archive, www.leefamilyarchive.org.

49. Griffin credits his time with the Egelis in the early 1990s. See an interview with the artist by Ann Dorbin-Frock, "Easton Artist's 9-Year Streak," *Tidewater Times* (July 2013), https://issuu.com/tidewatertimes/docs/july_2013_ttimes_web_magazine, accessed July 2020.

Maps

KATIE MCKINNEY

Virginia, Maryland,
Pennsilvania,
1773–94.
Cat. 105

To BUILD HIS MAP COLLECTION, FURLONG Baldwin focused on maps featuring the Eastern Shore of Virginia that identify the town of Cheriton, located just southeast of Eyre Hall at the end of Eyre Hall Creek. Though there is no evidence that maps were used as wall decoration or otherwise, generations of the Eyre family owned books containing maps. The library also included educational texts on geography such as William Guthrie's *A New System of Modern Geography* (1794), which is stamped with William Eyre's name.[1] Several focused on early American geography, such as the English edition of Antonio de Herrera's *The General History of the Vast Continent and Islands of America,*

commonly called the West Indies (1725-26) and Antoine-Simon Le Page du Pratz's *The History of Louisiana, or of the western parts of Virginia and Carolina, containing a description of the countries that lye on both sides of the Mississippi* (1763). Both books carry Eyre's 1794 bookplate, but could have been purchased much earlier. Beyond the maps in these publications, the texts themselves contained valuable information related to trade, politics, and agriculture. In 1764, Landon Carter, planter, fellow Burgess, and contemporary of Littleton Eyre, consulted Du Pratz's book to compare information about Louisiana with his observations about the climate, soil, and ideas to improve crops on his plantation in Virginia.[2]

105

Virginia, Maryland, Pennsilvania, East & West New Jersey
Published by John Mount (1725–1786) and Thomas Page III (1730–1781)

Published by John Mount and Thomas Page
London, 1773-94[3]
Line engraving on laid paper
H. 20 in., W. 31½ in.; frame 28 × 39 in.

The English Pilot: The Fourth Book, a sea atlas first published by William Fisher and John Thornton in 1689, would be published in 30 editions over the course of the next century.[4] The maps and charts contained in this book were essential to mariners and merchants with North American interests, and it appears in the inventories of several mariners and ship's captains in the Chesapeake.[5] Fisher and Thornton first published a version of this chart of the Chesapeake and Delaware Bays, which was largely based on an earlier map made by Augustine Herman in 1673. A

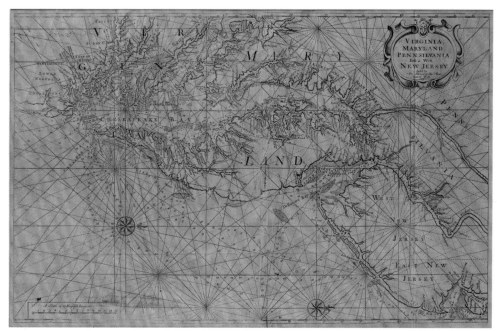

Dutch merchant who arrived in New Amsterdam in 1644, he was involved in trade from New England to the Caribbean. He owned land in Northampton County by the mid-seventeenth century, and utilized his extensive knowledge of the region to create his detailed map which became the standard source of cartographic information into the eighteenth century.[6] Given Thornton's position as hydrographer to the East India Company, he had access to manuscript maps and descriptions of the American coast and was able to provide additional hydrographic information to that depicted on the earlier

map. In 1743, publishers John Mount and Thomas Page (who published the book after Thornton's death in 1708) re-engraved the map on a new copperplate—the older one being perhaps worn out from extensive wear.

This version of the chart likely results from a state published between 1773 and 1794, when the plate was revised to change "New Jarsey" to "New Jersey" and the publishers' names were added.[7] The overall longevity of the map is a testament to its usefulness to mariners in the area, who turned to it for over one hundred years.

106

A Draught of Virginia from the Capes to York in York River and Kuiquotan or Hamton in James River

Compiled by Mark Tiddeman (fl. 1730)
Published by William (1688–1769) and John Mount (1725–1786) and Thomas Page II (1704–1762)
London, ca. 1773
Line engraving and etching on laid paper
H. 18½ in., W. 23 in.; frame 25 × 30 in.

When Mark Tiddeman's chart of the waters of Hampton Roads was added to *The English Pilot: The Fourth Book* in 1729, it was the first map dedicated exclusively to one particular region within the colony of Virginia.[8] The map provided the most detailed soundings that were available for the Hampton Roads area and that would have been of great interest to anyone navigating between the Eastern Shore and the mainland. Tiddeman collected his data first hand while serving as master of the *Tartar*, a Royal Navy ship that was sent to patrol American waters, cruising back and forth along the coastline from the waters of Hampton Roads to New York between February 8, 1724 and August 2, 1728.[9] Though he did not include hydrographic surveys of the Eastern Shore, nor is there evidence that he set foot there, he did name three areas that were, at one time or another, Eyre family properties: Golden Quarter, Old Plantation, and Cheriton. He most likely borrowed these location names from Thornton's map which lists these same locations.[10]

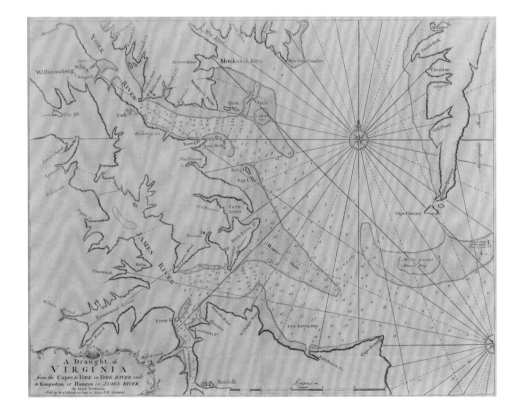

107

A New Map of Virginia Mary-land And the Improved Parts of Pennsylvania & New Jersey

Engraved and designed by John Senex (1678–1740)
after the work of Christopher Browne (fl. 1684–1712)
London, 1719
Hand-colored line engraving on laid paper
H. 19½ in., W. 22¼ in.; frame 26¼ × 29 in.

Although Christopher Browne originally published an earlier version of this map in 1685, it was popularized by John Senex, one of England's leading mapmakers. Senex purchased Browne's copperplate, made adjustments, added his imprint, included a dedication to George Hamilton, Earl of Orkney (absentee governor of Virginia between 1710 and 1737), and republished it in 1719.[11] The map was separately issued and also included in Senex's *A New General Atlas*, published in 1721. The map met with enormous commercial success, and this modified version of Browne's plate went on to be the more successful of the two. The map is a derivative of the Herrman map; it includes some of the same place names, including Cheriton, misspelled "Cherriton," and hydrographic information about depths from the Thornton map.

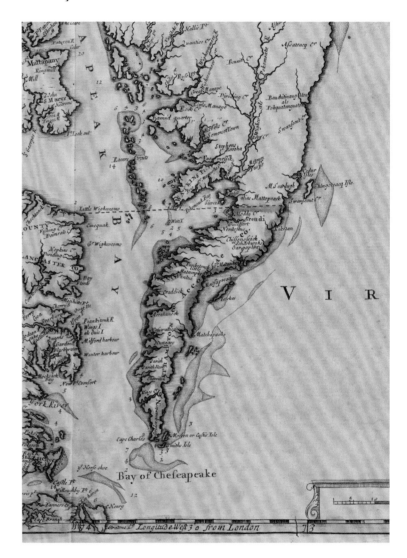

NOTES

1. William Guthrie, *A New System of Modern Geography; or, A Geographical, Historical, and Commercial Grammar; and Present State of the Several Nations of the World* (Philadelphia: Printed by Matthew Carey, 1794). First American edition in two volumes, 1: 1794, 2: 1795. No notations in first volume; in second volume, rubber stamp "W Eyre."

2. See entry for February 25, 1764 in *The Diary of Landon Carter of Sabine Hall, 1752–1778*, ed. Jack P. Greene (Charlottesville: University Press of Virginia, 1965), 1:256–58.

3. This is plate II, state 2, according to Coolie Verner, *A Carto-Bibliographical Study of The English Pilot: The Fourth Book. With Special Reference to the Charts of Virginia* (Charlottesville: University of Virginia Press, 1960), 39.

4. Verner, *A Carto-Bibliographical Study of The English Pilot.*

5. See the inventories of John Jones, 1734, Maryland Register of Wills Records, 1629–1999, Kent County Inventory Accounts 1732–1740, 129-30 and Captain James Gough, July 1767, Norfolk County, Virginia, Appraisements, No. 1, 1755–1783, 115–16.

6. Christian J. Koot, "The Merchant, the Map, and Empire: Augustine Herrman's Chesapeake and Interimperial Trade, 1644–73," *William and Mary Quarterly*, 3rd ser., 67, no. 4 (October 2010): 603–44. And see also Part I, chapter 1, "Golden Quarter," regarding Herrman's background and connection to the Eastern Shore.

7. Philip D. Burden, *The Mapping of North America: A List of Printed Maps*, vol. 2, *1671–1700* (Rickmansworth, U.K.: Raleigh Publications, 2007), 361, no. 667.

8. William C. Wooldridge, *Mapping Virginia: From the Age of Exploration to the Civil War* (Charlottesville: University of Virginia Press, 2012), 98, no. 94.

9. Verner, *A Carto-Bibliographical Study of The English Pilot*, 51–53.

10. Wooldridge, *Mapping Virginia*, 98.

11. Wooldridge, *Mapping Virginia*, 90, no. 84.

Prints

KATIE MCKINNEY

The Portraiture of Sir
Charles Sidley's Bay
Gelding True Blew,
1753.
Cat. 109

FRAGILE AND RELIANT ON FASHION AND TASTE, prints can be ephemeral objects. They are often worn out when exposed to elements, dispersed, repurposed, or discarded. Prints that survive with evidence that they were used as furnishings, rather than being bound into books or kept in portfolios, in early America, particularly the South, are extremely rare. Rarer still are prints with intact family histories, making the relatively large number of eighteenth-century prints that remain at Eyre Hall exceptional. They were first documented in Severn Eyre's 1774 inventory. Forty prints of varying sizes appear grouped together in the 1774 inventory, listed as "pictures," which was how prints were commonly referred to in the period.[1] Prints are often difficult to identify with certainty in inventories, as is the case in Severn's inventory:

> 13 large pictures @ 15 shillings (a total of £9.15.0)
> 1 doz (on) small do @ 10 shillings (a total of £6)
> 15 ditto (small pictures) at 75 each (a total of £3.15.0)[2]

Out of the forty prints mentioned in the inventory, at least 14 with histories at Eyre Hall survive, making up three thematic groupings of prints: six racing prints, four English landscapes, and four featuring Roman ruins.

The Eyre Hall prints were likely ordered through a factor in England or could have been obtained through the Eyres' mercantile connections in Philadelphia and New England. The original publication dates range between 1745 and 1754, though some might have remained in publication or on the market much longer. Engraved copperplates for popular prints were frequently sold between publishers and might be reused long after their original imprint. Newspaper advertisements and auction records also reveal an active second-hand market for prints in the colonies. Severn might have brought them with him when he inherited Eyre Hall, though given the early publication dates of the prints it is also possible his father purchased them, and they were never hung.

Prints used for decoration were usually sold in sets because, when hung together framed, they filled the space as well as more expensive paintings or smaller, less expensive prints.[3] It is possible that "13 large pictures" refer to the landscapes and views of Rome, in addition to other prints no longer extant. The high value suggests that the prints were expensively framed and glazed, which raised the price of a loose print considerably. The racing prints, six of which survive from what would originally have been a set of 12, are housed in original eighteenth-century frames with sanded gilt liners. A 1772 invoice from London framer John Overlove to the merchant firm John Norton and Sons, which exported goods like prints to Chesapeake merchants, reveals the expense for framing similar prints:

> To 12 Large Prints of Gentlemans Seats in Peartree Frames; glass 22 x 16 6:16:6
>
> To 6 Large fine Prints of Horses framed in Partree [sic] frames and glasses 22 x 16 3:3:0
>
> To 6 Landskips in Carv'd gilt Frames 5:2:0[4]

These costs reflect both the price of the prints and framing, revealing variations in price, size, and types of frames, with gilding raising the price considerably.

Based on their location in Severn's inventory, it is likely that all 40 prints hung in the front hall of the house. A photograph dating to the period when the last Severn (1831–1914) and his wife Margaret S. Parker (1840–1899) summered at Eyre Hall shows that the horse prints and some of the landscapes or antiquities were on display in the front hall (see Fig. 28). This photograph offers insights into how pictures were arranged on the wall in the nineteenth century and offers tantalizing clues regarding how these prints might have been placed when they were first purchased. A photograph of the parlor dating from that same period shows two small engraved portraits of prominent lawyer William Wirt and congressman John

Fig. 234. Photograph
of second-floor best
chamber, ca. 1900.

The prints at Eyre Hall are a reflection of the interests and personalities of their owners as the house has transformed over generations. Some of these interests have remained constant across the years while others have come and gone, but today, as an assemblage, this important collection of rare prints in their original frames is a true treasure.

Dennis by Charles Balthazar Julien Févret de Saint-Mémin. Today they remain in the same location, flanking the fireplace. Another early photograph (Fig. 234) depicts four framed sentimental prints (three of which survive today) hanging over the fireplace in the best chamber, including two romantic French lithographs which were published by the French artist Julien Vallou de Villeneuve.[5] One of these prints, *The Miniature* (Cat. 108), was reframed at some point in an églomisé frame that bears the inscription "RUN a WAY LOVE," which was likely the title of another print.[6] French lithographs that reproduced the works of famous artists were imported in large numbers into the United States by the 1840s and were at the height of fashion. It is likely that fashion-conscious William L. Eyre purchased such prints to decorate Eyreville and they were later brought to Eyre Hall by his son.[7]

Musical talent and appreciation is shared by generations of women of the Eyre family, including Margaret Eyre Taylor Baldwin, who possibly purchased the genre print *The Old Old Song*, which features a line of notes and lyrics for Auld Lang Syne along the lower margin. The print was published around 1920, after the work of English artist Walter Dendy Sadler, and depicts men at dinner raising a glass to one another.[8] The desire for (or popularity of) sporting and equestrian prints endured into the twentieth century, clustered in the upstairs back hall, which includes several racing and foxhunting prints dating to the late eighteenth and mid-nineteenth centuries after the work of French artists Carle and Horace Vernet, who were famous for their representations of horses.

108

The Miniature

Julien Vallou de Villeneuve (1795–1866), after T. Harper
Published by Charles Louis Constans, France or England, ca. 1825
Lithograph
H. 12½ in., W. 10¼ in.; frame 17 × 14¾ in.

109

The Portraiture of Sir Charles Sidley's Bay Gelding True Blew

Henry Roberts (ca. 1710–ca. 1790), after James Roberts (1725–1799)
Published by Henry Roberts, London, 1753
Hand-colored etching and line engraving on laid paper
H. 9¾ in., W. 13⅞ in.; frame 13 × 17 in.

Reminders of the family's longheld interest in equestrian pursuits include a set of six portraits of racehorses. Originally, they were part of a set of twelve published between 1752 and 1754 by English printmaker and music publisher Henry Roberts. They feature famous English racehorses of the 1740s and early 1750s including Othello, Whynot, Antelope, Victorious, True Blew, and Grenadier.[9] It is likely that these prints were the one dozen "small" pictures that cost 10 shillings each listed in Severn Eyre's 1774 inventory.[10] In London, Roberts advertised that unframed copies of these prints sold for a shilling apiece, or his customers could purchase them, "neatly fram'd in Pear-tree, carv'd and gilt Edges, from 6 s. each, to 10 s."[11] The Eyre Hall horse prints all retain their original carved pear-tree frames with sand gilt liners. A photograph of the entry hall ca. 1900 shows seven of the these prints arranged above five of the larger views.

This incredibly rare set might have only been in publication for a brief period. Roberts was not completely honest when he advertised that his prints were "more accurately done than any of these like Sort; yet attempted."[12] The format—with a title surmounting a portrait of a horse, with details about their pedigree, owners, and performance flanking either side, and heraldry below—was almost directly lifted from a series of prints published by Thomas Butler after the works of James Seymour.[13] Butler responded to Roberts's cheaper and nearly identical set, calling them "Spurious" and insisting that "only them by me are authentick."[14] To avoid copyright laws, Roberts changed some of the wording and altered the central image, but their rarity suggests Butler put a stop to his competitor. Sometime before 1775, Roberts teamed up with prolific printseller Robert Sayer to market a set of the same 12 racehorses in a sparse and much reduced format.[15]

The Portraiture of Othello, the Property of Mr. Prior, late Sr. Ralph Gores

Published by Henry Roberts (ca. 1710–ca. 1790), after James Roberts (1725–1799)
London, 1752
Hand-colored etching and line engraving on laid paper
H. 9¾ in., W. 13⅞ in.; frame 13 × 17 in.

Horsemanship, breeding, racing, and hunting were popular in eighteenth-century England, and these prints reflect an extension of those interests shared by the Eyre family and other members of the Virginia and Maryland gentry. One foreign visitor to Williamsburg in the 1770s noted Virginians' love of horses, writing: "Virginians, of all ranks and denominations, are excessively fond of horses, especially those of the race breed. The gentlemen of fortune expend great sums on their studs, generally keeping handsome horses."[16] Roberts's prints were appealing because they depicted famous horses, but, more importantly, they served as documents of expensive equestrian pedigrees. For colonists in the Chesapeake, the importation of English horses and capitalizing on prestigious bloodlines was just as much a pastime as watching these horses run. One of the horses depicted in the prints, Othello, was imported to Maryland by Deputy Governor Horatio Sharpe in the late 1750s. After Othello's career as a racer ended, he went on to stand stud in the colonies for about 13 years.[17] Severn Eyre's inventory includes "1 English Horse" at £40—more than any other horse on the inventory by far.[18]

Roman Antiquities: The Nile in the Vatican Gardens, Arch of Constantine, Temple of Janus, Temple of Bacchus, Vase at the Villa Borghese

Johann Sebastian Müller (1715–1792), after Giovanni Paolo Pannini (1691–1765)
Published by Arthur Pond, London, 1746
Etching with line engraving
H. 17¾ in., W. 23 in.; frame 24¾ × 29¾ in.

Originally published in 1745, Arthur Pond's series *Roman Antiquities* reflected the increased interest in ancient culture, thought, and art fueled by the popularity of the Grand Tour, as wealthy English aristocrats trekked through Europe visiting ancient ruins, collecting replicas of sculptures, and commissioning copies of paintings.[19] The set was engraved by Johann Sebastian Müller after compositions by Giovanni Paolo Pannini, which were a pastiche of Roman ruins, buildings, and sculptures—fantastically arranged out of context—that were familiar to the Grand Tourist or those who aspired to such travels.[20] The main attractions are labeled for clarity and include such sites as the Apollo Belvedere, Trajan's Column, and the Coliseum. An integral part of liberal education for men of the period was an understanding of Roman architectural orders, as well as knowledge of Greek and Roman sculpture, which taught restraint and comportment. This rare full set consisted of five prints (there are four at Eyre Hall) that measured 18 by 24 inches, a size that would have been just as substantial as any painting.[21] These commercially successful prints, which were sold by Pond between 1745 and 1754, delighted customers in London, as well as in America.[22] Artist John Smibert, who retailed these prints in Boston, reported that "ye View of Greenwich & Antiquities by P. Panini please more here than ye others and I hope to some number of them will sell."[23] Prints of Roman and Greek antiquities, not specifically attributed to Pond, are found in other Virginia inventories of the period, though it can be difficult to determine if they were those by Pond or some of his many imitators.[24]

Fig. 235. Detail from *Roman Antiquities: Basilica of Antoninus, Temple of Fortuna Virilis, Mausoleum Vase*, Johann Sebastian Müller, after Giovanni Paolo Pannini, published by Arthur Pond, London, 1746, etching with line engraving.

A View in Exton Park belonging to the R:ᵗ Hon:ᵇˡᵉ the Earl of Gainsborough; to whom this Plate is inscrib'd by his Lordships most dutiful & most obed:ᵗ Serv:ᵗ T. Smith

James Mason (1710–1783), after Thomas Smith of Derby (1715–1767)
Published by François Vivares (1709–1780), London, after 1749
Etching and line engraving
H. 15 in., W. 21 in.; frame 21⅝ × 27⅝ in.

By the mid-century, Britons began to reflect on their national landmarks, architectural marvels, and landscapes.[25] In 1746, engraver François Vivares, who had previously worked with Arthur Pond, copied the formula used in the *Roman Antiquities*, announcing that he would publish "[f]our perspective Views of the most considerable Antique Ruins, in or near Rome" and a companion set of "four of the principal English ruins."[26] Though the set of four landscape prints at Eyre Hall[27] are not that set of English ruins, they reflect the contemporary interest in creating landscapes and structures inspired by antiquity. Eyre Hall's set of four landscape prints feature the parklands of four estates (Hagley Park, Exton Park, Newstead Park, and Belton) from the north of England after paintings by Thomas Smith of Derby. The plates were engraved by James Mason and François Vivares in 1749, though these particular prints are weak impressions and were likely published after that date.[28]

English nobility employed landscape designers and architects to design fantastic and thematic garden landscapes punctuated by follies such as replicas of Greek and Roman temples, grottos, hermitages, castle ruins, and elaborate water features like those featured in the four landscape prints at Eyre Hall.[29] Smith's paintings and Vivares's prints helped promote the careers of landscape architects and elevate the prestige of their patrons. The print of Hagley Park shows figures looking on in awe at the stately home's famous deer park, while the newly built replica of imagined castle ruins looms in the distance. The Ruined Castle, designed for Sir Thomas Lyttleton (1686–1751) and built at Hagley in 1747–48, helped to launch the career of Sanderson Miller.[30] The rusticated water feature at Belton was a carefully constructed ruin that also included a small hermitage at far center-left, featuring an actual hermit. The purpose of these elaborately designed structures was to create an immersive experience that supplied entertainment at every angle, round every turn, and over every carefully crafted vista.

113 and 114

John Dennis (1771–1806)

Charles Balthazar Julien Févret de Saint-Mémin (1770–1852)
Washington, D.C., 1803–5
Etching and engraving
Diam. 2½ in.; frame 6⅜ × 6⅜ in.

William Wirt (1772–1834)

Charles Balthazar Julien Févret de Saint-Mémin (1770–1852)
Richmond, 1807–8
Etching and engraving
Diam. 2⅛ in.; frame 6¼ × 6¼ in.

These two small engraved portraits of John Dennis (1771–1806) and William Wirt (1772–1834) were engraved by Charles Balthazar Julien Févret de Saint-Mémin (1770–1852), a French portraitist working in America around the turn of the nineteenth century. The engravings were based on life-sized chalk profile portraits that Saint-Mémin would take using a device called a physiognotrace, which traced outlines of the subject's face, with the details subsequently rendered by the artist.[31] Saint-Mémin would then reduce the image and engrave a small copperplate using a combination of engraving and etching techniques to create a circular engraving ten times smaller than the original image.[32] These bespoke engravings were not retailed separately during the period and clients could order a number of them, usually 12, to send to friends and family to give as gifts, and the copperplate was saved for future use.[33] Wirt's and Dennis's portraits are both framed in apparently bespoke gilt frames made from moldings meant for larger portraits and set with a fitted round liner.[34] The frame moldings feature a leaf-and-dart course, which was popular during the 1790s and through to the 1820s.[35]

It is unknown how the portraits came to Eyre Hall, but there are several direct and indirect connections between the sitters and John Eyre. John Dennis, whose portrait was completed between 1803 and 1805 in Washington, D.C., was a Federalist politician from the lower Eastern Shore of Maryland near Pocomoke, who served four terms in the United States House of Representatives.[36] John Eyre's brother-in-law Littleton Dennis Teackle was Dennis's nephew, and their homes—the Teackle Mansion and Beckford—were adjacent to one another in Princess Anne, Maryland.[37] In 1817, Dennis's daughter Elizabeth married Judge Abel Parker Upshur of Vaucluse (1790–1844), cousin of John's wife, Ann Upshur Eyre. Sadly, Elizabeth died that same year, at the age of 22, and is buried at Vaucluse.[38]

Before his marriage to Elizabeth, Abel Parker Upshur studied law in Richmond with the prominent lawyer William Wirt (1772–1834), who would go on to become the longest-serving United States attorney general in the country's history.[39] Between 1803 and 1806, Wirt had served on the bar in Norfolk with Robert Barraud Taylor.[40] Wirt was asked by President Thomas Jefferson to serve as prosecutor in the treason trial of Aaron Burr, launching him to prominence.[41] Quickly seeking to capitalize on the public exposure from the trial, Wirt published transcripts of his arguments in 1808 and included his recently completed engraved portrait by Saint-Mémin in the frontispiece.[42] It is possible that the portrait engraving at Eyre Hall was cut from this book and framed, or perhaps was given as a token to his young student. Abel P. Upshur had a successful political and legal career, though it was cut short at its peak. He died in 1844 in an accident while serving as secretary of state.[43] Having just lost one of their most prominent citizens, John Eyre chaired a meeting held in honor of deceased wife's first cousin in Eastville on March 23, 1844.[44] Eyre brought a copy of the resolves of the meeting to the family of Mr. Upshur.

115

No. 38 (Au Galop)

Charles François Gabriel Levachez
(ca. 1760–ca. 1820), after Carle Vernet
(1758–1836) and Horace Vernet (1789–1863)
Hand-colored aquatint with engraving
Originally published in Paris, ca. 1811
H. 12 in., W. 14½ in.; frame 19½ × 22 in.

The Eyre family had an interest in horses and sport that endured from the eighteenth century into the twentieth. Several rare French equestrian prints after the famous equestrian painters Carle and Horace Vernet survive in the house. William L. Eyre, a noted horse enthusiast with a knowledge of fashion, might have collected these imported prints that showcase the French fascination with English sporting culture. They include two aquatints[45] featuring racehorses that belong to a five-part series of horses in various sporting poses and situations published in Paris and engraved by Charles François Gabriel Lechavez around 1811.[46] There is another set of prints after Carle Vernet and engraved in color by Philibert-Louis Debucourt entitled *Le Chasseur au renaud*.[47]

NOTES

1. Prints were often referred to as "pictures" indiscriminately with paintings during the period; for more on print collecting and the use of the term, see Timothy Clayton, *The English Print, 1688–1802* (New Haven: Yale University, 1997), 3.
2. Inventory of the estate of Severn Eyre, February 27, 1774, Northampton County Wills & Inventories, No. 25, 1775–1777, 391.
3. Louise Lippincott, *Selling Art in Georgian London: The Rise of Arthur Pond* (New Haven and London: Yale University Press for the Paul Mellon Centre for Studies in British Art, 1983), 144.
4. Invoice from John Overlove to John Norton & Son, June 30, 1772, John Norton & Sons Papers, John D. Rockefeller Jr. Library, Colonial Willamsburg.
5. John Hannavy, *Encyclopedia of Nineteenth-Century Photography* (London: Routledge, 2013), 1435.
6. There was a lithograph entitled *Run Away Love* made by Charles Knight after the work of Thomas Stothard, published in 1792; see British Museum, London, 1917,1208.2363.
7. Firms like Maison Goupil (which opened an outlet in New York in 1848) sold reproductive prints after contemporary artists working in the Romantic style. For a history of the Maison Goupil see DeCourcy McIntosh, "The Origins of

the Maison Goupil in the Age of Romanticism," *The British Art Journal* 5, no. 1 (Spring/Summer 2004): 64–76. Perhaps these prints were also acquired when Elizabeth Upshur Teackle stayed at Eyre Hall in the 1830s before her marriage. She lived in the house prior to her marriage in 1839 to Aaron Balderson Quinby.

8. Engraved by James Dobie after Walter Dendy Sadler, published by L. H. Lefèvre, London, 1920. There is also another print by Walter Dendy Sadler in the house, entitled *The New Will*.
9. The prints are dated as follows: Othello (1752), Whynot (1753), Antelope (1753), Victorious (1753), True Blew (1753), and Grenadier (1754). The publication of a print of the horse named Silver Leg was announced in January 1753, though Roberts noted that "Little Driver, Othello, or Black and all Black" were also available for purchase, suggesting that they were published prior to this announcement. The prints of Little Driver and Silver Leg do not remain at Eyre Hall. Advertisement, *London Evening Post*, January 9–11, 1753.
10. Inventory of the estate of Severn Eyre, 391.
11. *London Evening Post*, May 12–15, 1753.
12. Roberts advertised originality with "genuine

Pedigrees, Performances, Colours, Marks, and Arms." *London Evening Post*, May 12–15, 1753.
13. In 1751 Henry Roberts engraved a horse portrait of Othello by Seymour for Butler that was part of a large set of horse portraits. A year later, Roberts published a riderless *Othello*: a wine bottle rests in the foreground, and the name of the horse's new owner, Sir Ralph Gore, has been added. Timothy Clayton, *The English Print, 1688–1802* (New Haven: Yale University Press, 1997), 141.
14. It seems possible that Butler put a stop to Roberts's equestrian prints, capping the set at 12, with the latest date being 1754. See Clayton, *English Print*, 142.
15. Robert Sayer and John Bennett's 1775 catalogue lists that second set of prints as "24. A Collection of the most famous and high bred Running Horses, with an account of their pedigrees, and number of matches won by them. Engraved from the originals of Wotton and Seymour, by H. Roberts." *Sayer and Bennett's Enlarged Catalogue of New and Valuable Prints* (London: Holland Press, 1775), reproduced in facsimile as *Sayer and Bennett's Catalogue for 1775* (London and Trowbridge: Redwood Press, 1970), 91.
16. Smyth also noted that some Virginia horses could claim the bloodlines of several well-known

English racehorses: J. F. D. Smyth, *A Tour in the United States of America, containing an account of the present situation of that country* (Dublin: G. Perin, 1784), 1:13–14.

17. Fairfax Harrison, *The Belair Stud: 1747–1761* (Richmond, Va.: Old Dominion Press, 1929), 31–34.

18. Inventory of the estate of Severn Eyre, 391.

19. Jeremy Black, *Italy and the Grand Tour* (New Haven: Yale University Press, 2003), 174.

20. Lippincott, *Selling Art in Georgian London*, 142–43.

21. Lippincott, *Selling Art in Georgian London*, 143.

22. According to Lippincott (*Selling Art in Georgian London*, 143), only 81 of the 544 sets were hand-colored and framed in Pond's shop; none were bound into portfolios.

23. Lippincott, *Selling Art in Georgian London*, 143.

24. The following two references are not to Pond's prints but to those of his imitators: Jane Vobe, proprietress of the Kings Arm Tavern in Williamsburg, purchased "6 ruins of Rome" from the printing office on February 5, 1765: *Virginia Gazette* Daybooks, 1750–1766, Tracy W. McGregor Library Accession #467, Albert and Shirley Small Special Collections, University of Virginia Library, Charlottesville. Joseph Royle of York County, Virginia, owned "6 ruins of Rome" valued at £1.15.0, as well as two more prints of Rome in its "Original Splendour" listed at 12 shillings: Inventory and appraisement of the estate of Joseph Royle, May 26, 1766, York County Wills & Inventories 21, 1760–1771, 271–76.

25. Peter Clayton attributes the growth of appreciation for picturesque landscapes to this type of print, which seems to have inspired domestic British artists to seek or create similar landscapes in Britain; see Clayton, *English Print*, 155–57.

26. Lippincott, *Selling Art in Georgian London*, 145.

27. *A View in Exton Park belonging to the R:t Hon:ble the Earl of Gainsborough* (engraved by James Mason); *A View in Newstead Park, belonging to the R.t Hon.ble the Lord Byron* (engraved by François Vivares, dated 1749); *A View of the New Waterworks &c at Belton in Lincolnshire belonging to the R.t Hon.ble the Lord Vis(t) Tyrconnel* (engraved by Mason, not dated on print); and *A View in Hagley Park belonging to R.t Th.s Lyttleton Bar:t* (engraved by Vivares, not dated on print).

28. The 1803 Boydell catalogue includes these four prints together in its list of prints of "Views of the Peak after the work of Smith." John and Josiah Boydell, *An Alphabetical Catalogue of Plates, engraved . . . after the finest pictures and drawings of the Italian, Flemish, German, French, English, and other schools, which compose the stock of John and Josiah Boydell, etc.* (London: W. Bulmer & Company, 1803), 44.

29. Rachel Kennedy, "Who Led Taste?," in *Design & the Decorative Arts: Britain 1500–1900*, ed. Michael Snodin and John Styles (London: V&A Publications, 2001), 218–23.

30. Michael Cousins, "Hagley Park, Worcestershire," *Garden History* 35 (2007): 19.

31. Both drawings for Dennis and Wirt are unlocated. See Ellen G. Miles, *Saint-Mémin and the Neoclassical Profile Portrait in America* (Washington, D.C.: National Portrait Gallery, 1994), "Catalogue

of Portraits and Other Works," 288, no. 251, and 433–34, no. 962.

32. Miles, *Saint-Mémin*, 72–76.

33. Public figures, like the two subjects, might have had more than the usual number of copies printed—Thomas Jefferson ordered four dozen engravings from the artist—or, as in the case of William Wirt in 1808, included them as frontispieces for a book: Alexander Smyth of Richmond, for example, published his portrait by Saint-Mémin as a frontispiece in two separate publications. See Miles, *Saint-Mémin*, 205.

34. There is evidence of Saint-Mémin engravings being placed into albums, enclosed in lockets, or framed and hung in drawing rooms, such as the portrait at Eyre Hall; Miles, *Saint-Mémin*, 205.

35. According to Chris Swan, Senior Conservator of Wooden Artifacts at the Colonial Williamsburg Foundation, this style of frame molding was popular in America as early as the 1790s, but the profile also continues into the 1820s. It is also possible that an older frame could have been cut down. Email to the author, April 27, 2020.

36. John Eyre and John Dennis were both descended from Colonel Southey Littleton (1645–1679). Dennis was born at Beverly near Pocomoke in Worcester County, Maryland, to Littleton Dennis (ca. 1728–1774) and Susanna Upshur (1733–1784). His mother was the sister of Arthur Upshur IV who married Leah Custis, and aunt of Abel Upshur II, whose daughters were Ann Upshur (married John Eyre) and Elizabeth Upshur. Though Dennis voted for Aaron Burr in 1800, he was one of six Federalists to abstain from voting in the tiebreaker between Burr and Thomas Jefferson, therefore granting Jefferson victory. In 1804, he was appointed to the House Committee to oversee the impeachment of Supreme Court justice Samuel Chase. After four terms as a representative for Maryland, he retired from the House of Representatives in 1805, and died the following year while in Philadelphia. See J. Jefferson Looney and Ruth L. Woodward, *Princetonians, 1791–1794: A Biographical Dictionary* (Princeton: Princeton University Press, 1991), 4–42.

After completing engravings, Saint-Mémin kept several proof copies to show prospective clients. The sets were compiled, and they are the main source of identifying and dating portraits by the artist. In the collection at the National Portrait Gallery, this portrait is identified as "Th: Gilpin," but this identification was reattributed based on inscriptions by Elias Dexter, who identified the sitter as "John Dennis" in his publication *St.-Memin Collection of Portraits, Consisting of Seven Hundred and Sixty Medallion Portraits, principally of Distinguished Americans* (New York, 1862). Based on Dexter's reattribution, the catalogue raisonné of the work of Saint-Mémin by Ellen Miles identifies the sitter as John Dennis. See Miles, *Saint-Mémin*, 206–13, "Catalogue of Portraits and Other Works," 288, no. 251.

37. John Dennis's sister Elizabeth married John Teackle, whose son, Littleton Dennis Teackle, married Elizabeth Upshur, sister of Ann Upshur Eyre. Beckford was deeded in 1803 by George Jackson to John Dennis who built the house. There are a number of similarities in construction

details between the Teackle Mansion and Beckford. Anna E. Hill, "Beckford, Princess Anne, Somerset County, Maryland," National Register of Historic Places Inventory – Nomination Form, Annapolis, Maryland, 1973. Looney and Woodward, *Princetonians*, 42.

38. Anne Parker's brother George married Margaret Eyre on October 12, 1786. Jean Mihalyka, *Marriages, Northampton County, Virginia, 1661–1854* (Bowie, Md.: Heritage Books, 1991), 82.

39. Upshur was apparently one of his star students: in 1816, he even recommended him to James Madison for the position of U.S. district attorney for Virginia, but Madison chose Wirt instead. Though a lawyer, Wirt's politics leaned Democratic-Republican for most of his life, he was viewed as someone with the ability to set aside partisanship in order to mediate between two factions. Galen N. Thorp, "William Wirt," *Journal of Supreme Court History* 33, no. 3 (November 2008): 236; Joseph C. Robert, "William Wirt, Virginian," *The Virginia Magazine of History and Biography* 80, no. 4 (October 1972): 440.

40. Anya Jabour, "'No Fetters But Such as Love Shall Forge': Elizabeth and William Wirt and Marriage in the Early Republic," in *Constructing a Revolution: Women and Gender Roles in Virginia*, special issue, *The Virginia Magazine of History and Biography* 104, no. 2 (Spring 1996): 216; Robert Alonzo Brock, *Virginia and Virginians: Eminent Virginians* (Richmond: H. H. Hardesty, 1888), 1:167–68.

41. Thorp, "William Wirt," 236.

42. In 1807 Wirt sent his friend Ninian Edwards a copy of *The Two Principal Arguments of William Wirt, Esquire, on the Trial of Aaron Burr, for High Treason, and on the Motion to Commit Aaron Burr and Others, for Trial in Kentucky* (Richmond, 1808). In the accompanying letter, he wrote, "I suspect my face has altered so much since you saw me that you will scarcely see the likeness of the plate in the frontispiece. It is done by a very eminent artist here." Wirt to Ninian Edwards, December 26, 1807, Edwards Papers, Chicago Historical Society.

43. John Andrew Upshur, *Upshur Family in Virginia* (Richmond, Va.: The Dietz Press, 1955), 165–67.

44. At the meeting of those gathered, John Eyre expressed the common sentiment of "the melancholy bereavement sustained by our whole community" for the loss of "the lamented Upshur – the pride and boast of our county, the friend and companion of our daily walks." *Daily National Intelligencer* (Washington), March 23, 1844.

45. They are plates from "Quatrième suite de chevaux, dessinés par Carle et Horace Vernet et gravés par Levachez," published originally between 1794 and 1807.

46. John B. Podeschi, *Books on the Horse and Horsemanship: Riding, Hunting, Breeding & Racing 1400–1941: A Catalogue* (London: Tate Gallery for the Yale Center for British Art, 1981), 99; Jules Thiébaud, *Bibliographie des ouvrages français sur la chasse illustrée de quarante fac-similés* (Paris: E. Nourry & Librairie cynégétique, 1934), 928–29.

47. This aquatint is likely to be from a republication of late eighteenth- and early nineteenth-century prints by Debucourt after Vernet that were published ca. 1920.

Books

BENNIE BROWN

Laws of Virginia,
1794.
Cat. 124

A LIBRARY IS NEVER FIXED IN STONE WITH A one-time list. Books were a very fluid commodity, and were regularly borrowed, sold, or traded. The books at Eyre Hall were acquired by many methods: by direct purchase from local booksellers or through English agents, as gifts from family or friends, or through borrowings. Just as common—and this also holds true for Eyre Hall—was the purchase of books from neighbors or through family connections by marriage or family associations.

The present library contains over 300 titles in 800 surviving volumes dating from 1638 to 1911, which, if they were complete sets, would number more than 900 volumes. For organizational purposes, the collection is divided into three portions based upon the date of publication. The first portion comprises books dated and probably collected before 1789 by the first three owners of Eyre Hall, Littleton the builder (d. 1768), son Severn (d. 1773), and oldest grandson Littleton (d. 1789). The second groups those published between 1789 and 1855 when the library exploded in size under John, another grandson of the builder (d. 1855), and his nephew William L. Eyre of Eyreville (d. 1852). The third portion consists of the remaining volumes accumulated up to 1911, a few years before the death of the last Severn Eyre (d. 1914), the son of William L. Eyre and inheritor of Eyre Hall in 1855.[1] Most works carry personalized inscriptions and ownership markings linking them to many of the Eastern Shore's prominent citizens and members of the family.

Few early libraries were inventoried or catalogued. But we do have several family estate inventories which reflect the growth of the library. The inventory for Thomas Eyre (1719), the brother of the first Severn Eyre (d. 1728) who was the father of Littleton Eyre the builder, gives us a glimpse of the composition of his library, listing as it does "1 old Large Bible £ .5.0, 1 Athenian Mercury in folio £ .10.0." and "Parcel old books £ .6.0." Severn's inventory (1728) cites a few more

books but not necessarily those in his brother's estate: "1 Large book titl'd the new Testam' according to the Catholick Church £1.5.0, 1 Large Bible £ 0.10.0," and an early Virginia legal book, "1 Abridgemt of the Laws of Virga £ 0.3.6." The 1768 probate inventory of Littleton Eyre, the builder of Eyre Hall, only gives the usual obscure "a parcel of books."[2] At least the estate inventory of his son, Severn, in 1774 gives added information. In the dining room that Severn added there is mention of a mahogany desk and bookcase valued at £10. The inventory notes "1 Library 300 volumes £75.0.0," which would have been a sizable library for the day. Aside from the slaves, the item is the most expensive single entry in the inventory.[3] This citation indicates that the bulk of the library was kept in Severn's chamber and study, which was the northeast room on the ground floor. A logical place for these books is in the northeast closet next to the fireplace, where some original pine shelves still survive and hold some of the collection today. It parallels other Virginia estate inventories where large collections of books are listed as being housed in closets, as for example at Corotoman in 1732.[4]

The present count of books indicates how the collection was built. The first generation at Eyre Hall was Littleton Eyre, who built the house. His portion of the library numbered 36 titles in 162 volumes. The second generation was Littleton's son Severn, who added 17 titles in 84 volumes. The total number of books for these two generations comes to 246 volumes (as complete sets), which means the majority of the 300 books inventoried in 1774 are still there. The third generation was Severn's eldest son Littleton, who added an additional nine titles in 50 volumes. Collectively, the three generations compiled a library of 62 titles in 306 volumes.

Books dated between 1789 to 1855 fall within the long tenure of John Eyre, a younger brother of the short-lived Littleton who greatly expanded the library. He added 185 volumes (205 if complete sets) to the library. He commissioned a printed bookplate which is pasted down

116
Bookplate

Engraved and printed bookplate of John Eyre, who inherited Eyre Hall in 1789. He commissioned them in 1794 and used them to mark the books that he had inherited from his father and grandfather.

117
Bookplate

Printed bookplate of William L. Eyre of Eyreville, the family estate adjoining Eyre Hall. William L. Eyre was the son of William, who was the younger brother of John Eyre. William L. Eyre's son Severn Eyre inherited Eyre Hall from the childless John and incorporated his father's extensive library into the family library. William L. Eyre wrote the number of each book on his bookplate.

in 59 titles comprising 229 volumes dating from before 1796. He did not use a bookplate after that date (Cat. 116). However, an equal number of books came from the library of John Eyre's nephew, William L. Eyre of nearby Eyreville. He inherited Eyreville on the death of his father William, the younger brother of John. A collection of 113 titles in 340 surviving volumes (430 volumes if complete sets) bear the printed bookplate of William Littleton Eyre (Cat. 117). William died in 1852 and his son, Severn, inherited Eyre Hall from the childless John Eyre in 1855, thereby adding his father's collection into the main family collection. William L. Eyre created his own library from scratch, since the volumes all date to the first quarter of the nineteenth century. The remainder of the books date up to 1911, as gifts to the family. They reflect the transition of Eyre Hall from the permanent primary residence to a secondary abode.

COMPOSITION OF THE LIBRARY

The different phases of the library's growth reflect contemporary tastes and usages. For the rural and isolated part of the colony that the Eastern Shore was, books were more than a luxury to entertain, but a vital lifeline connecting the family to the outside world. For the self-reliant rural community at Eyre Hall, books were a necessity covering many critical issues facing the family: from commerce, education, agriculture, religion, and government, to medicine, history, and manners. The same is true of the additions from later generations. Following the Revolution, reading matter became more readily available, with the explosion of printing presses and publishers across Virginia and the other states; books now came not only from publishers in England, but from American bookmen in Baltimore, Philadelphia, New York, and Charleston.

In addition, tastes in literature were changing, and the establishment of private library companies opened people

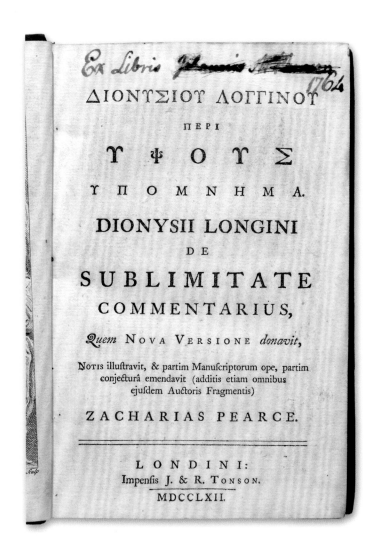

118

De sublimitate commentarius

Dionysius Longinus, *De sublimitate commentarius*
London: J.and R. Toxson, 1762
Octavo

Title page of this Latin/Greek classic popular in schools as a text for students. Many books were bought and sold among the local community, and this volume with its unknown crossed-out signature is typical.

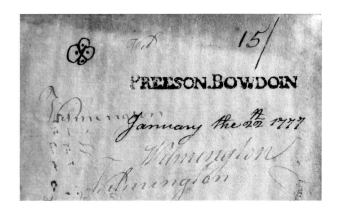

Fig. 236. Uncommon ink-stamped bookplate of Preeson Bowdoin, inscribed "January the 27th 1777," the date he purchased Longinus's *De sublimitate commentarius* for his classes at William and Mary (Cat. 118).

to additional opportunities for new books. The focus of household libraries was also changing. In the eighteenth century, books were for edification, instruction, and self-improvement, and the taste for fiction or "belles lettres" was just beginning to appear on the market with works by Alexander Pope and Jonathan Swift. In the nineteenth century, taste for fiction vastly increased in popularity, with the emergence of many of the new authors familiar to us today such as Washington Irving and James Fenimore Cooper in America and Sir Walter Scott and Charles Dickens in England. All these authors are present in the Eyre Hall collection.

CATEGORIES OF BOOKS

Classics

The classics were the backbone of any gentleman's education, and the Eyre family owned the standard English translations of many key Latin and Greek works. Alexander Pope's English translation of Homer's duo of the *Iliad* and *Odyssey* (London, 1750 and 1752) is the best example. Two titles printed in both Latin and Greek are Isocrates's *Opera* (London, 1769) and Longinus's *De sublimitate commentarius* (London, 1762) edited by Zachary Pearce (Cat. 118). Three

Waverley

Walter Scott, *Waverley; or, 'Tis Sixty Years Since*
Philadelphia: J. Crissy, 1825, 2 vols.
Octavo

Front cover of *Waverley*, with the gold-stamped name "Wm. L. Eyre, E. S. Va." for William L. Eyre of Eyreville in Northampton County, near Eyre Hall. Usually reserved for special books, this is a rare instance of a gold-stamped ownership signature on the front of a leather book board.

titles no longer extant were purchased by Colonel Littleton Eyre from the *Virginia Gazette* in Williamsburg between 1750 and 1752: Justinus's *Historia Philippicae* (1732) to be rebound, and two translations by John Clarke from Latin of Ovid's *Metamorphoses* and Virgil "in usum Delphini."[5] Titles added in the nineteenth century that were popular in America after the Revolution include Anacreon's *Odes* (London, 1802). Other classical works include Josephus's *Genuine Works* (New York, 1822–24), an edition revised by Samuel Butler from the Reverend William Whiston's translation, as well as Livy's *History of Rome* (Philadelphia, 1823), and Plutarch's *Lives* (New York, 1822).

English Literature

Literature makes up the lion's share of the library, encompassing criticism, essays, poetry, plays and so on. John Eyre collected sets of works by leading authors including Joseph Addison (1753), Abraham Cowley (1721), Henry Fielding (1783), Alexander Pope (1751 and 1767), William Shakespeare (1757), Jonathan Swift (1765), and James Thomson (1766). In addition to the sets, there is also a considerable number of individual works, such as Samuel Butler's satirical poem *Hudibras* (London, 1761) illustrated by William Hogarth, a popular novel by Charlotte Lennox entitled *The Female Quixote; or, The Adventures of Arabella* (London, 1752), and Laurence Sterne's best-known novel *The Life and Opinions of Tristram Shandy, Gentleman* (Glasgow, 1767).

The practice of collecting sets continued into the nineteenth century, and most were from William L. Eyre at Eyreville, who added sets by Oliver Goldsmith (1811 and 1835), Samuel Johnson (1823), and John Milton (1824). Individual titles include Mark Akenside's *Pleasures of the Imagination* (New York, 1819), Samuel Johnson's *Lives of the Most Eminent Poets* (London, 1800–1), and Thomas Percy's collection of ballads and songs originally published in 1765 as *Reliques of Ancient English Poetry* (Philadelphia, 1822).

The Eyres added collected sets by popular authors such as Robert Burns (1821) and Lord Byron (1821 and 1825). Individual volumes of such collections include two of Charles Dickens's major works: *The Posthumous Papers of the Pickwick Club* (Philadelphia, 1837) and *Sketches by Boz* (Philadelphia, 1839) illustrated by George Cruikshank. Works by Edward Lyttleton are legion, comprising six titles in 12 volumes of his lesser-known novels. English author Frederick Marryat's novels were just as popular, with six titles in ten volumes. The best-represented author in the library is Walter Scott, with his Waverley series of novels, which encompasses 18 titles in 48 volumes including *Ivanhoe* (Philadelphia, 1823) and *Waverley* (Philadelphia, 1825) (Cat. 119).

The few American literary contributions come from the leading authors of the first half of the nineteenth century: the Eyres collected six titles in 12 volumes of James Fenimore Cooper and five titles in 10 volumes of Washington Irving. There is a smattering of other titles, with the best-known example being James Paulding's *Letters from the South* (New York, 1817), a fictitious popular travel journal.

120
History of the Roman Republic

Adam Ferguson, *The History of the Progress and Termination of the Roman Republic*
London: W. Strahan, 1783
Quarto

Title page with ownership signature of "William Stith, Novr. 1788." Stith was a longtime friend, legal associate, and relative of John Eyre's.

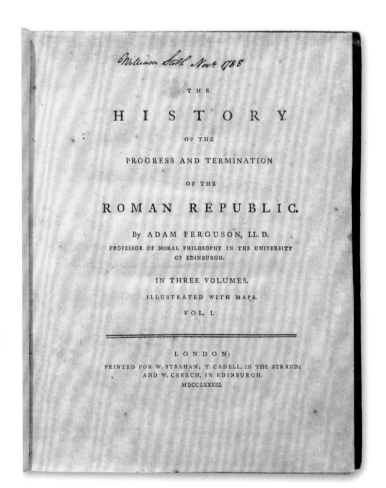

121
Description of the East

Richard Pococke, *A Description of the East and Some Other Countries*
London: W. Boyer, 1743–45, 2 vols. in 3 parts
Folio

Title page from Volume I, with elaborate engraved vignette, of a description of the eastern Mediterranean before Englishmen regularly traveled there. The title page of each volume in the set gives different information and ornamental details.

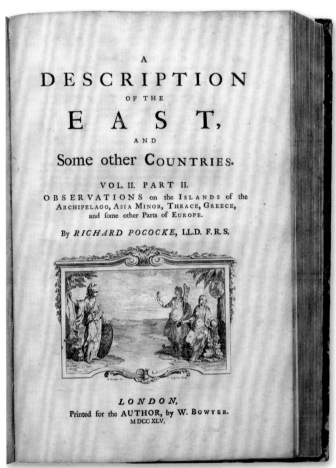

Ancient History

Every gentleman's library carried the standard works on ancient history, and the Eyres' library is no exception. The best examples are Charles Rollin's *Antient History* (London, 1754) and his other classic text, *Roman History* (London, 1754). Another title is Adam Ferguson's *History of the Progress and Termination of the Roman Republic* (London, 1783) (Cat.

120). A rare work in the library, more a travel journal, is Richard Pococke's *Description of the East and Some Other Countries* (London, 1743–45), an account of an English clergyman's trip to Greece, Egypt, and the Levant well before members of the Society of Dilettanti traveled to the Middle East to explore and study the largely unexplored Greek and Roman ruins and sites (Cat. 121 and Fig. 237). His work was a rare item in the colony. The only copy documented

Fig. 237. Finely engraved plate from Pococke's book (Cat. 121) of the uniquely designed semicircular Roman ruin called the Temple of Venus at Baalbek. The discovery and recording of Palmyra's Roman ruins shortly after Pococke's book was published greatly influenced classical architectural design in mid-eighteenth-century Britain and Europe.

in Virginia is in the Alexandria Library Company. However, wealthy Maryland merchant Edward Lloyd at nearby Wye House in Talbot County, Maryland, also kept a copy in his extensive library.[6] The primary contributions from the post-1789 period include a full set of Edward Gibbon's landmark *History of the Decline and Fall of the Roman Empire* (Philadelphia, 1804–5) and Pons Alletz's *History of Ancient Greece* (Edinburgh, 1794).

European and English History

Histories of England were prevalent in libraries, with Tobias Smollett's classic *Complete History of England* and his *Continuation* (London, 1758–60 and 1760–65) being a key example. As a counter to Smollett's "Whiggish" interpretation of English history, the library also contains David Hume's more "Tory" interpretation, *History of England* (London, 1763). Other titles include James Welwood's *Memoirs* (London, 1749) and William Robertson's *History of Scotland* (London, 1781). A nineteenth-century addition is Robert Bisset's *History of the Reign of George III* (Philadelphia, 1822). Among other European histories are James Boswell's *Account of Corsica* (London, 1769) and Robertson's *History*

of the Reign of the Emperor Charles V (London, 1781). Further titles include Washington Irving's *History of the Life and Voyage of Christopher Columbus* (New York, 1828), Philippe de Ségur's *History of the Expedition to Russia* (Philadelphia, 1825), and Adolphe Thiers's *History of the French Revolution* (Philadelphia, 1840).

American and Virginian History

Many of the titles in the library relate to the Americas and Virginia. The best eighteenth-century works include Antonio Herrera y Tordesillas's *General History of the Vast Continent and Island of America* (London, 1725–26), Antoine-Simon Le Page de Pratz's *History of Louisiana* (London, 1763), Guillaume Raynal's *Philosophical and Political History of the Settlements and Travel of Europeans in East and West Indies* (London, 1763), and William Robertson's *History of America* (London, 1783).

There was an explosion of new titles in the nineteenth century focusing on Revolutionary American history, including Paul Allen's *History of the American Revolution* (Baltimore, 1822) and Jared Sparks's *Life of Gouverneur Morris* (Boston, 1832). Other works added were *Memoirs of Charles Lee* (Dublin, 1792), John Sanderson's *Biography of the Signers of the Declaration of Independence* (Philadelphia, 1823–27), and John Marshall's classic work, *The Life of George Washington* (Philadelphia, 1805–7), the first definitive biography of Washington.

Surprisingly, there are few works on Virginia and all from the nineteenth century. The best ones are Henry Howe's *Historical Collections of Virginia* (Charleston, 1845) and the Richmond 1819 first American reprint of John Smith's famous seventeenth-century account of his journeys around Europe, Africa, and the founding of Virginia in *True Travels, Adventures and Observations*. The library also contains two sets of Bishop William Meade's *Old Churches, Ministers and Families of Virginia* (Philadelphia, 1857 and 1891) with early observations on Virginia's old families, homes, and churches.

122
Family Bible

The Holy Bible containing the Old Testament and the New Testament
Cambridge: Thomas Buck and Roger Daniel, 1638
Folio

The family Bible lacks its original title page, but the title page from the New Testament gives us the printing date and thus proof that it is the oldest book in the library. In addition, the volume also incorporated a Book of Common Prayer and Psalter.

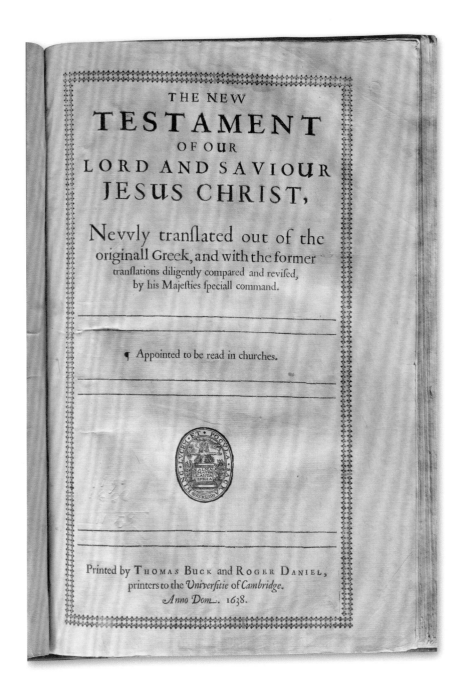

Religion

The typical Virginia library contained many religious works. The jewel of the collection is the seventeenth-century family Bible published in London in 1638. It is a well-worn folio missing its first few leaves (Cat. 122). It is the oldest book in the library and may be the one cited in Severn Eyre's inventory in 1728. It might have been brought to Virginia by the first Thomas Eyre in the seventeenth century. There are some early inscriptions by Littleton Eyre (dated 1733) and artwork that includes a sketch of a boat. Littleton Eyre did add a Book of Common Prayer for £0.6.15 from the printer William Hunter in Williamsburg in 1750, which does not survive.[7] Further religious items acquired in the nineteenth century include an additional Bible (Boston, 1831–32) and a New Testament (Philadelphia, 1830). There is also the American edition of the Book of Common Prayer published in Baltimore in 1834.

123

Acts of Assembly

The Acts of Assembly Now in Force, in the Colony of Virginia
Williamsburg: W. Rind, A. Purdie, and
J. Dixon, 1769
Folio

Title page of the only Williamsburg imprint still in the Eyre Hall library when Littleton Eyre, the builder, served in the House of Burgesses.

124

Stamped Bookplate

Rare personalized example of a leather gilt-stamped plate, "John Eyre, Northampton," on the front cover of *A Collection of All Such Acts of the General Assembly of Virginia* (Richmond: Augustine Davis, 1794, folio). The fifth printed Acts of Assembly for Virginia, and the second one from Richmond when John Eyre was a member of the state Senate.

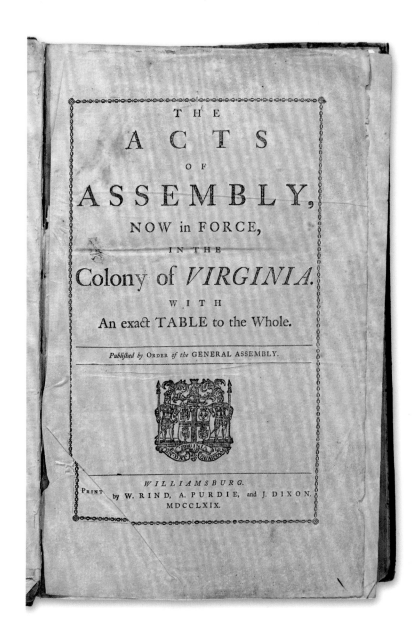

THE
ACTS
OF
ASSEMBLY,
NOW in FORCE,
IN THE
Colony of *VIRGINIA*.
WITH
An exact TABLE to the Whole.

Published by ORDER of the GENERAL ASSEMBLY.

WILLIAMSBURG.
Print by W. RIND, A. PURDIE, and J. DIXON.
MDCCLXIX.

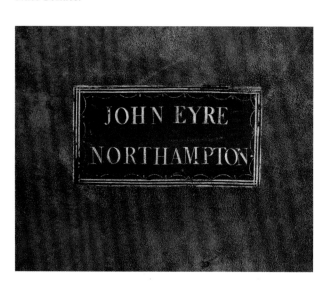

Philosophy

The study of philosophy was an important field in the eighteenth century, and Eyre Hall contains the works of four of the most important thinkers in Britain, starting with Henry St. John, Viscount Bolingbroke, a leading Tory politician in the first half of the eighteenth century and prolific political philosopher, with two of his works, *Letters on the Study and Use of History* (London, 1752) and *Philosophical Works* (London, 1754–77). Next is Edmund Burke, an Anglo-Irish statesman and Enlightenment philosopher, with two contributions, *A Philosophical Enquiry into the Origin of Our Ideas of the Sublime and Beautiful* (London, 1762), which made him a household name in the field of aesthetics and arts, and *Works* (Dublin, 1793). The third author is David Hume, a Scottish Enlightenment philosopher, considered a conservative and outright Tory by Thomas Jefferson, with his *Essays and Treatises* (London, 1762). The last is also a Scottish Enlightenment philosopher, Henry Home, Lord Kames, with two of his works, *Elements of Criticism* (Edinburgh, 1769) and *Sketches of the History of Man* (Dublin, 1774–75). Two European authors are represented at Eyre Hall as well. Claude Helvétius is an early eighteenth-century French philosopher and adversary of Voltaire with his *Treatise on Man* (London, 1777). The primary work by Voltaire at Eyre Hall is his *Philosophical Dictionary* (London, 1785).

Law

Considering the regular contributions the Eyres made to local and colonial government as vestrymen, county justices of the peace, and members of the House of Burgesses in Williamsburg, and, after the Revolution, the House of Delegates in Richmond, not to mention Littleton Eyre's attendance at the constitutional ratifying convention in 1788, their legal volumes are scant. Two editions of the published Acts of Assembly are extant: the *Acts of Assembly* published by William Rind and other Williamsburg printers in 1769, the only Williamsburg imprint still in the library (Cat. 123), and the later 1794 *Collection of All Such Acts*, published by Augustine Davis in Richmond when John Eyre served in the Senate of Virginia, with a distinctive embossed nameplate on the front board, "John Eyre, Northampton" (Cat. 124). The 1752 *Acts of Assembly* published by William Hunter in Williamsburg was once in the library as well.

Estate inventories reveal that the family also owned several law staples. The first Severn (d. 1728) owned a "book called Daltons Justice," which is Michael Dalton's *The Country Justice, Containing the Practice, Duty and Power of the Justices of the Peace* (London, 1727), a book mandated by the General Assembly that all county justices own.[8] According to his 1728 inventory, Severn also possessed an early "Abridgemt of the Laws of Virga," probably William Beverley's *Abridgment of the Publick Laws of Virginia* (London, 1728). In addition, all county justices were also required by the General Assembly to own John Mercer's *Abridgement* (Glasgow, 1759).[9]

Political Science

The library contains many of the important works in the field of political science. The primary works are John Locke's *Essay Concerning Human Understanding* (London, 1764), Charles Montesquieu's *Spirit of Laws* (London, 1758), John Trenchard's *Cato's Letters; or, Essays on Liberty* (London, 1755), and James Steuart's *Inquiry into the Principles of Political Oeconomy* (Dublin, 1770). Another related important work is Adam Smith's *Inquiry into the Nature and Causes of the Wealth of Nations* (London, 1783), his revolutionary new economic theory which radically changed the world and was quickly added to libraries across the colony.

125

Treatise on Electricity

Tiberius Cavallo, *A Complete Treatise on Electricity, in Theory and Practice, with Original Experiments*
London: C. Dilly, 1795, 3 vols.
Octavo

Title page from Volume I of Cavallo's scientific treatise on electricity. Eyre Hall has two copies from different family sources. This copy is from John A. Parker, whose extended family married into the Eyre family.

Fig. 238. Printed ornamental bookplate of "John A. Parker, Eastern Shore, Virginia," from the Cavallo set (Cat. 125).

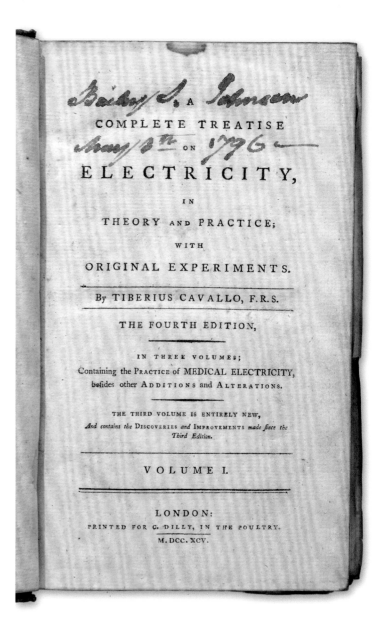

Science and Math

Surprisingly, there are few scientific books, and all acquired after 1790. The primary examples are two works by the Italian physicist and natural philosopher Tiberius Cavallo: his *Complete Treatise on Electricity* (London, 1795), with two sets that were added through different family marriages—one from Dr. James Lyon, and the other from John A. Parker with his printed bookplate (Cat. 125 and Fig. 238); and his *Elements of Natural or Experimental Philosophy* (Philadelphia, 1813). Jefferson recommended both for the University of Virginia library.[10] For a man

whose main sources of income were the productivity of his land, the absence of gardening and farming titles is surprising, especially since John Eyre built his own orangery and expanded the formal garden.

Schoolbooks

Many books were acquired as textbooks, and several have markings delineating where the students attended. The best examples include Charles Rollin's *History of the Arts and Sciences of the Ancients* (London, 1737–39), inscribed "William Littleton Eyre, August 17th domini 1778, William and Mary

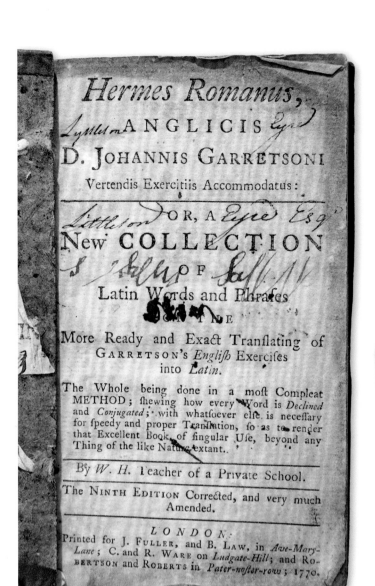

126

Hermes Romanus

William Hamilton, *Hermes Romanus . . . or,*
A New Collection of Latin Words and Phrases
London: J. Fuller and B. Law, 1770
Duodecimo

Title page from book with inscribed
name, "Littleton Eyre Esq." A prime
example of a textbook in the library
that was much used by the family.

Fig. 239. Leather binding for *Hermes*
Romanus with ink inscription on the front,
"Littleton Eyre Ex Lib, Anno Domini 1774,"
before he enrolled as a student at William
and Mary (Cat. 126).

College." Rollin also published a *Roman History* (London, 1754), which is inscribed "Ex Libris Severn Eyre, Domini 1762," which postdates his attendance at the college in the early 1750s. One of the most interesting examples is a small volume edited by William Hamilton entitled *Hermes Romanus . . . or, A New Collection of Latin Words and Phrases* (London, 1770) filled with scribbled names of former students including Preeson Bowdoin and Littleton Eyre; it is a well-used volume, with the front leather board inscribed "Littleton Eyre Ex Lib, Anno Domini 1774," perhaps dating to his schooling just before he enrolled at William and Mary (Cat. 126 and Fig. 239).

Lady's Monthly Museum

The Lady's Monthly Museum; or, Polite Repository of Amusement and Instruction
London: Verner and Hood, 1798–1803, vols. 1–7 and 9–10
Octavo

Engraved and decorated title page of this periodical—with the inscription "Wm. Eyre, 1824"—added to the Eyre Hall library by William Eyre's son Severn when he inherited the family estate in 1855.

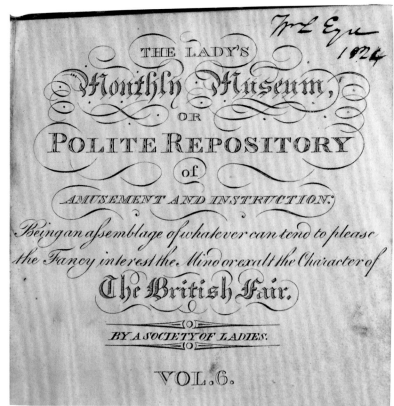

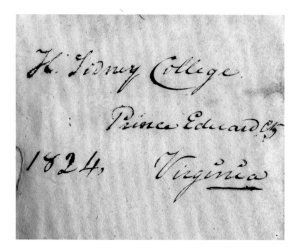

Fig. 240. Manuscript inscription from inside the *Lady's Monthly Museum* (Cat. 127), "H. Sidney College, Prince Edward Cty, Virginia, 1824," the college that William L. Eyre attended in southern Virginia.

Later volumes include *Lord Chesterfield's Advice to his Son* (Chiswick, 1823) inscribed "Wm. L. Eyre, Hampton-Sidney, 1825," as well as the *Lady's Monthly Museum* (London, 1798–1803) inscribed "H. Sidney College, Prince Edward Cty, Virginia, 1824" (Cat. 127 and Fig. 240). One of the best-known works is Fénelon's *Les Aventures de Télémaque* (Philadelphia, 1821), which is the only French work in the library, inscribed "Wm. L. Eyre, Hampton Sidney, January 25, 1825." Another title from this group, Robert Walsh's *Works of the British Poets* (Philadelphia, 1822), includes several interesting inscriptions starting with "William Madison Taylor, Yale College, 1824" and later "Wm. Eyre swapped with Wm. M. Peyton at the Sidney College for Boccacio's [sic] Works 1825." Another later work, Oliver Goldsmith's *Poetical Works* (Baltimore, 1816), traveled the farthest from home to Harvard, and is inscribed "Severn

Eyre Eyreville, Cambridge Mass, June 185[2]," the year he attended law school there.

Reference Works

Periodicals were the lifeblood of a plantation: they connected the planters to the outside world, with news on government, politics, business, society, culture, world events, and the latest published works. A valuable reference work was the *Encyclopaedia; or, A Dictionary of Arts, Sciences, and Miscellaneous Literature* (Philadelphia, 1791–98) with *Supplement* (1804). The first American edition was based on the original *Encyclopaedia Britannica* adapted for America. The work was popular in Virginia and was owned by Thomas Jefferson and George Washington, among others.

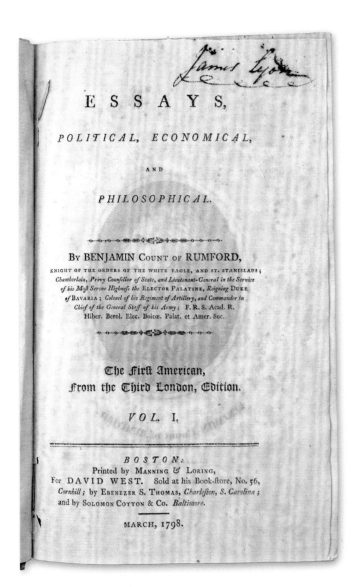

Essays

Baron Rumford, *Essays, Political, Economical, and Philosophical*
Boston: Manning & Loring, 1798–1802, 2 vols.
Octavo

Plain title page from Volume I of the set, with the signature of James Lyon, who married Sarah, the daughter of Severn Eyre. James acquired the Rumford volumes in 1802.

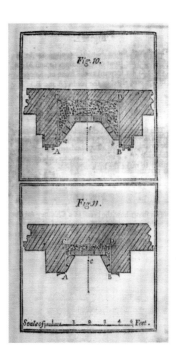

Fig. 241. Printed plate of fireplace designs from Volume I of Rumford's *Essays* (Cat. 128). Rumford's research into ventilation and efficient air flow revolutionized the design of fireplaces, and all the fireplaces at Eyre Hall reflect this radical and efficient change in design at an early time.

A work comparable in subject, but much more specialized, is Count Rumford's *Essays, Political, Economical, and Philosophical* (Boston, 1798–1804) (Cat. 128 and Fig. 241). This is the first American edition of a collection of essays, first published in London in 1796, on a wide variety of practical and scientific topics, food, thermodynamics, and the efficiency of chimney design, and was a popular title—appearing in the collections of Jefferson and Washington, as well as the Library of Virginia and the University of Virginia.[11] Another educational publication, and more fitting the reference category, is a work by Hugh Blair, a noted Scottish minister and teacher, *Lectures on Rhetoric and Belles Lettres* (London, 1793), a series of lectures published as guidelines for students. Blair's work had a significant influence on early American education, with copies in the libraries of Jefferson and Wythe, among others.[12] Samuel

Johnson's classic work, *Dictionary of the English Language* (Philadelphia, 1818), was not added to the library until after Severn Eyre settled at Eyre Hall in 1855.

Miscellanies

There are always some titles in a library that do not easily fit into the above categories or are too unique and must be listed separately, such as music, gift books, or specialty titles. Examples include Johann Georg Zimmermann's *Solitude; or, The Effects of Occasional Retirement on the Mind, the Heart. . .* (London, 1780), a study on health that has not been identified in Virginia before. Another specialized work is the first American unauthorized edition of William Combe's *Tour of Doctor Syntax* (Philadelphia, ca. 1814), a poem satirizing the fashion for publishing travel journals illustrated with colored plates copied from Thomas Rowlandson, one of the leading political illustrators in late eighteenth- and early nineteenth-century England, considered the Hogarth of his day.

The library includes several musical titles, including a composite work with added pieces of music under the title *Journal of Musick, Composed of Italian, French and English Songs* (Baltimore, 1819), Thomas Moore's *Irish Melodies* (London, 1849) with a handwritten note "Severn – . . . remember the one whose acquaintance with you has made him sincerely your friend Geo. R. Locke, Louiseville [sic] KY, July 21 '52," and *Songs of Home* (New York, 1870) by a range of different composers inscribed "Aunt Annie – with the love of J. W. P., Christmas 1870." Gift books and other ephemera were popular in the nineteenth century. Select examples include John Galt and Susanna Moodie's *Friendship's Offering: A Literary Album and Christmas and New Year's Present* (London, 1831), a Christmas present for 1831 inscribed "E. Savage, Va.," and William Hone's *Every-Day Book; or, Everlasting Calendar of Popular Amusement, Sports. . .* (London, 1826–27).

PROVENANCE OF THE BOOKS

Aside from the two major contributors to the library, John Eyre and his nephew William L. Eyre, who each had his distinctive bookplate, many of the books came into the library in smaller select numbers from a variety of sources. Twenty-one titles are identified as coming from Littleton Eyre. However, with a few exceptions, it is difficult to determine which books came from which generation. These books date from 1638 (the family Bible) to 1770 (Hamilton's *Hermes Romanus*). Five titles are directly attributable to the elder Littleton Eyre (d. 1768), such as a Bible and four titles he purchased from Williamsburg printers. A total of six titles can be firmly traced to his grandson Littleton Eyre (d. 1789) and are clearly dated, such as the two Latin and Greek works—the *Hermes Romanus* and Isocrates's *Opera*—as

Inscription

Manuscript notations and names on the blank leaf inside Samuel Pratt's *The Pupil of Pleasure* (Philadelphia: Robert Bell, 1778, octavo). The inscription "Littleton Eyre Ejus Liber, Anno Domini August 17. 1778" indicates incorporation of the book into the library at the time of publication.

well as Smollett's *Continuation of the Complete History of England* and Voltaire's *Works*. Another work, classified as a textbook, is Samuel Pratt's *Pupil of Pleasure* (Philadelphia, 1778), which bears the inscription "Littleton Eyre Ejus Liber, Anno Domini August 17. 1778" (Cat. 129). The remaining 11 titles without any signatures date early enough to be either generation.

For Severn Eyre (d. 1773, son of the builder), there are 15 identified titles dating from 1721 (Cowley's *Works*) to 1771 (Blackstone's *Commentaries*). Severn marked his books

130

New Universal Gazetteer

Jedidiah and Richard C. Morse, *A New Universal Gazetteer of
Geographical Dictionary*
New Haven: S. Converse, 1823
Octavo

Title page signed by "Wm. E. Lyon, 1824," the son of
Dr. James Lyon and Sarah Eyre Lyon.

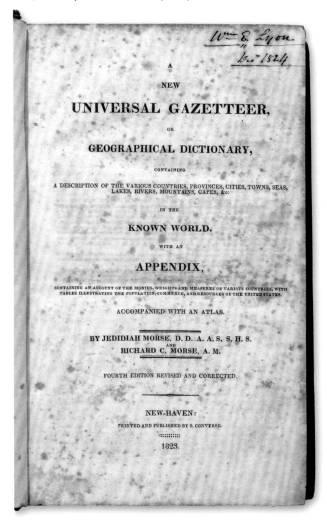

not only with his signature but also with the purchase
date: Charles Rollin's *Roman History* (London, 1754), for
example, is inscribed "Severn Eyre, Jan 7, 1762, 16 vols,
Roman History."

Many of the volumes came through friends and business
associates, such as the collection from Griffin Stith, noted
clerk of Northampton County court and associate of both
Littleton and Severn and Eyre. Fourteen titles bear his
signature or those of family members. At least one was
purchased by Dr. James Lyon, who married into the Eyre
family: Robertson's *History of Scotland*, and possibly his
History of the Reign of the Emperor Charles V. John Eyre bought
another Stith book, Michel de Montaigne's *Essays* (London,
1759): "Purchased from the Estate of Wm. Stith, . . . John
Eyre 1794." The Stith books encompass a wide spectrum
of eighteenth-century intellectual thought and date from
1752, with Bolingbroke's *Letters on the Study and Uses of
History*, to 1790, with Alletz's *History of Ancient Greece.*

A couple of classical language textbooks bear the
distinctive ink-stamped bookplate of first cousin Preeson
Bowdoin, who was a classmate with Littleton Eyre (d. 1789)
at William and Mary: Longinus, *De sublimitate commentarius*
(London, 1762), which is also inscribed "January the 27th
1777" (see Fig. 236) and previously mentioned above under
Littleton. Preeson's father, also named Preeson, had married
Severn's sister Sarah, the daughter of Littleton the builder.
Unfortunately, she died in late 1760 when young Preeson
was only six months old.

Dr. James Lyon married Sarah, the daughter of Severn
Eyre, in 1799. He and his son added eight titles, which date
from 1781, with Robertson's *History of Scotland* mentioned
earlier in connection with Stith, to 1825, with Ségur's *History
of the Expedition to Russia*, added by James's son William E. Lyon
in 1826. The context of his collecting was in the sciences and
travels including both scientific titles by Cavallo, Rumford's
Essays, and Jedidiah and Richard C. Morse's *New Universal
Gazetteer* (New Haven, 1823) (Cat. 130).

Three books came as gifts from a family friend in
Norfolk, William Tazewell Nivison, a local lawyer who
also owned land in Northampton County. Two have his
printed bookplates and two personal inscriptions from
Nivison as gifts to Ann Eyre, John's wife. All are works by
Walter Scott including *Ballads and Lyrical Pieces*, and *The
Lay of the Last Minstrel.*

The women at Eyre Hall made their contributions,
too. Margaret Eyre, wife of Severn, signed four titles in

Gilt-Stamped Bookplate

A rare gilt-stamped bookplate, "Ann M. Eyre,"
on the front cover of Volume IV, "Ann M. Eyre
Collection," one of four bound volumes of Ann
Eyre's collection of sheet music at Eyre Hall.

the library, probably her personal favorites. They include Dodsley's *Collection of Poems by Several Hands*, and Lennox's *Female Quixote*, with her inscription "Margaret Eyre's Female Quixote." Ann Matilda Upshur, who married John Eyre in 1800, left her imprint on three titles, with the earliest being Zimmermann's *Solitude* of 1784 and the latest being a composite of loose sheet music that includes a work titled *Journal of Musick* (1810); both have leather personalized bookplates stamped with her name, "Ann M. Eyre," something that is rarely seen in early Virginia (Cat. 131). Other members of her family also contributed to the family collection, including Caleb B. Upshur, with Wilson's *Reports of Cases*, and a later family member, Arthur Upshur, with Johnson's *Lives of the Most Eminent Poets*.

Margaret S. Parker, who married the last Severn Eyre in 1865, and several members of her family over several generations left volumes that made their way into the library. Cavallo's *Complete Treatise on Electricity* was owned by John S. Parker, Margaret's father, who lived at Eyreville in the 1870s and '80s. The Upshur family contributed eight titles that date from 1795, with the Cavallo set, to the last book added into the library in 1911, Jennings Cropper Wise's *Ye Kingdome of Accawmacke*, added by Alfred P. Upshur.

Several books came through Mary Burton Savage and her family. She married William L. Eyre of Eyreville in 1828. All told, there are seven titles, from Pratt's *Pupil of Pleasure* of 1778 to Galt's *Friendship's Offering* of 1831. Two were gifts to Mary Savage prior to her marriage. Shortly before they were married, William L. Eyre gave her Henry Kollock's *Sermons* as a Christmas gift in 1827 (Cat. 132). Grace Eyre, daughter of the last Severn Eyre, married Richard B. Taylor of Norfolk in 1897, and through this line came four older books dated between 1770 and 1845. The oldest one,

Stuart's *Inquiry into the Principles of Political Oeconomy*, came through Robert B. Taylor. In the middle of the nineteenth century, another Taylor, Robert E. Taylor, gave two books, Howe's *Historical Collections of Virginia* and Gough's *System of Practical Arithmetick*.

One common method used by publishers to help defray costs was to advertise the sale of subscriptions for upcoming publications; such was the case with the 1752 *Acts of Assembly*, published in Williamsburg by William Hunter and to which the first Littleton subscribed. His son Severn did the same by purchasing a subscription to the Philadelphia edition of Blackstone's *Commentaries* on the eve of the Revolution.[13] In the next generation, both John and William Eyre continued the practice by purchasing subscriptions for Marshall's *Life of George Washington*, which is the only surviving subscribed title still in the library.

The overall caliber of the library is practical and not scholarly, and parallels the literary interests of Robert Skipwith, Thomas Jefferson's brother-in-law, who wrote a letter to Jefferson in 1771 asking advice on building a book collection and to which the latter responded: "I would have them suited to the capacity of a common reader who understands but little of the classics and who has not leisure for any intricate or tedious study. Let them be improving as well as amusing and among the rest let there be Hume's history of England, the new edition of Shakespear [sic], the short Roman History you mentioned and all Stern's works."[14] The extensive list of books Jefferson sent his kinsman parallels many of the titles in Eyre Hall.

The library at Eyre Hall is impressive by its survival. However, it reveals more about itself by what is not there than what has survived. We know that many volumes are missing, as often happens in old libraries. The evidence

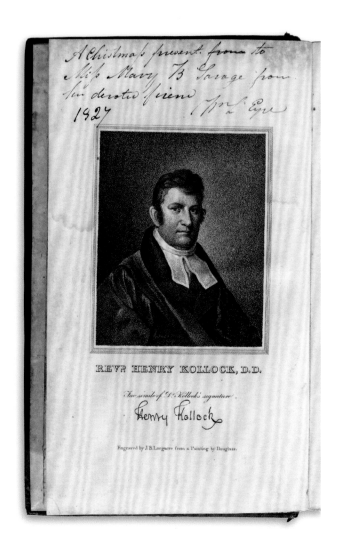

Sermons

Henry Kollock, *Sermons on Various Subjects*
Savannah: S.C. and L. Schenck, 1822
Octavo

The frontispiece, with its engraved portrait of the author, carries a personal inscription: "A Christmas present [from crossed out] to Miss Mary B. Savage from her devoted friend Wm. L. Eyre, 1827." William L. Eyre married Mary three months later, in March 1828.

found in family records and public documents show that the library was more extensive, with other unknown works once filling in the gaps. It was not intended to compete with the great libraries of William Byrd at Westover or Thomas Jefferson at Monticello. It was more typical of the eighteenth-century gentleman's library with later nineteenth-century additions, and it is imprinted with the Eyre family's wants and needs. It tells the story of this house and family, revealing many of their secrets in the kinds of books they purchased, borrowed, and read.

NOTES

1. The library we are examining consists of the surviving original books up to 1911. The collections of the last two owners of Eyre Hall—Margaret Baldwin, owner 1914–79, and her son Furlong Baldwin, 1979–present—are not included in this survey, nor were they integrated into the catalogue that was made by Furlong's sister Mary Peacock. It should be stressed that, while the books are listed in artificial categories based upon publication date, they may not have been added to the library at that time. One such example is *The Proceedings of the House of Representatives . . . on the Impeachment of the Hon. Samuel Chase* (Washington, 1805); although it is found in the second portion of the library (1789–1855), personal inscriptions prove it was a much later addition to the collection. The inscriptions begin in 1932 and end with one that reads "given by Mrs. Eunice Jenkins Page . . . to Mary Eyre Peacock, circa 1975."

2. Inventory of the estate of Thomas Eyre, October 28, 1719, Northampton County Wills, etc., No. 15, 1717–1725, 73–76; Inventory of the estate of Severn Eyre (d. 1728), August 14, 1728, Northampton County Wills, Deeds, etc., No. 26, 1725–1733, 151–54; Inventory of the estate of Littleton Eyre, October 14, 1769, Northampton County Wills & Inventories, No. 24, 1766–1772, 224–26.

3. Inventory of the estate of Severn Eyre (d. 1773), February 27, 1774, Northampton County Wills & Inventories, No. 25, 1772–1777, 392–93.

4. Inventory of the estate of Robert Carter, [November?] 1733, Carter Papers, Virginia Historical Society, Richmond.

5. William Hunter, *Virginia Gazette* Journals 1750–1752, 7, 66, 101, John D. Rockefeller Jr. Library, Colonial Williamsburg. The phrase "ad usum Delphini" may refer to an expurgated version of Virgil's *Aeneid*.

6. Edwin Wolf, Jr., "The Library of Edward Lloyd, IV of Wye House," *Winterthur Portfolio* 5 (1969): 110; *A Catalog of the Books belonging to the Alexandria Library Company* (Alexandria, Va.: Cottom and Stewart, 1801), 14.

7. William Hunter, *Virginia Gazette* Journals 1750–1752, August 3, 1750.

8. Addenda to the inventory of Severn Eyre, April 9, 1735, Northampton County Wills & Inventories, No. 18, 1733–1740, 82. Warren Billings, "English Legal Literature as a Source of Law and Legal Practice of Seventeenth Century Virginia," *Virginia Magazine of History and Biography* 87, no. 4 (October 1979): 141.

9. Bennie Brown, "John Mercer, Merchant, Lawyer, Author, Book Collector," in *"Esteemed Bookes of Lawe" and the Legal Culture of Early Virginia*, ed. Warren M. Billings and Brent Tarter (Charlottesville: University of Virginia Press, 2017), 101–2.

10. *1828 Catalogue of the Library of the University of Virginia* (Charlottesville: University Press of Virginia, 1945), 30.

11. *A Catalog of the Library of the State of Virginia* (Richmond, Va.: Samuel Shephard, 1831), 34; William Bainter O'Neal, *A Fine Arts Library: Jefferson's Selections for the University of Virginia, together with his Architectural Books at Monticello* (Charlottesville: University Press of Virginia, 1976), 307–9; *A Catalogue of the Washington Collection in the Boston Athenaeum* (Cambridge, Mass.: University Press, 1897), 551.

12. Bennie Brown, "The Library of George Wythe of Williamsburg and Richmond," unpublished typescript, 2017, 37; Millicent E. Sowerby, *Catalogue of the Library of Thomas Jefferson* (Washington, D.C.: Library of Congress, 1959), 5:19.

13. "Subscribers in Virginia to Blackstone's Commentaries on the Laws of England, Philadelphia, 1771–1772," *William and Mary Quarterly*, 2nd ser., 1, no. 3 (July 1921): 183–85.

14. Julian P. Boyd, ed., *The Papers of Thomas Jefferson*, vol. 1, *1760–1776* (Princeton: Princeton University Press, 1950), 74–75.

Musical Instruments

JOHN WATSON

Physharmonica,
1830–45.
Cat. 135

MUSICAL INSTRUMENTS AND THE EYRES

A WALK THROUGH THE HOUSE GIVES THE IMPRESSION that music played an exceptional role at Eyre Hall. The ephemeral sounds have faded but the evidence of a musical past is unmistakable. Six musical instruments are longtime furnishings of the house, all but one from the first half of the nineteenth century during the ownership of John Eyre and his wife Ann Upshur Eyre, covering the 66 years from 1789 to 1855. How did a special relationship with music begin at Eyre Hall? Who was responsible? In gentry households of the period children are typically involved, often a father purchasing a fine pianoforte for a teen daughter to burnish her social skills and add to a de facto dowry ahead of attracting a suitable husband.[1] Then the other children demand their due: an English guitar for a sister, a flute or fiddle for a brother. The situation at Eyre Hall during the period in which most of the instruments were purchased, however, offers no such tale. John Eyre and his wife Ann were childless.

To understand the origins of musical life at Eyre Hall, we must start with an instrument that is absent and long forgotten. Could that familiar story of a father providing an instrument for his daughter have occurred in the previous generation? The evidence suggests that is precisely what happened. Ann Upshur brought a pianoforte into her marriage with John Eyre in 1800 and she continued to sing and play the instrument, purchasing music regularly for most of her life.[2] Besides a surviving collection of printed music, the existence of a piano in the early part of that century is proven in the tax records beginning in 1815. In that year, a luxury tax on "Pianos harpsichords organs and harps" was levied to replenish funds after the War of 1812, and John Eyre was taxed for owning one such instrument.[3] Ann Eyre, the matriarch of the house for three decades, thus brought with her a piano and a love of music when she arrived in 1800, and ultimately left a musical legacy that is palpable.

Of the several musical instruments that survive at Eyre Hall two are imported flutes, called "German flutes" in the period to distinguish them from "common" or "English flutes," which are known today as recorders. Along with fiddles, flutes were the most common musical instruments to be found in inventories in the region and were also the two most often called upon to accompany dance.[4]

A large and finely made hand-cranked barrel organ from London had been purchased soon after 1806. It too could accompany dance even in the absence of a skilled musician, but it also offered music in many styles for any occasion. Six barrels, of which four survive, are pinned with ten tunes each, providing devotional music, patriotic tunes, marches, and popular songs from musical theater. Mechanical organs were precursors to the Victrola and to today's profusion of audio devices before which music had to be made before it could be heard.

Finally, and more reliant on the presence of appropriately skilled musicians, are two remarkable mid-nineteenth-century keyboard instruments. Most exotic and rare of the collection is a physharmonica, an early form of continental European reed organ with an unusual capacity for nuances of volume depending on the player's control in pumping the foot-operated bellows. The other keyboard is a combination square piano and organ from New York. Made in 1846 when the invention was at its peak of popularity, the "aeolian attachment" is a reed organ playable separately or together with the piano from a shared keyboard.

The latest musical instrument to arrive at Eyre Hall is a Steinway grand piano from 1928, now covered by a forest of family photos as if to proclaim a different kind of harmony. After the advent of the Steinway, attention turned to the restoration and preservation of the earlier instruments.

The American musical instrument-making industry was among the largest in the world by the end of the nineteenth century, but that status was slow in coming, as the Eyre Hall collection illustrates. Of the five nineteenth-century instruments in the house, only the latest, the Nunns & Clark piano, was made in America. Two, the barrel organ and Astor flute, were made in London, which had been the dominant source of musical instruments from the beginnings of British America until the 1830s. Not surprisingly, many of the first-generation American makers were immigrants from London, including Robert Nunns and John Clark who made the square piano.

Perhaps surprisingly, a major foreign influence on the musical instruments of Eyre Hall comes from Germany. Two of the six instruments were made in German-speaking Europe including the Klemm flute (stamped "Phila." by its American importer), and very likely the physharmonica. A fourth, the Astor flute, was made by a German immigrant in London, and finally the 1926 Steinway piano was made in a New York factory still dominated by the heritage of its German founders. The strong German connection is not a fluke. An unusual aptitude and inclination for musical-instrument making in German culture accounted not only for exported instruments to America but also the immigration of instrument makers, especially to Pennsylvania—resulting in that region becoming the cradle of the American piano industry.[5]

Fig. 242. View of the physharmonica (Cat. 135) in the north passage, ca. 1890.

133

Flute

George Astor & Co.
Marked "ASTOR / LONDON."
London, 1785–1815
Boxwood with ivory ferrule rings and end cap and silver keys
L. 24 in.

This four-key boxwood flute is stamped on all four sections with the maker's mark consisting of a unicorn surmounted by the words "ASTOR / LONDON." The flute has four sections with decorative ivory ferrule rings, and an ivory end cap. The keys are silver with square heads.

After their immigration from Germany, George Peter Astor (1752–1813) partnered with his brother John Jacob Astor (1763–1848) to establish a flute and pianoforte manufactory in London in about 1778. Five years later, John Jacob moved to America to retail his brother's instruments and, by 1809,

famously discovered the much greater profit potential of the fur trade, becoming the richest man in America at his death. Meanwhile, George continued manufacturing pianos, organs, and many other types of instruments, selling printed music, and other musical merchandize in London, trading under the name Astor & Co. from 1784 to 1826, by which time his widow Elizabeth had taken over the firm. It is not known if the Eyre Hall flute passed through John Jacob Astor's New York retail music store.

134

Flute

Probably by Johann Gottlieb Schuster
Marked "KLEMM & BRO / PHILA." [retailers]
Probably Markneukirchen, Germany, 1820–50
Black-stained wood with ivory ferrule rings and pewter keys
L. 24½ in.

The five-section flute of turned, black-stained wood has four pewter keys with "salt-spoon" heads and six single-bead ivory ferrule rings. The head joint terminates in an adjustable tuning stopper with turned head. The flute is stamped on the barrel section by the retailers "Klemm & Bro / Phila." John George Klemm (1795–1835) and his brother August Klemm (1797–1876) were music publishers and merchants of musical merchandise in Philadelphia, the firm continuing under that name from 1819 to 1879.

The Klemm brothers imported woodwind instruments manufactured by their brother-in-law, Johann Gottlieb Schuster, in Markneukirchen, Germany.[6] Known as Neukirchen until 1858, the area was and remains a supplier to the world for woodwind and brasswind musical instruments. Some scholars speculate that the Klemm brothers may have been related to Johann Gottlob Klemm (1690–1762), maker of the earliest surviving keyboard instrument made in America.[7]

135
Physharmonica

Unknown maker
Probably Germany or Austria, 1830–45
Elm carcass, various unidentified woods, ivory, paper, copper alloy, various leathers
H. 32 in., W. 37 in., D. 27 in.

The most unusual instrument in the collection is an early form of harmonium called a physharmonica. It is a type of European reed organ that differs from the typical American varieties in using positive air pressure to blow air through the reeds. The familiar and somewhat later "pump organ" or "parlor organ" that reached enormous popularity in late nineteenth- and early twentieth-century America operates on negative air pressure, that is by sucking air through the reeds.

Another difference between the European harmonium and its stateside counterpart—widely termed simply "American organ"—is its potential for expression, meaning the control of volume independent of how many stops are pulled. The harmonium achieves this by giving the player direct control over the wind pressure through how fast the bellows are pumped. In the American organ, expression can only be achieved by knee-operated flaps that cover the ranks of reeds, thus controlling how much sound escapes.

The keyboard of this instrument is three notes short of five octaves (C to A). Two walnut hand stops operate the two

ranks of reeds, the right knob for normal pitch and the left knob controlling a stop one octave higher for a more brilliant tone. Two pedals operate the bellows, and, unlike later types of harmonium, there is no reservoir to even out the wind pressure, requiring the player to have considerable skill to pump smoothly. Later harmoniums evened out the air pressure by including a reservoir, which could also be bypassed on demand to give full control of wind pressure and musical expression to the player.

The simple elm-wood case with clear coating stands on four tapered square-section legs. The area surrounding the keys is painted black, and a removable dust board is perforated at one end with fret-sawn f-holes. A pedal lyre holds two brass pumping pedals. The internal surfaces of the wind chest are sealed with pages from the complete works of poet and writer Christoph Martin Wieland (1733–1813) published in several editions between 1794 and 1858.[8] The timing and circumstances that brought such a rare instrument to Eyre Hall are not known (Fig. 242).

136

Barrel Organ

George England
Marked "G. P. England / Londini, fecit."
London, 1806–10
Mahogany, copper alloy, iron, lead alloy, leather, skin drumhead,
gold leaf, various woods, silk, paper
H. 76 in., W. 31 in., D. 33 in.

What Fanny Fielding called in her 1867 salute to Eyre Hall "an immense organ which plays forty tunes, more beguiling to the juveniles than the 'forty thieves' in story" is indeed the most visually impressive of the musical artifacts at Eyre Hall.[9] Standing over 6 feet tall, the mahogany instrument demands attention with an eye-catching façade of 19 gilded faux pipes flanked by reeded pilasters topped by urn finials of brass. The base with its central oval and corner carvings serves as storage for additional pinned drums.

A painted black rectangle with indented corners bears the maker's formal inscription in gold lettering, "G. P. England / Londini, fecit." The last in a family dynasty of important church and chamber pipe organ builders in London, George Pike England (ca. 1768–1815) was called by historian David C. Wickens "the epitome of English organ building at the end of the eighteenth century." Wickens went on to describe G. P. England's style as "without the excesses to be found in [Samuel] Green's work; tonally, it was a conservative, understated style, firmly rooted in the work of its antecedents but showing some of the trends of the time."[10]

As mechanical instruments that required only turning a crank to produce a full musical sound, barrel organs differed from other musical instruments by removing the need for musical training. In that way, it was a predecessor first to the Victrola and eventually to today's profusion of audio playback devices. In its time, it must have also given its untrained operator the sensation of being a virtual musician with the competence to perform a large repertoire of diverse musical styles. But unlike a simple crank-operated music box, this type of barrel organ gives the operator some discretionary control for less or more volume, or to create one effect for a pastoral hymn and another for an energetic march. Stop knobs offer a choice of sonorities. Five stops control the organ pipes themselves: Open Diapason, Stopped Diapason, Principal, Twelfth, and Fifteenth. Two more engage the percussion stops: Drum and Triangle.

According to the hand-lettered list of tunes framed on the side of the case, the organ originally had six barrels of which four are extant.[11] Each barrel is capable of playing ten tunes that can be selected by positioning the barrel's protruding pivot accordingly. Possibly indicating the organ's

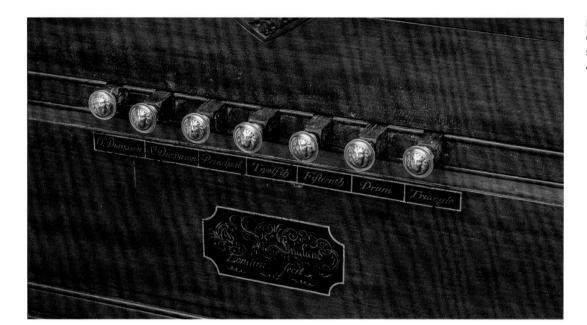

Fig. 243. Detail of Cat. 136 showing seven stop knobs and maker's mark.

principal use in the house is a preponderance of dance tunes, including jigs, reels, hornpipes, and waltzes. One barrel is devoted to religious music including hymns and devotional tunes. Another offers marches, and, yet another, songs (airs) for singing or listening. The rest are stocked with tunes from musical theater, popular, traditional, patriotic and fiddle tunes, and some art music, such as portions of the then wildly popular *Battle of Prague* by Frantisek Kotzwara.[12] Not surprisingly, several of the tunes including that last are also to be found in Ann Eyre's contemporaneous collection of vocal and piano sheet music.

Fig. 244. Detail of Cat. 136 with façade removed showing (bottom to top) stop knobs, pinned barrel, pipes, triangle, and drum.

137
Piano

With aeolian (reed organ) attachment
Marks: "R. Nunns & Clark" engraved on silver plaque; "5334" (serial number) stamped near tuning pins; "O.M. COLEMAN'S / PATENT"
internally on aeolian attachment; "R. CLARK / Sept. 22 – 1846" on side of top key
New York, 1846
Rosewood, various hard and soft woods, ivory, copper alloy, silver, iron, cast iron, various felts and cloth, leather
H. 35½ in., W. 71¼ in., D. 33½ in.

The last instrument to be added to Eyre Hall in the musically active nineteenth century was a fine rosewood square piano with an aeolian attachment (reed organ) by the New York firm of Nunns & Clark. Its arrival is reflected in the property taxes paid by John Eyre, whose piano tax jumped from $200 in 1846 to $350 the next year, presumably also indicating that Ann's old piano remained until the arrival of its replacement.[13] We can only speculate about why a new piano was required. The most familiar musical sounds in Eyre Hall during the first three decades of the nineteenth century must have been Ann Eyre's voice and the piano she brought with her from Philadelphia. By the time the piano was replaced in 1846, almost 20 years after her death, it would have been well over 50 years old.[14] The transformation that had occurred during that span in the

technological evolution of the piano would have rendered Ann's instrument unusable if for no other reason than because its eighteenth-century keyboard would not have had enough keys for the new music.

Besides the old piano becoming inadequate in musical resources and probably also its mechanical fitness, it remains to be asked what or who provoked the purchase of a new piano in the late 1840s, so long after Ann Eyre's death. Fanny Fielding wrote of the widower John Eyre that he was "especially interested in young people, he never omitted an opportunity to bring them pleasantly together." A new piano may have been a magnet to help attract visits from extended family. The provocation for a new piano might also have involved James Marshall (d. 1848), about whom Fanny Fielding wrote in 1867, "many years resided here, a sort of dependent friend who presided over the destinies of all the musical instruments about the establishment,—(he was ingenious and skillful)."[15] Until recently, James Marshall was the only non-family member to be buried in the Eyre graveyard, which surely means he was an important part of the family and, by Fielding's account, also of its musical life.

The Nunns & Clark piano came equipped with an invention at the peak of its popularity. The "aeolian attachment" was a reed organ built into the piano and playable from the same keyboard. It was patented in 1844 by Obed Mitchell Coleman. Use rights were sold to Nunns & Clark who exhibited one at the 1851 Great Exhibition in London.[16] Efforts to provide stringed keyboard instruments with organ stops already had a long history as a way of compensating for the natural decay of sound after a note is played on a harpsichord or piano. Four hundred years earlier, King Henry VIII owned four claviorgans (harpsichord-type instruments with added organ pipes).[17] Much closer to the time and place of Eyre Hall, a combination upright grand piano and six-stop pipe organ was purchased by St. George Tucker of Williamsburg in 1799 for his daughter Anne Frances (Fanny) Bland Tucker, who was born one year before Ann Upshur.[18] By the time the new Nunns & Clark piano arrived at Eyre Hall, the popular new and much cheaper free-reed type of organ had replaced pipes in piano-organ combination instruments.

The Eyre Hall piano's organ bellows can be pumped either by the player by means of a foot pedal, or by an assistant using a pumping handle provided on the right side of the piano. It is possible to play the piano alone or with the organ depending on whether the bellows are being pumped. To play the organ alone, a knob provided at the bass end of the keyboard can be pushed forward, lifting all the hammers close to the strings, effectively stopping the effect of the keys on them. The first of the four pedals (on the left) is for pumping the organ. The second is a moderator stop, which softens the tone by inserting tabs of cloth between the hammers and the strings. The third pedal, common to nearly all pianos, is for the dampers. The fourth is an expression pedal that opens and closes a cover over the reeds to vary the volume of the organ.

Fig. 245. Detail of Cat. 137 showing portion of interior and knob at left end of keyboard for disengaging piano to allow use of organ alone.

STEINWAY PIANO

After the arrival of the 1846 square piano, it would be 82 years before a new musical instrument arrived at Eyre Hall. With 12 years of music lessons from her youth, Margaret Eyre Taylor Baldwin is said to have sold her wedding gifts in 1928 to purchase the ebony-finish Steinway & Sons grand piano that has been in the house ever since (see Fig. 230). The 6-foot-2-inch "Model A" was first manufactured by Steinway in 1878 and remains in production. Steinway pianos have enjoyed the endorsement of many touring artists and have been widely regarded as among the finest available.

Besides the long-absent late eighteenth-century piano that Ann Eyre brought to Eyre Hall in 1800, there were at least two other instruments in the house that survive only in documentary sources. The earliest mention of a musical instrument is "1 Violin Bow and Case" in the 1774 probate inventory that followed Severn Eyre's death.[19] A violin is also mentioned in Fielding's 1867 comment about James Marshall, "the thrilling sounds of whose violin seem almost audible now."[20] The fiddle or violin shared with the flute a gender connection in America and Britain as the most appropriate choice for a man or boy. In grand estates like Eyre Hall, both instruments were also popularly employed for the musical accompaniment of country dances.

Another instrument that existed at the time of Fielding's report was a guitar. The strong female association of this type of instrument especially in the eighteenth century may suggest that the guitar was also one of Ann Eyre's possessions from her youth. Some pieces in her extensive collection of printed music included parts for guitar, violin, or flute.

NOTES

1. Several examples of this scenario in Virginia include George Washington providing a piano in 1789 and a harpsichord in 1793 for his then ten-year-old step-granddaughter Eleanor Parke Custis, "Nelly," (1779–1854); Thomas Jefferson providing harpsichords to each of his daughters, Martha (1772–1836) age 14 in 1786 and Maria (1778–1804) at age 20 in 1798. Helen Cripe, *Thomas Jefferson and Music* (Charlottesville, Va.: Thomas Jefferson Foundation, 2009). St. George Tucker of Williamsburg provided a large combination pipe organ–grand piano to his daughter Anne Frances Bland Tucker, "Fanny," in 1799 as well as a Broadwood grand piano for his step-daughter Mary Walker Carter Tucker, "Polly," (1785–1863) in 1803. John Watson, "The 1799 Organized Upright Grand Piano in Williamsburg: A Preliminary Report," *Journal of the American Musical Instrument Society* 40 (2014): 9–28.

2. See Gary Stanton's essay on Ann Upshur Eyre's sheet music collection in this volume. Assuming Ann (b. 1780) received her piano at a typical age for piano instructions to begin, around ten to 12 years, it can be estimated that the piano was from about 1790–92. Nelly Custis, whose music collection included many of the same pieces as Ann's, was born a year earlier and received her piano from George Washington in 1789 at age ten.

3. Northampton County Property Tax Lists.

4. David Hildebrand, "Musical Instruments: Their Implications concerning Musical Life in Colonial Annapolis" (master's thesis, George Washington University, 1979), 83.

5. See Laurence Libin, "Pennsylvania, Cradle of American Piano Making," in *The Square Piano in Rural Pennsylvania 1760–1830* (Bethlehem, Pa.: Payne Gallery of Moravian College, 2001), 2–11.

6. James Kopp, "Two Bassoons Marked "Klemm / Philada," *Newsletter of the American Musical Instrument Society* 42, no. 2 (Fall 2013): 16–18.

7. Laurence Libin, *American Musical Instruments in the Metropolitan Museum of Art* (New York: The Metropolitan Museum of Art, 1985), 164; Dorothy Potter, *Food for Apollo: Cultivated Music in Antebellum Philadelphia* (Bethlehem, Pa.: Lehigh University Press, 2011), 117.

8. The papers were identified by Thomas Snyder in a 2015 organ conservation report.

9. Fanny Fielding [pseud.], "Southern Homesteads. Eyre Hall," *The Land We Love* 3, no. 6 (October 1867): 507.

10. David C. Wickens, "England (ii)" (on the England family of organ builders), in *Grove Music Online*, accessed August 15, 2019 [subscription access through Early Music America].

11. Presumably the two missing barrels were already absent at the time Fanny Fielding described the organ in her 1868 account, which mentions its "forty tunes." The two missing barrels would have added 20 more to the total. Fielding, "Southern Homesteads. Eyre Hall," 507.

12. Barrel organ tunes as listed in pen on two papers attached to the exterior of the organ casework: Barrel 1: *Sally Montgomery's Reel, Lady Harriet Hope's Reel, Sir David Hunter Blair's Reel, Speed the Plough, Back of the Charge House, The Honey Moon, Lady Nelson's Reel, Laura Lizner, Master Pitwell Virginia Reel*; Barrel 2: *Lord Nelson's Hornpipe, The Parisian Roy, Molly Put the Kettle On, Lady McDonald's Reel, Lady Campbell's Reel, St. Patrick's Reel, Sir Doublass [Douglas's?] Reel, Col. McBain's Reel, The Isle of Thanot, I'll Go No More to Your Lair*; Barrel 3: *Peace and Plenty, Murphy Delaney, Off She Goes, The Courant, The Trumpeter's Gate, Irish Washerwoman, Lord Nelson's Waltz, Lady Carolina Lee's Waltz, Haymaker's Waltz, Lauretto*; Barrel 4 (barrel lost): *The Willow, No More the Same, The Horn, In my Cottage, Spanish Guittarre, Old Fowler, Fair Ellen, Far from me my Love Flies, Lady Lindsay's Minuet, God Save the King*; Barrel 5 (barrel lost): *Lord Cornwallis' March, Queen's March, March in the Battle of Prague, Quick Step in the Battle of Prague, Westminster March, Duke of York's New March, March in Blue Beard, March in Pizarro, March in The Caravan*; Barrel 6: *The 100th Psalm, The 104th Psalm, Bedford, Morning Hymn, Abingdon, Evening Hymn, [...] German Hymn, His Loving Pasture, A Voluntary.*

13. Northampton County Property Tax Lists, 1846, 1847.

14. This estimated construction date for Ann's piano is based on her 1780 birth year and the most likely age at which she would have begun music lessons being around 10–12. Her piano was thus probably made within a couple years of 1791.

15. Fielding, "Southern Homesteads. Eyre Hall," 508.

16. According to the Clinkscale online database of historic pianos, most of the known surviving pianos with aeolian attachment are by Timothy Gilbert, a Boston piano manufacturer who also bought rights to the invention. The aeolian attachment was patented in America (No. 3548, dated April 17, 1844) and in Britain (No. 10341, dated October 10, 1844). For a contemporary account of the inventor and the success of the aeolian attachment, see "Coleman and his Eolian [sic] Attachment," in Charles Cist, *The Cincinnati Miscellany*, vol. 1 (Cincinnati: Caleb Clark, Printer, 1845), 98. Available online at https://play.google.com/store/books/details?id=kFEVAAAAYAAJ&rdid=book-kFEVAAAAYAAJ&rdot=1 (accessed October 30, 2019).

17. Eleanor Smith, "The History and Use of the Claviorgan" (PhD diss., University of Edinburgh, 2013), 13.

18. The Tucker instrument is in the collections of the Colonial Williamsburg Foundation, accession no. 2012-150. See John R. Watson, "The 1799 Organized Upright Grand Piano in Williamsburg: A Preliminary Report," *Early Keyboard Journal* (2014): 9–28.

19. Inventory of the estate of Severn Eyre, February 27, 1774, Northampton County Wills & Inventories, No. 25, 1772–1777, 393.

20. Fielding, "Southern Homesteads. Eyre Hall," 508–9.

Sheet Music

GARY STANTON

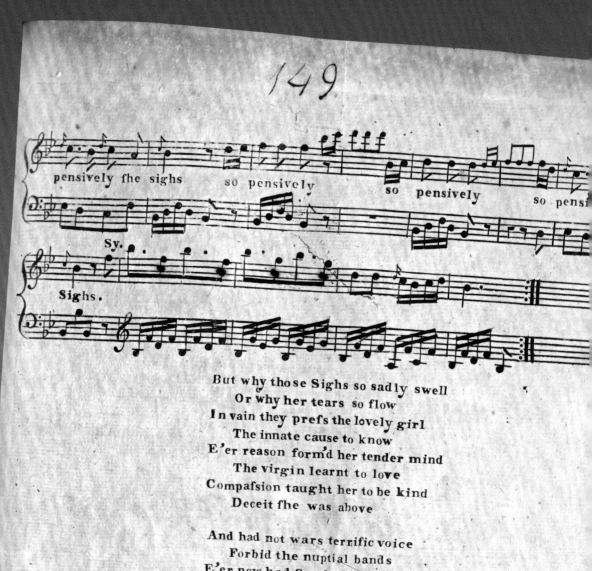

"The Caledonian Maid."
Cat. 143

138

"Comely Ned that Died at Sea"

From Volume I, "A Collection of New and Favorite Songs."

AMONG THE MANY BOOKS OF ART, LITERATURE, and history at Eyre Hall are four bound volumes of sheet music originally published between 1793 and 1824. The 304 pieces preserve a mix of popular vocal and instrumental works, entirely secular and individually arranged for performance on the pianoforte. After actively purchasing and sharing broadside (single sheet), subscription, and collected settings for more than 20 years, the Eyre family gathered together, organized, and bound these musical materials to create a remembrance of past associations (Cat. 138). For these reasons, the volumes are of interest both for the music they embrace and for the aesthetic of their preservation. The goal of this brief essay will be to explain the popular musical impulses for which this sheet music was created and the social conditions the music satisfied.

Ann Matilda Upshur Eyre was the musician and principal collector of this musical library. The dates of publication and errata inscribed on the sheets give evidence that she accumulated notated music as loose sheets and published collections from which these bound volumes were created. The music was used for sight-read performances much like poetry recitations within her own home. There is no evidence that Ann ever aspired to play in public beyond her parlor, nor was she a composer of music. Near the end of her life she began the process of conversion (including repair, trimming, and mounting damaged pages) of the various musical pieces into bound and indexed volumes that commemorated her lifelong passion. After her death, her niece Elizabeth Ann Upshur Teackle (or John Eyre, Ann's husband) completed the project of arranging and binding the music (see Cat. 131). It is clear that Mrs. Eyre did not seek to restore the page order of the music. In arranging the music in these volumes she ignored the printed page numbers of original collections, but retained some cover sheets of collections as they had survived.

Ann Eyre's lifelong interest in acquiring and sharing this popular music was sustained by a network of similar-minded women with whom she circulated printed sheet music and handwritten copies.[1] In the early 1790s, Ann Upshur and her sister Elizabeth were sent to Philadelphia where they boarded and almost certainly took music

139

Inscription

The names of Mary Bassett and Ann Upshur on the back of a piece of sheet music that probably circulated in Philadelphia when Ann was in school there with her sister in the 1790s. Volume I, "A Collection of New and Favorite Songs."

140

"My Marie's E'es o' the Deep Deep Blue"

Last stanza of handwritten lyrics and music of "My Marie's E'es o' the Deep Deep Blue," with signature of Emily A. Eyre (1805–1832). After her parents, William and Grace Eyre of Eyreville, died in 1808 and 1809 respectively, Emily probably lived with her aunt and uncle, Ann and John Eyre, at Eyre Hall. Volume IV, "Ann M. Eyre Collection."

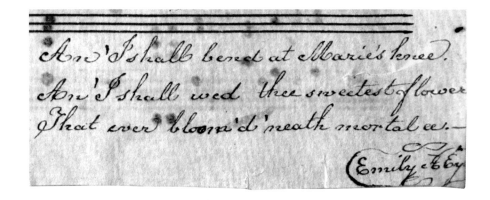

141

Inscription

One of two pieces of sheet music addressed and mailed from Littleton Dennis Teackle, Princess Anne, Maryland, to his wife "Mrs. Teackle, now at Eyre-Hall Northampton, ES Virga." Volume IV, "Ann M. Eyre Collection."

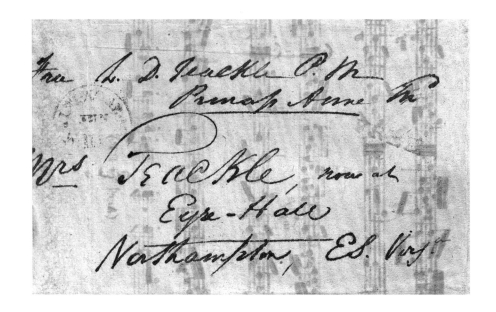

"The Baron of Maubray"

Manuscript copy, transcribed by Elizabeth Ann Teackle.
From Volume IV, "Ann M. Eyre Collection."

and other finishing lessons in the home of Mrs. Fullerton.[2] Ann's music collection began at this time, and several pieces of sheet music she retained are signed Miss Ann M. Upshur, or Ann Upshur, Esq. On the back cover of "The Caledonian Maid," there are two names in script, Miss Mary Bassett Esq. and Miss Ann Upshur (Cat. 139). Clearly the music was being shared among musicians beyond the family. After her marriage to John Eyre in 1800 and the beginning of her residence at Eyre Hall, Ann continued to share music among her family and friends on the Eastern Shore. Music circulated among these musicians in both published formats and lined foolscap sheets notated by hand. Among the handwritten copies of scores are "My Marie's E'es o' the Deep Deep Blue" signed by Emily A. Eyre, John Eyre's niece (Cat. 140). The score "If I were Yonder Wave, My Dear" is marked "For Miss Ann Jackson" on the back cover; and "Just

Like Love" is inscribed "To Miss Margaret Parramore" on the first page. In addition, pieces of sheet music were sent to Ann's sister Elizabeth Upshur Teackle while she was visiting Eyre Hall. "The Favorite Pas de Deux" and "The Celebrated Shawl Dance and Broad Sword Hornpipe" as performed by the Misses Abercrombie in the New Theatre [Philadelphia] and arranged by Thomas Carr were folded and posted to her at Eyre Hall from her husband Littleton Dennis Teackle from their home in Princess Anne, Maryland (Cat. 141).

The quality of the hand-written copies varies from quick scratches on lined paper to the very carefully drawn "The Baron of Moubray" that William Gaskins suggests was rendered by Elizabeth Ann Teackle (Cat. 142). Sheet music of this "favorite new ballad" was published by G. E. Blake in Philadelphia in around 1816, with no credit given to the composer Charles Edward Horn.[3] The music is notated very accurately with the title shadow-lettered in imitation of the printed form. With the music and first verse so legible, verses two and three are quickly scribbled on the remaining page. With only one exception, the handwritten pieces contained in these volumes are clearly reproductions of printed material.[4] Copyright would not come into the world of the consumer until the twentieth century.

The four volumes are consistent in appearance, each having marbled boards and leather binding; the sheet music has been trimmed, or backed, to fit the folio size. Upon closer inspection the volumes differ in pagination and indexing. This variation suggests that the bound volumes were created at slightly different times. In order to reference specific volumes in this writing, they have been assigned volume numbers I–IV corresponding to date ranges of the most recent music publications. Volume I ("A Collection of New and Favorite Songs") contains 105 separate pieces, beginning with the song "Comely Ned that Died at Sea" and ending with "Jockey and Jenny." Volume II ("Journal of Music, Part 1") contains 49 pieces beginning with the "Overture to the Opera L'Auberge de Bagnères" and ending with the song "Henry and Anna." Volume III contains 86 pieces beginning with "Ah, little Blind Boy!" and ending with "Sweetly in Life's Jocund Morning." Volume IV is embossed on the face "Ann M. Eyre" and contains 64 pieces beginning with "Hail La Fayette" and ending with "Believe Me, Sir."

American popular music at the close of the eighteenth century was quintessentially British music.[5] The styles, forms, narratives, and allusions all overtly reference historic, comic, or tragic predecessors in England, Ireland, and Scotland. Exotic settings are archetypically the settings of Spain, Italy, ancient Greece, and the Levant. The lack of New World settings would not have been remarkable to the theater and home audiences of popular music in the cities of the United States at that time. Indeed, the majority of the musical artists, composers, and publishers in Philadelphia, New York, and Baltimore were first-generation immigrants

from London, Dublin, or other British centers of artistic production. The outliers and important change agents in American musical tastes were French entrepreneurs adrift from the revolutionary disturbances in Paris and the bloodshed of rebellion in the French Caribbean.

The sheet music collected in these four volumes reflects the intentions of the performers. Ann M. Eyre and her circle of friends and family who shared an interest and ability to play these pieces were principally collecting songs with pianoforte accompaniment. Less than 10 percent (24) of the pieces in these volumes are instrumentals.[6] The small number of handwritten pieces bound within the volumes are all songs (or just lyrics). Settings of the music were arranged to be playable by pianists of modest ability. From selections published in the 1790s to the 1810s, the most frequent setting incorporates the vocal line into the right hand of the accompaniment. The bass often plays single notes. Increasingly, arrangements were printed as a three-staff form, separating the voice from the piano accompaniment. Separate notation for flute or guitar was common among the music of Volume I, as the pianoforte had not yet achieved the supremacy it would hold by the 1840s (Cat. 143). In Volume I, for example, there are 25 songs with separate flute accompaniment (17 separate accompaniments for guitar).[7] In Volume IV there are only two flute accompaniments. No preference for one or a cluster of keys can be seen, but the flute and guitar accompaniments were never written in a flat key. What is striking is how infrequently the melody is set in a minor mode. Of the 304 pieces in these volumes, only ten employ a minor mode, and no setting uses a minor key throughout.

Peopling the poetry of these songs are male archetypes of theater and print—sailors, shepherds, swains, and soldiers. The roles assigned to women are much more circumscribed and pivot about their attachment to men, as unmarried maids, wives, mothers, and widows. Poignant tableaux more often structure the songs, emotion triumphs over

"The Caledonian Maid"

With flute accompaniment. From Volume I,
"A Collection of New and Favorite Songs."

narrative. The purpose of song in British comic opera was not to advance the story, but to linger on the mood of the moment. Scottish ballads are the exception to this formula, "Lochinvar" or "The Chieftain" being among those scores that are action-driven.

The popular music pieces of the late eighteenth and early nineteenth century collected here are overwhelmingly the products of stage performance. This helps to explain the awkwardness of the titles—many titles are the opening line, not a summary affectation.[8] The head notes of sheet music often include the name(s) of the singer and the place of performance, for example "sung by Mr. Webster at the Sons of Apollo, Philadelphia."[9] Alternatively, the banner will announce the singer and the name of the production in which the ballad or song appears—"sung by Mrs. Marshall in 'The Spoiled Child.'"[10] Composers of melody and the poets of lyrics might also appear in the banner: "words by Thomas Moore, Esquire, composed by Sir John Stevenson."[11] Of increasing importance in the popular sheet music of the early nineteenth century was the acknowledgment of patronage through the dedication of music to an individual, one such example being "La Grange Waltz," composed by Thomas Palmer and dedicated to General La Fayette in 1824.

The music in these volumes, whether a set of compositions or a single piece, has banners that include the name

144
Copyright Notice

Notice of Victor Pelissier's publication copyright of "Pelissier's Columbian Melodies," Philadelphia, 1811. From Volume IV, "Ann M. Eyre Collection."

and address(es) of the printer, engraver, or publisher. Many domestic publishers are represented, and there is also a healthy smattering of songs published by music houses in London and Dublin.[12] These imports were almost certainly purchased through musical emporiums in Boston, New York, Philadelphia, or Baltimore.[13]

Immediately apparent is the extent to which the music-publishing industry was concentrated in mid-Atlantic and New England cities. The corollary to this concentration is that music publishing is very specialized. The value of the name and location of the publisher for researchers is important. The publisher was the nodal figure in the production of sheet music; the firm either had in-house engraving capacity, or the publishing house contracted with engravers to deliver the plates for printing. As creator of the physical object, the publisher was most often the agent who deposited copies of the music with the clerk of the United States District Court to register the music for copyright (Cat. 144).[14] Publishers' place of business, firm name, and partnerships change over time, providing rough dating tools for establishing when a particular piece may have become available for purchase.

This exploration of the business of music publishing obscures the primacy of performance in an age with limited mechanical reproduction. Composers and arrangers created scores that were translated into sounds by the singers and musicians who accompanied them. The stage performance was never accompanied solely by the pianoforte. Arrangers (again sometimes the composer) reworked the music from the stage performance and translated as best they could the ensemble sounds of an orchestra into a playable piece for piano. Authenticity of reproduction was never an issue because it was impossible to achieve. Ann Eyre bought, shared, sang, and played from the printed page or from memory. But the sounds for her satisfaction and delight were limited to the sheet music she had available, and lasted only as long as she performed.

Volume I of the Eyre Hall sheet music collection is the most organized and annotated of the four volumes, with an initial alphabetical index and a final serial index. The pages are hand-numbered as a collection (1–185 total pages including index, banner engraving, or blank pages yields 200 pages of music) without any correlation to the printed numbers of individual pieces. The greatest number of previously assembled pieces (40) come from "Young's Vocal and Instrumental Musical Miscellany" Parts 1–6, printed in Philadelphia and sold by subscription by the author, John Young, at 117 Race Street in 1793. Another major group is "The favorite Songs Sung at Vauxhall Gardens 1795," ten songs composed by James Hook. Thirty-two different operas contributed at least one song to this volume. Of the 105 titles, those with traceable publication dates (found through publisher information in secondary sources) were published prior to 1800—in other words, pieces that Ann M. Upshur obtained prior to her marriage to John Eyre in 1800. Neither the accumulation of sheet music nor the binding of diverse materials into bound volumes was unusual for women in gentry families of the federal period. A comparison with three albums owned by Nelly Custis Lewis and dating from 1797 to 1809 (in the Harvard Theatre Collection) shows remarkable overlap in content and classes of music.

Volume II of the collection consists of 49 pieces bound with frontispiece pages from the *Journal of Musick* part one, arranged by Madame Le Pelletier, Baltimore, and deposited for copyright February 15, 1810 (Cat. 145). The *Journal of Musick* contributes 30 pieces to the total bound collection (205 pages).[15] The music in Volume II is hand-numbered sequentially, by piece, not by page (in contrast to Volume I) but does not include a table of contents or index. The publication dates for pieces in this volume cluster between 1802 and 1812. The settings of the music, on balance, are more complex, more frequently separating the vocal line from the righthand accompaniment. Arrangements and settings published by Madame Le Pelletier bring French and Italian popular pieces into the mixture, with vocal scores commonly in French or Italian (rare in Volume I). Walter Scott's "Lady of the Lake," published in 1810, is virtually contemporary with the musical settings in the *Journal of Musick* composed by Sir John Stevenson and Dr. John Clarke. Volume II includes two settings of Scott's canto iii, stanza 23 of "Lady of the Lake," one under the title "Norman's Song" and the other under the rendered title "The Soldier Bridegroom's Song."

Volume III of the collection contains 86 songs, or short instrumental selections. As in Volume II, the pieces are hand-numbered (beginning with 2) not the pages. The volume starts with the frontispiece for the *Journal of Musick* part two—a confusing insertion given that none of the music included is from that publication. Nestled in this otherwise unordered miscellany of theater pieces are 39 songs and instrumental selections from the ballad opera *Love in a Village* by Dr. Thomas Arne (Cat. 146).[16] Another ten of the included pieces were published by Benjamin Carr and George Schetky in *Carr's Musical Journal*, a serial publication issued between 1804 and 1812 and sold by a chain of music

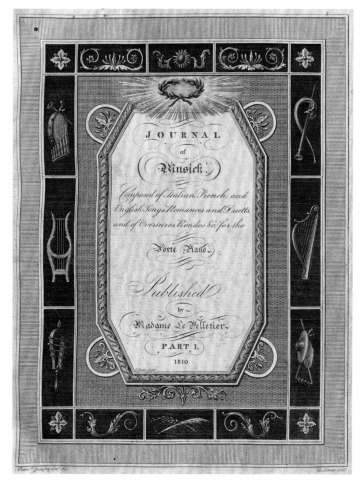

145

Journal of Musick

Frontispiece of Madame Le Pelletier's *Journal of Musick*. From Volume II, "Journal of Music, Part 1."

"Let Rakes and Libertines, [Resign'd]"

From the English ballad opera, *Love in a Village*. The libretto was by Isaac Bickerstaffe and the music—which included older music from a number of composers including Handel—was arranged by Thomas Arne. First staged in London during the 1762–63 season, the role of Lucinda was performed by Isabella Hallam. On May 1, 1771, the American Company of Comedians performed the play in the Douglass Theater in Williamsburg. Thomas Jefferson and George Washington were both in the audience and watched Isabella Hallam's cousin Nancy Hallam on the stage. Was Severn Eyre also in the audience along with his fellow members of the House of Burgesses?

stores in Baltimore, Philadelphia, New York, and Boston. The remaining musical selections are principally theater music from the British and American stage, including the work of popular composers (William Shield, James Hook, Joseph Mazzinghi, John Braham, Benjamin Carr), poetry by Thomas Moore, R. B. Sheridan, Charles and Thomas Dibdin, and a host of other sources.

Volume IV of the collection contains 64 songs, poetry, or instrumentals (163 pages). This volume is embossed on the face "Ann M. Eyre," but has no numbering of the included pieces. The visit of the Marquis de Lafayette to the United States in 1824 is the subject of the most recent pieces in the collection. Beyond these patriotic marches and quicksteps, the remainder of the pieces have no discernible organization, though most songs were published between 1810 and 1824.

Only a single ballad, "Jessie the Flow'r o' Dumblane" was published in London, although several pieces are reprinted from the London stage, including the 1823 "Home! Sweet Home!" written by Henry Rowley Bishop composed on a Sicilian air. Scottish ballads by Sir Walter Scott ("Allen-a-dale," "The Cypress Wreath," and several from "Rokeby") and others are frequent.

Beyond these four bound volumes of sheet music, Eyre Hall has a small collection of loose sheet music scores brought by Margaret Eyre Baldwin when she started using the house as a summer home in the early 1930s. Mrs. Baldwin purchased a Steinway grand piano for the parlor of Eyre Hall, and a collection of loose sheet music survives associated with the piano (see Fig. 230). A single volume of nineteenth-century opera scores arranged for piano, *Grand*

Opera at Home, edited and arranged by Albert E. Wier, is certainly a vestige of Mrs. Baldwin's lengthy experience as a piano student. A similar compendium by Albert E. Wier titled *Songs the Children Love to Sing* is a mixed bag of simple melodies published in 1916. Twenty-four of the remaining (34) scores are popular songs collected from Broadway musicals and the emerging motion picture soundtracks of Disney Studios, among others. Mrs. Baldwin's son recalls that in summer months she would play piano and sing with the windows open, and that the head gardener would join her in duet. Their most likely source of collaboration would have been music from the Protestant Episcopal hymnal (1913), but her son recalls the gardener singing popular songs and spirituals as well.[17] What is unexplained is Eyre Hall's connection to the world of machine music. Neither a radio nor record player have ever been present.

NOTES

1. All discussion of the sharing of music among Ann M. Eyre, her family, and friends is informed by and derived from the research done by William Gaskins as part of "The Eyre Hall Project," a William and Mary research seminar directed by Carl Lounsbury, spring 2017. Gaskins's report, "Ann Upshur Eyre's Binder's Volumes: An Annotated Guide to the Handwritten Notes," March 17, 2017, is the source for unexplained associations.

2. In a letter to her stepfather, Ann Upshur noted the increased charges for lodging and classes. Ann Upshur to John Upshur, April 10, 1795, Upshur Family Papers, Special Collections Research Center, Swem Library, College of William and Mary, Williamsburg.

3. [Charles E. Horn], *The Baron of Moubray, a Favourite New Ballad* (Philadelphia: G. E. Blake, ca. 1816). Available online at https://www.loc.gov/ item/2014565962/.

4. That the unknown source of the reproduced "Absence" was printed is suggested by the careful treatment of the title and the very accurate rendering of the stanzas.

5. There are both American and English operas and other stage compositions treating New World themes in the late eighteenth century, but they are not represented in the Eyre family volumes and were few in comparison with other productions.

6. The instrumental pieces sought by Mrs. Eyre may have been considerably less. Almost half of the instrumental pieces were acquired in sets of music not as single purchases. Five of the pieces celebrated Lafayette's return to Philadelphia in 1824.

7. Volume III includes separate flute accompaniment for ten pieces, and 16 separate guitar accompaniments. These are almost entirely for the sheet music of the ballad opera *Love in a Village*, which was printed by Longman & Co., Cheapside, London. The business was dissolved in 1804 after the death of James Longman.

8. Confusion between title and text led to the inclusion of two printings of the same song from the opera *The Siege of Calais* in Volume I. "Pauvre Madelon" and "Would go with you all the world over" are the same song words by George Colman, composed by Samuel Arnold.

9. "When She Smiles!" composed by John Bray, words by James Nelson Barker. Published by G. E. Blake, No. 1 South 3rd St., Philadelphia, [1808], from Barker's first performed score, *Tears and Smiles*, a comedy in five acts.

10. "Since Then I'm Doomed", words by Bickerstaff, [n.d.]. Published at B. Carr's Musical Repository, Market St., Philadelphia, and William St., New York, and by J. Carr, Baltimore.

11. "Donna Donna Donna Della, A Favorite Song," composed by Mr. Hook, [1797 99]. Printed and sold at J. Hewitt's Musical Repository, 131 William St., New York, B. Carr's, Phila & at J. Carr's Baltimore.

12. This assessment ignores the 39 scores, virtually the catalogue of songs from the comic opera *Love in the Village*, written and arranged by Thomas Arne, published by Longman & Co., Cheapside, London. See note 8 above.

13. This chart does not separately list variations of firms, nor does it cluster successive owners of a publishing company.

14. Printed copyright notice was required under the amendment of the Copyright Act of 1790, passed April 29, 1802. Dated copyright notices become much more typical in the 1820s. Sheet music published from the British stage was derivative and not available for copyright. Only the collections of music from the 1790s to 1810s were copyrighted in the Eyre Collection. The copyrighted broadsides only appear in Volume IV.

15. The Eyre Volume II includes all the published pieces from the *Journal of Musick*, Part 1, with the exception of "Fantaisie sur un Air Russe." See Elise K. Kirk, "Charlotte Le Pelletier's *Journal of Musick* (1810): A New Look at French Culture in Early America." *American Music* 29, no. 2 (Summer 2011): 203–28.

16. *Love in a Village* by Dr. Thomas Arne, first performed in London in 1762, created a vogue for pastiche opera that endured into the nineteenth century. See Todd Gilman, *The Theatre Career of Thomas Arne* (Lanham, Md.: Rowman & Littlefield, 2013), 1.

17. Furlong Baldwin interview with Gary Stanton, March 22, 2017.

Costume and Textiles

NEAL T. HURST

Baby's Pin Pillow,
1790.
Cat. 147

THE EYRE FAMILY, AND THE GENERATIONS OF enslaved people they owned, used textiles every day of their lives. From the mundane huckaback linen towel to dry a washed face, to the imported English broadcloth made into a greatcoat to keep warm, or the fine, domestically made Virginia cloth bed curtains, the Eyres consumed large quantities of textiles.[1] Unlike furniture, ceramics, or metals, textiles and clothing rarely survive, but period probate inventories help to fill in the gaps. In many ways, the Eyre family during the eighteenth century epitomizes the typical wealthy Virginia planter class; however, written evidence provides clues to a truly unique economy not seen in the mainland Tidewater region. Over the years, Eyre Hall became the repository for its family's material past. Many of the textile objects and clothing accessories such as lace fragments, collars, and fans dating to the nineteenth century remain completely anonymous. Other objects mark important family events.

147

Pin Pillow

Northampton County, Virginia, 1790
Silk, linen, iron, tin, saw dust, sand

Discovered packed away in a trunk in the attic of Eyre Hall, a baby's pin pillow—with the name Nathaniel Littleton Savage written with the heads of pins—is the earliest textile object to survive from the Eyre family. During the eighteenth century, mothers often received, as gifts for their newborn, small pillows with inscriptions of names, initials, flowers, birth dates, or sayings such as "Welcome Little Stranger." These pillows, while often beautiful works of art, were meant as practical gifts for the baby's mother. The maker created the design with the heads of pins. Throughout the eighteenth and nineteenth centuries,

most infants' clothing fastened with pins, and this gift provided the mother with an ample supply.[2]

Born on March 2, 1790, Nathaniel Littleton Savage was the first son of Thomas Littleton Savage and Mary Burton. Thomas and Mary's family continued to grow, with the birth of two more daughters: Maria Teackle in 1792 and Leah Littleton in 1794. Unfortunately, tragedy struck on March 25, 1795; after a very short illness, five-year-old Nathaniel died. Four months later, the young family also lost their mother.

At some point, Maria Teackle received the pin pillow made for her deceased older brother. On July 13, 1811, Maria married Severn Eyre Parker, the son of Margaret Eyre, sister to John Eyre, the owner of Eyre Hall at that time. The very worn white silk satin pin pillow with fraying tassels in the corner returned to Eyre Hall, probably in the nineteenth century, as a memento of the untimely death of the young Nathaniel Littleton Savage.

148

Wallets

Wallet (James Lyon)
Carlisle, Pennsylvania, 1795
Leather, ink

Wallet (W. E. Lyon)
Northampton County, Virginia, before 1826
Leather, gilt

On July 16, 1799, Sarah Eyre, daughter of Severn Eyre, the second owner of Eyre Hall, married Dr. James Lyon, a physician from Carlisle, Pennsylvania. They had two children, William Eyre Lyon and Margaret Alice Lyon. Two wallets survive from this line of the family. One red Moroccan leather wallet with various swag tooling, inscribed in ink on the inner flap "James Lyon, Nov 1795," and a plain brown leather wallet with heavy tooling around the edges and stamped in gold with the name "W. E. Lyon," for Captain William Eyre Lyon. Captain Lyon lived a short life, passing away at age 23 in 1826.

Men and women used wallets and pocketbooks much as we do today. Typical examples, like the surviving Lyon wallets, are divided and subdivided into pockets in the interior to hold paper money, bills of exchange, receipts, notes, and other flat paper items. Many pocketbooks included small blank paper books and integral holders for pencils and port crayons to write notes throughout the day. For physicians, merchants, and sea captains, these small objects proved practical and valuable in daily life, perhaps suggesting why they survive to this day.

Fig. 246. Detail of inside
flap of James Lyon wallet.

149

Fragment of Margaret Parker Eyre's Gown or Under Petticoat

Gown or Petticoat
Northampton County, Virginia, 1865
Cotton

Another small grouping of clothing survives from the children and grandchildren of William Eyre, the youngest son of Severn Eyre. In 1828, William Littleton Eyre, his only son to live to adulthood, married Mary Burton Savage. A surviving white-worked shirt with a label that reads "Shirt of William L. Eyre of Eyre Ville" documents the wearer and perhaps the shirt he wore on his wedding day. The white cotton shirt has fine pleats and a very narrow ruffle to either side of the center front opening and is further embellished with whitework vines and flowers. Overall, it is exquisitely sewn and a remarkable survival. Several of these white-worked shirts have histories of being worn at weddings and survive in both public and private collections.

William L. Eyre and Mary Burton Savage Eyre had two sons, John and Severn Eyre. In 1865, Severn married Margaret S. Parker. A fragment of a white cotton gown or under-petticoat survives, with a note stating, "Dress of Margaret P. Eyre, wife of Severn Eyre (belonging to her trousseau)." Perhaps when descendants packed away this piece it remained intact as a full dress, but only a small scrap now remains. Packed together and with notes pinned to them written with the same hand, there is no doubt that these pieces came back to Eyre Hall in the twentieth century.

TEXTILES, LEATHER, AND BALEEN

Extant textile objects from Eyre Hall provide a very limited view of the household's consumption and usage over time. The series of inventories taken in the eighteenth century provide a better glimpse of the over one hundred different types of fabrics found within the home along with insights into the well-established tanning and whaling industries found on the properties between 1719 and 1790. Like most members of the Virginia gentry, the Eyres imported large quantities of textiles from or through Great Britain. The names of many of these fabrics reference their place of manufacture, among them Lancaster sheeting, Striped Holland, Devonshire cloth, or Irish linen. The Eyres also produced large amounts of fabric domestically on their plantations, such as Virginia striped linen, Virginia cloth, and Virginia linen. The inventories show well-appointed homes that employed both domestic and imported fabrics.

Unlike other regions within the Tidewater, the Eastern Shore of Virginia's unique location fostered the development of early industries. Starting in the 1630s, government officials promoted the cultivation of flax and hemp and, by the 1650s, encouraged silk production, with monetary bounties for yardage.[3] In 1666, the Virginia Assembly ordered each county to provide a weaver and loom at public expense to help produce fabrics for servants living in Virginia.[4] Along with flax, hemp, and silk, plantations across the Eastern Shore steadily increased their flocks of sheep for woolen textiles. Northampton and Accomack Counties established and followed these colony-wide recommendations.

Three of the five eighteenth-century Eyre family inventories date prior to the building of Eyre Hall, but show a well-established family. John Eyre's 1719 inventory lists many pieces of fiber-processing equipment and raw materials, including four linen spinning wheels, six pounds of picked cotton, a parcel of unbroken flax, a loom, two pairs of sheep shears, 60 pounds of unwashed wool, a wool spinning wheel, and 50 head of sheep. In his home, John Eyre also had, not surprisingly, 14 yards of Virginia cloth, a set of Virginia cloth bed curtains and valances, and an old pair of Virginia cloth breeches.

John's brother Thomas Eyre II had three sons: Neech, who died ca. 1709; Thomas III, who died in 1719; and Severn, who died in 1728. The inventories of the latter two listed similar textiles and showed evidence of similar domestic production. Thomas owned 62 sheep and had 138 pounds of wool stored for spinning with his wool wheel. He also owned a linen spinning wheel and a parcel of unbroken flax. Other textiles listed on the inventory include a very early and rare set of red and white calico curtains and valances for one of his bedsteads and another set of bed hangings described as flowered. He also owned a cotton hammock and a very expensive £5 broadcloth suit.

Thomas's brother Severn also produced textiles on his plantation. The equipment on his inventory was substantial and included 22 pairs of tow cards, nine wool cards, a hackle, a flax break, 48 sheep, two spinning wheels, one loom with two sets of harnesses, and a wool wheel. His inventory also showed substantial use of domestic textiles including Virginia cloth blankets, Virginia striped linen, and two sets of Virginia linsey-woolsey bed curtains.

Severn's son and the builder of Eyre Hall, Littleton Eyre, continued the practices established by earlier generations. His impressive inventory includes 16 linen and wool spinning wheels, 157 pounds of tow thread, parcels of picked and unpicked cotton, two looms with warping bars and gears, three flax breaks, sheep shears, and over 200 sheep. Although his inventory does not go into as much detail as his father's and uncle's, Littleton certainly produced domestically manufactured textiles.

As early the mid-seventeenth century, the Virginia Assembly promoted the leather tanning industry. In 1661, the assembly ordered that each county erect tan houses for the processing of leather, primarily for shoes.[5] Accomack County resident Hugh Yeo sent a letter to his brother in 1666 requesting him to find more workmen for his tan house. Yeo said that he had the tan house for seven years and had no problems procuring hides and tanning over 200 annually. With more workmen, he told his brother, he could easily increase production to over 500 hides.[6] Large plantations and property owners like the Eyres also established tanning vats.

Thomas Eyre's 1719 inventory suggests a well-established tanning industry on his properties at the time of his death. The gentlemen assigned to take the inventory listed "twelve sides sole leather in ye fats (vats)." Eyre's inventory also included 50 pounds and 32 sides of sole leather and 42 sides of uppers leather. Additionally, Eyre owned over 40 cows, calves, bulls, and steer, keeping ready supply of food for his table and skins for his tanning operation.

The inventory taken in 1728 of the possessions of Thomas's brother Severn similarly lists large quantities of leather and completed shoes, including 18 sides of sole leather, 20 pairs of leather-heeled shoes, nine pairs of wooden-heeled shoes, and two pairs of women's shoes. Littleton Eyre carried on this industry on the Eyre Hall property. His inventory from 1768 details 58 sides in tan vats, 46½ sides of upper leather, 39 sides of sole leather, and over 130 cattle. The inventory also included a set of shoemaker's tools and 12 pairs of "Negro" shoes.[7]

With easy access to the Chesapeake and Atlantic Ocean, the Eyres engaged with the local whaling industry. Whales provided a wide variety of raw materials that workmen could further process into oils, waxes, and boning for garments. Thomas Eyre's inventory taken on October 28, 1719 included one whaleboat and oars along with three whale lances and two iron harpoons. It also listed 80 pounds of whalebone or baleen at 12 pence per pound and later four casks of old whalebone and an old joint. A joint, possibly referencing a junk, was a whaler's term for a series of five to ten baleen fins together when removed from the jaw of the whale. Thomas's uncle John also included a small three-pound parcel of baleen in his inventory.

While often referred to as whalebone, baleen is not truly bone. Baleen whales, such as the fin, humpback, or right whales, belong to this group due to the stiff keratin plates that grow down from the gums along either side of the upper jaw. Baleen grows in long fins, up to 13 feet in some species, and terminates on the interior of the mouth with fringes. These types of whales take in great mouthfuls of water and use their tongues to push the water through the baleen, catching zooplankton and krill in the baleen's dense fringe.

Tradesmen employed baleen or whalebone in many ways. Throughout the seventeenth and eighteenth centuries, stay makers produced structured boned garments for women to wear in order to support the bust and gain a fashionable shape. Bodies or stays covered the women from the fullness of the bust to the waist. Made of multiple layers of linen, wool, and/or silk, the stay maker stitched channels in which they inserted the baleen. The keratin-based baleen made it easy to shape the stays to the woman's body and yet remained stiff and ridged. Baleen is also a very poor conductor of heat.[8]

Historic clothing and textiles rarely survive in great quantities from a single family. Objects made from linen, cotton, wool, silk, hemp, or leather faced constant use and remaking until worn out, succumbing to the test of time or the feasting of insects. The Eyre family kept clothing and textile objects to remember or memorialize significant events from the past, whether happy times (as with the gown fragment of Margaret S. Parker Eyre's 1865 wedding trousseau) or sadder times (as in the case of the 1790 pin pillow commemorating the death of five-year-old Nathaniel Littleton Savage). Extant objects tell only a few stories, while eighteenth-century inventories indicate sizable textile and leather production along with baleen processing—probably for both consumption on their plantations by free and enslaved people, and also retailing to local merchants and tradesmen. The Eyres purchased textiles and clothing from England, as typically practiced by Virginia gentry, but, unlike most upper-class homes, seemingly more than supplemented them with domestically made fabrics. As merchants located on the somewhat secluded and fertile Eastern Shore of Virginia, the Eyre family imported, traded, and produced textiles and clothing and further saved those precious items for posterity.

NOTES
1. For textile definitions used throughout this section, see Florence M. Montgomery, *Textiles in America, 1650–1870* (New York: W. W. Norton & Company, 2007).
2. For further discussion of pin pillows, see Susan Burrows Swan, *Plain & Fancy: American Women and their Needlework, 1750–1850* (New York: Holt, Rinehart and Winston, 1977), 119–22.
3. William Waller Hening, *The Statutes at Large, being a Collection of all the Laws of Virginia* (New York, Richmond, and Philadelphia, 1819–23), 1:115, 218, 336, 425, 469–70, 487.
4. Hening, *Statutes at Large*, 2:238.
5. Hening, *Statutes at Large*, 2:128.
6. Hugh Yeo to Justinian Yeo, March 27, 1666, Accomack County Deeds, Wills, etc., 1676–1690, 127–28.
7. For more on early leather production in Virginia specifically, see Harold B. Gill, Jr., *Leather Workers in Colonial Virginia*, Colonial Williamsburg Foundation Library Reach Report Series (Williamsburg: Colonial Williamsburg Foundation, 1966). For more information on early Eastern Shore industry, see Susie M. Ames, *Studies of the Virginia Eastern Shore in the Seventeenth Century* (Richmond, Va.: The Dietz Press, 1940), 109–46.
8. For more on baleen and its use in the fashion industry, especially stays, see Lynn Sorge-English, *Stays and Body Image in London: The Staymaking Trade, 1680–1810* (London: Pickering & Chatto, 2011).

Ironwork and Arms

ERIK GOLDSTEIN

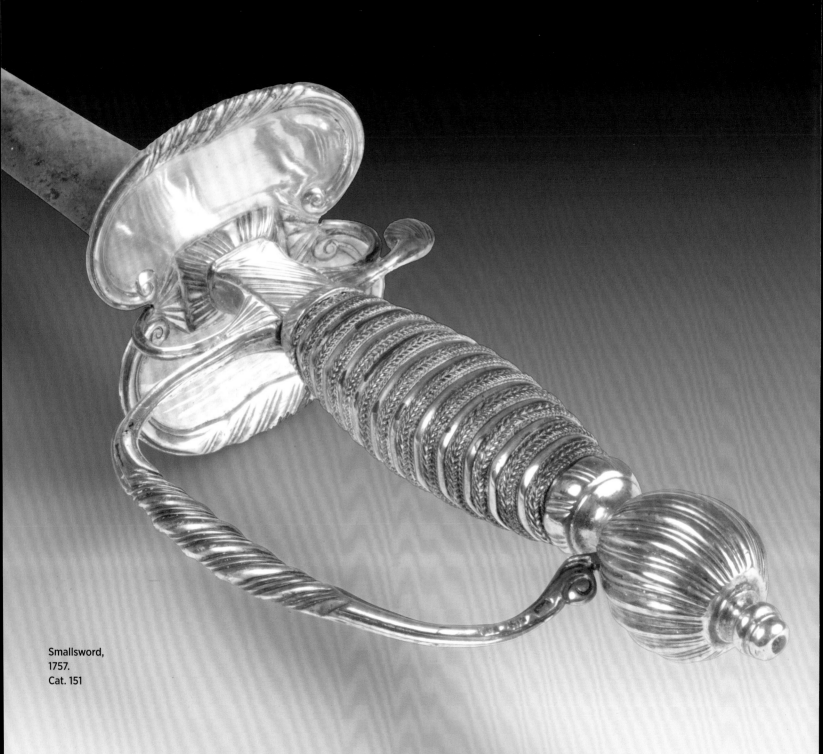

Smallsword,
1757.
Cat. 151

150

Fireback

Sited in the second-floor southeast bedchamber firebox
Grymes Forge
Benjamin Grymes (1725–ca. 1776)
Massaponax, Spotsylvania, Virginia, November 5, 1758
Cast iron
H. 26½ in., W. 23½ in.

Like the andirons, shovel, and tongs, the fireback was an essential component of the colonial fireplace. A singular piece of robust cast iron, it commanded the firebox and served a number of clever purposes. It was primarily intended to protect the bricks and mortar at the back of the firebox from the disintegrative effects of the inferno set before it. Being a thick slab of metal it would also retain heat and radiate it back into the room long after the fire had died down. In the case of many produced in the American colonies, the fireback could also be a decorative piece, adding some beauty to the dirtiest and most inhospitable part of the hearth.

However, that is not true for this remarkable fireback. It takes the shape of the pattern from which it was produced, being a vertically oriented rectangular board, only embellished by raised molding on its three visible sides. The field carries the name of the iron-master of the foundry that cast the piece, "B. GRYMES," and the date it was poured, "NOVᴿ 5ᵀᴴ 1758." Though many pre-Revolutionary American firebacks bear the year they were created, the Eyre Hall fireback is exceptional for including the month and day too.

Plain matrices like Grymes's traded extensive embellishment for flexibility in the fireback-creating process known as "puddle casting." In this method, mold sand was set into the floor in front of an iron furnace's tap hole. After the pattern was pressed into the sand to form the mold cavity, any inscription desired by the proprietor or patron could be imparted directly into the sand. When the furnace's dam stone was knocked aside, molten iron flowed from the tap, filling the channels and molds arranged before it. Once solidified and cooled, the new fireback castings were broken free, lightly cleaned up, and were now ready to be installed in a customer's fireplace.

Ironworks like Grymes's were as plentiful in eighteenth-century Virginia as the ore they converted into salable products. On the date the Eyre Hall fireback was cast, Benjamin Grymes (1725–ca. 1776) was new to the game, having only acquired the facility and its adjoining 6,300 acres the previous May. His success as an iron master, perhaps coupled with other business ventures, propelled him to prominence in the 1760s when he served as a justice of the county. Grymes also represented Spotsylvania in the House of Burgesses at various times between 1761 and 1771. On August 15, 1770, he sold the works and 800 acres for £1,250 (Virginia currency), ending his tenure in the iron-manufacturing business.[1]

Assuming this November 5, 1758 dated fireback was originally installed in the principal (southeast) bedchamber as part of the room's finish, it reinforces the 1759 date of Eyre Hall's completion perfectly. It is therefore logical to assume that the other three original fireboxes in the house may have also had firebacks made at Grymes Forge in Massaponax. Only this example survives.

151
Smallsword

Unknown maker
London, 1757
Steel, iron, silver, wood
L. (overall) 38¼ in., L. (hilt) 6½ in., L. (blade) 31⅞ in., H. 1⅛ in.

Evolving from the cumbersome and overlong rapier of the seventeenth century, British smallswords of the early Georgian era were light, elegant, beautiful, and deadly. Though they differed little in basic architecture and varied greatly in style, they can be recognized by the little finger loops called *pas d'âne* set between the grip and counterguard of the hilt. Smallswords were mounted with a straight blade of one configuration or another and became the choice weapon to adorn the left hip of a well-dressed gentleman.

Since British and American officers were gentlemen too, a smallsword was frequently adopted as an essential part of his uniform, though it wasn't very combat-worthy. Regardless, they had become immensely popular with those serving on both land and sea by the middle years of the eighteenth century, and the Eyre Hall smallsword typifies a fashionable design carried by many such warriors.

This enduring style appeared in the mid-1740s and remained in vogue until the early 1770s. These are easily identified by panels of "gadrooning," a writhen fluted embellishment, used with tasteful restraint on all components of their cast and chased silver hilts. The Eyre Hall smallsword's wooden handle still retains its original wrap composed of a spiraling band of silver tape flanked by contrasting strands of twisted silver wire. This binding is meant to improve the user's grip while presenting a visual effect which mimics gadrooning.

The sword's silver components were made in 1757 by an unknown London hilt-maker, whose mark was not applied in conjunction with the usual date, city, and fineness hallmarks struck into the upper end of the knucklebow near the pommel. It is mounted on a lozenge-sectioned double-edged blade which abruptly narrows a few inches below the hilt, in imitation of the idiosyncratic "colichemarde" profile. As the true colichemarde blade is of a hollow triangular section and meant strictly for thrusting, this double-edged version seeks to combine the former's swanky look with the ability to both slash and stab. Possibly a product of Solingen (Germany), it

is now very worn, but still exhibits traces of etched decoration on both sides.

To find a parallel with undeniable provenance, we can look at the silver-hilted smallsword of 1753 owned by George Washington and now in the collections of Mount Vernon.[2] Also a product of London, it is believed to have been ordered by Washington when he received his first commission, as district adjutant of the Virginia militia with the rank of major, in February of 1753. Family tradition maintains that this sword went into the wilderness with young George during the French and Indian War. Thus, it was likely a witness to the ambush of Jumonville's party on May 23, 1754, Washington's humiliating surrender of Fort Necessity the following July 4, and the disastrous expedition to take Fort Duquesne in the summer of 1755, now referred to as "Braddock's Defeat."

Though it is unknown how this silver-hilted smallsword came to be at Eyre Hall, there are some clues that can't be ignored. With a military cutting and thrusting blade and mounted with the same hilt style chosen by Washington for his service in the Virginia militia, it is tempting to associate it with Littleton Eyre (1709–1768), builder of the home and county lieutenant of Northampton. In this role, Eyre received command of the Northampton County militia in November of 1754.[3] Could it be that Littleton Eyre acquired this specific pattern of sword during the French and Indian War because it was popular with Virginia's militia officers?

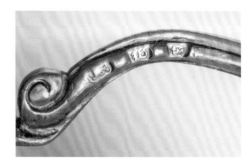

Fig. 247. Detail of the hallmark on hilt, Cat. 151.

152
Officer's Saber

Unknown maker
Great Britain, 1770–85
Steel, iron, wood, copper
L. (overall) 32⅞ in., L. (hilt) 6¼ in., L. (blade) 26⁹⁄₁₆ in., H. 1³⁄₁₆ in.

Also known as a "hanger" for hanging by its wearer's left hip, these light military swords were frequently chosen by officers fighting on both sides of the Revolutionary War as a required part of their uniform.[4] With a broad counterguard and a cutting and thrusting blade, sabers like this were still useful in an age when the sword was losing its prominence as the go-to combat weapon for most infantry officers.

These hangers first appeared in Britain in the late 1760s, borrowing traits from a number of other popular sword types.[5] Taking its cue from the hilt design of a light cavalry sword of the late 1750s, the steel hilt on this saber is simple and elegant.[6] Its major component is commonly referred to as a four-slot "D" guard, embellished by flutes tapering up the knucklebow from the apertures. A plain ovoid pommel is mounted by an inverted acorn-shaped capstan, through which the tang of the blade is peened, thereby holding the sword together. The spiraling wooden grip has a copper tape running down its channel, secured by the foot of the pommel at its top and a beaded ferrule at its base.

Fullered and curved blades like the one on the Eyre Hall hanger were also used on "cuttoes," a type of delicate hunting sword that was also popular with American and British officers serving in the Revolutionary War. Since the blade is unmarked, it could have been made in either Solingen or Birmingham.

Though this sword survives at Eyre Hall without any provenance, it appeared over the front door crossed with the silver-hilted smallsword of 1757 in a late nineteenth-century photograph of the hall interior, where it is displayed today (Fig. 249).

Fig. 248. Detail of hilt, Cat. 152.

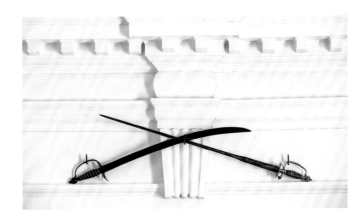

Fig. 249. Crossed swords over the south doorway of the entrance hall.

NOTES

1. For information on Benjamin Grymes, see "Grymes of Brandon Etc.," *The Virginia Magazine of History and Biography* 28, no. 2 (April 1920): 187–88.
2. Erik Goldstein, Stuart C. Mowbray, and Brian Hendelson, *The Swords of George Washington* (Woonsocket, R.I.: Mowbray Publishing, 2016), 45–50.
3. No sword, or any of the trappings of a militia colonel were listed in Littleton Eyre's inventory of October 14, 1769. However, "1 silver hilted sword" valued at 60 shillings (Virginia currency), appeared in his son Severn's inventory in 1774, and may well have been this one. Inventory of the estate of Severn Eyre, February 27, 1774, Northampton County Wills & Inventories, No. 25, 1772–1777, 393.
4. This common hanger type is illustrated in numerous portraits from the Revolutionary War era.
5. George Neumann, *Swords and Blades of the American Revolution* (Harrisburg, Pa.: Stackpole Books, 1973), 106–11.
6. Neumann, *Swords and Blades*, 54, no. 279.S.

Index

Photo credits